ALEXANDER THE GREAT

Alexander the Great's vast conquests have captivated people for centuries, and have led to the development of an almost legendary status. But is this status deserved, and can we penetrate his legend to understand the man and his actions? This exciting new edition is an indispensable guide to the study of Alexander, showing the problems of the ancient source material, and making it clear that there is no single approach to be taken to the study of Alexander and his achievements.

Twelve thematic chapters contain a broad selection of the most significant published articles about Alexander, revised to include the most up-to-date scholarship, and examine the main areas of debate and discussion:

- The Sources
- Alexander's Influences and the Macedonian Background
- Alexander's Aims
- Alexander's Battles and Generalship
- Alexander and the Greeks
- Alexander and the Persian Empire
- Alexander, India and the Gedrosian Desert
- From Mass Marriage to Death
- Alexander and the 'Unity of Mankind'
- Alexander and Deification
- Alexander and Conspiracies
- Alexander: The 'Great'?

With translations of a substantial number of primary sources, and prefacing each chapter with an overview of the subject, this new Reader is a vital tool for students of classics and ancient history, and anyone with an interest in one of history's most famous conquerors.

Ian Worthington is Professor of History at the University of Missouri. He has published 15 sole-authored and edited books and over 100 articles and essays on Greek history, epigraphy and oratory. In 2005 he won the Chancellor's Award for Outstanding Research and Creativity in the Humanities, in 2007 the Student-Athlete Advisory Council Most Inspiring Professor Award and in 2010 the William H. Byler Distinguished Professor Award. In 2011 he was awarded the CAMWS Excellence in University Teaching Award.

ALEXANDER THE GREAT

A Reader

Second Edition

Ian Worthington

Routledge
Taylor & Francis Group

LONDON AND NEW YORK

First published 2012
by Routledge
2 Park Square, Milton Park, Abingdon, Oxon, OX14 4RN

Simultaneously published in the USA and Canada
by Routledge
711 Third Avenue, New York, NY 10017

Routledge is an imprint of the Taylor & Francis Group, an informa business

British Library Cataloguing in Publication Data
A catalogue record for this book is available from the British Library.

Library of Congress Cataloging-in-Publication Data
A catalogue record for this book has been requested.

ISBN: 978-0-415-66742-5 (hbk)
ISBN: 978-0-415-66743-2 (pbk)
ISBN: 978-0-203-80435-3 (ebk)

Typeset in Garamond by
Saxon Graphics Ltd, Derby.

MIX
Paper from
responsible sources
FSC® C004839

Printed and bound in Great Britain by
TJ International Ltd, Padstow, Cornwall

CONTENTS

CONTENTS

REVISED PREFACE

Alexander the Great of Macedonia is one of the best known and most fascinating figures from antiquity. In his thirteen-year reign (336–323), he defeated the vast Persian empire and invaded what the Greeks called India (what is today Pakistan), thus establishing a Macedonian empire that stretched from Greece in the west to 'India' in the east. His fighting prowess and brilliant strategy and tactics were combined with a fierce intellect and appreciation of learning, and he was quick to see the value of integrating Asians into his administration and army to improve the fighting capabilities of his army and help maintain Macedonian rule over the subject peoples. He was the type of man that legends are made of, and therein lies the major problem in any study of Alexander: separating the legendary Alexander from the historical.

In the generations, indeed centuries, after his death stories were written about Alexander in the west which were unhistorical. Some of these, such as the king's dealings with a tribe of headless men (in the literary *Alexander Romance*) can easily be dismissed. Others not so, for during Alexander's lifetime and in the generations after his death many works were written about him, all with shortcomings and biases, which have not survived in their entirety today. These contemporary works were used by the later writers centuries after Alexander's death, who give us our connected narratives of his reign. The problem is obvious: how reliable are sources written so long after the events they describe, how critically did their writers evaluate the earlier works and decide which account to prefer over another, and how do their own political, social and moral backgrounds affect their presentation of Alexander? Indeed, there is no actual evidence that later writers such as Arrian and Plutarch read the earlier works in their entirety, thereby compounding the problem.

Ought we then to accept the (western) picture of a dashing king enjoying spectacular successes and establishing a great empire, or the understandably hostile picture presented by non-western sources of Alexander the Accursed? Indeed, when we consider the downsides to Alexander's kingship, we can wonder whether he even deserves to be called 'Great' nowadays.

The aim of the Routledge Reader series as told to me is to provide translations of more inaccessible contemporary sources, with minimal notes, followed by a selection of modern scholars' works in English. The contemporary works we have for Alexander are often passed over in favour of the later ones (in which they are quoted or paraphrased), yet they are the foundation stones of the later connected histories of the reign, and provide valuable information on many aspects of the areas through which Alexander marched. Thus in keeping with this series' format I give a selection of contemporary inscriptional and especially literary material, which allows readers to set it next to the more readily available later accounts (which should be read in their entirety).

Translations of the epigraphical material are my own; translations of the fragments of the contemporary writers are those of C.A. Robinson, *The History of Alexander the Great* 1 (Providence: 1953). I am very grateful to Brown University Library for granting permission to reprint.

This book is divided into twelve chapters. The first chapter deals with the problem of the source material for him. His background and influences are the subject of Chapter 2, and his aims of Chapter 3. The main events of his life and reign in chronological order are the focus of Chapters 4–8. Four thematic chapters on controversies associated with events in his reign and his character follow: the 'unity of mankind' (Chapter 9), his pretensions to personal divinity (Chapter 10), conspiracies against him (Chapter 11), and his 'greatness' (Chapter 12). Each chapter has a brief introduction to set the scene, selections from modern scholars' works and a list of additional readings.

I have tried where possible to select modern scholars' works that focus on the nature of the source material and in the process give different interpretations of the same topic. My aim is to show that there is no single approach to Alexander, that there can be substantial disagreement, and that consensus of opinion might never be reached. There are thus no right or wrong answers, and it is up to readers, based on their critical evaluation of the sources and arguments of modern scholars, to reach their own conclusions – as indeed it should be. I know that not everyone will agree with my selections (ancient or modern), but if I gave a translation of all sources along with everything that has been written on Alexander, the Reader would run to 100 volumes, and I would be criticised for not being selective. I hope that my critics will see my rationale for what I included, and leave it at that. There are some chapters where I wanted to reprint more modern works, but high reprint fees disallowed that. On pp. xi–xiv, I list ancient writers and some modern books (in English), which should be consulted in the first instance. Those who wish to read more as well as foreign works should consult the bibliographies in these books and in the notes of the articles cited in the additional reading lists.

Second edition

The opportunity to prepare a second edition of this reader allowed me to make a number of changes and improvements to the first edition (first published in 2003). Most important is a rearrangement of some chapters and inclusion of new ones to allow more coverage of Persia in this period (Chapter 6) and of Alexander's death, its manipulation and aftermath (Chapter 8). The chapter on Alexander's generalship in the first edition is the present Chapter 4 (now titled 'Alexander's battles and generalship'), as it is better suited there to set the scene for the chapters that follow. I also made changes to the selections from the modern scholars' works in many chapters, removing some and adding new ones (especially those published after the first edition). The lists of additional readings in all chapters are greatly expanded and updated, the introductions to the chapters are likewise expanded, and I provide detailed maps for Alexander's campaigns in Persia. Finally, I rearranged the fragmentary ancient sources in some chapters, deleted some sources and added new ones, and provided sub-headings throughout to aid readers. Occasionally for the sake of convenience I repeated a contemporary source in a later chapter where it was especially relevant.

One of the publisher's readers suggested I add a chapter on material culture in the age of Alexander. The problems with this type of chapter are what contemporary (literary) sources to include in it and whether its worth could be affected by new archaeological evidence. Hence, I refrained from adding such a chapter, and direct readers (no bias intended) to the various material culture and evidence chapters in Joseph Roisman and Ian Worthington (eds), *The Blackwell Companion to Ancient Macedonia* (Oxford: 2010).

I am grateful to Matthew Gibbons and Lalle Pursglove at Routledge for their help and patience in putting up with me. I would like to thank Richard Stoneman again for inviting me to compile the first edition of this reader. Finally, I am grateful to my family, as always, for its support and endurance – more than I (or Alexander) deserve.

Ian Worthington
University of Missouri
November 2010

ANCIENT SOURCES
AND MODERN BOOKS

Contemporary inscriptions

P.E. Harding, *From the End of the Peloponnesian War to the Battle of Ipsus* (Cambridge: 1985), nos. 102–122 – English translation and notes.

A.J. Heisserer, *Alexander the Great and the Greeks* (Norman: 1980) – Greek text, English translation and commentary.

L. Moretti, *Inscrizioni Storiche Ellenistiche* (Florence: 1967) – Greek text and Italian commentary.

P.J. Rhodes and R. Osborne, *Greek Historical Inscriptions, 404–323 BC* (Oxford: 2003), nos. 76, 83–101 – Greek text, English translation and commentary.

M.N. Tod, *Greek Historical Inscriptions* 2 (Oxford: 1948), nos. 183–203 – Greek text and English commentary.

Collected fragments of the contemporary sources

F. Jacoby, *Die Fragmente der griechischen Historiker* (*FGrH*) IIB, nos. 117–153 (Berlin: 1927), Greek texts, with a German commentary on them in IID (Berlin: 1927), pp. 403–542, and IIIB nos. 742–742 (Berlin: 1930).

Ian Worthington (editor-in-chief), *Brill's New Jacoby* (*BNJ*) (Leiden: 2004–), will include all of the fragmentary writers in *FGrH* I–IIII with English translations and new, critical commentaries on them.

All of the fragmentary sources are translated in C.A. Robinson, *The History of Alexander the Great* 1 (Providence: 1953), pp. 30–276; see also Volume 2 for events dealt with by ancient writers and as found in the extant historians.

See also: L. Pearson, *The Lost Histories of Alexander the Great* (New York: 1960).

Principal later writers

Diodorus Siculus, *The Library of History* Book 17; Arrian, *Campaigns of Alexander*; Quintus Curtius Rufus, *The History of Alexander the Great of Macedonia*; Plutarch, *Life of Alexander* (see too the lives of Demosthenes and Phocion); Plutarch, *On the Fortune or the Virtue of Alexander*; Justin, *Epitome of the Philippic History of Pompeius Trogus*; Strabo, *Geographica* Books 15–17.

The above are translated in the Loeb Classical Library, with the exception of Justin, for which see J.C. Yardley and W. Heckel, *Justin. Epitome of the Philippic History of Pompeius Trogus 1, Books 11–12: Alexander the Great* (Oxford: 1997). Arrian, Curtius and Plutarch's *Lives* are also translated in the Penguin Classics series. See also J.E. Atkinson and J.C. Yardley, *Curtius Rufus, Histories of Alexander the Great, Book 10* (Oxford 2009).

Other sources

The Greek Alexander Romance, translated by R. Stoneman, Penguin Classics (Harmondsworth: 1991).

Legends of Alexander the Great, translated by R. Stoneman, Everyman Library (London: 1994).

W. Heckel and J. Yardley, *Alexander the Great. Historical Sources in Translation* (Malden: 2003), for translated extracts of various ancient sources with comments.

J. Roisman, *Alexander the Great: Ancient and Modern Perspectives* (Lexington: 1995), for translated extracts of the source material, together with some modern views (abridged) on aspects of Alexander's reign.

Modern source studies

E. Baynham, *The Unique History of Quintus Curtius Rufus* (Ann Arbor: 1998).

A.B. Bosworth, *From Arrian to Alexander* (Oxford: 1988).

A. Cohen, *The Alexander Mosaic: Stories of Victory and Defeat* (Cambridge: 1997).

K. Dahmen, *The Legend of Alexander the Great on Greek and Roman Coins* (London: 2007).

T. Duff, *Plutarch's Lives. Exploring Vice and Virtue* (Oxford: 1999).

N.G.L. Hammond, *Three Historians of Alexander the Great* (Cambridge: 1983), for Diodorus, Curtius and Justin.

——, *Sources for Alexander the Great* (Cambridge: 1993), for Arrian and Plutarch's *Alexander*.

A.J. Heisserer, *Alexander the Great and the Greeks* (Norman: 1980).

K. Sacks, *Diodorus Siculus and the First Century* (Princeton: 1990).

D. Spencer, *The Roman Alexander: Reading a Cultural Myth* (Exeter: 2002).

P. Stadter, *Arrian of Nicomedia* (Chapel Hill: 1980).

R. Stoneman, *Alexander the Great: A Life in Legend* (New Haven and London: 2008).

J.C. Yardley, *Justin and Trogus. A Study of the Language of Justin's Epitome of Trogus* (Toronto: 2003).

For commentaries on some ancient sources, see A.B. Bosworth, *A Historical Commentary on Arrian's History of Alexander* 1 (Oxford: 1980), covering Books 1–3, and 2 (Oxford: 1995), covering Books 4–5.29, J.E. Atkinson, *A Commentary on Q. Curtius Rufus' Historiae Alexandri Magni* (Amsterdam: 1980), covering Books 3–4, and *ibid.* (Amsterdam: 1994), covering Books 5–7.2, and J.R. Hamilton, *A Commetary on Plutarch's Life of Alexander* (Oxford: 1969).

Some modern biographies and works on Alexander in English

A.B. Bosworth, *Conquest and Empire, the Reign of Alexander the Great* (Cambridge: 1988).

——, 'Alexander the Great', Chapters 16 and 17 in the *Cambridge Ancient History* 6[2] (Cambridge: 1994), pp. 791–875

——, *Alexander and the East* (Oxford: 1996).

P. Briant, *From Cyrus to Alexander*, trans. P.T. Daniels (Winona Lake: 2002).

——, *Alexander the Great and his Empire*, trans. A. Kuhrt (Princeton: 2010).

P. Cartledge, *Alexander the Great* (London: 2003).

D. Engels, *Alexander the Great and the Logistics of the Macedonian Army* (Berkeley and Los Angeles: 1978).

P.M. Fraser, *Cities of Alexander the Great* (Oxford: 1996).

Major General J.F.C. Fuller, *The Generalship of Alexander the Great* (repr. New Brunswick: 1960).

J.D. Grainger, *Alexander the Great Failure: The Collapse of the Macedonian Empire* (London: 2007).

P. Green, *Alexander of Macedon* (Harmondsworth: 1974).

J.R. Hamilton, *Alexander the Great* (London: 1973).

N.G.L. Hammond, *Alexander the Great*: *King, Commander and Statesman*[2] (Bristol: 1989).

——, *The Genius of Alexander the Great* (London: 1997).

W. Heckel, *The Marshals of Alexander's Empire* (London: 1992).

——, *Who's Who in the Age of Alexander the Great* (Oxford: 2006).

F.L. Holt, *Alexander the Great and Bactria* (Leiden: 1985).

——, *Alexander the Great and the Mystery of the Elephant Medallions* (Berkeley and Los Angeles: 2003).

R. Lane Fox, *Alexander the Great* (London: 1973).

——, *The Search for Alexander* (Boston and Toronto: 1980).

R.D. Milns, *Alexander the Great* (London: 1968).

C. Mossé, *Alexander: Destiny and Myth*, trans. J. Lloyd (Baltimore: 2004).

J.M. O'Brien, *Alexander the Great*: *The Invisible Enemy* (London: 1992).

N.V. Sekunda and J. Warry, *Alexander the Great: His Armies and Campaigns, 334–323 BC* (London: 1998).

R. Stoneman, *Alexander the Great* (Lancaster: 1997).

——, *Alexander the Great: A Life in Legend* (New Haven and London: 2008).

W.W. Tarn, *Alexander the Great*, 2 vols (Cambridge: 1948).

C.G. Thomas, *Alexander the Great in His World* (Malden: 2006).

U. Wilcken, *Alexander the Great*, translated by G.C. Richards (New York: 1967).

M. Wood, *In the Footsteps of Alexander: A Journey from Greece to Asia* (Berkeley and Los Angeles: 1997).

Ian Worthington, *Alexander the Great: Man and God*, rev. ed. (London 2004).

Articles in collections dealing with different aspects of Alexander, his influences and the period

W.L. Adams and and E.N. Borza (eds), *Philip II, Alexander the Great, and the Macedonian Heritage* (Lanham: 1982).

A.B. Bosworth and E.J. Baynham (eds), *Alexander the Great in Fact and Fiction* (Oxford: 2000).

E. Carney and D. Ogden (eds), *Philip II and Alexander the Great: Lives and Afterlives* (Oxford: 2010).

G.T. Griffith (ed.), *Alexander the Great: The Main Problems* (Cambridge: 1966).

W. Heckel and L.A. Tritle (eds), *Crossroads of History. The Age of Alexander* (Claremont: 2003).

——, L. Tritle and P. Wheatley (eds), *Alexander's Empire: Formulation to Decay* (Claremont: 2007).

—— and L. Tritle (eds), *Alexander the Great: A New History* (Oxford: 2009).

J.M. Muir and E.R.A. Sewter (eds), *Alexander the Great, Greece and Rome*[2] 12 (1965).

J. Roisman (ed.), *A Companion to Alexander the Great* (Leiden: 2003).

—— and Ian Worthington (eds), *The Blackwell Companion to Ancient Macedonia* (Oxford: 2010).

L. Tritle (ed.), *The Greek World in the Fourth Century* (London: 1997).

P. Wheatley and R. Hannah (eds), *Alexander and His Successors* (Claremont: 2009).

Ian Worthington (ed.), *Ventures into Greek History. Essays in Honour of N.G.L. Hammond* (Oxford: 1994).

Macedonia before Alexander and the reign of Philip II

E.N. Borza, *In the Shadow of Olympus. The Emergence of Macedon* (Princeton: 1990).

——, *Before Alexander: Constructing Early Macedonia* (Claremont: 1999).

E. Carney, *Women and Monarchy in Macedonia* (Norman: 2000).

G.L. Cawkwell, *Philip of Macedon* (London: 1978).

J.R. Ellis, *Philip II and Macedonian Imperialism* (London: 1976).

R.M. Errington, *A History of Macedonia*, trans. C. Errington (Berkeley and Los Angeles: 1990).

N.G.L. Hammond, *The Macedonian State: Origins, Institutions, and History* (Oxford: 1989).

——, *Philip of Macedon* (London: 1994).

—— and G.T. Griffith, *A History of Macedonia*, vol. 2 (Oxford 1979).

R. Sealey, *Demosthenes and His Time: A Study in Defeat* (Oxford: 1993).

Ian Worthington, *Philip II of Macedonia* (New Haven and London: 2008).

See also the edited works cited above by Adams and Borza, Carney and Ogden, Roisman, Tritle, Roisman and Worthington, and Worthington.

ALEXANDER'S LIFE AND REIGN
The main events

356   Birth of Alexander, son of Philip II and Olympias of Epirus (July)

342   Commences studying under Aristotle at Mieza

340   Regent of Macedonia while Philip in Thrace (sieges of Perinthus and Byzantium); defeats Maedians on the Upper Strymon river (in Thrace); founds Alexandropoulos

338   Commands the Macedonian left flank at the Battle of Chaeronea; overcomes the Theban Sacred Band; leads diplomatic mission to Athens (August)

337   Philip's seventh marriage (to Cleopatra) causes rift with Alexander; Alexander and Olympias leave Pella for a time

336   Assassination of Philip II at Aegae (summer); Alexander succeeds to the throne of Macedonia as Alexander III; ends a revolt of the Greeks

335   Campaigns successfully in the north against the Triballi and in the Danube (spring); campaigns against the Illyrians (summer); revolt of Thebes, razed to the ground on Alexander's orders (late summer–autumn)

334   Crosses the Hellespont to invade Persia (spring); throws a spear into soil before disembarking to show Asia is his spear-won territory; Battle of the Granicus River (May); campaigns in Asia Minor; sieges of Miletus and Halicarnassus (late summer)

333   'Unties' the Gordian knot at Gordium (spring–summer); near-fatal illness at Tarsus; Battle of Issus; calls himself 'Lord of Asia' (November)

332   Sieges of Tyre (January–July) and Gaza (September?); marches into Egypt and becomes its pharaoh (November)

331   Founds Alexandria (officially on 7 April); visits the Oracle of Zeus Ammon in the Oasis of Siwah (Libyan desert); Agis III of Sparta's war against Macedonia (autumn); Battle of Gaugamela (1 October); takes Babylon, Susa and Persepolis

330   Burns Persepolis (May); death of Darius III (July); arrives in Zadracarta and begins wearing Persian dress; Bessus declares himself Great King; orders executions of Philotas and Parmenion (September); arrives at the Hindu Kush (winter)

329   Crosses the Hindu Kush; crosses Oxus river (spring); captures and orders execution of Bessus (summer); arrives at Maracanda (Samarkand), revolts of Bactria and Sogdiana

328   Intense guerrilla fighting in Sogdiana; capture of Rock of Arimazes (winter–spring); murders Cleitus at Maracanda after a drunken argument (November)

327   End of the Bactrian campaign; captures the Sogdian Rock and Rock of Chorienes (spring); marries Roxane (daughter of Oxyartes of Bactria); attempts to

ALEXANDER IN QUOTES

The stories that have been spread far and wide with a view to glorifying Alexander are not accepted by all; and their fabricators were men who cared for flattery rather than truth.

(Strabo 11.5.5)

Of the three philosophers remaining, the one who was asked how someone might become a god from being a man said: 'By doing what is impossible for a man to do.'

(Plut. *Alexander* 64.9)

Demades urged [the Athenians] to pay no heed to the report [of Alexander's death], since, had it been true, the whole world would long ago have been filled with the smell of the body.

(Plut. *Phocion* 22.3)

Tranio: Alexander the Great and Agathocles, so I've heard say, were the two foremost champion wonder-workers of the world. Why shouldn't I be a third; aren't I a famous and wonderful worker?

(Plautus, *The Ghost Story* 775–778)

The storie of Alisaundre is so commune
That every wight that hath discrecioun
Hath herd somwhat or al of his fortune

(Chaucer, *The Monk's Tale* 2361–2363)

Alexander has often been worshipped, by biographers ancient and modern, for virtues he lacked. He deserves greater credit for those he possessed.

(E. Badian, 'The Administration of the Empire',
Greece and Rome[2] 12 (1965), p. 182)

The king's name and image were invoked as his conquests were renounced and dismembered. The debate over legitimacy lasted a mere generation. After that Alexander was a symbol and nothing else. For subsequent ages he typified the world conqueror, and his territorial acquisitions were a standing inspiration and challenge to successive dynasts.

(A.B. Bosworth, *Conquest and Empire*, p. 181)

Alexander was in most things a Macedonian through and through ... and primarily a man of war whose genius is seen most clearly on the field of battle.

(N.G.L. Hammond, *Alexander the Great*, p. v)

Determined to astound contemporaries and awe future generations with his unique *arete*, Alexander exploited mankind and god with relentless perseverance. In the process, his hybris offended a deity capable of revealing and expiating mortal deficiencies with artful brutality. Dionysus chose wine as the vehicle through which he would unveil and magnify the defects of a brilliant man who was spiritually blind.

(J.M. O'Brien, *Alexander the Great: The Invisible Enemy*, pp. 229–230)

Alexander was fortunate in his death. His fame could hardly have increased; but it might perhaps have been diminished. For he died with the real task yet before him. He had made war as few have made it; it remained to be seen if he could make peace.

(W.W. Tarn, *Alexander the Great* 1, p. 121)

... when evaluating Alexander it is essential to view the 'package' of king as a whole; i.e., as king, commander and statesman. All too often this is not the case. There is no question that Alexander was spectacularly successful in the military field, and had Alexander only been a general his epithet may well have been deserved. But he was not just a general; he was a king too, and hence military exploits form only a percentage of what Alexander did, or did not do – in other words, we must look at the 'package' of him as king as a whole.

(Ian Worthington, 'How "Great" was Alexander?',
Ancient History Bulletin 13 (1999), p. 39)

SPECIAL NOTES AND ABBREVIATIONS

It should be emphasised that the literary sources in all chapters are fragments from works and are not connected texts; they have survived because later writers quote or paraphrase them. At the end of each fragment, the name of the contemporary writer is given, followed by the later writer.

The modern scholars' works in each of the chapters are printed as they were published, hence they will have differences in punctuation and spelling (English and American), as well as style of referencing. An individual list of references follows selections in which an author has used an abbreviated title of a modern work that is not immediately obvious or a referencing system that does not supply full details of the work cited.

The lists of additional readings at the end of the chapters does not include the books cited on pp. xi–xiv, otherwise almost all of them would appear in every list. However, I have at times included essays from the edited books given above when they are especially relevant to the topic of the chapter.

All dates are BC unless otherwise indicated.

The abbreviations below are used in my own notes to the introductions and translated sources as well as by most scholars whose works are reprinted; some use different abbreviations for ancient authors, but these are easily recognisable.

Ancient sources

Aes.	Aeschines
Arr.	Arrian, *Campaigns of Alexander*
Athen.	Athenaeus
Curt.	Quintus Curtius Rufus
Dem.	Demosthenes
Din.	Dinarchus
Diod.	Diodorus
Hyp.	Hyperides
Plut.	Plutarch
Plut. *Alex.*	Plutarch, *Life of Alexander*
[Plut.] *Mor.*	Pseudo-Plutarch, *Moralia*

Modern works

BNJ	Ian Worthington (editor-in-chief), *Brill's New Jacoby* (Leiden: 2004–)
FGrH	F. Jacoby, *Die Fragmente der grieschischen Historiker* (Berlin: 1927–)
R–O	P.J. Rhodes and R. Osborne, *Greek Historical Inscriptions, 404–323 BC* (Oxford: 2003)
Tod	M.N. Tod, *Greek Historical Inscriptions* 2 (Oxford: 1948)

LIST OF MAPS

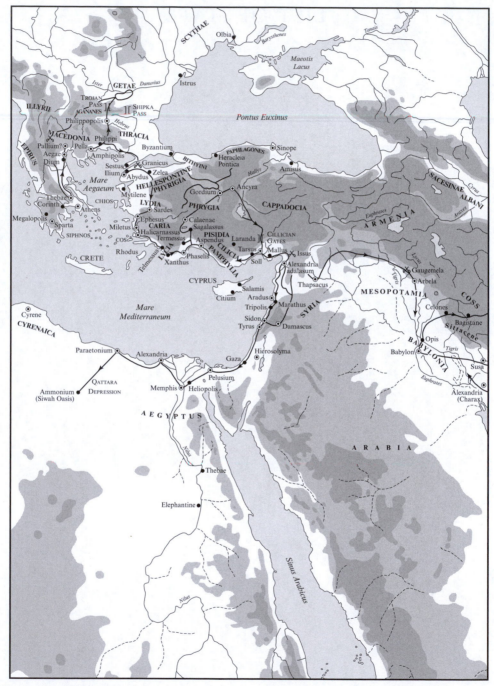

Map 1. Alexander's empire

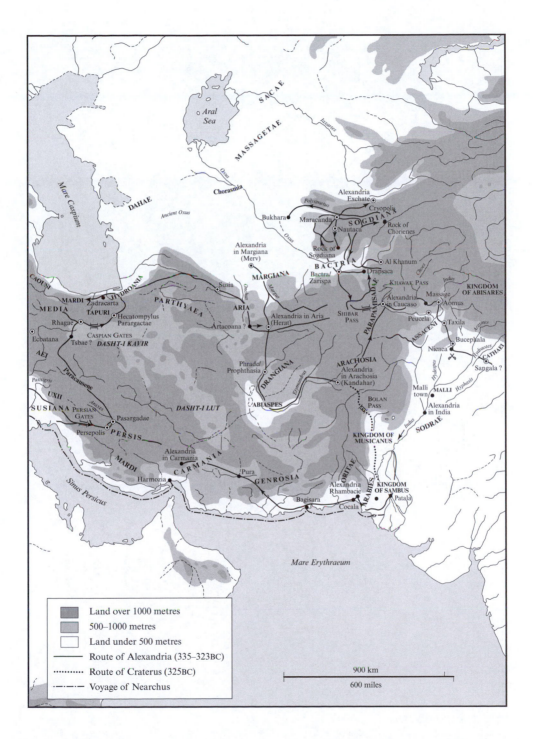

Aral
Sea

SACAE

MASSAGETAE

Mare Caspian

DAHAE

Chorasmia

Ancient Oxus

Alexandria
Exchate

Cryopolis

Polytimetus

Bukhara   Maracanda   Rock of
Nautaca   Chorienes

SOGDIANA

Alexandria
in Margiana
(Merv)

Rock of
Sogdiana

Al Khanum

BACTRIA

Bactra/
Zarispa

Drapsaca

KHAWAK PASS

KINGDOM
OF ABISARES

Susia

Oxus

MARGIANA

Massage

CAOUSI   Ochus   Marpius   Aornus

MARDI   Zadracarta   PARTHYAEA   ARIA   Alexandria
in Caucaso   Peucela

HYDROANIA

MEDIA   TAPURI   Hecatompylus   Artacoana ?   Alexandria in Aria   SHIBAR   Taxila

Rhague   Parargactae   (Herat)   PASS   Bucephala

Ecbatana   CASPIAN GATES   ASSACENI   Nicaea

AEI   Tsbae ?   *DASHT-I KAVIR*   Hydraotes   CATHAEI

Pasitigris   Parizeuscene   Phrade/   ARACHOSIA   Sangala ?

Prophthasia   Alexandria   Malli   Hyphasis

UXII   Arexes   DRANGIANA   in Arachosia   town   MALLI

SUSIANA   PERSIAN   *DASHT-I LUT*   (Kandahar)   Alexandria

Arexes   GATES   in India

Pasargadae   ABIASPES   BOLAN   SODRAE

Persepolis   PERSIS   PASS

MARDI   Alexandria   KINGDOM OF
in Carmania   MUSICANUS

CARMANIA   Pura

Sinus Persicus   Harmozia   GENROSIA   ORITAE   KINGDOM
OF SAMBUS

Alexandria   ARBES

Rhambacie   Patala

Bagisara   Cocala

Mare Erythraeum

Legend:

- Land over 1000 metres
- 500–1000 metres
- Land under 500 metres
- —— Route of Alexandria (335–323BC)
- ·········· Route of Craterus (325BC)
- —·—·— Voyage of Nearchus

900 km

600 miles

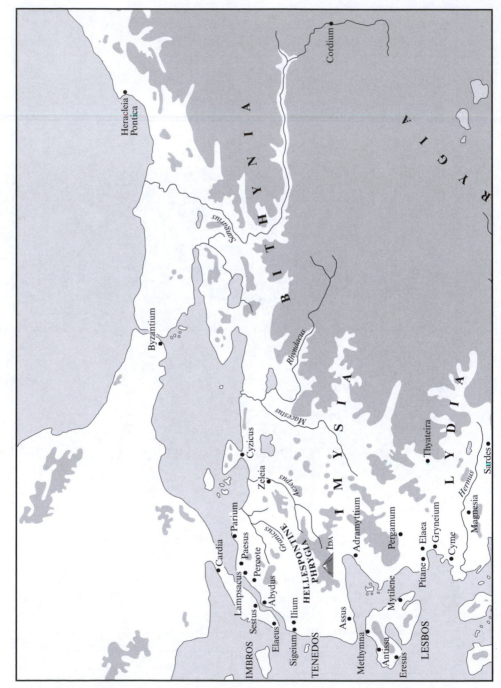

Map 2. Western Asia Minor

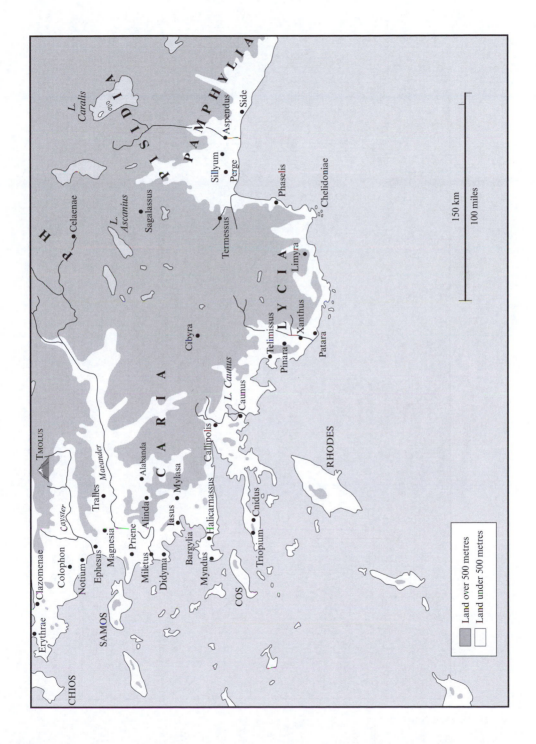

CHIOS

Erythrae

Clazomenae

Colophon

Notium

SAMOS

Ephesus

Magnesia

TMOLUS

Cayster

Tralles

Maeander

Priene

Miletus

Alinda

Didyma

Iasus

Bargylia

Myndus

Mylasa

Halicarnassus

Callipolis

Alabanda

C A R I A

Cibyra

Triopium

Cnidus

Caunus

L. Caunus

COS

RHODES

Telmissus

Pinara

Xanthus

Patara

L Y C I A

Limyra

Chelidoniae

Phaselis

Termessus

Sagalassus

L. Ascanius

Celaenae

L. Caralis

P H R

P I S I D I A

P A M P H Y L I A

Sillyum

Perge

Aspendus

Side

150 km

100 miles

Land over 500 metres

Land under 500 metres

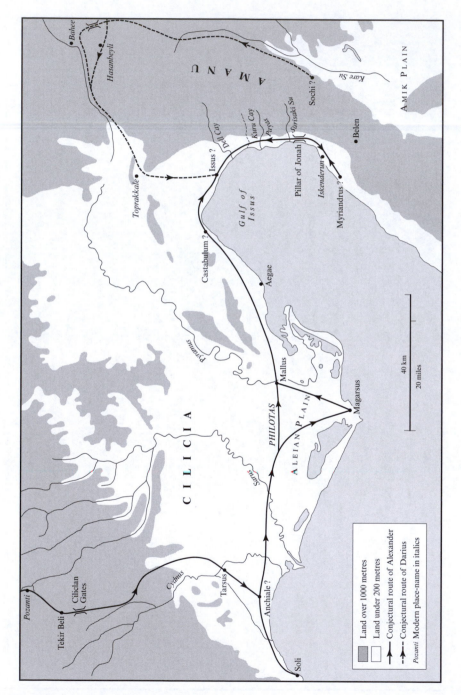

Map 3. Cilicia and Northern Syria

Map 4. Assyria and Babylonia

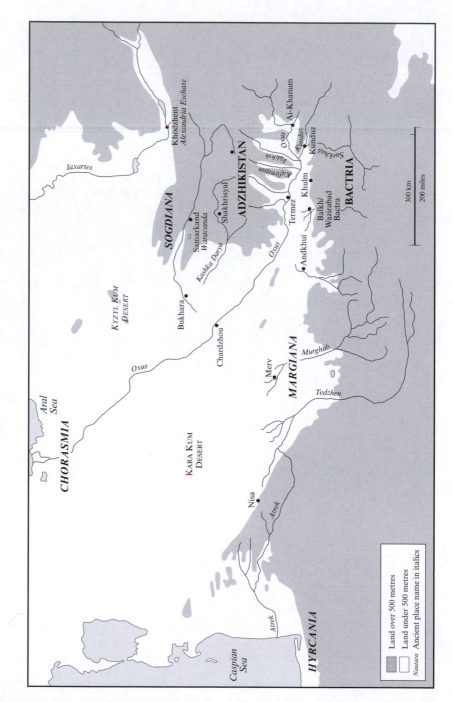

Map 5. Chorasmia, Margiana, Sogdiana and Bactria

1

THE SOURCES

Introduction

Different authors have given different accounts of Alexander's exploits, and there is no one about whom more have written, or more at variance with each other.

(Arr. *Preface* 2)

The stories that have been spread far and wide with a view to glorifying Alexander are not accepted by all; and their fabricators were men who cared for flattery rather than truth.

(Strabo 11.5.5)

The study of Alexander is challenging and frustrating because of the nature of the source material. 'In short, one turns the barrel of a kaleidoscope one way and the glittering pieces form a particular, attractive pattern. But turn the barrel again and they fall another way. So it is with Alexander sources ... the individual will always tune into the harmony of voices that he or she finds plausible and pleasing.'[1] Never a truer word was spoken, for the surviving contemporary literary evidence, all of which is fragmentary, affects the presentation of Alexander by those earlier writers as well as by modern ones.

There is also the added complication that our narrative of Alexander's reign is drawn from western writers, who have given us (as is to be expected) the heroic, legendary, and ever-successful Alexander 'the Great'. However, non-western accounts are fewer and (equally to be expected) present a very different Alexander. Both types of source material need to taken into account when evaluating Alexander's exploits, especially in Asia.

As far as western sources are concerned, we have only a small number of inscriptions,[2] numismatic evidence, and occasional comments in some of the later Greek orators[3] that are contemporaneous. Although much was written about Alexander during his life (356–323) and in the generation or two after his death, these contemporary works have not survived in their entirety to the present day.[4] What remains of them are to be found quoted or paraphrased by much later authors in their own histories of Alexander (see below). Of those contemporary writers, we have the most number of fragments from works by Aristobulus of Cassandria (*FGrH* 139), Callisthenes of Olynthus (*FGrH* 124), Chares of Mytilene (*FGrH* 125), Cleitarchus of Alexandria (*FGrH* 137), Nearchus of Crete (*FGrH* 133 – now *BNJ* 133), Onesicritus of Astypalaea (*FGrH* 134 – now *BNJ* 134), and Alexander's general Ptolemy, son of Lagus (*FGrH* 138). All these earlier writers raise problems: did each one deal with the reign in full, or did some concentrate on only aspects of it or just on the person of the king? We cannot answer these types of questions properly, but just because what we have quoted of, say, Baeton's work (*FGrH* 119) does not mean that he was only concerned with geographical and social matters.

We also have information on aspects of Alexander's kingship in other writers, of which the most important are Strabo (first century BC) and Athenaeus (second/early third century AD). These writers also furnish valuable information on such things as the topography, culture, wealth, fauna, natural resources, and the peoples of the areas through which Alexander marched.[5] Three other sources may also be mentioned. First, the *Ephemerides* (*FGrH* 117), supposedly a daily journal kept throughout the reign, but apart from a fragment about Alexander's hunting practices what survives today tells of Alexander's excessive drinking habits and the manner of his death (Arr. 7.25.1–26.3, Plut. *Alex.* 76–77.1; see, further, Chapter 8). Second, *On the Fortune or Virtue of Alexander*, a treatise attributed to Plutarch which depicted Alexander as a warrior king and philosophical idealist. Third, the *Alexander Romance*, a mostly fictitious account of Alexander's reign which began its life in the third or second century BC and was reworked and expanded for many centuries to come (in the mediaeval period, for example, it was translated into every language, and each culture developed and imposed its own version of Alexander on it).

It is not until several centuries after the king's death that we get a connected narrative of the reign by Diodorus Siculus (first century BC), Quintus Curtius Rufus (first century AD), Arrian (second century AD), and Justin (third century AD), who epitomized Pompeius Trogus' history of the world (first century AD). To these may be added Plutarch's biography of Alexander, and to a lesser extent his biographies of Demosthenes and Phocion (second century AD). Our knowledge of what the earlier, contemporary writers said is derived from these later writers. Whether they had access to the early works in their entirety is unknown, but presumably they had more to read than we do. For example, Nearchus' account of his voyage around India was used extensively by Arrian and Strabo, Ptolemy's essentially unromantic and military account of Alexander's reign lay at the heart of Arrian's account, and Cleitarchus was the principal source for Diodorus, Curtius, and Plutarch. Athenaeus quoted many earlier accounts, though he is less interested in facts and more in anecdotes (not a surprise since his work was set at a banquet at which guests discussed various intellectual and artistic matters).

As already stated, the early accounts need to be viewed with caution, not just because we do not have them in their entirety. Additionally, for example, as the official court historian Callisthenes was biased towards Alexander, and Ptolemy and Aristobulus exaggerated their own roles and achievements when on campaign with Alexander (cf. Sources 8 and 10), in the process embellishing those of Alexander – for their own as well as his sake (cf. Source 1). Moreover, the early writers are often in dispute with each other; for example over the numbers of Alexander's invasion force in 334 (cf. Sources 19 and 20), matters of geography (cf. Sources 36–37, 60–61) matters affecting conspiracies (cf. Sources 108–110), and the death of Callisthenes (cf. Sources 111–113). Caution needs also to be exercised towards the *Ephemerides*, *On the Fortune or Virtue of Alexander*, and the *Alexander Romance*. Although Arrian and Plutarch cited the *Ephemerides* for Alexander's last days, their authenticity is disputed – although the reports of Alexander's excessive drinking appear in many writers' accounts and are not likely to be inaccurate. *On the Fortune or the Virtue of Alexander* is essentially a rhetorical exercise, much influenced by the background, especially philosophical, in which it was written. Finally, the *Alexander Romance* is riddled with exploits attributed to Alexander that are unhistorical.

Some of these may be dismissed without hesitation, such as Alexander's encounter with the tribe of headless men, but others not so – did Alexander meet the Amazons and have sex with their queen, Thalestria, for example? The contemporary writers are divided on this event (see Source 3).

The shortcomings of the early accounts clearly affect the later ones. We can only presume that the latter had access to the full contemporary accounts, whereas we do not, but if so, then how accurately did the later authors interpret the earlier material? How and why did they decide that one account was to be preferred over another (cf. the quotations from Arrian and Strabo at the start of this chapter)? On what was their selectivity of earlier works based? To what extent did they impose their own social, political, and moral backgrounds on their subject matter? How the sources are interpreted has affected many generations of modern scholars, whose images of Alexander range from the philosophical idealist to a cynical and pragmatic king.

Then there are the non-western sources, which also add to our knowledge of Alexander but which are also of questionable historical reliability – Alexander in the *Talmud*, for example, not to mention Islamic and mediaeval Christian authors. It is not a surprise that ancient Persian writers detested Alexander for burning their sacred books, and hence give a very hostile view of him (Alexander the Accursed). There are also contemporary documents commonly called the Babylonian astronomical diaries (written in cuneiform). These record monthly astronomical observations and phenomena, as well as events in Babylonia, and so are of help in determining the chronology of Alexander's moves in Asia. Thus in many respects these types of Middle Eastern accounts, and indeed the later traditions of the *Alexander Romance* (especially the Iranian and Arabic) are a negative 'balance' to our western literary tradition.

At the end of the day, perhaps only one safe conclusion can be advanced, despite its defeatist tone: we will never truly get to the historical Alexander.

Ancient sources

Manipulation of geography

1   Many false notions were also added to the account of this sea (the Hyrcanian) because of Alexander's love of glory; for, since it was agreed by all that the Tanais separated Asia from Europe, and that the region between the sea and the Tanais, being a considerable part of Asia, had not fallen under the power of the Macedonians, it was resolved to manipulate the account of Alexander's expedition so that in fame at least he might be credited with having conquered those parts of Asia too. They therefore united Lake Maeotis, which receives the Tanais, with the Caspian Sea, calling this too a lake and asserting that both were connected with one another by an underground passage and that each was a part of the other. Polycleitus goes on to adduce proofs in connection with his belief that the sea is a lake (for instance, he says that it produces serpents, and that its water is sweetish); and that it is no other than Maeotis he judges from the fact that the Tanais empties into it. From the same Indian mountains, where the Ochus and the Oxus and several other rivers rise, flows also the Iaxartes, which, like those rivers, empties into the Caspian Sea and is the most northerly of them all. This river, accordingly, they named Tanais; and in addition to so naming it they gave as proof that it was the Tanais mentioned by Polycleitus that the country on the far side of this river produces

the fir tree and that the Scythians in that region use arrows made of fir wood; and they say that this is also evidence that the country on the far side belongs to Europe and not to Asia, for, they add, Upper and Eastern Asia does not produce the fir tree. But Eratosthenes says that the fir tree grows also in India … (Polycleitus, *FGrH* 128 F 7 = Strabo 11.7.4).

2   Ctesias … says that India is equal to the rest of Asia, but he talks nonsense; and so does Onesicritus, saying that it is the third part of all the earth (Onesicritus, *FGrH* 134 – now *BNJ* 134 – F 6 = Arrian, *Indica* 3.6, Strabo 15.1.12).

The Amazon queen

3   Here the queen of the Amazons came to see him as most writers say, among whom are Cleitarchus (*FGrH* 137 FF 15–16), Polycleitus (*FGrH* 128 F 8), Onesicritus, Antigenes (*FGrH* 141 F 1), and Ister; but Aristobulus (*FGrH* 139 F 21), Chares the royal usher (*FGrH* 125 F 12), Ptolemy (*FGrH* 138 F 21), Anticleides (*FGrH* 140 F 12), Philo the Theban, and Philip of Theangela, besides Hecataeus of Eretria, Philip the Chalcidian, and Duris of Samos, say that this is a fiction. And it would seem that Alexander's testimony is in favour of their statement. For in a letter to Antipater which gives all the details minutely he says that the Scythian king offered him his daughter in marriage, but he makes no mention of the Amazon (Onesicritus, *FGrH* 134 – now *BNJ* 134 – F 1 = Plut. *Alex.* 46.1–3).

Alexander and alcohol

4   There was a report about Alexander … that he did not drink much, but spent much time over his drink conversing with his friends. Philinus, however, has shown from the Royal Ephemerides that such persons talk nonsense, since it is continually and very often written there that 'he slept through the day from drinking' and sometimes 'the next day too' (*Ephemerides, FGrH* 117 F 2c = [Plut.] Mor. 623e).

Journey to Siwah

5   Ptolemy, son of Lagus, says that two serpents went in front of the army, uttering a voice, and Alexander ordered the guides to follow them, trusting in the divine portent. He says too that they showed the way to the oracle and back again. But Aristobulus (*FGrH* 139 F 14), whose account is generally admitted as correct, says that two ravens … (Ptolemy, *FGrH* 138 F 8 = Arr. 3.3.5).

Varia *from Alexander's reign*

6   To provision these forces,[6] Aristobulus (*FGrH* 139 F 4) says he had not more than seventy talents; Duris (*FGrH* 70 F 40) speaks of maintenance for only thirty days; and Onesicritus says he owed two hundred talents as well (Onesicritus, *FGrH* 134 – now *BNJ* 134 – F 2 = Plut. *Alex.* 15.2, [Plut.] *Mor.* 327d).

7   Aristobulus says that Callisthenes was carried about with the army bound with fetters, and afterwards died a natural death; but Ptolemy, son of Lagus, says that he was stretched upon the rack and then hanged. Thus not even did these authors, whose narratives are very trustworthy, and who at the time were in intimate association with Alexander, give accounts consistent with each other of events so well known, and the circumstances of which could not have escaped their notice (Ptolemy, *FGrH* 138 F 17 = Arr. 4.14.3).

8   The whole of the naval force was under the command of Nearchus; but the pilot of Alexander's ship was Onesicritus, who, in the narrative which he composed of Alexander's campaigns, falsely asserted that he was admiral, while in reality he was only a pilot (Onesicritus, *FGrH* 134 – now *BNJ* 134 – F 27 = Arr. 6.2.3).

9   How Alexander constructed his bridge over the river Indus is explained neither by Aristobulus nor Ptolemy (*FGrH* 138 F 19), authors whom I usually follow (Aristobulus, *FGrH* 139 F 34 = Arr. 5.7.1).

10   Cleitarchus, as well as Timagenes, represents Ptolemy, who was subsequently a sovereign,[7] to have been present at this assault (at a town of the Sudracae);[8] but Ptolemy, truly no detractor from his own glory, relates that he was absent (*FGrH* 138 F 26), detached on an expedition (Cleitarchus, *FGrH* 137 F 24 = Curt. 9.5.21).

11   Moreover, in regard to those who covered Alexander with their shields in his peril,[9] all agree that Peucestas did so; but they no longer agree in regard to Leonnatus or Abreas, the soldier in receipt of double pay for his distinguished services. Some say that Alexander, having received a blow on the head with a piece of wood, fell down in a fit of dizziness; and that having risen again he was wounded with a dart through the corselet in his chest. But Ptolemy, son of Lagus, says that he received only this wound in the chest. However, in my opinion, the greatest error made by those who have written the history of Alexander is the following. There are some who have recorded that Ptolemy, son of Lagus, in company with Peucestas, mounted the ladder with Alexander, that Ptolemy held his shield over him when he lay wounded, and that he was called Soter on that account. And yet Ptolemy himself has recorded that he was not even present at this engagement, but was fighting battles against other barbarians at the head of another army. Let me mention these facts as a digression from the main narrative, so that the correct account of such great deeds and calamities may not be a matter of indifference to men of the future (Ptolemy, *FGrH* 138 F 26a = Arr. 6.11.7–8).

12   [No Romans have recorded a Roman embassy to Alexander] nor of those who have written an account of Alexander's actions, has either Ptolemy, son of Lagus (*FGrH* 138 F 29), or Aristobulus. With these authors I am generally inclined to agree (Aristobulus, *FGrH* 139 F 53 = Arr. 7.15.6).[10]

Modern works

In the following selection, A.B. Bosworth, Emeritus Professor of Classics at the University of Western Australia, discusses some of the problems associated with the nature of the ancient sources.

A.B. Bosworth, *From Arrian to Alexander* (Oxford University Press: 1988), Chap. I, 'Introduction: Some Basic Principles', pp. 1–15.[11]

Additional reading

J.E. Atkinson, 'Originality and Its Limits in the Alexander Sources of the Early Empire', in A.B. Bosworth and E. Baynham (eds), *Alexander the Great in Fact and Fiction* (Oxford: 2000), pp. 307–326.

E. Baynham, 'Who Put the Alexander in the *Alexander Romance*? The *Alexander Romance* Within Alexander Historiography', *Ancient History Bulletin* 9 (1995), pp. 1–13.

——, 'The Ancient Evidence for Alexander the Great', in J. Roisman (ed.), *Brill's Companion to Alexander the Great* (Leiden: 2003), pp. 3–29.

E.N. Borza, 'An Introduction to Alexander Studies', in U. Wilcken, *Alexander the Great*, transl. G.C. Richards (New York: 1967), pp. ix–xxviii.

A.B. Bosworth, 'The Death of Alexander the Great: Rumour and Propaganda', *Classical Quarterly*[2] 21 (1971), pp. 112–136 (reprinted in Chapter 8).

——, *Alexander and the East* (Oxford: 1996), chapters 1 and 2.

P.A. Brunt, 'Persian Accounts of Alexander's Campaigns', *Classical Quarterly*[2] 12 (1962), pp. 141–155.

——, *Arrian, History of Alexander*, Loeb Classical Library 1 (Cambridge, Mass. and London: 1976), pp. xviii–xxxiv.

——, 'On Historical Fragments and Epitomes', *Classical Quarterly*[2] 30 (1980), pp. 477–494.

E.D. Carney, 'Artifice and Alexander History', in A.B. Bosworth and E. Baynham (eds), *Alexander the Great in Fact and Fiction* (Oxford 2000), pp. 263–285.

A. Chugg, 'The Journal of Alexander the Great', *Ancient History Bulletin* 19 (2005), pp. 155–175.

A.M. Devine, 'Alexander's Propaganda Machine: Callisthenes as the Ultimate Source for Arrian, *Anabasis* 1–3', in Ian Worthington (ed.), *Ventures Into Greek History. Essays in Honour of N.G.L. Hammond* (Oxford: 1994), pp. 89–102.

R.M. Errington, 'Bias in Ptolemy's History of Alexander', *Classical Quarterly*[2] 19 (1969), pp. 233–242.

J.R. Hamilton, 'Cleitarchus and Diodorus 17', in K. Kinzl (ed.), *Greece and the Ancient Mediterranean in History and Prehistory. Studies Presented to F. Schachermeyr on his Eightieth Birthday* (Berlin 1977), pp. 126–146.

——, *A Commetary on Plutarch's Life of Alexander* (Oxford: 1969), pp. lix–lxx.

N.G.L. Hammond, 'The Royal Journal of Alexander', *Historia* 37 (1988), pp. 129–150.

——, 'Aspects of Alexander's Journal and Ring in his Last Days', *AJPh* 110 (1989), pp. 155–160.

J.M. Mossman, 'Tragedy and Epic in Plutarch's *Alexander*', *Journal of Hellenic Studies* 108 (1988), pp. 83–93.

Powell, J.E. 'The Sources of Plutarch's Alexander', *Journal of Hellenic Studies* 59 (1939), pp. 229–240.

H.P. Ray and D.T. Potts (eds), *Memory as History. The Legacy of Alexander in Asia* (New Delhi: 2007).

J. Roisman, 'Ptolemy and his Rivals in his History of Alexander', *Classical Quarterly*[2] 34 (1984), pp. 373–385.

A.J. Sachs and H. Hunger, *Astronomical Diaries and Related Texts from Babylonia* 1 (Vienna: 1988).

K. Sacks, 'Diodorus and his Sources: Conformity and Creativity', in S. Hornblower (ed.), Greek Historiography (Oxford: 1994), pp. 213–232.

S. Shabaz, 'Iranian Interpretations of Alexander', *American Journal of Ancient History*[2] 2 (1977), pp. 5–38.

R.J. van der Spek, 'Darius III, Alexander the Great and Babylonian Scholarship', *Achaemenid History* 13 (2003), pp. 289–346.

R. Stoneman, 'The Alexander Romance: From History to Fiction', in J.R. Morgan and R. Stoneman (eds), *Greek Fiction. The Greek Novel in Context* (London: 1994), pp. 117–129.

D. Spencer, 'You Should Never Meet Your Heroes: Growing Up with Alexander, the Valerius Maximus Way', in E.D. Carney and D. Ogden (eds), *Philip II and Alexander the Great: Lives and Afterlives* (Oxford: 2010), pp. 175–191.

Notes

1 E. Baynham, 'The Ancient Evidence for Alexander the Great', in J. Roisman (ed.), *Brill's Companion to Alexander the Great* (Leiden: 2003), p. 29.

2 See Sources 26–30, a selection of more important inscriptions that involve Alexander.

3 For example, Dem. 18.270 (wide-ranging power of Philip and Alexander), Aes. 3.133 (fate of Thebes in 335 and of Spartan hostages after Agis III's war of 331–330 being sent to Alexander), 3.160–164 (Alexander's first few years as king and that Demosthenes hoped that he would be defeated at the Battle of Issus in 333), 3.165 and Din. 1.34 (mistakenly have it that Alexander was in India during Agis III's war).

4 For information on where these works (and translations of them) can be found, see pp. x–xi.

5 See Chapters 6 and 7.

6 For the invasion of Persia in 334.

7 He founded the Ptolemaic dynasty in Egypt, and ruled at Alexandria as Ptolemy I from 323 to 283 (from 285 jointly with his son, Ptolemy II).

8 During the siege of Malli in India; see Sources 11, 70 and 71.

9 At the siege of Malli, when an enemy arrow punctured Alexander's lung: see Sources 70 and 71.

10 On the Roman embassy to Alexander at Babylon, see, however, Source 115.

11 Reprinted by permission of Oxford University Press.

INTRODUCTION:
SOME BASIC PRINCIPLES

A.B. Bosworth

The period of Alexander the Great is at first sight well attested.[1] There is an apparent abundance of narrative material: full-length histories of the reign by Arrian and Curtius Rufus, a formal biography by Plutarch, a whole book of Diodorus Siculus' *Bibliotheca*, two books of Justin's epitome of Pompeius Trogus, and substantial passages in the latter books of Strabo's *Geography*. This wealth of documentation is misleading, for all the primary sources are late. The earliest of our extant authorities, Diodorus, composed his work in the third quarter of the first century BC. Strabo wrote in the late Augustan period, Curtius at a still undefined date in the early Empire,[2] Plutarch and Arrian in the second century AD, and Trogus' work, composed under Augustus, is known through the third-century epitome of Justin. There is, then, a hiatus of close to three centuries between the death of Alexander in June 323 and the first connected narrative of the reign. The problem of transmission therefore becomes acute. What sources did our extant authorities use and how faithfully did they report the substance of what they read? Both questions are clearly important. A careless and perfunctory epitome by a secondary author can be as rich a source of historical error as conscious mendacity and distortion in a contemporary historian. On the other hand a derivative history based on reliable authorities, carefully selected and meticulously reported, may be more trustworthy than any single first-generation source.

The main thrust of modern scholarship has been to attempt to isolate the contemporary or near-contemporary historians of Alexander and to reconstruct as far as possible the outline and characteristics of each work. This approach has had major and permanent results. Its most tangible product is the two hundred pages of fragments of lost Alexander historians which Felix Jacoby compiled in his monumental *Fragmente der griechischen Historiker*.[3] We have a fair knowledge of the names and the general sequence of the primary historians and a sample, largely random, of the content of their work. Contemporary history began in the king's lifetime, with Anaximenes' work *On Alexander*[4] and, more importantly, the *Deeds of Alexander* by Callisthenes of Olynthus, who lived at court from the beginning of the campaign in Asia until his dramatic death in 327 and gave a first-hand narrative of events down to 330 at least.[5] Callisthenes' work was the only history known to be exactly contemporaneous with the events, but after the king's death there was a great efflorescence of memoirs by senior and not-so-senior members of his staff. Onesicritus and Nearchus wrote early in the period of the Successors, and at some indeterminate date before his own death (in 283 BC) came the work of Ptolemy.[6] Some time after the battle of Ipsus (301) the ageing Aristobulus of Cassandreia composed his history of the reign, and during the first generation after Alexander (so it is now generally agreed[7]) Cleitarchus of Alexandria wrote what was probably the most widely read of the early histories of the reign. There was also less formal material: pamphlets of differing political persuasions, such as the treatises on the deaths of Alexander and Hephaestion by Ephippus of Olynthus, and works of a documentary or pseudo-documentary nature like the *stathmoi* of the Royal surveyors and the Royal *Ephemerides* which Eumenes allegedly compiled.[8] These sources, contemporary or near-contemporary, provided a rich field for the historian of antiquity, and it is tempting to trace their effect on the extant tradition, using the preserved fragments as a basis. The method is to examine the texts and testimonia and extrapolate characteristic attitudes and biases which can then be identified in the secondary tradition. It is an approach which can be fertile when one has some external evidence for the sources used,[9] as is the case with Arrian, but there are major drawbacks when the identification is merely speculative.

The principal and besetting problem is that the majority of Alexander's early historians are only known through brief citations, and it is rare that one can examine any single author *in extenso*. Nearchus is the chief exception to the rule. His account of his voyage from South India to Susa is the narrative base for the second half of Arrian's *Indike*, and we have a fair idea of the content of his work in outline and detail. For some passages, Strabo acts as a control source and provides an independent record of the original.[10] As a result portions of Nearchus' work are well attested and capable of analysis. The same is true, to a more limited degree, of Aristobulus,[11] but there is no extended extract which can compare with Arrian's digest of Nearchus. Most often the lost histories are known from a scattering of citations, usually short, indirect, and uncharacteristic. The vast majority of the verbatim quotations come from the *Deipnosophistae* of Athenaeus of Naucratis, but their value is largely impaired by the content, which, thanks to Athenaeus' avowed interests, is concentrated upon the pleasures of the flesh and the table and cannot be expected to give a representative sample of the authors cited. In some cases, such as the pamphlets of Ephippus and Nicobule, the rather lurid passages quoted by Athenaeus may indeed be characteristic of those productions, but it is hard to think that his excerpts from the works of Alexander's surveyors (a comment on the Tapurians' addiction to wine and descriptions of the natural produce of the East) are in any sense typical of their general tenor.[12] Other authors are no less selective in their citation, and usually they are not concerned to reproduce the wording of their original. In any case the sources are usually named because there is something suspect in what is recorded. Ancient writers tend to refer to their authorities by name primarily to criticize – to point out falsehood or to indicate information the veracity of which they are not prepared to guarantee. As a result the preserved citations naturally highlight the colourful and the erroneous. Material which was sober and informative would be exploited without comment.

Callisthenes of Olynthus makes an interesting case study. One would naturally expect him, as Alexander's first historian, to have been widely used and cited, but there are no more than a dozen identifiable references to his *Deeds of Alexander*. Those references are a scattered bunch. Observations on the mythology of Asia Minor, reported by Strabo, comprise the majority.[13] Otherwise there is a Homeric scholion citing his description of the Pamphylian Sea doing obeisance before Alexander (F 31), two vignettes from his account of Gaugamela, retailed by Plutarch (F 36–7), and finally the two major fragments. Both these fragments are critical. Polybius examines his description of the battle of Issus, concentrating on the figures he gives for both sides and proving their incompatibility with the terrain as described.[14] The passage is designed to prove Callisthenes' incompetence, and indeed Polybius does isolate real faults in his account – gross exaggeration of Persian numbers and a eulogistic bias towards Alexander and his Macedonians.[15] But on the other hand much of Polybius' criticism is demonstrably wrong-headed, vitiated by the false assumption that all Alexander's infantry was contained in his phalanx and by the equally false conviction that the phalanx at Issus was as clumsy and inflexible as the phalanx of his own day.[16] Polybius' attempt to convict

Callisthenes of ignorance and military incompetence largely fails, and most of the details he singles out have been taken as axioms for modern reconstructions of the battle-site.[17] We should be grateful for Polybius' minuteness of criticism, for all its petty-mindedness. Had he merely stigmatized the description as false without argument, his statement would have been unhesitatingly accepted, and had he quoted the Persian numbers out of context Callisthenes would surely have been dismissed as worthless. As it is, the detail given helps rectify the criticism and allows a broad, if sketchy, reconstruction of Callisthenes' narrative. In most cases we have a single detail, isolated from its context, and there is no way of telling whether or not it is characteristic of the author, or even correctly reported. The other major fragment concerns the journey to Siwah. Once again the context of the citation is critical. Strabo refers to Callisthenes' narrative as a classic example of historical flattery. The motif of adulation first occurs with the story of the two ravens acting as guides to the oasis, and Strabo states that it persists throughout the consultation of the oracle. There was an equally suspect sequel in the report of the formal delivery at Memphis of oracles from Branchidae and Erythrae.[18] Now Strabo is not pretending to give a full reproduction of Callisthenes' narrative. He is emphasizing details which he considered biased to flatter Alexander, and there is every indication that he was retailing standard criticisms. Plutarch also singled out the episode of the guidance by ravens,[19] and long before, early in the third century, Timaeus of Tauromenium had arraigned Callisthenes as an example of unphilosophical adulation for his concentration on ravens and frenzied women (i.e. the Sibyl of Erythrae).[20]

Callisthenes' account of the consultation of Ammon was clearly a well-known passage and regularly cited as an illustration of partial and interested writing. It fell within the wider context of his general picture of the king, which was widely denounced as flattery. Both Timaeus and Philodemus[21] stated that his historical work amounted to an apotheosis of Alexander, and several of the fragments illustrate the theme. Plutarch highlights his prayer to Zeus at Gaugamela.[22] The Homeric scholia depict the Pamphylian sea offering *proskynesis* to its new lord (F 31). Most importantly, Strabo's passage on the visit to Siwah is an extended essay on the subject, culminating in the priest's statement that Alexander was son of Zeus and appending the oracles from Asia Minor which also declared his divine sonship. This was a genuine and undeniably important feature of Callisthenes' work,[23] but it was only one feature. Polybius' critique of his description of Issus reveals that he gave quite detailed statements of numbers and movements which, coming from a contemporary and eyewitness, have every likelihood of being correct.[24] But this is not the material for which Callisthenes is quoted. Such facts were absorbed into the secondary historical tradition without acknowledgement, and the named citations concentrate upon the eulogistic and the bizarre.

As a result Callisthenes' work is totally lost for us. His style, like that of most of the prose writers of his day, was reprobated by later generations as inflated and clumsy, and he had no chance of survival as a literary model. But he certainly influenced the early tradition of Alexander history. The main lines of his description both of Issus and of the Siwah visit were repeated and developed by later writers. Even the exaggerations were echoed and embellished.[25] The same must have been true of his narrative as a whole, but the vast bulk of his work is irretrievable. One facet alone is preserved for us in a sharp and lurid light.

The problem is especially acute in the case of Cleitarchus. It is clear that he was a popular author in the Roman period, the only historian between Ephorus and Timagenes to be included in Quintilian's canon.[26] He is cited by a wide range of authorities, and he may have been the most generally read of all the Alexander historians. Unfortunately, the 36 fragments which Jacoby accepts as authentic deal exclusively with trivialities. The most extensive come from Aelian of Praeneste, who excerpted several of Cleitarchus' descriptions of the animal curiosities of India,[27] and Strabo (probably echoing the strictures or Eratosthenes) comments critically on the geographical errors in his description of Central Asia.[28] Indeed most of the citations are critical. Demetrius focuses on his stylistic impropriety (F 14), Curtius Rufus on exaggeration and invention (F 24–5), Cicero on rhetorical mendacity (F 34). The general impression conveyed by the fragments alone is therefore far from favourable. It suggests a taste for the tawdry and colourful, a predilection for sensationalism, a preoccupation for rhetoric which encouraged exaggeration and preferred imaginative fiction to sober truth.[29] Unfortunately we have no easy way of testing these criticisms. The handful of verbatim quotations that survive amounts to five lines in all and can scarcely be representative. There is no extensive appreciation of any part of his work, nothing comparable to Polybius' detailed critique of Callisthenes.

The general impression conveyed by the fragments may be correct, as far as it goes, but it is unlikely to be the whole story. If, for instance, our knowledge of Herodotus were limited to the citations in Athenaeus and Plutarch's essay *On the Malice of Herodotus,* we should have a much larger body of testimony than exists for Cleitarchus and it would give the same general impression, a sensational and trivial concentration on curiosities and a penchant for bias and historical deformation. The extant criticisms of Cleitarchus may be similarly misleading. It would certainly be erroneous to conclude that everything he wrote was sensational, biased, or fictional. What is needed is a more extensive sample of Cleitarchus' work than that provided by the named fragments.

That sample is probably provided by the so-called 'vulgate tradition'. One of the few established results of the source-criticism of the Alexander period has been the extrapolation of a common tradition at the root of several of the extant sources. It is undeniable that large segments of Diodorus and Curtius Rufus run parallel, retailing the same information and supplementing each other to a degree that is only explicable if both authors were ultimately working from the same source.[30] The same material is detectable in Justin's epitome of Trogus and in the *Metz Epitome* (a late compilation following roughly the same tradition as Curtius but extant only for the campaign between Hyrcania and South India). There is obviously a common tradition, and the term 'vulgate', despite a certain clumsiness, is a useful shorthand. It is sometimes misunderstood,[31] and for the reader's convenience I should state that when I refer to the 'vulgate tradition' I am referring to the body of material which is multiply attested (in Diodorus and Curtius and often in Justin and the *Metz Epitome*) and can reasonably be attributed to a common source. 'Vulgate sources' is perhaps a more questionable expression, but once again it can be useful shorthand to denote the sources which *on a given occasion* reflect the common tradition. There is no implication that these sources use the vulgate and nothing else. Plutarch, for instance, is eclectic.[32] He may follow the common tradition of Diodorus and Curtius but more often he uses material that is quite distinct. What is denoted as the vulgate may come from different sources at different times, but the nucleus is usually agreement in Diodorus and Curtius, corroborated, as the case may be, by one or more other sources. 'Vulgate' nicely encapsulates the idea of a shared tradition without begging the question of its authorship.

But there is a very strong probability that the vulgate tradition is based ultimately on Cleitarchus. The key passage is provided by Curtius (ix. 8. 15), who refers to Cleitarchus as his source for the number of Indians killed during Alexander's campaign in the kingdom of Sambus. The information is no variant. It is a figure taken out of the general narrative and comes in a context that is exactly paralleled in Diodorus.[33] We therefore have an instance of a common tradition with a direct attribution to Cleitarchus. That establishes a strong probability that the rest of the shared tradition goes back ultimately to the same source. The other alternative, that Diodorus and Curtius used two or more common sources independently, is far less plausible and founders on what is known of Diodorus' approach to historical composition. Where cross-comparison is possible, it is demonstrable that Diodorus followed a single source for chapters on end, transferring only when he came to the end of his subject-matter.[34] There are occasional inserts from other sources, but such inserts are largely digressions, short and limited in scope. Within each book Diodorus tends to change sources as he moves from area to area, particularly when he reverts to the history of his native Sicily, and he adds chronographic material from a separate date-table.[35] But Book xvii is unusually homogeneous. The narrative focus is exclusively on Alexander and there is no material on the history of the Greek west, nor is there any chronographic information.[36] It is overwhelmingly probable that his material derives from a single major source and that there is a single source for the tradition shared with Curtius.

Now Diodorus himself takes us back to Cleitarchus. In a digression in Book ii he gives Cleitarchus' figures for the dimensions of the walls of Babylon and presents them as a variant, contrasting with the description of his main source, Ctesias.[37] This information is paralleled in Curtius' description of Babylon, which otherwise corresponds to Diodorus' narrative in Book xvii.[38] It looks as though Diodorus extrapolated the material relating to the city walls and used it in his mythological exordium, to set off the information in Ctesias. There may well be a similar digression later. After describing the death of Themistocles, following his main source for Greek affairs in Book xi, Diodorus adds a variant from an unnamed source (ἔνιοι ... τῶν συγγραφέων).[39] That variant is the story of Themistocles drinking bull's blood, an episode which we know was rhetorically treated by Cleitarchus.[40] Once more, it looks as though Diodorus has drawn upon his general knowledge of Cleitarchus to embellish his earlier historical narrative.[41]

In that case it can hardly be doubted that Cleitarchus provided the narrative base for his account of Alexander, and that Cleitarchus is the ultimate source of the vulgate tradition. The attribution has, of course, been challenged, largely on the ground that several of the extant fragments of Cleitarchus are not found in any of the so-called vulgate sources. In fact the points of detail contained in the fragments are in general so trivial that their omission is only to be expected. The two most striking absences (the Roman embassy and the story of Ptolemy's presence at the Malli town) are more difficult to explain,[42] but given Diodorus' extreme selectiveness it is not too surprising that he passed over both incidents. On the other hand there is a reasonably strong correlation between many of the preserved fragments and the common tradition of Diodorus and Curtius; and it remains the strongest probability that the vulgate tradition in general and Diodorus' account in particular is derived ultimately from the single source, Cleitarchus.

In that case there is a large corpus of material which can be traced back to Cleitarchus, and in theory the broad characteristics of his work should be capable of reconstruction.

That is easier said than done. The material in the vulgate covers a wide spectrum, from wild and colourful zoological fantasy to sober and apparently well-informed campaign reports. A recent analysis has concluded that there is not a single common source for Diodorus and Curtius but two, a baroque and sensation-hungry author, hostile to Alexander and his Macedonians (Cleitarchus), and a better-informed, more impartial historian, not prone to sensationalism and fiction (Diyllus?).[43] It is perhaps more profitable to ask whether the same source cannot be both Jekyll and Hyde, capable both of objective reporting and emotional bathos (one need only reflect on the almost infinite variety of material in Herodotus).

A more pertinent question is the amount of distortion that has taken place in transmission. All the extant sources of the vulgate tradition are highly erratic and second-rate authors, and they may be assumed to have altered their material for the worse. Contraction is a serious problem. Cleitarchus' work was fairly voluminous. In Book xii he described the Indian ascetics and their disregard for death.[44] That presumably came in the context of Calanus' self-immolation in Persis late in 325. The period to Alexander's death, one assumes, would have required several more books. By contrast Diodorus covers the entire reign in a single book (admittedly of unusual length) and Justin is even more grossly abridged. Given such a drastic précis it is not surprising that some episodes in Diodorus are abbreviated to near gibberish, and the distortion in Justin is such that one often needs other texts to infer even what was in his immediate exemplar, Trogus.[45] There is also the problem of embellishment and exaggeration in the immediate source. That is a particular danger with Curtius Rufus, whose work is deeply infused with rhetoric.[46] His narrative is punctuated by a running commentary, with highly subjective attributions of motive, and there is no doubt that his source material is reworked, often a mere vehicle for descriptive rhetoric or moralizing comment. Even Diodorus is prone to impose his own personality. The style of his original is watered down and reduced to flat monotony. More seriously, he has an eye for the sensational and has favourite themes, usually banalities such as epic pictures of slaughter and fighting in relays.[47] That accounts for the unbalanced nature of such episodes as the battle of the Granicus. Diodorus' interest is attracted by the single combat between Alexander and the Persian commanders and he spends a disproportionate amount of his battle narrative expatiating upon it. The remaining details are scattered and drastically abbreviated, so as to obscure the strategy and defy any rational reconstruction of the engagement.[48] There is no control source, and we cannot assume that Diodorus' original was as unbalanced as his epitome of it.

Cleitarchus, then, is elusive. Is he also irretrievable? My feeling is that it *is* possible to reconstruct something of his work, but the exercise of doing so is particularly arduous. One must begin with an appreciation of the methods of the major extant sources. In the case of Diodorus this is not too difficult, for there is an abundance of material for comparison outside Book xvii. Curtius is far more difficult, for his work is confined to the Alexander period, the text is lacunose and often corrupt, and there are no extant sources to provide a direct check on his methods of excerpting. One can only rely on cross-comparison, where the material is attested in other contexts. That is the crux. The starting-point should be examination of extended passages which are reported by Diodorus and Curtius (preferably other sources as well).[49] Then one can build up a composite narrative and gain some idea of what is omitted or distorted in each individual writer. The more focuses that can be brought to bear on the vulgate, the more illumination of the common base will accrue. But the illumination will come from the continuous narrative of the extant works, not from the scattered and unrepresentative 'fragments' to which Cleitarchus' name is explicitly attached.

The importance of Arrian is now clear. His work is the most complete and the most sober account of Alexander's reign and at the same time it provides explicit information about the sources used. The seven-book *History of Alexander* was based on Ptolemy son of Lagus and Aristobulus son of Aristobulus. That is stated explicitly in the Preface and confirmed by the narrative which refers repeatedly to the authority of both men.[50] From Book vi the narrative range is expanded by the inclusion of Nearchus and there are explicit borrowings from the geographical work of Eratosthenes. The companion work, the *Indike*, dealing with the natural curiosities of India and the voyage of Alexander's fleet in the southern Ocean, is equally candid about its use of sources: the material comes from Eratosthenes, Megasthenes, and Nearchus.[51] In the case of Arrian we have the entire range of primary sources spelt out for us, and they are exciting and contemporary. Ptolemy, Nearchus, and Aristobulus were all eyewitnesses of the campaigns, and the first two at least were major actors in the great events they described. It is not surprising that the primary sources have occupied the centre stage of research. The text of Arrian is often read as though it were practically the same as Ptolemy, and Ptolemy/Arrian is a traditional shorthand used to characterize that part of Arrian's narrative that is commonly believed to be based on Ptolemy. Ernst Kornemann even subjected Arrian's text to a detailed stylistic analysis, extrapolating what he thought were distinctive thumb-prints of Ptolemaic phraseology.[52] The assumption, usually implicit, is that one may go direct from Arrian to his sources and that Arrian himself may be disregarded, a simple solider who paid his tribute to the memory of Alexander by selecting the best possible sources and reproducing them with patient fidelity.

The object of this exercise is wholly commendable. Arrian's sources *are* of fundamental importance, far more so for the modern historian than Arrian himself. In particular Ptolemy's picture of Alexander is of consuming interest, an account of the reign by one of its great architects and beneficiaries. But whatever results are obtained, they are necessarily distorted unless they are based on a careful study of Arrian as a writer. It is obvious from the most perfunctory reading of Arrian and the most superficial study of his career that he was a sophisticated and experienced writer, with the highest claims to stylistic excellence. To put it mildly, he is unlikely to have transcribed his sources without reshaping them and adding his own comments. The methodology outlined for approaching Cleitarchus will therefore hold good for Arrian's sources also. Arrian's pretensions as a historian need to be elucidated, in particular his aims in composing a history of Alexander. His modes of citing sources should also be studied and, where possible, his version should be contrasted with other writers' use of the same source material. Finally his own contribution should be delineated, the degree to which he comments on his material, whether parenthetically or in formal digressions and set speeches. That is the object of this book and explains its somewhat pretentious title. One cannot examine the history of Alexander without a study of the primary sources and the primary sources themselves are embedded in secondary and derivative works like those of Arrian.

Notes

1 For modern bibliography the two surveys by Jakob Seibert are indispensable: *Alexander der Grosse* (Erträge der Forschung 10; Darmstadt, 1972); *Das Zeitalter der Diadochen* (Erträge der Forschung 185; Darmstadt, 1983). Both volumes present an exhaustive survey of modern literature from the middle of the nineteenth century and obviate the need for extensive references to secondary works. I shall attempt to limit my annotations to what is most important or most recent.

2 The controversy about the date is unresolved and continuing. J. E Atkinson, *A Commentary on Q, Curtius Rufus' Historiae Alexandri Magni Books 3 and 4* (Amsterdam, 1980) 19–57, has presented the strongest case yet for the reign of Claudius (see further, Syme, *HSCP* 86 [1982] 197f.), and there are more arguments in support of the Claudian dating in H. Bodefeld's dissertation, *Untersuchungen zur Datierung der Alexandergeschichte des Q. Curtius Rufus* (Düsseldorf, 1982). The problem is far from settled (for some counter-arguments see *CP* 78 [1983] 151–4), but it is largely irrelevant to the study of Alexander. Most scholars would concede that Curtius was later than Diodorus and earlier than Plutarch or Arrian.

3 Jacoby, *FGrH* ii.B 618–828 (nos 117–53; commentary ii.D 403–542). A few additional fragments, mostly insignificant, are printed at *FGrH* iii.B 742–3 and in H. J. Mette, *Lustrum* 21 (1978) 18–20. For a sensible and readable appraisal of the principal fragments see L. Pearson, *The Lost Histories of Alexander the Great* [*LHA*]. There is also a recent compendium by P. Pédech, *Historiens campagnons d'Alexandre* (Paris, 1984), which deals extensively with Callisthenes, Onesicritus, Nearchus, Ptolemy, and Aristobulus.

4 *FGrH* 72 F 15–17, 29. The work is too scantily attested to support any conclusions on its nature or purpose.

5 *FGrH* 124. The last datable fragments (F 36–7) deal with Gaugamela, late in 331. See further Jacoby, *RE* x. 1674–1707 (still fundamental); Pearson, *LHA* 22–49 (cf. Badian, *Studies in Greek and Roman History* 251–2); Pédech (above, n. 3) 14–69.

6 The date is elusive. For a sceptical survey of arguments for both early (post 320) and late (*c.*285) dates see J. Roisman, *CQ* 34 (1984) 373–85.

7 Cf. Schachermeyr, *Alexander in Babyon* 211–24; Badian, *PACA* 8 (1965) 1–8.

8 Cf. *FGrH* 126 (Ephippus), 119–23 (surveyors [/ηματισται]), 117 (*Ephemerides*). On the latter see ch. 7 [in Bosworth, *Arrian to Alexander*].

9 The best example of the genre is probably Hermann Strasburger's early monograph, *Ptolemaios und Alexander* (Leipzig, 1934 = *Studien zur alten Geschichte* [Hildesheim, 1982] 83–147).

10 Arr. *Ind.* 18–42 = *FGrH* 133 F 1 (Jacoby interweaves seven extracts from Strabo).

11 See ch. 2. [in Bosworth, *Arrian to Alexander*].

12 Athen. x. 442B = Baeton, *FGrH* 119 F 1; ii. 67A, xi. 5ood = Amyntas, *FGrH* 122 F 4, 1. See also Brunt, *CQ* 30 (1980) 485–6 on the extant fragments of Chares of Mytilene (*FGrH* 125).

13 *FGrH* 124 F 28–30, 32–3, 38(?).

14 Polyb. xii. 17. 1–22. 7 = *FGrH* 124 F 35. There are detailed commentaries by P. Pédech, *Polybe xii* (Budé 1961), 104 ff. and Walbank, *HCP* ii. 364 ff.

15 On the exaggerated numbers (of cavalry and mercenaries) see Polyb. xii. 18. 2 ff., and for exaggeration of the difficulties of the terrain to enhance the Macedonian achievement see particularly 18. 11–12.

16 Cf. xii. 19. 1–4, 21. 2–10 (calculation of phalanx numbers); 20. 6–8, 22. 4 (criticism of phalanx movements).

17 xii. 17. 4–5. For the modem literature see Seibert, *Alexander der Grosse* 98–102; *HCArr.* i. 198 ff. For the adaptation and embellishment of Callisthenes in the later tradition see *Entretiens Hardt* 22 (1976) 25–32.

18 Strabo xvii. 1. 43 (814) = *FGrH* 124 F 14a. For some of the specific problems of the passage see Pearson, *LHA* 33–6 and my own observations in *Greece & the E. Mediterranean* 68–75.

19 Plut. *Al.* 27. 4 = *FGrH* 124 F 14b.

20 Polyb. xii. 12b. 2 = *FGrH* 566 F 155.

21 Philod. π. κόλακ. i².4 = *FGrH* 124 T 21.

22 Plut. *Al.* 33. 1 = *FGrH* 124 F 36. See further *Greece & the E. Mediterranean* 57–60.

23 For Callisthenes' view of his own importance (which was not unlike Arrian's own) see Arr. iv. 10.2. On his panegyric tendencies see Jacoby, *RE* x. 1701–4.

24   Polyb. xii. 19. 1–2, 5–6, 20. 1.

25   For details see *Entretiens Hardt* 22 (1976) 26 f.; *HCArr* i. 31, 212, 217, 272–3.

26   Quint. *Inst*. x. 1. 74 = *FGrH* 137 T 7. Cf. Jacoby, *RE* xi. 654: 'In Rom war er . . . im 1. Jhdt. v. Chr. die grosse Mode.'

27   *FGrH* 137 F 18–19, 21–2.

28   F 13, 16.

29   For thoroughgoing condemnation see Tarn, *Alexander* ii. 54–5; Hammond, *Three Historians*, esp. 25–7. Jacoby, *RE* xi. 645, was (typically) more measured and judicious.

30   A list of parallels, far from complete, was compiled by Eduard Schwartz (*RE* iv. 1873f.). For a survey of modern literature see Seibert, *Alexander der Grosse* 26–8 and J. R. Hamilton, *Greece & the E. Mediterranean* 126–46 (additional parallels 127 n. 7).

31   For criticisms of the use of the term see Hammond, *Three Historians*, esp. 2.

32   See the excellent appreciation by Hamilton, *Plut. Al*. xlix–lii. Hammond, *Three Historians* 170 n. 5. has taken me to task for inconsistency in references to Plutarch, including him sometimes in the vulgate, sometimes not. All the references which include him as a vulgate source are instances where he corroborates the shared tradition of Diodorus and Curtius. Where he stands apart from that shared tradition, he cannot be classed as part of the vulgate. The same is of course true of Curtius. He is to a great extent dependent on the common tradition, but he undeniably uses a multiplicity of other sources.

33   Diod. xvii. 102. 5–7. Diodorus gives 80,000 as the number of victims, whereas the manuscripts of Curtius vary between 800 and 800,000. Given the general concordance, it is usually assumed that the numerals in Curtius are (as so often) corrupt. The common source is not in doubt.

34   The most illuminating segment of narrative is Diod. iii. 12–48, where the source is Agatharchides of Cnidus (cf. iii. 11. 2). The same material is digested by Photius (*Bibl*. cod. 250), and there is impressive agreement both in economy and vocabulary. For parallel texts see Müller, *GGM* i. 123–93 and, for discussion, D. Woelk, *Agatharchides von Knidos: Über das Rote Meer* (diss. Bamberg, 1966); J. Hornblower, *Hieronymus of Cardia* 27–32. See further, Seibert, *Das Zeitalter der Diadochen* 30–2.

35   These passages are usefully listed by Schwartz, *RE* v. 666–9.

36   The same is true of Book xviii, which is largely (if not wholly) based on Hieronymus of Cardia. Sicilian history resumes emphatically at XIX. 1 with the tyranny of Agathocles (cf. xviii. 1. 6, 75.3); notes on Roman history continue from XIX. 10. 1, and the chronographic information emerges again in Book xx.

37   Diod. ii. 7.3 = *FGrH* 137 F 10.

38   Curt. v. 1. 10–45 (esp. 26); cf. Diod. xvii. 64. 3–6. Hammond (*Three Historians* 190 n. 25) mentions only the figure of 365 stades for the circuit of the walls, which he suggests might have been reported by sources other than Cleitarchus. He omits the rest of the correspondences which make the hypothesis of a common source compelling. See, however, Hamilton, in *Greece & the E. Mediterranean* 138–40.

39   Diod. xi. 58. 2–3.

40   Cic. *Brut*. 42–3 = *FGrH* 137 F 34.

41   This was suggested by Schwartz, *RE* v. 684 and accepted by Jacoby, *FGrH* ii.D 497.

42   See ch. 4 [in Bosworth, 1988].

43   Hammond, *Three Historians*, esp. 12–51. See now the critical observation of Badian, *EMC* n. s. 4 (1985) 461–3.

44   Diog. Laert. i. 6 = *FGrH* 137 F 6. The other book numbers are unhelpful. The sack of Thebes came (as we would expect) in Book i (F 1), the Sardanapalus saga (perhaps a digression based on Alexander's visit to Anchiale in 333) in Book iv (F 2), the Adonis cult at Byblus (332?) in Book v, and a dissertation on the upright tiara in Book x (F 5). The book number in F 4 is contracted and possibly corrupt. One can hardly reconstruct the outlines of Cleitarchus' history, but its volume is not in doubt.

45   For some examples see *HCArr*. i. 358 (on Justin xii. 4. 12); *Antichthon* 17 (1983) 42 (on Justin xiii. 4. 20).

46   Cf. Atkinson (above, n. 2) 67–73, with my comments in *CP* 78 (1983) 157–9. W. Rutz, *Hermes* 93 (1965) 370–82.

47 On this, see R. K. Sinclair, *CQ* 16 (1966) 249–55. For a general appreciation of Diodorus see Hornblower (above, n. 34) 22 ff.

48 The *aristeia* monopolizes the narrative from xvii. 20. 1 to 21. 3. The rest of the narrative is a series of commonplaces, the opening sentence (19.3) a celebrated historical crux. For a mordant critique of the tradition see Badian, in *Ancient Macedonia* ii. 272–4. See also Hammond, *JHS* 100 (1980) 73 f., *Three Historians* 16f.

49 The method has been well employed by Hamilton, in *Greece & the E. Mediterranean* 129–35, comparing Curtius ix with Diod. xvii. 89–104.

50 See the exposition in *HCArr.* i. 16–34 for details.

51 See ch. 2 [in Bosworth, 1988].

52 E. Kornemann, *Die Alexandergeschichte des Königs Ptolemaios I. ron Aegspien* (Leipzig, 1934). The method is here at its most extreme and was rightly criticized from the outset (see Strasburger's review in *Gnomon* 13 [1937] 483–92); but its basic assumptions are pervasive in modern scholarship.

References

Entretiens Hardt = E. Badian (ed.), *Alexandre le Grand, Image et Réalité*, Fondation Hardt, *Entretiens* 22 (Geneva: 1976).

Greece & the Eastern Mediterranean = K.H. Kinzl (ed.), *Greece and the Eastern Mediterranean in History and Prehistory: Studies Presented to Fritz Schachermeyr* (Berlin: 1977).

Hamilton, *Plut. Al.* = J.R. Hamilton, *Plutarch Alexander: A Commentary* (Oxford: 1969).

Hammond, *Three Historians* = N.G.L. Hammond, *Three Historians of Alexander the Great* (Cambridge: 1983).

HCArr. = A.B. Bosworth, *A Historical Commentary on Arrian's History of Alexander* (Oxford: 1980–).

Hornblower, J. *Hieronymus of Cardia*

RE = *Realencyclopädie der classischen Altertumswissenschaft*, ed. Pauly, Wisowa, Kroll (Stuttgart: 1893–).

Tarn, *Alexander* = W.W. Tarn, *Alexander the Great* I–II (Cambridge: 1948).

Walbank, *HCP* = F.W. Walbank, *A Historical Commentary on Polybius* I–III (Oxford: 1957–79).

2

ALEXANDER'S INFLUENCES AND THE MACEDONIAN BACKGROUND

Introduction

There was a distinction in the ancient Greek world between those who lived south of Mount Olympus and those who lived to its north, the Macedonians. The proper term for these people was 'Makedones', a name that is Greek in root and ethnic terminations, and may have meant 'highlanders'. However, the Greeks referred to them as 'barbarians' as late as the last quarter of the fourth century (Din. 1.24), which indicates that they did not see them as Greek speaking and hence not as Greek. Yet many of the Macedonian proper names and toponyms are Greek; the people had the same Greek pantheon of gods, we never hear of interpreters being needed when Greek embassies visited the Macedonian court and vice versa, and literary sources, spanning centuries, wrote of the Macedonians as Greek. Much has been written on the 'ethnicity' of the Macedonians, which is an issue that will never be properly solved. However, there is no question that the Greeks south of Mount Olympus considered themselves superior to the Macedonians politically (they thought a people ruled by a king were unintelligent and had no individuality) and socially (for example, they derided Macedonian customs such as polygamy and drinking wine unmixed). This attitude must have influenced all Macedonian kings in their dealings with the Greeks, but especially Philip and Alexander, who conquered and dominated them.

When Philip II was assassinated in 336 Alexander became king at the age of 20,[1] he inherited a Macedonian empire that already controlled Greece and was ready to invade Persia, the legacy of his father Philip II (359–336).[2] The Macedonian kingship was already powerful: the king had semi-divine power, performed certain state sacrifices, sat as final judge in any cases of appeal, and his person was protected at all times. He was one-half of the government of Macedonia, the other being the Assembly, composed of Macedonian citizens, which amongst other things met to acclaim a king and to judge cases of treason. While it was a powerful organ, in reality it was the king that had the final say in all matters, and he ruled as an autocrat (cf. Curt. 6.8.25). Before Philip there was disunity between Upper and Lower Macedonia, and the people living in the former owed no allegiance to the king in his capital at Pella, situated in Lower Macedonia. This lack of unity was a fundamental weakness to Macedonia's security, allowing numerous incursions from neighbouring peoples that could never be properly repulsed by the largely ill-equipped conscript army.

Philip would change all that. He developed Macedonia's mining, agriculture and trade, and changed it from a near-feudal tribal type of society into a wealthy, united and powerful state, with a centralized monarchy. For the first time in Macedonia's history he united Upper and Lower Macedonia after defeating the Illyrian tribes in the former early in his reign, and it was this success that led to his achievements in the areas just mentioned. Further, he created a powerful and superbly trained army, which was the best in the ancient world until the time of the Romans. His military reforms revolutionized not only the army but also the state, for the army's continued success and the subsequent expansion of Macedonian power created a feeling of national unity and nationalistic pride. Philip's achievements laid the foundations for Alexander's successes: without them, Alexander could not have achieved what he did.

Alexander was born in July 356 (Arr. 7.28.1, Plut. *Alex*. 3.5), the son of Philip's fourth wife Olympias, a princess from Epirus, situated to Macedonia's west. When Alexander was 14 in 342 his father hired Aristotle as his tutor (Plut. *Alex*. 7.2–3), who built on Alexander's literary accomplishments by probably introducing him to philosophy, rhetoric, zoology and geometry. Although he was not Philip's eldest son (his brother Arrhidaeus, son of Philip and his third wife Philinna of Larissa, was born a year before him), Alexander was intended to succeed Philip, and he was called upon to perform duties consistent with an heir apparent. In 340, at age 16, when his father was busy with the sieges of Perinthus and Byzantium, Alexander acted as regent (Plut. *Alex*. 9.1), and successfully led troops against the Maedians on the upper Strymon river. In 338 he played an important role in the battle of Chaeronea, where he commanded the left flank of the Macedonian cavalry that annihilated the crack 300-strong Theban Sacred Band (Plut. *Alex*. 9.2; cf. Diod. 16.86.3–4), and afterwards he led an important diplomatic mission to Athens.

Alexander was brought up to believe in the Homeric notion of personal success (*arete*) for the sake of honour (*time*) and glory (*kudos*); he was an avid reader of poetry, tragedy and historiography, and allegedly slept with a copy of the *Iliad* (and a knife) under his pillow (see Source 15). Throughout his life, Alexander emulated his two heroes Heracles and Achilles, both of whom were his ancestors,[3] and he also tried to outdo the exploits of Dionysus (cf. Source 69). However, his greatest role model was his father. He would have attended the symposia at which copious amounts of alcohol were drunk and stories of valour were related, which perhaps played a role in his later heavy drinking (Sources 85–90, 117–119). The person who had the most to boast about at such gatherings was Philip, and Alexander strove hard to match him. However, in his later teen years a rift developed between father and son. They never fully reconciled, and that rift may even have led to Alexander playing a role in a conspiracy that led to his father's assassination. As his reign progressed, Alexander strove to eclipse the exploits of Philip, a motive perhaps in his pretensions to personal divinity while alive.

Ancient sources

Birth

13 Be that as it may, Alexander was born early in the month Hecatombaeon, the Macedonian name for which is Lous, on the sixth day of the month, and on this day the temple of Ephesian Artemis was burnt. It was *apropos* of this that Hegesias the Magnesian made an utterance frigid enough to have extinguished that great conflagration. He said, namely, it was no wonder that the temple of Artemis was burnt down, since the goddess was busy bringing Alexander into the world. But all the Magi who were then at Ephesus,

looking upon the temple's disaster as a sign of further disaster, ran about beating their faces and crying aloud that woe and great calamity for Asia had that day been born. To Philip, however, who had just taken Potidaea, there came three messages at the same time: the first that Parmenion had conquered the Illyrians in a great battle, the second that his race-horse had won a victory at the Olympic Games, while a third announced the birth of Alexander. These things delighted him, of course, and the seers raised his spirits still higher by declaring that the son whose birth coincided with three victories would always be victorious (Hegesias, *FGrH* 142 F 3 = Plut. *Alex.* 3.5–9).

Interests and influence of Homer

14   Often, too, for diversion, he would hunt foxes or birds, as may be gathered from the *Ephemerides* (*FGrH* 117 F 1 = Plut. *Alex.* 23.4).

15   He (Alexander) was also by nature a lover of learning and a lover of reading. And since he thought and called the *Iliad* a viaticum of the military art, he took with him Aristotle's recension of the poem, called the *Iliad of the Casket*, and always kept it lying with his dagger under his pillow, as Onesicritus informs us; and when he could find no other books in the interior of Asia, he ordered Harpalus to send him some (Onesicritus, *FGrH* 134 – now *BNJ* 134 – F 38 = Plut. *Alex.* 8.2).

16   We read that Alexander the Great carried in his train numbers of epic poets and historians. And yet, standing before the tomb of Achilles at Sigeum,[4] he exclaimed, 'fortunate youth, to have found in Homer a herald of your valour!' (*Relating to the History of Alexander*, *FGrH* 153 T 1 = Cicero, *Pro. Archia poet.* 24).

Less interested in females as a youth?

17   But Alexander ... neither laid hands upon these women, nor did he know any other before marriage, except Barsine. This woman, Memnon's widow, was taken prisoner at Damascus (Aristobulus, *FGrH* 139 F 11 = Plut. *Alex.* 21.7–9).

Relations with Philip II

18   For this man (Harpalus) at first had been banished, while Philip was still king, because he was an adherent of Alexander;[5] as also was Ptolemy, son of Lagus, for the same reason; likewise Nearchus, son of Androtimus, Erigyius, son of Larichus, and his brother Laomedon. For Alexander fell under Philip's suspicion when the latter married Eurydice and treated Alexander's mother Olympias with dishonour. But after Philip's death those who had been banished on Alexander's account returned from exile and were received into favour. He made Ptolemy one of his confidential bodyguards ... Nearchus also was appointed viceroy of Lycia and of the land adjacent to it as far as Mount Taurus (Nearchus, *FGrH* 133 – now *BNJ* 133 – T 4 = Arr. 3.6.5–6).

Modern works

In the following selections, Ian Worthington, Professor of History at the University of Missouri, summarizes the evidence on the question of Macedonian ethnicity, arguing that the Macedonians were Greek. C.J. King, Assistant Professor of Classics at Sir Wilfred Grenfell College, discusses the nature of the kingship in Macedonia, and shows that the king was autocratic in all areas, with no limits on his authority. N. Sawada,

Associate Professor of History at Shizuoka University, discusses aspects of Macedonian society (necessarily limited to the elite because of the information we have), some of which set the people apart from Greeks.

1   Ian Worthington, *Philip II of Macedonia* (Yale University Press: 2008), Appendix 2, 'The Question of Macedonian Ethnicity', pp. 216–219.[6]
2   C.J. King, 'Macedonian Kingship and Other Political Institutions', in J. Roisman and Ian Worthington (eds), *A Companion to Ancient Macedonia* (Wiley-Blackwell: 2010), pp. 374–391.[7]
3   N. Sawada, 'Social Customs and Institutions', in J. Roisman and Ian Worthington (eds), *A Companion to* Ancient *Macedonia* (Wiley-Blackwell: 2010), pp. 392–408.[8]

Additional reading

E.M. Anson, 'The Meaning of the Term *Makedones*', *Ancient World* 10 (1984), pp. 67–68.
——, 'Philip II and the Transformation of Macedonia: A Reappraisal', in T. Howe and J. Reames (eds), *Macedonian Legacies: Studies in Ancient Macedonian History and Culture in Honor of Eugene N. Borza* (Claremont: 2008), pp. 17–30.
Sulochana R. Asirvatham, 'Perspectives on the Macedonians from Greece, Rome, and Beyond', in J. Roisman and Ian Worthington (eds), *A Companion to Ancient Macedonia* (Oxford: 2010), pp. 99–124.
E. Badian, 'Greeks and Macedonians', in B. Barr-Sharrar and E.N. Borza (eds), *Macedonia and Greece in Late Classical and Early Hellenistic Times* (Washington: 1982), pp. 33–51.
E.N. Borza, 'The Symposium at Alexander's Court', *Ancient Macedonia* 3 (Thessaloniki 1983), pp. 44–55.
——, 'Greeks and Macedonians in the Age of Alexander. The Source Traditions', in W. Wallace and E.M. Harris (eds), *Transitions to Empire. Essays in Honor of E. Badian* (Norman: 1996), pp. 122–139.
E.D. Carney, 'Hunting and the Macedonian Elite: Sharing the Rivalry of the Chase', in D. Ogden (ed.), *The Hellenistic World: New Perspectives* (Swansea: 2002) pp. 59–80.
——, 'Drinking and the Macedonian Elite: The Unmixed Life', *Syllecta Classica* 18 (2007), pp. 129–180.
——, 'The Role of the *Basilikoi Paides* at the Argead Court', in T. Howe and J. Reames (eds), *Macedonian Legacies: Studies in Ancient Macedonian History and Culture in Honor of Eugene N. Borza* (Claremont: 2008), pp. 145–164.
J.E. Engels, 'Macedonians and Greeks', in J. Roisman and Ian Worthington (eds), *A Companion to Ancient Macedonia* (Oxford: 2010), pp. 81–98.
E.A. Fredricksmeyer, 'Alexander and Philip: Emulation and Resentment', *Classical Journal* 85 (1990), pp. 300–315.
G.T. Griffith, 'The Macedonian Background', *Greece and Rome*[2] 12 (1965), pp. 125–139.
J. Hall, 'Contested Ethnicities: Perceptions of Macedonia within Evolving Definitions of Greek Identity', in I. Malkin (ed.), *Ancient Perceptions of Greek Ethnicity* (Cambridge: 2001), pp. 159–186.
J.R. Hamilton, 'Alexander's Early Life', *Greece and Rome*[2] 12 (1965), pp. 117–124.
J. Heskel, 'Macedonia and the North, 400–336', in L. Tritle (ed.), *The Greek World in the Fourth Century* (London: 1997), pp. 167–188.

F. Pownall, 'The Symposia of Philip II and Alexander III of Macedon: The View from Greece', in E.D. Carney and D. Ogden (eds), *Philip II and Alexander the Great: Lives and Afterlives* (Oxford: 2010), pp. 55–65.

M.B. Sakellariou, 'The Inhabitants', in M.B. Sakellariou (ed.), *Macedonia, 4000 Years of Greek History and Civilization* (Athens: 1983), pp. 48–63.

C.G. Thomas, 'The Physical Kingdom', in J. Roisman and Ian Worthington (eds), *A Companion to Ancient Macedonia* (Oxford: 2010), pp. 65–80.

R.A. Tomlinson, 'Ancient Macedonian Symposia', *Ancient Macedonia* 1 (Institute for Balkan Studies, Thessaloniki: 1970), pp. 308–315.

G. Weber, 'The Court of Alexander as Social System', in W. Heckel and L. Tritle (eds), *Alexander the Great: A New History* (Oxford: 2009), pp. 102–120.

Ian Worthington, 'Alexander, Philip, and the Macedonian Background', in J. Roisman (ed.), *A Companion to Alexander the Great* (Leiden: 2002), pp. 69–98.

M. Zahrnt, 'The Macedonian Background', in W. Heckel and L. Tritle (eds), *Alexander the Great: A New History* (Oxford: 2009), pp. 7–25.

Notes

1   Diod. 16.91.1–94.4, Arr. 1.1.1, Plut. *Alex.* 10.6.
2   The start of Philip's reign may be dated to 360 and not 359: M.B. Hatzopoulos, 'The Oleveni Inscription and the Dates of Philip II's Reign', in W.L. Adams and E.N. Borza (eds), *Philip II, Alexander the Great, and the Macedonian Heritage* (Lanham: 1982), pp. 21–42; see also Ian Worthington, *Philip II of Macedonia* (New Haven and London: 2008), pp. 20–22 on Philip's accession.
3   The Argead clan traced its ancestry back to Heracles via Temenus, a hero of Argos (Herodotus 5.20, 22, Thucydides 2.99.3, 5.80.2); Achilles and Andromache were ancestors of his mother, Olympias (cf. Plut. *Alex.* 2.1).
4   Alexander visited the tomb of Achilles at Troy when he first landed in Asia in 334.
5   The context is the aftermath of the Pixodarus affair in 337. Earlier that year, Philip married for the seventh time (his bride was Cleopatra) as the extract mentions.
6   Reprinted by permission of Yale University Press.
7   Reprinted by permission of Wiley-Blackwell.
8   Reprinted by permission of Wiley-Blackwell.

THE QUESTION OF MACEDONIAN ETHNICITY

Ian Worthington

There is no consensus on the issue of Macedonian ethnicity: whether the Macedonians were of Greek or mixed descent; for example, a Slavic people who later adopted Greek culture. This confusion is a consequence of the nature of the ancient source material[1] and the influence of modern politics, especially after 1991 when the 'new state' of the Republic of Macedonia was formed.[2] One theory is that the Macedonians were a Balkan people, hence members of a different ethnic group that only gradually became influenced by Greek culture through contact (cultural and otherwise) with the Greeks. However, this is flawed, for it fails to explain the Greek words (especially the names of towns) common to both Greek and Macedonian cultures well before the Greeks began to have dealings with their neighbours. Moreover, almost all of the literary sources and archaeological evidence, spanning several centuries, point to the Macedonians speaking Greek, hence (importantly) being Greek, as the following survey shows.

The epic poet Hesiod of Boeotia (eighth century) gives us the genealogy of the Macedonians' ancestors. He tells us that Deucalion had a son, Hellen, from whom the Greeks derived the name they used for themselves, 'Hellenes'. Hellen had three sons and a daughter, Thyia. The latter was impregnated by Zeus and gave birth to two sons, Macedon and Magnes. Macedon and his descendants lived in Pieria and around Mount Olympus (giving the name of Macedonia to the region), and Magnes and his descendants lived in Thessaly (to the south). Macedon and Magnes were thus nephews of Hellen's sons and grandsons of Hellen, and so part of the same family. Since Hellen's three sons were supposed to represent three dialect groups of Greece (Doric, Ionic and Aeolic) and Magnes settled in Thessaly, which was Greek-speaking, it follows that Macedon (and hence the Macedonians) must also have been Greek-speaking.

In the mid-fifth century, Herodotus, the 'father of history', who visited Macedonia, traced the ethnicity of the Macedonians to Perdiccas.[3] The latter was a member of the royal house of the Temenidae at Argos in the north-eastern Peloponnese; he came to Macedonia in the seventh century.[4] The house was descended from Temenus, whose ancestor was Heracles (son of Zeus), and who founded Argos in the twelfth century. Hence Perdiccas and his people would have spoken the Doric dialect of Greek. Thus was established the Temenid dynasty, taking its name from Temenus. Herodotus also tells us that Alexander I, who was the king at the time of the Persian Wars (of 480–479), took part in the Olympic Games, finishing equal first in the 200-yard (185 m) race.[5] (Herodotus may well have learned this information from Alexander himself since the two of them likely met.)[6] Now, only Greeks could compete at these games, and apparently Alexander was able to do so because he successfully argued that the ruling house of Macedonia came originally from Argos.

Other writers followed suit. Thucydides, writing in the later fifth century, and often critical of his predecessors, especially Herodotus, also accepts the arrival of the new dynasty led by Perdiccas from Argos. Under that king, the newcomers pushed back Illyrian influence in many areas of Macedonia and settled in places such as Pieria, Bottia the Axius valley and even Aegae. All together, goes on Thucydides, the places were called Macedonia.[7] The Athenian orator Isocrates, who repeatedly urged Philip to invade Asia, had no trouble in accepting that the king was a descendant of Argos: 'Argos, for one, is your ancestral home, and it is right that you have as much regard for it as you would for your own ancestors.'[8] And even later Strabo, writing around the time of Christ, said succinctly that 'Macedonia is Greece'.[9]

Of course, literature is not history. Hesiod's genealogy has been accused of indulging in make-believe, and mythical descendants are common among Greek nobility. Herodotus and Thucydides also have their shortcomings when it comes to factual accuracy, and the grounds for Alexander I's eligibility to compete in the Olympic Games are anchored only in a tradition that at some time a new dynasty of the Macedonian royal house came from Argos. Moreover, Alexander's name does not appear on the list of victors kept at Olympia. However, in 408 we know that Archelaus was victorious in the four-horse chariot race (*tethrippon*),[10] and Philip II's chariot teams won races there in 356, 352 and 348 (after the first triumph he issued commemorative coinage).[11] Moreover, in 346 Philip was elected President of the Pythian Games at Delphi, another Olympic festival, for which he minted a commemorative gold stater. Thus, even if we discount the opposing arguments, what is common to all accounts is the arrival of the new ruling dynasty from Argos in the Peloponnese and participation in the Olympic Games, both of which facts point to the 'Greekness' of the Macedonians.

In terms of language, the proper name for the Macedonians was 'Makedones', a Greek word meaning 'highlanders'.[12] The names of the months, the names of the people and (especially significant) the names of the towns were all Greek.[13] Thus, the first known king (in the mid-seventh century) was Perdiccas, a Greek word that may have something to do with justice (*peridikaios*). While we are told that the Greeks could not understand the Illyrians without an interpreter,[14] no source says that Athenian envoys to the Macedonian court needed them, and Aeschines indicates that Macedonian ambassadors spoke before the Athenians without interpreters: '[Demosthenes] called Antipater to the platform and put a question to him (having told him in advance what he would say and coached him in the reply he must give against the interests of the city).'[15]

Archaeological evidence, such as inscriptions in Greek, has been found at Dium (the main religious sanctuary), Vergina, Pella and Amphipolis, and Greek was used widely on Macedonian coins. Also, the style of Macedonian theatres was Greek (that at Dium has the only underground access tunnel between the centre of the *orchestra*, or performance area, and buildings at the rear). It would also have made little sense for the late fourth-century king Archelaus to invite Euripides and Socrates from Athens to his court if no one could understand them. Socrates declined the invitation, but Euripides wrote at least two plays at Pella and died there (he was buried at Arethousa). He was granted citizenship, for the Macedonians refused to hand over his corpse to the Athenians.

If the Greeks called non-Greek-speaking people 'barbarians', it is important to note that so also did the Macedonians. In 324 Alexander the Great was faced with a mutiny at Opis. He delivered a passionate speech to his men that included a eulogy of his father Philip. In it, Alexander says that Philip 'made you [the Macedonians] a match in battle for the barbarians on your borders'.[16] He is talking here of tribes such as the Illyrians and Paeonians, who had had a habit of expanding their territories and invading Macedonia before Philip put an end to the practice.[17] The content of the speech may be questioned, although its general context must be accepted, and it is hard to accept that Alexander's use of the word 'barbarian' is make-believe. Hence, if 'barbarian' refers to someone who does not speak Greek, the person using the word must by definition be Greek-speaking.

Religion also shows many commonalities. Macedonia was home to the twelve Olympian gods and the nine Olympian Muses, the daughters of Zeus and the goddess Memory (who gave birth to them not far from Olympus' peak), as well as to Dionysus and Orpheus, all deities found in Greece, Asia Minor, Crete and Thrace. The Thracian poet Orpheus, the god of poetry and music, gave his name to the Orphic religion (whose initiates believed in life after death). The Macedonians were said to have killed him and buried him at Dium, and the earliest Orphic hymn was found in a fourth-century tomb at Derveni (central Macedonia). Like Zeus and Heracles, Dionysus (god of fertility, vegetation and wine) enjoyed a special place in the Macedonian pantheon, and there was a cult to him. Towards the end of his reign, Alexander the Great came to identify himself more with Dionysus than with his heroes Heracles (an ancestor on his father's side) and Achilles (an ancestor on his mother's). During a procession through Carmania in 324, Alexander, who by then most likely believed in his own divinity, dressed as the god.[18]

The gods whom the Makedones worshipped were all members of the Greek pantheon. These included Zeus, Athena (as protectress of cattle), Heracles Patrous (Heracles the Father – that is, of the royal family), Artemis, Hermes, Poseidon, Pluto, Persephone and Apollo – it was not just for the political leverage in central Greece that Philip II involved himself in the Third Sacred War (355–346) when Phocis seized Delphi, home of the oracle of Apollo (see Chapter 6). At Aegae, for example, there was a cult of the Mother of the Gods and of Eucleia, and at Pella of Aphrodite and Cybele. One of the king's daily duties was to perform religious sacrifices to Heracles Patrous. He was the ancestor of the Temenids, for Temenus was one of the sons of Heracles, himself a son of Zeus and a mortal woman, who had been deified on death. The Temenids were replaced by the Argead dynasty (of which Philip and Alexander were members) in about 540, when Amyntas I became king. Thus, the Macedonian kings could trace their lineage back to Zeus, who was the Macedonians' principal god.

We have nothing today that was written in what might be called 'ancient Macedonian', and it is implausible that if these people did write in another language every example of it has been lost. Thus, the Macedonians probably did not have an entirely different language (as the Persians did, for example), but, just as their material culture had local or regional styles, they probably had a local dialect, most likely a version of Aeolic Greek.[19] We know, for example, that names beginning with Bil- and Bilist- are the Macedonian equivalent of the more widespread and common Greek Phil- and Philist-.[20] Also, in 330, for example, Philotas, the commander of Alexander's Companion Cavalry, was put on trial for treason and reprimanded by Alexander for not speaking Macedonian in his defence. Alexander also resorted to what is referred to as Macedonian to prompt a quick response from his guards during his drunken and fatal exchange with Cleitus at Maracanda in 328.[21] The existence of the dialect hardly comes as a surprise: there were different dialects south of Mount Olympus as well. However, Macedonia's separation from the Greeks by Mount Olympus and the numerous tribes living on its borders probably contributed to its development. Greeks presumably could not understand it and so called the people there 'barbarians' (non-Greek-speakers). Therefore, there is enough evidence and reasoned theory to indicate that the Macedonians were Greek.

Appendix 2: The question of Macedonian ethnicity

1   The ancient evidence is exhaustively collected and discussed by M.B. Sakellariou, 'The Inhabitants', in M.B. Sakellariou (ed.), *Macedonia, 4000 Years of Greek History and Civilization* (Athens: 1983), pp.48–63 and E.N. Borza, 'Greeks and Macedonians in the Age of Alexander: The Source Traditions', in R.W. Wallace and E.M. Harris (eds), *Transitions to Empire: Essays in Honor of E. Badian* (Norman, OK: 1996), pp. 122–39; cf. J. Vokotopoulou, 'Macedonia in the Literary Sources', in J. Vokotopoulou (ed.), *Greek Civilization: Macedonia, Kingdom of Alexander the Great* (Athens: 1993), pp. 71–3. For a succinct overview of the problem, see E.N. Borza, *Before Alexander: Constructing Early Macedonia* (Claremont, CA: 1999), pp. 27–43 and his *Shadow of Olympus*, pp. 77–97.

2   On this latter vexed issue, see, for example, L.M. Danforth, *The Macedonian Conflict* (Princeton, NJ: 1995); cf. his 'Alexander the Great and the Macedonian Conflict', in J. Roisman (ed.), *Brill's Companion to Alexander the Great* (Leiden: 2003), pp. 347–64; H. Poulton, *Who Are the Macedonians?* (Bloomington, IN: 2000).

3   Herodotus 1.56, 5.22.1, 8.43, 8.137–9.

4   See further N.G.L. Hammond, *A History of Macedonia* 1 (Oxford: 1972), pp. 432–34 and Borza, *Shadow of Olympus*, pp. 80–4 and 110–13.

5   Herodotus 5.22; cf. P. Roos, 'Alexander I in Olympia', *Eranos* 83 (1985), pp. 162–8. See the cautionary remarks of Borza, *Shadow of Olympus*, pp. 111–12; *contra* Hammond, *Macedonia* 2, pp. 4–5. See further R. Scaife, 'Alexander I in the Histories of Herodotus', *Hermes* 117 (1989), pp. 129–37, questioning Herodotus' portrayal of Alexander I, and hence his Greek descent; cf. E. Badian, 'Herodotus on Alexander I of Macedon; A Study in Some Subtle Silences', in S. Hornblower (ed.), *Greek Historiography* (Oxford: 1994), pp. 107–30.

6   Hammond, *Macedonia* 2, p. 98.

7   Thucydides 2.99.2–6; cf. 5.80.2 on the Argive connection.

8   Isocrates 5.32; cf. 6.17–18. The translation is that of T.L. Papillon, *Isocrates* 2 (Austin, TX: 2004), *ad loc.*

9   Strabo 7.8.

10 L. Moretti, *Olympionikai: i vincitori negli antichi agoni Olimpici* (Rome: 1957), pp. 110–11.

11 *Ibid.*, p. 124.

12 See further, on the word, E.M. Anson, 'The Meaning of the Term *Makedones*', *Anc. World* 10 (1984), pp. 67–8.

13 See further F. Papazoglou, *Les Villes de Macédoine à l'époque romaine* (Paris: 1988), Hammond, *Macedonia* 2, pp. 39–54; cf. Hammond, *Macedonian State*, pp. 12–15.

14 Polybius 28.8.9.

15 Aeschines 3.72.

16 A longer extract from this speech is given at the start of Chapter 1.

17 Cf. Hammond, *History of Macedonia* 1, pp. 420–3.

18 See D. Gilley, 'Alexander the Great and the Carmanian March of 324 BC', *AHB* (2007), pp. 9–14.

19 See especially Sakellariou, 'The Inhabitants', pp. 54–9.

20 See the discussion of B. Millis in his commentary on F1 of the anonymous author no. 311 in *Brill's New Jacoby* (Leiden: 2008).

21 Plutarch, *Alexander* 51.6. On these episodes, see A.B. Bosworth, *Conquest and Empire: The Reign of Alexander the Great* (Cambridge: 1988), pp. 101–3 (Philotas) and 114–15 (Cleitus), and Ian Worthington, *Alexander the Great, Man and God*, rev. and enl. edn (London: 2004), pp. 164–9 (Philotas) and 184–6 (Cleitus).

MACEDONIAN KINGSHIP AND OTHER POLITICAL INSTITUTIONS[1]

Carol J. King

Kingship is the earliest attested political structure in ancient Macedonia. Legend has it firmly established before recorded history and it continued to be the political heart of Macedonia until the Roman settlement in 167. This much is understood from sources such as political treatises, narrative histories, speeches, inscriptions, and other material remains. However, by no means does the evidence give a comprehensive picture of how kingship functioned in relation to other identifiable political bodies. Even Aristotle, who was in a position to know the inner workings, in his extant writings refers to the Macedonians and their kingship only in general terms. A dearth of sources for some periods and for others ambiguous accounts have led to much theorizing, with no consensus among scholars on the overall structure of the state. Close examination of the evidence, encumbered as it is by difficulties of interpretation, may leave as many questions as answers. Those questions, however, can and should be pointed and informed.

The nature of the evidence has shaped all scholarly debate. Evidence for the period before Philip II is scarce and non-Macedonian.[2] It consists chiefly of comments in Herodotus, Thucydides, Diodorus and Justin, and also a few inscriptions from Greek *poleis*. For the reign of Philip II there is considerable contemporary evidence but this too is non-Macedonian and largely hostile. The later *sine ira* universal history of Diodorus thus may be preferred over Demosthenes' contemporary vitriolic oratory.[3] Evidence for the reign of Alexander III ('the Great') is copious, but the five surviving narrative histories are all late; the earliest, Diodorus, was written 300 years after Alexander's death. However, Diodorus' account and those of Curtius, Plutarch, Arrian and Justin are largely based on lost accounts of Macedonians and others who campaigned with Alexander. Diodorus' narrative survives into the wars of the Successors. Then narrative sources peter out for nearly a century. For the later period of Macedonian independence we have the contemporary – though again non-Macedonian – narrative of Polybius, and where he fails Livy, alongside a larger body of epigraphic evidence from Macedonia as well as from Greek *poleis*. These sources suffice to confirm hereditary kingship and the existence of several other institutions, 'institution' herein qualified as being an established law, custom, or practice, which may or may not be part of a constitutional framework.

Along with the *basileus* (king), from the time of Philip II sources refer to the *basilikoi paides* (royal pages), the *somatophylakes* (bodyguards), the *hetairoi* (companions) or *philoi* (friends), to an assembly usually of the army, and especially in the Hellenistic period to several magistracies. Evidence is insufficient, however, to confirm the origins of the various institutions, their longevity, or their authority relative to the king. Moreover, mere mention of such bodies with supposed political functions does not prove that they were institutions with constitutional authority. On this point hinges an ongoing debate questioning the nature of kingship and also the degree of political participation of other bodies.

Admittedly one can only theorize about the functions or even existence of institutions apart from kingship before Philip II. Therefore, in order to reflect the limitations of our sources as well as those major changes brought about first by the grand expansion in the third quarter of the fourth century and subsequently by the fragmentation of the empire (cf. Livy 45.9), the present discussion observes three chronological divisions: (1) the period before Philip II, (2) the period of Philip II and Alexander III and (3) the period after Alexander III. But first, background for the ongoing scholarly debate must be outlined in brief.[4]

1 Constitution versus autocracy

Scholarly views on the structure of the Macedonian state fall generally into two schools of thought: the 'constitutionalist' position and that of monarchic 'autocracy'. The 'constitutionalist' position, first proposed by Granier in 1931 and subsequently revised by many scholars (see bibliographical essay), holds that the Macedonian state from before Philip II was run according to established traditions or laws that granted customary rights to groups within the state. Granier proposed an evolution from a Homeric society of many minor 'kings' of relatively equal authority, with a dominant nobility, to a sovereign military state in which an army of citizen soldiers supported the central king against a rival class of nobles.[5] The army had the right to choose the king (or regent) and to judge cases of treason. All 'constitutionalists' following Granier insist on the latter two 'rights'. The chief weakness of this position is that the bulk of evidence for the army choosing a new king and judging cases of treason comes from the reign of Alexander III. And that evidence is not conclusive that these were in fact 'rights'.

The position of 'autocracy' put forward by de Francisci in 1948 and again followed by many (see bibliographical essay) holds that the monarch ruled supreme and that the perceived authority of any other body, such as the army assembly, was only conferred by the whim of the ruler.[6] The arguments are largely refutations of the constitutionalist position, so again much of the evidence comes from the reign of Alexander III. If in the East it does appear to have been Alexander's whim that ruled supreme, we should keep in mind the anomaly of his army court traveling far from Macedonia. In Macedonia proper Antipater ruled as regent from 334 until 319 (four years after Alexander's death).

The scholarly debate has subsided since the publication in 1996 of Hatzopoulos' epigraphic study *Macedonian Institutions under the Kings*. Nevertheless, the few reactions to his work indicate that the questions, both major and minor, are not definitively settled (see bibliographical essay).

2 Kingship before Philip II (about 510–359)

The only political institution positively attested before the reign of Philip II is the kingship. Our earliest sources use the title *basileus*,[7] a Greek term for a nondescript lord, prince, or king. The title alone offers no precise view to the duties or powers of the Macedonian kings since it can denote positions of varying authority. Greek historians of the Classical period apply the term not only to the kings of Macedonia but also to the autocratic 'great king' of Persia, to the dual military kings of oligarchic Sparta, and to one of the nine archons in democratic Athens. There is virtually no evidence, however, for Macedonian kings calling themselves *basileus* before Alexander III.[8] The title appears to be imposed from outside Macedonia yet with welcome connotations.

The position held by the *basileus* derives from the tribal system of early times when it represented an office granted to an individual of a prominent family deemed sufficiently worthy by virtue of skill or wisdom to lead the tribe, especially in warfare. In many ancient (and medieval) societies the office evolved into a hereditary position, and this may be how kingship evolved in Macedonia too; at any rate, by the archaic period kingship was hereditary. How much the Macedonians were influenced by Mycenaean civilization is questionable, yet early Macedonian kingship does evoke Homeric aristocratic structures. According to Thucydides 2.99, in early times several Macedonian tribes, those in Lower Macedonia in the region of Pieria and Mount Olympus near the sea, as well as the Lyncestae and Elimiotae of Upper (inland) Macedonia, were all ruled by *basileis*. Eventually, though they retained a local *basileus*, the Lyncestae, Elimiotae, and other inland tribes became subject to the *basileus* of Lower Macedonia. One cannot avoid the echo of Homer's Agamemnon as overlord of Menelaus of Sparta, Odysseus of Ithaca, Achilles of Phthia, and so on.

Hereditary kingship in Macedonia followed one family line descending from the archaic king Perdiccas I down to Alexander IV, the posthumous son and co-successor of Alexander III 'the Great'. In the Hellenistic period the Antigonids established another royal dynasty. The kings of the earlier dynasty are variously called Temenids (Temenidae) or Argeads (Argeadae). Both Herodotus (8.137–139) and Thucydides (2.99.3) claim that the Macedonian kings were descended from Temenus of Argos. As Herodotus tells the story, three brothers, descendants of Temenus, as exiles from Argos came to Upper Macedonia through Illyria. They worked as servants for the local *basileus* until an omen involving the youngest brother, Perdiccas, warned the king and he expelled all three men. They moved on to another part of Macedonia and settled near the Gardens of Midas under Mount Bermium (Vermion in Lower Macedonia), and from there gradually took control of all Macedonia (as it was known in Herodotus' day).

Some scholars regard Herodotus' story about the Temenids – through Temenus descendants also of Heracles and Zeus – as a foundation myth to provide the ruling house of Macedonia with Greek ancestry.[9] Yet it is a story not without weight, for in the fifth century it seems to have been generally believed. We hear of the officials at Olympia allowing Alexander I to compete in the footrace (Hdt. 5.22) and the usually skeptical Thucydides accepts the Argive connection without reserve (2.99.3, 5.80.2). Those who reject the Argive origin of the Macedonian royal house prefer the term Argeads, descendants of Argeas son of Macedon son of Zeus from Orestis (Hesiod, *Eoeae* F 7, Appian 11.63). Both origin stories take the royal house back to Zeus, thus establishing divine ancestry and, by implication, a divine right to rule. Homeric echoes are apparent both in the association with Agamemnon's Argos and with Zeus, from whose divine will kings derived their authority.

As background to the Persian invasion of Greece via Macedonia Herodotus establishes seven generations of royal lineage in father-to-son succession from Perdiccas I of Argos to Alexander I, who fought with Mardonius against the Greeks at Plataea in 479. We know little else but the names of the first five Argead kings (Justin 7.2 gives a slightly different succession). Hence our understanding of Macedonian political structure does not begin to emerge until the Classical period with Amyntas I and Alexander I. Thucydides, Diodorus, and Justin continue our record of the Argead royal line from Alexander I through Perdiccas II to Archelaus' minor successor Orestes, who was murdered in 396. Then a number of dynastic disputes interrupt father-to-son succession. These challenges for the throne – some certainly and perhaps all – by members of the extended Argead house, coupled with outside intervention and arbitration (Plut.,

Pelopidas 26–7), confound an answer to the question of whether succession was based on primogeniture or on some other criterion, perhaps merit or the king's choice.[10] The question is important for it bears on the larger question of the Macedonian constitution: was the choice of a new king the 'right' of an assembly of the army or people, or was there merely public approval for a predetermined choice?

Evidence for established rules of succession is weak. Most often sons succeeded fathers, but primogeniture is far from confirmed by the sources. Amyntas III (about 392–370) is said to have been succeeded by his 'eldest' son, Alexander II (so Diod. 16.2.4, Justin 7.4.8), who is named along with his father in a treaty between Amyntas and the Athenians.[11] This strongly suggests that he was designated heir before his father's death. But Amyntas had six sons by two wives and Alexander was eldest by the second wife. An attempt to reconcile this with primogeniture proposes that when a king had several sons, one or more being born before he came to power, that succession fell to the eldest son born *after* the king came to the throne.[12] When Perdiccas III (about 365–360) was killed in battle, succession probably, but not certainly, fell to his (only) infant son Amyntas IV (Justin 7.5.8–9) rather than to a capable adult. In such cases the designated regent seems to have been the nearest male relative – the deceased king's brother if he had one. But herein lays a spawning ground for dynastic rivalry since the child or youth was at the mercy of his guardian-regent and, in practice, more vulnerable than one might expect if constitutional law was in place. Archelaus' successor-son Orestes is said to have been murdered by his regent Aeropus II (Diod. 14.37.6). Another theory proposes that the ruling king chose from his sons the one best suited to rule, which is inspired by the succession of Philip II.[13]

Other questions regarding succession remain unanswered. What constituted 'legitimate' male offspring? Archelaus is said by a contemporary source (Pl., *Gorgias* 471), to have been Perdiccas II's son by a slave woman and to have seized the throne from 'Perdiccas' legitimate son, a child of seven', whom he threw down a well. The Macedonian kings' practice of polygamy may have been, in part, for the purpose of securing succession through male offspring, but as is evident from the many wives of Philip II the practice of polygamy had other important political significance since most marriages sealed foreign alliances.[14] Whatever the benefits reaped from the practice, it could well have complicated succession more than aided it. Problems of succession tell against a highly developed infrastructure in Macedonia before Philip II's reign. Nevertheless, the Macedonian throne did remain in the same line for at least 300 years, from Perdiccas I in the mid-seventh century until the murder by Cassander of Alexander IV in about 310.

The Macedonian kings of the classical period appear most often in the historical record as constituting the 'state'. This perception is due to the tendency of historians when describing political developments in the north Aegean region to use the name of the current king rather than the ethnic designation as is typically used for Greek city-states (for example, the Athenians, the Lacedaemonians) and other peoples, both Greek and non-Greek (for example, the Thessalians, the Thracians – the latter also ruled by monarchs). Bearing in mind that before Alexander we have an almost entirely non-Macedonian viewpoint, and that Greeks recorded information about a people *they* perceived as foreign (even if the ruling house of Macedonia claimed Greek ancestry), this usage may have had no political connotation. Hammond points to some references to the kings that also include the 'Macedones', whom he claims are citizens, and concludes that the state consisted of the king and the Macedonians equally.[15] But arguments from the 'constitutionalist' position that the king alone does not constitute the state are not conclusive. In support of Hammond's conclusion Hatzopoulos has brought to attention considerable epigraphic evidence. However, Hammond's evidence – much of it literary – and nearly all the inscriptions cited by Hatzopoulos are later than the fifth century. One exception, an inscription concerning Perdiccas II's alliance with Athens perhaps during the Peloponnesian War (*IG* 1[3] 89), lists some of the king's relatives and many other leading men, at least 85 in total, as oath-takers together with Perdiccas.[16] Errington, arguing a date in the 440s for the treaty, suggests that the reason for so many witnesses to Perdiccas II's alliance with Athens was the weakness of his position in the early years of his reign.[17] Further confusion arises from inconsistency within the epigraphic evidence for a treaty between Amyntas III and the Chalcidians (dated to 393 or 391) names only 'Amyntas son of Arrhidaeus' in its preamble.[18]

In foreign relations the king, if he is not himself 'the state', appears to be at the head of it. From earliest times it was his prerogative to entertain foreign envoys (Hdt. 5.17–22) and he also negotiated foreign policy and alliances, both on his own behalf (for example, Thuc. 4.132) and, in the case of Alexander I, for the Persians (Hdt. 8.136, 140–4). Following the Persian defeat at Salamis, Mardonius sent the Macedonian king to Athens to negotiate a Persian–Athenian alliance for two reasons: Alexander I had a formal relationship with Athens and he was related by marriage to a prominent Persian. Both of these suggest that the kingship had a strong personal nature. The marriage confirms the early establishment of the policy of Macedonian kings to form alliances through marriage, a policy that would be continued throughout their history. Macedonian kings gained much through diplomacy. However, Perdiccas' many alliances made – and broken – with Athens (for example, Thuc. 2.29, 2.80), Sparta (for example, Thuc. 4.78–83) and others earned him a reputation for perfidy, or at least this is the Athenian perspective (Thuc. 1.57–63). Indeed, Perdiccas' backroom deals with Sparta and Argos in the midst of the Peloponnesian War (Thuc. 5.80, 83) hardly seem the result of a vote in the assembly – and could have provoked the need for many witnesses to his treaties.

The king controlled and owned the natural resources of the Macedonian territory such as timber, silver, and gold as well as royal land.[19] Thus he was able to grant sizable gifts of land and money and offer bribes to win support both domestic and foreign (for example, Xen., *Hellenica* 5.2.38, Diod. 14.92.3, 15.19.2, Plut., *Pelopidas* 27). Alexander I made a kingly display of wealth by dedicating a gold statue at Delphi (Hdt. 8.121, Dem. 12.21). Most important, wealth financed military activity. From earliest times the Macedonian king served as the supreme commander in warfare. Tradition holds that the archaic infant king Aeropus I was placed at the rear of the Macedonian battle-line so as to inspire the troops and to bring good auspices (Justin 7.2.5–12), and Alexander I was 'king and commander' of the Macedonian forces with Mardonius at Plataea (Hdt. 9.44). During the revolt of Potidaea from the Delian League the allies supporting Potidaea chose Perdiccas II as 'overall commander' of the cavalry (though not of the infantry, Thuc. 1.62). Archelaus' innovations to both cavalry and infantry strengthened Macedonia's own military capacity (Thuc. 2.100), this at a time when most of the Greek *poleis* were embroiled in or still reeling from the Peloponnesian War at the close of the fifth century. Thus, the military aspect of Macedonian kingship, so well known from the reigns of Philip II and Alexander III, is a point of continuity in all periods.

If there were any political institutions other than kingship before the reign of Philip II they are not firmly attested by the sources. Hammond would trace institutions attested in the fourth century back to the fifth but he admits that this is only an assumption.[20] One reference to a body of attendees on the king, the *paredroi* (literally, 'those who sit beside', Hdt. 8.138.1), suggests the early (archaic) existence of a council of advisors. No similar body is heard of again until Alexander III. We have no evidence for the function of assemblies, either civic or army, before Philip II. The king's role as military commander would necessitate appointing a deputy in charge of other affairs (Thuc. 1.62), but otherwise the evidence, perhaps misleadingly, since it is an argument from silence, suggests that the king acted according to his own inclination.

3 Institutions under Philip II and Alexander III (359–323)

If the early Argeads, looking for Hellenic favor, 'invented' Argive ancestry, it is ironic that by the time it emerges from the murk of pre-history the principal Macedonian political institution, kingship, is fundamentally objectionable to most Greeks. In the fifth century, when the Athenians were fiercely protecting their democracy through the practice of ostracism and the Spartans continued to elect five annual ephors to keep their two kings in check, Macedonian kingship appears extremely outdated. For some Greeks kingship held a greater appeal in the fourth century when its virtues found expression in political theory, particularly in Plato's philosopher kings and in Aristotle's favorable discussion. Aristotle (*Politics* 5.1310b) distinguishes between two kinds of monarchy or 'the rule of one': tyranny, usually established and maintained by force, is an ignoble rule, whereas kingship is a position of merit, either by virtue or birth or good deeds or the capacity to do good deeds. He refers explicitly to the Macedonians as an example of kingship-monarchy – in other words Macedonian kingship was not a rule by force (cf. Arr. 4.11.6). Of Aristotle's five subcategories of kingship (*Politics* 3.1284b35–1285b33), heroic kingship fits closely with our literary view of the Macedonians (Arr. 7.9.1–10.7). Aristotle was intimately acquainted with Macedonian kings, having educated one successor to the throne, Alexander III (and perhaps also at the same time several future Hellenistic kings). But how much his discussion of kingship was influenced by his time at the Macedonian court, or how much Alexander might have been influenced by Aristotle's political views, is unknown. It has been theorized that Philip II's rule was influenced by Plato's Academy,[21] but this too is a matter of speculation.

Kingship under Philip II and Alexander III was much more inclined toward the heroic warrior than to the philosopher king, although both kept philosophers at court. Coming to power at a time of serious external threat, Philip revitalized the military organization and in one campaign after another led the army in conquest and expansion, fighting in the van (Diod. 16.4.5) and suffering the same risks as his men (Diod. 16.34.5). It was a style of kingship that was most effective for winning the loyalty of the soldiers, whom he generously rewarded (for example, Diod. 16.53.2–3). Diodorus (16.60.3) claims he won a reputation for both excellent generalship and piety. The Macedonian kingship was in part a priesthood, for the king offered daily sacrifices and presided over religious festivals. Alexander emulated his father's style of kingship, and not until after his defeat of Darius and the adoption of aspects of Persian kingship – unpalatable to Macedonians because they were accustomed to a king who was their comrade-in-arms rather than their lord and master – did he meet with serious discontent.[22]

Both kings through gift-giving and land grants sought support among the most prominent families of what is generally regarded an aristocratic society. Through several institutions these leading families were closely associated with the royal court and dominated the high posts. Arrian 4.13.1 states that 'from Philip's [II] time' sons of leading Macedonians, when they reached adolescence, were conscripted for service to the king as royal pages (*basilikoi paides*). Whether Arrian means *beginning* with Philip or *at least from the time of* Philip is open to interpretation,[23] and Curtius' language at 8.6.2 may suggest that this 'custom' (*mos*) was longstanding. At any rate, there are no certain references to the institution prior to Alexander's Asian campaign. The royal pages are discussed by N. Sawada in chapter 19 [of the original], and there is no need to duplicate her discussion here except to say that ultimately the pages were more in training for political life than actively participating in it.

An elite body of adult men held the prestigious honor of being appointed the king's bodyguards and were called *somatophylakes*. Two categories of bodyguards are mentioned in the sources: the elite *agema* of the *hypaspists* (for example, Arr. 3.17.2, 4.3.2, 30.3) and the smaller group of highborn contemporaries of Alexander who belonged to his innermost court circle.[24] The former was a 'special forces' military unit numbering in the hundreds. The latter was evidently only seven until 325 when Alexander appointed an eighth honorary bodyguard for having saved his life in India. Of the bodyguards named at this time by Arrian (6.28.4), two, significantly, were of royal blood (Leonnatus and Perdiccas), and also significantly three were from Orestis and Eordaea, the two most powerful cantons in the territory of Macedonia. By selecting his elite bodyguards from the most influential Macedonian families in the kingdom the king paid due respect to their birth (and perhaps diffused potential rivalry). It was also at the king's discretion to remove (Arr. 3.27.5) or reappoint (Arr. 2.12.2) bodyguards and to replace them with other men of high birth.

The royal bodyguards held some of the highest military commands in Alexander's army. But because they commanded individual units they could not, as a group, physically shield the king at all times. When Alexander came under heavy fire in an attack on a Mallian town along the Indus (Arr. 6.9–11, Curt. 9.4.26–5.30, Plut., *Alexander* 63), only two or three men were there to protect him, and of these possibly only one, Leonnatus, was a bodyguard. In practice, then, the role of the bodyguards was more a mark of honor for the highest born men than an effective unit for protecting the king's life. On the night that Cleitus was murdered in 328 in Maracanda several bodyguards intervened trying to separate Alexander and Cleitus (Arr. 4.8.8–9, Curt. 8.1.45, 48, Plut., *Alexander* 51.8), but since in the end they did not prevent the king from killing his cavalry commander, one wonders how they could have prevented the reverse outcome. And as with the pages, the king was somewhat vulnerable. In Bactria a bodyguard was implicated in an alleged plot on Alexander's life and was either dismissed or executed (Arr. 3.27.5, Curt. 6.11.35–8, 7.15, 9.5), and Philip II's assassin Pausanias was one of his own bodyguards (Diod. 16.93.3).

The bodyguards were only a small number of the king's court circle. Companions (*hetairoi*) or friends (*philoi*) in large number, by invitation, attended the king at home in Macedonia and on campaign. Although the two terms are used somewhat interchangeably in the late sources (where they clearly indicate the same group),[25] technically speaking 'friends' is a later Hellenistic designation, which under the monarchs in Egypt and Syria took on some different characteristics. For the period of Philip II and Alexander III 'companions' is the more appropriate term. It is doubtless an archaic designation for the king's highborn associates, akin to the *hetairoi* of Achilles (Homer, *Iliad* 1.345), but evidence does not reveal how early the institution was established.[26] *Hetairoi* came to be applied as well to the elite Macedonian Companion Cavalry (for example, Arr. 3.11.8) and to some of the Macedonian foot, the *pezhetairoi* (for example, Dem. 2.17). That the designation 'companion' was not restricted to Macedonians – Philip II cultivated foreign *hetairoi* (Polyb. 8.9.6–13) and Alexander III admitted Greeks (Arr. 7.4.6) as well as Orientals (Plut., *Alexander* 47.3) – is a factor telling against the companions being a constitutional institution.

However, references to Alexander III's Council of Companions (for example, *ho syllogos ton hetairon*, Arr. 2.25.2; *consilium amicorum*, Curt. 6.8.1) indicate that some at least served as an advisory body to the king. Probably this was a much smaller group of men than the whole companionate. At Susa in 324 Alexander took two royal Persian wives and at least 80 of his companions were also married to Persian high noble women (Arr. 7.4.6; cf. Athen. 12.538b–539, 92), a number suggestively comparable to the approximately 85 'oath-takers' named in Perdiccas II's treaty with Athens (*IG* 1³ 89). The companions together with military commanders (many companions were themselves commanders) were summoned before engagements either to hear the king's speeches or for consultation (for example, Arr. 2.16.8, 3.9.3–4). On other political matters they met with the king alone and were summoned and dismissed by him. They evidently had the right to speak freely (Diod. 17.54.3, Polyb. 5.27.6) but there is no indication that they held a formal vote or that the king was bound to heed their opinions.[27] Reports of their meetings leave no clear picture. When evidence surfaced in 334 implicating Alexander of Lyncestis in a treasonous plot the summoned companions opined that they distrusted the Lyncestian and the king had him arrested (Arr. 1.25.4–5). But the fact that the Lyncestian's two brothers had been executed for involvement in the assassination of Philip II may have been a greater determinant than the opinions of the companions; in other words, Alexander may have been seeking support for a decision toward which he already inclined. When Alexander reported to the Council of Companions the settlement offered by Darius following the battle at Issus in 333 (Arr. 2.25.2, Curt. 4.11.1, Plut., *Alexander* 29.8, Diod. 17.54.2), he is reported as *not* taking the advice offered by his second-in-command Parmenion. This conflict of opinion appears as a *topos*, yet it would seem that Alexander was not bound to heed advice given in council. But when in 330 Alexander summoned the council for consultation in the 'Philotas affair', although according to one source the king formally forgave Philotas his failure to inform on an alleged plot, several prominent fellow companions of Philotas aggressively pressed the accusation, arrest, torture, and prosecution (Curt. 6.8.1–15, 17, 11.9–10). Does this mean that Alexander, because of his council's opinion, was effectively coerced into condemning the commander of the Companion Cavalry? As doubtful as this is,[28] the opinions of those companions dearest to him, such as Craterus and Hephaestion, surely were not inconsequential. The episode, at any rate, suggests fierce rivalry within the circle of Alexander's closest companions.

As a counterpoint, Justin's comment at 12.6.12 that Alexander had caused fear and resentment of himself among his friends with the murder of Cleitus – all the more horrific because it occurred when king and companions were conversing freely at dinner – ought not to be dismissed. It seems that the companions did speak less freely thereafter (Arr. 5.27.1) and their advisory body may have lost some political influence. Alexander's reprimand of the quarrelling Hephaestion and Craterus, his two dearest companions (Plut., *Alexander* 47), shows the king in complete control. More than slight is the evidence for an increasingly autocratic king, who became more difficult of access.

It was nonetheless the companions acting as a council who took command of the situation in the turmoil immediately after Alexander's death, albeit very briefly. That council quickly dissolved in dispute and rivalry, while the highest ranking companions soon scattered to their allotted satrapies. Later Eumenes would subject his authority to a council of sorts when he, a non-Macedonian, became general of the royal army in the war against Antigonus (Diod. 18.60.4–61.2, Plut., *Eumenes* 13.3–4), but this was a concession to the Macedonian commanders not contented under his authority. So whether the Council of Companions by tradition held political power counter to the king remains an open question.[29] One must consider also the role of the larger body of the populace, both the rank and file of the army and the common people at home: did they come together for the purpose of decision-making and did they serve as counter-balance to the kingship by forming half of the Macedonian state, as Hammond claims?[30]

Assemblies are not attested before Philip II's accession to the kingship in 359.[31] After the Macedonians were seriously defeated in battle by the Illyrians and more than 4,000 of their ranks, along with king Perdiccas III, lay dead, Philip called them together in a number of assemblies and made speeches in order to rebuild their morale (Diod. 16.3.5, 4.3). Perhaps we should take this much at face value. The majority of the assemblies called by Alexander III during the Asian campaign were likewise for the purpose of encouragement, which went hand-in-hand with popular support, and for broadcasting information.[32] Despite a lack of evidence it is reasonable to suppose that Philip was not the first Macedonian king to assemble his army and make encouraging speeches; no less would be expected of a king who serves as military commander. Thus I would posit that the traditional purpose of an assembly of Macedonian soldiers was so that the king, through speeches of persuasion, could boost morale and win popular support for his enterprises as well as disseminate information. However, scholars who argue for a 'constitutionalist' Macedonian state believe that in times of war an 'Army Assembly' or in times of peace a 'People's Assembly' held specific rights, chiefly (as mentioned above) the right to choose the successor to the throne, whether king or regent, and the right to judge in cases of treason.[33] For the reigns of Philip II and Alexander III there is some evidence to support this claim, but a look at three situations will suffice to demonstrate the problems of interpretation.

At Alexander III's accession to the throne in 336 it seems that some form of assembly met. But the literary evidence is hardly explicit about the rights of that assembly in the selection of the king and far from proves Hammond's generalization that 'we know that the Assembly [that is, of 'Macedones'] elected a king, deposed a king, and chose the guardian of a king who was a minor.'[34] Justin, the poorest and latest of the five extant Alexander historians, states at 11.1.8 that Alexander alleviated the fears of Philip's army when he addressed 'the entire army' in an assembly after Philip's murder. Surely 'alleviating fears' constitutes persuasion. And if Alexander had not already succeeded before an assembly met, why was he addressing it in such a manner? Justin adds at 11.2.2 that Alexander of Lyncestis was spared whereas two of his brothers were executed in the purge of Philip's alleged assassins because he had been first 'to acknowledge' Alexander as king. Curtius 7.1.6, perhaps following the same (unidentifiable) source as Justin, makes the same claim. Arrian 1.25.2 says the Lyncestian was 'among the first of

Alexander's friends' to support him, and putting on his cuirass he accompanied Alexander into the palace. Diodorus 17.2.1–2 states that Alexander 'succeeded to the kingship' and that he won over 'the mass of people' with befitting words. In order to infer that an assembly *chose* Alexander as Philip's successor one must stretch these sources and ignore the fact that Alexander had been groomed for succession! But if one takes Diodorus at face value again, then Alexander used persuasion to win popular support for what had been his father's choice. Those military men who made a public display of their support for Alexander as Philip's (already established) successor perhaps did so, as in the case of Alexander of Lyncestis, because their loyalty might have been in question.

Hammond's inference leans heavily on the succession clash following the death of Alexander III in Babylon in June 323. It must be emphasized that this situation is exceptional since in point of fact Alexander had no legitimate living son or brother capable of ruling at the time of his death. Curtius 10.6.1 claims that when Alexander died the king's bodyguards summoned to the royal quarters two groups of people, 'the most eminent of [Alexander's] friends' and 'the commanders of the troops'. A 'throng of soldiers' followed desiring 'to know' – not 'to decide' – to whom the fortune (that is, empire) of Alexander would be transferred. By this account the initial gathering was not an assembly of the entire army for only the leading companions and officers of the king were summoned while those soldiers who could crowded into the royal quarters in disregard of the invitation-only order (Curt. 10.6.2) – natural enough given their vested interest. The elite group of officers, which then proceeded in the presence of some of the rank and file to debate the succession, appears synonymous with the council of advisors. In a series of speeches put into the mouths of the leading men,[35] the 'contenders' for the throne are proposed: Roxane's unborn child should it be male, Heracles, Alexander's illegitimate son by the captive Barsine, and Arrhidaeus, a reputedly mentally deficient son of Philip, Alexander's half brother (Curt. 10.6.8–7.2, Justin 13.2.4–14). These were the Argead males, notably all requiring a regent. It was also suggested that the council of advisors assume rule on the authority of Alexander's throne. If this council had been a constitutional body, surely the suggestion was sound, at least as a temporary measure in the given circumstances. That it was rejected is telling.

One may infer from Curtius' account that the choice of succession was traditionally the king's (as argued above). But upon Alexander's untimely death it fell to the high command because the late king had broken with tradition by not naming a 'next of kin' successor. And how could he since there was no realistic 'legitimate' successor to be named prior to Roxane giving birth? Thus on his deathbed Alexander very likely had handed his royal seal to Perdiccas, a man of proven ability and evidently descended from another branch of the Argeads.[36] However, Justin claims at 13.3.1 that the infantry, furious 'at being left no say in the matter', declared Arrhidaeus king. Should we infer from this that the infantry was enforcing a constitutional right, which had been denied, in the process of selecting a king? Anson has argued that we should rather see in the succession clash evidence for the army's progressive assumption of power in decision making, which was *not* constitutional, toward the end of Alexander's reign, apparent also at the Hyphasis river mutiny in 326, when Alexander was forced to turn back, and in the mutiny at Opis in 324.[37]

Although the ancient sources are clear that the leading men were in serious disagreement on the question of Alexander's succession and that the infantry backed Arrhidaeus, they are not explicit about who had the 'right' to make a choice. When

Perdiccas says to those assembled, 'it is in your power to name a head' (Curt. 10.6.8), the meaning of 'power' (*potestas*) is ambiguous: is it 'right' or 'ability'? The fact is that if an army assembly at Babylon enforced a tradition in choosing the adult male next of kin,[38] it did so only with the threat of violence (Curt. 10.7.16–20, Diod. 18.2.2). Moreover, given Arrhidaeus' mental incapacity for leadership and blatant reluctance to take up the crown, the choice was unwise. Perhaps Alexander's succession was volatile and anomalous for the very reason that tradition *had* to be reinvented. Ultimately, once Roxane gave birth to a male, for the first time two successors were acknowledged.

As for Hammond's evidence for the army assembly's 'acclamation' of the king by the clashing of spears on shields,[39] this too is inconclusive. When Meleager donned his cuirass in chief support of Arrhidaeus, the phalanx soldiers approved by clashing spears on shields as a sign that they stood ready to shed the blood of any 'illegitimate' challenger to the throne (Curt. 10.7.14). The cuirass was evidently a symbolic gesture, for Alexander of Lyncestis similarly donned his cuirass in support of Alexander III in 336 (Arr. 1.25.2). However, at Babylon the phalanx soldiers also clashed their shields when Barsine's son Heracles was proposed (Curt. 10.6.12), in this case clearly indicating the army's *dis*approval.

The third situation is that of the trials for treason conducted during Alexander's Bactrian campaign, of Philotas in 330 and the pages in 327. Here the difficulties of interpreting the texts are compound. The 'constitutionalist' position rests heavily on a statement of Curtius 6.8.25 that it was an ancient Macedonian custom (*vetusto Macedonum modo*) for the king (*rex*) to investigate (*inquirebat*) in capital cases and for the army (*exercitus*) – in peace time the people (*vulgus*) – to pass judgment (*iudicabat*), and that the power (*potestas*) of the king had no influence unless his prior personal authority (*auctoritas*) had been influential. Is this proof that the army assembly held the constitutional right to judge in cases of treason? It is not. Most editors have accepted an emendation and added *rex* and *iudicabat*. If one does not emend the text (and rather follows most manuscripts), then we should read that it was an ancient Macedonian custom for the army to investigate in capital cases; the right 'to judge' does not enter into the statement (although Curtius uses this verb later at 9.34).[40] However, sources leave little doubt but that some form of army assembly was gathered to hear Philotas' case, and again three years later to hear the case of Hermolaus and the pages. Advocates of the 'autocracy' position argue that Curtius cannot be trusted, that these trials were the exception rather than the rule, or simply show pieces whereby Alexander could test his power.[41] The trial of Philotas in particular was extremely controversial because of his position of high command and his loyal following, not to mention the authority of his father Parmenion. The trial of the pages was perhaps in part a smoke screen for the elimination of Callisthenes and others vehemently opposed to Alexander's 'orientalization' – chiefly to changes in the nature of kingship.

Curtius' terminology also presents a difficulty. His no doubt well-considered use of *potestas* and *auctoritas*, potent terms in the early Principate, reveals a contemporary bias in his writing, a bias evident in his descriptions of the treason trials in general. Errington's interpretation of Curtius' text is that Alexander needed to test his authority (*auctoritas*) before exercising his power (*potestas*).[42] And the power rested with the king. Moreover, if Curtius was referring to a constitutional 'law' (*lex*), why did he use a term for 'tradition' or 'practice' (*modus*)? Or was tradition as good as written law in ancient Macedonia? If one were to accept Aymard's arguments for *nomos*,[43] one still must reconcile this with practice: the king could and did act without the army's judgment (Diod. 17.2.4–4.2, 5.1). The execution without trial of Attalus, and arguably of Parmenion (though Curtius suggests he was tried *in absentia* with Philotas), was carried out on the orders of a king acting autocratically. And, in the case of Parmenion, soldiers who expressed objection to the execution (after the fact) were disciplined (Curt. 7.2.35–38, Diod. 17.80.4, Justin 12.5.3–8). It seems the only recourse for the army or people in the case of the king overturning a tradition, even if it was as good as law, was verbal objection.

These situations should make clear the complexity of the source problems, which leave open to debate the important question of the authority of the Macedonian king relative to an assembly of soldiers or citizens. Most assemblies we hear about in the extant historians were not decision-making gatherings; the treason trials appear to be exceptions, whereas generally the king called assemblies for the purpose of making speeches of encouragement or disseminating information. And we are still left with the crucial question of the composition of these assemblies. We are told that 6,000 gathered for the trial of Philotas (Curt. 6.8.23), but these were evidently not all Macedonians since both Alexander and Philotas are said to have addressed the assembly in Greek rather than Macedonian (Curt. 6.9.35, albeit Attic Greek seems to have been the *lingua franca* of the Macedonian court).[44] And who does Perdiccas address in Babylon: only the summoned companions and officers or the 'uninvited' soldiers as well? How many were gathered we do not know. By this time many Persians had been admitted into Alexander's circle of friends and officer class, while Persian youths trained in Macedonian tactics had been incorporated into the ranks (Arr. 7.6.1–2). Would not, therefore, a Macedonian army assembly have included a number of Persians and how would they fit into a Macedonian constitution? One must conclude that Alexander's traveling court necessitated changes to Macedonian traditions – whatever they had been when the army set out in 334 and whatever remained intact in Macedonia itself under Antipater's regency.

4 Institutions after Alexander III (323–167)

After the death of Alexander III kingship was necessarily altered. As Mooren puts it, 'in Alexander the Macedonian, Achaemenid and Pharaonic legacies had been briefly united.'[45] This brief union, resulting in Alexander's 'orientalization' of his kingship, left a lasting mark on the Successors outside Macedonia. Macedonians were still to be found in the courts and armies of the Hellenistic rulers, but since the latter were ruling mostly foreign peoples kingship needed to be adapted to its context. The process was gradual. In 306 Antigonus Monophthalmus and his son Demetrius Poliorcetes assumed the title *basileus* in Asia Minor, and other Successors outside Macedonia soon adopted the title themselves. These self-styled *basileis*, as Aymard argues, developed 'personal' kingships in their respective territories in contrast to what he describes as a 'national' kingship of the homeland.[46] Neither the Ptolemies nor the Attalids adopted traditional Macedonian institutions, and the Seleucids did so only in part.[47] Within Macedonia, however, some traditions held a strong political force. The Argead dynasty survived another dozen years, although Arrhidaeus-Philip III was never more than a pawn and the juvenile Alexander IV, following the death of Olympias in 316, was kept under house arrest. Then Cassander's extinction of the Argead line by his murder of Alexander IV left no one, not even himself (though he did marry Alexander's half sister), with a 'legitimate' claim to the Macedonian kingship. Cassander therefore may have avoided the title *basileus* or perhaps used it only in a domestic context.[48] Clearly he intended succession to continue to be hereditary (Justin 16.1.1–6, Plut., *Pyrrhus* 6), but it was not until 277, when Antigonus Gonatas secured the Macedonian throne, that a new dynasty was established and the kingship restored in that traditional sense.

Meantime, between Cassander's death in 297 and the accession of Gonatus, Macedonian kingship changed hands nearly a dozen times. Those who held the throne, however briefly, did so by exploiting the nature of kingship, namely the close relationship between the king and his chosen companions: in addition to force of arms, they relied heavily on the cultivation of 'friends' or the 'first men' (*protoi*, Plut., *Pyrrhus* 12.10) – that is, men of birth and worth. As an indication of just how important the 'first men' were to a bid for the throne, in her attempt to destroy Cassander's rising power Olympias struck at the heart of his support system by killing 100 of the most eminent Macedonians from among his 'friends' (Diod. 19.11.8).

Antigonus Gonatas' evident consolidation and foreign policy suggest that he was the author of significant reforms in Macedonia. Unfortunately, a dearth of sources for his reign leaves us guessing. Errington sees in Gonatas' reign a return to authoritarian kingship, which he claims had been interrupted by the heirless death of Alexander and continued through the succession struggles of the Diadochi.[49] Hatzopoulos favors continuity from the days of the Argeads.[50] He proceeds on the assumption that a Macedonian 'commonwealth' existed. In his view, before Philip II political power was shared between the king and companions. The latter were the king's counselors and comrades-in-arms. Philip expanded the number of companions, who as an advisory body formed a council. We have seen the council in action during the reign of Alexander III. Hatzopoulos ascribes to the council a probouleutic role; whatever it decided had to be ratified by the assembly, which he argues developed as a counter-balance to the political authority of the aristocratic companions. He insists that the assembly was civilian and that an assembly meeting was *mandatory* to try cases of treason and to appoint a new king or regent; he infers that consultation on matters of foreign policy, such as the declaration of war and the conclusion of treaties, was optional. In the contexts in which we have observed the assemblies, however, they are clearly military and summoned *ad hoc*.

Evidence for trials and succession in the period following Alexander III does not settle our questions. In 218 Philip V, evidently without trial, executed Leontius, commander of the *peltasts* (Polyb. 5.27.4–8). Leontius' troops requested that the king not try the case until they were present, but he ignored their request to hear the charge and executed their commander before they could arrive. Was this a 'slight', as Polybius says, or an infringement of their right? The question has been argued on both sides.[51] As for succession, Demetrius I is said to have been acclaimed king by the royal army upon the death of Cassander's son Alexander V in 294 (Plut., *Demetrius* 37.3–2, Justin 16.1.8–18). However, Demetrius had been the one responsible for Alexander's death and the royal army had little choice in their present circumstance with Demetrius' forces having the upper hand. Livy's detailed account (40.9.8–16.1) of the rivalry between Perseus and his brother Demetrius for the succession to Philip V suggests three factors determining succession: rules of succession, the will of the previous king, and, lastly, the will of the Macedonians.[52] From this Hatzopoulos concludes that the 'right' of the

Macedonians to elect a king was mostly theoretical – or a last resort. The record of Antigonus III Doson's 'will' (Polyb. 4.87.6–8) also points to the king's right to name his successor. The evidence is inconclusive on these important questions regarding the relative powers of king and council or assembly.

Other institutions identified during the reign of Alexander III are also attested in the later period. Pages were attending Demetrius I at the time when he was seeking the throne (Plut., *Demetrius* 36), and bodyguards appear as late as 182 (Livy 40.6, 8). Apart from these bodies of the royal court, under the Antigonids a complex network of magistracies efficiently ran the state. At the regional level, the epigraphic evidence reveals the administration of individual Macedonian cities and provides the titles and roles of many city magistrates: *strategos*, *gymnasiarch*, *politarch*, *exetastai* and, most important, the *epistates*, eponymous alongside or in lieu of a priest.[53] These positions, though of political weight in their own context, could not collectively pull down the king from his throne. It was left to the Romans to do this. Their eventual abolition of the kingship in 167 speaks to the longevity as well as to the authority vested in Macedonian kingship as the principal political institution of the state.

Bibliographical essay

A good introduction to the institutions and scholarly debate is E.N. Borza, *In the Shadow of Olympus* (Princeton 1990), pp. 231–52. For the historical development of Macedonia, N.G.L. Hammond, *The Macedonian State* (Oxford 1989) is a more accessible synthesis of the seminal work N.G.L. Hammond and G.T. Griffith, *A History of Macedonia* 2 (Oxford 1979), and N.G.L. Hammond and F.W. Walbank, *A History of Macedonia* 3 (Oxford 1988), and see also R.M. Errington, *A History of Macedonia* (Berkeley and Los Angeles 1990), pp. 218–50. The most thorough study of the epigraphic evidence is M.B. Hatzopoulos, *Macedonian Institutions under the Kings*, 2 vols. (Athens 1996). On the 'constitutionalist' position, see also F. Granier, *Die makedonische Heeresversammlung: Ein Beitrag zum antiken Staatsrecht* (Munich 1931), the following articles by A. Aymard: 'Le protocole royal grec et son évolution', REA 50 (1948), pp. 232–63, '*Basileus Makedonon*', RIDA 4 (1950), pp. 61–97, 'Sur l'assemblée macédonienne', REA 52 (1950), pp. 115–37, 'L'institution monarchique', Relazioni del X Congresso di Scienze Storiche (Florence 1955), pp. 215–34, P. Briant, *Antigone le Borgne: Les débuts de sa carrière et les problèmes l'assemblée macédonienne* (Paris 1973), P. Goukowsky, 'Antigone, Alexandre et l'assemblée macédonienne (336–270 av. J.-C.)', *Rev. Phil.* 49 (1975), pp. 263–77, and N.G.L. Hammond, 'Some Passages in Arrian Concerning Alexander', CQ^2 30 (1980), pp. 455–76. For contrary arguments and the position of 'autocracy', see P. de Francisci, *Aracana Imperii* 2 (Milan 1948), R.M. Errington, 'The Nature of the Macedonian State under the Monarchy', *Chiron* 8 (1978), pp. 77–133 and 'The Historiographical Origins of Macedonian "Staatsrecht"', *Ancient Macedonia* 3 (Thessaloniki 1983), pp. 89–101, R. Lock, 'The Macedonian Army Assembly in the Time of Alexander the Great', CP72 (1977), pp. 91–107, E. Lévy, 'La monarchie macédonienne et le mythe d'une royauté démocratique', *Ktema* 3 (1978), pp. 201–25, and E.M. Anson, 'Macedonia's Alleged Constitutionalism', CJ80 (1985), pp. 303–16 and 'The Evolution of the Macedonian Army Assembly (330–315 B.C.)', Historia 40 (1991), pp. 230–47. On the nature of kingship, see F. Hampl, *Der König der Makedonen* (Weida 1934), F.E. Adcock, 'Greek and Macedonian Kingship', *Proceedings of the British Academy* 39 (1953), pp. 163–80,

L. Mooren, 'The Nature of the Hellenistic Monarchy', in E. Van't Dack, P. Van Dessel, and W. Van Gucht (eds.), *Egypt and the Hellenistic World* (Lovanii 1983), pp. 205–40, W.L. Adams, 'Macedonian Kingship and the Right of Petition', *Ancient Macedonia 4* (Thessaloniki 1986), pp. 43–52, and R.A. Billows, *Kings and Colonists, Aspects of Macedonian Imperialism* (Leiden 1995). For studies of the individual institutions, see N.G.L. Hammond, 'Royal Pages, Personal Pages, and Boys Trained in the Macedonian Manner during the Period of the Temenid Monarchy', *Historia* 49 (1990), pp. 261–90, W. Heckel, '*SOMATOPHYLAKIA*. A Macedonian cursus honorum', *Phoenix* 40 (1986), pp. 279–94 and 'King and "Companions": Observations on the Nature of Power in the Reign of Alexander', in J. Roisman (ed.), *Brill's Companion to Alexander the Great* (Leiden 2003), pp. 197–225, and G. Stagakis, 'Observations on the Hetairoi of Alexander the Great', *Ancient Macedonia 1* (Thessaloniki 1970), pp. 86–102. For magistracies, see C. Schuler, 'The Macedonian Politarchs', CP 55 (1960), pp. 90–100, N.G.L. Hammond, 'Some Macedonian Offices c. 336–309 B.C.', JHS 105 (1985), pp. 156–60, and Hatzopoulos, *Macedonian Institutions*, pp. 372–429. For some reactions to Hatzopoulos' study, see Z.H. Archibald, 'Review: Macedonian Administration', CR 49 (1999), pp. 163–5, N.G.L. Hammond, 'The Continuity of Macedonian Institutions and the Macedonian Kingdoms of the Hellenistic Era', *Historia* 49 (2000), pp. 141–60, and R.M. Errington, 'König und Stadt im hellenistischen Makedonien', Chiron 32 (2002), pp. 51–63.

Notes

1 I wish to express my gratitude to Ian Worthington and Joseph Roisman for their kind invitation to contribute to this volume. Also I am indebted to James Greenlee, whose close reading of an early draft of the chapter led me to greater clarity in thought and phrasing. Any shortcomings remaining are entirely my own.

2 On the literary and epigraphic source material, see P.J. Rhodes, chapter 2.

3 On the pitfalls of oratory as a historical source, see Ian Worthington, *Philip II of Macedonia* (New Haven 2008), appendix 1, pp. 213–14.

4 On the history of the periods discussed in this chapter, see part IV 'History'.

5 F. Granier, *Die makedonische Heeresversammlung: Ein Beitrag zum antiken Staatsrecht* (Munich 1931), pp. 4–28, 48–57.

6 P. de Francisci, *Aracana Imperii* 2 (Milan 1948), pp. 345–435.

7 Herodotus uses *basileus* for the ruler of Macedonia encountered by the Temenid brothers from Argos (8.137–8) and for Alexander I in the context of the battle at Plataea in 479 (9.44). Thucydides calls Perdiccas II, son of Alexander I, *basileus* (2.99).

8 On the term *basileus* and its use, see R.M. Errington, 'Macedonian "Royal Style" and its Historical Significance', *JHS* 94 (1974), pp. 20–37.

9 For example, Borza, *Shadow of Olympus*, pp. 81–4 and 100–13; *contra* Hammond and Griffith, *History of Macedonia* 2, pp. 3–13, and Hammond, *Macedonian State*, p. 19. See also J. Engels, chapter 5.

10 N.G.L. Hammond, *The Miracle that was Macedonia* (London 1991), p. 35, M.B. Hatzopoulos, 'Succession and Regency in Classical Macedonia', *Ancient Macedonia* 4 (Thessaloniki 1986), pp. 286–7.

11 M.N. Tod, *Greek Historical Inscriptions* 2 (Oxford 1948), no. 129. For this and the following cases, see also J. Roisman, chapter 8.

12 Hatzopoulos, 'Succession and Regency', p. 282.

13 J.R. Ellis, 'The Assassination of Philip II', in H.J. Dell (ed.), *Ancient Macedonian Studies in Honor of Charles F. Edson* (Thessaloniki 1981), pp. 115–16.

14   For a different view of polygamy and with a bibliography, see M.B. Hatzopoulos, *Macedonian Institutions under the Kings* 1 (Athens 1996), pp. 278–9, n. 7.

15   Hammond, *Macedonian State*, pp. 58, 166.

16   For a brief summary of the controversy over the restored text of the inscription and the date of the alliance (dates range from the 440s to about 413), see Borza, *Shadow of Olympus*, pp. 153–4, and Errington, *History of Macedonia*, p. 267, n. 3.

17   Errington, *History of Macedonia*, pp. 15–16.

18   Rhodes and Osborne, *Greek Historical Inscriptions*, no. 12.

19   Borza, *Shadow of Olympus*, p. 56 (with further bibliography).

20   Hammond, *Macedonian State*, p. 53.

21   Hatzopoulos, *Macedonian Institutions* 1, pp. 158–60.

22   On the uprisings at the Hyphasis and Opis, see E.D. Carney, 'Macedonians and Mutiny: Discipline and Indiscipline in the Army of Philip and Alexander', *CP* 91 (1996), pp. 19–44, and D.B. Nagle, 'The Cultural Context of Alexander's Speech at Opis', *TAPA* 126 (1996), pp. 151–72.

23   Hammond and Griffith, *History of Macedonia* 2, p. 155, n. 2: 'formalized' rather than initiated by Philip II. For a full discussion, see N.G.L. Hammond, 'Royal Pages, Personal Pages, and Boys Trained in the Macedonian Manner during the Period of the Temenid Monarchy', *Historia* 49 (1990), pp. 261–90. See also A.B. Bosworth, *A Historical Commentary on Arrian's History of Alexander* 2 (Oxford 1995), pp. 90–1.

24   A.B. Bosworth, *A Historical Commentary on Arrian's History of Alexander* 1 (Oxford 1980), p. 72. On the *somatophylakes*, see W. Heckel, *The Marshals of Alexander's Empire* (London 1992), pp. 237–44;, and on the *hypaspists*, see N.V. Sekunda, chapter 22.

25   Arrian usually but not always uses *hetairoi* (for example, 1.25.1, 2.16.8, 7.4.4 but not 1.25.2), whereas Diodorus almost always but not exclusively uses *philoi* (for example, 17.57.1, 100.1 but not 114.2).

26   See G. Stagakis, 'Observations on the *Hetairoi* of Alexander the Great', *Ancient Macedonia* 1 (Thessaloniki 1970), pp. 86–102, Hammond and Griffith, *History of Macedonia* 2, pp. 158–60, and more recently W. Heckel, 'King and "Companions": Observations on the Nature of Power in the Reign of Alexander', in J. Roisman (ed.), *Brill's Companion to Alexander the Great* (Leiden 2003), pp. 197–225.

27   Bosworth, *Historical Commentary* 1, p. 162.

28   [Alexander was] 'certainly not unwittingly manipulated by his men' so Heckel, 'King and "Companions"', p. 218. Further, on Curtius' account of the trial of Philotas, see the discussions of J.E. Atkinson, *A Commentary on Q. Curtius Rufus' Historiae Alexandri Magni Books 5 to 7.2* (Amsterdam 1994), pp. 212–46, noting Curtius' evident experience with *maiestas* trials in the Roman Senate, and E. Baynham, *Alexander the Great: The Unique History of Quintus Curtius* (Ann Arbor 1998), pp. 171–80.

29   For the political weight of the Council of Companions, see R.M. Errington, 'The Nature of the Macedonian State under the Monarchy', *Chiron* 8 (1978), pp. 99–133. For a factional view of the companions, see Heckel, 'King and "Companions"', pp. 197–205.

30   For Hammond's 'Macedones', see Hammond, *Macedonian State*, pp. 60–4.

31   For the view that he was made king and not regent by the assembly in 359, see Worthington, *Philip II*, pp. 20–2.

32   For example, no fewer than six assemblies reported by Curtius are for the purpose of encouragement (cf. 6.2.21, 9.1.1, 9.2.12, 9.4.19, 10.3.6, 5.10), while those for trials are the exception (cf. 6.9.1, 7.1.5).

33   'Army Assembly': chiefly Granier, *Die makedonische Heeresversammlung*, A. Aymard, 'Sur l'assemblée macédonienne', *REA* 52 (1950), pp. 115–37, and Hammond and Griffith, *History of Macedonia* 2, pp 160–2. 'People's Assembly': P. Briant, *Antigone le Borgne: Les débuts de sa carrière et les problèmes l'assemblée macédonienne* (Paris 1973), especially pp. 286–343, but rejected by Errington, 'Nature of the Macedonian State', pp. 91–9, as well as by Hammond and Griffith, *History of Macedonia* 2, pp. 160–2.

34   Hammond, *Macedonian State*, p. 60.

35   Curtius' term for the context of the speeches (10.7.1 and 3) is *contio*, which in Rome is a non-voting assembly, but whether Curtius meant to make this distinction is questionable: see the

discussions in Errington, 'Nature of the Macedonian State', pp. 94–6, E.M. Anson, 'The Evolution of the Macedonian Army Assembly (330–315 B.C.)', *Historia* 40 (1991), pp. 232, 236–7, and Hatzopoulos, *Macedonian Institutions* 1, pp. 276–9.

36 For Alexander's choice of Perdiccas, see Curt. 10.5.4, 6.4–5, Diod. 17.117.3, Justin 12.15.12–13. For further references and bibliography, see J.C. Yardley and W. Heckel, *Justin Epitome of the Phillipic History of Pompeius Trogus Books 11–12: Alexander the Great* (Oxford 1997), p. 292.

37 E.M. Anson, 'Macedonia's Alleged Constitutionalism', *CJ* 80 (1985), pp. 310–11, following Errington, 'Nature of the Macedonian State', pp. 115–16. In support of his claim, see n. 22 above.

38 Curt. 10.7.1–2: 'if you seek a next of kin, [Arrhidaeus] is the only one'.

39 Hammond, *Macedonian State*, p. 22.

40 L. Mooren, 'The Nature of the Hellenistic Monarchy', in E. Van't Dack, P. Van Dessel, and W. Van Gucht (eds.), *Egypt and the Hellenistic World* (Lovanii 1983), pp. 227–31.

41 On the *un*reliability of Curtius as an authority on Macedonian customs, see R. Lock, 'The Macedonian Army Assembly in the Time of Alexander the Great', *CP* 72 (1977), pp. 95–7, and R.M. Errington, 'The Historiographical Origins of Macedonian "Staatsrecht"', *Ancient Macedonia* 3 (Thessaloniki 1983), pp. 91–101; *contra* W.W. Tarn, *Alexander the Great* 2 (Cambridge 1948), pp. 106–7. On Macedonian treason trials in general, see recently E.M. Anson, 'Macedonian Judicial Assemblies', *CP* 103 (2008), pp. 135–49.

42 Errington, 'Nature of the Macedonian State', pp. 90–1.

43 Aymard, 'Assemblée macédonienne', p. 127. Arr. 4.11.6: Argead rule 'not by force but by law'.

44 Anson, 'Judicial Assemblies', pp. 144–5.

45 Mooren, 'Hellenistic Monarchy', pp. 207–8.

46 Aymard, 'Assemblée macédonienne', pp. 119–22.

47 J. Ma, 'Kings', in A. Erskine (ed.), *A Companion to the Hellenistic World* (Oxford 2003), pp. 192–3.

48 Errington, 'Nature of the Macedonian State', pp. 125–6. Cassander also saw to the elimination of Heracles, who seems not to have been considered a 'legitimate' Argead.

49 Errington, 'Nature of the Macedonian State', pp. 132–3.

50 For the arguments here presented, see Hatzopoulos, *Macedonian Institutions* 1, pp. 261–98.

51 For trials after the reign of Alexander III, see Lock, 'Army Assembly', p. 93, Hatzopoulos, *Macedonian Institutions* 1, pp. 271–6, and Anson, 'Judicial Assemblies', especially pp. 139–43, 145–6, 148–9.

52 Hatzopoulos, *Macedonian Institutions* 1, pp. 279–80, n. 4: 'Thus, although election was more often than not theoretical, the awareness of this right never became extinct and was revived whenever an appropriate case presented itself.'

53 Hatzopoulos, *Macedonian Institutions* 1, p. 156; for a detailed discussion of these magistracies, see especially pp. 372–429.

References

Borza, *Shadow of Olympus* = E.N. Borza, *In the Shadow of Olympus. The Emergence of Macedon* (Princeton: 1990).

Errington, *History of Macedonia* = R.M. Errington, *A History of Macedonia*, trans. C. Errington (Berkeley and Los Angeles: 1990).

Hammond, *Macedonian State* = N.G.L. Hammond, *The Macedonian State: The Origins, Institutions and History* (Oxford: 1992).

Hammond and Griffith, *History of Macedonia* 2 = N.G.L. Hammond and G.T. Griffith, *A History of Macedonia* 2 (Oxford: 1979).

IG = *Inscriptiones Graecae*.

Rhodes and Osborne, *Greek Historical Inscriptions* = P.J. Rhodes and R. Osborne, *Greek Historical Inscriptions, 404–323 BC* (Oxford: 2003).

SOCIAL CUSTOMS AND INSTITUTIONS:
ASPECTS OF MACEDONIAN ELITE SOCIETY

Noriko Sawada

The overwhelming majority of original literary sources of information about Macedonian society comes from the reigns of Philip II and Alexander III.[1] Indeed, Philip's reign was a period of great change in Macedonian history.[2] His conquests provided Macedonia with a dramatic increase in both territory and prosperity and led to rapid urbanization; his court at Pella became a venue for international diplomacy, and Hellenization proceeded much faster than ever before. Thus, we must be cautious about applying the picture of Macedonian society provided by these sources to pre-Philip Macedonia. In addition, most of the information is about the royals and elites, the upper strata of Macedonian society. Naturally, their way of life and their customs differed fundamentally from those of the common people. Those who comprised the Macedonian elite were usually called 'Companions' (*hetairoi*).[3] They served as the retinue and primary associates of the king and enjoyed power at court. They had grown up with him through the institution of the *paides*, or royal pages, in which the sons of the elite lived with and served the king.[4] The Companions accompanied the king in fighting, hunting, and feasting, and were often given lavish tracts of land as a reward for faithful service.

Given the limitations of the sources, this chapter deals with Macedonian elite society during the monarchical period, with special emphasis on the reigns of Philip and Alexander.[5] I focus on three features that provided a venue for regular interaction between the king and his Companions and that characterized Macedonian elite society: court *symposia*, royal hunting, and the institution of the *paides*.

1 Court *symposia*[6]

Participation in communal eating and drinking is an essential part of social life in many societies. The *symposia* in Greek *poleis* have been well studied, and scholars generally agree that they gave the world of archaic Greece its characteristic qualities.[7] Murray asserted that without the *symposia*, we could not begin to understand early Greek society.[8] They offer the key to an understanding of Macedonian elite society as well. Indeed, as we shall see, Macedonian court *symposia* embodied the elite society and culture.

An investigation of Macedonian *symposia* is handicapped by the limitations of relevant sources. Not only do the great majority of the surviving literary accounts of them come from the reigns of Philip and Alexander, but political and personal prejudices permeate the sources, making analysis of Macedonian drinking practices sometimes difficult. Writers contemporary with Philip, such as Demosthenes and Theopompus, make frequent reference to the Macedonian *symposium*, emphasizing it as a symbol of barbaric tyranny.[9] Although literary accounts of Alexander's *symposia* abound, the writers were much more likely to recount those at which traumatic events occurred and to exaggerate the degree of disorder and violence; thus, this propensity distorts our understanding of what was normal for and at Macedonian *symposia*. Archaeological evidence, especially the extraordinary number and variety of drinking vessels from the royal and elite tombs, confirms the picture, drawn from literary sources, that the Macedonian kings and elite were truly heavy drinkers,[10] and the remains of the banquet rooms (for example, in the Vergina palace) provide valuable information about the architectural setting of court *symposia*.

Any discussion of *symposia* before Philip's reign is mostly speculative. Hegesander's account (*apud* Athen. 1.18a), which is often cited as evidence for early Macedonian *symposia*, states that Macedonians were not permitted to recline at them until they had killed a wild boar without using a net, and that Cassander allegedly remained seated at *symposia* at the age of 35. This account has usually been taken to mean that both *symposia* and hunting were the major activities of the elite in early Macedonia. Hegesander's language, however, reveals only that the custom existed in the days of Cassander, and it is entirely unclear how far back it can be traced.

Literary sources preserve two well-known stories about early court *symposia*, both of which are probably fictional. The earliest one is from Herodotus (5.17–21), who told a tale about a *symposium* held by Amyntas I for the Persian ambassadors, which ended with their murder by the king's son. His account of the *symposium*, however dubious, offers some evidence that it was an important court activity.[11] The second one is from Plato (*Gorgias* 471a–c), who claimed that Archelaus entertained his uncle Alcetas and his uncle's son Alexander at his court *symposium*, got them drunk, and killed them in order to gain the throne. Although the historicity of this claim is often doubted,[12] it suggests that regicide and conspiracy were possible in a sympotic context, as in the reigns of Philip and Alexander.

In addition, Aelian (*Varra Historiae* 13.4) told a tale about a *symposium* held by Archelaus at which Euripides drank too much and kissed Agathon. Archelaus is known to have attracted many leading Greek writers and artists to his court (see below), and Aelian's story shows that these Greek intellectuals were often invited to court *symposia*. Carystius of Pergamon (*apud* Athen. 11.508e) reports that in the reign of Perdiccas III Euphraeus, a pupil of Plato, stayed at the Macedonian court as a political adviser and permitted only those who practiced geometry and philosophy to dine with the king. Although it is hard to believe that such a rigid sympotic criterion was enforced at the Macedonian court,[13] this story suggests that court *symposia* had an intellectual tone to them, as did those in Greece (south of Mount Olympus).

We have more evidence from Philip's reign showing that the Macedonian kings and elite were heavy drinkers and that drinking and court *symposia* were their major activities. From his reign on, literary sources emphasize, sometimes with exaggeration, the excessive drinking of the kings and elite. As proof of their excessive drinking, it has usually been argued that Macedonians, unlike Greeks, drank their wine unmixed (*akratos*) and that this custom was regarded as a sign of barbaric excess by Greeks. Although there are in fact no general assertions in the sources that Macedonians drank pure wine,[14] it seems at least clear that it was much more common for the Macedonian kings and elite to drink unmixed wine than others.[15]

We know of four specific *symposia* held by Philip: the state banquet held after the fall of Olynthus in 348 (Dem. 19.192, Diod. 16.55.1–2), the *symposium* where he entertained the Greek ambassadors during the peace negotiations in 347/6 (Aes. 1.168–169, 2.41–42, 51–52), the drinking party held after the Macedonian victory at Chaeronea (for example, Theopompus, *FGrH* 115 F 236, Diod. 16.86.6–87.1), and the wedding banquet celebrating the marriage of Philip and his last wife Cleopatra in 337 (Plut., *Alexander* 9.6–10, Athen. 13.557d–e). Brief literary accounts of these *symposia* do not clarify their actual significance for the king and the elite, the latter being rarely mentioned in the accounts of Philip's *symposia*.

Alexander's *symposia* are much more frequently described in the literary sources, especially the very large ones with hundreds or even thousands of guests. For example, there is the great celebration at Dium on the eve of his departure for Asia in 334, where he used a dining tent holding 100 couches, meaning that there were probably 200 guests (Diod. 17.16.3–4). At the famous mass wedding banquet at Susa in 324, Alexander invited 9,000 guests and spent 9,800 talents (Plut., *Alexander* 70.3, Athen. 12.538b–539a), and at the reconciliation banquet after the mutiny at Opis in 324, he again invited 9,000 guests (Arr. 7.11.8–9). Also recounted are his *symposia* where there were sympotic disorder and violence, including the famous drinking party that led to the destruction of Persepolis in 330, the drunken brawl that ended with Alexander stabbing Cleitus to death in 328, the defiance of Callisthenes to Alexander's attempt to introduce *proskynesis* at court in 327 that alienated Callisthenes from Alexander, the *symposium* in India at which Meleager publicly criticized Alexander's behavior in 326, that at Ecbatana in which Hephaestion consumed great quantities of wine, fell sick, and finally died in 324, and Alexander's final drinking party in Babylon in 323, which caused his ultimate demise.[16] It was the Companions who regularly attended *symposia*, and they were major events both for them and the king. As we shall see later, the sons of the Companions, the *paides* or pages (hence the future Companions), were brought up at court and were also present at *symposia*, for one of their duties was to serve the king at them.

The *symposium* had several important functions.[17] For one thing, it was a relief from the rigors of a march, particularly during Alexander's campaigns, and no doubt a wide variety of entertainment was offered at it that contributed to the relief. The entertainment took the form of singing, dancing, and conjuring, as evidenced by the mass wedding banquet at Susa (Athen. 12.538e–539a). Dramatic and literary performances were among the most popular entertainment at *symposia*; Alexander is known to have held a dramatic contest in Phoenicia in 331, and he particularly enjoyed a comparison of favorite verses from Homer (Plut., *Moralia* 331d, 334e). Also common were sophisticated debates among the court intellectuals, involving his Companions and which often had a professional, competitive edge.

The *symposia* also provided a structure and venue for regular interaction between the king and the elite. For the king, a *symposium* was an excellent platform for him to display his power and superiority, particularly through his drinking prowess, the luxurious furnishings of his banquet rooms, and the lavishness of his entertainment. For the Companions, it was an arena in which they had to compete with one another for the king's attention and favor and to struggle to maintain or improve their position at court, since he was in complete control of promoting or demoting them. As the Macedonian court became a venue for international diplomacy from Philip's reign on, court *symposia* possibly came to assume a further role – international display.

Moreover, and more importantly, the *symposium* served a quasi-constitutional function in the decision-making process, at least during Alexander's reign.[18] We have no evidence to suggest the existence of a formal royal advisory council or assembly in Macedonia. In fact, the sources provide a number of indications that Alexander carefully discussed matters of policy and strategy with his Companions during his campaigns and held what could be called a council with them.[19] Although there was no obligation on his part to follow their advice, the Companions did play an informal advisory role. The king sometimes tried out new policies on them, using the *symposia* as a testing ground. In this sense, they were a regular social gathering for the king and his Companions, and informally a context for decision making at court. For the Companions, the *symposia* were vital to their welfare, all the more so because they had a quasi-constitutional function.

Macedonian *symposia* had several similarities with those of Greece.[20] Greek *symposia*, which are thought to have evolved from the Homeric feasting tradition under the influence of the Near East, had four characteristic features: (1) they were a largely male elite activity, (2) there was egalitarianism in a sympotic context, (3) there was a clear distinction between the activities of feasting and drinking, with an emphasis on the latter, and (4) the guests generally reclined on couches, rather than sitting on them.[21] Of these features, the first two were attested already in Homeric feasts, and the last was apparently imported from the Near East in the eighth or seventh century.

In fact, the introduction of couches represented a fundamental change in Greek commensality as it determined the size of the sympotic group. The typical Greek *symposium* thus involved between 14 and 30 male guests in a comparatively small banquet room (*andron*) of the private house of a member of the elite, with two guests reclining on each couch, which were positioned along the walls of the room. Both Greek and Macedonian *symposia* were often a setting for erotic relationships between male guests; both provided venues for dramatic performances and intellectual debates, and, as evidenced by the Vergina palace, they were held in a traditional Greek-style *andron*, a square and closed room with couches along the walls.

Given these similarities, can we identify any Greek influences on Macedonian *symposia*? Of course, one should not automatically assume that similarity signifies influence. Nevertheless, it is safe to assume that the Greek-style *andron* was imported from Greece, together with the practice of reclining on couches, and probably the forms of entertainment were also imported from Greece through the Hellenization of the court. Since a *symposium* was a court event, where Greek intellectuals were present, Greek influences on the sympotic performances are undeniable.

Additionally, the principle of egalitarianism, which was found in Homeric feasts and strengthened in Greek *symposia*, is also found in Macedonian *symposia* in the form of sympotic freedom of speech (*parrhesia*); for instance, Cleitus, Callisthenes, and Meleager criticized Alexander in sympotic situations. Since egalitarianism intrinsically contradicts monarchy, the tradition of *parrhesia* at Macedonian *symposia* was likely the result of reconciling the Greek tradition of equality among participants at *symposia* with the realities of a royal court.[22] The king, who was the 'chief drinker', also assumed the role of fellow drinker under the principle of equality.[23] In fact, this dual role often led to cases of sympotic disorder and violence (see below).

There were, however, also marked differences between Greek and Macedonian *symposia*, one being related to their size. Those held in the banquet rooms of the palace of Vergina (each accommodating 15–19 couches[24]) were probably closer to Greek norms. However, during Alexander's campaigns there were a number of huge *symposia* with thousands of guests. They were usually held in the royal pavilion or in the open air, such as the mass wedding banquet at Susa mentioned above. In addition to this gigantic scale, sympotic extravagance and material excess were characteristics of the Macedonian *symposia*. Given that banquets in a monarchy are always an excellent stage for the display of royal power and distinction, it is no wonder that Macedonian *symposia* were markedly different from those of the Greek democratic *poleis*. Indeed, the Macedonian kings and elite demonstrated a taste for conspicuous display through their luxurious couches and splendid drinking vessels. In the later years of Alexander's reign, unlike in Greek *symposia* that idealized order and moderation, gold and silver were used extravagantly at *symposia*, as attested by both literary and archaeological evidence.[25] This sympotic gigantism and extravagant luxury indicate possible Persian influence following Alexander's campaigns.[26]

Another significant difference is the political and social importance of *symposia* for the participants. Since the Macedonian ones served as a context for the Companions to compete for the king's favor and to advance their welfare, they served as a locus for the competition vitally important in their life.

Moreover, unlike the peaceful *symposia* of Greek *poleis*, Macedonian ones are known to have been arenas in which quarrels, drunken brawls, and even murders frequently occurred (though we should always bear in mind the great propensity of the sources to recount the more unruly banquets). What caused this sympotic violence? First, the excessive, disorderly drinking. The potential for physical violence is naturally increased by the consumption of great quantities of wine. For instance, it was the intoxicated Alexander who stabbed Cleitus to death. Second, the agonistic element was particularly strong in Macedonian *symposia*, even in the entertainment. The egalitarian ethos at *symposia* provided opportunities for the participants to assert themselves, whether against the king or others, and made *symposia* a venue for competition not only among the elite but also between the king and his Companions. The uneasy coexistence of egalitarianism and keen competitiveness increased the potential for violence.[27] These factors are not found in the *symposia* of Greek *poleis*, hence the Macedonian ones represented a world of feasting very different from the Greek ones.

Violence and conspiracy at *symposia* did not end with the Argeads, for Demetrius Poliorcetes and Alexander V, son of Cassander, plotted to murder each other at a *symposium* (Plut., *Demetrius* 36.3–5). Antigonus Gonatas, who is known to have loved banquets, enjoyed drinking with Persaeus of Cition, a pupil of Zeno and the author of *Sympotika Hypomnemata* (Athen. 13.603e, 607b–f). Since Antigonus Gonatas, like Archelaus and Philip, attracted many Greek intellectuals to his court (see further below), they must have frequently attended his court *symposia*, and so it seems certain that the highly intellectual mood of Argead court *symposia* survived at least until the reign of Antigonus Gonatas. Although we have little information for evaluating which functions of Argead *symposia* discussed above endured in the Antigonid period, they undoubtedly formed part of the royal court life there. In addition, Hippolochus (*apud* Athen. 4.128e–130d) gives a detailed account of the Macedonian marriage feast of Caranus in the early third century, though not of a court *symposium* but of a private one with 20 guests.[28] His vivid description of an amazingly splendid feast provides us with valuable information about the sympotic luxury of the Macedonian elite in the Hellenistic period. Macedonian sympotic extravagance, which characterized the later years of Alexander's reign, continued in the other Hellenic dynasties as well, as attested by the detailed accounts of the pavilion of Ptolemy Philadelphus at Alexandria (Athen. 5.196a–197c).

2 Hunting

Most of the characteristics of Macedonian elite society that we have observed in a sympotic context apply also to hunting, although the evidence is more limited. Direct literary accounts of hunting do not pre-date Alexander, and almost all of the extant iconographic evidence for royal hunts comes from the period of Alexander and the Successors. Since these sources provide information about only royal hunting, we have no way of knowing what hunting meant for Macedonians in general or how we should place hunting in Macedonian society.

Evidence for royal hunting before Alexander's reign is minimal. The custom described by Hegesander (*apud* Athen. 1.18a), already referred to, might provide evidence that puts it into the context of court life, but the origin of the custom remains uncertain. The evidence begins with the royal coinage of the fifth century: a magnificent octadrachm of Alexander I shows a horseman, probably the king himself, allegedly riding to the hunt, though disagreement persists about whether the rider represents a hunter.[29] A silver stater of Amyntas III also portrays on the obverse a horseman with a spear and on the reverse a lion pierced by a broken spear.[30] In addition, two passages contain allusions to hunting prior to Alexander's reign: Diodorus 14.37.6 reports that Archelaus was accidentally killed by his lover Craterus during a hunting expedition,[31] and Polyaenus 4.2.16 tells a story of Philip using hunting dogs to find enemies in hiding (which suggests hunting). Although we have no direct information about hunting during Philip's reign, one of the duties of the *paides* at his court was to attend him while hunting (see below). It is thus certain that he and the elite did hunt during his reign.

In contrast, both iconographic and literary evidence of royal hunting abounds for Alexander's love of hunting. Plutarch recounts many episodes of his hunts (for example, *Alexander* 4.11, 23.3–4), and he often sponsored big hunting competitions during his campaigns: for instance, a hunt in Syria, where Lysimachus distinguished himself by killing a large lion though he was severely wounded; a hunt in Syria, where Craterus saved Alexander from the charge of a lion; a big hunt in a game park of Bazeira in Sogdiana, where Alexander shoved Lysimachus aside and killed a charging lion with a single blow; and a hunt where Hermolaus struck a wild boar before Alexander could do so and was flogged by the outraged king.[32]

The sources on Alexander emphasize his lion hunts, however the motif of most of the extant hunting iconography is lion hunting: for instance, the relief frieze of the so-called Alexander Sarcophagus from Sidon; the Craterus monument at Delphi in commemoration of the lion hunt in Syria where Craterus saved Alexander; a floor mosaic in a private house in Pella of the late fourth century showing two Macedonians (probably Alexander and Craterus) hunting a lion on foot; and the Messene relief depicting a lion hunt of the late fourth or early third century, possibly dedicated by one of the Successors, which was the last of the monumental representations of Alexander's lion hunts.[33]

The most intriguing of the lion-hunt iconography is the hunting fresco on the facade of Tomb II at Vergina.[34] It shows three hunters on horseback and seven on foot, and scenes of the hunting of two deer, a wild boar, a bear, and a lion, probably in a large game park. It is suggested that images of lion hunting disappear from Greek art after the seventh century until its revival after Alexander's campaigns, with the exception of Heracles' killing of the Nemean lion.[35] In addition, mounted hunting was completely unheard of in Greece.[36] The fresco thus represents elements unknown in contemporary Greece: lion hunting, mounted hunting, and a large game park.

The identification of the male occupant of Tomb II is a hotly debated issue.[37] The long controversy about whether Tomb II is the burial place of Philip (buried in 336) or of Philip III Arrhidaeus (buried in 316) has been connected to a debate about when the elements depicted in the hunting fresco (among other things lion hunting) were introduced in Macedonia, namely before or after Alexander's campaigns.[38] In fact, the origin of lion hunting in Macedonia is not known. Herodotus (7.126), Aristotle (*Hist. an.* 579b6, 606b14), and Pausanias (6.5.4–5), report that lions existed in Macedonia in the classical period, and some scholars see the disputed rider coins of Amyntas III as proof that Macedonian kings hunted lions at least starting in his reign. Even if lion hunting was not new to Macedonia, it seems reasonable to suppose that only in Alexander's reign did it acquire a symbolic significance. In the Near East, lions were symbols of kingship and royalty, and Persian kings are known to have engaged in lion hunts and have depicted themselves hunting lions in their royal art.[39] Alexander, determined to become the successor to Persian kings and to rule the Near East, was likely to have borrowed the symbolic significance of the lion hunt and its iconography from the East. The disputed hunting fresco of Tomb II aside, the lion-hunt motif was in fact first used by Alexander himself, for Diodorus 17.115.1–5 tells us that the elaborate funeral monument Alexander ordered for his closest friend Hephaestion, who died at Ecbatana in 324, included a hunting scene.[40] The lion-hunt theme gained sudden popularity during the struggles of the Successors, who were eager to justify their legitimacy as successors to Alexander.[41] Undoubtedly, it is the symbolic significance conferred on lion hunting by Alexander himself that explains why several of them emphasized the lion-hunt theme.[42] The enthusiasm of the Macedonian elite for hunting survived the period of the Successors, for we know Cassander and Demetrius Poliorcetes hunted on a number of occasions (Diod. 18.49.3, Plut., *Demetrius* 3.1, 50.5, 52.1), however it was never as popular as during the earlier period of the Successors.

What were the functions of the royal hunt?[43] First, it was a court event for the king, his Companions, and the *paides*, and like the *symposia* it was a relief from the rigors of the campaigns. It was also a good way to train for warfare during periods of peace, as Xenophon claims (*Cyn.* 1.18, *Eq.* 8.10). Moreover, it provided another venue for interaction between the king and the elite. Hunting promoted egalitarian values in the form of comradeship among fellow hunters and cooperation in pursuing a common quarry. In the egalitarian context of hunting, the king himself was a fellow hunter, but, as the 'chief hunter', he had to show himself the best at the hunt and to display his individualistic distinction. The royal wrath bestowed on Lysimachus and Hermolaus for anticipating Alexander's strikes exemplifies this. For the Companions, hunting with the king signaled their privileged status. Indeed, royal hunting was a locus for their intense competition as they pursued both the king's favor and hunting success, which conferred on them the mark of excellence.

These observations reveal several similarities between *symposia* and royal hunting. Both were major social events that provided entertainment and comradery for the king, his Companions, and the *paides*. In both, the elite competed for the king's favor and for distinction. The king, while demonstrating his personal excellence, played the dual role of chief and fellow. This ambivalence – during *symposia* with the tradition of *parrhesia* and during royal hunting in pursuit of a common prey – caused vicious competition not only among the elite but also between the king and his Companions, which had the potential for creating clashes and ultimately led to explosions of violence.[44] In fact, the intense enthusiasm for the pursuit of personal prowess was an enduring feature of the Macedonian kings and elite, who were highly competitive in virtually everything. *Symposia* and royal hunting, I believe, embodied this hardy, tough, and intimate world of the Macedonian elite, characterized by agonistic Homeric values.

As mentioned above, several of the Successors eagerly associated themselves with Alexander's famous royal hunts, with particular stress on lion hunts, to emphasize their intimacy with Alexander and to confer legitimacy on their aspirations to rule. That is why the lion tales of Craterus and Lysimachus survived well, as did the lion-hunt iconography. Craterus commissioned a great bronze group erected at Delphi, while Lysimachus commemorated his daring against lions on his coins when he was a king.[45] The Argead hunting tradition endured in the Antigonid period, for the royal cult of Heracles Kynagidas (Heracles the Hunter) was practiced throughout Macedonia,[46] and Philip V's hunting prowess was praised by the poets (*Anth. Pal.* 6.114–116). Polybius' account of how the Romans found game parks in Macedonia after the Battle of Pydna in 168 shows that the Antigonid kings maintained royal game parks until the end of their dynasty (31.29.3–5). In fact, evidence for the Antigonid hunting is focused on the king, and we have little information about the elite's competition or interaction with the king in the context of hunting.[47] Quite possibly, the Macedonian enthusiasm for hunting continued in the other two major Hellenistic dynasties as well, as is shown by the many anecdotes about the enthusiasm displayed by Ptolemaic and Seleucid rulers for hunting.[48]

Although hunting was more important as a locus for competition in the life of the Macedonian elite than athletics, a quick look at athletics is suggestive because it provided one of the main contexts for competition in Greece. Athletics apparently did not become a major activity of the Macedonian elite until the Hellenistic period.[49] In fact, we know almost nothing about the elite's interest in competitive athletics prior to Alexander's reign. Both Alexander I and Archelaus may have participated in the Olympic Games (Hdt. 5.22, Solinus 9.16), and Philip did, for he won at least three equestrian victories at Olympia and commemorated them by issuing coinage (Plut., *Alexander* 3.8, 4.9). For their reigns, however, all we find is evidence of royal interest in international competition, mainly equestrian, not of elite interest in athletics. Alexander himself was physically strong and muscular, but he is known to have disdained athletics and never competed in the Olympics. During his campaigns, however, he regularly sponsored athletic contests for his troops, some of his courtiers, Craterus, Leonnatus, and Perdiccas, are said to have been athletic enthusiasts,[50] and Alexander's action led to the spread of Greek athletics to the east. It seems likely that during Alexander's campaigns athletics became an important pastime and, at the same time, began to provide another locus for competition among the elite.

3 The institution of the paides

The institution of the *paides*, the third feature that characterized Macedonian elite society, provided the context for early indoctrination of young males in the distinctive practices and values of Macedonian elite society, including those discussed above. The *paides* were the sons of the elite, who were brought up at court in the immediate entourage of the king to become Companions in due course. Since they played a prominent role in the so-called 'Pages Conspiracy' in 327 (Curt. 8.6.1–8.23, Arr. 4.12.7–14.4), when Hermolaus, one of their number, was publicly flogged by Alexander for anticipating the king's strike against a wild boar during a hunt and plotted to kill Alexander in revenge,[51] most of the surviving literary evidence comes from Alexander's reign.

The origin of the institution of the *paides* is not clear. Arrian 4.13.1 says, in recounting their duties, that it was a practice going back to Philip's reign, but it remains unclear whether Philip himself established the institution. Curtius' language (8.6.2, 8.3), as well as that of Valerius Maximus (3.3. *ext.* 1), may mean that it was a custom of long standing. The circumstances of the death of Archelaus, whose killers might have been members of the *paides*,[52] seem to suggest that the institution existed already in his reign. Although we have no certain knowledge about its origin, it seems reasonable to suppose that Philip extended or systematized an existing practice.[53] In fact, the elite stratum was dramatically increased by Philip when he enlarged the scope of his Companions to include the nobility of the cantons of Upper Macedonia and many able Greeks. It is thus likely that, along with the increase in the number of Companions, the number of *paides* was also increased and that the institution was redefined. Since the sons of Persian nobles were raised at the court of the Great King, as Xenophon remarks (*Anabasis* 1.9.2–5), their institution may have, to some degree, been inspired by a similar practice at the Persian court.[54]

Only two *paides* from Philip's reign are known by name. Aelian (*Varra Historiae* 14.48) mentions that Philip flogged Aphthonetus and executed Archedamus for infractions of military discipline. Alexander of Epirus, who was brought up at Philip's court, and Pausanias of Orestis, who assassinated Philip, could have been among his *paides*, both of whom are alleged to have had sexual relationships with him. His *paides* also included those who are said to have been Alexander's *syntrophoi* (foster-brothers), such as Hephaestion, Marsyas of Pella, and Leonnatus.[55] Lysimachus, Craterus, Perdiccas, Ptolemy, and Seleucus, who all distinguished themselves in the age of Alexander and the Successors, were probably *paides* as well.[56]

We are well informed about the duties of the *paides*. Curtius (8.6.2–6) and Arrian (4.13.1) give detailed accounts of them in their description of the Pages Conspiracy, and there is little contradiction between their accounts. According to them, their duties included attending to the king's personal needs and keeping him company; they guarded him while he slept, served him at *symposia*, handed him his horse and helped him to mount, and accompanied him on the hunt. Curtius (5.1.42, 8.6.4) also described them accompanying the king in battle. Yet there is no actual record of the *paides* being present in battle, though Aelian's account (*Varra Historiae* 14.48) indicates they had military training.[57]

Although no source clearly states their age range, it is generally agreed that they were in their mid- to late teens. It is unlikely that they were any younger because their duties included the defense of the person of the king and because both Philip and Alexander treated them like adults.[58] We also lack certainty about their number. It is not known whether all sons of the Companions served as *paides* or whether they were selected from the entire body of the elite. Nor are we told whether the number was fixed.[59] It seems safe to assume that, during the reigns of Philip and Alexander, a period of great change in Macedonia, the number fluctuated over time, just like the number of Companions.

The institution of the *paides* was significant, first of all, because it was a kind of training school for future generals and governors, as Curtius observed (5.1.42, 8.6.6), and it served as an institutionalized rite of passage for the young elite.[60] The *paides'* regular participation in court *symposia* and royal hunting led to their early indoctrination in the values of elite Macedonians. In short, the institution constituted the beginning of the *paides'* lifelong paths as members of the elite. The institution also served to tie them securely to the king, and, in particular, those who became the *syntrophoi* of the king's son developed intimate personal ties with him. The early attachment of the elite boys to the king and the prince resulted in the close interdependence between the king and his Companions. Moreover, the *paides* were instructed in all branches of a liberal education and met and conversed with the leading Greek intellectuals who stayed at court. As a result, the Macedonian elite was fully integrated into the cultural development at court. Among the former *paides* of Philip are several distinguished men of letters, such as Ptolemy and Marsyas. Furthermore, the *paides* served as hostages to an extent so as to ensure their fathers' good behavior, especially after the nobility of the cantons of Upper Macedonia became Companions during Philip's reign. The institution of the *paides* thus further strengthened the loyalty of the elite to the king.

Significantly, the institution of the *paides* just like the *symposia* and royal hunting, was marked by contradictory elements.[61] On the one hand, the *paides* were distinguished by their prominent background and their closeness to the king and his son. On the other hand, their duties were not much different from those of slaves, as Curtius specifically notes (8.6.2), and as is exemplified by the fact that punishment for misconduct was usually flogging. Archelaus' death (if Decamnichus was a member of the *paides*) and certainly Hermolaus' conspiracy were triggered by revenge for having been flogged. It appears that the king, who alone had the right to flog them (Curt. 8.6.5), sought to imbue the sons of the elite with the idea of his superiority through this demeaning and humiliating punishment.

In addition, the institution of the *paides* often provided a locus for erotic relationships at the Macedonian court, where homosexuality was common. We know that there were pairs of lovers among the *paides*, or involving *paides* and older members of the elite, and sometimes the king himself. Examples of these include the two couples in the conspiracy of Hermolaus (Hermolaus and Sostratus, Epimenes and Charicles), Dimnus and Nicomachus in the Philotas affair (they were probably alumni), Archelaus and Crataeus (or Craterus), Archelaus and Hellanocrates, Philip and Alexander of Epirus,[62] and Philip and Pausanias of Orestis. The alleged sexual relationship between Alexander and Hephaestion may have begun when they were *syntrophoi*. In fact, the somewhat institutionalized homosexuality at the Macedonian court, which began when the elite were *paides* and was maintained later in sympotic situations, sometimes formed the background for regicide and conspiracy.[63]

In the later years of Alexander's reign, evidence about the *paides* is poorer. After Hermolaus' conspiracy, nothing more is heard of them individually or collectively until they re-emerge in Babylon after Alexander's death (Curt. 10.5.8, 7.16), and it may well be that they were greatly reduced in number after the conspiracy.[64] During the period of the Successors, each general recruited his own guards in imitation of Alexander and probably had his own system of *paides* as well, for Eumenes, Alcetas, Seleucus, and Antigonus are known to have had their own *paides*.[65] Although we have scant direct information about the *paides* in the Antigonid period, the institution seems to have endured until the end of the dynasty, as is shown by Livy's account of Perseus being accompanied by *paides* when he fled to Samothrace after the Battle of Pydna (45.6.7).[66]

4 Conclusion

The life of the Macedonian elite was highly agonistic. It has been frequently observed that the Macedonian monarchy was very personal in nature, that the king's power was conceived as personal rather than institutional, and that personal relationships with the king determined almost everything. For the Companions status, wealth, and fame came from the king only. While he lavishly entertained them at *symposia* and engaged with them in hunting, he also fostered intense competition among them for his favor.

The Macedonian court, which provided a stage for their regular interaction and competition, is known to have been increasingly integrated into the cultural life of Greece. Argead kings attracted many leading Greek intellectuals to their court, and it was Archelaus who promoted its intense Hellenization, although he was not the first king to invite Greek intellectuals. Alexander I's connections with Herodotus and Pindar are well known, and Perdiccas II probably entertained Melanippides and Hippocrates at his court. Archelaus invited a number of major Greek artists and intellectuals to his court, including Euripides, Agathon, Zeuxis, Choerilus, and Timotheus, and he sought to make his court a focus for Greek intellectual life. Royal interest in Hellenic high culture continued in the fourth century as Amyntas III employed Nicomachus, father of Aristotle, as his court doctor, and Perdiccas III, whose devotion to philosophy is well known, used the Platonic philosopher Euphraeus as his political adviser. Philip II continued this tradition on an even larger scale by attracting a great number of Greek intellectuals to Pella, among whom were Aristotle, Anaximenes, Theopompus, and Python. During his reign, which was characterized by growing Hellenization, these intellectuals competed for royal patronage. At the court of Alexander, who himself had grown up under the tutelage of Aristotle and was a lover of Greek culture, Callisthenes and Anaxarchus were major figures. Indeed, Hellenization and royal patronage did not cease with the end of the Argead dynasty. In the period of the Successors both Antipater, who himself was a distinguished man of letters, and Cassander, who was known as a patron of fine arts, had intimate connections with the Peripatetic school at Athens. In the Antigonid period, Pella once more became a center of Greek culture under Antigonus Gonatas, who himself had been a pupil of Menedemus and of Zeno. In Gonatas' reign, Greek intellectuals again frequented the Macedonian court, including Hieronymus, Aratus, Persaeus, and Timon. As a result of this ongoing Hellenization of the court, not only the kings but also the Companions and the *paides* were imbued with Hellenic culture and were fully integrated into the Greek intellectual world.[67]

It is thus clear that the upper strata of Macedonian society were highly Hellenized. The fact that the Macedonian kings and elite nevertheless retained their own distinctive practices and values, discussed above, at least until Alexander's reign is noteworthy. Although we have little evidence about how the Macedonian kings and elite saw themselves because of the lack of Macedonian literary accounts, their retention of distinctive practices and values provides hints for exploring their self-perceptions.[68]

Bibliographical essay

A good starting point for the study of the Macedonian *symposium* is E.N. Borza, 'The Symposium at Alexander's Court', *Ancient Macedonia* 3 (Thessaloniki 1983), pp. 45–55, which emphasizes the significance of the *symposium* as a social institution at the

Macedonian court. The most recent and fullest treatment is E.D. Carney, 'Symposia and the Macedonian Elite: The Unmixed Life', *Syllecta Classica* 18 (2007), pp. 129–80. Also useful and suggestive are O. Murray, 'Hellenistic Royal Symposia', in P. Bilde et al. (eds.), *Aspects of Hellenistic Kingships* (Aarhus 1996), pp. 15–27, and A. Kottaridi, 'The Symposium', in D. Pandermalis (ed.), *Alexander the Great* (New York 2004), pp. 65–87. Important studies of the physical setting of *symposia* are R.A. Tomlinson, 'Ancient Macedonian Symposia', *Ancient Macedonia* 1 (Thessaloniki 1970), pp. 308–15, and I. Nielsen, 'Royal Banquets: The Development of Royal Banquets and Banqueting Halls from Alexander to the Tetrarchs', in I. Nielsen and H.S. Nielsen (eds.), *Meals in a Social Context: Aspects of the Communal Meal in the Hellenistic and Roman World* (Aarhus 1998), pp. 102–33. K.A. Wardle et al., 'The Symposium in Macedonia: A Prehistoric Perspective', *AEMTH* 15 (2003), pp. 631–43, offers a valuable survey of the archaeological evidence for Macedonian drinking practices in pre-Argead times.

On Macedonian royal hunting, P. Briant, 'Chasses royales macédoniennes et chasses royales perses: Le thème de la chasse au lion sur *la chasse de Vergina*', *DHA* 17 (1991), pp. 211–55, and 'Les chasses d'Alexandre', *Ancient Macedonia* 5 (Thessaloniki 1993), pp. 267–77, remain indispensable works. A recent important study of hunting is E.D. Carney, 'Hunting and the Macedonian Elite: Sharing the Rivalry of the Chase (Arrian 4.13.1)', in D. Ogden (ed.), *The Hellenistic World: New Perspectives* (Swansea 2002), pp. 59–80, which treats hunting in the context of the interaction between the king and the elite. Also of note is R. Lane Fox, 'Ancient Hunting: From Homer to Polybios', in G. Shipley and J. Salmon (eds.), *Human Landscapes in Classical Antiquity: Environment and Culture* (London 1996), pp. 119–53. On the hunting iconography, O. Palagia, 'Hephaestion's Pyre and the Royal Hunt of Alexander', in A.B. Bosworth and E.J. Baynham (eds.), *Alexander the Great in Fact and Fiction* (Oxford 2000), pp. 167–206, is excellent, showing how integral lion hunting is to Macedonian ideology. Two valuable books on hunting in ancient Greece, J.K. Anderson, *Hunting in the Ancient World* (Berkeley and Los Angeles 1985), and J.M. Barringer, *The Hunt in Ancient Greece* (Baltimore 2001), also contain fine treatments of the Macedonian hunting tradition.

On the institution of the *paides*, the most comprehensive study is N.G.L. Hammond, 'Royal Pages, Personal Pages, and Boys Trained in the Macedonian Manner during the Period of the Temenid Monarchy', *Historia* 39 (1990), pp. 261–90. W. Heckel, *The Marshals of Alexander's Empire* (London 1992), provides a useful overview of *paides* in Alexander's reign on pp. 237–44. Most recently there is E.D. Carney, 'The Role of the *Basilikoi Paides* at the Argead Court', in T. Howe and J. Reames (eds.), *Macedonian Legacies: Studies in Ancient Macedonian History and Culture in Honor of Eugene N. Borza* (Claremont 2008) pp. 145–64. All of these topics are also suggestively treated by J. Roisman, 'Honor in Alexander's Campaign', in J. Roisman (ed.), *Brill's Companion to Alexander the Great* (Leiden 2003), pp. 279–321.

Notes

1 On these sources, see P.J. Rhodes, chapter 2.
2 On Philip II, see S. Müller, chapter 9.
3 On the Companions, see Hammond and Griffith, *History of Macedonia* 2, pp. 395–400, Hammond, *Macedonian State*, pp. 53–7, 140–7, and W. Heckel, 'King and "Companions"', in J. Roisman (ed.), *Brill's Companion to Alexander the Great* (Leiden 2003), pp. 197–225.

4   In the Alexander-historians these youths are officially called *paides* or *paides basilikoi*: W. Heckel, *The Marshals of Alexander's Empire* (London 1992), p. 241. The usual English label for them is 'pages', although this is misleading given its medieval context, as E.D. Carney, 'The Conspiracy of Hermolaus', *CJ* 76 (1980–1), p. 227, and 'The Role of the *Basilikoi Paides* at the Argead Court', in T. Howe and J. Reames (eds.), *Macedonian Legacies: Studies in Ancient Macedonian History and Culture in Honor of Eugene N. Borza* (Claremont 2008), pp. 145–6, notes, so I tend to use the term *paides* in this chapter.

5   On Alexander, see D.L. Gilley and Ian Worthington, chapter 10.

6   On the usage of the term *symposium*, see E.N. Borza, 'The Symposium at Alexander's Court', *Ancient Macedonia* 3 (Thessaloniki 1983), pp. 45–6.

7   On the culture of Greek *symposia*, see, for example, O. Murray, 'The Symposion as Social Organization', in R. Hägg (ed.), *The Greek Renaissance of the Eighth Century B.C.* (Stockholm 1983), pp. 195–9, 'Sympotic History', in O. Murray (ed.), *Sympotica* (Oxford 1990), pp. 3–13, and 'Forms of Sociality', in J.-P. Vernant (ed.), *The Greeks* (Chicago 1995), pp. 218–53.

8   Murray, 'Symposion as Social Organization', p. 196.

9   For example, Dem. 2.18–19, Theopompus, *FGrH* 115 FF 81, 224, 225, 236, 282.

10 Many of the tombs of the female elites also contain drinking items. Although female sympotic activity has been controversial, material evidence certainly associates women with drinking: see A. Kottaridi, 'The Symposium', in D. Pandermalis (ed.), *Alexander the Great* (New York 2004), p. 69, and E.D. Carney, 'Symposia and the Macedonian Elite: The Unmixed Life', *Syllecta Classica* 18 (2007), pp. 143–4. On Macedonian women, see E.D. Carney, chapter 20.

11 On the dubious historicity of this tale, see R.M. Errington, 'Alexander the Philhellene and Persia', in H.J. Dell (ed.), *Ancient Macedonian Studies in Honor of Charles F. Edson* (Thessaloniki 1981), pp. 139–43, and Borza, *Shadow of Olympus*, pp. 101–3.

12 F. Geyer, *Makedonien bis zur Thronbesteigung Philipps II* (Munich 1930), pp. 84–5, Hammond and Griffith, *History of Macedonia 2*, pp. 135–7, and Borza, *Shadow of Olympus*, pp. 161–2.

13 On the inaccuracy of Carystius on Euphraeus, see Hammond and Griffith, *History of Macedonia 2*, p. 206; see also J. Roisman, chapter 8, p. 163.

14 This point is made by O. Murray, 'Hellenistic Royal Symposia', in P. Bilde et al. (eds.), *Aspects of Hellenistic Kingships* (Aarhus 1996), p. 18; see Carney, 'Symposia and the Macedonian Elite', pp. 153–9, for full discussion.

15 For a discussion of why Greeks needed to dilute their wine with water and why the Macedonians did not, see Borza, 'Symposium at Alexander's Court', pp. 48–9, and J. Davidson, *Courtesans and Fishcakes: The Consuming Passions of Classical Athens* (London 1997), pp. 46–8.

16 For discussion and reference on these unruly banquets, see J. Roisman, 'Honor in Alexander's Campaign', in J. Roisman (ed.), *Brill's Companion to Alexander the Great* (Leiden 2003), pp. 318–21, and Carney, 'Symposia and the Macedonian Elite', pp. 167–9.

17 On the functions of the *symposia*, see Borza, 'Symposium at Alexander's Court', pp. 54–5, *Shadow of Olympus*, pp. 241–2, and Carney, 'Symposia and the Macedonian Elite', pp. 161–2, 172–3.

18 See Borza, 'Symposium at Alexander's Court', p. 55, and *Shadow of Olympus*, p. 242.

19 See references in Hammond and Griffith, *History of Macedonia 2*, pp. 397–8, and Hammond, *Macedonian State*, pp. 143–4.

20 See Murray, 'Hellenistic Royal Symposia', pp. 16–18, and Carney, 'Symposia and the Macedonian Elite', pp. 142–63, for general discussion.

21 Murray, 'Sympotic History', pp. 6–7, and 'Forms of Sociality', pp. 224–34.

22 Murray, 'Forms of Sociality', p. 243, and 'Hellenistic Royal Symposia', p. 25.

23 See Roisman, 'Honor in Alexander's Campaign', p. 317, and Carney, 'Symposia and the Macedonian Elite', p. 173.

24 I. Nielsen, 'Royal Palaces and Type of Monarchy', *Hephaistos* 15 (1997), pp. 157–8.

25 For example, Plut., *Alexander* 70.3, Curt. 9.7.15, Athen. 1.17f, 12.537d, 538c–d, and see Carney, 'Symposia and the Macedonian Elite', pp. 148–51.

26 Persian official banquets were quite splendid and luxurious, sometimes with as many as 15,000 guests (Athen. 4.145a–146c): see Murray, 'Hellenistic Royal Symposia', pp. 18–19.

27 For a discussion of these contradictory elements in the Macedonian *symposia*, see Roisman, 'Honor in Alexander's Campaign', pp. 316–18.

28   See the discussion and references in A. Dalby, 'The Wedding Feast of Caranus the Macedonian by Hippolochus', *Petits Propos Culinaires* 29 (1988), pp. 37–45.

29   See Hammond and Griffith, *History of Macedonia* 2, p. 156, Borza, *Shadow of Olympus*, p. 130, and E.D. Carney, 'Hunting and the Macedonian Elite', in D. Ogden (ed.), *The Hellenistic World* (Swansea 2002), pp. 60–1.

30   See W.S. Greenwalt, 'The Iconographical Significance of Amyntas III's Mounted Hunter Stater', *Ancient Macedonia* 5 (Thessaloniki 1993), p. 515, and Carney, 'Hunting and the Macedonian Elite', p. 61. The same hunting motif appears on the coins of Perdiccas III and Cassander.

31   Aristotle (*Politics* 1311b) claims that Archelaus was intentionally killed by his lover 'Crataeus', in cooperation with Decamnichus (who had been flogged by the king) and Hellanocrates; cf. Ael., *Varra Historiae* 8.9. Hammond and Griffith, *History of Macedonia* 2, pp. 167–8, prefers Aristotle's account.

32   See the evidence collected by P. Briant, 'Les chasses d'Alexandre', *Ancient Macedonia* 5 (Thessaloniki 1993), pp. 267–70.

33   On these representations of Alexander's lion hunts, see A. Stewart, *Faces of Power* (Berkeley and Los Angeles 1993), pp. 270–7, 294–306, O. Palagia, 'Hephaestion's Pyre and the Royal Hunt of Alexander', in A.B. Bosworth and E.J. Baynham (eds.), *Alexander the Great in Fact and Fiction* (Oxford 2000), pp. 184–9, 202–6, and J.M. Barringer, *The Hunt in Ancient Greece* (Baltimore 2001), pp. 185–7.

34   See P. Briant, 'Chasses royales macédoniennes et chasses royales perses', *DHA* 17 (1991), pp. 211–14, and Palagia, 'Hephaestion's Pyre', pp. 189–200.

35   Palagia, 'Hephaestion's Pyre', p. 167, and Barringer, *Hunt in Ancient Greece*, p. 1.

36   Palagia, 'Hephaestion's Pyre', p. 177, and Carney, 'Hunting and the Macedonian Elite', p. 62.

37   For convenient summaries of this controversy and arguments for and against the occupant being Philip II, see E.N. Borza and O. Palagia, 'The Chronology of the Macedonian Royal Tombs at Vergina', *JDAI* 122 (2007), pp. 81–125, and Ian Worthington, *Philip II of Macedonia* (New Haven 2008), pp. 234–41.

38   Since there is no evidence to suggest that game parks existed in Macedonia before Alexander, they may well have been introduced after his campaigns. On the vast game parks in the Persian Empire, see Xenophon, *Cyropaedia* 1.4.5–11, 6.28–29. Briant, 'Chasses royales macédoniennes', pp. 232–4, and 'Chasses d'Alexandre', pp. 272–3, assumes that they were introduced from Thrace during Philip's reign.

39   See J.K. Anderson, *Hunting in the Ancient World* (Berkeley and Los Angeles 1985), pp. 63–70, Briant, 'Chasses royales macédoniennes', pp. 217–22, and Palagia, 'Hephaestion's Pyre', p. 181.

40   On Hephaestion's pyre, which has been the subject of controversy, see Palagia, 'Hephaestion's Pyre', pp. 167–75.

41   On the struggles, see W.L. Adams, chapter 11.

42   See Briant, 'Chasses royales macédoniennes', p. 241, Palagia, 'Hephaestion's Pyre', pp. 167, 183–4, Carney, 'Hunting and the Macedonian Elite', pp. 65, 67.

43   On the functions of the royal hunt, see Greenwalt, 'Iconographical Significance', p. 518, R. Lane Fox, 'Ancient Hunting', in G. Shipley and J. Salmon (eds.), *Human Landscapes in Classical Antiquity* (London 1996), pp. 141–3, Carney, 'Hunting and the Macedonian Elite', pp. 59, 62, 68, and Roisman, 'Honor in Alexander's Campaign', pp. 313–16.

44   The ambivalence between egalitarian and competitive values in Alexander's *symposia* and hunting is discussed by Roisman, 'Honor in Alexander's Campaign', pp. 313–21, especially pp. 314 and 317.

45   H.S. Lund, *Lysimachus* (London 1992), pp. 160–1.

46   C.F. Edson, 'The Antigonids, Heracles and Beroea', *HSCP* 45 (1934), pp. 226–9, and 'Macedonica', *HSCP* 51 (1940), pp. 125–6, Hammond and Griffith, *History of Macedonia* 2, p. 155, n. 4.

47   Carney, 'Hunting and the Macedonian Elite', p. 68.

48   For references, see Anderson, *Hunting in the Ancient World*, pp. 81–2, Lane Fox, 'Ancient Hunting', p. 144.

49   See E.D. Carney, 'Elite Education and High Culture in Macedonia', in W. Heckel and L. Tritle (eds.), *Crossroads of History* (Claremont 2003), p. 60, n. 44 and p. 62.

50   Plut., *Alexander* 40.1, Athen. 13.539c, Ael., *Varra Historiae* 9.3.

51 On the conspiracy of Hermolaus, see Carney, 'Conspiracy of Hermolaus', pp. 223–31, and 'Role of the *Basilikoi Paides*', pp. 150–7, A.B. Bosworth, *A Historical Commentary on Arrian's History of Alexander* 2 (Oxford 1995), pp. 90–101, E. Badian, 'Conspiracies', in A.B. Bosworth and E. Baynham (eds.), *Alexander the Great in Fact and Fiction* (Oxford 2000), pp. 70–2.

52 Those who are said to have killed Archelaus (Arist., *Politics* 1311b, Diod. 14.37.6; see also n. 31 above), Crataeus (or Craterus), Decamnichus, and Hellanocrates, may have been among his *paides*. Hammond and Griffith, *History of Macedonia* 2, pp. 167–8, and N.G.L Hammond, 'Royal Pages, Personal Pages, and Boys Trained in the Macedonian Manner during the Period of the Temenid Monarchy', *Historia* 39 (1990), p. 263, despite the skeptical remarks of Heckel, *Marshals of Alexander's Empire*, p. 239, and Bosworth, *Commentary on Arrian* 2, p. 94.

53 See Hammond and Griffith, *History of Macedonia* 2, p. 401, Hammond, 'Royal Pages, Personal Pages, and Boys', pp. 261–4, Heckel, *Marshals of Alexander's Empire*, pp. 239–40, Bosworth, *Commentary on Arrian* 2, p. 91, Worthington, *Philip II*, p. 30.

54 Heckel, *Marshals of Alexander's Empire*, p. 239, and 'King and "Companions"', p. 205, Carney, 'Role of the *Basilikoi Paides*', p. 146.

55 Carney, 'Elite Education and High Culture in Macedonia', pp. 57–9, cautions against considering *syntrophoi* as synonymous with *paides*.

56 See Hammond and Griffith, *History of Macedonia* 2, pp. 401–2, Heckel, *Marshals of Alexander's Empire*, p. 238.

57 See Bosworth, *Commentary on Arrian* 2, p. 93.

58 Carney, 'Conspiracy of Hermolaus', p. 228, and 'Role of the *Basilikoi Paides*', pp. 147–8.

59 H. Berve, *Das Alexanderreich auf prosopographischer Grundlage* 1 (Munich 1926), p. 37, n. 3, assumes a figure of about 100, Hammond and Griffith, *History of Macedonia* 2, p. 401, about 85, and Hammond, 'Royal Pages, Personal Pages, and Boys', p. 266, some 200. None of their assertions is warranted by the evidence.

60 On the significance of the institution, see Hammond and Griffith, *History of Macedonia* 2, p. 401, Heckel, 'King and "Companions"', p. 206, Roisman, 'Honor in Alexander's Campaign', p. 303, Carney, 'Role of the *Basilikoi Paides*', p. 147.

61 On the ambiguity of their status, see Roisman, 'Honor in Alexander's Campaign', pp. 302–3.

62 It is doubtful that Philip had this sort of liaison with Alexander of Epirus, which is based on a hostile tradition: see Worthington, *Philip II*, p. 70.

63 See E.D. Carney, 'Regicide in Macedonia', *PP* 38 (1983), p. 272.

64 Carney, 'Conspiracy of Hermolaus', p. 231, Bosworth, *Commentary on Arrian* 2, p. 92.

65 For references, see Hammond, 'Royal Pages, Personal Pages, and Boys', pp. 270–1, Heckel, *Marshals of Alexander's Empire*, pp. 240–1. See also Hammond and Walbank, *History of Macedonia* 3, p. 195, n. 2.

66 On Perseus' flight, see Hammond and Walbank, *History of Macedonia* 3, p. 558, Hammond, *Macedonian State*, p. 378.

67 For discussion and references, see Carney, 'Elite Education and High Culture in Macedonia', pp. 50–7. See also F.W. Walbank, 'Macedonia and Greece', *CAH²* 7.1 (Cambridge 1984), pp. 228–9.

68 This is related to the vexed question of Macedonian ethnic identity. For a detailed discussion of this issue, see J. Engels, chapter 5.

References

CAH² = *Cambridge Ancient History²*.

FGrH = F. Jacoby, *Die Fragmente der grieschischen Historiker*.

Borza, *Shadow of Olympus* = E.N. Borza, *In the Shadow of Olympus. The Emergence of Macedon* (Princeton: 1990).

Hammond, *Macedonian State* = N.G.L. Hammond, *The Macedonian State: The Origins, Institutions and History* (Oxford: 1992).

Hammond and Griffith, *History of Macedonia* 2 = N.G.L. Hammond and G.T. Griffith, *A History of Macedonia* 2 (Oxford; 1979).

Hammond and Walbank, *History of Macedonia* 3 = N.G.L. Hammond and F.W. Walbank, *A History of Macedonia* 3 (Oxford: 1988).

3

ALEXANDER'S AIMS

Introduction

Alexander's aim in invading Asia and then his aims in Asia are as controversial as any other aspect of his life. When he became king in 336 on the assassination of Philip,[1] his aims were apparently clear: to succeed his father as king and hegemon of his League of Corinth,[2] and to fulfil Philip's last ambitious plan, the invasion of Persia (Diod. 16.89.2, Arr. 2.14.4, 3.18.12). Although the Greeks revolted when Philip died, Alexander swiftly reimposed Macedonian hegemony (Diod. 17.3–4, Arr. 1.1.1–3), and in early spring 334 he led his army into Persia (Arr. 1.11.3).

Precisely why Philip had set his sights on Asia is not fully known, but a factor may well have been the need for money given he practised a rolling economy, with the spoils of one campaign funding the next.[3] Some sources suggest that Alexander was hard-pressed for revenue when he invaded Persia, indicating that he also inherited a debt from his father (see Sources 19 and 20). However, the official reason – as put forward by Philip in 337 – was to inflict revenge on the Persians for their sacrilegious looting of Athens in 480 during the Persian War (cf. Source 21) and to liberate the Greek cities under Persian rule in Asia Minor. This was the 'mandate' that the League of Corinth would bestow on Alexander in 336, and it presumably followed that once he achieved it he would return home. He did not; after the empire fell to him he turned eastwards into India. There his army mutinied on him at the Hyphasis river in 326,[4] an action which forced him finally to turn back west (Source 76). Even then, he did not plan to return to Greece, but set in motion his next campaign, the invasion of Arabia.

Philip may have intended to campaign only in the western part of the Persian empire,[5] but Alexander intended to bring down the entire empire (Sources 43, 44 and 50). The question is whether Alexander had that goal in mind when he became king (hence an attempt to outdo the plans of his father) or whether his spectacular military successes brought with them the desire to continue advancing as Alexander grew to know nothing other than fighting. If the latter, how did that relate to the mandate of the League of Corinth, and what sort of empire was Alexander envisaging?

Another question is the effect Asia would have on Alexander.[6] His visit to the Oracle of Zeus Ammon at Siwah in 330 (Sources 98–103),[7] at which he had apparently been confirmed as a son of Zeus, was a turning point not only in his attitude to his own divinity but also in his aims (cf. Source 106). As Alexander continued further east into Bactria and Sogdiana, and then India, he underwent a drastic transformation, appearing in his dress and manners more like an oriental potentate than a Macedonian warrior king. His desire to outdo the exploits of his heroic ancestors Heracles and Dionysus is one reason why he decided to invade India (cf. Source 69).[8] He may even have decided to move the capital of his kingdom from Pella to Babylon, or perhaps Alexandria. But again, was all this – and how he came to perceive himself – the result of his continued time in Asia, or something that he been contemplating at the start of his campaign? To what extent did his aims change, if at all, from the time he invaded Asia, and how did he come to see his empire?

Ancient sources

The need for money?

19   To provision these forces,[9] Aristobulus (*FGrH* 139 F 4) says he had not more than seventy talents; Duris (*FGrH* 70 F 40) speaks of maintenance for only thirty days; and Onesicritus says he owed two hundred talents as well (Onesicritus, *FGrH* 134 – now *BNJ* 134 – F 2 = Plut. *Alex.* 15.2, [Plut.] *Mor.* 327d).

20   [Alexander went to Asia] trusting only to the strength of thirty thousand foot and four thousand horse. For so many there were, by the account which Aristobulus gives; by the relation of King Ptolemy (*FGrH* 138 F 4), there were thirty thousand foot and five thousand horse … Now the glorious and magnificent sum which Fortune had raised up to supply the necessities … was no more than seventy talents, according to Aristobulus (Aristobulus, *FGrH* 139 F 4 = Plut. *Alex.* 15.1–2, [Plut.] *Mor.* 327d–e, 342d).

Never forgetting the reason for the invasion?

21   Of his campaign against Porus[10] he himself has given an account in his letters. But the Hydaspes, made violent by the storm and dashing high against its bank, made a great breach in it, and a large part of the stream was setting in that direction; and the shore between the two currents gave his men no sure footing, since it was broken and slippery. And here it was that he is said to have cried: 'O Athenians, can you possibly believe what perils I am undergoing to win glory in your eyes?' This, however, is the story of Onesicritus; Alexander himself says that they left their rafts and crossed the breach with their armour on, wading breast-high in water (Onesicritus, *FGrH* 134 – now *BNJ* 134 – F 19 = Plut. *Alex.* 60.1, 5–7).

Modern works

In the following selections, the late P.A. Brunt, formerly Camden Professor of Roman History at the University of Oxford, talks of Alexander's invasion of Persia as simply his inheritance from Philip and his advance to India as something of a natural extension of Alexander's military campaigning and the product of his own growing religiosity. W. Heckel, Professor of Ancient History at the University of Calgary, argues that Alexander intended to conquer the Persian empire, but only that, and deliberately did not venture beyond the boundaries of his empire.

1   P.A. Brunt, 'The Aims of Alexander', *Greece and Rome*[2] 12 (Cambridge University Press: 1965), pp. 205–215.[11]

2   W. Heckel, 'Alexander the Great and the "Limits of the Civilised World"', in W. Heckel and L. Tritle (eds), *Crossroads of History, The Age of Alexander* (Regina Books: 2003), Chap. 8, pp. 147–174.[12]

Additional reading

M.M. Austin, 'Alexander and the Macedonian Invasion of Asia', in J. Rich and G. Shipley (eds), *War and Society in the Greek World* (London: 1993), pp. 197–223.

E.A. Fredricksmeyer, 'On the Final Aims of Philip II', in W.L. Adams and E.N. Borza (eds), *Philip II, Alexander the Great, and the Macedonian Heritage* (Lanham: 1982), pp. 85–98.

D.L. Gilley and Ian Worthington, 'Alexander the Great, Macedonia and Asia', in J. Roisman and Ian Worthington (eds), *The Blackwell Companion to Ancient Macedonia* (Oxford: 2010), pp. 186–207.

N.G.L. Hammond, 'The Kingdom of Asia and the Persian Throne', *Antichthon* 20 (1986), pp. 73–85.

Ian Worthington, *Philip II of Macedonia* (New Haven and London: 2008), pp. 166–171.

Notes

1 Diod. 16.91.1–94.4, Arr. 1.1.1, Plut. *Alex.* 10.6.
2 On this, and on Alexander's dealings with the Greeks, see Chapter 5.
3 See Ian Worthington, *Philip II of Macedonia* (New Haven and London: 2008), pp. 166–171, on Philip's aims.
4 Diod. 17.94.3 ff., Arr. 5.25.2 ff., Curt. 9.3.3–5.
5 Worthington, *Philip II of Macedonia*, pp. 169–171.
6 See Chapter 6.
7 Strabo 17.1.43, Arr. 3.3–4, Plut. *Alex.* 27.8–10, cf. Diod. 17.51, Curt. 4.7.25, Justin 11.11.2–12.
8 On India, see Chapter 7.
9 For the invasion of Persia in 334.
10 The Indian prince, whose defiance of Alexander in 326 led to the Battle of the Hydaspes river: see Sources 72–75.
11 Reprinted with the permission of Cambridge University Press.
12 Reprinted by permission of Regina Books.

THE AIMS OF ALEXANDER[1]

P. A. Brunt

Sir William Tarn wrote that 'the primary reason why Alexander invaded Persia was, no doubt, that he never thought of *not* doing it; it was his inheritance'. The invasion had been planned and begun by Philip. It was, in name, a Panhellenic enterprise, to exact retribution for the devastation wrought by Xerxes in Greece and to liberate the Greeks of Asia Minor.[2] These aims Alexander faithfully fulfilled. From the spoils of the Granicus he dedicated three hundred Persian panoplies to Athens' tutelary goddess; he sent back to Athens the statues of Harmodius and Aristogiton which Xerxes had carried off to Susa; and he excused the burning of Persepolis as a reprisal for the sack of Athens.[3] The Panhellenic war was then over, and Alexander sent the Greek contingents home (A. iii. 19. 5). In general he freed the Greek cities of Asia from the control of satraps; they were to pay no taxes, to receive no garrisons and to live under their own laws.[4] By expelling tyrants or oligarchs and setting up democratic governments, he not only removed the partisans of Persia from power but did homage to the growing tendency in Greece to equate freedom with democracy.[5] The gratitude of the liberated cities was long-enduring; it was here that his cult survived into Roman times.[6] In reality of course they were as much subject to his will as less privileged subjects. And to Greek cities that opposed him he was less accommodating. Halicarnassus and Aspendus, which certainly counted as Greek, were subjected to his satraps.[7] They could be treated as disloyal to the Panhellenic cause, like the captive mercenaries who fought against him at the Granicus and who were sent back in chains to forced labour in Macedon. But Alexander was not always so merciless. He spared the mercenaries who were holding out against him on an island in the harbour of Miletus, and enlisted them in his own army; it would not have been easy to take the island by force.[8] Sentiment and principle gave way to his own interests, as they always did.

Polybius says that Philip launched the crusade against Persia to win goodwill in the Greek world.[9] If he entertained such a hope, it was plainly delusory. The persistent propaganda of Isocrates for a national war against Persia had fallen on deaf ears. Since 412 all the leading Greek cities had vied with each other in seeking Persian subsidies or diplomatic support. None had any reason to fear Persian aggression; like the Romans after Augustus' death, the Persian kings were content with their *fines imperii*; bent on restoring control over Asia and Egypt, they had been very willing to promote internal discords among the Greek cities under the name of 'the freedom and autonomy of every city, great or small'. The sense of natural antagonism between Greeks and barbarians can easily be exaggerated,[10] and in any event to Greeks of the fourth century, even to Isocrates, Macedonians too were barbarians (though the ruling dynasty had a recognized claim to be regarded as Greek),[11] and it was they, not Persia, whose power menaced Greek freedom. Demosthenes and king Agis took Persian gold,[12] and the Thebans in 335 called on their fellow Greeks to fight for liberty in concert with the great king.[13] They were right; in his last year Alexander showed that he meant to be master in Greece. Between 336 and 322 most Greek cities were in arms at one time or another against the Macedonian power.[14] Alexander himself suffered no illusions;[15] he knew that he could not in 334 rely on a Greek fleet to dispute the mastery of the seas with the Persians, and the Greek contingents in his army played only a subordinate role in the fighting, apart from the Thessalians who owed Philip special gratitude for restoring peace and order in their country. The Panhellenic crusade was a fiction for everyone but modern scholars who suppose that Isocrates' pamphlets were widely admired for anything but their languid eloquence.

Even Isocrates had envisaged a war with a different purpose. Retribution for long distant wrongs hardly interested him;[16] he even showed surprisingly little concern for the 'enslaved' Greeks in Asia.[17] In the *Panegyricus* he had urged that it was folly for the Greeks to contend with each other over a few barren acres, when the wealth of the Persian empire was theirs for the taking. In 346 he had recommended Philip to win fame by conquering lands in Asia for the surplus population of Greece. Philip had sufficient power and wealth already; his reward was to be glory, and the material fruits of his victories were to enure to the Greeks.[18] At Pella this can only have evoked ridicule. For attacking Persia Philip had a Macedonian as well as a Panhellenic pretext, that by aiding Perinthus in 340 the Persians had broken a treaty concluded with him,[19] and he surely intended to annex Persian territory himself. Certainly this was Alexander's purpose from the first. As soon as he had won the battle of the Granicus, he appointed satraps and imposed tribute on the king's Asiatic subjects.[20]

We cannot say how far Philip intended to go. Perhaps he could not have said himself. In 332 Darius offered to cede all his territory west of the Euphrates. Parmenio declared that he would close with the offer, if he were Alexander. 'So would I', replied Alexander, 'if I were Parmenio.'[21] It is often supposed that Philip would have agreed with his old general rather than with his son. There is no warrant for this belief. Philip was an opportunist and his ambitions expanded with his successes. Wilcken thought that he would have been content to make his existing possessions secure by conquering the whole or the greater part of the seaboard of the eastern Mediterranean. But the Macedonians were not a maritime or commercial people, and it was natural for their king to entertain continental ambitions. All his contemporaries knew that the Persian empire was weak in everything but money. Outside Iran, where the nobility shared in the imperial government, the king's subjects in general were discontented, or at best indifferent to a change of masters; kings and satraps had depended heavily on Greek mercenaries who might be seduced by Panhellenic propaganda and were in any event not superior to the Macedonian phalanx; the chief strength of native armies lay in the Iranian cavalry, which had threatened the survival of the Ten Thousand and limited the successes of Agesilaus, but which Alexander's Macedonian and Thessalian horse had a good chance of beating easily; and no one with a distant recollection of the triumphs of Cyrus the Great, whose forces were probably no more numerous at first than Alexander's, could assert that the army Alexander inherited from Philip, well-trained, confident, and by ancient standards large, was incapable of doing what Cyrus had once done.

There is then no difficulty in supposing that when Alexander cast a spear on the Asian shore, he meant to symbolize his intention of conquering Asia, that is to say, the whole Persian empire;[22] to Isocrates (v. 76; 100) 'Asia' is a synonym for the king's dominion. The story indeed comes from Diodorus and the source is poor. But it was Aristobulus, a well-informed authority,[23] who told how early in 333 Alexander untied the Gordian knot and offered sacrifice in thanksgiving to the gods for manifesting by this sign that he was destined to rule over Asia. All the evidence suggests that Alexander was a deeply religious man, sedulous in performing the ceremonies sanctioned by custom,[24] and that he came to believe that he was upheld in his victorious career by the favour of the gods.[25] After Gordium then he can have been in little doubt that he was destined to rule over Asia. He proclaimed this aim before Issus, in his negotiations with Darius in 332, and again before Gaugamela. That victory seemed decisive, and he was then apparently acknowledged as king of Asia by the army.[26] A change soon came over his attitude to Darius. In 332 he had castigated him as a usurper; after his death, he paid him respect as the legitimate ruler, and seems to have represented himself in some peculiar way as the heir of the Achaemenids, whose tombs he was zealous to restore.[27] This was natural enough; he had seen the loyalty and courage of the Iranian nobility in defending their king, and he wished to bind them to himself by similar sentiments.

It is not likely indeed that Alexander was guided at any time in his life by purely rational calculations. Devoted to the reading of Homer, he conceived himself as a second Achilles,[28] born

αἰὲν ἀριστεύειν καὶ ὑπείροχον ἔμμεναι ἄλλων.

The spirit of heroic adventure mingled with an insatiate curiosity. The oft-recurring phrase that he was seized with a longing to do or see things that no one or only a few had done or seen before seems to come down from Ptolemy and Nearchus, who were among his most intimate companions.[29] His almost uninterrupted successes engendered in him the conviction that he was permitted to achieve what was denied to ordinary mortals. More than once we are told that the more impracticable a project appeared, the more he was determined to undertake it;[30] though at other times, it is true, he was ready to adopt the prudent courses that caution recommended,[31] this unparalleled audacity served him well by making enemies surrender at the mere terror of his name. In the Indian campaigns a new motif comes to the fore in the emulation of Heracles and Dionysus. The Macedonians, misinterpreting what they heard of local legends, thought that they had found traces that Heracles and Dionysus had preceded Alexander on his march. This idea was very congenial to Alexander. At the rock of Aornus he even found himself able to do what Heracles had failed to do. When he heard of Dionysus' presence at Nysa, and of his foundation of the city, he *wanted* the story to be true and conceived the hope that he might also outstrip the god. Many such stories come from inferior sources and may be disbelieved; but the particular incidents mentioned (and indeed others) were recorded by the best authorities and must be credited.[32] Tarn indeed ridicules the whole tradition on the ground that it makes Alexander into an imitative character.[33] This is a very curious view. To excel the achievements of beings who were thought to have attained godhead by their terrestrial beneficence was an ambition that could be entertained only by a man conscious of his own transcendent powers, and to Greeks might well have been the basis of a charge of *hybris*. Again, it was Nearchus who told that Alexander sought to outdo Cyrus and Semiramis by traversing the desert of Baluchistan; and this must be believed against the official apologia for an enterprise probably hardly less disastrous than Napoleon's Russian campaign. Here *hybris* was indeed attended by *ate* and *nemesis*.[34]

Long before this, Alexander had been addressed at Siwah by the prophet of Ammon as 'son of Zeus' and, if we may adopt a plausible suggestion of Tarn, had been told within the sanctuary the sense in which he, the new Pharaoh, was of divine filiation.[35] As son of Zeus or Ammon – the identification was not new[36] – he did not cease to be the son of Philip; he never denied his earthly paternity. But he had heard that there was some mystical sense in which he could claim a divine origin too. Perhaps he was not at once convinced; but at Gaugamela he prayed for the help of the gods 'if indeed he was the son of Zeus', and the help came.[37] The prayer is attested by Callisthenes, and (despite his final quarrel with Alexander) that court historian must be supposed to have written either what was true or what he knew would please the king; whichever hypothesis we adopt, we must conclude that the claim to be the son of Zeus was one that Alexander made, if not before the battle, then at least by the time that Callisthenes wrote. Callisthenes also recorded that Apollo at Branchidae and the Sibyl of Erythrae confirmed the prophet of Ammon; we may surmise that Callisthenes gave the interpretation placed officially on ambiguous responses.[38] Probably Alexander's prolonged victories made him more and more certain that he was in some sense divine. There is indeed no proof of this in his unsuccessful attempt to impose *proskynesis* on his Macedonian and Greek entourage; this was an act of respect due in Persian society from inferior to superior, and, living in the country, Alexander cannot have continued to share the mistaken view prevalent in Greece that it was a recognition of divinity. His aim must here simply have been to establish uniformity in court etiquette.[39] But his deification at the end of his reign is another matter. The evidence that he himself demanded acknowledgement of his godhead from the Greeks, slender as it is, seems to me sufficient in the absence of any directly conflicting testimony;[40] and it ought not to be rejected simply on the ground that he had no rational motive for such a demand; Tarn was certainly wrong in holding that as a god a king could have a legitimate excuse for intervening in the affairs of cities whose autonomy he had guaranteed.[41] But the evidence from Greece is powerfully confirmed by what we know of his emulation of Heracles and Dionysus, by the statement of Eratosthenes that the Macedonians were apt to invoke τὸ θεῖον to please Alexander,[42] and above all by the explicit testimony of Aristobulus that Alexander expected to be acknowledged, like 'Dionysus', as a god by the Arabians.[43]

The Greeks did not make the sharp distinction between the divine and the human which we have derived from Jewish thought. But the traditional view that it was proper for mortals θνητὰ φρονεῖν was not extinct; it was only after Alexander that apotheosis became a conventional honour for kings or benefactors in Greece, and in Macedon it was not claimed by later kings. Even if we make the initiative for Alexander's deification come from Greeks who felt gratitude to him or wished to flatter him, it is hard to explain the choice of this still strange mode of doing him honour except on the assumption that it was believed to correspond to his own desires. Arrian's conjecture that he sought apotheosis to enhance his dignity (vii. 29) is not satisfying. A man so devout would hardly have aspired to divinity unless he had felt that he had a religious justification. Long ago Empedocles, one of the most religious of Greek thinkers, had written: 'I go among you as an immortal god, no mortal now, honoured among all as is right, crowned with fillets and flowery garlands.'[44] Why should we not suppose that Alexander too was imbued with a sense of divine inspiration, power and beneficence, sown in his mind by the teaching of Ammon and other oracular responses and confirmed by his superhuman achievements which made him feel himself to be the equal of Dionysus, entitled to the adoration of mankind? He knew of course that he would die, or rather quit this life;[45] but that had been the fate of Heracles and Dionysus. At any rate the belief in his divinity was accepted even by his proud Macedonian officers; for after his death his former secretary, Eumenes, induced them to set up a golden throne in the camp, before which they all did daily sacrifices and obeised themselves to Alexander as a god, taking counsel from his divine will and ever-living spirit.[46] Like Caesar,[47] and unlike any other deified king, Alexander commanded genuine veneration.

To a god upon earth the allegiance of all mankind was rightly due. In India Alexander expected universal submission and treated resistance as revolt,[48] even when he had passed beyond the confines of the empire the Achaemenids had once ruled.[49] Some held that he aimed at reaching the mouth of the Ganges and the encircling Ocean stream.[50] Even on Eratosthenes' later reconstruction of the eastern hemisphere he was not seemingly so far distant from this objective when he had reached the Hyphasis.[51] Here mutiny turned him back; but he had not forsworn conquests, and took his army homewards by a devious route that involved more fighting and brought him to the Ocean at the Indus delta. Certainly he did not (as Tarn holds) abandon any of his Indian acquisitions; the principalities of Porus and Taxilas were still regarded as parts of the empire after his death, and their status was not different in principle from the kingdoms of Cyprus and Phoenicia.[52] After his return to Mesopotamia he was still bent on more wars; he promised his veterans at Opis to give them rewards enough to incite the new Macedonian drafts to be ready to share the same dangers and exertions.[53] His immediate projects comprised the exploration of the Caspian, surely as a prelude to the deferred campaign against the Scyths,[54] and the conquest, not the mere circumnavigation, of Arabia; Aristobulus said that he intended to take possession of the country and found colonies there as part of a design to be 'lord of all'.[55] We are told that he left behind him memoranda for a gigantic plan of conquest in the west that would have taken him along the southern shore of the Mediterranean to the Ocean at Gibraltar (where Heracles once again had preceded him) and then along the northern shore back to Macedon.[56] Arrian has nothing of this, but then he has nothing about *any* plans of Alexander (except for the Caspian and Arabian projects). And Arrian himself had no doubt that Alexander would never have been content with what he had already conquered.[57] The authenticity of Alexander's reputed memoranda has been questioned, but in my view on quite insufficient grounds. The plan attributed to him is in keeping with all that we know of his character. It would have marked a new stage in the attempt to reduce the whole inhabited world, bounded by the Ocean, a world which in the west as in the east appeared much smaller than we know it to be.[58]

A prudent ruler, governed by rational calculations, would clearly not have embarked on such an enterprise. Large tracts of the old Persian empire were still not pacified.[59] Whatever administrative changes in its ramshackle structure be ascribed to Alexander, the conduct of some of his satraps during his long disappearance behind the barrier of the Hindu-Kush had shown that their independence could still, as under the Achaemenids, threaten the stability and unity of the empire. Greece was smouldering with discontent; even the loyalty of Macedon and its vice-gerent, Antipater, who did not comply with Alexander's summons to his court in 324, could not be counted on.[60] To secure the gains he had already made, Alexander needed decades of patient organizing work. It was not enough to remove or punish (as he did) officials whom he suspected of infidelity or oppression. But there is no sign that he had any taste for the humdrum routine of administration.

Not that he lacked statesmanlike views. He sought to turn nomads into settled, peaceful cultivators of the soil,[61] to foster economic development[62] and to create cities as centres of civilization.[63] In some, but not all, of his foundations there were Greek and Macedonian settlers; as, even in these, natives were brought within the walls and the

Greeks and Macedonians were no doubt expected to solace themselves with native wives, mixed communities were likely to be formed, in which the culture would surely be Hellenic, as in the older ethnically mixed cities of Ionia,[64] and from which Hellenic ideas would radiate to barbarians, as in fourth-century Caria and Lycia.[65] Alexander himself was devoted to Greek culture, and I suspect that he never thought of his realm as being other than fundamentally Hellenic; it is said that he had Greek taught to Darius' family and to the children his soldiers had had by native women.[66] Not that he despised barbarians. We are told that he rejected Aristotle's advice to treat barbarians as enemies and to behave to them as a master might towards slaves; experience showed him, as indeed it showed Aristotle, that the distinction between natural masters and slaves was not to be equated with that between Greeks and barbarians.[67] Phoenicians, Iranians, Indians, all rendered him valuable services; he needed Orientals to fill the ranks of his army and to administer subjects with whose languages and customs they were familiar. He recognized local laws, left natives to manage local affairs, and even appointed Iranians to satrapies and admitted them to his entourage. To reconcile them to his rule, he progressively adopted Persian dress and court ceremonial. All this aroused opposition among old-fashioned Macedonians. Alexander was prepared to crush it without mercy, but he wished also to effect a genuine union of hearts. The notion of Tarn that he originated the concept of the brotherhood of men is indefensible; the concept was not new and it was not Alexander's.[68] What he prayed for at Opis was harmony between the old ruling class of the Persian empire and the Macedonians; it was *their* lives, customs, and marriages he proposed 'to mix as in a loving-cup'.[69] He approved of his soldiers having children by native women, though they were to be brought up in Macedonian ways.[70] He himself married two Iranian princesses and virtually forced his chief officers to do likewise.[71] Overriding all resentment, he went ahead with plans to incorporate Orientals both in the Companion cavalry and in the phalanx.[72] He always assumed that his invincible will would surmount every obstacle, of sentiment no less than of armed resistance. His colonies illustrate this: established in sites carefully chosen for strategic or commercial value, they were designed to become great cities and by their names to perpetuate his own; for the feelings of conscribed settlers who 'yearned for the Greek way of life and had been cast away in the extremities of the kingdom'[73] he cared nothing. Admirable as these aims were, one may yet feel that he did not possess 'le tact des choses possibles'. But who can say what his iron resolution might not have achieved, if fate had not denied him the long life needed to bring his purposes to fruition?

His early death would have mattered less if he had had an able successor to carry on his work. The rise of Macedon to power had long been retarded by disputes over the succession and by the turbulence of the nobility. Philip had attached the great nobles more closely to the court,[74] but the danger of dynastic quarrels remained, and it was not unreasonable for Demosthenes and other Greeks to hope, after 346 and even after 338, that Macedonian power would disintegrate. Alexander's old advisers, Antipater and Parmenio, had pressed him not to invade Persia before he had married and begotten an heir.[75] He rejected the advice, and at his death he still had no child. Roxane was indeed pregnant, and her unborn son was recognized as the future king. But like all minors who ascended the Macedonian throne, Alexander IV was not suffered to survive for long. The chief Macedonian generals were bent on securing their own power, if necessary at the expense of the unity of the empire; no less independent and ambitious than their ancestors, in the world that Alexander had transformed, they could aim at the acquisition of kingdoms or empires rather than petty principalities. But they had to take more account than Alexander had done of the prejudices of the common soldiers on whose support they relied, prejudices which indeed most of them probably shared; and if some of them adopted his plan of settling Greeks and Macedonians in the east, it was to assure themselves of a supply of fighting men rather than to promote the diffusion of a common and mainly Hellenic culture in their kingdoms, though Hellenization was naturally a result of their policy. The deliberate attempt to found a world-empire based on reconciliation and unity between Macedonians and Iranians faded in their incessant wars.

According to Plutarch Alexander had sought to be 'a governor from God and a reconciler of the world; using force of arms against those whom he failed to bring together by reason, he united peoples of the most varied origin and ordered . . . all men to look on the *oikoumene* as their fatherland, the army as their citadel and guardian, good men as kin, and wicked as foreigners; he taught them that the proof of Hellenism lay in virtue and of barbarism in wickedness.'[76] This objective could be achieved only by blood and iron, and by the will of a despot who was prepared to override the sentiments of his subjects; and though the world was to be united in government and culture, there is no concept here of the brotherhood of all men as sons of a common Father, but at best only of those who possessed *arete*. Neither Alexander nor anyone else realized the objective, and it may be doubted if in his own mind it was so clearly defined as in Plutarch's ideal description. But his work tended in this direction and helped to inspire not only perhaps Stoic philosophers but the Romans, who were also to transcend national differences and to conceive that Italy had been marked out to unite scattered empires, to humanise customs, to give mankind a common speech and to become 'una cunctarum gentium in toto orbe patria'.[77]

Notes

1   I thank Professor Badian for comments on an earlier draft; any errors or misinterpretations are my own. I have sought in general to illustrate statements in the text with references to sources that depend on undoubtedly contemporary authorities; this does not imply that I regard the 'inferior' tradition as worthless, or the contemporary authorities such as Ptolemy as reliable at all points. Plutarch is cited from the Loeb edition.
2   Polyb. iii. 6.8 ff.; D. xvi. 89. 2; 91.2; xvii. 24. 1; A. ii. 14. 4.
3   A. i. 16. 7; iii. 16. 7–8; 18. 11–12; vi. 30. 1.
4   Cf. Badian, [*Greece and Rome*² 12 (1965)] p. 169.
5   A. H. M. Jones, *The Greek City from Alexander to Justinian* (Oxford, 1940), ch. x.
6   *Inschr. von Priene* 108, 75; *OGIS* 3.
7   A. i. 23. 8; 27. 4. Halicarnassus Greek (*contra* Tarn ii. 218), Hdt. ii. 178; vii. 99.
8   A. i. 16. 6; 19.6.
9   Polyb. iii. 6. 8 ff.
10 The grant of privileges to Sidonians at Athens and the foundation of cults of Isis there (Tod 139; 189) are revealing.
11 Isocr. v. 107–8 (cf. Hdt. v. 20–22; viii. 137–9). Arrian's sources also distinguish Greeks and Macedonians, e.g. *Ind.* 18. 6–7 (Nearchus).
12 Aeschin. iii. 239 ff.; Dinarch. i. 10; 18; Plut. *Dem.* 20; A. ii. 13. 6.
13 D. xvii. 9. 5; cf. 62 (Agis).
14 Some cities saw in Philip or Alexander a protector against powerful and aggressive neighbours, cf. Polyb. xviii. 14; thus Argos and Messene were pro-Macedonian from fear of Sparta, but they too rose against Macedon in the Lamian war, when Sparta was prostrate, as did the Thessalians (D. xviii. 11).
15 A. i. 18. 8; 29. 6; ii. 17, etc.

16 But see iv. 155; 183; 185; v. 124–6 (?).
17 But see iv. 181; xii. 103; *ep.* ix. 8.
18 iv. 131–3; 174; 182; 187; v. 9; 84–85; 107–8; 112; 120–2; 129–45.
19 A. ii. 14. 2.
20 A. i. 17. 1 and 7.
21 A. ii. 25.
22 D. xvii. 17. 2. For another view cf. Badian, [*Greece and Rome*[2] 12 (1965)] pp. 166 ff.
23 Cited in A. ii. 3. 7.
24 A. iii. 16. 9; 25. 1; vi. 3. 1, &c.
25 A. ii. 7. 3; 14. 7; iii. 3. 4; v. 3. 1; 29. 1. The story in Callisthenes (Jacoby, *Fragm. d. griech. Hist.* no. 124) F 31 that the Pamphylian sea miraculously receded to allow Alexander's march past Mount Climax was in all histories of Alexander (Jos. *Ant. Jud.* ii. 348), cf. A. i. 26. 2, and obviously found favour with him.
26 A. ii. 7. 6; 12. 5; 14. 8–9; iii. 9. 6; P. 34.
27 Contrast A. ii. 14. 5 with iii. 22. 1; vi. 29, &c.
28 A. i. 12. 1.
29 V. Ehrenberg, *Alexander and the Greeks* (Oxford, 1938), ch. ii.
30 A. ii. 26. 3; iv. 21. 3; vi. 6. 3; 24. 3.
31 A. i. 18; ii. 17; iii. 9. 1 and 4; but Arrian's own reflections in iii. 10. 3–4 illustrate how Alexander's conduct should *not* be interpreted, in view of the evidence in 10. 2.
32 A. ii. 16; iii. 3; iv. 28; 30. 4; v. 2; 3. 2; vi. 3. 4–5; 14. 2; vii. 20 (all from Ptolemy or Aristobulus or both). Tarn ii. 45 dismisses A. v. 2 as a mere *logos* of the inferior tradition, but wrongly; the first section in *oratio recta* guarantees what follows down to section 7 in *oratio obliqua* as coming from one or both of the main sources (cf. ii. 12. 3–6 for their account in the form of a *logos* in *oratio obliqua*); in section 7 a change of source in explicit.
33 Tarn ii. 51 ff. wrongly ascribing the tradition to Clitarchus.
34 A. vi. 24. 2 f., cf. Strabo xv. 1. 5. On the Gedrosian march cf. H. Strasburger, *Hermes* lxxx (1952), 456 ff. A. vi. 21. 3–22. 3; 23. 1–24. 1; 27. 1 come from an official, apologetic source (presumably Ptolemy) which rationalized Alexander's motives and minimized the disaster; 22. 4–8 from Aristobulus, and 24. 1–26. 5 either from him or, as Strasburger argues, from Nearchus, a reliable source whichever view be adopted, whose account agreed with all others and with modern travellers' descriptions of the desert; Strasburger reckons that Alexander lost three-fourths of the army that went with him.
35 Strabo xvii. 1.43 (Callisthenes), cf. Tarn ii. 353 ff.
36 Tarn's objections (ii. 348 ff.) cannot stand against the texts of Pindar he cites and Hdt. ii. 42; 55. A Greek could not be certain of the true name of Zeus, cf. Aesch. *Agam.* 160 ff.
37 P. 33.
38 Strabo xvii. 1.43.
39 J. P. V. D. Balsdon, *Historia* i (1950), 353 ff.
40 See esp. Dinarch. i. 94; Hyper. *contra Dem.* 31; *epitaphios* 21 (on which cf. E. Bickermann, *Athenaeum* xli (1963), 70 ff.; in my view the present ἀναγκαζόμεθα relates not to Athens, but to Greece generally, or rather cities not yet freed).
41 E. Bickermann, *CPh.* xlv (1950), 43 (review of Tarn).
42 A. v. 3. 1.
43 A. vii. 20. 1; Strabo xvi. 1. 11; cf. L. Pearson, *Lost Histories of Alexander the Great* (New York, 1960), 184.
44 Diels, *Fragm. d. Vorsokratiker* I[6] B 114.
45 μεταλλάττειν, *OGIS* 4; D. xviii 56. 2.
46 D. xviii. 60–61; Plut. *Eumenes* 13.
47 Suet. *Caes*. 88.
48 A. vi. 15. 5; 17. 1–2, &c.
49 Persian rule had once extended to the Indus (Hdt. iv. 44; A. *Ind.* 1), not beyond; nor in Alexander's time so far (Strabo xv. 1. 26); even the Indus country was no longer known, A. vi. 1; *Ind.* 20; 32.
50 A. iv. 15. 5–6; v. 26 (but the reliability of this speech is called in grave doubt by D. Kienast, *Historia* xiv (1965), 180 ff.).
51 J. O. Thomson, *Hist. of Anc. Geography* (Cambridge, 1948), 135.

52 A. v. 29. 4–5; C. x. 1. 21; D. xviii. 3. 2; 39. 6; xix. 14. 8.

53 A. vii.8. 1.

54 A. vii. 16, cf. iv. 15.

55 A. vii. 19. 3 ff., cf. Strabo xvi. 1. 11.

56 D. xviii. 4; C. x. 1. 17–19. Tarn's criticisms are answered by F. Schachermeyr, *Jahreshefte der österr. arch. Inst.* (1954), 118 ff.

57 A. iv. 7. 5; vii. 1. 4.

58 Thomson, op. cit. 139 ff.

59 Perdiccas conquered Cappadocia after Alexander's death (D. xviii. 16); Armenia remained unsubdued.

60 E. Badian, *JHS* lxxxi (1961), 16 ff.

61 A. *Ind.* 40. 7–8 (Nearchus). For the motive cf. Tac. *Agr.* 21.

62 A. iii. 1. 5 (cf. P. 26); iv. 25. 4; vi. 15. 2; 21. 5; vii. 21; Strabo ix. 2. 18; xvi. 1. 9–11.

63 Jones (op. cit. in n. 5, p. 51), ch. 1. Native towns, e.g. A. ii. 27. 7; iv. 28. 4.

64 Hdt. i. 146.

65 Tod 138 (Caria); A. T. Olmstead, *Hist. of the Persian Empire* (Chicago, 1948), 348–50; 360; 391–2; 405–6 (Lycia).

66 D. xvii. 67. 1; P. 47. 3 (cf. A. vii. 12). For Alexander's culture see P. 4. 1 and 6; 7–8; 10. 4; 11. 6 (= A. i. 9. 10); 26. 1; 29. 1–3 (cf. A. iii. 6. 1); A. i. 12. 1, &c.

67 E. Badian, *Historia* vii (1958), 440 ff.

68 Badian, op. cit. 425 ff.; P. Merlan, *CPh.* xlv (1950), 161 ff.

69 A. vii. 11. 8–9; Plut. *Mor.* 329.

70 A. vii. 12.

71 A. iv. 19; vii. 4.

72 A. vii. 6; 11; 23.

73 D. xviii. 7.

74 e.g. Alexander the Lyncestian, Leonnatus, and Perdiccas (cf. Berve's biographies); see also A. iv. 13. 1.

75 D. xvii. 16.

76 P. 329.

77 Pliny, *NH* iii. 39.

ALEXANDER THE GREAT AND THE 'LIMITS OF THE CIVILISED WORLD'[1]

Waldemar Heckel

The legend of Alexander the Great, as it develops from the histories of the first, contemporary historians to the sensational accounts of the Greek and medieval romances, transforms the Macedonian king from a relatively conservative leader into a 'world conqueror' (*kosmokrator*) driven by the urge to explore strange new worlds, to push into the great unknown.[2] Most serious scholars are quick to note the limited nature of Alexander's undertaking: he had adopted Philip's war with Persia in Asia Minor, but extended it to include the whole of the Achaemenid empire; he employed the propaganda of political writers like Isocrates and claimed to lead a 'Panhellenic war of vengeance' against the barbarian; and he followed in the footsteps of the Persian kings themselves – his, to quote Gareth Fowden ([1993:] 138), 'was an off-the-rack empire, ready-made when he conquered it'. But two elements of Alexander's developing legend interfered with this sober view, both in ancient and later times: his alleged 'final plans' or 'future plans', contained in his *Hypomnemata*, and the pronouncement of his adoptive father, Amun, that 'he was being promised victory in all his wars and possession of the whole world' (*victoriam omnium bellorum possessionemque terrarum dari respondetur*: Justin 11.11.10). For the worst historians, prophecy is quickly transmuted into fact, and Justin (whether he is accurately representing Trogus' views, we cannot say) adds that Alexander, 'succeeding to the throne, gave orders that he be called the king of all lands and of the world' (*Accepto deinde imperio regem se terrarum omnium ac mundi appellari iussit*: Justin 12.16.9).[3]

Now, of course, 'the world' or even 'the whole world' in antiquity meant considerably more as time progressed, though still representing far less than what we understand by such terms. Only at one point in his expedition does Alexander appear to deviate from his limited conquest of the Persian empire – if one can truly call such a large-scale undertaking 'limited' or 'modest' – and that was in India. Hermann Bengtson remarks (in E.F. Bloedow's translation):

> Alexander's Indian expedition can scarcely be justified on military grounds. The plan for this conquest sprang much more from the romantic nature of the young king. He wanted to reach the eastern frontier of the inhabited world, the shores of Ocean, thought to be in the East, in India. It was *the urge for remote regions and infinite expanses*, which gave him direction at a decisive moment in his life.[4]

I have supplied the italics in the preceding passage; for the words, 'the urge for remote regions and infinite expanses', illustrate how the legend of Alexander begins to supplant the historical evidence. Alexander was indeed famous for his *pothos* ('yearning').[5] And this was to do specific things, like follow in the footsteps of his ancestors, or to succeed where others had failed. But, in fact, the evidence at hand suggests that to push into 'remote regions and infinite expanses' was not one of the king's driving characteristics.[6]

It is, however, in India (at the Hyphasis, or Beas, river) that Alexander's actions (which constituted, primarily, *inaction*) appear to give some credence to this notion. Arrian makes Alexander say:

For my part, I set no limit to exertions for a man of noble spirit, save that the exertions themselves should lead to deeds of prowess. Yet if any one longs to hear what will be the limit of the actual fighting, he should understand that there remains no great stretch of land before us up to the river Ganges and the eastern sea. This sea, I assure you, will prove to be joined to the Hyrcanian sea; for the great sea encircles all the land. And it will be for me to show Macedonians and allies alike that the Indian gulf forms but one stretch of water with the Persian Gulf, and the Hyrcanian Sea with the Indian gulf. From the Persian gulf our fleet shall sail round to Libya as far as the Pillars of Hercules; from the Pillars all the interior of Libya then becomes ours, just as Asia is in fact becoming ours in its entirety, and the boundaries of our Empire are becoming those which god set for the whole continent.[7]

The sentiments expressed here are not found in the other extant Alexander historians – they were doubtless absent from the lost, primary sources – and are attributable to Arrian himself.[8] Alexander is thus depicted in the developing legend not only as a man knowledgeable of world geography (as befits a former student of Aristotle),[9] but also as world-conqueror, or world-ruler (*kosmokrator*), whose only defeat comes at the Hyphasis, as a result of his own men's unwillingness to follow him into the unknown.

In truth, Alexander's expedition was relatively 'conservative' and avoided senselessly thrusting into the unknown. Conquest of the 'known world' was his primary object, rather than adding to the ancients' knowledge of the world by conquering the unknown. For the ancient Greeks, who had colonised the Mediterranean and Black Seas, Persia did in fact represent the remainder of the known world (cf. also n. 1). Xenophon makes Cyrus the Younger say to his Greek mercenaries that his ancestral empire 'extends southwards to where heat and northward to where cold make it impossible for men to live'.[10] And even in Roman sources Alexander, if he does not conquer 'the whole world', certainly becomes master of 'the entire East', while his brother-in-law (and uncle) Alexander of Epirus tries to establish a corresponding western empire (Justin 12.2.1).

In the histories of Alexander, the Hyphasis mutiny is thus an important turning-point (the pun is almost unavoidable). At the last of the five rivers of the Punjab, Alexander is told of numerous and fierce enemies to the east. But what fires the king's desire dampens the spirit of the common soldier. Arrian tells us (5.25.2): 'This report stirred Alexander to a desire for further advance; but the Macedonians' spirits were flagging by now, as they saw the king taking on one hard and dangerous task after another' (ταῦτα δὲ ἐξαγγελλόμενα Ἀλέξανδρον μὲν παρώξυνεν ἐς ἐπιθυμίαν τοῦ πρόσω ἰέναι· οἱ Μακεδόνες δὲ ἐξέκαμνον ἤδη ταῖς γνώμαις, πόνους τε ἐκ πόνων καὶ κινδύνους ἐκ κινδύνων ἐπαναιρουμενον ὁρῶντες τὸν βασιλέα). It is perhaps worth considering what Alexander's actual policy was and to ask ourselves if his reluctance to turn back was, in fact, genuine. How did Alexander approach the question of 'the frontier'?

Upon closer examination, we find that Alexander had very clear ideas about the boundaries of his empire. In the north he conducted both punitive and preemptive strikes against the barbarians on the marches of the Macedonian kingdom. He pursued the Triballians and their king, Syrmus, towards the Danube and then launched a campaign against the Getae on the north side of the river. These he defeated in a quick campaign, designed rather for show than for lasting effect. And he conducted sacrifices, in a manner that would become all too familiar, at the first of several natural boundaries.

> He himself … sacrificed on the bank of the Ister to Zeus the Preserver and Heracles and Ister himself, for permitting the passage. Then the same day he took all his force safe and sound back to the camp.[11]

It will hardly have escaped Alexander's notice (or anyone else's for that matter) that the Getic and Scythian presence on the borders of the 'empire' had been accepted long ago by a reluctant, and indeed lucky, Darius I, who had found safety on the Danube's southern shore after a disastrous campaign farther north. Hence, far from breaking new ground, Alexander contented himself with maintaining the boundaries of the former Persian satrapy. The king was doubtless aware of his predecessor's failure, for, at the Tanais, he is alleged to [have] responded to Aristander's warning that he should not expose himself to danger and fight the Scythians by saying 'that it was better to go to any extremity of danger than, after subduing almost the whole of Asia, to be a laughing-stock to the Scythians, as Darius the father of Xerxes had been long ago' (Arr. 4.4.3: ὁ δὲ κϱεῖσσων ἔφη ἐς ἔσχατον κινδύνου ἐλθεῖν ἢ κατεστϱαμμένον ξύμπασαν ὀλίγου δεῖν τὴν Ἀσίαν γέλωτα εἶναι Σκύθαις, καθάπεϱ Δαϱεῖος ὁ Ξέϱξου πατὴϱ πάλαι ἐγένετο).[12]

Two interesting (recurring) elements are seen in the Danubian campaign for the first time: Alexander's practice of setting up altars or conducting sacrifices at the 'edges of the world' (particularly to Zeus and Heracles, his ancestors – but also to Athena Nike or Minerva Victoria[13] – and to the natural elements themselves: here the Danube), and, second, the motif of 'great powers' coming to Alexander to recognise his authority. Arrian reports the latter, allowing himself a bit of a laugh at his hero's expense:

> At this juncture ambassadors came to Alexander from Syrmus, King of the Triballi and from the other self-governing tribes near the Ister; others from the Celts settled on the Ionian gulf. The Celts were of great height and had a high conceit of themselves; but all professed to have come in desire for Alexander's friendship, and with all he exchanged pledges. Of the Celts he enquired what mortal thing they most dreaded, hoping that his own great name had reached the Celts and gone still farther, and that they would say that they dreaded him more than anything else. Their answer, however, was not what he expected, for, living in difficult country far from Alexander, and seeing that his aim lay elsewhere, they said that their greatest dread was that the sky would fall upon them, and that, while they admired Alexander, neither fear nor interest had prompted their embassy. He declared them his friends, made them his allies and sent them home, only remarking, 'What braggarts Celts are!'[14]

Similarly, Alexander, after conducting sacrifices and games to Zeus at the ancient Macedonian city of Dium (Arr. 1.11.1; Diod. 17.16.3–4), marks off another boundary, the Hellespont, after crossing which he has truly embarked upon his Panhellenic expedition.

Arriving at Elaeus, he sacrificed to Protesilaus at his tomb, since he was thought to be the first to disembark on Asian soil of the Greeks who fought with Agamemnon against Troy. The intention of the sacrifice was that his own landing on Asian soil might be luckier than that of Protesilaus.[15]

The Trojan War parallels are old, and obvious, and had been used already by Agesilaus – though his ceremony was turned to fiasco by the Boeotian cavalry at Aulis.[16] More important are the sacrifices, again described in detail by Arrian:

According to the prevalent story Alexander made from Elaeus for the Achaean harbour, and steered the admiral's ship himself when he crossed, sacrificing a bull to Poseidon and the Nereids in the midst of the Hellespont strait, and pouring into the sea a drink offering from a golden bowl. They also say that he was the first to disembark on Asian soil ... , that he set up altars both where he started from Europe and where he landed in Asia to Zeus of Safe Landings, Athena, and Heracles.[17]

Thus we see again the importance attached by Alexander to important landmarks. Before we investigate this further, it may be useful to add a third feature of Alexander's propaganda, or, at least, of the propaganda of the Alexander historians, which delighted in casting the king in the role of *kosmokrator*. When Alexander does not come to the physical edge of the world, and when he is not visited by peoples who live 'beyond the edge' but who are cowed by his power or curious to see the man in person because the glory of his reputation[18] has reached even the uncivilised areas, he encounters places with mythical connexions: the cave of Typhon (Curt. 3.4.10),[19] the place of Prometheus' imprisonment (Diod. 17.83.1; cf. Arr. 5.3.2), or any number of places visited by Perseus, Heracles or Dionysus.

But again, in truth, he does not wander far from the beaten track, from the Royal Road of the Persians. His route through Asia Minor takes him around Mt Climax, where the sea is said to have recognised his greatness and to have performed *proskynesis* to him (just as, as contemporaries were doubtless aware, the Euphrates had done obeisance to Cyrus the Younger in 401 at Thapsacus).[20] He goes to Gordium, where he exploits the oracle associated with the Gordian knot, and perhaps also the Macedonian connexions with Midas and the Brygi (Brygians). Possibly he made a slight detour in the direction of Cappadocia, but, in fact, the territory which had held out against Persia remained independent in Alexander's day as well.[21] From here Alexander returned to the well-known route of Cyrus and the Ten Thousand, which led via the Cilician Gates to Tarsus and eventually the gulf of Issus.[22] Even when he came to Egypt, he moved to Memphis, but not farther south. There was no repeat of Cambyses' allegedly ill-fated Ethiopian campaign, nor was there any attempt to succeed where the Persian had failed. Perhaps the desert journey to the Ammonium at Siwah could be said to have surpassed Cambyses' failure[23] and to have followed in the footsteps of Perseus and Heracles, but it took Alexander over well-travelled sands. Here there was not even an attempt to establish altars on the southern limits of the empire, though Alexandria on the western edge of the Nile Delta might have been intended as a marker of some sort. We might remember here too that Alexandrias were planted in strategic locations throughout the empire, either on the lines of communication or on the marches (cf. Alexandria in the Caucasus; Alexandria Eschate; Alexander's Harbour or Portus Macedonum).[24]

And so the campaign continued until Alexander reached Parthia and Hyrcania, where he was met, it was said, by a delegation of the Amazons, and particularly by Queen Thalestris, who had come to 'breed' with the greatest of men.[25] But, despite the inhabitants of the 'other' world coming to Alexander, he showed no enthusiasm for entering theirs. Arrian, who rationalises the Amazon story (4.15; cf. 7.13), alleges that Alexander was met by Pharasmenes, king of the Chorasmians, who offered to help him in a campaign against the Amazons, but Alexander dismissed him after concluding a pact of friendship and alliance, saying that now was a convenient time for such a campaign (καὶ Φαρασμάνην ἐπαινέσας τε καὶ φιλίαν καὶ ξυμμαχίαν πρὸς αὐτὸν ξυνθέμενος αὐτῷ μὲν τότε οὐκ ἔφη ἐν καιρῷ εἶναι ἐλαύνειν ἐπὶ τὸν Πόντον: Arr. 4.15.5).

In 330, when Alexander was in Hyrcania, such a campaign could easily be dismissed as inopportune, since Alexander had to deal with Bessus and the rebels who had fled to Bactria. But Pharasmenes' proposal came at a better time, and it was far from urgent for Alexander to proceed into India. In fact, we see that the king had already established another of his boundary markers at the Iaxartes (Tanais),[26] that is, at the place where many in antiquity thought that Cyrus the Great had met his end against the Scythian queen, Tomyris. Alexander thus took and resettled the population of Cyropolis and conducted a preemptive strike against the Scythians north of the river. The scene is strongly reminiscent of the trans-Danubian campaign.

> Not many days later, envoys came to Alexander from the Abian Scythians, as they are called, whom Homer praised in his epic by calling them 'most just of men'; they live in Asia, and are independent, chiefly through their poverty and their sense of justice. Envoys came too from the European Scythians, the largest nation dwelling in Europe. Alexander sent some of the Companions to them, pretending it was an embassy to conclude a friendly agreement; but the idea of the mission was rather to spy out the nature of the Scythians' land, their numbers, their customs and the arms they use on their warlike expeditions.[27]

In Curtius' account (7.8.8ff.), the Scythians send ambassadors to Alexander, and their arrogance reminds us of the boasting Celts at the Danube. The actual campaign against the Scythians north of the river is brief, as the Scythians flee before him, and Alexander's success is cut short, not by dysentery (as in Arr. 4.4.9; cf. *Itiner. Al.* [38] 85) but by the advent of darkness and the ill effects of a neck wound suffered shortly before in Sogdiana (7.9.11–14). But significantly, Curtius points out:

> By now they [the Macedonians] had crossed the bounds of Father Liber [i.e. of Dionysus], the markers of which were stones set out at frequent intervals and tall trees with ivy-covered trunks.[28]

And, not surprisingly, word of his great achievement induces the barbarians to surrender:

> People had believed the Scythians invincible, but after this crushing defeat they had to admit that no race was a match for Macedonian arms. So the Sacae sent a delegation to promise submission, prompted to do so less by the king's valour than by his clemency towards the defeated Scythians.[29]

This is clearly a case of making the most of very little. Again, Alexander's feeble campaign beyond the Iaxartes – surely he must have remembered also the fate of Cyrus the Great,[30] who had placed the river at his back – is depicted in 'glamorous' terms by making the King reach yet another of the world's boundaries. Wilcken (1967: 159) puts the episode into perspective: 'By reason of the endless steppes on the other side, Alexander had no more idea of moving the frontier further north than he had before at the Danube; he had reached the limit of the "inhabited world" (*oikoumene*), which was bounded not merely by the Ocean but also by deserts. Nevertheless, as at the Danube, he now made a single victorious advance over the Jaxartes, to inspire these barbarians with respect for his arms.'

So too at the Hyphasis, Alexander did not venture beyond territory that was known to him from earlier accounts or from local guides. He had indeed advanced beyond the Persian satrapy of Gandhara, and thus beyond the eastern limits of the Persian Empire. But he was also aware that the Indus river-system formed a natural boundary, just like the Danube, the Hellespont, and the Tanais. And, indeed, the Macedonians had already begun to assemble a new fleet in India for the purpose of following the Indus to the Ocean.[31] Rumour had it that the natives beyond the Hyphasis, and beyond the desert, were 'ripe for the picking', that the Nanda dynasty was faltering – as the rise of Chandragupta would prove shortly afterwards.[32] Nevertheless, the Macedonian king did not advance. Now it was no longer possible to claim preoccupation with a more pressing problem. Now the decision had to be fobbed off on the men. For everyone knows that Alexander was itching to find a new enemy and a new fight. So it was the men, exhausted and lacking the king's energy and courage, who prevailed upon the 'world-conqueror' to turn back.[33] Alexander had come to another 'edge' of the world, though he knew well that it was not so.

> Then he divided the army into twelve parts and ordered each to set up an altar as high as the greatest towers, and in breadth even greater than towers would be, as thank-offerings to the gods who had brought him so far as a conqueror, and as memorials of his own exertions. When the altars had been built for him, he performed the customary sacrifices on them, and held athletic and equestrian games.[34]

Arrian's account is, of course, favourable to Alexander. Not surprisingly, the popular tradition[35] is less kind: Alexander is depicted as attempting to deceive posterity.

> [He] gave orders to break camp. But when he did so he devised a number of ruses and deceptions to impress the inhabitants of the region. For example he had arms, horses' mangers and bits prepared, all of which exceeded the normal size or height or weight, and these were left scattered about the country. He also set up altars for the gods.[36]

> [H]is intention was to make everything appear greater than it was, for he was preparing to leave to posterity a fraudulent wonder.[37]

In fact, Alexander's alleged 'Quest for Ocean', which lay to the East, was not seriously jeopardised. In his speech to the men at the Hyphasis, Alexander makes his view (unless it is a later one, attributable to Eratosthenes) known: from the Ganges to the Eastern Ocean is not a great distance, and the Indian, Persian and Hyrcanian seas are all connected (Arr. 5.26).[38] At any rate, Alexander knew from the expedition of Scylax of Caryanda, conducted on behalf of Darius I, that the Indus river-system led to the Ocean, and that the mission to the Persian Gulf, on which he would later send Nearchus, was possible.[39] The preparations for the descent of the Indus are thus strongly reminiscent of the crossing of the Hellespont:

> When everything had been got ready by Alexander, at dawn the army began its embarkation, and Alexander sacrificed to the gods according to custom, and to the river Hydaspes according to the instructions of the seers. After embarking he poured a libation into the river out of a golden bowl from the bows, calling upon the Acesines as well as the Hydaspes, since he had learned that it was the largest of the other rivers and joined the Hydaspes, and also that the meeting of the waters was not far away; and he also called upon the Indus, into which the Acesines runs with the Hydaspes. When he had poured a libation to Heracles his ancestor, to Ammon and to the other gods to whom he usually made offering, he bade the bugle sound for departure.[40]

And, when Alexander reaches the final 'corner' of his empire (and thus the last corner of the world),[41] the mouth of the Indus and the Ocean, he repeats the by now familiar ceremony. At the mouth of the Indus, Alexander came to an island and,

> anchoring by its headland [he] sacrificed to the gods to which, he used to say, Ammon had enjoined him to sacrifice. Next day he sailed down to the other island in the sea, put in there, and sacrificed there too, performing different sacrifices to different gods with different ceremonial; these sacrifices also, he said, he offered in accordance with the oracle given by Ammon.[42]

From [there] he sails into the open Ocean and:

> sacrificed bulls to Poseidon, and cast them into the sea, and after the sacrifice poured a libation and cast into the sea the cup made of gold and golden bowls as thank-offerings, praying that Poseidon would safely convoy the naval force he intended to despatch with Nearchus towards the Persian Gulf and the mouths of the Euphrates and Tigris.[43]

Alexander had come into possession of the Persian Empire, which he added to the regions subjugated by his father Philip II. Only in India had he stepped over the threshold of established 'world boundaries', and here only slightly. Not surprisingly, the Indian satrapies were the first to be lost, and one wonders whether Alexander had any firm hopes of holding the Punjab. Already before his departure from India there were ominous signs of rebellion. The peace between Taxiles and Porus, though sealed by marriage, was scarcely assumed to outlast the honeymoon.[44]

Hence we return to the question of Alexander's decision to turn back at the Hyphasis. In the popular tradition, Alexander learns about the lands to the east from a certain

'King Phegeus' – the name is probably a Graecism of a regional title associated with the river Begas-Ganga[45] – who reports that the Indians beyond the Hyphasis are ruled by a certain Xandrames (Aggrammes in Curt. 9.2.3) and can field an army of 20,000 cavalrymen, 200,000 infantry, 2,000 chariots and 4,000 war-elephants.[46] Phegeus' report is, by any account, one of gross exaggerations, designed, we might think, precisely to intimidate the Macedonians. Was this the intention of Porus and his fellow dynasts in India? To dissuade Alexander from continuing? Hardly. For it would have been in the best interests of these Indian rajahs to have Alexander continue eastward, where he would, if they were lucky, subdue the hostile tribes who threatened them from that direction, or, if they were luckier (for they could not have known of Chandragupta's unexpected rise to greatness), Alexander might perish together with his army. Arrian, by contrast, says nothing of either Phegeus or enemy numbers. He restricts himself to some general observations:

> On the other side of the Hyphasis, so it was reported to Alexander, the country was fertile, the men good labourers of the soil and valiant warrior[s], who managed their own affairs in an orderly manner; most of them were under aristocracies, yet these made no demands other than reasonable. These people also had a number of elephants, a good many more than the other Indians, and these were, moreover, very large and courageous.
>
> (Arr. 5.25.1)

Challenging, but not insurmountable, odds. But Arrian is trying to put his hero in a good light. The reader will have little regard for Alexander's leadership, if he believes that the king planned to take a suffering and demoralised army against an overwhelmingly superior enemy.

The report of Phegeus must have been intended by Alexander to reach the ears of his Macedonian troops; for he could surely have suppressed the information. Greek history has no shortage of examples of leaders suppressing the truth so that they would not enter a battle or a campaign demoralised; indeed, Polyaenus has a section devoted to the importance of lying to one's own troops for their own good (*Excerpta* 30). Xenophon reports how Agesilaus learned that Conon had defeated the Spartan fleet under Peisander at Cnidus shortly before he himself was to engage the Athenians and Thebans at Coronea (394 BC). The messengers were told to return to the Spartan camp wearing fillets and rejoicing, claiming (contrary to fact) that Peisander had been victorious.[47] And we need only look at Alexander's own speeches before Issus and Gaugamela, which downplayed the strengths and manliness of the enemy.[48]

I contend that Alexander wanted his men to know the worst (and, if possible, more than the worst), so that they could make the decision for him. He would be forced, seemingly against his will, to return to the west, to content himself with the spoils of his Persian campaign. His sulking, his disappointment, these were all for show. Probably there was no one happier to return to the Hydaspes in 326 than Alexander himself. He had established another boundary-stone on the 'edge of the world', and he had not imitated his Persian predecessors by foolishly overextending himself. What if the army had not resorted to *secessio*? Would Alexander have led back a ragged army in ignominious defeat, like Cambyses or Darius? Or would he perhaps have departed from history with his head in a sack of blood, like that other 'Great' ruler of the East?[49]

We need only look at Alexander's own actions and preparations in order to see that the proposed invasion of India beyond the Hyphasis was a sham. The clearest indications that Alexander believes he has completed the conquest of the Persian Empire, and thus achieved his goal, are the sacrifices at the Hydaspes and the building of the Indus fleet. These are clearly spelled out in the popular tradition but Arrian's account obscures Alexander's true intentions somewhat, and I believe this obfuscation is intentional.

Diodorus 17.89.3 reports that Alexander sacrifices to Helios ('who had given him the eastern region to conquer': αὐτὸς δὲ Ἡλίῳ ἔθυσεν ὡς δεδωκότι τὰ πρὸς ἀνατολὴν μέρη καταστρέψασθαι). Lane Fox (1974: 363) interprets the action in the following way: 'Alexander paid a sacrifice to the Sun. His choice of god was a symbol of his ambitions: his march was to take him eastwards, out towards the sunrise.' But Arrian, who does not mention Helios in this context, does say that Alexander made 'the customary victory sacrifices' (τὰ νομιζόμενα ἐπινίκια), and Bosworth (1995: 316) recognises that 'the sacrifice according to Diodorus and Curtius had a wider significance. It marked the end of the conquest in the east, and is evidently connected with the tradition that Alexander considered the Ocean close at hand and easily accessible from the Hydaspes.' Although Bosworth does not accept this 'Cleitarchean' view, it is, in my opinion, the correct one. The sacrifice to Helios was a thank-offering, for things already accomplished, rather than votive. And the preparation of the fleet at this point makes it clear that any advance to the east was to have a limited purpose. Arrian, of course, depicted Alexander as one who desired to push into the unknown, and attributed to him a view of eastern geography which we cannot be certain that the king himself held. Hence, it was necessary to omit the reference to the building of the fleet in order to make his ambition to conquer the entire east seem plausible.

Diodorus 17.89.4–5 goes on to say that Alexander learns of vast forests from which he can take sufficient wood for shipbuilding. He intends to reach the borders of India (τὸ τέρμα τῆς Ἰνδικῆς) and then to sail down the Hydaspes to the Ocean. Again, this has led some scholars to assume that the king intended to reach the eastern ocean, which he believed was nearby, and then to return to the Hydaspes. Bosworth thus speaks of the 'Indus voyage [as] a secondary objective, to take place after the penetration of India to its eastern limits'.[50] But it is not at all clear what the sources, or Alexander himself, regarded as the boundary of India. If such a campaign entailed reaching the Eastern Ocean, then why not say so?[51] In fact, it is only in the later extant sources, where there is clearly a fair degree of authorial comment, that the king's goal is presented in a general and grandiose manner. It is likely that a more precise definition of Alexander's objectives reflects the wording (or at least intention) of the primary source.

What then did Cleitarchus or some other lost comtemporary writer mean by India? The answer is that we simply do not know. Nevertheless, it is doubtful that, for the Macedonians, India meant much more than those areas adjacent to the Indus River (in the broad sense of the term), and thus in the north, the Punjab.[52] Certainly, the subcontinent was unknown to the Greeks, and it is likely that Alexander learned about the extent of the Punjab from Taxiles. The desert lay beyond the last of its rivers, the Beas,[53] and it is reasonable to assume that Alexander considered this stream, like the Iaxartes in the north, the eastern limits. Now this, of course, leads to the much-debated question of whether Alexander had previous knowledge of the Gangetic region – the river and the Nanda kingdom.[54] If the Macedonians were aware of its existence, then Alexander must be faulted for the way in which he conducted the campaign east of the

Hydaspes; for he was neither prepared to continue the conquest, nor had he prepared his men. This was clearly not something that could be approached in such a cavalier manner. It makes more sense that Alexander only learned about the extent of Indian territory as he approached the Beas, after he had already made plans to sail down the Hydaspes.

After the Hydaspes battle, no additional territory was annexed to the Macedonian Empire. All campaigns were conducted against the neighbours and enemies of Porus, for the security of that ruler's kingdom. No permanent cities or garrisons were established that were not manned by natives or mercenaries and turned over to Porus – most notably Hephaestion's recent foundation at the Acesines.[55] Is it conceivable that Alexander planned to advance to the Eastern Ocean without winning another square mile of territory for himself? Or that he intended to leave a vassal astride his lines of communication? Breloer recognised long ago that Alexander was interested in securing Porus' kingdom, which would act as a buffer zone on the edge of his own empire, an empire that extended as far as the Hydaspes.[56]

Alexander's aims in the northeastern Punjab can be understood in the following terms. In terms of grand strategy, it was necessary to secure the frontier in the way that I have described above. The army, after a rest of thirty days (Diod. 17.90.6), had to remain occupied while the construction of the Indus fleet was taking place, and it was necessary that a large army obtain its supplies from enemy territory so that it would not be a burden on a recently acquired ally. The effect of an extended period of idleness in Porus' realm during the monsoon season would have been even more demoralising for the army than the campaigning that followed.[57]

At this point, we may turn again to Arrian's account – in part, because there are still those who believe that sources can simply be sorted into 'good' and 'bad', and who accept information uncritically because it comes from what is regarded as the best of the 'good' sources. For example, Eggermont finds it necessary to remind us that Arrian 'had the best military source, Ptolemaeus, and the best technical one, Aristobulus, at his disposal'.[58] But, Arrian does not disguise his admiration for the king, and in numerous places he goes out of his way to whitewash his actions. Arrian's version of the events after the battle with Porus is noteworthy for its failure to mention the building of the Hydaspes fleet in its proper context. Now Arrian does mention this project elsewhere, both in the *Indica* (which relates the activities of this fleet) and in the Alexander history, at the beginning of Book Six – that is, *after the Hyphasis 'mutiny'*. The army, having made the decision to turn back, reaches the Hydaspes and finds that the fleet, which Alexander had ordered to be prepared for the journey downriver, was all but completed. Why did Arrian not mention this earlier? Well, perhaps he forgot. Or, what is more likely, he realised that he could not make a persuasive argument concerning Alexander's desire (*epithymia*) to march ever eastward, if he had already informed his reader that the king had every intention of proceeding downriver to the *southern* Ocean. Arrian clearly was trying to portray Alexander as a man driven by curiosity and an urge to thrust into the unknown, as a man capable of conquering the entire world. Alexander's real purpose in the campaign of 326 was, by contrast, rather mundane.

Scholars have nevertheless been prepared to accept the arguments that Arrian puts into his hero's mouth at the Hyphasis. That he believed he was nearing the eastern end of the world, that the Ocean was not far away, that he was truly desirous of continuing eastward. The Hydaspes fleet is dismissed as irrelevant. First of all, the fleet would not be ready to sail for some time, since it would take time for the wood to dry.[59] This, of course, ignores the fact that, when Alexander returned to the Hydaspes (where this 'soggy' fleet was located), he set sail downriver almost immediately, waiting only long enough to build a few additional ships – from wood that also had no time to dry! We should remember, too, that the felling of the trees and the preparation of the timber occurred during the monsoon season (July to September). Nevertheless, in October/November the fleet sailed south without difficulty.

Second, it is argued by J.R. Hamilton that Alexander had his entire army with him at the Hyphasis and was preparing to advance in full strength in the direction of the Ganges.[60] This is surely not the case. To begin with, there were those who had been left behind at the Hydaspes to oversee the construction of the fleet – sailors, shipwrights, and a military guard.[61] And a good portion of the army had been dispersed (in part because of problems of supply): Hephaestion and his forces were fortifying a strategic position at the Acesines;[62] and Coenus (and presumably Craterus) had only joined the king after an extend[ed] foraging campaign. The last point is also used in favour of the proposed march to the east: the supplies were intended for that campaign. As if the army would not need to eat unless it continued eastward! As I have already noted, the foraging in the eastern Punjab was desirable because it transferred the burden of supplying the Macedonian army from Porus, who was now an ally, to Porus' enemies, including the Cathaeans whom Alexander had only recently defeated. Furthermore, by the time the men reached the Hyphasis, they were a ragged and tired bunch, ill prepared to finish their work in the Punjab, let alone embark upon a new mission of conquest.

So, if all the indicators point to a right turn at the Hydaspes, what are the dramatics at the Hyphasis all about? In all likelihood, when Alexander came to the kingdom of Phegeus (the land between the Ravi and the Beas, and the only part of what is modern-day India that the Macedonians entered), he learned that he had not indeed reached the end of the civilised world. How can he continue to style himself *kosmokrator* and ignore these new regions? The decision has to be fobbed off on the army. Hence, he does what no competent general with serious intentions of continuing the campaign would do in such a situation: he allows rumours of the exaggerated strength of the Gangetic kingdom to circulate through the army. But Alexander is anything but incompetent. He knows full well that such reports will cause his troops to become dispirited, and for that very reason does nothing to suppress the rumours. In his speeches (as reported by Arrian and Curtius) he does not dismiss this information, but rather confirms it. And, when the army reacts in predictable fashion,[63] he sulks for a while and then pretends that he is still determined to go ahead (without them, if he has to). When the army refuses to relent, he conducts sacrifices, which, to no one's surprise, turn out to be unfavourable (Arr. 5.28.4).

Defeated by the army and the gods, he agrees to turn back. On the Hyphasis altars are established and a camp of superhuman proportions, to serve as a fraudulent wonder for posterity. When he returns to the Hydaspes, as the monsoon season ends, no one is surprised to see him. Reinforcements arrive, along with 25,000 new suits of armour. Would it not have been prudent to wait for these at the Hyphasis before setting out for the Ganges? Why did Alexander not tell his weary troops that he expected substantial reinforcements, and new equipment? The answer is that he did not want them to know.

Only when Alexander returns from the Beas does Arrian mention the Hydaspes fleet. Alexander now makes preparations to sail down the river to the Great Sea (ὡϑ ἐπὶ τὴν μεγάλην θάλασσαν). And, at the beginning of Book 6, Arrian writes:

Since Alexander had ready for him on the banks of the Hydaspes many *triakontoroi* and *hemioliai* and many transports for horses and other vessels useful for the conveyance of an army by river, he determined to sail down the Hydaspes to the Great Sea (6.1.1).[64]

Now this sounds like a coincidence, an afterthought: since the king suddenly discovers that he has all these ships, he decides that he might as well use them to sail to the south! It is, however, clear from a reading of Diodorus and related sources that Alexander had intended all along to establish the Hydaspes as the limits of the Macedonian Empire and that the brief campaign east of that river was intended to secure the buffer kingdom of Porus. No further Macedonian garrisons were established, and a substantial contingent of the army was left behind to prepare for the river expedition. The sacrifice to Helios at the Hydaspes, far from indicating that Alexander intended to continue into the lands of the rising sun, marked the completion of Alexander's eastward expansion.

Alexander's purpose had clearly been to make himself master of the Persian Empire, not to blaze new trails or create new frontiers. He employed the network of roads established by his Achaemenid predecessors: men, money and equipment moved quickly through Asia, and even when Alexander was in its remotest parts, various contingents managed to hook up with him with relative ease. Despite Aeschines' rhetorical comment about Alexander disappearing over the horizon and beyond the *oikoumene* (ἔξω τῆς ἄρκτου καὶ τῆς οἰκουμένης ὀλίγου δεῖν πάσης μεθειστήκει: 3.165), the Macedonian army was always easy to find and knew where it was going. The king did not allow himself to be drawn into campaigns beyond the frontiers, but instead remained focused on his primary goal. It became the task of his historians, to many of whom flattery had become, quite literally, a way of life, to rescue some aspects of the expedition from 'Dullsville'. They were the ones who depicted Alexander as everywhere on the frontiers, as surpassing the greatest heroes of the historical[65] and mythical past, as the world-conqueror whose very name brought the uncultivated and hitherto feared barbarians to his camp or to his Court to make submission.

Notes

1 Fowden 1993: 13: 'By such expressions as *orbis terrarum* and *oikoumene*, educated Greeks and Romans basically meant the *Kulturländer*, the useful parts of the world, which they defined with rather self-conscious broad-mindedness as what lay between, in the West, the Atlantic Ocean where Heracles had set the bounds of the earth; in the East, the remotest Indians who had been visited by Heracles together with Dionysus; in the North, the Scythians; and in the South, the Blemmyes and Ethiopians.'
A version of this paper was accepted for presentation to the Rocky Mountain History Conference in Salt Lake City, Utah, in the fall of 1996. I wish to thank Professor Gene Borza who, when I was unable to attend, offered to read the paper on my behalf; though it should not be assumed that he agrees with the arguments presented here. Subsequently, Philip O. Spann published an article (Spann 1999), which was based on a paper given when he was a graduate student (referred to by Green 1974: 555 n. 109). Spann also believes that Alexander had no desire to advance beyond the Hyphasis (Beas) and engineered the so-called mutiny in order to save face. What Spann's paper does not do is to put the episode into the context of the limitations set upon his conquest by Alexander himself.

2 See, for example, a Latin version of Alexander's *Letter to Aristotle Concerning India*, where Alexander comments: 'I gave orders that we should circumnavigate the leftward part of India. I wanted there to be no place that remained unknown to me' (translated by Richard Stoneman 1994: 11).

For a discussion of Alexander as *kosmokrator* see Goukowsky 1978: 149–65; cf. also Bosworth 1993.

3 Throughout this paper, unless otherwise indicated, I have used the translations of Brunt 1976 and 1983 (Arrian); Yardley 1984 (Curtius) and 1997 (Justin); Scott-Kilvert 1973 (Plutarch).

4 Bengtson 1988: 214. We might add Stoneman 1998: 1, who comments that Alexander was 'campaigning in hitherto unexplored regions'.

5 On Alexander's *pothos* see Ehrenberg 1938; for further literature see Seibert 1972: 183–6.

6 See the highly sensible refutation of Ehrenberg's thesis by Kraft 1971: 81–118.

7 Arr. 5.26.1–2: Πέρας δὲ τῶν πόνων γενναίῳ μὲν ἀνδρὶ οὐδὲν δοκῶ ἔγωγε ὅτι μὴ αὐτοὺς τοὺς πόνους, ὅσοι αὐτῶν ἐς καλὰ ἔργα φέρουσιν. εἰ δέ τις καὶ αὐτῷ τῷ πολεμεῖν ποθεῖ ἀκοῦσαί ὅ τι περ ἔσται πέρας, μαθέτω ὅτι οὐ πολλὴ ἔτι ὑμῖν ἡ λοιπὴ ἐστιν ἔστε ἐπὶ ποταμόν τε Γάγγην καὶ τὴν ἐῴαν θάλασσαν· ταύτῃ δέ, λέγω ὑμῖν, ξυναφὴς φανεῖται ἡ Ὑρκανία θάλασσα· ἐκπεριέρχεται γὰρ γῆν πέρι πᾶσαν ἡ μεγάλη θάλασσα. καὶ ἐγὼ ἐπιδείξω Μακεδόσι τε καὶ τοῖς ξυμμάχοις τὸν μὲν Ἰνδικὸν κόλπον ξύρρουν ὄντα τῷ Περσικῷ, τὴν δὲ Ὑρκανίαν <θάλασσαν> τῷ Ἰνδικῷ· ἀπὸ δὲ τοῦ Περσικοῦ εἰς Λιβύην περιπλευσ–θήσεται στόλῳ ἡμετέρῳ τὰ μέχρι Ἡρακλέους Στηλῶν· ἀπὸ δὲ Στηλῶν ἡ ἐντὸς Λιβύη πᾶσα ἡμετέρα γίγνεται καὶ ἡ Ἀσία δὴ οὕτω πᾶσα, καὶ ὅροι τῆς ταύτῃ ἀρχῆς οὕσπερ καὶ τῇ γῆς ὅρους ὁ θεὸς ἐποίησε.

8 Thus Bosworth 1995: 347; Bosworth 1988: 129 ff.

9 See Endres 1924; Berve 1966: 334–5. Endres argues that, until Alexander reached the Punjab and saw the situation for himself, he believed that India represented the eastern edge of the continent, next to which was the sea. But Alexander must have known about the voyage of Scylax of Caryanda (in the reign of Darius I), either from Herodotus or from informants. The route from the Indus delta to the straits of Hormuz, which was later followed by Nearchus and the Macedonian fleet, had long been known to sailors (cf. Casson 1991: 8–9). If the Alexander historians know nothing of Scylax, it may be because Nearchus and Onesicritus themselves omitted all mention of him in order not to detract from their own achievements.

10 Xen. *Anab.* 1.7.6: πρὸς μὲν μεσημβρίαν μέχρι οὗ διὰ καῦμα οὐ δύνται οἰκεῖν ἄνθρωποι, πρὸς δὲ ἄρκτον μέχρι οὗ διὰ χειμῶνα.

11 Arr. 1.4.5: αὐτὸς δὲ ... θύει τε ἐπὶ τῇ ὄχθῃ τοῦ Ἴστρου Διὶ Σωτῆρι καὶ Ἡρακλεῖ καὶ αὐτῷ τῷ Ἴστρῳ, ὅτι οὐκ ἄπορος αὐτῷ ἐγένετο, καὶ ἐπανάγει αὐτῆς ἡμέρας σώους σύμπαντας ἐπὶ τὸ στρατόπεδον. Cf. also the comments of Wilcken 1967: 67.

12 For Darius I's disastrous Scythian expedition in 513 see Hdt. 4. 118–142; cf. also Arr. 4.11.9. See also Bosworth 1995: 28: 'there is every reason to believe that, like Cyrus' defeat in 530, it was constantly in Alexander's mind.' The uncivilised Scythians form a buffer between the more familiar world of the Thracians and the mythical Hyperboreans to the north. See Romm 1992: 75 n. 72.

13 Though these are more common at the battle-sites.

14 Arr. 1.4.7–8: Ἐνταῦθα ἀφίκοντο πρέσβεις ὡς Ἀλέξανδρον παρά τε τῶν ἄλλων ὅσα αὐτόνομα ἔθνη προσοικεῖ τῷ Ἴστρῳ καὶ παρὰ Σύρμου τοῦ Τριβαλλῶν βασιλέως· καὶ παρὰ Κελτῶν δὲ τῶν ἐπὶ τῷ Ἰονίῳ κόλπῳ ᾠκισμένων ἧκον· μεγάλοι οἱ Κελτοὶ τὰ σώματα καὶ μέγα ἐπὶ σφίσι φρονοῦντες· πάντες δὲ φιλίας τῆς Ἀλεξάνδρου ἐφιέμενοι ἥκειν ἔφασαν. καὶ πᾶσιν ἔδωκε πίστεις Ἀλέξανδρος καὶ ἔλαβε· τοὺς Κελτοὺς δὲ καὶ ἤρετο, ὅ τι μάλιστα δεδίττεται αὐτοὺς τῶν ἀνθρωπίνων, ἐλπίσας ὅτι μέγα ὄνομα τὸ αὐτοῦ καὶ ἐς Κελτοὺς καὶ ἔτι προσωτέρω ἥκει καὶ ὅτι αὐτὸν μάλιστα πάντων δεδιέναι φήσουσι. τῷ δὲ παρ' ἐλπίδα ξυνέβη τῶν Κελτῶν ἡ ἀπόκρισις· οἷα γὰρ πόρρω τε ᾠκισμένοι Ἀλεξάνδρου καὶ χωρία δύσπορα οἰκοῦντες καὶ Ἀλεξάνδρου ἐς ἄλλα τὴν ὁρμὴν ὁρῶντες ἔφασαν δεδιέναι μήποτε ὁ οὐρανὸς αὐτοῖς ἐμπέσοι, Ἀλέξανδρόν τε ἀγασθέντες οὔτε δέει οὔτε κατ' ὠφέλειαν πρεσβεῦσαι παρ' αὐτόν. καὶ τούτους φίλους τε ὀνομάσας καὶ ξυμμάχους ποιησάμενος ὀπίσω ἀπέπεμψε, τοσοῦτον ὑπειπὼν ὅτι ἀλαζόνες Κελτοὶ εἰσιν. Cf. Strabo 7.3.8, based on Ptolemy (*FGrH* 138 F 2). Similar stories are told about the Ethiopians (in response to Cambyses' campaigns) and the Scythians beyond the Tanais (Iaxartes).

15 Arr. 1.11.5: ἐλθὼν δὲ ἐς Ἐλαιοῦντα θύει Πρωτεσιλάῳ ἐπὶ τῷ τάφῳ τοῦ Πρωτεσιλάου, ὅτι καὶ Πρωτεσίλαος πρῶτος ἐδόκει ἐκβῆναι ἐς τὴν Ἀσίαν τῶν Ἑλλήνων ἅμα Ἀγαμέμνονι ἐς Ἴλιον στρατευσάντων. καὶ ὁ νοῦς τῆς θυσίας ἦν ἐπιτυχεστέραν οἷ

γενέσθαι ἢ Πρωτεσιλάῳ τὴν ἀπόβασιν. Protesilaus was also the first of Agamemnon's men to be killed in Asia.

16 Xenophon, *HG* 3.4.3–4; Plut. *Ages.* 6. For Alexander's sacrifices at Ilium see Plut. *Alex.* 15.7–9; Arr. 1.12.1–2; Diod. 17.17.3; Justin 11.5.12.

17 Arr. 1.11.6–7: Ἀλέξανδρον δὲ ἐξ Ἐλαιοῦντος ἐς τὸν Ἀχαιῶν λιμένα κατᾶραι ὁ πλείων λόγος κατέχει, καὶ αὐτόν τε κυβερνῶντα τὴν στρατηγίδα ναῦν διαβάλλειν καί, ἐπειδὴ κατὰ μέσον τὸν πόρον τοῦ Ἑλλησπόντου ἐγένετο, σφάξαντα ταῦρον τῷ Ποσειδῶνι καὶ Νηρηίσι σπένδειν ἐκ χρυσῆς φιάλης ἐς τὸν πόντον. λέγουσιν ... βωμοὺς ἱδρύσασθαι ὅθεν τε ἐστάλη ἐκ τῆς Εὐρώπης καὶ ὅπου ἐξέβη τῆς Ἀσίας Διὸς ἀποβατηρίου καὶ Ἀθηνᾶς καὶ Ἡρακλέους. Cf. Justin 11.5.10–11; Diod. 17.17.2. For the importance of the Hellespont, cf. Arrian's comment (1.13.6): 'Alexander had his answer: "Yes, Parmenion," he said, "but I should be ashamed of myself if a little trickle of water like this" (a very derogatory way of referring to the Granicus!) "were too much for us to cross without further preparation, when I had no difficulty whatever in crossing the Hellespont".'

18 For *terror nominis* see Justin 12.13.2. Cf. the notion of 'fame' and/or 'reputation' in Curtius (8.13.2; 10.5.37; and 5.13.14, with Atkinson 1994: 161, for the role of 'reputation' in imperial panegyric). Although Arrian 1.4.8 (quoted above), following Ptolemy (*FGrH* 138 F 2), claims that the Celts did not come to Alexander out of fear, Strabo 7.3.8 (C302) says that the Celts, although they claimed not to fear anyone, 'set as their highest priority the friendship of great men' (φιλίαν δὲ περὶ παντὸς τίθεσθαι μεγάλων ἀνδρῶν). Thalestris, the Amazon Queen, recognises that Alexander through his deeds has proved himself the best of all men (Diod. 17.77.3: ἐκεῖνον μὲν γὰρ τῶν ἁπάντων ἀνδρῶν διὰ τὰς πράξεις ἄριστον ὑπάρχειν).

19 The original account seems to go back to Callisthenes: where Strabo mentions Corycus, Lyrnessus, Thebe and Typhon, he makes reference to Callisthenes (Strabo 13.4.6 = *FGrH* 124 F 28; 14.4.1 = *FGrH* 124 F 32). Atkinson 1980: 143 notes significant differences in Curtius' version. These may be due to Curtius himself, or else to an intermediary source (e.g. Cleitarchus).

20 For Mt Climax see Plut. *Alex.* 17.6–7; cf. Arr. 1.26.1–2, with Bosworth 1980: 164–6. For the younger Cyrus at Thapsacus see Xen. *Anab.* 1.4.18; recognised by J. Rufus Fears in Badian 1976: 28).

21 Perdiccas conquered the region in 322 or 321 (Justin 13.6.1; Diod. 18.16.1–3; cf. Diod. 18.22.1; App. *Mithr.* 8 = *FGrH* 154 F3).

22 For Alexander's decision to return to the coastal area as a reaction to the activities of Darius III see Kraft 1971: 88–90.

23 The comparison is, indeed, made by Plut. *Alex.* 26.12. Note also Alexander's sacrifice to Apis (Arr. 3.1); although the story of Cambyses' killing of the Apis calf is now regarded by many scholars as fictitious (see, for example, Olmstead 1948: 89–90; Cook 1983: 49; Briant 1996: 67–8), Alexander will have been familiar with Herodotus' version (2. 27–28), which he no doubt considered to be true.

24 For Alexander's foundations see Fraser 1996.

25 Diod. 17.77; Curt. 6.5.24ff.; Justin 12.3.5–7. The episode is rejected by Plutarch (*Alex.* 46), who provides an impressive list of authors who either believed or dismissed the story. See now Baynham 2001, who examines various historiographical aspects of Alexander's meeting with Thalestris, including its significance for Alexander's *Verschmelzungspolitik*, and drawing attention to the fact that Alexander's mythical ancestors (Heracles and Achilles) had both had encounters with Amazons.

26 Arr. 3.30 recognises that the Iaxartes, which some of the primary Alexander historians called the Tanais, was not identical with the Tanais mentioned by Herodotus. Nevertheless, he does speak of an embassy from the European Scythians and this reflects the contemporary (late 4th century view) that the Iaxartes also divided Asia from Europe (cf. Hamilton 1971).

27 Arr. 4.1.1–2: οὐ πολλαῖς δὲ ἡμέραις ὕστερον ἀφικνοῦνται πα'ρ Ἀλέξανδρον πρέσβεις παρά τε Σκυθῶν τῶν Ἀβίων καλουμένων (οὕς καὶ Ὅμηρος δικαιοτάτους ἀνθρώπους εἰπὼν ἐν τῇ ποιήσει ἐπήνεσεν· οἰκοῦσι δὲ ἐν τῇ Ἀσίᾳ οὗτοι αὐτόνομοι, οὐχ ἥκιστα διὰ πενίαν τε καὶ δικαιότητα) καὶ παρὰ τῶν ἐκ τῆς Εὐρώπης Σκυθῶν, οἳ δὴ τὸ μέγιστον ἔθνος [Σκυθικὸν] ἐν τῇ Εὐρώπῃ ἐποικοῦσιν. καὶ τούτοις ξυμπέμπει Ἀλέξανδρος τῶν ἑταίρων, πρόφασιν μὲν κατὰ πρεσβείαν φιλίαν ξυνθησομένους, ὁ δὲ νοῦς τῆς πομπῆς

ἐς κατασκοπήν τι μᾶλλον ἔφερε φύσεώς τε τῆς χώρας τῆς Σκυθικῆς καὶ πλήθους αὐτῶν καὶ νομαίων καὶ ὁπλίσεως, ἥντινα ἔχοντες στέλλονται ἐς τὰς μάχας.

28 Curt. 7. 9. 15: Transierant iam Liberi Patris terminos, quorum monumenta lapides erant crebris interuallis dispositi arboresque procerae, quarum stipites hedera contexerat. Cf. *Metz Epit.* 12.

29 Curt. 7.9.17–18: Inuictos Scythas esse crediderant; quibus fractis nullam gentem Macedonum armis parem fore confitebantur. Itaque Sacae misere legatos, qui pollicerentur gentem imperata facturam. Mouerat eos Regis non uirtus magis quam clementia in deuictos Scythas.

30 Arr. 4. 4. 3 draws attention not to the case of Cyrus but rather Darius I's Scythian campaign in 513.

31 Cf. Hamilton 1973: 'The order given by Alexander immediately after Porus' defeat for the construction of a fleet indicates that he had made up his mind to sail down the Indus to the sea' (117).

32 Thus Plut. *Alex.* 62.9; cf. Curt. 9.2.6–7; Diod. 17.93.3. See also Justin 15.4.13–19. Even the details about the lowly origins of the Nanda king (a barber's son) are confirmed by independent Indian sources (cf. Bosworth 1996: 76–7).

33 Spann 1999: 68: 'This, of course, was precisely what Alexander realized that he had to do. He simply did not want to be responsible for proposing it. ... The failure to conquer all of Asia, to reach the eastern Ocean was indeed a defeat, but the army was responsible for it. His speech at the Beas, indeed his behavior as a whole, was a disingenuous fiction.' Bosworth 1996: 80, accepts Arrian's view: 'For him it [sc. news of Gangetic kingdom] was an inspiring challenge, but for his troops it came as the last straw, a promise of misery without end.'

34 Arr. 5.29.1–2: ἔνθα δὴ διελὼν κατὰ τάξεις τὴν στρατιὰν δώδεκα βωμοὺς κατασκευάζειν προστάττει, ὕψος μὲν κατὰ τοὺς μεγίστους πύργους, εὖρος δὲ μείζονας ἔτι ἢ κατὰ πύργους, χαριστήρια τοῖς θεοῖς τοῖς ἐς τοσόνδε ἀγαγοῦσιν αὐτὸν νικῶντα καὶ μνημεῖα τῶν αὑτοῦ πόνων. ὡς δὲ κατεσκευασμένοι αὐτῷ οἱ βωμοὶ ἦσαν, θύει δὴ ἐπ' αὐτῶν ὡς νόμος καὶ ἀγῶνα ποιεῖ γυμνικόν τε καὶ ἱππικόν.

35 Generally referred to as the 'Alexander Vulgate', a term which is beginning to lose some of its meaning, and the tendency in recent years to speak of 'the so-called "vulgate"' is no more helpful. I refer here to those extant Alexander historians who make extensive, if not exclusive, use of a common lost source (probably Cleitarchus) and I include in this number not only Diodorus, Curtius and Justin-Trogus, but also the *Metz Epitome* and Plutarch, who in his *Life* uses much 'Cleitarchean' information for his 'historical' narrative.

36 Plut. *Alex.* 62.6–7: ἐπικλασθεὶς ἀνεζεύγνυε, πολλὰ πρὸς δόξαν ἀπατηλὰ καὶ σοφιστικὰ μηχανώμενος. καὶ γὰρ ὅπλα μείζονα καὶ φάτνας ἵππων καὶ χαλινοὺς βαρυτέρους κατασκευάσας ἀπέλιπέ τε καὶ διέρριψεν ἱδρύσατο δὲ βωμοὺς θεῶν... .

37 Curt. 9.3.19: ut speciem omnium augeret, posteritati fallax miraculum praeparans.

38 See Bosworth's comments on 5.26 (Bosworth 1995: 347–8).

39 Cf. Romm 1992: 84 ff. I must agree with Wirth 1971: 629, who comments: 'Daß Alexander von der Fahrt des in Werken seines eigenen Lehrers Aristoteles zitierten Skylax nichts wußte, kann ich nicht glauben.'

40 Arr. 6.3.1–2: ὡς δὲ ξύμπαντα αὐτῷ παρεσκεύαστο, ὑπὸ τὴν ἕω ὁ μὲν στρατὸς ἐπέβαινε τῶν νεῶν, αὐτὸς δὲ ἔθυε τοῖς θεοῖς ὡς νόμος καὶ τῷ ποταμῷ Ὑδάσπῃ ὅπως οἱ μάντεις ἐξηγοῦντο. καὶ ἐπιβὰς τῆς νεὼς ἀπὸ τῆς πρώρας ἐκ χρυσῆς φιάλης ἔσπενδεν ἐς τὸν ποταμόν, τόν τε Ἀκεσίνην ξυνεπικαλούμενος τῷ Ὑδάσπῃ, ὅντινα μέγιστον αὖ τῶν ἄλλων ποταμῶν ξυμβάλλειν τῷ Ὑδάσπῃ ἐπέπυστο καὶ οὐ πόρρω αὐτῶν εἶναι τὰς, ξυμβολάς, καὶ τὸν Ἰνδόν, ἐς ὅντινα ὁ Ἀκεσίνης ξὺν τῷ Ὑδάσπῃ ἐμβάλλει. ἐπὶ δὲ Ἡρακλεῖ τε τῷ προπάτορι σπείσας καὶ Ἄμμωνι καὶ τοῖς ἄλλοις θεοῖς ὅσοις αὐτῷ νόμος σημῆναι ἐς ἀναγωγὴν κελεύει τῇ σάλπιγγι.

41 For Alexander and the 'corners' of the world see also Pearson 1960: 13–16.

42 Arr. 6.19.4: καὶ πρὸς τοῖς ἄκροις αὐτῆς καθορμισθεὶς θύει τοῖς θεοῖς Ἀλέξανδρος ὅσοις ἔφασκεν ὅτι παρὰ τοῦ Ἄμμωνος ἐπηγγελμένον ἦν θῦσαι αὐτῷ. ἐς δὲ τὴν ὑστεραίαν κατέπλει ὡς ἐπὶ τὴν ἄλλην τὴν ἐν τῷ πόντῳ νῆσον, καὶ προσχὼν καὶ ταύτῃ ἔθυε καὶ ἐνταῦθα ἄλλας αὖ θυσίας ἄλλοις τε θεοῖς καὶ ἄλλῳ τρόπῳ· καὶ ταύτας δὲ κατ' ἐπιθεσπισμὸν <ἀέφασκε> τοῦ Ἄμμωνος.

44 For the marriage alliance see Curt. 9.3.22; cf. 10.1.20. One of the Indian satraps, Philip son of Machatas, was killed by mercenaries (Curt. 10.1.21; Arr. 6.27.2); his replacement Eudamus was

serving in India and perhaps at the court of Taxiles – Arrian says that Alexander sent letters to both men. Eudamus later murdered Porus (Diod. 19.14.1), possibly with the support of Taxiles.

45 Thus Anspach 1903: 2.38 n. 245.

46 Diodorus, Curtius and *Metz Epitome* all give the same number of horse, infantry and chariots. Diod. 17.93.2 has 4,000 elephants, Curt. 9.2.4 says 3,000; *Metz Epitome* 68 is corrupt but seems to record 180 elephants. Justin 12.8.10 is also corrupt and only traces of the 200,000 infantry remain. Plut. *Alex.* 62.3 gives different figures: 200,000 infantry; 80,000 cavalry, 8,000 chariots and 6,000 elephants. The higher figures are hard to explain.

47 Xenophon, *HG* 4.3.10–14; cf. Plut. *Agesilaus* 17. The Spartans were at Chaeronea at the time and the bad news was compounded by the superstition associated with a partial eclipse of the sun.

48 See, for example, Curt. 3.10.6, 10; 4.14.1–7.

49 Hdt. 1.214.3–5.

50 Bosworth 1993: 422. Cf. Hamilton 1973: 115: 'At this time, too, he gave orders for the building of a fleet on which he planned, *after his eastern campaign* [my italics], to sail down the Jhelum to the Indus and thence to the sea.'

51 Curt. 8.9.5–8 draws a rather confusing picture of Indian geography: he asserts that the Ganges flowed in a southerly direction, joining its waters with that of another river – the text of 8.9.8 is corrupt – before reaching the Red Sea (which we may take to mean the Indian Ocean, but certainly not the Bay of Bengal).

52 If the Alexander historians regarded India as substantially more than the Punjab, the source of Diodorus 17.93.1 could scarcely have referred to Hephaestion's conquest of the kingdom of 'Bad (or Cowardly) Porus' as 'a big part of India' πολλὴν τῆς Ἰνδικῆς καταπεπολεμηκώς. Curtius 8.9.2 says that India is longer than it is wide. This view of India must have been formed *before* Megasthenes' visit to the court of Chandragupta (Sandracottus).

53 Alexander appears to have known nothing of the Sutlej.

54 See the full discussion in Bosworth 1996: 186–200.

55 Arr. 5.29.2–3. Here Alexander settles natives and *mercenaries* no longer fit for service. Some scholars have, of course, seen the assignment of this territory to Porus as an afterthought. Thus Green 1974: 412 writes: 'Alexander's sudden loss of interest in northern India was largely due to circumstances beyond his control. To save time and trouble, all conquered territory as far as the Beas was simply made part of Porus' kingdom.' So, too, Tarn 1948: 2.394 observes that 'when [Alexander] turned back at the Beas he *abandoned* a hard-won conquest: he formally handed over the Punjab east of the Jhelum to Porus' [my italics]. Cf. Lane Fox 1974: 375: 'Only Porus benefited from the new despair. The "seven nations and two thousand towns" between the Jhelum and the Beas were added to his kingdom; they had lost their interest now that the march to the east had been cancelled.' But this ignores the fact that Alexander did not establish Macedonian garrisons or phrourarchs or officials of any sort in the course of the campaigning that brought him to the Hyphasis. Arr. 5.24.8 makes it clear that Porus himself was to garrison the cities of the Cathaeans (καὶ Πῶρον μὲν ξὺν τῇ δυνάμει ἀμφ' αὐτὸν ἐκπέμπει ἐπὶ τὰς πόλεις αἳ προσκεχωρήκεσαν, φρουρὰς εἰσάξοντα εἰς αὐτάς).

56 Breloer 1941: 75: 'Der Zug an den Hyphasis ist kein Frontalangriff gegen das Gangesgebiet, sondern eine Flankendeckung des Zuges abwärts des Indus zum Meere hin.' P.A. Brunt's remark that Breloer's works 'may be neglected with special advantage' (1983: 443) is unnecessarily (and one would hope uncharacteristically) malicious and does nothing to further the cause of scholarship.

57 In fact, Curtius 9.1.2–3 suggests that Alexander promised his men the opportunity of enriching themselves through plunder in the Punjab.

58 Eggermont 1993: 13.

59 Thus Hamilton 1973: 117.

60 Hamilton 1973: 117.

61 Whether Nearchus and/or Onesicritus remained at the Hydaspes is not clear. Neither is mentioned in the accounts of these months and only two fragments of Onesicritus suggest that he may have accompanied Alexander. *FGrH* 134 FF21–22 record Onesicritus' views on the Cathaeans, but these do not include observations that could not have been made during the descent of the Indus river-system. Certainly F9, which speaks of the position of the sun at the

'Hypasis' (= Hyphasis) at the solstice must be an error for the Hydaspes, since the battle with Porus occurred at the time of the summer solstice (Arr. 5.9.4) and the advance to the east began more than a month later. There is nothing in the fragments of Nearchus to suggest that he advanced east of the Hydaspes.

62 Diod. 17.93.1–2 shows that Hephaestion rejoined Alexander at the Hyphasis, but this may have been to report the completion of the Acesines project. If the place was strategically important, we must assume that he left a substantial force there to guard it.

63 Coenus son of Polemocrates acted as spokesman for the soldiery, and Spann 1999: 68–9 suggests that he did so by pre-arrangement with Alexander, though perhaps 'he may have divined the king's wishes without prompting'. The suggestion of one scholar, that Coenus may have been eliminated for his outspoken opposition to the king, has found support in recent literature, but the idea is rightly dismissed by Holt 2000.

64 Ἀλέξανδροῦ δέ, ἐπειδὴ παρεσκευάσθησαν αὐτῷ ἐπὶ τοῦ Ὑδάσπου ταῖϑ ὄχθαιϑ πολλαὶ μὲν τριακόντοροι καὶ ἡμιόλιαι, πολλὰ δὲ καὶ ἱππαλωλὰ πλοῖα καὶ ἄλλα ὅσα ἐϑ παρακομιδὴν στρατιᾶϑ ποταμῷ εὔπορα, ἔλνω καταπλεῖν κατὰ τὸν Ὑδάσπην ὡϑ ἐπὶ τὴν μελάλην θάλασσαν.

65 For example, Cyrus (at the Iaxartes, in the land of the Ariaspians, and in the Gedrosian desert, where there is emulation also of Semiramis).

References

Anspach 1903 = A.E. Anspach, *De Alexandri Magni expeditione Indica* (Leipzig: 1903).

Atkinson 1980 = J.E. Atkinson, *A Commentary on Q. Curtius Rufus'* Historiae Alexandri Magni, *Books 3 and 4* (Amsterdam: 1980).

Atkinson 1994 = J.E. Atkinson, *A Commentary on Q. Curtius Rufus'* Historiae Alexandri Magni, *Books 5 to 7.2* (Amsterdam: 1994).

Badian 1976 = E. Badian, 'The Deification of Alexander the Great', in H.J. Dell (ed.), *Ancient Macedonian Studies in Honour of C.F. Edson* (Thessaloniki: 1981), pp. 27–71.

Baynham 2001 = E. Baynham, 'Alexander and the Amazons', *CQ²* 51 (2001), pp. 115–126.

Bengtson 1988 = H. Bengtson, *History of Greece from the Beginnings to the Byzantine Era*, trans. E.F. Bloedow (Ottawa: 1988).

Berve 1966 = H. Berve, 'Alexander der Grosse als Entdecker', *Gestaltende Kräfte der Antike* (Munich: 1966), pp. 333–353.

Bosworth 1980 = A.B. Bosworth, *A Commentary on Arrian's History of Alexander* 1 (Oxford: 1980).

Bosworth 1988 = A.B. Bosworth, *Conquest and Empire: The Reign of Alexander the Great* (Cambridge: 1988).

Bosworth 1993 = A.B. Bosworth, 'Aristotle, India and the Alexander Historians', *TOPOI* 2–3 (1993), pp. 407–24.

Bosworth 1995 = A.B. Bosworth, *A Commentary on Arrian's History of Alexander* 2 (Oxford: 1995).

Bosworth 1996 = A.B. Bosworth, *Alexander and the East. The Tragedy of Triumph* (Oxford: 1996).

Breloer 1941 = B. Breloer, *Alexanders Bund mit Poros. Indien von Dareios zu Sandrokottos* (Leipzig: 1941).

Briant 1996 = P. Briant, *Histoire de l'empire perse. De Cyrus à Alexandre* (Paris: 1996).

Brunt 1976 = P.A. Brunt, *Arrian, History of Alexander* 1, Loeb Classical Library (Cambridge: 1976).

Brunt 1983 = P.A. Brunt, *Arrian, History of Alexander* 2, Loeb Classical Library (Cambridge: 1983).

Casson 1991 = L. Casson, *The Ancient Mariners* (Princeton: 1991).

Cook 1983 = J.M. Cook, *The Persian Empire* (London: 1983).

Ehrenberg 1938 = V. Ehrenberg, 'Alexander and the Greeks', in G.T. Griffith (ed.), *Alexander the Great: The Main Problems* (Cambridge: 1966), pp. 74–83.

Endres 1924 = H. Endres, *Geographischer Horizont und Politik bei Alexander d. Gr. in den Jahren 330/323* (Würzburg: 1924).

Fowden 1993 = G. Fowden, *Empire to Commonwealth. Consequences of Monotheism in Late Antiquity* (Princeton: 1993).

Fraser 1996 = P.M. Fraser, *Cities of Alexander the Great* (Oxford: 1996).

Goukowsky 1978 = P. Goukowsky, *Essai sur les origines du mythe d'Alexandre (336–270 av. J.-C.)* (Nancy: 1978).

Green 1974 = P. Green, *Alexander of Macedon, 356–323 B.C. A Historical Biography* (London: 1974).

Hamilton 1971 = J.R. Hamilton, 'Alexander and the Aral', *CQ*[2] 21 (1971), pp. 106–111.

Hamilton 1973 = J.R. Hamilton, *Alexander the Great* (London: 1973).

Holt 2000 = F.L. Holt, 'The Death of Coenus: Another Study in Method', *AHB* 14 (2000), pp. 49–55.

Kraft 1971 = K. Kraft, *Der 'rationale' Alexander* (Frankfurt: 1971).

Lane Fox 1974 = R. Lane Fox, *Alexander the Great* (London: 1973).

Olmstead 1948 = A.T. Olmstead, *History of the Persian Empire* (Chicago: 1948).

Pearson 1960 = L. Pearson, *The Lost Histories of Alexander the Great* (Philadelphia: 1960).

Romm 1992 = J.S. Romm, *The Edges of the Earth in Ancient Thought* (Princeton: 1992).

Scott-Kilvert 1973 = I. Scott-Kilvert, *Plutarch. The Age of Alexander*, Penguin Classics (Harmondsworth: 1973).

Seibert 1972 = J. Seibert, *Alexander der Grosse* (Darmstadt: 1972).

Spann 1999 = P.O. Spann, 'Alexander at the Beas: Fox in a Lion's Skin', in F. Titchener and R.F. Moorten (eds), *The Eye Expanded* (Berkeley: 1999), pp. 62–74.

Stoneman 1994 = R. Stoneman, *Legends of Alexander the Great*, Penguin Classics (London: 1994).

Stoneman 1998 = R. Stoneman, *Alexander the Great* (London: 1998).

Tarn 1948 = W.W. Tarn, *Alexander the Great* (Cambridge: 1948).

Wilcken 1967 = U. Wilcken, *Alexander the Great*, trans. G.C. Richards (New York: 1967).

Wirth 1971 = G. Wirth, 'Nearchos der Flottenchef', *Acta Conventus XI, 'Eirene'* (Warsaw: 1972), pp. 615–639.

Yardley 1984 = J.C. Yardley, *Quintis Curtius Rufus. The History of Alexander*, Penguin Classics (Harmondsworth: 1984).

Yardley 1997 = J.C. Yardley and W. Heckel, *Justin. The Epitome of* the Philippic History *of Pompeius Trogus 1: Books 11–12: Alexander the Great* (Oxford: 1997).{

4

ALEXANDER'S BATTLES AND GENERALSHIP

Introduction

Alexander's military successes extended the Macedonian empire from the Greek mainland to as far east as what the Greeks called India but today is Pakistan. There is no question that he was a spectacularly successful general, and that he had a demonstrated brilliance for battle and siege tactics (cf. Sources 51 and 52 on Tyre). His own willingness to lead from the front and fight with his men rather than hold back until battles were over was both commendable in a general and an inspiration to his troops; it was also what the people expected of a Macedonian warrior king. Like his father, Alexander was often wounded, sometimes near-fatally (cf. Sources 11, 23, 24, 70), but bore his scars with pride and as a symbol of his fighting prowess. Like any good general and king, he was also quick to identify with his men, and to suffer the same hardships as they did (see Source 79); nor would he abandon them, often risking great personal danger in the process (cf. Source 23).

Although Alexander battled against various tribes and peoples on so many occasions, some of which were minor and nothing more than skirmishes, four major or 'set' battles from his reign are especially important and represent his military prowess at its best. These are the three battles against the Persians at Granicus (334), Issus (333) and Gaugamela (331),[1] and the battle against the Indian prince Porus at the Hydaspes river (326).[2] He also waged a number of sieges, of which his most spectacular were those of Tyre (332) and the Rock of Aornus (327–326), and we should also acknowledge his adaptability and resilience in the intense guerrilla fighting his army waged in Bactria and Sogdiana (329–327). For a very good overview of Alexander's major military actions and his tactics, see B. Strauss, 'Alexander: The Military Campaign', in J. Roisman (ed.), *Brill's Companion to Alexander the Great* (Leiden: 2003), pp. 133–156.

Yet the Homeric nature of the battles and the magnitude of the military victories, always against vastly superior numbers with surprisingly small (by comparison) Macedonian casualties, may be questioned, and were perhaps the products of his own propaganda. He very likely told the court historian Callisthenes of Olynthus what to say about his victory over Darius III at the battle of Issus in 333,[3] after which he started to call himself Lord of Asia. Indeed, that battle becomes part of an exaggerated Alexander tradition, still manifesting itself in Roman times as the so-called Alexander mosaic shows. Yet, after Issus Alexander allowed Darius to escape from the battlefield, and rather than pursue him to consolidate his gains and bring down the Great King he pushed south into Egypt (cf. Source 114), thereby allowing Darius to regroup his forces and bring Alexander to battle again at Gaugamela in 331.

After the defeat of Porus Alexander had struck a commemorative coinage that exaggerated his victory. Certainly his crossing of the swollen river Hydaspes, during which he lost the element of surprise, was commendable, but once on the opposite bank his speed and tactical superiority were always going to bring about the rout of Porus' army that happened. We should also remember that Alexander's men twice mutinied on him (326 and 324), and that Alexander blundered badly when he led part of his army westwards through the Gedrosian Desert for his own personal reasons (in 325). Thus, Alexander's obvious prowess on the battlefield and strategic and tactical genius must be weighed against this downside as general and king.[4]

Ancient sources

22   At Issus he (Alexander) was run through the thigh with a sword by Darius (as Chares relates), who encountered him hand to hand. Alexander also himself, writing the truth with all sincerity to Antipater, said, that it was my fortune to be wounded with a poniard in the thigh, but no ill symptoms attended it either when it was newly done or afterwards during the cure (Chares, *FGrH* 125 F 6 = [Plut.] *Mor.* 341c).

23   While the siege of the city was in progress,[5] he made an expedition against the Arabians who dwelt in the neighbourhood of Mount Antilibanus. On this occasion he risked his life to save his tutor, Lysimachus, who insisted on following him, declaring himself to be neither older or weaker than Phoenix. But when the force drew near the mountains, they abandoned their horses and proceeded on foot, and most of them got far on in advance. Alexander himself, however, would not consent to abandon the worn and weary Lysimachus, since evening was already coming on and the enemy were near, but sought to encourage him and carry him along. Before he was aware of it, therefore, he was separated from his army with a few followers, and had to spend a night of darkness and intense cold in a region that was rough and difficult. In this plight, he saw far off a number of scattered fires which the enemy was burning. So, since he was confident in his own agility, and was ever wont to cheer the Macedonians in their perplexities by sharing their toils, he ran to the nearest camp-fire. Two barbarians who were sitting at the fire he dispatched with his dagger, and snatching up a fire-brand, brought it to his own party. These kindled a great fire and at once frightened some of the enemy into flight, routed others who came up against them, and spent the night without further peril. Such, then, is the account we have from Chares (*FGrH* 125 F 7 = Plut. *Alex.* 24.10–14).

24   Alexander himself also was wounded with an arrow under the breast through the breast-plate in the chest, so that Ptolemy says air was breathed out from the wound together with the blood (Ptolemy, *FGrH* 138 F 25 = Arr. 6.10.1).

25   But the truth was, it seems to me, that Alexander was insatiably ambitious of ever acquiring fresh territory (Aristobulus, *FGrH* 139 F 55 = Arr. 7.19.6).

Modern works

In the following selection, Major General J.F.C. Fuller considers Alexander's battles in their broad contexts to assess the king's abilities as strategist, tactician and leader, and hence his overall military prowess.

J.F.C. Fuller, *The Generalship of Alexander the Great* (repr. Rutgers University Press: 1960), Chap. 10, 'Alexander's Generalship', pp. 284–305.[6]

Additional reading

M.M. Austin, 'Alexander and the Macedonian Invasion of Asia', in J. Rich and G. Shipley (eds), *War and Society in the Greek World* (London: 1993), pp. 197–223.

E. Badian, 'The Battle of Granicus: A New Look', *Ancient Macedonia* 2 (Institute for Balkan Studies, Thessaloniki: 1977), pp. 271–293.

E.F. Bloedow, 'The Siege of Tyre in 332 BC: Alexander at the Crossroads in his Career', *La Parola del Passato* 301 (1998), pp. 255–293.

A.R. Burn, 'The Generalship of Alexander', *Greece and Rome*[2] 12 (1965), pp. 140–154.

A.M. Devine, 'Grand Tactics at Gaugamela', *Phoenix* 29 (1975), pp. 374–385.

——, 'The Strategies of Alexander the Great and Darius III in the Issus Campaign (333 BC)', *Ancient World* 12 (1985), pp. 25–38.

——, 'Grand Tactics at the Battle of Issus', *Ancient World* 12 (1985), pp. 39–59.

——, 'Demythologizing the Battle of the Granicus', *Phoenix* 40 (1986), pp. 265–278.

——, 'The Battle of Gaugamela: A Tactical and Source-Critical Study', *Ancient World* 13 (1986), pp. 87–115.

——, 'The Battle of Hydaspes; A Tactical and Source-Critical Study', *Ancient World* 16 (1987), pp. 91–113.

——, 'A Pawn-Sacrifice at the Battle of the Granicus: The Origins of a Favorite Stratagem of Alexander the Great', *Ancient World* 18 (1988), pp. 3–20.

——, 'The Macedonian Army at Gaugamela: Its Strength and the Length of Its Battle-Line', *Ancient World* 19 (1989), pp. 77–80.

——, 'Alexander the Great', in J. Hackett (ed.), *Warfare in the Ancient World* (New York: 1989), pp. 104–129.

D. Engels, *Alexander the Great and the Logistics of the Macedonian Army* (Berkeley and Los Angeles: 1978).

G.T. Griffith, 'Alexander's Generalship at Gaugamela', *Journal of Hellenic Studies* 67 (1947), pp. 77–89.

N.G.L. Hammond, 'The Battle of the Granicus River', *Journal of Hellenic Studies* 100 (1980), pp. 73–88.

——, 'Alexander's Charge at the Battle of Issus in 333 BC', *Historia* 41 (1992), pp. 395–406.

W. Heckel, 'King and "Companions": Observations on the Nature of Power in the Reign of Alexander', in J. Roisman (ed.), *Brill's Companion to Alexander the Great* (Leiden: 2003), pp. 197–225.

——, 'King and Army', in W. Heckel and L. Tritle (eds), *Alexander the Great: A New History* (Oxford: 2009), pp. 83–103.

F.L. Holt, '*Imperium Macedonicum* and the East: The Problem of Logistics', *Ancient Macedonia* 5 (Institute for Balkan Studies, Thessaloniki: 1993), pp. 585–592.

R.D. Milns, 'The Army of Alexander the Great', in E. Badian (ed.), *Alexandre le Grand, image et réalité*, Fondation Hardt, *Entretiens* 22 (Geneva: 1976), pp. 87–136.

C.L. Murison, 'Darius III and the Battle of Issus', *Historia* 21 (1972), pp. 399–423.

P. Romane, 'Alexander's Siege of Tyre', *Ancient World* 16 (1987), pp. 79–90.

——, Alexander's Siege of Gaza', *Ancient World* 18 (1988), pp. 21–30.

B. Strauss, 'Alexander: The Military Campaign', in J. Roisman (ed.), *Brill's Companion to Alexander the Great* (Leiden: 2003), pp. 133–156.

W.W. Tarn, *Alexander the Great* 2 (Cambridge: 1948), pp. 135–198.

Notes

1   On Alexander in Persia, see Chapter 6.
2   On Alexander in India, see Chapter 7.
3   On the problem of the source material, see Chapter 1.
4   On this aspect, see Chapter 12.
5   The siege of Tyre in 332; for what comes before this passage, see Source 51.
6   © 1960 by John Frederick Charles Fuller. Reprinted by permission of Rutgers University Press.

AS STRATEGIST

J.F.C. Fuller

At the opening of the eighteenth century the word 'strategy' – 'the art of the general (*strateges*)' – was added to the military vocabulary to denote the methodical manoeuvres, marches and counter-marches prevalent in the age of strictly limited wars. Today, in most dictionaries, it is defined as the science or art of projecting and directing military movements, and after the Napoleonic wars, which, unlike the wars of the twentieth century, were still simple enough to bear some resemblance to Alexander's, Clausewitz defined strategy as follows:

> Strategy is the employment of battle to gain the end in war; it must therefore give an aim to the whole military action, which must be in accordance with the object of the war; in other words, strategy forms the plan of the war, and to this end it links together the series of acts which are to lead to the final decision, that is to say, it makes the plan for the separate campaigns and regulates the combats to be fought in each.

He adds that at its highest point 'strategy borders on political science, or rather ... the two become one'.[1]

Alexander was as fully aware as Clausewitz that strategy employs the battle to gain the end in war. But where he profoundly differs from him is in the definition of the end – that is, in the aim or object of the war. In Clausewitz's days the twentieth-century democratic conception that the object is to annihilate the enemy, not only militarily, but politically, economically and socially as well, had not yet fuddled man's mind. To Clausewitz war was a clash between armed forces which protected their respective civil populations; each contended for a political aim, and when one side gained a decisive victory, the vanquished automatically sued for peace, and the victor's political aim was gained in a negotiated treaty. But Alexander's aim was not to bring Darius to terms, it was to appropriate his empire, and, were his conquest to be of profit to him, he had not only to defeat the Persian army but win his acceptance in the eyes of the Persian peoples. There was no question of suing for peace, which after his crushing defeat at Issus Darius vainly attempted to do, nor of a negotiated treaty, because Alexander's aim was conquest, and at the minimum expenditure of force and the minimum dislocation and damage of the Persian empire: his policy limited and moderated his strategy.

This limitation is noticed by Polybius in a citation he makes from a speech delivered by Alexander Isius concerning Philip V of Macedon (221–179 B.C.). The orator said that Philip avoided meeting his enemies face to face, and instead employed his time in burning and plundering cities.

> Yet [he added] former kings of Macedonia had not adopted this plan, but one exactly the reverse: for they were continually fighting with each other in the open field, but rarely destroyed and ruined cities. This was shown clearly by Alexander's war in Asia against King Darius; and again in the contentions between his successors ... they had been prompt to war against each other in

the open field, and to do everything they could to conquer each other in arms, but had spared the cities, that they might rule them if they conquered, and be honoured by their subjects. But that a man should abandon war, and yet destroy that for which the war was undertaken, seemed an act of madness, and madness of a very violent sort.[2]

It was because Alexander's aim was conquest, and not vengeance or spoliation, that, according to Justin, when 'marching forward in quest of the enemy, he kept the soldiers from ravaging Asia, telling them that "they ought to spare their own property, and not destroy what they came to possess"'.[3] Wilcken points out that 'his extensive money gifts to his army were a compensation for the prohibition of plundering the conquered districts, which for political reasons he thought necessary'.[4] While the aim of his strategy was to win great battles, the aim of his policy was to pacify and not antagonize his enemy, so as to limit the number of battles he would have to fight. In idea it was not far removed from the policy which Themistocles recommended to the Athenians after Salamis: 'I have often myself witnessed occasions, and I have heard of many more from others where men who had been conquered by an enemy, having been driven quite to desperation, have renewed the fight, and retrieved their former disasters.'[5] The same advice was given by Jason of Pherae to the Thebans after Leuctra. 'It behoves you to reflect', he said, 'that the Lacedaemonians, if they be forced to relinquish the hope of life, will fight with desperation; and the divine powers, as it seems, often take delight in making the little great, and the great little.'[6]

It was because Alexander's aim was to achieve, as far as it was possible, a bloodless conquest, that he drew so distinct a line between the Persian army and the Persian peoples; the defeat of the army was his strategical aim; the winning over of the peoples his political aim. The first was the means to attain the second, because, as long as the Persian army held the field, there was no certain assurance that the people would willingly accept him. Alexander needed no telling that 'war is only a part of political intercourse, therefore by no means an independent thing in itself'.[7]

After he had defined strategy, Clausewitz turned to the more important strategical principles, and these are worth quoting because they show that, had Clausewitz enumerated them in the fourth century B.C., Alexander would have had little to learn from them; in fact he might have tendered the German military theorist some useful advice.

> There are three principal objects [he writes] in carrying on war:
> (*a*) to conquer and destroy the enemy's armed forces.
> (*b*) to get possession of the material elements of aggression, and of the other sources of existence of the hostile army.
> (*c*) To gain public opinion.[8]

The first object calls for no comment: to remember the battles of the Granicus, Issus, Arbela, and the Hydaspes is sufficient.

The second needs none either, because once Alexander had seized the Persian treasure at Susa and Persepolis, he deprived Darius of his most important means of recruiting another army, and it prevented Darius from fomenting rebellions in his enemy's rear by bribery. Gold and silver, and not 'principal towns, magazines and great fortresses', were the chief 'material elements' in Alexander's day.

The third object – public opinion – is, according to Clausewitz, 'ultimately gained by great victories, and by the possession of the enemy's capital'. Although in the eighteenth and nineteenth centuries the occupation of the enemy's capital more frequently than not brought war to an end,[9] in classical times, except for Rome,[10] strictly speaking there were no capital cities; instead there were city-states, or royal residences, such as Babylon, Susa and Persepolis.[11] With the exception of war between two city-states, because the occupation of cities and royal residences did not bring war to an end, as has several times been pointed out in these pages, Alexander substituted the ultramodern conception of subversion of the enemy's people. Russia is today the leading exponent of this.

Clausewitz next lays down five strategical principles.

The first, and in his opinion the most important, is: 'to employ *all* the forces which we can make available with the *utmost* energy'.

'The second is to concentrate our force ... at the point where the decisive blows are to be struck, to run the risk even of being at a disadvantage at other points, in order to make sure of the result at the decisive point. The success at that point will compensate for all defeats at secondary points'.

'The third principle is: not to lose time.... . By rapidity many measures of the enemy are nipped in the bud, and public opinion is gained in our favour'.

The fourth is surprise: '... it is the most powerful element of victory'.

And the last is: 'to follow up the success we gain with the utmost energy. The pursuit of the enemy when defeated is the only means of gathering up the fruits of victory.'[12]

After what we have recorded on Alexander's generalship, and because these principles will be discussed in the next section, it is unnecessary to point out here that the value of utmost energy, concentration at the decisive point, rapidity of movement, surprise and pursuit were as clearly apparent to Alexander as they were to Clausewitz.

In all strategical problems which embrace war, either in its entirety or in part, there are two outstanding strategical factors – the establishment of secure bases and secure communications. The first may be compared with the foundations of a house, they must be sufficiently substantial to bear the weight of the superstructure; the second is the scaffolding, which enables the builders to maintain contact with the ground (base), and progressively feed the masons with the materials they require. Should the foundations sink, the superstructure will be imperilled; should the scaffolding collapse, its erection cannot be continued until the scaffolding is restored.

When a war or campaign is compared with the superstructure, the importance of the base – its starting point – at once becomes apparent, and no general has understood this better than Alexander. First he established a secure home base – that is, his initial or main base – by his Danubian campaign and the destruction of Thebes. The Danubian campaign was a strategical operation, the establishment of a secure northern frontier; the destruction of Thebes a political operation, the establishment of a quiescent inner front. They were complementary; one removed a danger that might have been exploited by anti-Macedonian factions within Greece, the other resulted in the paralysis of these factions, and thereby deprived the Thracian and Illyrian tribesmen of all hope of being able to take advantage of revolt within Greece. Together they secured the Macedonian home base throughout Alexander's reign.

Next, Alexander established his base of operations against Persia on the eastern coast of the Aegean, which, before he moved eastward, he secured by his victory on the Granicus. It did not secure the sea-link between his base of operations and his home base, because naval command was in his enemy's hands. That was why, because there was no Persian army west of the Halys which could impede his advance, his strategy was to strike at his enemy's naval bases, the more important of which lay in Phoenicia and Cyprus. This strategy is so clearly revealed in his speech to his generals immediately before the siege of Tyre, that it is worth reverting to it. With his home base in mind, it will be remembered that Alexander said: 'I am apprehensive lest, while we advance with our forces toward Babylon and in pursuit of Darius, the Persians should again conquer the maritime districts, and transfer the war into Greece.' The offer of non-belligerence made to him by the Tyrians was insufficient; it was imperative that Tyre and Egypt should be occupied, for then, as he said, 'no anxiety about Greece and our land will any longer remain'. He also saw that, when the Phoenician cities were threatened, the high probability was that the Phoenician fleets would come over to him and give him 'absolute sovereignty of the sea'. The aim of his strategy, then, was not only to deprive his enemy of his sea power, but simultaneously to acquire it and thereby win the command of the eastern Mediterranean, and secure his home base and his conquests in Asia Minor for good and all. Only then did he consider that he would be free to renew his land operations against Darius.

Again, when he reached Arbela, he abandoned his pursuit to strike at the 'material' base of his enemy's military power; first he occupied Babylon, and next seized the treasure stored at Susa and Persepolis. With that in his hands, he was in a position of strength such as the French would have been in if, in 1940, they had decisively defeated the Germans, and, instead of pursuing them, had occupied the Ruhr – the material base of the German fighting forces. Here again, it will be seen that Alexander's strategy led to the augmentation of his own power, not by destroying the foundations of his enemy's power, but by appropriating them. As the Persian fleet had passed into his hands, so did the Persian treasure. He became financial master of Asia, and Darius a bankrupt.

After the death of Darius his first action was not to pursue the usurper Bessus, but to secure his rear – his most advanced base – by subduing the tribesmen of the Elburz mountains. As soon as this had been done, he set out after Bessus; but directly he learnt of the revolt of Satibarzanes, he broke off the chase to re-establish his authority over his rear before he continued. In Sogdiana he followed an identical strategy. After the capture of Bessus, suddenly he found himself in an extraordinary predicament; the revolt of Spitamenes not only threatened his base at Maracanda, but deprived him of Cyropolis and his frontier posts on the Jaxartes. He was between two forest fires – which should he extinguish first? Should he turn on Spitamenes, the leader of the revolt? No, he must first secure his base of operations against him, and this meant the reoccupation of Cyropolis, and the defeat of the Scythians. Once this had been done his rear was secure, and he was free to deal with Spitamenes. Later, the same basic strategy was followed. When he had occupied the tribesmen's cities in the Swat valley, he did not march on their stronghold at Aornus, but moved southward into the Peshawar valley to establish a firm base of operations from which he could operate against Aornus without imperilling his communications. Soon after this he established his advanced base at Taxila before proceeding against Porus.

It is important to remember that the means Alexander used to make secure the more important bases, that covered extensive territories, were more political than military. Their administration was carefully organized, peaceful conditions were restored, trade was stimulated, and the garrisons left in them were police forces and colonists rather than armies of occupation. As his conquests extended, his empire progressively took form; he won his peace as he waged his war,[13] and bound the whole into one by means of his communications.

Strategy today is so intimately related to communications – road, rail, river, canal, sea and air – that it is difficult to picture a strategical problem in which there are no maps, and movements are limited to a few caravan routes and an unknown number of pack-ways and trails connecting village with village.[14] In Greece there were no made-up roads, except in the vicinity of important sanctuaries, and no road-construction is recorded during the reigns of Alexander and his successors.[15] But, as described in chapter 4, [in Fuller], since the days of Darius I a number of main roads had existed in the Persian empire, and it was possible to travel by road from Ephesus, on the Aegean, by way of Sardes, Babylon, Ecbatana and Bactra to Taxila. This great thoroughfare was the axis of Alexander's communications – a kind of trans-Siberian railway.

In addition to this road, and a number which branched from it, Alexander had the sea, and at the beginning of the war it was one of Antipater's tasks to keep open the passage of the Dardanelles. After the fall of Tyre, when the threat to the Aegean was eliminated, this responsibility was delegated to Philoxenes who, according to Plutarch, was appointed 'governor of the coast-line of Asia Minor',[16] or what would seem a more appropriate title – Base Commandant. His headquarters were at Ephesus – the western terminus of the axial road – and there he collected supplies and reinforcements coming from Macedonia and Greece, and when required dispatched them in convoys to Alexander. When Susa was occupied, Alexander placed Menes, son of Dionysius, in command of sea communications between Phoenicia and the west,[17] and when the Thessalians' service was terminated, he was instructed to arrange for their transit by sea from Syria to Euboea.[18] Finally toward the close of his reign, Alexander was engaged on opening a sea-way from Patala on the Indus to Babylon on the Euphrates, to help him to hold India.

From west to east, with the axial road as its backbone, Alexander divided his land communications into sections, each under a responsible officer. The most westerly section included Asia Minor, and was allotted to Antigonus with his headquarters at Celaenae in Phrygia. East of it and to some undefined point eastward – possibly Meshed or Herat – came the next section, first under Parmenion and later under Cleander, with headquarters at Ecbatana. Then there was probably the Bactrian section, and possibly east of it the Indian, but of these sections nothing is known.

Although we have no details of the organization of Alexander's communications, because of the ease with which reinforcements constantly reached him, it is not difficult to supply them. Depots, at which supplies were collected from the surrounding country, and staging camps, each a day's march from the other, must either have been established or taken over from the Persians in each section along the axial road. Further, it would appear that the Persian postal relay system was retained and improved upon, because we are told by Plutarch that, when Alexander was at Samarkand, 'some people came bringing Greek fruit to the king from the sea-board'[19] – a distance of well over 3,000 miles. Incidentally, this fruit was the indirect cause of the death of Cleitus, because Alexander was so struck with its 'beauty and perfection' that he asked him to share some with him at the fatal supper.

In only one of his Asiatic campaigns did Alexander lose touch with his home base, and then only for twenty-four hours before the battle of Issus; only once is it recorded that his supply system broke down, and that was during his march across Gedrosia.[20] This is sufficient proof of the superb staff work of his headquarters.

His lack of maps was made good by what must have been a highly organized intelligence service. He always tried to obtain advance information about the country he decided to conquer, and there was nothing adventurous in his movements. Like Napoleon and Wellington, whenever possible he saw things for himself, and from his actions it may be judged that he held with Napoleon that, 'A general who has to see things through other people's eyes will never be able to command an army as it should be commanded.' And he could, with truth, have said with Wellington: 'The real reason why I succeeded ... is because I was always on the spot. I saw everything, and did everything myself.' When this was not possible, as happened repeatedly, he stepped into his enemy's shoes, looked at the situation through his enemy's eyes, and fathomed his intentions. Although he was one of the most audacious generals in history, the risks he accepted were seldom left to chance; they were carefully weighed and calculated probabilities.

As tactician

As a tactician, Alexander's greatest asset was the army he inherited from his father; without it, and in spite of his genius, his conquests would be inconceivable – it was an instrument that exactly suited his craft. Its composition has been dealt with in Chapter 2 {in Fuller}, here its organization will be briefly examined, because it was from its organization that Alexander was able to develop his tactics.

On the opening page of his great work *On War*, Clausewitz makes a very simple yet profound remark. It is that 'War is nothing but a duel on an extensive scale', and he likens it to a struggle between two wrestlers; between two pugilists would be a more apt comparison. If so, then the primary elements of tactics are to be seen in their simplest form in a fight between two unarmed men. They are: to think, to guard, to move and to hit.

Before a bout opens, each man must consider how best to knock out his adversary, and though as the fight proceeds he may be compelled to modify his means, he must never abandon his aim. At the start he must assume a defensive attitude until he has measured up his opponent. Next, he must move under cover of his defence towards him, and lastly by foot-play, and still under cover of his defence, he must assume the offensive and attempt to knock him out. In military terms, the four primary tactical elements are: the aim or object, security, mobility and offensive power.

If the two pugilists are skilled in their art, they will recognize the value of three accentuating elements. They will economize their physical force, so as not to exhaust themselves prematurely; they will concentrate their blows against the decisive point selected, the left or right of their opponent's jaw, or his solar plexus, and throughout will attempt to surprise him – that is, take him off-guard, or do something which he does not expect, or cannot guard against. In military terms these accentuating elements are: economy of force, concentration of force, and surprise.

With this elementary picture in mind, Philip's tactical organization can be considered. It was threefold, not merely a phalanx with protective bodies of cavalry on its flanks, as was then customary, but a phalanx with two fighting arms, each of which was more mobile than the trunk, each of which could be used either to guard or to hit, and of which the right was the more powerful, because Philip decided to concentrate his punching-power in it. His army – whether intentionally, accidentally, or experimentally does not matter – was a gigantic pugilist, and in the hands of a skilled leader it could fight as such.

The only extraneous point worth making is that, although in the inter-city wars the punching had been done almost entirely by infantry, Philip decided that it should be done by cavalry; not only because cavalry was more mobile than infantry, and so could be concentrated more rapidly against the point of decision, but also because throughout history there has been something irresistible and terrifying in the cavalry charge, and the foot soldier has always dreaded being trampled by horsemen – hence the value of mounted over foot police. In other words, provided that cavalry could charge, the moral effect produced by the combination of two living creatures – man and horse – coupled with mobility, was greater than anything the foot soldier could produce.

In most military text books, more particularly in those known as *Field Service Regulations,* a list of the principles of war will be found. Five, as propounded by Clausewitz, have already been given. There are several versions of these so-called principles, but they are no more than pegs on which to hang our tactical thoughts. There is nothing irrevocable about them; sometimes they may be discarded with impunity; but as a study of military history will show, they should only be discarded after deep consideration. They are very important guides rather than principles, and in the writer's opinion the simplest and most useful are derived from the seven tactical elements mentioned above – aim or object, security, mobility, offensive power, economy of force, concentration of force, and surprise. Further, they are as applicable to strategy (operations in plan) as to tactics (operations in action), two terms which should never be separated by a bulkhead, because their components flow into each other and together constitute the art of war, which, incidentally, was cleverly defined by Captain Cochegrue when he said: 'In great battles, he endeavoured always to give blows without receiving them, which is, and always will be, the only problem to solve in war.'[21] It is illuminating to examine the military activities of Alexander by applying to them, in turn, the seven principles cited.

The principle of the maintenance of the aim

'To conquer is nothing, one must profit from one's success'

Napoleon.

The first point to note in all Alexander's tactical operations is, that they were invariably subordinated to the strategical aim of their respective campaigns. For example, when he acceded to the throne of Macedonia and when Greece was in turmoil, because he planned war with Persia, his strategical aim was to establish his authority as rapidly and peacefully as he could, and he did so with such lightning-like speed, that a display of tactical force was sufficient to attain it without bloodshed. Soon after this, when the Thebans revolted, because his aim was still the same, he offered terms of surrender; but when they refused them, to paralyse their allies he obliterated Thebes, and attained his aim at the cost of one city. Again, after his victory at Issus, he abandoned his pursuit and laid siege to Tyre in order to maintain his strategic aim, which was then the elimination of his enemy's naval power. After Arbela, again he sacrificed pursuit in order to occupy Babylon and seize Susa and Persepolis, because the treasure stored in these cities was the mainstay of Persian political and military power. In all his campaigns it was the same; his strategical aim was subordinated to his political aim, and his tactical aim to his strategical aim, and the result was systematic and methodical conquest.

In each of his four great battles his aim was to assault from a secure base and annihilate his enemy's power of resistance; his base was his order of battle which, except in the battle of the Hydaspes, he never varied. With the phalanx as his chest, his left arm was his left wing, which he used defensively; and his right arm his right wing, used offensively to break through the enemy's front, and thereby disrupt his organization. Penetration was his tactical means, and he held fast to it in all his great battles. At the Granicus, he broke through the Persian cavalry at the head of his Companion cavalry; at Issus, he broke through the Persian infantry, and at Arbela he broke through a gap in the Persian front. Only at the Hydaspes, his most skilfully fought battle, did he make use of his phalanx to deliver the knock-out blow, and that was because his cavalry horses would not face the Indian elephants.

During the heat of the battle he never lost sight of his tactical aim. At the Granicus, once he had effected a penetration, he turned on the Greek mercenary infantry; he did the same at Issus; at Arbela, first – as assumed – he came to the help of his hard-pressed right wing, and then – as is known – he set out to rescue his left wing, which was hard pressed by Mazaeus, that is, where the battle was still in doubt. At the sieges of Tyre, Gaza and Aornus, once he had made up his mind, the tenacity with which he held fast to his tactical aim is remarkable. But he was not a pigheaded general. When he decided to capture the island of Peuce in his Danubian campaign, and he found that it would be both costly and difficult, he substituted for its capture a more profitable operation; at the Persian Gates he did the same, and when in his campaign against the Malli, with cavalry alone he attacked the Indians who were holding the opposite bank of the Ravi, directly it became apparent to him that they intended to stand up to his assault, he broke off the engagement, surrounded them with his horsemen, and awaited the arrival of his infantry. Although he was always ready to attempt the seemingly impossible, he was just as ready to avoid the obviously unprofitable.

The principle of security

'The whole art of war consists in a well-reasoned and extremely circumspect defensive, followed by rapid and audacious attack'

Napoleon.

Unfortunately, little has been recorded of the security measures adopted by Alexander while at rest, on the line of march, or in battle. Now and again it is recorded that he fortified his camp, ordered entrenchments to be dug, and picketed the road along which he marched, as he did in the Elburz mountains. On that occasion, Arrian writes, whenever he thought there was danger along the road, he posted pickets on its flanks to protect the marching troops from the hillmen on the heights above them.[22] Also, he frequently resorted to night movements to hide his intentions or to surprise his enemy, and notably so before the battles of Arbela and the Hydaspes and during the Persepolis campaign. The probable reason for the lack of information is that, unlike Julius Caesar, Alexander was not an entrenching general; the tactical conditions of his campaigns did not require him to be so, because the Persians seldom assumed the offensive, and the tribesmen he conquered did not indulge in night attacks.

In battle, the security of his army was guaranteed by its organization, coupled with its usual oblique approach. Its centre was impenetrable as long as the phalanx maintained its dressing, and its mobile wings, composed as they were of infantry and cavalry, were self-protective; they could adapt themselves to attack or defence as occasion demanded. Although reserves were hitherto unknown, at Issus Alexander is said to have held the Greek mercenaries in reserve, and because at Arbela the Macedonian front was far outflanked by the Persian, to secure his front from an attack in flank and rear he drew up a second, or reserve, phalanx behind it, which, when the two wings on the flanks of the forward phalanx were drawn backward, enabled a hollow square to be formed, a formation which offered all-round defence. Yet it is strange that, neither at Issus nor Arbela, did he attempt to overcome the one great danger to his phalanx. It was that, due to its oblique approach and the speed of his assault on its right, it was liable to break in half, as it did in both these battles. To rectify this, all that was necessary was to withdraw one battalion of the phalanx and post it in rear of the centre of the others, so that, should a gap occur in the ranks in front, it could at once be filled by the battalion in rear.

Of the various protective means used by Alexander, the most interesting is his use of the catapult as field artillery. Though for long used as a siege weapon, until his campaign in Illyria it had never been brought into the field. It was then that for the first time in the history of war catapults were deployed to cover a river crossing, as again they were in the battle with the Scythians on the Jaxartes. Also, they were used with considerable effect to cover the assaults on Aornus and elsewhere. Wherever Alexander went his field artillery accompanied him, and after his death, in the hands of his successors it became a recognized arm in every well-organized army, and remained the artillery of the world until the introduction of cannon. Alexander has the distinction of being the first field gunner in history.

The principle of mobility

'In the art of war, as in mechanics, velocity is the grand element between weight and force'

Napoleon.

Except for Napoleon, probably no other general appreciated as fully as Alexander the value of mobility in war. From the opening of his career until its close, speed dominated all his movements, and the result was that, by increasing the time at his disposal, in any given period he could proportionately accomplish more than his opponent.

In his first campaign his enemies were so completely paralysed by the rapidity of his advance that they were not allowed time enough to assemble their forces; in his advance on the Cilician Gates, although it was reported to Arsames, who held the pass, Arsames was so unhinged by his enemy's speed that he abandoned it. The dividends paid by speed, whether against an organized enemy on the plains, or hillmen in the mountains, were a long series of surprises, which enabled Alexander to accomplish with a fraction of his forces what at a slower pace might have demanded his whole army.

He was the first general in history to understand that the fruits of a great battle are to be gathered in the pursuit. At the battle of Arbela, directly he had assured himself of the safety of his left wing, he turned about his Companion cavalry, and in spite of their exhausted horses followed Darius, and pressed on to Arbela, thirty miles east of the battlefield. Alter his defeat of Ariobarzanes at the Persian Gates, in spite of a most fatiguing night march and the exertions of the battle, he pressed on to Persepolis, some eighty to one hundred miles away, and reached it at dawn on the following morning. Also, in the heat of a Persian summer and in a region largely devoid of water, his pursuit of Darius was kept up for seven days at the average daily speed of either thirty or thirty-six miles. As Tarn observes: he taught the West a lesson his successors did not forget, 'that in warfare distance was no longer a prohibitive factor'.[23] Also he taught the West the advantage of marching in two divisions; one composed of a selected body of troops marching light, and the other of the slower moving troops and the impedimenta.

That the velocity of his movements on occasion led him into difficulties is understandable. It seems to have done so during his Illyrian campaign, when Glaucias came up on his rear, and it certainly did so at Issus, when he lost his communications and was surprised. But during his twelve years of campaigning the exceptions are so rare that they prove the rule that he who can move twice as fast as his opponent doubles his operative time and thereby halves it for his opponent. As a winner of time Alexander has few equals.

The principle of the offensive

'In short, I think like Frederick, one should always be the first to attack'

Napoleon.

The reason why all the great Captains were offensively-minded was not only because battle is the tactical aim in war but also because, as Moltke pointed out in his *Instructions for the Commanders of Large Formations*: 'The offensive knows what it wants', whereas 'the defensive is in a state of uncertainty'. In other words: the initiative is more readily gained by offensive than by defensive action; not only does it enable a general to develop his plan, select his point of attack, and surprise his adversary, but it exalts the spirit of his troops – as Frederick said: 'To conquer is to advance'. Though Napoleon was forced on the defensive at Leipzig, La Rothière and Arcis, he never once set out to fight a defensive battle; nor did Alexander, and all his offensive battles were successful.

What is remarkable about them is, that he overcame his several opponents by a tactics shaped to fit each occasion. Thus, with same certainty with which he attacked his known opponents – Greek mercenaries or Persian cavalry – he overcame opponents who before he fought them were entirely unknown to him; the Scythians, Indian hillmen, and Porus with his elephants. In his many battles his tactical genius is apparent in the lightning-like speed with which he adapted his actions to novel circumstances; he never copied his former successes, and this was the main reason why success followed success.

Although in his great battles he relied on his Companion cavalry as his main offensive arm, he never brought it into action until he was certain that its assault would prove decisive. At the Granicus, because of the faulty deployment of the Persian cavalry, directly his feint against the Persian left began to tell, he charged instantly, and the battle was virtually won before the rest of his troops had crossed the river. At Issus he held back his assault until he had cleared his right flank, then in a headlong charge he burst through the Persian infantry; and at Arbela he fought a protracted defensive engagement with his right flank guard, which drew his enemy in and thereby created the opportunity for his decisive cavalry charge. When it came, in a flash he seized the initiative, and swept through the gap in the Persian front. The timing was perfect, and as Napoleon once said. 'The fate of a battle is a question of a single moment, a single thought ... the decisive moment arrives, the moral spark is kindled, and the smallest reserve force settles the argument.'[24] And again: 'There is a moment in engagements when the least manoeuvre is decisive and gives the victory; it is the one drop of water which makes the vessel run over.'[25] The last reserve in his right wing was his Companion cavalry, and its assault was decisive, as was the assault of his phalanx at the battle of the Hydaspes.

The principles of economy and concentration of force

'The art of war consists in bringing to bear with an inferior army a superiority of force at the point at which one attacks or is attacked'

Napoleon.

These two principles are closely related and their application is largely governed by the depth of the forces engaged. Today, it may run to many miles, with the bulk of the troops in reserve; because of this the battle is usually prolonged, and is decided by the reserves. Consequently, economy of force – the judicious expenditure of the reserves – is of vital importance. But when all troops are concentrated in the battle front, with no reserves in rear of them, economy of force is restricted to the troops immediately at hand, and in Alexander's day it was restricted to cavalry and light infantry because, when once engaged, the heavy infantry were unable to manoeuvre. Few better examples of this restricted form of economy of force are to be found than his handling of the right flank guard at Arbela. By judiciously feeding his light cavalry, squadron by squadron, into the action, he progressively enticed his enemy to denude his left wing of its main cavalry forces, and so to create the fatal gap that led to his ruin. Another and equally notable example is to be seen at the battle of the Hydaspes. Because the elephants forbade Alexander his usual cavalry assault, he was compelled to rely on his phalanx to penetrate his enemy's front. But, in order to secure its advance, it was first necessary to draw in the whole of the Indian cavalry, to prevent it from attacking the phalanx in flank or rear. This he did by a most skilful economy of his own cavalry.

When Clausewitz wrote that 'the greatest possible number of troops should be brought into action at the decisive point',[26] he had in mind the battles of the Napoleonic wars, in which the depths of the contending armies were already considerable. But in battles of the classical age depths were seldom more than one hundred paces, and frequently no more than that of a phalanx; so thin that, when a front was broken, it usually fell to pieces, and its men took to their heels. But to make certain of breaking a front, it was as necessary then as in Napoleon's day – and it still is necessary – to bring a superiority of force against the decisive point; but superior in quality rather than in quantity. Alexander did this by means of his superb Companion cavalry, coupled with his oblique order of approach, which automatically brought his offensive right wing opposite to the point in his enemy's front that he intended to penetrate, while his centre and left wing, though refused, were sufficiently close to the enemy's centre and right wing to threaten or hold them. Should the enemy attempt to overwhelm Alexander's left wing, which he could only do with cavalry, then he would have fewer cavalry to hold back Alexander's right wing. And should he concentrate the bulk of his cavalry against Alexander's right wing, he would risk penetration or envelopment of his own right wing by the Thessalian cavalry, who numerically were as powerful as the Companion cavalry and little inferior to them.

The only way out of this dilemma was to seize the initiative and attack first, and this Darius did at Arbela; he was frustrated by Alexander's application of the principle of economy of force. Coupled with the initiative, Alexander's oblique order of approach enabled him to concentrate a superiority of force against the decisive point, and at the same time, until he struck, economize – virtually hold in reserve – the rest of his army. First, the battering-ram assault, then *'tout le monde à la bataille'*. The assault preceded the general attack, a tactics which was reintroduced by the tank at the battle of Cambrai in 1917, and which characterizes so many of the tank offensives of the Second World War.

The principle of surprise

'The art of war is no more than the art of argumenting the chances which are in our favour'
Napoleon.

According to Clausewitz, 'surprise lies at the foundation of all [military] undertakings without exception', and of the means at the disposal of the general it is the most effective in attaining either physical or moral superiority. 'Without it', he writes, 'the preponderance at the decisive point is not properly conceivable'.[27] But where is the decisive point?

Throughout the history of war its position has remained constant; it is the will of the commander as expressed in his plan, coupled with the will of his soldiers to carry it out. All other points of decision should be related to this ultimate goal, because they are no more than stepping-stones toward it. Therefore the question: 'Where should the decisive point be sought?' does not arise; the question is, 'How best can a preponderance of force be brought against the enemy's will?'

There are two answers to this question: to do something which the enemy cannot prevent, and to do something which he does not suspect. The first action may be compared to surprising a man with his eyes open, in the other, the man has his eyes shut. At the Granicus, Issus and Arbela, the Persians were the victims of the first of these modes of surprise, because they were unprepared to counter Alexander's great cavalry assaults; at the Persian gates and the battle of the Hydaspes, Ariobarzanes and Porus respectively were victims because their eyes were shut. Though the battle of the Persian Gates was a rapidly improvised manoeuvre, and the Hydaspes a methodically prepared operation, both were based on a common factor, the fixing of the enemy's attention, therefore of his will, in a direction other than the one in which surprise was to be sought. In all these surprisals, whether the approach was direct and visible, or indirect and invisible, Alexander paralysed the will of his enemy by shattering his plan. But it should be remembered that, in the warfare of his age, the will of the commanding general was far more his personal property than it is now,[28] when he shares his responsibilities with his General Staff, and to a lesser extent with his subordinate commanders; therefore it was vastly more sensitive in Alexander's day.

As is to be expected, Alexander's small wars abound with surprisals, because – then as now – though tribesmen are adepts at ambushes and ruses, their lack of discipline and submission to authority make them particularly susceptible to surprisals. Alexander drew the Triballians into battle by a ruse; surprised the Getae by an unexpected crossing of the Danube; threw Glaucias off guard by a ceremonial parade; captured Pelion by an unlooked-for night attack; surprised the Uxian hillmen while asleep in their villages; re-took Cyropolis at an unsuspected point; lured the Scythians into battle by an inviting bait; captured the Sogdian Rock by scaling its most precipitous side; drew the Assacenians into battle by a feint withdrawal; and fell upon the Malli unexpectedly by crossing a waterless desert. Further, whenever it was possible, he attacked the hillmen during the winter months, when the snow kept them in their villages. The economy of force derived from these surprisals was enormous; without them his army would have rapidly melted away.

As leader

Battles now are so vast, so complex, and so dependent on the handling of reserves, that a general-in-chief can no longer lead his army into action; he directs it from an elaborately organized headquarters, which may be one hundred or more miles behind the battle front, and the leadership of his men is delegated, not to his more senior, but to his most junior officers.

In battles of the classical age the duties of the general and the subaltern coincided, and in consequence the personal leadership of the general-in-chief was of paramount importance. When Alexander took the field, he was both the thinking and fighting head of his army. In battle he invariably set his men an example of supreme personal bravery; on the line of march there was no toil that he did not share with them; in his sieges he laboured with them, and it was his presence among them that fired their imagination and awoke in them the mystical faith that led them to accept without question that there was nothing he would not dare, and nothing he could not do – to them, as to the priestess of Delphi, he was ΑΝΙΚΗΤΟΣ – the Invincible. There are many examples of this in the preceding chapters; here, that side of his leadership which won the devotion of his officers and the affection of his men will be considered.

The Macedonian army cannot have been easy to lead, particularly because the prestige it had won under Philip divided its officers into two age-categories: the elder, who had shared his successes, and the younger – the boyhood companions of Alexander – who at the outset of the war still had their spurs to win. This division led to the growth of what may be called the Parmenion and Alexander factions: the stubborn-minded Philippians, and the more liberal-minded Alexandrians, men like Hephaestion, Nearchus and Ptolemy, who had been Alexander's playmates. Because of the constitution of the Macedonian monarchy, elimination of jealousies was no easy task. The monarchy was still partly of the heroic type, in which the idea of the kin survived. The king was the hereditary military chief of the Macedonian tribes; he was acknowledged by the assembly of the armed people – the army – and limited in power by the other 'kings', the heads of the aristocracy, who were his kin or companions. According to Macedonian usage, the army, not the king and his council, was the supreme court before which capital charges, such as murder or treason, were brought, as happened with Philotas. Alexander, though an autocrat, was not a despot who could do exactly as he liked.

In spite of this limitation of power, Alexander treated his followers impartially, and his attitude towards them was seldom one of suspicion. In Egypt, when it was alleged that Philotas was implicated in a somewhat similar conspiracy to the one which led to his death, because of the long friendship between them Alexander did not believe it to be possible; when word was brought to him by Ephialtes and Cissus that Harpalus had absconded with 5,000 talents, he threw them into prison, because he could not believe it of Harpalus, who had been a friend of his boyhood. Invariably, it would appear, he treated all his followers alike, and lavished honours and presents upon them so extravagantly, that his mother complained that he made them the equals of kings. But at all times he was their master, and when in India a quarrel arose between Craterus and Hephaestion, he publicly called Hephaestion a fool and a madman for not knowing that without his favour he was nothing, and in private he sharply reproved Craterus. 'Then he brought them together and reconciled them, taking an oath ... that he loved them most of all men; but that if he heard of their quarrelling again, he would kill both or at least the one who began the quarrel.'[29]

This was no idle threat, for he would not tolerate any infringement of his authority. 'For instance', writes Plutarch, 'when a certain Menander, one of his companions, who had been put in command of a garrison, refused to remain there, he put him to death.'[30] And, at the close of his reign in Babylon when Cassander, one of Antipater's sons, saw Persians doing obeisance to him, and burst out laughing, Alexander was so enraged that with both hands he clutched him by the hair and dashed his head against the wall.

And in general [writes Plutarch], as we are told, Cassander's spirit was deeply penetrated and imbued with a dreadful fear of Alexander, so that many years afterwards, when he was now king of Macedonia and master of Greece, as he was walking about and surveying the statues at Delphi, the sight of an image of Alexander smote him suddenly with a shuddering and trembling from which he could scarcely recover, and made his head swim.[31]

Whether on the battlefield or in camp, Alexander dominated his companions. Through his overmastering personality and his genius for war he won their trust and devotion, and many of them were outstanding personalities, among whom Cassander was not the least.[32] When it is remembered that the Macedonians were a truculent and semi-barbaric people, not a few of whose kings had perished by the knife, it redounds to Alexander's leadership that, in spite of his pro-Persian policy, which was so deeply resented by Philip's old veterans, he was able to carry out his conquests with so few internal dissensions as those recorded.

To his men he was not only their king but their comrade in arms, and on the battlefield one of them. Their devotion to him and reliance on him are touchingly described by Arrian in the scene which followed his wounding in the assault on the Mallian citadel. His extreme heroism, coupled with the hesitation of his men to mount the wall, must have awakened in them a sense of guilt and rage, which is to be seen in their indiscriminate slaughter of the unfortunate Malli and Oxydracae. When rumours spread through the camp that Alexander had succumbed to his wound, they were thrown into the depths of fear and despair; surrounded as they were by warlike tribes, without him how could they hope to return to their homes? Next, a rumour was circulated that he was alive, but their despair was so great that they would not believe it, and as soon as his wound permitted, Alexander had himself carried to the river, placed on a boat and conveyed to the camp. But his soldiers still would not believe that he was alive until he raised his hand toward them, when a great shout burst from their lips. He was carried ashore and raised on to his horse, and when he dismounted at his tent and his men saw him walking, 'they all ran towards him from this side and that, some touching his hands, some his knees, some his garments; others just looked on him from near at hand, and with a blessing upon him went their way; some cast wreaths upon him, some such flowers as the country of India bare at that time'.[33]

This devotion was roused, not only by his heroism, but also by his daily concern in their welfare and happiness, and because of his deep understanding of how to stir their hearts. Before battle, he would ride down the ranks, and call aloud by name, not only the generals, but also those men who in previous battles had performed conspicuous deeds of valour; at such a moment to call a soldier by name is to electrify every soldier within hearing. After battle, his care for the wounded won the affection of all his men; 'and the dead he gathered together and gave them a splendid military funeral, the whole army marshalled in their finest battle array'. Then 'he praised all who, by his own personal witness, or by the agreed report of others, he knew had done valorous deeds in the battle; these men and all he honoured by a devotion suitable to their desert'.[34] At a prolonged halt, or after a notable success, he held games and festivals of all sorts to celebrate the prowess of his army.

What appealed to his men probably more than anything else, were his unexpected kindnesses toward them; such as when, after the capture of Halicarnassus, he sent his newly married men home to spend the winter with their families; the care with which he prepared the return journey of his Thessalians from Ecbatana; and when after the great reconciliation at Opis he not only rewarded his departing veterans in a princely way, but 'also ordained that the orphan children of those who had lost their lives in his service should receive their father's pay'.[35]

He never asked his men to do what he would not do himself. When, before he set out on his march to India, he found that the army train was cumbered with booty, he first ordered the contents of the wagons which belonged to him and his companions to be burnt. Also, he always placed the needs of his men before his own. When he led his men on foot to set an example to them during the march through Gedrosia, he was distressed by thirst and some of the light-armed troops found a little water in a water-hole and carried it in a helmet to the king.

He received it [writes Arrian], and thanked those who had brought it; and taking it poured it out in the sight of all his troops; and at this action the whole army was so much heartened that you would have said that each and every man had drunk that water which Alexander thus poured out. This deed of Alexander's above all I commend most warmly as a proof both of his endurance and his excellence as a general.[36]

Incidents such as these bound his men to him with invisible and unbreakable moral ties. They endowed them with particles of his invincible will, and, under his leadership, they obliterated dangers, smoothed away adversities, and enabled him to lead them to what for them appeared to be the ends of the world.

Notes

1 *On War*, vol. I, pp. 164, 167.
2 Polybius, XVIII, 3.
3 Justin, XI, vi.
4 *Alexander the Great*, p. 243.
5 Herodotus, VIII, 109.
6 Xenophon's *Hellenics*, VI, iv, 23. Aeneas Tacticus (xxxviii, 1–5) says much the same thing: 'But he who acts in a harsh and savage manner, immediately after becoming master of a city … makes other cities hostile, so that the war becomes laborious for him and victory difficult to attain … For nothing makes men so brave as to fear of what ills they will suffer if they surrender.' And Rabelais (bk. I, chap. XLIII) makes Gargantua proffer the following words of wisdom to Gymnast: '… according to right military discipline, *you must never drive your enemy unto despair*. For that such a strength doth multiply his force, and increase his courage, which was before broken and cast down. Neither is there any better help for men that are out of heart, toiled and spent, than *to hope for no favour at all*.'
7 Clausewitz, *On War*, vol. III, p. 121.
8 Ibid., vol. III, p. 209.
9 Though the occupation of Paris in 1870 failed to do so, in 1940 it immediately led to the capitulation of France.
10 Had Hannibal after the battle of Cannae (216 B.C.) occupied Rome, the probability is that he would have brought the second Carthaginian war to an end.
11 The occupation of Athens by Xerxes in 480 B.C. did not bring war to an end, nor did Alexander's occupation of Babylon, Susa, and Persepolis.
12 Ibid., vol. III, pp. 210–11
13 In the Civil War in Spain (1936–9) General Franco did the same; directly a district was won it was placed on a peace footing.
14 In recent times much the same difficulty faced the British command in the South African War of 1899–1902. Roads were not more than cart tracks, approximately shown on unreliable maps, and footpaths were known only to the local inhabitants. Only what may be called bee-line strategy was possible.
15 From an early date the Romans were aware of the importance of roads, but it was not until 312 B.C. that the earliest of the main roads, the Via Appia, which linked Rome and Capua, was built.
16 Plutarch's *Moralia*, 'On the Fortune of Alexander', 333A.
17 Arrian, III, xvi, 9.
18 Ibid., III, xix, 6.
19 Plutarch's 'Alexander', L.
20 Due largely to Apollophanes, who failed to forward supplies.
21 *Balzac's Droll Stories* (English trans. illustrated by Gustave Doré, 1874), 'The Devil's Heir', p. 111.
22 Arrian, III, xxiii, 3. Compare 'crowning the heights' in present-day mountain warfare.
23 *Hellenistic Military and Naval Developments*, p. 41.
24 *Mémorial de St Hélène*, Las Cases (1823), vol. II, p. 15.
25 *Correspondence de Napoléon I^ier^*, 'Précis des guerres de J. César', vol. XXXII, p. 27.
26 *On War*, vol. I, p. 194.
27 *On War*, vol I, p. 194.
28 An example of this is the conquest of Peru by Pizarro and 183 men. The Inca power was so highly centralized that when Atahualpa was eliminated the whole country was rapidly subdued.
29 Plutarch's 'Alexander', XLVIII.
30 Ibid., LVII.
31 Ibid., LXXIV.
32 He rebuilt Thebes, founded Cassandreia and Thessalonica (Salonika), was the slayer of Alexander's mother, son and widow, and had friends among the Peripatetics.
33 Arrian, VI, xiii, 3.
34 Ibid., II, xii, I.
35 Plutarch's 'Alexander', LXXI. Cf. Arrian, VII, xii, 2.

36 Arrian, VI, xxvi, 2–3. Plutarch ('Alexander', XLII) attributes this incident to the pursuit of Darius, and ends his account as follows: 'But when they beheld his self-control and loftiness of spirit, they shouted out to him to lead them forward boldly … declaring that they would not regard themselves as weary, or thirsty, or as mortals at all, so long as they had such a king.'

5

ALEXANDER
AND THE GREEKS

Introduction

In 338 Philip II defeated a Greek coalition at the Battle of Chaeronea that established Macedonian hegemony over the Greeks. In 337 he formalized that military control with a Common Peace, administered by an executive arm that is commonly called the League of Corinth (a modern term). A Common Peace bound all parties together on an equal basis, with each state, among other things, forbidden to wage war against another; if that happened, then all the other states could combine against the aggressor. Given the rivalries of the various states towards one another, Philip's exploitation of Common Peace (which he enforced, unlike previous ones, which had soon broken down) was an ingenious method to keep the Greeks passive while he campaigned in Asia. Macedonia was not a member of this Common Peace, but Philip bound the Greeks together under Macedonian rule by means of the league, for each state swore allegiance to the hegemon of the League, which turned out to be Philip, of course![1] Sparta refused to join the peace, but Philip could safely leave it be as it was encircled by Macedonian allies. This combination of Common Peace and league was completely new in Greek political life. Matters affecting the Greeks were to be discussed by the league and then implemented on its authority, thus giving the Greeks some semblance of autonomy. Thus, in 337 when Philip announced his intention to invade Persia on the pretext of avenging the Athenians for what they had suffered during the Persian War (cf. Source 21) and to liberate the Greek cities of Asia Minor, he did so at a league meeting (Diod. 16.89.2, Arr. 2.14.4, 3.18.12).

Alexander inherited both league and the plans to invade Asia when Philip was assassinated in 336, but at that time the Greek states revolted from Macedonian rule. Alexander quickly subdued them and resumed control of the Greeks by means of the League of Corinth; Sparta again remained aloof, and was left alone. The council of the league elected him the hegemon and also endorsed the invasion of Asia for the same reasons as his father. Alexander's departure was delayed for almost two years because of campaigns in the north, and then in 335 Thebes revolted (again) when news came that Alexander had died during his intervention in Illyria (Arr. 1.5.1), and called upon the Greeks to rise against Macedonian rule. The Thebans may also have been supporting his half-brother Amyntas (the true heir in 359 when the Macedonian Assembly acclaimed his uncle Philip as king) as a possible claimant to the throne. Alexander was far from dead, and far from forgiving, given the threat that the Theban revolt posed to Macedonian hegemony of Greece (and his own kingship if challenged by Amyntas). After a brief siege, he razed Thebes to the ground and either killed or enslaved the population (see

Sources 34 and 35).[2] This action was followed up by his demand for several Athenian statesmen (Source 33), although later he relented. Finally, in spring 334, Alexander departed to Persia, leaving behind Antipater as regent of Greece and deputy hegemon of the League of Corinth (Arr. 1.11.3).

Alexander had little to do with the mainland Greeks while he was in Asia. After liberating the Greek cities of Asia Minor from Persian rule in the early stages of his campaign, he probably gave orders that they and the neighbouring islands should join the League of Corinth. For his dealings with the Greeks, we are dependent largely on inscriptional evidence, and some examples are given as Sources 26, 27, 28 and 30; Source 29, dated after Alexander's death, attests to a decision he made in the context of his Exiles Decree (see below). Particularly significant are the king's dealings with the return of exiles to some states and the maintenance or creation of a democratic government. This shows his decision to involve himself in matters pertinent only to the state itself, as the details contained in the Mytilene (Source 28) and Tegea decrees illustrate (Source 30).

Antipater was not faced with any major problem from the Greeks until Agis III of Sparta declared war in 331.[3] This abortive attempt to free Greece from Macedonian rule had little support, and it ended in 330 with the Spartans' defeat at the hands of Antipater. As might be expected, the League of Corinth debated the punishment of the few states that had supported Agis, but significantly it referred the fate of the Spartans to Alexander himself.[4] It is plausible that after Agis' defeat Sparta was forced to join the Common Peace, and hence the League of Corinth.

If Alexander had intended the razing of Thebes to serve as a warning to the Greeks of what would happen to any state that revolted, it did the trick. Once Alexander left for Asia we hear of no attempt to defy Macedonian rule apart from the short, ill-fated and unsupported attempt of Agis of Sparta, until his death in 323. Another reason for the Greeks' passivity may well be that they had come to accept Macedonian hegemony, given the peace and prosperity it provided after decades of fighting and financial exhaustion. It is true that Demosthenes, Philip's principal opponent in Athens, had contacts at Alexander's court (Source 31), but these were merely diplomatic, and no plan of revolt was hatched. The League of Corinth continued to function, but Alexander came to view it, and the autonomy of the Greek states, as of decreasing importance.

The most explicit example of Alexander's attitude came in 324 when he issued his Exiles Decree, which ordered that all exiles (excluding Thebans and those guilty of murder) were to return to their native cities, and Antipater was ordered to use force against any unwilling city.[5] This unpopular measure was meant to solve the problem of roaming bands of mercenaries in Alexander's empire being hired by ambitious satraps or generals and to increase the king's support base in Greece as he prepared to invade Arabia. For Athens, the decree meant not only the return of the exiles but also the loss of the island of Samos, then populated by Athenian cleruchs (Source 29). To make matters worse, Greece was still recovering from a major famine during which many *poleis* had received donations of corn, and the influx of exiles would have caused more economic chaos. Technically, the decree was illegal since in theory only the Greek states could decide on a measure such as this, but the reality was that Alexander was long used to acting unilaterally, and preserving the pretence of Greek autonomy was not high on his list of priorities. His death the following year cancelled the decree, which explains why only one state, Tegea, received back its exiles (Source 30).

Alexander's divine status was also a matter of discussion among some Greek states in the final years of his reign, although it is implausible to see it originating in some form of 'deification decree' that Alexander sent out at the same time as the Exiles Decree because he wanted the Greeks to worship him.[6] Most likely is that the Exiles Decree caused the Greeks to send embassies to the king at Babylon to protest it, and they may have thought that if they appeared to recognize Alexander's divinity he would be less likely to enforce the decree. Finally, another factor on the Greek scene was the imperial treasurer Harpalus, who fled from Alexander with a significant number of ships and men, and a large amount of money, and sought asylum in Athens (Diod. 17.108.6, Curt. 10.2.1). He wanted to urge the Athenians to spearhead a Greek revolt against Macedonian rule. However, no such revolt came – at least not until after Alexander's death in June 323, when the Greeks once more rose against the Macedonian hegemony in what is commonly called the Lamian War. This would end the following year with Antipater's defeat of a Greek coalition force at Crannon, and Greece again fell under Macedonian rule.

Ancient sources

Alexander's dealing with Greeks throughout his reign

26   King Alexander dedicated the temple of Athena Polias (Tod, no. 184 = R–O no. 86A).[7]

27   In the prytany of Deisitheus, from King Alexander to the people of Chios.[8] All the exiles from Chios shall return home and the constitution in Chios shall be a democracy. Law-writers shall be chosen who will write and correct the laws in order that nothing may be contrary to the democracy or to the return of the exiles, and what has been written or corrected shall be referred to Alexander. The Chians shall provide twenty fully-equipped triremes at their own expense, and these shall sail as long as the other fleet of the Greeks sails with us. Of those who betrayed the city to the barbarians,[9] as many as have escaped shall be exiled from all the cities that share in the peace and are to be arrested in accordance with the resolution of the Greeks; all those who were left behind shall be returned and judged in the Council of the Greeks. If a dispute arises between those who have returned and those in the city, those people shall be judged about this before us. Until the Chians are reconciled, there shall be a garrison among them from Alexander the king, of a size that is sufficient; and the Chians shall maintain it (Tod, no. 192 = R–O no. 84A).

28   ... let the kings[10] be favorable to the restored exile, for the reason that the one who was previously in the city has been guilty of a fraud.[11] But if anyone of the returned exiles does not follow these reconciliations, let him no longer have any property from the city nor own anything given to him by those who were previously in the city, but let those who were previously in the city who gave them to him regain these properties, and let the generals again transfer the properties to the one who was previously in the city, for the reason that the restored exile has not accepted the reconciliation, and let the kings be favorable to the one who was previously in the city, for the reason that a fraud has been carried out by the restored exile. If anyone brings a lawsuit about these things, the *peridromoi* and the *dikaskopoi*[12] nor any other magistrate shall bring it to court. It shall be the responsibility of the generals and the kings and the *peridromoi* and the *dikaskopoi* and the other officials, if everything does not turn out as has been written in the decree, to condemn the man neglecting any of the terms written in the decree, so that nothing may come between the restored exiles and those who were in the city previously, but all might be reconciled to one another and live in harmony without intrigue and may abide by the inscribed edict and by the reconciliation written in this decree. And the people shall choose twenty men, ten from the returned exiles and ten from those who were previously in the city. Let these men zealously guard and make sure that nothing will be a source of disagreement forever between those who returned and those who were previously in the city, and concerning the contested properties that those who returned shall be reconciled especially with those who were in the city and with one another, but if not, that they will be as just as possible, and that everyone will abide by the reconciliations which the king judged in his edict and will live in the city and the country in harmony with one another. And concerning money, that the reconciliation may be carried out as much as possible, and concerning an oath that the citizens will swear, concerning all these things, the chosen men are to bring before the people whatever they agree among themselves, and the People, upon hearing, if they think it is beneficial, let them deliberate abut accepting what was agreed among themselves as beneficial, just as in the same way it was decreed previously for those who returned in the prytany of Smithinas. If something is lacking in this decree, let the decision about this lie with the Council. When this decree has been ratified by the People, the entire citizen body on the twentieth day of the month after the sacrifice will pray to the gods that the safety and prosperity of all the citizens will be on the reconciliation between those who returned and those who were previously in the city. All of the priests and the priestesses with public authority will open the temples and the people will assemble together for prayer. The sacrifices that the people vowed when it sent the messengers to the king shall be paid by the kings to the gods annually. And there shall be present at the sacrifice the whole citizen body and the messengers who were sent to the king, from those who were in the city and from those who returned. When the treasurers have inscribed this decree on a stone stele, they are to set it up in the temple of Athena[13] (Tod, no. 201 = R–O no. 85).

29   Decreed by the Council and People, Epicurus, son of Dracon, made the motion.[14] Since Gorgus and Minneon the Iasians,[15] sons of Theodotus, have been good and noble towards the Samians in their exile, and since Gorgus, while staying at the court of Alexander, showed much goodwill and zeal concerning the *demos* of the Samians, and worked eagerly so that the Samians might recover their land quickly, and when Alexander proclaimed in his camp that he would return Samos to the Samians,[16] and the Greeks crowned him because of this, and Gorgus crowned him and sent the news to Iasus to the archons that those of the Samians living in Iasus, when they returned to their native land, should carry away their possessions tax free and transport would be provided to them, the city of the Iasians meeting the cost, and now Gorgus and Minion (*sic*) promise to do whatever good they are able for the *demos* of the Samians, it has been decreed by the *demos* to bestow citizenship on them on fair and equal terms, both to them and to their descendants, and to assign them by lot to a tribe, both a thousand and a hundred and a clan, and to inscribe their names in the clan, whichever one they obtain by the lot, just as also the other Samians, and the five men who have been chosen shall attend to the inscribing, and this decree is to be inscribed on a stone stele and set up in

the temple of Hera, and the treasurer will attend to the cost (W. Dittenberger, *Sylloge Inscriptionum Graecorum*[3] [Leipzig: 1915–24], no. 312 = R–O no. 90B).

30 ... king Alexander,[17] the edict is to be inscribed in accordance with those terms corrected by the city that were objected to in the edict.[18] To the returned exiles shall be given the paternal property which they had when they went into exile, and the women the maternal property, as many as were unmarried and held possession of their property and happened not to have brothers. But if it befell any married woman that her brother, both himself and his offspring, has died, she also shall have the maternal property, and it will not be any more. In connection with the houses, each man shall have one in keeping with the edict. And if a house has a garden next to it, let him not take another. But if there is no garden next to the house but there is one nearby within the distance of a *plethron*, let him take the garden. But if the garden is more than a *plethron* away, let him take one half of it, as also it has been written about the other properties. As for the houses, let the price to be recovered for each house be two minas, and the appraisal value of the houses will be whatever the city decides. And double the value shall be recovered for the cultivated gardens than is stipulated in the law. Monetary claims do not involve the city, and it will not settle either with the exiles or with those who previously stayed at home as citizens. In connection with the festivals, from which the exiles have been absent, the city shall deliberate, and whatever the city decides is to be valid. The foreign court[19] is to judge suits for sixty days. All those who do not file suits within sixty days shall not be allowed to have legal recourse about the properties in the foreign court, but in the civic court ever after. If they later discover something (they may present it) within sixty days from the day that the court was established. If a person does not file suit within this time, it will be no longer possible for him to go to court. If later some people return from exile, when the foreign court is no longer convened, let them lay a claim with the generals of the properties within sixty days, and if there is any opposition to them, the court shall be Mantinea. But if they do not file their suits within these days, no longer shall they go to court. In connection with the sacred monies ... the debts, the city will make these right for the Goddess,[20] the one who has the property will give back half to the returned exile just as the others are to do. And all those who are themselves in debt to the Goddess as guarantors or otherwise, if the man holding the property clearly has discharged the debt with the Goddess, let him give back half to the returned exile, just as the others do, omitting nothing. But if he clearly has not discharged his debt with the Goddess, let him give back half to the returned exile and from his half himself discharge the debt. But if he does not wish to settle, let him give back to the returned exile the entire property, and let the man who has received it discharge the whole debt with the Goddess. As many of the wives of the exiles or daughters who stayed at home, married, or were in exile and later (returned and) married in Tegea, and remaining at home obtained their discharge, these shall not be subject to investigation about their paternal or their maternal property, nor their descendants, except that as many who later went into exile through compulsion and are heading back in the opportunity that currently exists, either themselves or their children, those shall be subject to investigation, both themselves and their descendants, concerning their paternal and maternal property in accordance with the edict. I swear by Zeus, by Athena, by Apollo, by Poseidon that I shall be well disposed towards the returned exiles whom it was decided by the city to receive back, and I shall not bear a grievance against any of them for whatever he may have plotted, from the day on which I swore the oath, and I shall not obstruct the safety of the returned exiles, neither in the … nor in the government of the city … edict … towards the returned exiles … to the city … the terms that have been written in the edict concerning … nor shall I plan against anyone (Tod, no. 202 = R–O no. 101).

Relations between Athens and Alexander

31 Aristion. Hyperides, *Against Demosthenes*. This man is a Samian or a Plataean, as Diyllus states (*FGrH* 73 F 2), and a friend of Demosthenes from childhood. He was sent by him to Hephaestion for a reconciliation, as Marsyas says (*FGrH* 135 F 2) in the fifth (book) of *Matters related to Alexander* (Harpocration, *Lexicon*, s.v. Aristion).

32 Margites: used by Aeschines in his speech *Against Ctesiphon*: 'and he gave Alexander the nickname Margites';[21] and Marsyas in the fifth book of his work *On Alexander* writes that Alexander was called Margites by Demosthenes (Marsyas, *FGrH* 135 F 3 = Harpocration, *Lexicon*, s.v. Margites).

33 Then straightway[22] Alexander sent to Athens a demand for the surrender to him of ten of their popular leaders, according to Idomeneus and Duris, but according to the most reputable writers, only eight, namely, Demosthenes, Polyeuctus, Ephialtes, Lycurgus, Moerocles, Demon, Callisthenes, and Charidemus. It was on this occasion that Demosthenes told the Athenians the story of how the sheep surrendered their dogs to the wolves, comparing himself and his fellow orators to dogs fighting in defence of the people, and calling Alexander 'the Macedonian arch wolf.' Moreover, he said further: 'Just as grain merchants sell their whole stock by means of a few kernels of wheat which they carry about with them in a bowl as a sample, so in surrendering us you unwittingly surrender also yourselves, all of you.' Such, then, is the account which Aristobulus of Cassandreia has given (Aristobulus, *FGrH* 139 F 3 = Plut. *Demosthenes* 23.4–6).

The siege of Thebes (335)

34 But Ptolemy, son of Lagus, tells us that Perdiccas, who had been posted in the advanced guard of the camp with his own brigade,[23] and was not far from the enemy's stockade, did not wait for the signal from Alexander to commence the battle; but of his own accord was the first to assault the stockade, and, having made a breach in it, fell upon the advanced guard of the Thebans. Amyntas, son of Andromenes, followed Perdiccas, because he had been stationed with him. This general also of his own accord led on his brigade when he saw that Perdiccas had advanced within the stockade. When Alexander saw this, he led on the rest of his army, fearing that unsupported they might be intercepted by the Thebans and be in danger of destruction. He gave instructions to the archers and Agrianians to rush within the stockade, but he still retained the guards and shield-bearing troops outside. Then indeed Perdiccas, after forcing his way within the second stockade, fell there wounded with a dart, and was carried back grievously injured to the camp, where he was with difficulty cured of his wound. However, the men of Perdiccas, in company with the archers sent by Alexander, fell upon the Thebans and shut them up in the hollow way leading to the temple of Heracles and followed them in their retreat as far as the temple itself. The Thebans, having wheeled round, again advanced from that position with a shout, and put the Macedonians to flight. Eurybotas the Cretan, the captain of the archers, fell with about seventy of his men; but the rest fled to the Macedonian guard and the royal shield-bearing troops. Now, when

Alexander saw that his own men were in flight, and that the Thebans had broken their ranks in pursuit, he attacked them with his phalanx drawn up in proper order, and drove them back within the gates. The Thebans fled in such a panic that being driven into the city through the gates they had not time to shut them; for all the Macedonians, who were close behind the fugitives, rushed with them within the fortifications, inasmuch as the walls also were destitute of defenders on account of the numerous pickets in front of them. When the Macedonians had entered the Cadmea,[24] some of them marched out of it, in company with those who held the fortress, along the temple of Amphion into the other part of the city, but others crossing along the walls, which were now in the possession of those who had rushed in together with the fugitives, advanced with a run into the market place. Those of the Thebans who had been drawn up opposite the temple of Amphion stood their ground for a short time; but when the Macedonians pressed hard upon them in all directions, Alexander presenting himself now in one place now in another, their cavalry rushed through the city and sallied forth into the plain, and their infantry fled for safety as each man found it possible. Then indeed the Thebans, no longer defending themselves, were slain, not so much by the Macedonians as by the Phocians, Plataeans and other Boeotians, who by indiscriminate slaughter vented their rage against them. Some were even attacked in the houses (a few of whom turned to defend themselves), and others as they were supplicating the protection of the gods in the temples; not even the women and children being spared (Ptolemy, *FGrH* 138 F 3 = Arr. 1.8).

35   Timoclea. Theagenes the Theban, who held the same sentiments with regard to his country's welfare with Epaminondas, Pelopidas, and the other most worthy Thebans,[25] was slain in Chaeronea,[26] in the common disaster of Greece, even then when he had conquered his enemies and was in pursuit of them. For it was he that answered one who cried out aloud to him, How far wilt thou pursue? Even (said he) to Macedonia. When he was dead, his sister survived him, who gave testimony that he was nobly descended, and that he was naturally a great man and excellently accomplished. Moreover, this woman was so fortunate as to reap a great benefit by her prowess, so that the more public calamities fell upon her, so much the easier she bore them. For when Alexander took Thebes and the soldiers fell aplundering, some in one part and some in another, it happened that a man, neither civil nor sober but mischievous and mad, took up his quarters in Timoclea's house. He was a captain to a Thracian company, and the king's namesake, but nothing like him; for he having no regard either to the family or estate of this woman, when he had swilled himself in wine after supper, commanded her to come and lie with him. Neither ended he here, but enquired for gold and silver, whether she had not some hid by her; sometimes threatening as if he would kill her, sometimes flattering as if he would always repute her in the place of a wife. She, taking the occasion offered by him, said: 'Would God I had died before this night came, rather than lived to it; that though all other things had been lost, I might have preserved my body free from abuse. But now seeing it is thus come to pass, and Divine Providence hath thus disposed of it that I must repute thee my guardian, lord, and husband, I will not hold any thing from thee that is thine own. And as for myself, I see I am at thy disposition. As for corporeal enjoyments, the world was mine, I had silver bowls, I had gold, and some money; but when this city was taken, I commanded my maids to pack it up altogether, and threw it, or rather put it for security, into a well that had no water in it. Neither do many know of it, for it hath a covering, and nature hath provided a shady wood round about it. Take then these things, and much good may they do thee; and they shall lie by thee, as certain tokens and marks of the late flourishing fortune and splendor of our family.' When the Macedonian heard these things, he stayed not for day, but presently went to the place by Timoclea's conduct, commanding the garden door to be shut, that none might perceive what they were about. He descended in his morning vestment. But the revengeful Clotho brought dreadful things upon him by the hand of Timoclea, who stood on the top of the well; for as soon as she perceived by his voice that he reached the bottom, she threw down abundance of stones upon him, and her maids rolled in many and great ones, till they had dashed him to pieces and buried him under them. As soon as the Macedonians came to understand this and had taken up the corpse, there having been late proclamation that none of the Thebans should be slain, they seized her and carried her before the king and declared her audacious exploit; but the king, who by the gravity of her countenance and stateliness of her behaviour did perceive in her something that savoured of the greatest worth and nobility, asked her first, What woman art thou? She courageously and undauntedly answered: Theagenes was my brother, who was a commander at Chaeronea, and lost his life fighting against you in defense of the Grecian liberty, that we might not suffer any such thing; and seeing I have suffered things unworthy of my rank, I refuse not to die; for it is better so to do than to experience another such a night as the last, which awaits me unless thou forbid it. All the most tender-spirited persons that were present broke out into tears; but Alexander was not for pitying her, as being a woman above pity. But he admired her fortitude and eloquence, which had taken strong hold on him, and charged his officers to have a special care and look to the guards, lest any such abuse be offered again to any renowned family; and dismissed Timoclea, charging them to have a special regard to her and all that should be found to be of her family (Aristobulus, *FGrH* 139 F 2b = [Plut.] *Mor.* 259d–260d).

Modern works

In the following selections, the late N.G.L. Hammond, formerly Professor of Greek at the University of Bristol, and the late F.W. Walbank, Emeritus Professor of Classics at the University of Liverpool, and E. Poddighe, Lecturer in Ancient History at the University of Cagliari, discuss Alexander's dealings with the mainland Greeks, together with those of the islands and Asia Minor. Poddighe goes into more detail, especially on the mainland Greeks, based on the nature and range of the evidence.

1   N.G.L. Hammond and F.W. Walbank, *A History of Macedonia* 3 (Oxford University Press: 1988), Chap. III, 'Alexander and the Greek States', Sec. 3, 'Relations with the Greek States', pp. 72–83.[27]
2   E. Poddighe, 'Alexander and the Greeks', in W. Heckel and L. Tritle (eds), *Alexander the Great. A New History* (Wiley-Blackwell: 2009), Chap. 6, pp. 99–120.[28]

Additional reading

E. Badian, 'Harpalus', *Journal of Hellenic Studies* 81 (1961), pp. 25–31.
——, 'The Administration of the Empire', *Greece and Rome*[2] 12 (1965), pp. 166–182.

——, 'Alexander the Great and the Greeks of Asia', in E. Badian (ed.), *Ancient Society and Institutions, Studies Presented to V. Ehrenberg* (Oxford: 1966), pp. 37–69.

——, 'Agis III: Revisions and Reflections', in Ian Worthington (ed.), *Ventures into Greek History. Essays in Honour of N.G.L. Hammond* (Oxford: 1994), pp. 258–292.

A.B. Bosworth, *Conquest and Empire, The Reign of Alexander the Great* (Cambridge: 1988), pp. 187–228 and 250–258.

S. Dmitriev, 'Alexander's Exile's Decree', *Klio* 86 (2004), pp. 348–381.

V. Ehrenberg, *Alexander and the Greeks* (Oxford: 1938).

M. Faraguna, 'Alexander and the Greeks', in J. Roisman (ed.), *Brill's Companion to Alexander the Great* (Leiden: 2003), pp. 99–130.

M.A. Flower, 'Alexander the Great and Panhellenism', in A.B. Bosworth and E. Baynham (eds), *Alexander the Great in Fact and Fiction* (Oxford: 2000), pp. 96–135.

W. Heckel, 'Resistance to Alexander the Great', in L. Tritle (ed.), *The Greek World in the Fourth Century* (London: 1997), pp. 189–227.

F. Mitchel, *Lykourgan Athens: 338–322, Semple Lectures* 2 (Cincinnati: 1970).

S. Perlman, 'Greek Diplomatic Tradition and the Corinthian League of Philip of Macedon', *Historia* 34 (1985), pp. 153–174.

E. Poddighe, 'Alexander and the Greeks: The Corinthian League', in W. Heckel and L. Tritle (eds), *Alexander the Great: A New History* (Oxford: 2009), pp. 121–140.

T.T.B. Ryder, *Koine Eirene* (Oxford: 1965), pp. 102–109.

G. Shipley, 'Between Macedonia and Rome: Political Landscapes and Social Changes in Southern Greece in the Early Hellenistic Period', *Annual of the British School at Athens* 100 (2005), pp. 315–330.

Ian Worthington, 'The Harpalus Affair and the Greek Response to the Macedonian Hegemony', in Ian Worthington (ed.), *Ventures Into Greek History. Essays in Honour of N.G.L. Hammond* (Oxford: 1994), pp. 307–330.

——, 'Alexander's Destruction of Thebes', in W. Heckel and L.A. Tritle (eds), *Crossroads of History. The Age of Alexander the Great* (Claremont: 2003), pp. 65–86.

——, 'Alexander the Great and the Greeks in 336? Another Reading of *IG* ii^2 329', *Zeitschrift für Papyrologie und Epigraphik* 147 (2004), pp. 59–71.

——, 'From East to West: Alexander and the Exiles Decree', in E. Baynham (ed.), *East and West in the World of Alexander: Essays in Honour of A.B. Bosworth* (Oxford: 2011).

Notes

1 Diod. 16.89.1–3, Justin 9.5.1–6; cf. [Dem.] 17.1. For discussion of the Common Peace, see Ian Worthington, *Philip II of Macedonia* (New Haven and London: 2008), pp. 161–163.

2 Diod. 17.8.3–14, Arr. 1.7.1–8.8, Plut. *Demosthenes* 23.1–3, Justin 11.3.8.

3 Aes. 3.165–166, Diod. 17.48.1, 62.6–63.4, 73.5, Curt. 6.1; cf. Arr. 2.13.4, 3.6.3 and 16.10.

4 Aes. 3.133, Diod. 17.63.1–3, 73.5–6, Curt. 6.1.19–21.

5 Hyp. 5.18, Diod. 18.8.2–7, Curt. 10.2.4, [Plut.] *Mor.* 221a, Justin 13.5.2; cf. Plut. *Demosthenes* 9.1 and [Plut.] *Mor.* 845c.

6 On Alexander's pretensions to personal divinity, see Chapter 10.

7 At Priene, in either 334 or 330.

8 Alexander's letter to the Chians has survived virtually complete, unlike most of the inscriptional evidence from the reign of Alexander. It is not part of the Exiles Decree of 324 (see above), and may be dated to either 334 or 332 (A.J. Heisserer, *Alexander the Great and the Greeks* (Norman: 1980), pp. 83–95).

9   The Persians.
10 Not kings in the sense of monarchs, but probably elected senior officials of the city.
11 This decree concerns returning exiles to Mytilene on the island of Lesbos. It is not part of the context of Alexander's Exiles Decree, as has often been thought (for example by Tod), but may be dated to 332: Heisserer, *Alexander the Great and the Greeks*, pp. 131–139, and Ian Worthington, 'Alexander the Great and the Date of the Mytilene Decree', *Zeitschrift für Papyrologie und Epigraphik* 83 (1990), pp. 194–214.
12 Officials with legal powers.
13 The end of the decree is missing, and this conclusion has been restored.
14 This decree may be dated to 321.
15 Iasus was south of Miletus on the coast of Asia Minor.
16 The context is the king's Exiles Decree of 324: see above. However, it was not until 322/1 that the Samian exiles were fully restored, and it was then that they honoured Gorgus and Minneon with citizenship for their efforts.
17 The name of the king is restored here to Alexander, but Cassander, one of the protagonists in the struggles for Macedonian power after the death of Alexander, would also fit here, although this is unlikely: see Ian Worthington, 'The Date of the Tegea decree (Tod ii 202): A Response to the *Diagramma* of Alexander III or of Polyperchon?', *Ancient History Bulletin* 7 (1993), pp. 59–64.
18 This decree concerns returning exiles to Tegea, and may be dated to 324 in the context of Alexander's Exiles Decree. The opening indicates that this is the second version of the Tegeans' plan for the return of exiles; clearly, Alexander had found the original plan unacceptable.
19 A foreign court, probably from Mantinea since this place is cited later in the decree.
20 Athena Alea.
21 Aes. 3.160; Margites is a nickname associated with stupidity.
22 After the razing of Thebes in 335.
23 The context is the revolt of Thebes in 335.
24 The citadel of Thebes.
25 During the so-called Theban hegemony of Greece, from 371 to 362.
26 The battle fought between Philip II and a coalition of some Greek states (notably Athens and Thebes) in 338; Philip was victorious and Greek autonomy came to an end; cf. Worthington, *Philip II of Macedonia*, pp. 147–151.
27 Reprinted by permission of Dorothy Thompson.
28 Reprinted by permission of Wiley-Blackwell.

RELATIONS WITH THE GREEK STATES

N.G.L. Hammond and F.W. Walbank

Relations between an island state and Alexander were based either on membership of the Common Peace or on a treaty of alliance (e.g. at Arr. 2. 1. 4 κατα συμμαίαν in the case of Mytilene). In consecutive chapters Arrian gives an example of each, Tenedos having its agreement 'with Alexander and the Greeks', and Mytilene in Lesbos simply 'with Alexander' (2. 2. 2 and 1. 4).[1] These agreements carried different obligations. For example, offenders from Chios as a member of the Common Peace were tried by the Court of the Common Peace (*GHI* 192, 15). On the other hand, some Lesbian offenders were tried by the court of their own state in the island (3. 2. 7; C. 4. 8. 11–13), others by Alexander (*GHI* 191, 99), and others under an agreed procedure which stemmed from Alexander's *diagramma* (191, 129–30 and *SEG* 12. 1 and 16, being lines 20 and 28 of Heisserer 123 f.). Again in Lesbos Alexander rewarded Mytilene with money and 'a large grant of territory' (C. 4. 8.13). This land was taken probably from the king's territory on the mainland. Such a grant of land was not within the competence of the Council of the Common Peace.

During the struggle between Macedonia and Persia the faction strife which was already endemic in many states of the eastern Aegean took on a new impetus. With each change a new faction took power. Thus Chios had fought against Macedonia in 341/0; but in 335, if not earlier, it was a member of the Common Peace and, as such, a member of a common alliance with Macedonia. Then in 333 it resisted Memnon, but fell through betrayal from within and became an ally of Persia (2. 1. 1). Finally the popular party invited the help of Hegelochus, in 332, who defeated the Persian garrison and took over the island. The regulations which were made then by Alexander as *hegemon* have survived (*GHI* 192).[2] There was to be a democratic constitution, a new code of laws, and a banishing of those responsible for betraying the island to Persia from all Common Peace territories. Further, any persons so responsible, but still in Chios, were to be tried 'before the Council of the Greeks', and any such elsewhere were to be liable to arrest 'in accordance with the decree of the Greeks'. Any dispute arising between those in Chios and the returning exiles was to be tried by Alexander, and the drafted code of laws was to be submitted to him. Here we see Alexander as *hegemon* trying to check victimization through discriminatory verdicts and laws. Those of the pro-Persian leaders who were subsequently caught by the Macedonian fleet were imprisoned that winter at Elephantine in Egypt, probably until they could be sent safely through the Aegean to the Greek mainland for trial by the Council of the Greeks. For Alexander insisted on the establishment of law and proper legal procedures, and he put a stop to lynching and persecution (as we see at Ephesus, 1. 17. 12). In a second letter to Chios he called a halt to indictments on the charge of Medism and requested honourable treatment for a Chian citizen whom he regarded as a personal friend and as a sincere patriot (*SEG* 22. 506).[3]

There had been faction strife also in Eresus, a city-state on the island of Lesbos, with which Alexander made a treaty of alliance, as with Mytilene. Here between *c.* 350 and *c.* 340 a tyranny headed by three brothers had been in power, and it had been succeeded by a democracy which set up altars to Zeus Philippius, presumably because Philip had had a hand in promoting the change. Its life was short; for before the agreement was made between Alexander and the Greeks in late 336 there was already another set of tyrants in power ([Dem.] 17. 7). They fled in 334, only to return with Memnon in 333, whereupon they committed a number of atrocities against their fellow citizens. In 332 the Macedonians gained control of Lesbos and brought the leader of the Eresus tyrants, Agonippus, to Alexander in Egypt, by whom he was sent back to be tried by a court of the restored democracy. He and his colleague were executed.[4] In accordance with normal Greek practice, reprisals were taken against the families of the condemned tyrants, and the relatives of both sets of tyrants were duly exiled. At an unknown date Alexander asked the democracy to consider in its court whether the descendants of the first set of tyrants should be restored or continue in exile; the verdict was the latter. The relatives of the second set were exiled by a judgement of Alexander, and this judgement was confirmed later by Philip Arrhidaeus. In the inscriptions which give us this information we can see that Alexander insisted on the democracy following legal procedures and instituting trials with a secret ballot.

Mytilene as an ally of Alexander defied Memnon in 333. When it was compelled to submit, Pharnabazus installed a garrison, made a restored exile tyrant, banished the previous leaders, and exacted a heavy financial penalty; and perforce the state allied itself with Persia and accepted the 'Peace of Antalcidas', a fossil some fifty years old (Arr. 2. 1. 2–5). A year later Mytilene was liberated by Hegelochus and was rewarded for its loyalty .... The exiles were recalled, the tyrant (if he survived) was tried in the local court and a democracy was set up. Alexander issued a *diagramma* which was expressly designed to bring the two factions of the Mytileneans into concord (Heisserer 123 ll. 28–30, with his restoration).

We may assume that Rhodes yielded to Memnon in 333; for we should have learnt from Arrian, were it otherwise. Then in 332 during the siege of Tyre ten Rhodian triremes made their way to Alexander (2. 20. 2), and after the fall of Tyre the city of Rhodes surrendered itself and its harbours into Alexander's hands (C. 4. 5. 9). Here too there must have been changes of faction, and probably a *diagramma* was issued by Alexander in favour of reconciliation; for a garrison was placed there, as at Chios, and it was removed later, probably after the end of the actions in Crete (C. 4. 8. 12). There is no sign that Rhodes became a member of the Common Peace. It simply remained an ally of Alexander, to the mutual satisfaction of both parties.

Greek cities on the Asiatic mainland formed a separate category. They were not admitted to membership of the Common Peace, and there is no evidence that the question of admission ever arose. Modern scholars have expressed surprise or disapproval, because they have associated liberation from Persian rule with membership of the Common Peace.[5] Greeks of the 330s probably had no such expectations. Athens and Sparta had 'liberated' Greek cities from Persian rule, not in order that they should become free members of the Hellenic League or the Peloponnesian League, but in order that they should enter the power system of the 'liberator'. So now the 'liberated' Greek cities entered Alexander's power system, the Kingdom of Asia, as subjects of the King, but by his grace with a preferential status, paying a 'contribution' for the war and not 'tribute' and dealing directly with the King. Such was the status of Aspendus, for instance. But when Aspendus went back on its obligations, it was made tributary both to Alexander as King of Asia and to Macedonia and also made subject to the orders of Alexander's deputy, the satrap; and at the moment it had to pay an indemnity, provide hostages for good conduct, and accept Alexander's ruling in a border dispute (Arr. 1. 27. 4). Athens had done no less to an 'ally' who broke her agreement in the 450s, and

Alexander's methods now served as a model for the treatment of Greek cities within a kingdom.

The Greeks of the islands and of the Asiatic mainland preferred the rule of Alexander to the rule of Persia,[6] particularly because Alexander favoured democracy, while Persia relied on cliques or tyrants, and because the restored democratic leaders obtained the general support of the electorate. The real centre of disaffection was on the Greek mainland, at Sparta, which stood outside the Common Peace and had good reason to hate Macedonia. Philip had had her excommunicated by the Amphictyonic Council in 346, had thwarted her attempts to reconstitute an alliance in the Peloponnese, and had finally deprived her of some border territories and maintained the independence of Messene and Megalopolis. When Sparta refused to recognize Philip, Alexander, and the Common Peace, she was left in proud, but impotent, isolation. When her hated rival, Thebes, was in danger, Sparta did not go to her aid either in 338 or in 335; and when she decided in 333 to side with Persia against Macedonia, she was too late to affect the course of the war at sea, as we have seen, but she did obtain what she had lacked, a large enough subsidy of Persian gold to hire eventually 10,000 Greek mercenaries (Dinarch. 1. 34) and maintain her own army on a war footing.

In the last months of 331 Sparta faced a difficult choice. More than a year of war in alliance with Persia against the forces of the Greek League and Macedonia at sea had ended in utter failure. Prudence might now have advised capitulation. But some factors seemed to favour the continuation of war, not at sea, but on the Greek mainland. Most important of all, Sparta had the military means; for her forces were more than twice as large as they had been for some generations thanks to the Persian subsidy, which would however become a wasting asset if they delayed. On the other hand, the forces of Macedonia were widely dispersed and over-strained: the army of Antipater, drained by the sending of 6,500 Macedonians to the East, was now at a low ebb, and Alexander himself was far away in Mesopotamia. The news of Memnon's large-scale rising in Thrace ... seemed to promise that Antipater's army would be further depleted and pinned down in the north. There were also political changes in some Peloponnesian states whereby anti-Macedonian leaders were coming into the ascendancy, and this might be a token that Greek opinion generally was moving towards a war of 'liberation' (D.S. 17. 62. 3–6). Yet Sparta must have realized that she had irreconcilable enemies in the Peloponnese – Messenia, Megalopolis, and Argos (cf. Isoc. 5. 74) – and that north-eastern Greece from Boeotia to Thessaly was likely to support the Common Peace and Macedonia. Much would depend upon the attitude of Athens and Aetolia, as at the time of Thebes' rising, and it was discouraging for Sparta that Athens had recently congratulated Alexander on his victories and he had released Athenian prisoners of war, captured at the Granicus river.

The news of Alexander's victory at Gaugamela on 1 October 331 and of his advance to Babylon may have contributed to the decision of the Spartan people; for it was clear he would not turn back to Greece. So they marched under the command of Agis and engaged the forces of the Macedonian commander Corragus, which represented the Greek League and Macedonia as keepers of the Common Peace. Sparta's full levy and her 10,000 mercenaries were completely victorious, and her success brought two states into alliance with her, Elis and Achaea apart from Pellene .... These states renounced their membership of the Common Peace, laid themselves open to attack by members of the Common Peace (*GHI* 177, 20 f.), and accepted the hegemony of Sparta, as in the days of the Peloponnesian League. Their example was followed later by Arcadia apart from Megalopolis. Elsewhere Sparta's approaches were rejected, and in particular Athens did not move from her membership of the Common Peace and her alliance with Macedonia.[7]

Early in 330 Sparta did not deploy the forces of her coalition against the Macedonian garrison of Acrocorinth or show the flag in central Greece, but instead she and her allies laid siege to Megalopolis, which was of particular concern to Sparta herself. Her strategy suited Antipater admirably. Having come to terms with Memnon and received a huge sum of money from Alexander (3. 16. 10), he reinforced his relatively small Macedonian army of some 1,500 cavalry and 12,000 phalanx infantry (D.S. 17. 17. 5) with perhaps some Balkan troops and certainly large numbers of Greeks, loyal to the Common Peace, who were willing to serve (Athenians not among them). It was probably April or May of 330 when Antipater led an army, reputedly of 40,000 men, into the Peloponnese (D.S. 17. 63. 1) and won near Megalopolis a hard-fought, but decisive, victory over an army numbering 2,000 cavalry, 20,000 citizen troops, and 10,000 mercenaries.[8] In particular the Macedonian pikeman outfought the Spartan hoplite, and Agis died fighting heroically. Losses of the Spartan coalition were 5,300 killed, and of Antipater's coalition 3,500 killed according to D.S. 17. 63. 3, but 1,000 and very many wounded according to C. 6. 1. 16. It was, in the words of Alexander 'a battle of mice'.[9]

Antipater, who had acted as deputy of the *hegemon*, now asked the Council of the Greek League to decide on the fate of the insurgents. Was Sparta to be destroyed, as Thebes had been? The Council imposed an indemnity of 120 talents on Elis and Achaea, which was to be paid to Megalopolis, arrested the ringleaders of the revolt in Tegea and probably other Arcadian cities (D.S. 17. 73. 5–6; C. 6. 1. 20), and referred the decision about Sparta to the *hegemon* himself, to whom Sparta was ordered to send fifty leading Spartiates to be held as hostages and also envoys to plead her case (Aeschin. 3. 133). Alexander showed surprising clemency; for he pardoned Sparta. It was also a sound piece of statesmanship, as Philip had realized .... For the course of the war had shown that the existence of Sparta was a source of disunity among those Greek states which might otherwise combine against him. On her side Sparta had shown more courage than intelligence in her continuation and conduct of the war; and Elis and Achaea were fortunate in escaping with a fine, as compared with what had happened to Thebes. It is probable that all three states and the Arcadian states were admitted to the Common Peace, Sparta for the first time.[10]

The failures of Greek resistance to Macedonia can be epitomized in the words 'united we stand, divided we fall.' Only a few mainland states fought at Chaeronea in 338, and none of them except Achaea fought again in 331/0. Thebes was abandoned even by the few states which had intended to help her in 335. Other Greek states fought against the resisting states in 335 and in 331/0. This situation was due to the long traditions of inter-state rivalry and warfare on the mainland and to the internal politics of individual states. Thus in 330, although Athens had not moved to help either side, Lycurgus in prosecuting Leocrates claimed that 'the freedom of Greece' was buried with the fallen at Chaeronea, and Aeschines failed to win even a fifth of the votes in his attack on the policy of Demosthenes. In fact, though not in spirit, the only form of unity lay still in the Common Peace.

Although Alexander could not command the allegiance of the Greek states to the spirit of the Common Peace, he could and, as far as we can tell, did respect the letter of the Agreement (*syntheke*) which he had made in 336 as *hegemon*. This was demonstrated particularly by the poor case which the speaker of the pseudo-Demosthenic speech, *On the Articles of Agreement with Alexander*, put forward late in 331. The omissions are highly significant. There was no raising of points which modern scholars might raise: the right of Macedonia to hegemony, the position of Alexander as *hegemon*, the destruction of Thebes, the disbanding and the recall of the Greek fleet, the non-admission of 'liberated' Greek states on some islands and in Asia to the Common Peace, and Alexander's treatment of pro-Persian Greeks, e.g. from Chios. We may conclude that in all these matters Alexander had not acted *ultra vires*. The charges actually made are trivial. They were based on the more or less tacit assumption that the *hegemon* was bound to observe the rules and regulations imposed on the member states by the Charter of the Common Peace. But the assumption was false; for the *hegemon* clearly had emergency powers. Thus just as he approved a change of government from oligarchy to democracy at Ambracia (D.S. 17. 3. 3), so he or his deputy approved or facilitated changes of government at Messene and Pellene, which the speaker represented, not necessarily with truth, as becoming close oligarchies or tyrannies ([Dem.] 17. 4 and 10).[11] As events were quickly to prove, these changes of government were in the interest of the Common Peace; for they were among the factors which kept Messene and Pellene loyal during the war of Agis.

As allies of Macedonia in the joint war against Persia, the members of the Common Peace had no grounds for complaint. Alexander was personally correct in his treatment of 'the Greeks'. Spoils were dedicated in the names of 'Alexander and the Greeks'; captured works of art were restored to their Greek owners; and large bounties were given to the allies at the end of their service in 330 (Arr. 1. 16. 7; 3. 16. 7–8 and 19.5). The war of revenge for the profanation of the Greek temples by Xerxes which 'the Greeks' had declared (D.S. 16. 89. 2) was brought to a dramatic conclusion by the burning of the Persian palace at Persepolis.

The dealings of Alexander with the Greek states did not begin or end with the members of the Common Peace. They began with the states of the Amphictyonic League. A list of the 'temple-building' delegates in 327 is remarkable for the large number of states which were represented; this surely indicates a high degree of recon-ciliation and co-operation. Argos had nine delegates out of forty-five. She may have taken a lead as the rival of Sparta and as the homeland of Alexander's family. Alexander's contacts with Greek states went far beyond those of the Common Peace. He was in treaty with probably all Greek states east of the Ionian and Sicilian Seas. While Alexander dealt with the Council of the Common Peace on all matters which fell within its competence, he did not use it as a channel of communication with Greek states in general. In his attempts to check the excesses of political faction and in his proposal that the Greek states should each recall and reinstate its own exiles, he preferred rightly to address the Greek states directly. For he was concerned with a problem which was not particular to the members of the Common Peace and did not fall within the sphere of competence of the Council of the Common Peace.

The announcement (*diagramma*) of Alexander's request that Greek states should recall all their exiles and restore to their exiled owners any confiscated territory, except for men under a curse and those exiled from Thebes, was made first at Susa to the army and later at Olympia to an audience at the Olympic festival which included more than 20,000 exiles. Alexander chose these occasions because he was addressing his request not to the members of the Common Peace alone, as Tarn and others have supposed, but to all states within his sphere of influence.[12] The announcement was not an 'order', as hostile critics suggested (e.g. Hyp. *Dem.* 18, *epitagmata*) but the starting-point for a dialogue, during which envoys were sent to Alexander, for instance at Babylon (D.S. 17. 113. 3).

Who would benefit from this restoration of exiles? It has sometimes been suggested that the return of the exiles would strengthen the pro-Macedonian parties in the states.[13] But a moment's reflection shows that this was not so. For those who had been exiled since the rise of Macedonia to power were not the supporters, but the enemies, of Macedonia. For example, the men in exile from Tegea had supported Sparta against Alexander. Yet, as we know from an inscription (*GHI* 202, 57–66), special steps were taken by Alexander to protect them from any victimization by loyal citizens of Tegea on their return; for his *diagramma* laid down strict principles which attest his humane concern for exiles (ibid. 2–3, 10–11, etc.). How greatly the modern world would benefit from such a measure! The reaction of the Greek world at the time may be summed up in the words of D.S. 18. 8. 6 (tr. R. M. Geer): 'people in general welcomed the restoration of exiles as a good thing', i.e. 'for a good purpose' (ὡς ἐπ' ἀγαθῷ γινομένην; cf. LSJ[9] s.v. ἐπί B III 2).

The restoration of confiscated territory to a dispossessed population (such as the Palestinian Arabs today) was likely to be resisted by the current owners. In particular Athens had expelled the population of Samos in 365 and seized the territory for her own citizens; and the Aetolians had acted similarly at Oeniadae in Acarnania. It would be absurd to suppose that the gratitude of the dispossessed would weigh more than the enmity of Athens and the Aetolian League in terms of power politics. That Alexander was prepared to incur that enmity is a measure of his sincerity and of his determination to establish more settled conditions in the Greek world of city-states. We do not hear of any attempt by Alexander to restore the survivors of Olynthus and Galepsus within the Macedonian kingdom to their original territories.[14] But it is probable that they had already been settled in new towns founded by Philip and Alexander.

Although Athens resented Alexander's plan, she behaved correctly in the matter of Harpalus. As one of Alexander's treasurers, this Macedonian officer had relieved a famine at Athens by sending shipments of grain, and for this he had been made an Athenian citizen. During Alexander's absence in India Harpalus embezzled funds and in the summer of 324 he fled with 6,000 mercenaries, thirty ships, and 5,000 talents to Sunium in Attica. The Assembly refused, on the recommendation of Demosthenes, to grant him asylum, and he moved on with his forces to Taenarum in the Peloponnese. From there he returned with the money but in a single ship, hoping to buy support. Once again he was disappointed. Indeed the Athenians arrested him, as the Macedonians had requested. However, he escaped and fled to Crete, where he met his death. These events at Athens took place between the announcement at Susa and the announcement at Olympia.[15]

In this year, 324, Alexander addressed two further requests to the Greek states in general. First, he asked that they should establish cults in honour of his dead friend Hephaestion as 'hero'. Such heroization of a dead man had been granted voluntarily in the past, for instance to Brasidas and Timoleon. Alexander's request was accepted.

Some cults were established in 323. Second, he asked that he himself should be granted 'divine honours'. Precedents were rare; but one was apposite for the would-be liberator of Samos, for his predecessor in that role, Lysander, had been worshipped at Samos *c.* 404. Moreover, some Greek cities in Asia in 334/3 and Thasos and Rhodes later had on their own initiative granted Alexander divine honours and established a cult with its own shrine, sacrifices, and games. But it was unique that the request was made by the would-be recipient. What were Alexander's motives? His chief motive was the desire for glory: to be recognized by the Greeks as a benefactor of exceptional degree.[16] To this may be added a political motive. A request from so powerful a person was likely to be accepted by many as a veiled order, and the general acceptance of him as a god would enhance his authority in the Greek world. This request, then, may be seen as a first, perhaps tentative step on the road towards establishing a ruler cult in the Greek world.

As Alexander had no doubt anticipated, the Greek states granted him 'divine honours', sometimes with sarcasm (e.g. Demosthenes at Athens remarking 'Let him be a son of Zeus . . . or Poseidon, for all I care') and sometimes no doubt with real gratitude. In 323 worship of him was inaugurated with shrines, altars, and statues (e.g. at Athens, Hyp. 1. 31, 6. 21), and games were held in his honour (by the Ionians, Str. 644).[17] Envoys came 'from Greece' to greet Alexander as a god. They were crowned and they crowned Alexander with golden crowns, as 'sacred envoys come to honour a god' (Arr. 7. 23. 2).[18] That was in Babylon shortly before his death. Had he lived to fulfil his plans, he would have built three great temples in Delos, Dodona, and Delphi and three more in Macedonia, all in honour of the leading gods whom Greeks and Macedonians shared. For whether he himself was recognized as a god or not, his duty to the Greek gods was his first priority, as he showed in his hearing of embassies at Babylon (D.S. 17. 113. 4). They repaid him in true Greek fashion: he died young.

Notes

1 The clear difference is obfuscated by E. Badian's assumption in 'Alexander the Great and the Greeks in Asia' in *Ancient Society and Institutions* (Oxford, 1966) 50 that Arrian's distinction is 'probably mere inaccuracy', or Bosworth's idea that the omission of 'and the Greeks' is a 'stylistic variation' (*C* 181). It is then easy for them to argue that A. broke his obligations to the Common Peace by using different methods of trial for persons from Chios and persons from Mytilene, for instance, as in Badian 53. Brunt, L. 124 n. 2, thinks Arrian mistaken. There is a better understanding of these passages in V. Ehrenberg, *Alexander and the Greeks* (Oxford, 1938) 20 ff., against whom Tarn's arguments were weak in 2. 201. n. 6. We do not know why some islanders joined the Common Peace and others did not, but it was probably due to preference on both sides and to opportunity when the Persian fleet was controlling most of the Aegean Sea. The verb ἐπανάγεσθαι in line 14 of *GHI* 192 is best explained like ἐπαναφέρεσθαι πρὸς ᾽Αλέξανδρον in line 7 as meaning 'be referred to A.', who was on the way to, or already in, Egypt.

2 This dating by Tod is preferable to that proposed by Heisserer 79–95, namely 334. Heisserer's view that Memnon took Chios in 335 (his pp. 83 and 93) overlooks the fact that Memnon campaigned only on land (D.S. 17. 7. 3 and 8–10); and if a Macedonian garrison was placed there in 334 and Chios was captured despite it in 333, as Heisserer supposes, Arrian would surely have mentioned that garrison, since he mentioned the garrison of A. at Mytilene (2. 1. 4). On my view Memnon 'won it over' (D.S. 17. 29. 2) through treachery from within (2. 1. 1) in 333. Thus from A.'s point of view Chios was then guilty of 'revolt' (*apostasis* 3. 2. 5) from the Common Peace.

3 Well discussed by Heisserer 96–116.

4 The order and the dating of events are disputed. Tod (*GHI* 191) has the above order, except that he puts the installation of the second set of tyrants early in A.'s reign (despite [Dem.] 17. 7, unless he means at the very start). Griffith in Volume II. 720 f. has the same order and dating down to the installation of the second set. Heisserer 27–78 carries the first down to 334, and introduces the second set in 333 (despite [D.] 17. 7). Bosworth 179 f. has tyrants continuously

until they meet with trouble in 332; this requires them to change political horses rapidly with impunity, which seems very unlikely.

5   In this controversial matter Ehrenberg, *Alexander and the Greeks* makes a better case than E. Badian in *Ancient Society and Institutions* (Oxford, 1966) 37 f.

6   As a change from enslavement to autonomy; see *SIG* 278. 3, Priene marking the new era with the words αὐτονόμων ἐόντων Πριηνέων.

7   The sequence of events is clearly given in Aeschin. 3. 165 and Dinarch. 1. 34, and there is no reason to rearrange them, as Tarn did in *CAH* 6. 445. For Athens' hostility to Sparta in the war see *IG* ii². 399 with *BSA* 79 (1984) 229 ff.

8   For the mercenaries see Dinarch. 1. 34; they are omitted by D.S. 17. 62. 7–8. The meaning of the latter passage is uncertain. If Diodorus' phrase 'most of the Peloponnesians' does not include the Lacedaemonians, then we may add Sparta's forces *pandemei*. This makes a total of almost 40,000. Berve 2. 9, much followed by others, is mistaken in putting Agis' forces at 22,000 in all; for he included the 10,000 mercenaries in the figure of 20,000 soldiers expressly recruited by 'most of the Peloponnesians' in D.S. 17. 62. 7. Thus the view of R. Lane Fox, *Alexander the Great* (London, 1973) 252, that the odds were 'two to one' in numerical strength in favour of Antipater, seems to be incorrect. For the size of Antipater's army we may compare that of Epaminondas, namely 40,000 hoplites, when he invaded the Peloponnese.

9   P *Ages* 15. 4 'myomachia', being contrasted with A.'s own epic fight against Darius, just as the 'batrachomyomachia' was contrasted with the Homeric epic.

10 The chronology of the war is much disputed, because Diodorus and Curtius are at variance. The *terminus post quem* is given by the arrival of Macedonian reinforcements between Babylon and Susa in November/December 331, they having set out before trouble broke out, and the *terminus ante quem* by the imminent journey of the Spartan envoys when Aeschines made his remark in 3. 133 in August 330. Diodorus is probably right in putting the final decision of Sparta after the news of Persia's defeat at Gaugamela (17. 62. 1). For various views see E. Badian, 'Agis III', *Hermes* 95 (1967) 190 f.; E. N. Borza, 'The end of Agis' revolt', *CP* 66 (1971) 230 f.; G. L. Cawkwell, 'The crowning of Demosthenes', *CQ* 19 (1969) 171 f.; Brunt, L 1. 480 ff.; G. Wirth, 'Alexander zwischen Gaugamela und Persepolis', *Historia* 20 (1971) 617 f. For the final settlement see E. I. McQueen in *Historia* 27 (1978) 53–8.

11 As regards the tyrants at Eresus in [Dem.] 17. 7 see p. 82.

12 A. Heuss, 'Antigonos Monophthalmos u. d. griech. Städte', *Hermes* 73 (1938) 135, accepts as genuine A.'s letter which was read out at Olympia (D.S. 18. 8. 4). It was addressed to τοῖς ἐκ τῶν Ἑλληνίδων πόλεων φυγάσι, i.e. to the exiles from the Greek states in general and not merely to those which participated in the Common Peace. That phrase may be genuine; but I do not think that A. would have committed himself and Antipater to the use of compulsion in advance (as the last sentence of the letter does). J. 13. 5. 2 had the exiles from all Greek states in mind: 'omnium civitatum exsules'.

13 As alleged in D. 18. 8. 2.

14 This point was hinted at by Demosthenes in speaking at Olympia (P *Demosth* 9. 1).

15 The chronology is in doubt. See D.S. 17. 108. 6–8; C. 10. 2. 2–4; P *Demosth* 25; and the discussion by E. Badian, 'Harpalus', *JHS* 81 (1961) 41 ff.

16 His desire to see Olympias deified after death (C. 9. 6. 26; 10. 5. 30) was to give her glory, not political power. Habicht 35 and C. F. Edson in *CP* 53 (1958) 64 stress A.'s desire for glory in this connection.

17 The second passage in Hyperides refers probably, but not necessarily, to Athens (see Habicht, *Studien* 28 f. and 246 f.) The people of Ephesus wrote of A. as 'a god' (Str. 641). A cult of A. as a god, son of Ammon, was probably established at Megalopolis in 323 before A.'s death (Paus. 8. 32. 1); see E. Fredricksmeyer, 'Alexander's deification', *AJAH* 4 (1979) 1 f. The evidence is well assembled by Berve 1. 96 ff. Lucian, *DMort* 391, said that some added A. in his life to the twelve gods, built him temples, and made sacrifice to him.

18 See Fredricksmeyer, op. cit. 3–5. The expression 'from Greece' takes its meaning from the context, namely Greece in general as A. was at Babylon (Arr. 7. 23. 2) rather than the Greek mainland in particular as Habicht *Studien* 22 argues ('die festländische Städte'). But Greece in general here did not include Asia Minor, parts of which were mentioned in Arr. 7. 23. 1.

References

A. = Alexander the Great.

Berve = H. Berve, *Das Alexanderreich auf prosopographischer Grundlage* (Munich: 1926).

Bosworth = A.B. Bosworth, *A Historical Commentary on Arrian's History of Alexander* (Oxford: 1980–).

Brunt, L. = P.A. Brunt, *Arrian, History of Alexander*, Loeb Classical Library 1 (Cambridge, MA and London: 1976).

Griffith = N.G.L. Hammond and G.T. Griffith, *A History of Macedonia* 2 (Oxford: 1979).

Habicht, *Studien* = C. Habicht, *Studien zur Geschichte Athens in hellenistischer Zeit* (Göttingen: 1982).

Heisserer = A.J. Heisserer, *Alexander the Great and the Greeks* (Norman, OK: 1980).

ALEXANDER AND THE GREEKS: THE CORINTHIAN LEAGUE

Elisabetta Poddighe

During Alexander's reign relations between the Greeks and the Macedonian kingdom were regulated by the charter of the 'Corinthian League.' This modern expression refers to the political and military pact between Philip II and the Greeks ratified at Corinth after the defeat of the allied Greeks at Chaeroneia, and then renewed by Alexander in 336. The pact set the seal on a design for establishing Macedonian hegemony that would insure control over Greece and unite it in a war against Persia. It achieved its purpose because Alexander, in his relations with the Greeks, constantly sought to emphasize the legitimacy of his leadership: on the basis of traditional Greek hegemonic practice, Alexander regulated his political activity in Greece and used key themes of Greek propaganda as a catalyst against his opponents, and by turning their opposition to tyranny and their concern for freedom to his own advantage.

Alexander's accession to leadership of the Corinthian League

After Philip's assassination at Aegae in 336, Alexander inherited, together with the Macedonian kingdom, his father's Panhellenic project to lead the Greeks in the conquest of Persia. Part of this legacy was the Corinthian League, founded for this purpose by Philip. This was a league of autonomous Greek states (excluding Sparta) that in early 337 proclaimed peace and autonomy for the Greeks who swore not to attack the kingdom of Macedonia. The peace required recognition of the conditions established in the postwar period, that is, the complete political and/or territorial reorganization of the cities that had challenged Macedonia for hegemony in Greece (Athens, Sparta, and Thebes), now policed by garrisons stationed in Corinth, Ambracia, Thebes, and Chalcis.[1] A common council (*koinon synedrion*) of the Greeks was established at Corinth, hence the name 'Corinthian League.' Voting rights were assigned to the member states on a proportional basis; these also conceded supreme command (*hegemonia*) to Philip (and to his descendants) in the event of war.[2] It had been agreed in advance that action must be taken against Persia, the common enemy, and predictably perhaps, the delegates consented to the proclamation of a war of revenge for the outrages committed against the Greeks in the Great Persian Wars of the fifth century, more than 150 years before (D.S. 16.89.2; Plb. 3.6.13).[3] This consent (*eunoia*), which confirmed the 'Greekness' of the war of revenge, legitimized the leadership role of the Macedonian kingdom, though Philip did not live to exploit it. Yet there can be no doubt that Philip's most important legacy, though always a fragile one, was Greek adherence to the Panhellenic project.

The lawful inheritance

In the meeting with the Greek delegations after Philip's death, Alexander demanded the consent of the Greeks as his paternal inheritance (D.S. 17.2.2), clearly *the* consent won by his father when he promised to lead the Greeks in a war against Persia. Later, when Alexander moved south into Greece, he demanded once again hegemony over Greece as part of his father's legacy (D.S. 17.4.1), and once again, as we shall see, he stressed the Panhellenic character of this undertaking. Both demands underlined a key concept: the Macedonian kingdom was the legitimate leader of the Greeks against the barbarians and Alexander, as Philip's heir in all respects, was determined to confirm the legitimacy of his leadership and status.[4]

Although the claim to Philip's position as leader of the Greeks was juridically founded, many Greeks did not intend to acknowledge it. The Athenians and the Thebans proclaimed that 'they did not want to concede hegemony over the Greeks to the Macedonians' (D.S. 17.3.2, 4). Athenian negotiations with the Persian king Darius III demonstrated that many Athenians saw the Macedonian king as a more dangerous and 'common' enemy than the Persian, a warning already delivered by Demosthenes ([Dem.] 10.33–4; D.S. 17.4.8). Peace appeared especially precarious in the places where, after the surrender to Philip, compliant regimes and military garrisons had been installed. It was these interventions in the cause of 'pacification' that surely precipitated the first revolt against Alexander (336): the Aetolians debated recalling the exiles proscribed by Philip; the Ambracians drove out the Macedonian garrison and set up a democratic regime; the Thebans decreed the removal of their garrison; and, probably at this stage, the Philiades were deposed at Messene (D.S. 17.3.3–5; [Dem.] 17.4).

Alexander's determination to follow Philip's path of mediation in the pursuit of supreme leadership in Greece is certainly indicated by his policy of intervening in the Greek world only on a firm legitimate basis. Diodorus strongly emphasized this when he pointed out how the Greeks had legitimized Philip's hegemonic aspirations, not only on the basis of Macedonian military superiority demonstrated at Chaeroneia (16.89.1), but also as a result of the discussions and meetings 'in the cities' that convinced the Greeks to endorse the Persian campaign (16.89.2–3). The contents of those discussions are unknown, but it is certain that the language used was precisely the Panhellenic rhetoric that claimed the Greek (and Macedonian) right to territorial expansion and to the civilizing of the non-Hellenic peoples (cf. Isoc. 5.16.111–16).[5] The Greeks could tolerate – sometimes defend – Macedonian leadership only in terms of 'antibarbarian' rhetoric (Aeschin. 3.132; Plu. *Phoc.* 17.7). Therefore, it was a foregone conclusion that Alexander would request a *formal* reconfirmation of his supreme command and undertake *formal* negotiations with the Greeks (D.S. 17.4.1–9) by reiterating the Panhellenic grounds for the anti-Persian crusade (Ael. VH 13.11).

The Panhellenic crusade and acknowledgment of hegemony over Greece

Negotiations with the Greeks insured, first of all, that the Thessalian and Delphic Amphictyonies (*koina*) recognized Alexander's hegemony (D.S. 17.4.1–2). According to the sources, Alexander persuaded the Thessalian League to grant him the double title of *hegemon* and *archon*. This he claimed by appealing to the common descent (*syggeneia*) of the Argeads and of the Aleuads, the ruling dynasty of Larissa, from Heracles and Achilles whose exploits prefigured the Asian campaign (D.S. 17.4.1; Just. 11.3.1–2).[6] It would seem that the Aleuad connection was also the basis for the Amphictyonic council's concession of hegemony over Greece to Alexander (D.S. 17.4.2). Indeed, a reevaluation of the Aleuads was linked to exploiting the myth of the Aeacidae[7] whose cult was an essential ingredient in Delphic propaganda. Alexander's visit to the sanctuary at Delphi, possibly confirmed by an inscription (*SIG*[3] 1. 251), is perfectly coherent with this diplomatic policy (Plu. *Alex.* 14.6).[8] Presumably the Panhellenic grounds for the war against Persia were also confirmed in negotiations with the Amphictyonies which, according to the *Alexander Romance*, were incited to make war against the 'barbarians' (Ps. Call. 1.25.1). In any case, their acknowledgment of the hegemony confronted the Corinthian *synedrion* with a *fait accompli* by emphasizing the principle of dynastic hegemony ratified at Delphi in 346 (D.S. 16.60.4–5) and at Corinth in 337, thereby legitimizing Macedonia's hegemonic role.[9] It is significant that the Panhellenic sanctuaries were delegated, later, to inform the allied Greek cities of federal decisions and to host the federal assemblies (see below).[10] This procedure would later be repeated in the League of 302 promoted by Antigonus I (Monophthalmus) and Demetrius, which attributed a kind of 'foundation act' to an amphyctictyonic *pse-phisma* (Lefèvre 1998: 97). This ordered too that, in peacetime, the federal assemblies were to be held during the sacred games (Moretti 1967, no. 44, ll. 65ff.).[11]

The glorification of cultural and religious themes most likely to promote Greek participation in the campaign was also a determining factor in negotiations with the states that refused to acknowledge Macedonian hegemony (D.S. 17.4.3–6). Once again, the criteria were the same as those adopted by Philip after Chaeronea. In Boeotia, Alexander ruled with an iron hand (D.S. 17.4.4; Just. 11.2.9), continuing Philip's policy which had imposed an oligarchic junta and a Macedonian garrison on this traditional hotbed of Persian sympathizers. At the same time, he favored the other Boeotian cities, especially Plataea, because its forefathers had provided the field of battle where the Persians were defeated in 479.[12] Now on the eve of the Panhellenic crusade, Plataea welcomed home its exiles. This was a decisive step for Macedonian propaganda which would soon portray Alexander as the champion of the Plataean cause (see below).

At Athens, which had hurriedly sent ambassadors to Boeotia to request pardon for not having conceded hegemony immediately,[13] favorable conditions for peace and the alliance sealed with Philip were confirmed (D.S. 16.87.3; Plu. *Phoc.* 16.5).[14] Ratification came under Athena's protection, to which anti-Persian propaganda reserved a determining role (Mari 2002: 260ff.). Macedonian officers 'in charge of the common defense' later set up an inscription in Athena's sanctuary at Pydna recording Athenian contributions to Alexander's army; a copy of this was, in turn, displayed on the Athenian acropolis (*IG* II² 329, ll. 12ff.).[15]

It must be noted that the agreements were reached without threat of sanctions. Thessaly's resolution to retaliate militarily against Athens (Aeschin. 3.161) would seem to belong to another context,[16] and it is highly improbable that Alexander, as *hegemon* of the League, would assume responsibility for a measure such as this. As long as the *synedrion* had not legitimized his role, Alexander was determined not to punish violations of the peace.

From Corinth 337 to Corinth 336:
the letter and the spirit of the agreements with Alexander

At Corinth the Greeks definitively recognized Alexander's legitimacy. The same delegates who had met in 337 confirmed Alexander's functions as *hegemon* and *strategos autokrator* (D.S. 17.4.9; Arr. 1.1.1–3; Plu. Alex. 14.1; Just. 11.2.5);[17] it seems that they also met in the same place, the city or the sanctuary of Isthmia,[18] symbolic sites associated with the first anti-Persian Greek federation of 480 (Hdt. 7.145). The roll of those taking the oath must also have included the cities and states of continental Greece (except

Sparta) together with some of the Aegean and Ionian islands (Rhodes–Osborne, no. 76b, 11. 2ff.).

Several clauses of the treaty (synthekai) are preserved in the Demosthenic oration *On the Treaty with Alexander,* possibly delivered by Hypereides.[19] There is general agreement that the treaty completely renewed the agreements with Philip (Buckler 2003: 516). The allies swore to guarantee the peace (eirene/koine eirene),[20] that is, the autonomy and freedom of the Greeks ([Dem.] 17.8), based on provisions tested in recent peace and alliance treaties such as the Peace of Antalcidas (387/6), the charter of the Second Athenian League (377), and the Athenian *koine eirene* of 371. The parameters of autonomy were defined with formulas preserved on inscriptions and in fourth-century historical accounts; on the negative side these stated what was forbidden: namely, not to attack states that had sworn to the peace and not to overthrow existing regimes (Rhodes–Osborne, no. 76, ll. 8–14; [Dem.] 17.10.14).[21] Other stipulations defined the right to political and territorial sovereignty[22] and obliged the Greeks to maintain the social status quo; illegal executions and banishment were prohibited as were the confiscation and redistribution of land, the remission of debts, the freeing of slaves, and the restoration of exiles to their home cities ([Dem.] 17.10, 15–16). Even in this case, however, the ban on fomenting revolution (neoterismos) was limited to improving a clause in the charter of the Second Athenian League that urged the allies 'to live at peace' (Rhodes–Osborne, no. 22, ll. 10–11). The result was that the Greeks guaranteed preservation of the status quo on the basis of principles elaborated during their long experience with hegemony and that the rights of the dominant state were safeguarded precisely on the basis of these formal guarantees.

Even the administrative machinery delegated to safeguard the regulations and their activation were regulated by criteria that gave only formal guarantees to the allies. The common council assigned the seats and votes to the delegates according to objective factors such as population and military strength;[23] it appears that councilors could not be prosecuted in their home states for their decisions (cf. Moretti 1967: no. 44, ll. 75ff.). The council's wide authority encompassed arbitration,[24] protection of the social order, and ratification of war but, in the crucial areas, it was firmly controlled by the Macedonian state. In maintaining social order, it was the Macedonian military, 'the board in charge of common defense,' that assisted the *synedrion* ([Dem.] 17.15; Bosworth 1992a: 148) and it was the role of the *hegemon* to propose to the council that it declare war against transgressors of the agreements.

In this case Greek diplomatic tradition also provided the principles that were to be followed. Armed intervention was regulated by a guarantee (or sanction) clause that had long been tested in fifth- and fourth-century treaties between the Greek states. In the Peace of Athens of 371 such a clause had demonstrated its potential, one capable of guaranteeing an alliance between signatories without ratification of a distinct treaty of symmachia (Alonso 2003b: 355ff.).[25] That the clause was to be activated only at the victim's request (Rhodes–Osborne, no. 76, ll. 18–19, Alonso 1997: 186) broadened its legitimate basis. The report of a clear abuse was sufficient for declaring war. The twofold role of the hegemon as advocate of peace (Arr. 2.14.6) and leader of the alliance, and the fact that peace was not guaranteed by the stamp of an external authority,[26] insured that the hegemon determined when sanctions would be declared.

Philip had activated the machinery for sanctions in 337: he had proposed that the synedrion declare war against the Persians in revenge for the sacrileges against the Greek temples in 480 (D.S. 16.89.2; Plb. 3.6.13), and declared afterward that he also wanted to liberate the Greeks in Asia (D.S. 16.91.2). Alexander repeated this procedure (Just. 11.5.6; D.S. 17.24.1). The Greeks and Macedonians could easily portray themselves as the victims of these earlier offenses that required punishment and thus the war could be interpreted as one of just retribution. In his letter to Darius III after Issus, Alexander referred to the offenses committed in 480 and denounced those of more recent date, namely, the plot against Philip and, after his death, the attempt to break up the peace among the Greeks (Arr. 2.14.4–6; Curt. 4.1.10–14).27 The transgression of law and decency (*paranomia*) by the Persians was evident in both cases (D.S. 16.89.2; Plb. 3.6.13): the violation of the laws of war regarding respect for sanctuaries (Ilari 1980: 258ff.) and the infringement of the norms regulating relations between states (Ryder 1965: 147). Even the Greek judgment that Greek autonomy in Asia entailed freedom for Greeks everywhere provided a legitimate basis for action against the Persians (Musti 2000: 176). There is no reason, however, to believe that the non-allied Greeks of Asia made a formal request for help;[28] rather it was the allies of Corinthian League who were the injured party (*adikoumenoi*).

Once war was declared, the prerogatives of the *hegemon* were renewed and everything was readied for the campaign. With an army of about 40,000 men Alexander renewed the expedition that Philip had earlier sent to Asia (D.S. 16.91.2). Less than a quarter of the army came from cities belonging to the League.[29] In this context, the *hegemon* had a legitimate basis for dealing with (predictable) Greek resistance. The *synedrion*'s resolution to punish any Greek who fought on the Persian side (Arr. 1.16.6, 3.23.8), a resolution inspired by the 'oath of Plataea' sworn at Corinth in 480,[30] would permit Alexander not only to punish the numerous[31] mercenaries recruited by Darius III, but all Persian sympathizers.

Modern scholars have often seen in Alexander's approach to the Persian sympathizers,[32] and in general his relations with the Greeks, evidence of an early and growing indifference to the League's charter.[33] Analysis of actual cases, however, demonstrates that the League was in fact what it claimed to be: an instrument for exercising control over the allies in the hands of the *hegemon* who used it according to his prerogatives throughout his entire reign.

Alexander and the Greeks of the Corinthian League in the context of the Persian War

The ideological profile of the campaign against the Persians and the network of relations with the allies justified the hegemonic role of the Macedonian king. As enforcer of the *eunoia* of the Greeks, Alexander's duty was to assert the primacy of civilization over barbarism; once elected *hegemon*, he was able to exercise his prerogatives in order to achieve his purpose.

On the other hand, many Greeks felt that Macedonian hegemony was an attack on the freedom of the *poleis*.[34] Although in hostile cities such as Athens reaction to these conditions took different forms, ranging from pragmatic acceptance of the new political reality (Aeschin. 2.164–5; Plu. *Phoc.* 16.7)[35] to pursuit of their own claims to hegemony (Dem. 18.60–72), the resolve to oppose the Macedonian tyrant usually prevailed. Opponents' demands followed a constant pattern that emphasized those elements of the treaty guaranteeing the freedom and autonomy of the allies, while obscuring the campaign, the alliance, and the powers ascribed to its leader. But it was precisely the "emergency powers"[36] decreed by the *synedrion* for conquering the Persian empire that were to be used against rebellious Greeks who, as Persian sympathizers, were the enemies of peace.

Panhellenism and the exercise of hegemony against Theban resistance

The war against Thebes is a striking example of resistance by the more hostile Greek allies (Thebes and Athens) to Macedonian leadership and the determination of the *hegemon* to oppose it on legal grounds. In the case of Thebes, sanctions had to demonstrate that defection from the accords would not be tolerated (D.S. 17.9.4; Plu. *Alex.* 11.17); at the same time it also had to emphasize that intervention was legitimate. Therefore, rebels had to be punished on the basis of League accords and wartime propaganda.

Late in the summer of 335, the exiles proscribed by Philip after Chaeroneia returned. After attacking and isolating the Macedonian garrison on the Cadmea, the Thebans installed a democratic regime, overthrowing the 300-member *politeuma* that had been set up two years before.[37] The rebels were convinced that Alexander had died in battle against the Illyrians. When this news turned out to be false, the majority of the Thebans resolved to hold fast to their original intentions.[38] The rebellion, which violated several clauses of the League charter, rapidly spread to the rest of Greece: the Arcadians revived their league and sent an army to the Isthmus; the Eleans exiled the pro-Macedonian party; the Athenians ordered the deployment of their forces. The rebellious Thebans invited the Greeks to return to the peace terms agreed in 387/6 with Persia which was financing the rebellion.

As *hegemon* Alexander intervened to punish the defection and collaboration with the Persians.[39] The legitimacy of the intervention took on a distinctive character as Greek forces joined Alexander's army during its march to Boeotia from Illyria where news of the rebellion had reached him (Arr. 1.7.5–7).[40] These forces included Phocians and Thessalians, but especially Orchomenians, Thespians, and Plataeans, all Boeotians and all enemies of Thebes. As the only Boeotians who had opposed the 'barbarian' during the Persians wars (Hdt. 7.132.1) they guaranteed legitimacy to federal sanctions. The support of these 'champions' of Greek liberty[41] compensated for the massive abstention of other allies in the war, the legality of which, in this and other cases, was no less serious an issue.[42] The case of the Arcadians demonstrates this: declaring themselves ready to support the Theban revolt, they were persuaded to accept the hegemon's decision by not being required to furnish troops (Din. 1.18–20).43

The exemplary purpose of sanctions required an exemplary use of the *hegemon*'s prerogatives and, in fact, this was guaranteed. The herald's proclamation that traditionally announced an ultimatum invited the Thebans to accept the offer of peace; this also emphasized the 'constitutionality' of the punitive war. Only after the Theban counter-proclamation, which invited violation of the accords, did punitive war (*timoria*) against the rebels begin.[44]

The *hegemon* also exercised his prerogatives after the battle which ended rapidly with the foreseeable defeat of the Thebans (Bosworth 1988a: 32ff.). On the basis of the rule that allowed the federal authority to select the *synedrion*'s meeting place, the allied council did not gather at Corinth as usual, but probably in Alexander's camp.[45] Here, the fate of the defeated, usually reserved to the *hegemon* (Alonso 2003a: 353), was delegated to the allies (Arr. 1.9.9); this was certainly intended to emphasize that Alexander would not be responsible for the anticipated vengeful decisions of Thebes' neighbors, and to use the *synedrion* against Persian sympathizers. Once military action had punished the defection, the campaign's propaganda apparatus conditioned debate among the allies about the final sentence. Thebes' earlier and more recent Persian sympathies, along with abuses committed against the Boeotian cities and Athens, placed the sentence firmly within a Panhellenic context. The decision to destroy Thebes, to sell the prisoners into slavery, and to banish the exiles from everywhere in Greece was just retaliation for the damage done by the Thebans to Plataea in 374/3 and Orchomenus in 364. The *synedrion*'s decision to link the destruction of Thebes with the reconstruction of Plataea, along with Alexander's pledge to carry this out, was an appropriate recognition of the Panhellenic status of the city that, in 479, had sacrificed its territory in the name of freedom.[46] The execution of a cruel sentence seemed legitimate from a Panhellenic point of view (Aeschin. 3.133), and the 'just' condemnation of Thebes echoes later in the *Alexander Romance* where a personified Mt. Cithaeron exults at the city's destruction (Ps. Call. 1.46.1; Gargiulo 2004: 109ff).

The Athenians, instigators of the revolt and Persian accomplices as well, paid a less drastic price for their crimes. Alexander directed the negotiations in person. The demand that those anti-Macedonian politicians most heavily involved in the revolt be turned over to the *synedrion* was reformulated in bilateral negotiations with Demades and Phocion (Arr. 1.10.3–6; Plu. *Phoc.* 9.10–17). Condemnation was reserved for those generals who had most compromised themselves with the Persians and who had fled Greece to fight on the side of Darius III.[47] The need to move quickly into Asia (Arr. 1.10.6) and to be moderate in his treatment of Athens convinced Alexander that he had to assume the role of final judge in deciding the fate of Persian sympathizers. This operating principle was used for the first time now and would be repeated at Chios and Sparta (see below).

Alexander's exercise of absolute sovereignty after his departure for Asia

Even after Alexander's arrival in Asia in spring 334, intervention among the allied cities appeared to be consistent with the League's mission. The visit to the tombs of the Greek heroes, Protesilaus, Ajax, and Achilles, leaders of the mythical first campaign in Asia, and sacrifices at the sanctuary of Athena Ilias, symbolically emphasized the significance of Alexander's presence in Asia and his campaign.[48] It was soon clear that Alexander was in a position to lead the alliance in pursuit of its objectives, not only in defeating the Persian army, but also by punishing those Greek mercenaries who fought for the Persians. He also exerted pressure on allied cities that impeded the war's success. In each case the appeal to the League's mission was formal in nature.

After the first victory over the Persians at the Granicus in summer 334, the 'spoils of war captured from the barbarians in Asia' were offered to Athena in the name of the League (Arr. 1.16.7; Plu. *Alex.* 16.17–18); captured Greek mercenaries were sentenced to hard labor in Macedonia for having fought 'against Greece' (Arr. 1.16.6, 1.29.5–6). Soon after, the imposition of pro-Macedonian regimes in the allied cities of the Peloponnesus and the Aegean islands followed. These, the anonymous Athenian orator tells, were based on ideological principles governing the League's actions: in Greece the principles of status quo and *homonoia* and, in Asia, the battle against despotism prevailed

([Dem.] 17.4, 7, 10). The anonymous orator went on to condemn constitutional upheavals that violated the accords – 'as if Alexander's absolute sovereignty extended over perjury also' (12) – and also pointed out that they did not even have a consistent ideological basis: on the one hand (at Messene) the installation of tyrants was legitimate because they were in power 'before' the accords (7); on the other hand (at Lesbos) the tyrants, though in power 'before' the accords, were deposed with the 'laughable' justification that they were detestable.[49] It is evident, however, that in both cases intervention punished defecting allies and helped achieve success in the war.

This intervention must be placed within the context of war against the attempted Persian reconquest of the Aegean;[50] this engaged Macedonian and League forces from the spring of 333 to the spring and summer of 332. The victories of the satraps Pharnabazus and Autophradates fed anti-Macedonian ferment in the island states of Chios and Lesbos, who now allied themselves with the Persians; on the Greek mainland Autophradates' support of Agis of Sparta resulted in certain counter-measures also mentioned by the anonymous Athenian orator ([Dem.] 17.4, 7, 10). Alexander's victory at Issus in the autumn of 333 helped considerably in rallying the temporary support of most mainland Greeks and placated their hostility. At the Isthmian Games in 332, the delegates of the Corinthian League decreed a golden crown for Alexander. In the same year, the king, in his letter to Darius III, officially confirmed the League's resolve to avenge fifth-century Persian offenses against the Greeks (see above), and dealt exemplary punishments to those island communities that had defected.

The hegemon and the allies Chios and Lesbos after their defection from the accords: the imposition of democracies and readmission to the League

The Macedonian reconquest of the islands (Arr. 3.2.3–7) was sanctioned by agreements defined by the sources as *homologiai*.[51] As reported by the anonymous orator, the oligarchs' treachery was punished by removal from office. The oligarchs had probably already been in power when the League was formed in 337. They were accepted at first and then deposed after their defection (Bosworth 1988a: 192; Lott 1996: 38). Removing the oligarchies as an effective anti-Persian measure had been demonstrated during the "liberation" of the Greek cities in Aeolia and Ionia. In the summer of 334, after the victory at the Granicus, Alexander had sent his agent Alcimachus to depose the oligarchies in those cities and install democratic regimes, thereby insuring their autonomy and remission from paying Persian tribute (Arr. 1.18.1–2). Obviously, it would be consistent to extend this measure to those allied cities that had left the alliance and joined the Persians. Experience with the non-allied cities of Ephesus, Priene, Aspendus, and Soli had already shown that institutional democratization did not necessarily guarantee effective freedom or a common juridical status; instead it satisfied in different ways the various military, propaganda, and financial needs of the war.[52] Furthermore, the democratic model was a part of Greek political culture and therefore ideal for reuniting the islands to the anti-Persian league.

Some inscriptions of uncertain date (c.332?) from Chios and Lesbos probably refer to this institutional reorganization.[53] The best evidence of the numerous juridical instruments at the disposal of the *hegemon* are Alexander's so-called first[54] and second letter to the Chians.[55] These contain, respectively, a constitutional plan for Chios and a message to its inhabitants regarding some questions arising from the first measure. The first letter probably referred to an edict (*diagmmma*) issued after the reconquest of the island.[56] The royal decree installed a democratic regime and reintegrated the pro-Macedonian exiles into civic life. The presence of a temporary garrison insured the application of the prescribed measures. A board of scribes was to draw up and revise the laws so that they would be in harmony with the democratic regime and the return of the exiles. These norms, whether amended or written, were to be submitted to Alexander. As king and supreme commander, Alexander would oversee the application of the measures. As supreme commander, he ordered that Chios provide twenty triremes as part of the 'fleet of the Hellenes,' this probably the fleet equipped by Hegelochus in 333.[57] Moreover, in conformity with the decrees already voted by the *synedrions*, he decided the fate of Persian sympathizers: he proclaimed the banishment and arrest of those who had fled the city; he deferred judgment of Persian sympathizers remaining on the island to the *synedrion*; and, finally, he mediated in the dispute between the Chians and Persian sympathizers who had returned home. In line with this role of direct mediation, already used in dealing with Athenian Persian sympathizers, Alexander decided the fate of the Persian sympathizers who had been captured on the island later. Taken to Egypt by Hegelochus (possibly after being judged by the *synedrion*), these were then sent by Alexander to Elephantine (Curt. 4.5.17; Arr. 3.2.3–7).[58]

The anonymous writer reports ([Dem.] 17.7), and the epigraphic record indirectly confirms, that intervention in the cities of Lesbos was equally drastic. A group of documents from Eresus[59] gives an account of the judicial proceedings against the tyrants Agonippus and Eurysilaus, guilty of collaborating with the Persians during the Aegean war, and then tried and exiled in 332. In this case, once again, a *diagramma* probably established the democratic regime that tried and exiled the two tyrants, a democratic regime whose judicial proceedings regarding the exile of Persian sympathizers had to conform to the decisions (*kriseis*) of Alexander and his successors.[60]

The installation of a democratic government and the forced civic reorganization at Mytilene (perhaps an ally since 337)[61] were probably also a result of the desertion in 333. Two decrees from the city[62] record the measures issued by the deliberative democratic organs (the *bolla* and the *damos*) installed by Alexander after Hegelochus' reconquest of Lesbos in 332 (Arr. 2.2.6; Worthington 1990: 207).[63] These measures were probably based on a *diagramma* (Bencivenni 2003: 47) that ordered, in the name of the king, the return of the exiles, the installation of a democratic regime, and civic reconciliation between the pro-Macedonian exiles and the Persian sympathizers. Once again Alexander oversaw the difficult civil reconciliation and the fate of the Persian sympathizers, apparently without the intervention of the *synedrion*.

The 'new' Peloponnesian tyrants and loyalty to the Corinthian accords

The constitutional changes in the Peloponnesian cities, coordinated by Antipater,[64] Alexander's deputy for Greek affairs, and in his absence, by Corrhagus the garrison commander of Acrocorinth, appear justified by the need to insure control over Greece in the years when Agis of Sparta was preparing war against Macedonia (see below). Both acted autonomously, that is, apparently without consulting the *synedrion*, and both appealed to the statutory principles of the status quo and (possibly) of civil concord (*homonoia*).

In about 333, during the first phase of negotiations between Agis and the Persians, the Philiades, tyrants overthrown in the disorders following Philip's death, were brought back to Messene ([Dem.] 17.7).[65] Their restoration to power was formally legitimate, but at this point it functioned especially to reinforce control over Sparta's eastern borders and, therefore, was linked to the measures adopted at Sicyon and Pellene for securing Sparta's northern borders. At Sicyon, an anonymous tyrant, known in Athens as 'the *paidotribes*' ('the professional trainer') was brought back from exile ([Dem.] 17.16; possibly he was Aristratus (Poddighe 2004: 187ff.)). His return had been imposed by an edict (*prostagma*), probably on the grounds of institutional continuity. At Pellene, however, soon before Agis' revolt and with the support of Corrhagus,[66] the tyrant Chaeron replaced the preceding regime which the anonymous Athenian orator thought democratic ([Dem.] 17.10). The historical circumstances of his installation are obscure, as Chaeron's supposed tyrannical ambitions derive from a *topos* elaborated by Athenian democratic propaganda, probably shaped by Demochares (Marasco 1985: 113ff.), and still recognizable in Pausanias in the second century AD (7.27.7).[67] The hypothesis based on Athenaeus (11.509b; cf. Marasco 1984: 163ff.), however, that the deposed regime was not democratic and that wide support for Chaeron's action resulted from serious social conflicts would suggest that intervention was based on the need to insure social order (*homonoia*) which would explain the *synedriot*'s silence. Moreover, it cannot be excluded that Alexander's intentions to suspend tyrannical regimes, once Asia had been conquered, had a reassuring effect on the *synedrion*. Furthermore, the consolidation of relations between Antipater and the Peloponnesian tyrants, though worrisome, could be tolerated for strategic reasons.[68] In any case, the effectiveness of the intervention at Pallene became evident when, soon afterward, Pellene was the only Achaean city that did not join Agis' anti-Macedonian revolt, the ultimate Greek threat to the war against Persia.[69]

Anti-Macedonian resistance during Alexander's absence

The territorial reorganization imposed on Sparta after Chaeroneia kept the city out of the League.[70] Alexander called attention to this when, in 334, he dedicated the arms taken at the Granicus to Athena for the Greeks 'except the Spartans' (Arr. 1.16.7; Plu. *Alex.* 16.17–18). Spartan determination to modify this territorial arrangement, secured by Macedonian garrisons, may well have helped spark Agis' revolt; but there were appeals also to antityrannical rhetoric and such slogans as 'freedom for the Greeks' (D.S. 17.62.1–63.3; Just. 12.1.6). Moreover, the agreements with the Persian king meant that the rebels were seen as enemies of peace and of the campaign against Persia. During the conflict, however, the league charter operated as it was set up and it is important to note these procedures.

We know from Arrian that after the battle of Issus, Agis obtained ships (ten triremes) and money (thirty talents) from Autophradates (2.13.4–6). Enlisting 8,000 mercenaries dismissed by Darius, he reestablished Persian control over most of Crete. Victory over Corrhagus, who commanded Macedonian forces in the Peloponnesus while Antipater was engaged in Thrace against Memnon, followed his operations on Crete (Aeschin. 3.165). At this point some of the allies joined the revolt: the Achaeans (except for Pellene), the Eleans, and the Arcadians (except for Megalopolis).[71] Yet the adherence of these and 'other' Greeks recorded by Diodorus (17.62.7) probably had no significant effect, and Agis began the siege of Megalopolis with an army totaling some 32,000 men.[72]

League sanctions brought the support of a number of Greek allies in this punitive war and these joined Antipater's army during its march to the Peloponnesus. The percentage and the composition of the Greek allies are much discussed (D.S. 17.63.1); the size of the Macedonian force Alexander entrusted to Antipater in 334, whether 12,000 or 4,000/5,000, is also uncertain.[73] The federal army, however, included troops from Corinth, Messenia, Argos, Megalopolis, as well as from Boeotia and Thessaly.[74] The composition of the *hegemon*'s de facto allies (and also Sparta's traditional enemies), and the fact that there was apparently no preliminary meeting of the *synedrion*, suggests that the response taken now followed that of the Theban crisis of 335. But unless we believe that the charter was non-operative from the beginning, we have no reason to consider the 331 intervention as anomalous. The absence of allies was common to both punitive wars. For most Greeks, but especially the more hostile Aetolians and Athenians (Aeschin. 3.165; D.S. 17.62.7), the option of neutrality seemed legitimate. The Aetolian decision to abstain was perhaps due to good relations with Antipater (Plu. *Alex.* 49.8) who, in exchange for neutrality in the face of Agis' revolt, tolerated the Aetolian occupation of Oeniadae (Mendels 1984: 132ff.; cf. below). In the case of Athens, however, the decision to respect the federal sanction was the outcome of heated debate. There has been a useless attempt to question this by accepting Diodorus' claim (17.62.7) that Athenian neutrality was a response to Alexander's benevolent treatment (Sawada 1996: 88ff.),[75] or by denying the strength of the interventionist position (Brun 2000: 88 ff.), or even by refusing to recognize the force of the Corinthian charter (Blackwell 1999: 58ff). Instead, respect for the treaty was the fundamental criterion for evaluating the legality of the assembly's decisions ([Dem.] 17.1, 5, 7, 11–12, 14, 17–19). These decisions determined the outcome of the revolt. Agis' army was defeated near Megalopolis (dated to spring 330) and Agis himself was killed.

Even when the war was over, the charter operated regularly. Antipater entrusted all decisions to the federal *synedrion* which met with its regular membership at Corinth (Curt. 6.1.19; D.S. 17.73.5). The fact that the meeting was not limited only to allies is evidence that Antipater was worried that an autocratic approach to the question would arouse Alexander's resentment, a concern indicated by the sources and which cannot be considered unfounded.[76] The *synedrion* legitimately discussed both the allies who had defected (Eleans, Achaeans, and Arcadians) and the Spartans. Those who had been in contact with the Persians (Arr. 2.15.2; Curt. 3.13.15) were guilty of treason. For this, the synedrion could take action against any Greek, even those who were not members of the League. After imposing a fine on the Eleans and the Achaeans (obliged to pay 120 talents for damage caused by the siege) and banishing only the guilty Tegeans, the *synedrion* also discussed at length the case of Sparta.[77] Because consensus among the delegates was impossible, in spite of the arguments for and against, the *synedrion* entrusted the matter to Alexander while giving the Spartans the option of sending their own delegates to the king to ask for pardon (D.S. 17.73.5–6; Curt. 6.1.20). This decision was based on precedents where the defendants were to be judged at the highest level: in the case of Athens as an alternative to the *synedrion*'s judgment and in the case of Chios apparently following the *synedrion*'s judgment. The intervention on the number and composition of the hostages handed over to Antipater pending the final sentence is consistent with the three-way negotiations from which the synedrion was excluded

(McQueen 1978: 53ff.). Alexander's decision is not recorded; but the hypothesis of Sparta's forcible enrollment in the League is probable and testifies to a strong interest in the League as late as 330.[78]

After Gaugamela: Alexander, the League, and 'Greek freedom'

The campaign's ideological profile and its relationship with the allies changed after Gaugamela when the conquest of the Persian capitals (Babylon, Susa, Persepolis, Ecbatana) and the discharge of the Greek contingents in Alexander's army signaled the end of the war of revenge.[79] The catalyst for rallying consent then became 'Greek freedom.' This principle satisfied several needs. Ideologically, it consolidated Greek association with the Asian campaign once the destruction of Persepolis had satisfied the desire for revenge (Flower 2000: 115ff.); it also governed relations with the allied states. In this latter area, although long empty of juridical content,[80] the principle of freedom supported Alexander's leadership aspirations more than the binding principle of autonomy. It was also a more effective answer to the antityrannical views of his Greek opponents.

If we are to believe Plutarch, immediately after his coronation as 'King of Asia,' Alexander provided factual proof that the principle of freedom was important for his political activity. He wrote to the Greeks informing them that tyranny had ended and autonomy had begun for the Greeks in Asia (*Alex.* 34.2; Hamilton 1969: 91). In this context, he promised the citizens of Plataea that he would rebuild their city as compensation for their forefathers' sacrifices in providing the battleground for the Greeks in the fight 'for freedom'; he sent a portion of the spoils of war to the Crotonians in Italy so that they could honor the memory of Phayllus, who had fought at Salamis (480) with the single ship given by western Greeks in the Hellenic cause (Hdt. 8.47; Plu. *Alex.* 34.2–4). Alexander rallied greater consensus in the years following 330 by exalting the principle of freedom for the Greeks (Flower 2000: 118ff.), and it is not surprising that this seems to be defended in the contemporary *Letter to Alexander* that has been attributed to Aristotle.[81] On two occasions the freedom of the Greeks was extolled with a public proclamation. The rebuilding of Plataea, that 'martyr' to freedom, was announced by a herald at the Olympic Games of 328 (Plu. *Arist.* 11.9; cf. Fredricksmeyer 2000: 138). In a similar manner, at the Olympic Games of 324, the return of the exiles was announced to the Greeks. This latter act is a striking example of the impact of the freedom principle on Alexander's Greek policy.[82]

The Exiles' Decree, Greek freedom, and the Corinthian League

At Opis in Mesopotamia, in the spring of 324, Alexander proclaimed the Exiles' Decree to his army in which many exiles were serving. One of the objectives of the Decree was to reinstate mercenaries in their native cities, a measure that took care of their needs and provided the king with a strong base of support in the Greek cities (Green 1991: 449ff.; Landucci Gattinoni 1995: 63ff.). The Decree's impact on life in the city-states was predictable and it also explains Craterus' return to Europe. He was given the task of bringing Macedonian veterans back home and a new assignment as Antipater's replacement as administrator of Macedonia, Thrace, Thessaly, and of 'Greek freedom' (Arr. 7.12.4).[83] It is possible that Alexander intended to extend the Asian experiment in 'liberation' to the mainland Greeks and that the exiles' return was a preliminary to the type of institutional democratization that took place in 319 following Polyperchon's *diagramma* (Heckel 1999: 492ff.).[84] But whatever Alexander's plans were, it is clear that the Exiles' Decree was intended as a reaffirmation of his *own* political procedures and an improvement on those of Philip and Antipater. This policy was consistent with his new role as King of Asia and ruler of all the Greeks ([Plu.] *Vit. X or.* 852d).[85]

The important fact, however, is that Alexander intended to adapt the juridical instrument at his disposal for this purpose, namely, the Corinthian League. Violating or ignoring its charter was neither useful nor necessary.[86] On the contrary, Alexander was anxious to legitimize the Decree: by insuring an effective flow of information and adjusting its content to previous decisions of the League, and by entrusting its application to recognized authorities, that is, Antipater and eventually to the allies (D.S. 18.8.4; Just. 13.5.7). The choice of the Olympic Games as a platform points to a hegemonic voice that permitted an exchange of information without any meeting of the *synedrion*.

The Decree was promulgated at the beginning of the Olympic Games between the end of July and the beginning of August. The emissary, Nicanor of Stageira, delivered an open letter to the winner of the herald's competition who read it to the more than 20,000 exiles present at Olympia (D.S. 18.8.2–5; Just 13.5.1–3).[87] Delegates from the cities, including Demosthenes, were also present in the audience (Din. 1.82).[88] The Decree ordered the return of all Greek exiles, with the exception of those guilty of sacrilege and murder, and required the cities to apply the measures under threat of military reprisal (D.S. 17.109.1, 18.8.2–4). In the text, as read by the herald, it appeared that everyone was to benefit from the Decree. But it is certain that the cases of application and exemption, as well as the procedures governing the exiles' reinstatement in their native cities, were contained in a more ample document than the proclamation, probably a *diagramma*. Plutarch clearly indicates that there were exceptions such as the Thebans (*Mor.* 221a); Diodorus also records categories of exiles that, in 324, did not benefit from the return because they had been proscribed by the generals (Antipater) after Alexander had crossed into Asia (18.56.4).[89] These few but significant exceptions confirmed the federal measures against Thebes, Tegea, and Pellene. Confirmation of these sentences created a dangerous difference in the fate of the cities in the regions to which they belonged (Arcadia, Achaea, and Boeotia), and, in view of possible resistance from the regional leagues, a second rescript was issued that Nicanor himself brought into Greece (Hyp. 5, col. 18). This might have been a warning to the Achaean and Arcadian (and possibly Boeotian)[90] leagues regarding debate about or military opposition to its application (Worthington 1986: 115ff.), or it might have been a measure ordering their dissolution (Bosworth 1988a: 77; Whitehead 2000: 415). In any case it was a measure conceived to insure the security of the return of the exiles (kathodos), as well as the office that had been entrusted to Antipater (D.S. 18.8.4).

Arcadian Tegea seems to be the 'exception to the exception' in that it allowed the return of exiles proscribed after 334; an inscription in Delphi, datable probably to 324, is evidence for this (Bencivenni 2003: no. 4; Rhodes–Osborne, no. 101). This exception can be explained by the concentration of hostile mercenaries on nearby Cape Taenarum.[91] This threat led to the reinstatement of most exiles including those recently condemned and who had been unable to attend public festivals (ll. 21–4),[92] and those of longer date (for whom Alexander was especially concerned) including possibly the Tegeans who had been proscribed during the civil war that brought the establishment of the Arcadian koinon (Xen. *Hell*. 6.5.10; D.S. 14.34.3, 5; McKechnie 1989: 26). The economic difficulties of integrating exiles[93] are evidence that the royal decree forced the integration of estranged groups and explains the decision to display the document at Delphi, a procedure usually reserved for interstate treaties (Bencivenni 2003: 97).

Athens, Samos, and Greek freedom

The Exiles' Decree arose from the determination to deal with different kinds of cases (Cargill 1995: 41–2; Bosworth 1998: 76). For some of these, Alexander was under strong pressure at court. Examples include the exiles from Oeniadae in Acarnania and from Samos, the victims respectively of Aetolian and Athenian colonialism. The fact that individual cases were not mentioned in the text of the Decree proves, according to some, that initially Alexander was indifferent;[94] but this is no argument since the text of the Decree, as read by the herald, did not mention any specific cases. The Oenidaean and Samian cases were, however, crucial from the Macedonian perspective. The exiles banished by the Aetolians and the Athenians belonged to the category of those whose exile was unjust and longstanding and whose reinstatement demanded the allies' support (D.S. 18.8.2–4; Just. 13.5.4, 7). In about 330 (D.S. 18.8.6–7; Jehne 1994: 241ff.), the Aetolians had occupied Oeniadae during a controversial campaign of expansion (Landucci Gattinoni 2004: 112ff.). Alexander certainly promised to punish this abuse and perhaps too the understanding between the Aetolians and Antipater (Plu. *Alex*. 49.8) who had tolerated their aggression (Mendels 1984: 131).

The Decree had an even stronger impact on Athens which was obliged 'to return Samos to the Samians' as we read on the cast of a now lost Samian inscription (*SIG*³ 312, ll. 11–14; Hallof 1999: 392ff.). The Samians had been expelled by Athenian cleruchs established on the island beginning in 365[95] and the Athenians were not disposed to allow their return (D.S. 18.8.7). Even when, shortly before the king's death, groups of Samian exiles tried to return to the island from their base on Anaea, Athenian reaction was very firm; clearly, the island was a possession not to be surrendered (Badian 1976: 289ff.). Alexander's position, strengthened by pressure from the supporters of the Samian cause such as Gorgus of Iasus, did not allow for indecision.[96] Alexander's hostility was already clear in the autumn of 324 when, during the annual sacrifice to Dionysus at Ecbatana, the prospect of a siege and war against Athens seems to have [been] discussed (Ephippus of Olynthus, *FGrH* 126 F5, preserved in Athen. 12.538a–b). Resentment grew further that summer when Harpalus, Alexander's treasurer, fled to Athens with a considerable portion of the royal treasury.[97] Harpalus was later mocked in a satyr play, which also reflected hostility toward Athens (Ath. 13.596a; Gadaleta 2001: 109ff.).

The Exiles' Decree was primarily intended for political exiles, but also for so many others who had been forced from their homes on account of poverty and who had, as in the case of a number of Athenians, taken up mercenary service (Landucci Gattinoni 1995: 61ff.). The prospect, however, of dispossessed Athenian cleruchs returning to Athens was upsetting, as these amounted to a third of all adult (male) Athenian citizens (Habicht 1996: 401). In this light, the Samian question is paradigmatic for understanding the social meaning of the Decree and the reasons for Athenian opposition to it on behalf of freedom.

According to Curtius (10.2.6), Athens claimed the role of *vindex publicae libertatis* against Alexander, emphasizing that the Decree's social consequences would be to bring back the 'dregs' (*purgamenta*) of the city. Athenian accusations against Alexander, expressed in typically antityrannical language, do not appear explicitly related to the return of the Samian cleruchs. This should not be surprising: the Samian issue was a clear case of colonialism (Shipley 1987: 166), embarrassing to the cause of freedom and therefore ignored, as seen in the total silence of the Athenian sources.[98] However, it is probable that Curtius' reference to the 'dregs' concerns the cleruchs of Samos whom the orator Demades (in Athenaeus) characterized as the 'deposit of the dregs' of the city (Ath. 3.99d; see Brun 2000: 105 n. 38; Poddighe 2007).

Alexander's death delayed the decision regarding Samos and only when Perdiccas raised the question again after the Lamian War (a war strongly motivated by the Exiles' Decree) were the Samians restored (D.S. 18.18.9).[99] But Alexander's conduct of the matter is evidence that he had a perfect grasp of the Greek interpretation of freedom. In a letter to the Athenians, Alexander 'returned to sender' the accusation of despotism when he called attention to the theme of Samian freedom in the following statement:[100] 'I would not have given you that *free* and admirable city: you have it, having received it from him ... who was said to be my father' (Plu. *Alex.* 28.2). Hypothetically, the context of the letter could be that referred to by Ephippus (see above). In both cases, there was a reference to the king's divine descent, a very topical issue in 324[101] in the context of the confrontation with Athens. Clearly, Alexander intended to defend the rights of the Samians by turning against Athens the very theme of freedom by which it claimed its right to the island.

Notes

1 The battle and postwar period: Hammond–Griffith 596–614; Buckler 2003: 500–11. Garrisons: D.S. 17.3.3, 8.7; Arr. 1.7; Plu. *Arat.* 23; Din. 1.18; Bosworth 1994a, 1994b; Buckler 2003: 511ff. The case of Chalcis (Plb. 38.3.3) is uncertain: Bosworth 1998: 48 n. 6; Faraguna 2003: 100 n. 4.

2 The oath sworn by the Greeks, preserved in a fragmentary inscription (Tod 1946: no. 177 = Rhodes–Osborne, no. 76), concedes hegemony to the Macedonian kingdom on a dynastic basis (1. 11; cf. Arr. 3.24.5): Perlman 1985: 170ff.; Hammond–Walbank 571; Hatzopoulos 1996: 297; Mari 2002: 113 n. 2.

3 Philip emphasized the prospect of the advantages involved in this (D.S. 16.89.3; Plb. 3.6.12): Hammond–Griffith 631. On the passage from Polybius: Walbank 1967: 307ff.; Seibert 1998: 27ff.

4 On Alexander's inheritance of authority, see Hammond–Walbank 16 n. 2; Squillace 2004: 20.

5 On Panhellenism in Macedonian propaganda see Seibert 1998: 7–58; Flower 2000: 96–135. On the invention of an ancient enmity between Macedonians and Persians see Brosius 2003. Her undervaluation, however, of the expansionistic aims of the undertaking is unacceptable. Cf. Sakellariou 1980: 136ff.; Fredricksmeyer 1982: 85ff.; Bosworth 1988a: 17ff; J.R. Ellis 1994: 784ff.; Seibert 1998: 28ff.

6 Sordi 1984a: 10 n. 5; Harris 1995: 175ff; Helly 1995: 59ff.; Sanchez 2001: 253; Squillace 2004: 47ff. For a different view: Heckel 1997: 90ff.

7 The symbols on a commemorative Larisean drachma are evidence of this: Sordi 1996: 38ff.; Squillace 2004: 48; cf. Just. 11.3.1.

8 Plutarch places the visit in 335: Sordi 1984a: 9.

9 Sordi 1984a: 9–13; Hammond–Walbank 14ff.; Lefèvre 1998: 94; Mari 2002: 221ff. Sanchez 2001: 253ff, however, distinguishes between Amphictyonic and Corinthian hegemony.

10 The reconstruction of Plataea and Thebes was announced at the Olympic (Plu. *Alex.* 34.2; see below) and Isthmean Games (Ps. Call. 1.47.1–7). The *synedrion* seems to have met at the Isthmus in 332 (D.S. 17.48.6; Curt. 4.5.11) and in 330 at the Pythian Games (Aeschin. 3.254).

11 Helly 1995: 66; Sanchez 2001: 246; Mari 2002: 222. The relevance of the League of 302 to Philip and Alexander remains under discussion: Moretti 1967: 116ff.; Bosworth 1988a: 190ff; Mari 2002: 135ff., 222ff.; Buckler 2003: 516 n. 26; Rhodes–Osborne 379.

12 D.S. 16.87.3, 17.8.3; Arr. 1.7.1; Just. 9.4.7–8; Paus. 4.27.10, 9.1.8, 6.5; *Anth. Pal.* 6.344; Dio Chrys. 37.42; Gullath 1982: 12ff.; Heckel 1997: 92.

13 According to Diodorus (17.4.5–8) Demosthenes was among them, but other sources give a different date for the episode (Aeschin. 3.160–1; Plu. *Dem.* 23.2–3).

14 The dissolution of the Second Athenian League (Paus. 1.25.3) was counterbalanced by the transfer of Oropus (Hyp. 3.16; [Demad.] *Concerning the Twelve Years* 9; [D.] 17.26; [Arist.] *Ath. Pol.* 61.6, 62.2; D.S. 18.56.6–7; Plu. *Alex.* 28.1–2; Just. 9.4–5; Plb. 5.10.1, 4; Paus. 1.34. 1; Brun 2000: 58 n. 11; Whitehead 2000: 207ff.; Faraguna 2003: 100 n. 4).

15 Heisserer 1980: 23; Voutiras 1998: 116; Rhodes–Osborne 379. Against: Tronson 1985: 15ff. On the "defense officers" see Hammond–Griffith 639ff; Culasso Gastaldi 1984: 67ff.

16 In 335, so Sanchez 2001: 245ff.; Mari 2002: 135; Hammond–Walbank 15.

17 The functions of *hegemon* and *strategos autokrator*, considered distinct by Diodorus (17.4.9; cf. Heckel 1997: 85ff.), appear to be interchangeable elsewhere and hegemony seems to include command of the expedition or campaign (*strateia*: Aeschin. 3.132; Arr. 1.1.2, 2.14.4, 7.9.5; Plu. *Alex.* 14.1; Just. 11.2.5). Even Philip is defined as *strategos autokrator* (D.S. 16.89.1–3; *FGrH* 255, ll. 24–5; Just. 9.5.4) or *hegemon* of the *strateia* (D.S. 16. 91.2; Plu. *Mor.* 240a; Plb. 9.33.7): Bosworth 1980b: 48ff.; Jehne 1994: 181ff; Hammond 1999a; Sisti 2001: 306ff.

18 D.S. 17.4.9; Just. 11.2.5 (Corinth); Plu. *Alex.* 14.1 (Isthmia, but in 335). The place chosen by Philip is uncertain (Mari 2002: 193 n. 3).

19 According to the traditional chronology of Demosthenes' speeches, the oration was given in 336/5 (Debord 1999: 469; some think 333 more probable: Will 1982: 202–3; Sordi 1984b: 23ff.) or 331 in the context of the debate following the revolt of Agis III (Cawkwell 1961; Bosworth 1994a: 847; Habicht 1997: 21; Blackwell 1999: 58 n. 79; Brun 2000: 78 n. 29). Differing are Culasso Gastaldi 1984: 159ff. (after 330) and Squillace 2004: 64 (335/4). Bosworth 1992a: 148 n. 17 attributes the oration to Hypereides, as does Whitehead 2000: 7 n. 26, on stylistic grounds. In the discussion below, the orator will simply be referred to as the "anonymous Athenian."

20 On the question of terminology: Buckler 1994: 114; Rhodes–Osborne 376.

21 Perlman 1985: 156ff; Lanzillotta 2000: 144ff.; Musti 2000: 172ff.; Buckler 2003: 511ff. See also Sakellariou 1980: 142; J.R. Ellis 1994: 784; Rhodes–Osborne 378.

22 Extended also to territorial waters: [D.] 17.19–21; Alonso 1997: 186ff.; Lanzillotta 2000: 152.

23 Hammond–Griffith 632ff.; Buckler 2003: 514; Rhodes–Osborne 378.

24 There is epigraphic evidence of arbitration between the islands of Melos and Cimolos for the possession of three islets in the Melos group (Tod 1946: no. 179; Ager 1997: no. 3; Magnetto 1997: no. 1; Rhodes–Osborne, no. 82). The verdict (in favor of Cimolos) seems to have been delivered by Argos on the authority of a '*synedrion* of the Hellenes' (ll. 3–5) that seems identifiable as the Corinthian *synedrion*; cf. Ager 1996: 40ff., Rhodes–Osborne 404.

25 The alliance, explicitly defined by Arrian (3.24.5), was provided for by the *synthekai* (Bosworth 1980b: 46–51; Hammond–Walbank 571ff.; Hatzopoulos 1996: 297; Blackwell 1999: 49; Buckler 2003: 513ff.). See also Magnetto 1994: 283ff. The absence of the term *symmachia* from the text of the Greeks' oath (Rhodes–Osborne 376), however, seems decisive for those who deny the existence of the alliance (Ryder 1965: 158; Hammond–Griffith 628; Jehne 1994: 157ff.; Faraguna 2003: 102), or else they admit it in a stage successive to the oath (Tod 1948: 177, 229; Heisserer 1980: 16; Sakellariou 1980: 145).

26 Differently from the Peace of 386: Schmidt 1999: 92ff.; Buckler 2003: 512.

27 Atkinson 2000: 332 defends the historicity of the letter. Cf. Bosworth 1980b: 277ff.; Squillace 2004: 102ff.

28 Thus Jehne 1994: 157ff. and Faraguna 2003: 102. Seibert 1998: 15ff. rightly emphasizes that the liberation theme only applied to operations undertaken in place (D.S. 16.1.5–6, 91.2; 17.24). Moreover, even once they were liberated the Ionian cities remained outside the League either as allies (Rhodes–Osborne 379) or as subjects (Bosworth 1998: 63).

29 D.S. 17.17.3–5; Just. 11.6.2; Plu. *Alex.* 15.1; Arr. 1.11.3.

30 Hdt. 7.132; Lycurg. *Leoc.* 81; D.S. 9.3.1–3; Bosworth 1988a: 189ff.

31 According to the sources (Curt. 5.11.5; Paus. 8.52.5) there were 50,000; Green 1991: 157ff.

32 Arr. 1.16.6, 19.6, 29.5; 3.6.2, 23.8; Curt. 3.1.9.

33 Already during the *strateia*: Prandi 1983: 32; Errington 1990: 82ff.; Blackwell 1999: 77ff. After 330: Heisserer 1980: 233ff. After 325/4: Bosworth 1988a: 220ff.; 1998: 73ff.

34 For an evaluation of the survival of the free *poleis* after Chaeroneia: Price 1988: 324ff.; Green 1990: xx–xxi, 24ff., 196ff.; Bencivenni 2003: 1ff.

35 On the views of Aeschines and Phocion: Tritle 1988: 123ff.; 1995. Against: Bearzot 1985: 135ff.

36 Hammond–Walbank 79; against: Blackwell 1999: 43 n. 37.

37 Just. 9.4.7–8 (Gullath 1982: 10; Heckel 1997: 92). Possibly the *politeuma* excluded manual workers (Arist. *Pol.* 1278a25; Poddighe 2002: 83, 98ff.).

38 The Thebans opposed to this were spared by Alexander after the battle (Plu. *Alex.* 11.12).

39 Aeschin. 3. 239–40; Din. 1.18–21; D.S. 17.8–14; Arr. 1.7–10; Just. 11.3.6–4, 8; Plu. *Alex.* 11; *Dem.* 20.4–5; Bosworth 1980: 73ff.; Gullath 1982: 20ff.; Hammond–Walbank 56ff.; Worthington 1992: 162ff.; Heckel 1997: 87ff.; Blackwell 1999: 46ff.; Brun 2000: 71ff.; Sisti 2001: 321ff.; Squillace 2004: 112ff.

40 Bosworth 1980b: 76ff.; Green 1991: 142; Sisti 2001: 323ff.

41 Hdt. 8.34, 8.50, 9.16, 25; Squillace 2004: 124ff.

42 The penalties imposed in 302 for failure to send a military contingent (Moretti 1967: no. 44, ll. 95ff.) are evidence that there was frequent abstention. The sanctions (20 drachmas per day for each hoplite) were imposed whenever a contingent was required from a city.

43 Only those who supported the revolt were punished (Bosworth 1980b: 92).

44 D.S. 17.9.5–6; Plu. *Alex.* 11.7–9; Alonso 1995: 211ff.; Squillace 2004: 122ff.

45 There is evidence for normal procedures only in 302 (Moretti 1967: no. 44, ll. 70ff.). The place (Borza 1989: 128; Blackwell 1999: 46) and composition of the meeting is uncertain; either the victorious (Arr. 1.9.9; Just. 11.3.8) or all the delegates to the *synedrion* (D.S. 17.14.1); Bosworth 1980b: 89ff.; Heckel 1997: 94.

46 Arr. 1.9.9; D.S. 17.14.2–4; Just. 11.3.9–11; Plu. *Alex.* 11.11. On Theban responsibility with respect to Athens, Plataea, and Orchomenus: Isocr. *Plat.* 31; Arr. 1.9.7; D.S. 15.46.5–6, 79.3–6. On the measures in favor of Plataea: Arr. 1.9.10; Plu. *Arist.* 11.3–9; *Alex.* 34. 2; Prandi 1988: 138ff. On the significance of the condemnation: Plu. *Alex.* 11.11; Plb. 4.23.8, 5.10.6, 9.28.8, 38. 2.13–4; Heckel 1997: 92ff.

47 The sources differ on the number and identity of the Athenians (Arr. 1.10.4; Plu. *Phoc.* 17.2; *Dem.* 23.4; *Suda* s.v. 'Antipater'; Heckel 1997: 102ff.; Sisti 2001: 334ff.) and on the final decisions (Arr. 1.10.6; Just. 1. 4.11; Landucci Gattinoni 1994: 60; Heckel 1997: 103; Brun 2000: 73ff.).

48 D.S. 17.17.1–3; Plu. *Alex.* 15.4; Arr. 1.11.3–7; Just. 11.5.12; Flower 2000: 108ff.

49 The pacts (*synthekai*) and the accords (*homologiai*) ratified in 336 and 332 (see below). Against: Debord 1999: 469ff.

50 Arr. 2.1.1–5, 13.4–5, 3.2.3–7; Curt. 3.1.19–20, 4.1.36–7, 5.14–21; D.S. 17.29.1–4; Bosworth 1988a: 52ff.; Debord 1999: 466ff.; Rhodes–Osborne 416ff.

51 [D.] 17.7; Arr. 3.2.6. See Rhodes–Osborne, no. 85b, 1. 35.

52 Bosworth 1998: 61ff.; Debord 1999: 476ff.; Mossé 2001: 52ff.; Faraguna 2003: 113ff. Epigraphic documentation on Alexander's intervention at Priene in Rhodes–Osborne, no. 86. Cf. Bosworth 1998: 64ff.; Debord 1999: 439ff.; Faraguna 2003: 109ff.; Squillace 2004: 155ff.; Hansen and Nielsen 2004: 1092ff. On Aspendos: Magnetto 1997: 24ff.; Bosworth 1998: 62ff.; Faraguna: 2003: 112.

53 Prandi 1983: 27; Bosworth 1988a: 192ff.; Hammond–Walbank 73ff.; Lott 1996: 26ff.; Brun 2000: 85ff.; Faraguna 2003: 109ff.; Hansen and Nielsen 2004: 1023ff., 1028, 1067ff. According to a different reconstruction (Heisserer 1980: 27ff; Labarre 1996 25ff.; Rhodes–Osborne 414ff.; Squillace 2004: 64), the inscriptions would be evidence for earlier constitutional changes. This theory is founded on the hypothesis that, on the islands allied to the League in 336 following the operations of Parmenio and Attalus (Diod. 16.91.2), democracies had already been installed, then deposed after the insurrection led by Memnon of Rhodes in 335 (D.S. 17.7.2–3, 8–10) and reinstated by Alexander in 334. It seems, however, that the islands were not involved in Parmenios' operations nor in Memnon's insurrection (Hammond–Walbank 73 n. 2; Green 1991: 139ff. Against: Labarre 1996: 24ff.).

54 *SIG3* 283 = Rhodes–Osborne, no. 84a = Bencivenni 2003: no. 1.

55 *SEG* xxii. 506 = Rhodes–Osborne, no. 84b.

56 Bencivenni 2003: 18ff. The hypothesis of a preventive document (Bosworth 1980b: 268) is discussed by Prandi 1983: 26ff. Cf. Bosworth 1988a: 193ff.; Debord 1999: 466ff.; Faraguna 2003: 113ff.; Hansen and Nielsen 2004: 1067ff.

57 Arr. 2.2.3; Curt. 3.1.19–20; Hauben 1976: 84ff.; Prandi 1983: 26 n. 10; Debord 1999: 466ff.

58 Bosworth 1980b: 268; 1988a: 193; Hammond, in Hammond–Walbank 74. Against: Prandi 1983: 28.

59 Rhodes–Osborne no. 83 = Bencivenni 2003: no. 3.

60 Bosworth 1988a: 192; Debord 1999: 468 ff.; Hansen and Nielsen 2004: 1023ff.

61 Arrian (2.1.4) records an alliance with Alexander (Bosworth 1980b: 181; Hammond–Walbank 73 n. 1) but this might be short for "alliance with Alexander and the Greeks" (as it is for Tenedos: Arr. 2.2.2.): Prandi 1983: 28; Sisti 2001: 395. Cf. also Badian 1966a: 50; Debord 1999: 472 n. 397.

62 Rhodes–Osborne, no. 85a–b = Bencivenni 2003: no. 2. Debord 1999: 467ff.; Hansen and Nielsen 2004: 1028.

63 For other dates (334, 324, or 319): Rhodes–Osborne 430; Bencivenni 2003: 45ff.

64 Arr. 1.11.3; D.S. 17.17.5; Blackwell 1999: 53 ff.

65 Bosworth 1988a: 188. For 333: Walbank 1967: 567. The years 336 and 335 are proposed respectively by Debord 1999: 469 and Squillace 2004: 64 n. 89.

66 *Acad. index Here.*, cols. 11, 28ff., 32ff; Culasso Gastaldi 1984: 54ff.; Bosworth 1988a: 194, 201.

67 Pausanias refers the *topos* to Alexander. For Pausanias' use of Demochares: Bearzot 1992: 11Iff.; Culasso Gastaldi 1984: 54ff., 159ff. attributes the pseudo-Demosthenic oration to Demochares.

68 Bosworth 1988a: 162; Badian 1994: 269; Baynham 1994: 343, 346; Blackwell 1999: 76.

69 Aeschin. 3.163, 165–7; Din. 1.34; D.S. 17.48.1–2, 62–3; Plu. *Mor.* 219b; *Dem.* 24.1; *Agis.* 3; Curt.4.1.39–40, 6.1.1–21; Arr. 2.13.4–6, 3.16.10; Just. 12.1.4–11; McQueen 1978: 40ff.; Bosworth 1988a: 198ff.; Badian 1994: 258ff; Baynham 1994: 339ff.; Heckel 1997:183ff.; Blackwell 1999: 53ff; Brun 2000: 85ff.; Worthington 2000: 189; Squillace 2004: 131ff. The much discussed chronology of the war places its outbreak in mid 331 (Bosworth 1988a: 200).

70 Laconia's borders were 'rearranged' to the advantage of the Argives, Arcadians, and Messenians (D. 18.64–5,295; Plb. 9.28.6–7, 33.8–12; Paus. 2.20.1, 38.5, 7.11.2, 8.7.4) and therefore Sparta remained outside the League (Just. 9.5.3; Arr. 1.16.7; Plu. *Alex.* 16.18; D.S. 17.3.4–5): McQueen 1978: 40ff.; Hammond–Griffith 613ff.; Magnetto 1994: 283ff.; Buckler 2003: 507ff.

71 Aeschin. 3.165; Din. 1.34; D.S. 17.62.6–63.4; Curt. 6.1.20; Paus. 7.27.7; Just. 12.1.6.

72 Din. 1.34; McQueen 1978: 52ff.; Bosworth 1988a: 203.

73 Badian 1994: 261ff. (12,000); Bosworth 2002: 65ff. (4,000/5,000).

74 Bosworth 1988a: 203; Baynham 1994: 340; Heckel 1997: 187; Blackwell 1999: 56.

75 Evidence of this is Iphicrates' mission to Darius III (Arr. 2.15.2; Curt. 3.13.15; Bosworth 1980b: 233ff.) and the ratification of an *epidosis* of 4,000 drachmas (Tod 1946: no. 198; Faraguna 1992: 256; Rhodes–Osborne, no. 94; against: Brun 2000: 88 n. 20). The abstentionist position, however, backed by Demosthenes and Demades prevailed: Badian 1994: 259; Blackwell 1999: 63.

76 Curt. 6.1.18–19; Baynham 1994: 341–2; Blackwell 1999: 72.

77 Differing: Bosworth 1988a: 203; Blackwell 1999: 70; Worthington 2000: 189.

78 McQueen 1978: 56; Bosworth 1988a: 204; Hammond 1989: 78.

79 Arr. 3.11.1–15.7, 19.5; Curt 4.12.1–16.9; Plu. *Alex.* 33.8–11; Bosworth 1980b: 329ff.; Sisti 2001: 518ff.

80 Karavites 1984: 191. On *eleutheria* and autonomy in the fourth century: Bosworth 1992a: 122ff.; Musti 2000: 176ff.; Bertoli 2003: 87ff.

81 Faraguna 2003: 116–18; Squillace 2004: 23ff. (with fuller bibliography).

82 Hyp. *Dem.*, cols. 18–19; Din. 1.81–2; D.S. 17.109.1–2, 18.8.2–7; Curt. 10.2.4–7; Just. 13.5.1–5; Bosworth 1988a: 220ff.; 1998: 73ff.; Hammond–Walbank 80ff.; Blackwell 1999: 145ff.; Flower 2000: 126ff.; Faraguna 2003: 124ff.

83 Bosworth 1994a: 856 n. 24; Sisti and Zambrini 2004: 610.

84 On the *diagramma* of Polyperchon (D.S. 18.56), cf. Poddighe 2002: 171ff.; Dixon 2007.

85 Culasso Gastaldi 2003: 69ff. (with fuller bibliography).

86   The following judge the Decree to be legitimate: Bikerman 1940: 29 n. 3; Hammond–Walbank 80ff.; Green 1991: 451ff. Against: Heisserer 1980: 233ff.; Errington 1990: 96ff.; Blackwell 1999: 146ff. suggests a provision that had nothing to do with the treaty.
87   Diodorus' source: for Hieronymus (Bosworth 1988a: 220; Heckel 1999: 491; Flower 2000: 127) or Duris (Prandi 1996: 89; Blackwell 1999: 146 n. 30). It is also discussed whether the 20,000 represented all of the beneficiaries (McKechnie 1989: 26) or only those present at Olympia (Worthington 1990: 201).
88   Din. 1.82–3, 103; Plu. *Dem.* 9. 1; Worthington 1992: 253; Landucci Gattinoni 1995: 70.
89   Bosworth 1988a: 224; Brun 2000: 104; Poddighe 2002: 186. Against: Jehne 1994: 248 n. 338.
90   The name of the Boeotians is not clearly legible: Bosworth 1988a: 222 n. 39.
91   Heisserer 1980: 221ff.; Worthington 1992: 63ff.; Blackwell 1999: 150; Bencivenni 2003: 95. On their composition: Green 1991: 449ff.; Landucci Gattinoni 1995: 66ff.
92   Probably sanctions for ceremonies that had not been paid for: Bencivenni 2003: 99.
93   *SIG*³ 312; Heisserer 1980: 182; Bosworth 1998: 75ff.
94   Mendels 1984: 147; Worthington 1992: 60.
95   Numbers and places of exile: Shipley 1987: 141ff.; Landucci Gattinoni 1997: 11ff.
96   *SIG*³ 312; Heisserer 1980: 182; Bosworth 1998: 75ff.
97   D.S. 17.108.4; Plu. *Dem.* 25.1–2; *Phoc.* 21.3; Curt. 10.2.1–3; Bosworth 1988a: 215ff.; Worthington 1994a: 307ff.; Blackwell 1999: 134ff.
98   In this perspective, silence does not prove either that the Athenians found the problem insoluble (Landucci Gattinoni 1995: 75ff.) or that it would arise later (Worthington 1992: 63).
99   Poddighe 2002: 186.
100 This is a text differently dated and translated (Rosen 1978: 20ff.; Hammond 1993: 174ff.; Jehne 1994: 254 n. 374). For 324: Hamilton 1969: 74; Heisserer 1980: 187 n. 44. For the proposed translation: Bikerman 1940: 34; Cargill 1995: 41.
101 Brun 2000: 104; Mari 2002: 239ff.

References

Ager 1996 = S. Ager, *Interstate Arbitrations in the Greek World, 337–90 BC* (Berkeley and Los Angeles: 1996).

Alonso 1995 = V. Alonso Troncoso, 'Ultimatum et déclaration de guerre dans la Grèce classique', in *Les Relations internationales: Actes du Colloque de Strasbourg 15–17 juin 1993* (Paris: 1995), pp. 211–295.

Alonso 1997 = V. Alonso Troncoso, Καθοτι αν επαγγελωσιν – παοαγγελωσιν: *Sobre una cláusula del derecho griego de los tratados*, in *Xaire: II reunión de historiadores del mundo griego antiguo* (Seville: 1997), pp. 181–191.

Alonso 2003a = V. Alonso Troncoso, *L'Institution de l'hégémonie entre la coutume et le droit écrit*, in *Symposion 1999: Vorträge zur griechischen und hellenistichen Rechtsgeschichte* (Cologne: 2003), pp. 339–354.

Alonso 2003b = V. Alonso Troncoso, 'La KOINH EIPHNH ateniese del 371 y el sistema griego de alianzas', *EC* 71 (2003), pp. 353–377.

Atkinson 2000 = J.E. Atikinson, *Curzio Rufo, Storie di Alessandro Magno* (Milan: 2000).

Badian 1966a = E. Badian, 'Alexander the Great and the Greeks of Asia', in E. Badian (ed.), *Ancient Society and Institutions: Studies Presented to Victor Ehrenberg on his 75th Birthday* (Oxford: 1966), pp. 37–69.

Badian 1976 = E. Badian (ed.), *Alexandre le Grande: image et realité* (Geneva: 1976).

Badian 1994 = E. Badian, 'Agis III: Revisions and Reflections', in Ian Worthington (ed.), *Ventures into Greek History. Essays in Honour of N.G.L. Hammond* (Oxford: 1994), pp. 258–292.

Baynham 1994 = E.J. Baynham, 'Antipater: Manager of Kings', in Ian Worthington (ed.), *Ventures into Greek History. Essays in Honour of N.G.L. Hammond* (Oxford: 1994), pp. 331–356.

Bearzot 1985 = C. Bearzot, *Focione tra storia e trasfiguazione ideale* (Milan: 1985).

Bearzot 1992 = C. Bearzot, *Storia e storiografia ellenistica in Pausania il Periegeta* (Venice: 1992).

Bencivenni 2003 = A. Bencivenni, *Progetti di riforme costituzionali nelle epigrafi greche dei secoli IV–II a.C.* (Bologna: 2003).

Bertoli 2003 = M. Bertoli, 'Sviluppi del concetto di "autonomia" tra IV e III secolo a.C.', in C. Bearzot, F. Landucci, and G. Zecchini (eds), *Gli stati territoriali nel mondo antico* (Milan: 2003), pp. 87–100.

Bikerman 1940 = E. Bikerman, 'La Lettre d'Alexandre aux bannis grecs', *REA* 42 (1940), pp. 25–-35.

Blackwell 1999 = C.W. Blackwell, *In the Absence of Alexander* (New York: 1999).

Borza 1989 = E. Borza, 'Significato politico, economico e sociale dell'impresa di Alessandro', in R. Bianchi Bandinelli (ed.), *Storia e civiltà dei Greci* 5 (Milan: 1989), pp. 122–167.

Bosworth 1980a = 'Alexander and the Iranians', *JHS* 100 (1980), pp. 1–21.

Bosworth 1980b = A.B. Bosworth, *A Historical Commentary on Arrian's History of Alexander* 1 (Oxford: 1980).

Bosworth 1988a = A.B. Bosworth, *Conquest and Empire: The Reign of Alexander the Great* (Cambridge: 1988).

Bosworth 1992a = A.B. Bosworth, '*Autonomia*: The Use and Abuse of Political Terminology', *SIFC* 10 (1992), pp. 122–152.

Bosworth 1994a = A.B. Bosworth, 'Alexander the Great, Part 2: Greece and the Conquered Territories', *CAH* 6 (Cambridge: 1994), pp. 846–859.

Bosworth 1994b = A.B. Bosworth, 'A New Macedonian Prince', CQ^2 44 (1994), pp. 57–65.

Bosworth 1998 = A.B. Bosworth, 'Alessandro: l'impero universale e le città greche', in S. Settis (ed.), *I Greci: Storia cultura arte società* 2 (Turin: 1998), pp. 47–80.

Bosworth 2002 = A.B. Bosworth, *The Legacy of Alexander: Politics, Warfare, and Propaganda under the Successors* (Oxford: 2002).

Brosius 2003 = M. Brosius, 'Alexander and the Persians', in J. Roisman (ed.), *Brill's Companion to Alexander the Great* (Leiden: 2003), pp. 169–193.

Brun 2000 = P. Brun, *L'Orateur Démade* (Bordeaux: 2000).

Buckler 1994 = J. Buckler, 'Philip II, the Greeks, and the King 346–336 B.C.', *ICS* 19 (1994), pp. 99–122.

Buckler 2003 = J. Buckler, *Aegean Greece in the Fourth Century B.C.* (Leiden: 2003).

Cargill 1995 = J. Cargill, *Athenian Settlements of the Fourth Century BC* (Leiden: 1995).

Cawkwell 1961 = G.L. Cawkwell, 'A Note on Ps. Demosthenes 17.20', *Phoenix* 15 (1961), pp. 74–78.

Culasso Gastaldi 1984 = E. Culasso Gastaldi, *Sul trattato con Alessandro (polis, monarchia macedone e memoria demostenica)* (Padua: 1984).

Culasso Gastaldi 2003 = E. Culasso Gastaldi, 'Eroi della città: Eufrone di Sicione e Licurgo di Atene', in A. Barzanò, C. Bearzot, F. Landucci, L. Prandi, and G. Zecchini (eds), *Modelli eroici dall'antichità alla cultura europea* (Rome: 2003), pp. 65–98.

Debord 1999 = P. Debord, *L'Asie Mineure au IVème siècle (412–323): Pouvoirs et jeux politiques* (Bordeaux: 1999).

Dixon 2007 = M.D. Dixon, 'Corinth, Greek Freedom, and the Diadochoi, 323–301 B.C.', in W. Heckel, L.A. Tritle, and P.V. Wheatley (eds), *Alexander's Empire: From Formulation to Decay* (Claremont: 2007), pp. 151–178.

Ellis 1994 = J.R. Ellis, 'Macedonian Hegemony Created', *CAH* 6 (1994), pp. 760–790.

Errington 1990 = R.M. Errington, *A History of Macedonia*, trans. C. Errington (Berkeley: 1990).

Faraguna 1992 = M. Faraguna, 'Atene nell'età di Alessandro: problemi politici, economici, finanziari', *Atti dell'Accademia Nazionale dei Lincei. Memorie* (1992), pp. 165–447.

Faraguna 2003 = M. Faraguna, 'Alexander and the Greeks', in J. Roisman (ed.), *Brill's Companion to Alexander the Great* (Leiden: 2003), pp. 99–130.

Flower 2000 = M. Flower, 'Alexander and Panhellenism', in A.B. Bosworth and E.J. Baynham (eds), *Alexander the Great in Fact and Fiction* (Oxford: 2000), pp. 96–135.

Fredricksmeyer 1982 = E.A. Fredricksmeyer, 'On the Final Aims of Philip II', in W.L. Adams and E.N. Borza (eds), *Philip II, Alexander the Great, and the Macedonian Heritage* (Lanham: 1982), pp. 85–98.

Fredricksmeyer 2000 = E.A. Fredricksmeyer, 'Alexander the Great and the Kingship of Asia', in A.B. Bosworth and E.J. Baynham (eds), *Alexander the Great in Fact and Fiction* (Oxford: 2000), pp. 136–166.

Gadaleta 2001 = A.P. Gadaleta, 'Efippo storico di Alessandro: testimonianze e frammenti', *AFLFB* 44 (2001), pp. 97–144.

Gargiulo 2004 = T. Gargiulo, 'E il Citerone esultava: una nota al Romanzo di Alessandro (I 46, 11)', *QS* 60 (2004), pp. 109–115.

Green 1990 = P. Green, *From Alexander to Actium: The Historical Evolution of the Hellenistic Age* (Berkeley: 1990).

Green 1991 = P. Green, *Alexander of Macedon, 356–323 BC: A Historical Biography* (Berkeley: 1991).

Gullath 1982 = B. Güllath, *Untersuchungen zur Geschichte Boiotiens in der Zeit Alexanders und der Diadochen* (Frankfurt: 1982).

Habicht 1996 = C. Habicht, 'Athens, Samos, and Alexander the Great', *PAPhS* 140 (1996), pp. 397–405.

Habicht 1997 = C. Habicht, *Athens from Alexander to Antony* (Cambridge: 1997).

Hallof 1999 = K. Hallof, 'Decretum samium *Syll.* 312 redivivum', *Klio* 81 (1999), pp. 392–396.

Hamilton 1969 = J.R. Hamilton, *Plutarch, Alexander: A Commentary* (Oxford: 1969).

Hammond 1989 = N.G.L. Hammond, *The Macedonian State* (Oxford: 1989).

Hammond 1993 = N.G.L. Hammond, *Sources for Alexander the Great* (Cambridge: 1993).

Hammond 1999a = N.G.L. Hammond, 'The Meaning of Arrian VII, 9, 5', *JHS* 119 (1999), pp. 166–168.

Hammond–Griffith = N.G.L. Hammond and G.T. Griffith, *A History of Macedonia* 2 (Oxford: 1979).

Hammond–Walbank = N.G.L. Hammond and F.W. Walbank, *A History of Macedonia* 3 (Oxford: 1988).

Hansen and Nielsen 2004 = M.H. Hansen and T.H. Nielsen, *An Inventory of Archaic and Classical Poleis* (Oxford: 2004).

Harris 1995 = E.M. Harris, *Aeschines and Athenian Politics* (New York: 1995).

Hatzopoulos 1996 = M.B. Hatzopoulos, *Macedonian Institutions under the Kings* (Athens: 1996).

Hauben 1976 = H. Hauben, 'The Expansion of Macedonian Sea-Power under Alexander the Great', *Anc. Soc.* 7 (1976), pp. 79–105.

Heckel 1997 = W. Heckel and J. Yardley, *Justin: Epitome of the Philippic History of Pompeius Trogus* (Oxford: 1997).

Heckel 1999 = W. Heckel, 'The Politics of Antipatros: 324–319 BC', *Ancient Macedonia* 6 (1999), pp. 489–498.

Heisserer 1980 = A.J. Heisserer, *Alexander and the Greek: The Epigraphic Evidence* (Norman: 1980).

Helly 1995 = B. Helly, *L'État thessalien: Aleus le Roux, les tétrades et les tagoi* (Lyon: 1995).

Jehne 1994 = M. Jehne, *Koine eirene: Untersuchungen zu den Befriedungs- und Stabilisierungsbemühungen in der griechischen Poliswelt des 4. Jahrhunderts v. Chr.* (Stuttgart: 1994).

Karavites 1984 = P. Karavites, 'The Political Use of Eleutheria and Autonomia', *RIDA* 31 (1984), pp. 178–191.

Labarre 1996 = G. Labarre, *Les Cités de Lesbos aux époques hellénistique et impériale* (Lyon: 1996).

Landucci Gattinoni 1994 = F. Landucci Gattinoni, 'I mercenari nella politica ateniese dell'età di Alessandro: i soldati e ufficiali mercenari ateniesi al servizio della Persia. Parte I', *Anc. Soc.* 25 (1994), pp. 33–62.

Landucci Gattinoni 1995 = F. Landucci Gattinoni, 'I mercenari nella politica ateniese dell'età di Alessandro. Parte II', *Anc. Soc.* 26 (1995), pp. 59–91.

Landucci Gattinoni 1997 = F. Landucci Gattinoni, *Duride di Samo* (Rome: 1997).

Landucci Gattinoni 2004 = F. Landucci Gattinoni, 'L'Etoliia nel protoellenismo: la progresiva centralità di una periferia semibarbara', in G. Vanotti and C. Perassi (eds), *In limine: ricerche su marginalità e periferia del mondo antico* (Milan: 2004), pp. 105–130.

Lanzillotta 2000 = E. Lanzillotta, 'Elementi di diritto costituzionale nelle iscrizioni greche del IV sècolo', *RFil* 128 (2000), pp. 144–154.

Lefèvre 1998 = F. Lefèvre, *L'Amphictionie pyléo-delphique: Histoire et institutions* (Paris: 1998).

Lott 1996 = J.B. Lott, 'Philip II, Alexander, and the Two Tyrannies at Eresos of *IG* XII. 2. 526', *Phoenix* 50 (1996), pp. 26–40.

McKechnie 1989 = P. McKechnie, *Outsiders in the Greek Cities in the Fourth Century B.C.* (London: 1989).

McQueen 1978 = E.I. McQueen, 'Some Notes on the Antimacedonian Movement in the Peloponnese in 331 B.C.', *Historia* 27 (1978), pp. 40–64.

Magnetto 1994 = A. Magnetto, 'L'intervento di Filippo nel Peloponneso e l'iscrizione *Syll* 665', in S. Alessandrì (ed.), Ιστοριη: *Studi offerti dagli allievi a G. Nenci in occasione del suo settantesimo compleanno* (Galatina: 1994), pp. 283–308.

Magnetto 1997 = A. Magnetto, *Gli arbitrati interstatali greci* (Pisa: 1997).

Marasco 1984 = G. Marasco, *Democare di Leuconoe: politica e cultura in Atene tra IV e III sècolo a.C.* (Florence: 1984).

Marasco 1985 = G. Marasco, 'Cherone di Pallene: un tiranno del IV sècolo a.C.', in F. Broilo (ed.), *Xenia: scritti in onore di Piero Treves* (Rome: 1985), pp. 111–119.

Mari 2002 = M. Mari, *Al di là dell'Olimpo: Macedoni e grandi santuari della Grecia dall'età arcaica al primo ellenismo* (Paris: 2002).

Mendels 1984 = D. Mendels, 'Aetolia 331–301: Frustration, Political Power, and Survival', *Historia* 33 (1984), pp. 129–180.

Moretti 1967 = L. Moretti, *Iscrizioni Storiche Ellenistiche* 2 (Florence: 1967).

Mossé 2001 = C. Mossé, *Alexandre: La Destinée du mythe* (Paris: 2001).

Musti 2000 = D. Musti, 'Il tema dell'autonomia nelle Elleniche di Senofonte', *RFIC* 128 (2000), pp. 170–181.

Perlman 1985 = S. Perlman, 'Greek Diplomatic Tradition and the Corinthian League of Philip of Macedon', *Historia* 34 (1985), pp. 153–174.

Poddighe 2002 = E. Poddighe, *Nel segno di Antipatro: l'eclissi della democrazia ateniese dal 323/2 al 319/8 a.C.* (Rome: 2002).

Poddighe 2004 = E. Poddighe, 'Una possibile identificazione del paidotriba di Sicione: Ps. Dem. XVII, 16', *QS* 59 (2004), pp. 183–196.

Poddighe 2007 = E. Poddighe, 'La questione samia tra Alessandro e Atene: libertà dei Greci', *QS* 66 (2007), pp. 29–45.

Prandi 1983 = L. Prandi, 'Alessandro Magno e Chio: considerazioni su *Syll.* 283 e *SEG* XXII, 506', *Aevum* 57 (1983), pp. 24–32.

Prandi 1988 = L. Prandi, *Platea: momenti e problema della storia di una polis* (Padua: 1988).

Prandi 1996 = L. Prandi, *Fortuna e realtà del'opera di Clitarco* (Stuttgart: 1996).

Price 1988 = S. Price, 'Greece and Hellenistic World', in J. Boardman, J. Griffin, and O. Murray (eds), *The Oxford History of the Classical World* (Oxford: 1988), pp. 309–331.

Rhodes–Osborne = P.J. Rhodes and and R. Osborne (eds), *Greek Historical Inscriptions, 404–323 BC* (Oxford: 2003).

Rosen 1978 = K. Rosen, 'Der "göttliche Alexander", Athen, und Samos', *Historia* 27 (1978), pp. 20–40.

Ryder 1965 = T.T.B. Ryder, *Koine Eirene: General Peace and Local Independence in Ancient Greece* (Oxford: 1965).

Sakellariou 1980 = M.B. Sakellariou, 'Panhellenism: From Concept to Policy', in M.B. Hatzopoulos and L.D. Loukopoulos (eds), *Philip of Macedon* (Athens: 1980), pp. 242–245.

Sanchez 2001 = P. Sanchez, *L'Amphictionie des Pyles et de Delphes* (Stuttgart: 2001).

Sawada 1996 = N. Sawada, 'Athenian Politics in the Age of Alexander the Great: A Reconsideration of the Trial of Ctesiphon', *Chiron* 26 (1996), pp. 57–74.

Schmidt 1999 = K. Schmidt, 'The Peace of Antalcidas and the Idea of the *Koine Eirene*: A Panhellenic Peace Movement', *RIDA* 46 (1999), pp. 81–96.

Seibert 1998 = J. Seibert, '"Panhellenischer" Kreuzzug, Nationalkrieg, Rachefeldzug oder makedonischer Eroberungskrieg? Überlegungen zu den Ursachen des Krieges gegen Persien', in W. Will (ed.), *Alexander der Grosse: Eine Welteroberung und ihr Hintergrund* (Bonn: 1998), pp. 5–58.

Shipley 1987 = G. Shipley, *A History of Samos 800–188 B.C.* (Oxford: 1987).

Sisti 2001 = F. Sisti (ed.), *Arriano: Anabasi di Alessandro* 1 (Milan: 2001).

Sisti and Zambrini 2004 = F. Sisti and A. Zambrini (eds), *Arriano: Anabasi di Alessandro* 2 (Milan: 2004).

Sordi 1984a = M. Sordi, 'Alessandro e l'Anfizionia nel 336/5', in M. Sordi (ed.), *Alessandro Magno tra storia e mito* (Milan: 1984), pp. 9–13.

Sordi 1984b = M. Sordi (ed.), *Alessandro Magno tra storia e mito* (Milan: 1984).

Sordi 1996 = M. Sordi, 'Larissa e la dinastia Alevade', *Aevum* 70 (1996), pp. 37–45.

Squillace 2004 = G. Squillace, *Filippo II e Alessandro Magno tra opposizione e consenso* (Soveria Mannelli: 2004).

Tod 1948 = M.N. Tod, *A Selection of Greek Historical Inscriptions* 2 (Oxford 1948).

Tritle 1988 = L.A. Tritle, *Phocion the Good* (London: 1988).

Tritle 1995 = L.A. Tritle, 'Review of E.M. Harris (1995)', *BMCR* 6 (1995), pp. 492–498.

Tronson 1985 = A. Tronson, 'The Relevance of IG II 329 to the Hellenic League of Alexander the Great', *Anc. World* 12 (1985), pp. 15–19.

Voutiras 1998 = E. Voutiras, 'Athéna dans les cités de Macédoine', *Kernos* 11 (1998), pp. 111–129.

Walbank 1967 = F.W. Walbank, *A Historical Commentary of Polybius* 2 (Oxford: 1967).

Whitehead 2000 = D. Whitehead, *Hypereides: The Forensic Speeches* (Oxford: 2000).

Will 1982 = W. Will, 'Zur Datierung der Rede Ps. Demosthenes XVII', *RhM* 125 (1982), pp. 202–212.

Worthington 1986 = Ian Worthington, 'Hyper. 5 *Dem.* 18 and Alexander's Second Directive to the Greeks', *C&M* 37(1986), pp. 115–121.

Worthington 1990 = Ian Worthington, 'Alexander the Great and the Date of the Mytilene Decree', *ZPE* 83 (1990), pp. 194–214.

Worthington 1992 = Ian Worthington, *A Historical Commentary on Dinarchus: Rhetoric and Conspiracy in Fourth-Century Athens* (Ann Arbor: 1992).

Worthington 1994a = Ian Worthington, 'The Harpalus Affair and the Greek Responses to the Macedonian Hegemony', in Ian Worthington (ed.), *Ventures into Greek History. Essays in Honour of N.G.L. Hammond* (Oxford: 1994), pp. 307–330.

Worthington 2000 = Ian Worthington, 'Review of Blackwell (1999)', *CR* 50 (2000), pp. 188–1.

6

ALEXANDER
AND THE PERSIAN EMPIRE

Introduction

Alexander invaded Persia in spring 334. He had with him an army of some 32,000 infantry and 5,000 cavalry (but note Sources 19 and 20), which grew to about 50,000 when it linked with an advance force (Arr. 1.17.11). He crossed the Hellespont, symbolically casting a spear into Asian soil before he disembarked to show he regarded Persia as 'spear-won' territory, and then immediately went to Troy to sacrifice at the tomb of his hero and ancestor Achilles.[1] Soon after Alexander advanced to the Granicus river in Hellespontine Phrygia, where he defeated a Persian army (cf. Sources 41 and 42).[2] This was not a Persian army proper but a hastily levied contingent and the Great King, Darius III, was not present at the battle. Alexander then journeyed down the coast of Asia Minor, dealing with any resistance (as at Miletus and Halicarnassus) and freeing Greek cities there from Persian rule, in accordance with one of the reasons for the invasion that he had laid before the League of Corinth. In Priene he dedicated the newly constructed temple of Athena Polias (Source 26). It is likely that the cities of Asia Minor joined the League of Corinth.

In 333, Alexander detoured to Gordium, where he untied (in controversial fashion) the famous Gordian knot (Sources 43 and 44). The symbolism of Alexander's act here was obvious, for it was written that whoever cut the knot would conquer Asia. There was some truth to this fable, for later in the same year the invaders again met the Persians, led by the Great King himself, in battle at Issus (Sources 46–49). Alexander won the battle, and Darius fled the battlefield, leaving behind his wife and daughters to fall into Macedonian hands. Alexander treated them with respect (cf. Source 50). Issus was a turning point for Alexander, for after it he began to refer to himself as Lord of Asia (although Darius was still alive), and the battle was quickly taken up by Alexander's propaganda machine.[3] Rather than pursue Darius after the battle, Alexander announced his intention to go to Egypt, which he reached in late 332 after being distracted for some time by the famous sieges of Tyre (Sources 51 and 52; cf. 86). The Egyptians welcomed him with open arms, and the Persian satrap surrendered the country to him. The following year he officially founded the great city of Alexandria (Source 114), which became so important in the Hellenistic and Roman periods, and he also visited the Oracle of Zeus Ammon at Siwah (see Sources 98–103), a visit that was a key turning point in his pretensions to personal divinity.[4]

Despite Alexander's preoccupation with the invasion of Asia he did not neglect the Greeks, nor they him, and in the 330s and 320s epigraphical evidence attests to various issues which they brought to his attention and his willingness to adjudicate at all levels. (See Chapter 5).

Darius was still alive, and had managed to regroup his forces. In spring 331, Alexander left Egypt and met Darius in battle at Gaugamela on 1 October 331 (Sources 53, 54 and 55), waging this battle as a son of Zeus (Source 104).[5] It was another Issus, with a Persian rout and Darius fleeing the battlefield. Again, Alexander did not pursue him, but marched to occupy the important palace capitals of Babylon, Susa and especially Persepolis. The last was the symbolic heart of the Persian empire, and as Alexander prepared to leave it (early spring 330) the palace burned to the ground (by accident or design cannot be completely determined; cf. Source 56).[6]

The destruction of the palace came to symbolize the end also of Darius and the Persian empire, for in the same year (330) the Great King was murdered at Hecatompylus. Bessus, Satrap of Bactria, succeeded him, proclaiming himself Artaxerxes V, and causing Alexander to march into Bactria and Sogdiana (in the northernmost parts of the old Persian empire) in 329 to hunt him down. The self-proclaimed Artaxerxes V was betrayed and executed in that year (cf. Sources 57 and 58). However, any thoughts that Alexander had conquered Bactria and Sogdiana were dashed when both revolted. Alexander faced over two years of intense guerrilla fighting before pacifying these regions, a campaign that culminated in his marriage to Roxanne of Bactria. Then towards the end of the same year (327) he invaded India.

During his time in Asia, Alexander began to change drastically as a king and as a man – hardly a surprise given not only his successes but also the wealth and splendour of the Persian court (see Sources 38 and 39). For example, in 330 at Zadracarta he began wearing Persian dress and the Persian upright tiara. Both actions caused dissatisfaction with his men, but to make matters worse after the visit to Siwah in 332 he called himself son of Zeus, and in 327 at Balkh attempted to enforce the Asian custom of *proskynesis* (genuflection) on his men, which was resisted (Sources 94 and 95).[7] Both of these actions can only be connected to his belief in his own divinity. The integration of Persians into his army and administration also caused dissatisfaction, although the Persian satraps he set up in various regions were never in control of the army or treasury. Because of growing discontent against him and then his growing paranoia, Alexander grew suspicious of those who were close to him. Thus at Phrada in 330 he had Philotas executed (who had allegedly plotted against him) and his father Parmenion assassinated (Source 107), and in 328 after a drunken quarrel he killed Cleitus at Maracanda for his undue (in Alexander's opinion) praise of Philip (Source 59). The conspiracy of the Pages in 327 was the most serious attempt on his life he faced (see Sources 108–113), and in dealing with it he implicated Callisthenes, who had defied him in his attempt to introduce *proskynesis*, in it. (On conspiracies, see Chapter 11).

However it was not merely Alexander's 'orientalism', paranoia and divine leanings that were distancing him from his men: the campaign itself was a factor. The army expected Alexander would announce a return to Greece when Darius was found dead at Hecatompylus in 330. Instead, Alexander persuaded the men to march after Bessus, thus initiating a new phase, not one sanctioned by the League of Corinth, in the Macedonian invasion of Asia. And in 327, when Alexander was at the farthest limits of the old Persian empire, there was every reason then to return to Greece. However, for personal reasons Alexander had no such intention, for India beckoned (on India, see Chapter 7).

Alexander's military exploits in Asia are less controversial than the questions they raise. Why did Alexander not want to return to Greece? What were his aims now?[8] How did he see himself, as Macedonian king, Great King, or some combination of both? What sorts of problems beyond the military did Alexander face in the administration of his empire, how did he try to deal with them, and how successful was he? Again, the nature of our sources and their presentation of Alexander pose problems. (On Alexander's administrative measures in India, see Chapter 7).

Ancient sources

Geography

36　As we pass from Europe to Asia in our geography, the northern division is the first of the two divisions to which we come; and therefore we must begin with this. Of this division the first portion is that in the region of the Tanais River, which I have taken as the boundary between Europe and Asia. This portion forms, in a way, a peninsula, for it is surrounded on the west by the Tanais River and Lake Maeotis as far as the Bosporus and that part of the coast of the Euxine Sea which terminates at Colchis; and then on the north by the Ocean as far as the mouth of the Caspian Sea; and then on the east by this same sea as far as the boundary between Albania and Armenia, where empty the rivers Cyrus and Araxes, the Araxes flowing through Armenia and the Cyrus through Iberia and Albania; and lastly, on the south by the tract of country which extends from the outlet of the Cyrus River to Colchis, which is about three thousand stades from sea to sea, across the territory of the Albanians and the Iberians, and therefore is described as an isthmus. But those writers who have reduced the width of the isthmus as much as Cleitarchus has, who says that it is subject to inundation from either sea, should not be considered even worthy of mention. Poseidonius states that the isthmus is fifteen hundred stades across, as wide as the isthmus from Pelusium ... 'And in my opinion,' he says, 'the isthmus from Lake Maeotis to the Ocean does not differ much therefrom' (Cleitarchus, *FGrH* 137 F 13 = Strabo 11.1.5).

37　Parthia's capital, Hecatompylus itself, is 133 miles distant from the Caspian Gates. Thus the kingdom of the Parthians also is shut out by these passes. As soon as one leaves these gates one meets the Caspian nation; this extends to the shores ... from this nation back to the river Cyrus the distance is said to be 225 miles; if we go from the same river to the Caspian gates, it is 700 miles. It was these Gates that they made the central point of Alexander's marches, setting down the distance from the Gates to the frontier of India as 15,680 stades; to the city of Bactra, which they call Zariasta, as 3,700 stades; from there to the river Iaxartes, as 5,000 stades. But, in order that the topography of the region may be understood, we are following Alexander the Great's tracks. Diognetus (*FGrH* 120 F 1) and Baeton, the surveyors of his expeditions, have written that from the Caspian Gates to Hecatompylus, the city of the Parthians, there are as many miles as we have said; from there to Alexandria of the Arii, a city which Alexander founded, the distance is 575 miles; to Prophthasia, a city of the Drangae, 199 miles; to the town of the Arachosii, 565 miles; to Hortospanus, 175 miles; from there to Alexander's town, 50 miles – in certain copies different figures are found – and this city is placed at the foot of the Caucasus itself; from it to the river Cophes and to Peucolatis, a town of India, 237 miles; from there to the river Indus and the town of Taxila, 60 miles; to the famous river Hydaspes, 120 miles; to the Hyphasis, a river no less famous, 390 miles – which was the terminus of Alexander's marches, although he crossed the river and dedicated altars on the opposite side (Baeton, *FGrH* 119 F 2a = Pliny, *Natural History* 6.44–45, 61).

Wealth and customs

38   But Chares of Mytilene, in the fifth book of his *History of Alexander*, says: 'The Persian kings had come to such a pitch of luxury, that at the head of the royal couch there was a supper-room laid with five couches, in which there were always kept five thousand talents of gold; and this was called the King's pillow. And at his feet was another supper-room, prepared with three couches, in which there were constantly kept three thousand talents of silver; and this was called the King's footstool. And in his bedchamber there was also a golden vine, inlaid with precious stones, above the King's bed' – and this vine, Amyntas says in his *Stages* (*FGrH* 122 F 6),[9] had bunches of grapes, composed of most valuable precious stones – 'and not far from it there was placed a golden bowl, the work of Theodorus of Samos' (Chares, *FGrH* F 2 = Athen. 12.514e–f).

39   Perhaps also the following, mentioned by Polycleitus, is one of their customs. He says that in Susa each one of the kings built for himself on the acropolis a separate habitation, treasure houses, and storage places for what tributes they each exacted, as memorials of his administration; and that they exacted silver from the people on the sea board, and from the people in the interior such things as each country produced, so that they also received dyes, drugs, hair, or wool, or something else of the kind, and likewise cattle; and that the king who arranged the separate tributes was Darius, called the Long-armed, and the most handsome of men, except for the length of his arms, for they reached even to his knees; and that most of the gold and silver is used in articles of equipment, but not much in money; and that they consider those metals as better adapted for presents and for depositing in storehouses; and that so much coined money as suffices their needs is enough; and that they coin only what money is commensurate with their expenditures (Nicobule, *FGrH* 127 F 3a = Strabo 15.3.21).

40   Now in early times the Sogdians and Bactrians did not differ much from the nomads in their modes of life and customs, although the Bactrians were a little more civilized; however, of these, as of the others, Onesicritus does not report their best traits, saying, for instance, that those who have become helpless because of old age or sickness are thrown out alive as prey to dogs kept expressly for this purpose, which in their native tongue are called 'undertakers', and that while the land outside the walls of the metropolis of the Bactrians looks clean, yet most of the land inside the walls is full of human bones; but that Alexander broke up the custom (Onesicritus, *FGrH* 134 – now *BNJ* 134 – F 5 = Strabo 11.11.3).

Battle of Granicus river

41   Of the Barbarians, we are told, twenty thousand footmen fell (at the Granicus), and twenty-five hundred horsemen. But on Alexander's side, Aristobulus says there were thirty-four dead in all, of whom nine were footmen (Aristobulus, *FGrH* 139 F 5 = Plut. *Alex*. 16.15).

42   They fight. Fearing then that they might some time be rebuked as having betrayed the cause to Alexander, they stayed and made ready for battle. Now Alexander encamped

on the edge of the Granicus and the Persians on the side opposite. When they joined in battle, Alexander won. He took much booty from the Persians and sent it to Greece, astounding the Greeks even in this manner; he also sent gifts to his mother Olympias. After this he proceeded to the next region (*Anonymous History of Alexander, FGrH* 151 F 1).

The Gordian knot

43   When Alexander arrived at Gordium, he was seized with an ardent desire to go up into the citadel, which contained the palace of Gordius and his son Midas. He was also desirous of seeing the wagon of Gordius and the cord of the yoke of this wagon. There was a great deal of talk about this wagon among the neighbouring population. It was said that Gordius was a poor man among the ancient Phrygians, who had a small piece of land to till, and two yoke of oxen. He used one of these in ploughing and the other to draw the wagon. On one occasion, while he was ploughing, an eagle settled upon the yoke, and remained sitting there until the time came for unyoking the oxen. Being alarmed at the sight, he went to the Telmissian soothsayers to consult them about the sign from the deity; for the Telmissians were skillful in interpreting the meaning of Divine manifestations, and the power of divination has been bestowed not only upon the men, but also upon their wives and children from generation to generation. When Gordius was driving his wagon near a certain village of the Telmissians, he met a maiden fetching water from the spring, and to her he related how the sign of the eagle had appeared to him. As she herself was of the prophetic race, she instructed him to return to the very spot and offer sacrifice to Zeus the king. Gordius requested her to accompany him and direct him how to perform the sacrifice. He offered the sacrifice in the way the girl suggested, and afterwards married her. A son was born to them named Midas. When Midas was grown to be a man, handsome and valiant, the Phrygians were harassed by civil discord, and consulting the oracle, they were told that a wagon would bring them a king, who would put an end to their discord. While they were still deliberating about this very matter, Midas arrived with his father and mother, and stopped near the assembly, wagon and all. They, comparing the oracular response with this occurrence, decided that this was the person whom the god told them the wagon would bring. They therefore appointed Midas king; and he, putting an end to their discord, dedicated his father's wagon in the citadel as a thank-offering to Zeus the king for sending the eagle. In addition to this the following saying was current concerning the wagon, that whosoever could loosen the cord of the yoke of this wagon, was destined to gain the rule of Asia. The cord was made of cornel bark, and neither end nor beginning of it could be seen. It is said by some that when Alexander could find out no way to loosen the cord and yet was unwilling to allow it to remain unloosened, lest this should exercise some disturbing influence upon the multitude, he struck it with his sword and cutting it through, said that it had been loosened. But Aristobulus says that he pulled out the pin of the wagon-pole, which was a wooden peg driven right through it, holding the cord together. Having done this, he drew out the yoke from the wagon-pole. How Alexander performed the feat in connection with this cord, I cannot affirm with confidence. At any rate both he and his troops departed from the wagon as if the oracular prediction concerning the loosening of the cord had been fulfilled. Moreover, that very night, the thunder and lightning were signs of its fulfillment; and for this reason Alexander offered sacrifice on the following day to the gods who had revealed the signs and the way to loosen the cord (Aristobulus, *FGrH* 139 F 7a = Arr. 2.3).

44   And after he had taken the city of Gordium, reputed to have been the home of the ancient Midas, he saw the much-talked-of wagon bound fast to its yoke with bark of the cornel tree, and heard a story confidently told about it by the Barbarians, to the effect that whosoever loosed the fastening was destined to become king of the whole world. Well, then, most writers say that since the fastenings had their ends concealed, and were intertwined many times in crooked coils, Alexander was at a loss how to proceed, and finally loosened the knot by cutting it through with his sword, and that when it was thus smitten many ends were to be seen. But Aristobulus says that he undid it very easily, by simply taking out the so-called 'hestor' or pin, of the wagon-pole, by which the yoke-fastening was held together, and then drawing away the yoke (Aristobulus, *FGrH* 139 F 7b = Plut. *Alex.* 18.2–4).

Alexander and the river Cydnus

45   While he was still in Cilicia, he fell sick of a very serious attack of illness for the reason following: The river Cydnus flowed through the middle of Tarsus, a city of Cilicia. Its waters are crystal clear and its flow perfectly calm. On account of the heat Alexander plunged in and was swimming more than he should, when for this very reason he was seized with convulsions and fell sick and after the seventh day all despaired of his life. The doctors saved him with difficulty (*Anonymous History of Alexander, FGrH* 151 F 6).

Battle of Issus

46   I mean Alexander's battle with Darius in Cilicia. Callisthenes tells us that Alexander had already passed the narrows and the so-called Cilician Gates, while Darius had marched through the pass known as the Gates of Amanus and had descended with his army into Cilicia. On learning from the natives that Alexander was advancing in the direction of Syria he followed him up, and when he approached the pass, encamped on the banks of the river Pinarus. The distance, he says, from the sea to the foot of the hills is not more than fourteen stades, the river running obliquely across this space, with gaps in its banks just where it issues from the mountains, but in its whole course through the plain as far as the sea passing between steep hills difficult to climb. Having given this sketch of the country, he tells us that Darius and his generals, when Alexander turned and marched back to meet them, decided to draw up the whole phalanx in the camp itself in its original position, the river affording protection, as it ran close past the camp. After this he says they drew up the cavalry along the sea shore, the mercenaries next them at the brink of the river, and the peltasts next the mercenaries in a line reaching as far as the mountains. It is difficult to understand how they posted all these troops in front of the phalanx, considering that the river ran close past the camp, especially in view of their numbers, for as Callisthenes himself says, there were thirty thousand cavalry and thirty thousand mercenaries. ... Where, then, were the mercenaries posted, unless indeed they were drawn up behind the cavalry? This he tells us was not so, as they were the first to meet the Macedonian attack. We must, then, of necessity, understand that the cavalry occupied that half of the space which was nearest to the sea and the mercenaries the half nearest the hills, and from this it is easy to reckon what was the depth of the cavalry and how far away from the camp the river must have been. After this he tells us that on the approach of the enemy, Darius, who was half way down the

line, called the mercenaries himself from the wing to come to him … Lastly, he says that
the cavalry from the right wing advanced and attacked Alexander's cavalry, who received
their charge bravely and delivering a counter charge fought stubbornly. He forgets that
there was a river between them and such a river as he has just described. Very similar are
his statements about Alexander. He says that when he crossed to Asia he had forty
thousand foot and four thousand five hundred horse, and that when he was on the point
of invading Cilicia he was joined by a further force of five thousand foot and eight
hundred horse. Suppose we deduct from this total three thousand foot and three hundred
horse, a liberal allowance for those absent on special service, there still remain forty-two
thousand foot and five thousand horse. Assuming these numbers, he tells us that when
Alexander heard the news of Darius' arrival in Cilicia he was a hundred stades away and
had already traversed the pass. In consequence he turned and marched back through the
pass with the phalanx in front, followed by the cavalry, and last of all the baggage-train.
Immediately on issuing into the open country he re-formed his order, passing to all the
word of command to form into phalanx, making it at first thirty-two deep, changing
this subsequently to sixteen deep, and finally as he approached the enemy to eight deep.
These statements are even more absurd than his former ones. From all this it is quite
plain that when Alexander made his army sixteen deep the line necessarily extended for
twenty stades, and this left all the cavalry and ten thousand of the infantry over.

After this he says that Alexander led on his army in an extended line, being then at a
distance of about forty stades from the enemy … A single one mentioned by Callisthenes
himself being sufficient to convince us of its impossibility … For he tells us that the
torrents descending from the mountains have formed so many clefts in the plain that
most of the Persians in their flight perished in such fissures. But, it may be said,
Alexander wished to be prepared for the appearance of the enemy … But here is the
greatest of all his mistakes. He tells us that Alexander, on approaching the enemy, made
his line eight deep … But he tells us that there was only a space of less than fourteen
stades, and as half of the cavalry were on the left near the sea and half on the right, the
room available for the infantry is still further reduced. Add to this that the whole line
must have kept at a considerable distance from the mountains so as not to be exposed to
attack by those of the enemy who held the foothills. We know that he did as a fact draw
up part of his force in a crescent formation to oppose these latter … It would be too long
a story to mention all the other absurdities of his narrative, and it will suffice to point
out a few. He tells us that Alexander in drawing up his army was most anxious to be
opposed to Darius in person, and that Darius also at first entertained the same wish, but
afterwards changed his mind (Callisthenes, *FGrH* 124 F 35 = Polybius 12.17–22).
47 (3) When he reached Cilicia and passed over the Cilician Taurus Range, he
encamped at Issus, a narrow spot in Cilicia and hard on the cavalry because it is rough
ground. (4) Darius was not willing to wait for Alexander in Persia nor to risk all his
power. He therefore raised an army and came to meet him. When he heard that
Alexander was in camp at Issus, he realised well how unsuitable for battle the place was.
But he did not want to appear as if he were choosing his ground, so with Persian vain-
glory he came to the Issus himself and pitched his camp there. The armies met in battle
and Alexander won the day. (5) Darius despairing for his safety fled, leaving his dearest
ones behind him. Alexander caught his wife prisoner, his mother, his daughters Stateira
and Drypetis and his son Ochus. Darius wished to ransom them and sent envoys to
Alexander asking for a truce and peace and offering him all the lands within the river

Halys and whichever one of his daughters Alexander might choose to marry and a dowry of 20,000 talents. But Alexander rejected the offer and went on, subjugating the barbarian nations next in his course (*Anonymous History of Alexander, FGrH* 151 FF 3–5).

48 At Issus he (Alexander) was run through the thigh with a sword by Darius (as Chares relates), who encountered him hand to hand. Alexander also himself, writing the truth with all sincerity to Antipater, said, that it was my fortune to be wounded with a poniard in the thigh, but no ill symptoms attended it either when it was newly done or afterwards during the cure (Chares, *FGrH* 125 F 6 = [Plut.] *Mor.* 341c).

49 Of the Persians were killed Arsames, Rheomithres, and Atizyes, three of the men who had commanded the cavalry at the Granicus. Sabaces, viceroy of Egypt, and Bubaces, one of the Persian dignitaries, were also killed, besides about 100,000 of the private soldiers, among them being more than 10,000 cavalry. So great was the slaughter that Ptolemy, son of Lagus, who then accompanied Alexander, says that the men who were with them pursuing Darius, coming in the pursuit to a ravine, passed over it upon the corpses (Ptolemy, *FGrH* 138 F 6 = Arr. 2.11.8).

The Persian royal family

50 Nor did he treat the mother, wife, and children of Darius with neglect; for some of those who have written Alexander's history say that on the very night in which he returned from the pursuit of Darius, entering the Persian king's tent, which had been selected for his use, he heard the lamentation of women and other noise of a similar kind not far from the tent. Enquiring therefore who the women were, and why they were in a tent so near, he was answered by someone as follows: 'O king, the mother, wife, and children of Darius are lamenting for him as slain, since they have been informed that thou hast his bow and royal mantle, and that his shield has been brought back.' When Alexander heard this, he sent Leonnatus, one of his Companions, to them, with injunctions to tell them: 'Darius is still alive; in his flight he left his arms and mantle in the chariot; and these are the only things of his that Alexander has.' Leonnatus entered the tent and told them the news about Darius, saying, moreover, that Alexander would allow them to retain the state and retinue befitting their royal rank, as well as the title of queens; for he had not undertaken the war against Darius from a feeling of hatred, but he had conducted it in a legitimate manner for the empire of Asia. Such are the statements of Ptolemy and Aristobulus (*FGrH* 139 F 10). But there is another report, to the effect that on the following day Alexander himself went ... (Ptolemy, *FGrH* 138 F 7 = Arr. 2.12.3–6).

The siege of Tyre

51 But Tyre he besieged for seventh months with moles, and engines-of-war, and two hundred triremes by sea. During this siege he had a dream in which he saw Heracles stretching out his hand to him from the wall and calling him. And many of the Tyrians dreamed that Apollo told them he was going away to Alexander, since he was displeased at what was going on in the city. Whereupon, as if the god had been a common deserter caught in the act of going over to the enemy, they encircled his colossal figure with cords and nailed it down to its pedestal, calling him an Alexandrist. In another dream, too, Alexander thought he saw a satyr who mocked him at a distance, and eluded his grasp when he tied to catch him, but finally, after much coaxing and chasing, surrendered.

159

The seers, dividing the word 'satyros' into two parts, said to him, plausibly enough, 'Tyre is to be yours'. And a spring is pointed out, near which Alexander dreamed he saw the satyr (Chares, *FGrH* 125 F 7 = Plut. *Alex.* 24.5–9).[10]

52   When he was out of Cilicia and came to Sidon, he attacked Tyre, a city of Sidon, and laid siege to it. Because he could not take it after a long siege, he was in a dilemma: neither did he wish to leave it unconquered nor to wait in his hurry to overtake Darius. He formed a plan as follows: Along the wall he saw a place constructed of several stones built in together. He ordered his subordinates to dig under them and when the place was dug through he and his army entered the city. In this manner he became master of Tyre and indignant for the Tyrians' long resistance he had in mind to kill all from the youth upwards. After the death of some he ceased this excessive cruelty, both due to his friends' intercession and to his reverence for Heracles, who was preeminently honoured by the Tyrians (*Anonymous History of Alexander*, *FGrH* 151 F 7).

Battle of Gaugamela

53   But those authors who make Arbela most distant say that it is 600 stades away from the place where Alexander and Darius fought their last battle, while those who make it least distant, say that it is 500 stades off. But Ptolemy and Aristobulus (*FGrH* 139 F 16) say that the battle was fought at Gaugamela near the river Bumodus. As Gaugamela was not a city, but only a large village, the place is not celebrated, nor is the name pleasing to the ear; hence, it seems to me, that Arbela, being a city, has carried off the glory of the great battle (Ptolemy, *FGrH* 138 F 10 = Arr. 6.11.5).

54   (12) After his defeats in two battles Darius was preparing for a third engagement.[11] He mustered all the hosts under his sway, till they aggregated one million. A large portion of his army was cavalry and archers, especially since the barbarians had not trained themselves in Greek war-practice. He also had elephants brought to him from India, the equipment of which was as follows: wooden towers suitably fashioned were placed on their backs, from which men fought with weapons, the result being that opponents were destroyed both by the men in the towers with their arms and by the elephants that trod them underfoot. Besides these Darius had scythe-bearing chariots drawn by four horses each and built as follows: On their wheels in the felloes were fashioned scythes, so that when these chariots rolled forward the ranks would break up and the men who fell would meet a most horrible death; because, with the motion of the scythes, some were caught by the arms, others by their legs and others by their armour and were dragged a long way till they were killed. (13) When they engaged in the fight Alexander devised the following weapon against the elephants: he had bronze caltrops made of extreme sharpness and cast on the ground where the animals were. The elephants would be pricked and would not come forward; they were pinned by the caltrops and fell (*Anonymous History of Alexander*, *FGrH* 151 FF 12–13).

55   However, it is thought that he (Darius) would not then have made his escape, had not fresh horsemen come from Parmenion summoning Alexander to his aid, on the grounds that a large force of the enemy still held together there and would not give ground. For there is general complaint that in that battle Parmenion was sluggish and inefficient, either because old age was now impairing somewhat his courage, or because he was made envious and resentful by the arrogance and pomp, to use the words of Callisthenes, of Alexander's power. At the time, then, although he was annoyed by the

summons, the king did not tell his soldiers the truth about it, but on the grounds that it was dark and he would therefore remit further slaughter, sounded a recall; and as he rode towards the endangered portion of his army, he heard by the way that the enemy had been utterly defeated and was in flight (Callisthenes, *FGrH* 124 F 37 = Plut. *Alex.* 33.9–11).

The burning of the Persepolis palace

56 And did not the great Alexander keep Thais about him, who was an Athenian courtesan? And Cleitarchus speaks of her as having been the cause that the palace of Persepolis was burnt down (Cleitarchus, *FGrH* 137 F 11 = Athen. 13.576d–e).

The hunt for Bessus

57 After passing over the river Oxus, he made a forced march to the place where he heard that Bessus was with his forces; but at this time messengers reached him from Spitamenes and Dataphernes, to announce that they would arrest Bessus and hand him over to Alexander if he would send to them merely a small army and a commander for it; since even at that very time they were holding him under guard, though they had not bound him with fetters. When Alexander heard this, he gave his army a rest, and marched more slowly than before. But he dispatched Ptolemy, son of Lagus, at the head of three regiments of the Companion cavalry and all the horse-javelin-men, and of the infantry, the brigade of Philotas, one regiment of 1,000 shield-bearing guards, all the Agrianians, and half the archers, with orders to make a forced march to Spitamenes and Dataphernes. Ptolemy went according to his instructions, and completing ten days' march in four days, arrived at the camp where on the preceding day the barbarians under Spitamenes had bivouacked. Here Ptolemy learned that Spitamenes and Dataphernes were not firmly resolved about the betrayal of Bessus. He therefore left the infantry behind with orders to follow him in regular order, and advanced with the cavalry till he arrived at a certain village, where Bessus was with a few soldiers; for Spitamenes and his party had already retired from thence, being ashamed to betray Bessus themselves. Ptolemy posted his cavalry right round the village, which was enclosed by a wall supplied with gates. He then issued a proclamation to the barbarians in the village, that they would be allowed to depart uninjured if they surrendered Bessus to him. They accordingly admitted Ptolemy and his men into the village. He then seized Bessus and returned; but sent a messenger on before to ask Alexander how he was to conduct Bessus into his presence. Alexander ordered him to bind the prisoner naked in a wooden collar, and thus to lead him and place him on the right hand side of the road along which he was about to march with the army. Thus did Ptolemy. When Alexander saw Bessus, he caused his chariot to stop, and asked him, for what reason he had in the first place arrested Darius, his own king, who was also his kinsman and benefactor, and then led him as a prisoner in chains, and at last killed him? Bessus said that he was not the only person who had decided to do this, but that it was the joint act of those who were at the time in attendance upon Darius, with the view of procuring safety for themselves from Alexander. For this Alexander ordered that he should be scourged, and that the herald should repeat the very same reproaches which he had himself made to Bessus in his enquiry. After being thus disgracefully tortured, he was sent away to Bactra to be put to death. Such is the account given by Ptolemy in relation to Bessus;

but Aristobulus (*FGrH* 139 F 24) says that Spitamenes and Dataphernes brought Bessus to Ptolemy, and having bound him naked in a wooden collar betrayed him to Alexander (Ptolemy, *FGrH* 138 F 14 = Arr. 3.29.6–30.5).

58   But Aristobulus says that Spitamenes and Dataphernes brought Bessus to Ptolemy, and having bound him naked in a wooden collar betrayed him to Alexander (Aristobulus, *FGrH* 139 F 24 = Arr. 3.30.5).

The murder of Cleitus

59   Aristobulus does not say whence the drunken quarrel originated, but asserts that the fault was entirely on the side of Cleitus, who, when Alexander had got so enraged with him as to jump up against him with the intention of making an end of him, was led away by Ptolemy, son of Lagus, the confidential bodyguard, though the gateway, beyond the wall and ditch of the citadel where the quarrel occurred. He adds that Cleitus could not control himself, but went back again, and falling in with Alexander who was calling out for Cleitus, he exclaimed: 'Alexander, here am I, Cleitus!' Thereupon he was struck with a long pike and killed (Aristobulus, *FGrH* 139 F 29 = Arr. 4.8.9).

Modern works

In the following selections, P. Briant, Professor of History at the Collège de France, outlines and discusses what the Persian empire was like during Darius III's kingship and considers Alexander's invasion and its impact on the Persians from their perspective. F.L. Holt, Professor of History at the University of Houston, argues against an aspect of Alexander's administration that is commonly taken as successful in maintaining control – the foundation of cities – from the perspective of Alexander's settlements in Central Asia, describing them as failures in Macedonian foreign policy. Ian Worthington, Professor of History at the University of Missouri, discusses the problems Alexander faced in ruling and administering a large, multi-cultural empire, together with the approaches and strategies he took to reconcile the subject peoples to Macedonian rule.

1   P. Briant, 'The Empire of Darius III in Perspective', in W. Heckel and L. Tritle (eds), *Alexander the Great. A New History* (Wiley-Blackwell: 2009), Chap. 8, pp. 141–170.[12]
2   F.L. Holt, 'Alexander's Settlements in Central Asia', *Ancient Macedonia* 4 (Institute for Balkan Studies, Thessaloniki: 1986), pp. 315–323.[13]
3   Ian Worthington, 'Alexander the Great, Nation Building, and the Creation and Maintenance of Empire', in V.D. Hanson (ed.), *Makers of Ancient Strategy: From the Persian Wars to the Fall of Rome* (Princeton University Press: 2010), Chap. 5, pp. 118–137.[14]

Additional reading

M.M. Austin, 'Alexander and the Macedonian Invasion of Asia', in J. Rich and G. Shipley (eds), *War and Society in the Greek World* (London: 1993), pp. 197–223.
E. Badian, 'Alexander the Great and the Loneliness of Power', in E. Badian (ed.), *Studies in Greek and Roman History* (Oxford: 1964), pp. 192–205 (reprinted in Chapter 11).

——, 'The Administration of the Empire', *Greece and Rome*[2] 12 (1965), pp. 166–182.

——, 'Alexander the Great and the Greeks in Asia', in E. Badian (ed.), *Ancient Society and Institutions. Studies Presented to Victor Ehrenberg on his 75th Birthday* (Oxford: 1966), pp. 37–69.

——, 'Alexander in Iran', *Cambridge History of Iran* 2 (Cambridge: 1985), pp. 420–501.

——, 'Alexander the Great and the Scientific Exploration of the Oriental Part of his Empire', *Ancient Society* 22 (1991), pp. 127–138.

——, 'Darius III', *Harvard Studies in Classical Philology* 100 (2000), pp. 241–268.

——, 'Conspiracies', in A.B. Bosworth and E.J. Baynham (eds), *Alexander the Great in Fact and Fiction* (Oxford: 2000), pp. 50–95.

E.N. Borza, 'Fire from Heaven: Alexander at Persepolis', *Classical Philology* 67 (1972), pp. 233–245.

——, 'Ethnicity and Cultural Policy at Alexander's Court', *Ancient World* 22 (1991), pp. 21–25 (reprinted in Chapter 9).

A.B. Bosworth, 'Alexander and the Iranians', *Journal of Hellenic Studies* 100 (1980), pp. 1–21 (reprinted in Chapter 9).

——, *Conquest and Empire, the Reign of Alexander the Great* (Cambridge: 1988), pp. 229–245.

M. Brosius, 'Alexander and the Persians', in J. Roisman (ed.), *Brill's Companion to Alexander the Great* (Leiden: 2003), pp. 169–193.

E.A. Fredricksmeyer, 'Alexander, Zeus Ammon, and the Conquest of Asia', *Transactions of the American Philological Association* 121 (1991), pp. 199–214.

——, 'Alexander the Great and the Kingship of Asia', in A.B. Bosworth and E.J. Baynham (eds), *Alexander the Great in Fact and Fiction* (Oxford: 2000), pp. 136–166.

E. Garvin, 'Darius III and Homeland Defense', in W. Heckel and L.A. Tritle (eds), *Crossroads of History. The Age of Alexander* (Claremont: 2003), pp. 87–111.

J.R. Hamilton, 'Alexander's Iranian Policy', in W. Will and J. Heinrichs (eds), *Zu Alexander d. Gr. Festschrift G. Wirth* 1 (Amsterdam: 1988), pp. 467–486.

N.G.L. Hammond, 'The Kingdom of Asia and the Persian Throne', *Antichthon* 20 (1986), pp. 73–85.

——, 'The Archaeological and Literary Evidence for the Burning of the Persepolis Palace', *Classical Quarterly*[2] 42 (1992), pp. 358–364.

W. Heckel, 'Resistance to Alexander the Great', in L. Tritle (ed.), *The Greek World in the Fourth Century* (London: 1997), pp. 189–227.

——, 'Alexander the Great and the "Limits of Civilised World"', in W. Heckel and L. Tritle (eds), *Crossroads of History, The Age of Alexander* (Claremont: 2003), pp. 147–174 (reprinted in Chapter 3).

W.E. Higgins, 'Aspects of Alexander's Imperial Administration: Some Modern Methods and Views Reviewed', *Athenaeum* 58 (1980), pp. 129–152.

F.L. Holt, '*Imperium Macedonicum* and the East: The Problem of Logistics', *Ancient Macedonia* 5 (Institute for Balkan Studies, Thessaloniki: 1993), pp. 585–592.

——, *Alexander the Great and Bactria* (Leiden: 1988).

M.J. Olbrycht, 'Macedonia and Persia', in J. Roisman and Ian Worthington (eds), *The Blackwell Companion to Ancient Macedonia* (Oxford: 2010), pp. 342–369.

S. Shabaz, 'Iranian Interpretations of Alexander', *American Journal of Ancient History*[2] 2 (1977), pp. 5–38.

B. Strauss, 'Alexander: The Military Campaign', in J. Roisman (ed.), *Brill's Companion to Alexander the Great* (Leiden: 2003), pp. 133–156.

Notes

1   Diod. 17.17.3, Arr. 1.12.1, Plut. *Alex.* 15.7–8, Justin 9.5.12.
2   Diod. 17.19–21, Arr. 1.13–16, Plut. *Alex.* 16; cf. Curt. 2.
3   On sources, see Chapter 1.
4   See, further, Chapter 10.
5   Diod. 17.56–61, Arr. 3.11–15, Plut. *Alex.* 31–33, Curt. 4.14–16.
6   Diod. 17.70–72, Arr. 3.18.10–12, Plut. *Alex.* 37.6–38, Curt. 5.7.3–11.
7   See, further, Chapter 10.
8   On Alexander's aims, see also Chapter 3.
9   'In this bedroom above the bed was a golden vineyard set with precious stones – and Amyntas says in his *Stages* that it has grape-clusters consisting of the most precious gems' (Amyntas, *FGrH* 122 F 6 = Athen. 12.514f).
10   For what comes after this passage, see Source 23.
11   This is incorrect, for Darius was not present at the Battle of the Granicus river, and so had met Alexander only once before in battle, at Issus in 333.
12   Reprinted by permission of Wiley-Blackwell.
13   Reprinted by permission of The Institute for Balkan Studies.
14   Reprinted by permission of Princeton University Press.

THE EMPIRE OF DARIUS III IN PERSPECTIVE

Pierre Briant

1 Sources and problems:
the empire in short- and middle-term perspective

1.1 *Darius and his empire*

Until recently, Achaemenid historiography did not show much interest in the reign of Darius III, or in the state of the empire at the time Alexander set foot in Asia Minor. It sufficed to explain everything by the convenient thesis of the 'colossus with feet of clay' that had become irreversibly undermined by disorganization, overtaxation, and rebellious subjects.[1] This thesis was, in itself, deemed sufficient to explain the Persian defeat in confrontations with the Macedonian armies.[2] From its origins, Alexander historiography has developed two visions on the Persian adversary. One is found in handbooks and the most recent conference proceedings: that the Achaemenid empire is evanescent to such a degree that it does not even represent one of two players in the game about to be played on the Near Eastern chessboard: time passes 'as if Alexander were alone … when he faced his personal quest.'[3] In contrast, other historians have attempted to reevaluate the military and strategic capacities of the last Great King.[4]

This double orientation in modern historiography is, to some extent, the latest avatar of a double-sided image of Darius handed down by the Greco-Roman tradition and continuously running through modern European historiography: Darius is either portrayed as a despot characterized by weakness and lack of drive, a man incapable of facing the danger that the Macedonian invasion presented to his throne and his empire; or he is glorified as a king possessing virtues and all kinds of admirable qualities, yet confronted by an enemy of such overwhelming strength that he stood no chance of gaining victory over him.[5] This second image, of a man both capable and courageous but overcome by a peerless adversary (presented by Bossuet as early as 1681), was adopted by Droysen from 1833 on, and the same conclusion is reached by a recent study by Badian (2000b: 265).[6]

This observation certainly does not imply that since Bossuet the historian's attitude toward his sources has not been redefined in terms of methodological rigor. It simply illustrates that, when scholars keep posing the same questions concerning Darius' 'merit,' there is a risk of falling into an epistemological trap, that is, to be obliged to choose between the 'vices' and the 'virtues' of Darius, a choice preconditioned by the ideological presuppositions and literary attitudes of the Classical authors.[7] Today, the historian's task should not be to 'rehabilitate' Darius, nor to summon Alexander before an international court of justice to charge him with his 'crimes.'[8]

The question of the political aptitude and strategic abilities of Darius should indeed not be ignored and, apart from a few exceptions (e.g., Strauss and Ober 1990), there is nowadays agreement among scholars that the king was not an incapable strategist. Yet, on the one hand, such an observation reduces the historical analysis to its military aspects, at the cost of the political aspects of the Persian–Macedonian conflict, while, on the other hand, the analysis may not be subordinated to a teleological approach predetermined by the Achaemenid defeats. The empire lived its own life and its rulers did not have their eyes fixed on what Classical and modern historiography has presented as a conquest that, if not determined by fate, was in any case inevitable. Consequently, it is better to avoid the term 'pre-Hellenistic' (German: *Vorhellenismus*), informed as it is by an a priori vision (*RTP* 320–3). Contrary to what a celebrated Iranian philologist in a commentary on the Xanthus Trilingual asserts, Asia Minor in the third quarter of the fourth century BC was not situated 'between the death throes of the Persian Empire and the Hellenistic Spring,' or 'in a dying world, plunged into the shadows,' a world waiting for 'the charismatic, still uncertain light of Alexander.'[9] When interpreted without such prejudices, the epigraphical document suggests a rather different assessment of the state of the empire (see below §3.1).

In order not to reduce a complex and evolving reality to the "shadow of Alexander," and to avoid an Aegeocentric approach,[10] it is helpful to analyze the Achaemenid empire, in geographical terms, as an entity stretching from Central Asia to the Aegean and, in terms of chronology, from a middle-term perspective, that is, the period roughly defined by the last part of Artaxerxes II's reign and the death of Darius III (*c.*365–330).[11] By reinserting Darius' short reign into the imperial context that precedes it, and from which it proceeds, one creates the conditions necessary for understanding the distinctiveness of the empire's internal situation.[12]

Evidently, an analysis of the kind just described would exceed the bounds of a chapter like the present one. I shall therefore only point out a number of particularly notable historical and methodological features, more precisely with evidence that, though still not fully published, [is] accessible to the historians of the empire. Many of these corpora continue into the beginnings of the Hellenistic period, but rather than treating the entire period of transition (see Briant and Joannès 2006), I aim simply to shed light on a period sometimes characterized as a Dark Age.

1.2 Greco-Roman literary sources

The Greco-Roman sources are, it should be stressed, a constituent part of the documentation that we have at our disposal. But they must be considered within the context of Achaemenid reality. Such evidence is so deeply enshrined in the Greco-Roman perspective that it is severely distorted. To give only one especially striking example: new analysis of Greco-Roman texts relating to the inhabitants of the Zagros (Uxians and Cossaeans) and to the καταρράκται in the Tigris demonstrates that, contrary to long established opinion based on superficial evaluation, the royal residences in the empire's core were not in Darius III's time at risk from the double threat of mountain 'brigands' and Persian Gulf 'pirates.'[13]

At the same time, and despite grave omissions and biases, it is clear that the historian should not minimize the testimonies of the Classical authors, as long as necessary methodological precautions are taken.[14] It is by these sources, for example, that we are informed about the violent dynastic conflicts that emerged, one after another, between the murder of Artaxerxes III (end of 338) and that of Darius III (July 330), including the brutal elimination of Arses by Bagoas followed by the rise of Codomannus/Artašata under the name of Darius (end of 336). When comparing such episodes with the numerous comparable cases since the death of Cambyses (522), it is easy to appreciate that they do not allow the conclusion of increasing decadence in Persian politics (Briant 2002b). The very same documentation clearly suggests that the accession of Darius occurred along familiar lines, with the new king assuming the robe of Cyrus, as

Artaxerxes II had done before (*HPE* 769–80, 1033–4). Also, it is generally implied in the sources that Darius managed to impose his authority: it is under his supreme command that Arsites was charged, in 334, with the command of the satrapal contingents from Asia Minor (*HPE* 820–3); from that moment until the fall of the royal residences (November 331–January 330) and the subsequent conspiracy instigated by Bessus under very special circumstances (331/30) no internal crises are detectable, nor any revolt within the Persian and Iranian nobility who held the reins of royal power.[15] One need only follow the ancient testimonies step by step to realize that, on the contrary, the leading officers, with very few exceptions (Mithrenes at Sardes), displayed an exemplary loyalty toward the crown, even after the first two defeats at the Granicus and at Issus (*HPE* 780–3, 842–52).

The Greco-Roman texts also allow, albeit only partially, the reconstruction of a relief map of Achaemenid lands, showing their specific aspects and traits at the moment they were crossed and conquered by Alexander's armies: they show that there were satrapies, palaces, treasuries, and fortresses, plains, streams, and natural resources, populations, villages, and towns, but also regulations and administrations at the level of cities and regions, tribute and taxes, as well as an overarching system of managing expenses and revenues. From this perspective, especially when considering the period under discussion, one cannot emphasize enough the importance of Ps.-Aristotle's *Oeconomica*.[16]

It is also thanks to the same sources that we have access to information on the military organization, on the mustering of the royal armies, on the rites that precede the entry and exit of the king's retinue, on many other aspects of Achaemenid aulic practice, and on the composition of the highest ranks in the imperial government. In general, it cannot be denied that our knowledge about the last phase of Achaemenid history would be diminished if we did not possess the conqueror's perspective, if only because we lack the perspective of the conquered.

1.3 The Achaemenid documentation: illuminating life in the provinces

Still, a type of documentation like that offered by the Greco-Roman sources could never suffice; one is obliged to gather, as far as possible, a range of sources from the lands that formed the Achaemenid empire, whether they are textual (in whatever language and script), archaeological, numismatic, or iconographic. Until recently, the period under discussion ranked among the most unknown of Achaemenid imperial history. The reign of Darius II (424–405/4) is the last one that is relatively well documented, and even this reign stands out much less distinctly than the reigns of Darius I (522–486), Xerxes (486–465), and Artaxerxes I (465–425/4).[17] In the case of Darius II, royal presence and activity is attested at Persepolis (inscriptions and constructions), Ecbatana, and Susa. Life in the provinces can be studied in detail on the basis of the abundant Babylonian documentation (in particular the corpus of tablets from the Murašû firm), the exceptional Aramaic documentation from Egypt, biblical and a number of Anatolian sources (*HPE* 600–11, 981–4). The study of the reign of Artaxerxes II (405/4–359/8) still profits from a reasonably favorable documentary situation, particularly through the epigraphical and archaeological sources from Susa (construction of the Palace of Chaour) and the other royal residences.[18] At the same time one has to observe that Aramaic documentation from Egypt has disappeared (the Nile valley became independent again *c.*400) and that the Babylonian documentation has become both less abundant and more difficult to use as a result of the frequent difficulty of distinguishing between the different kings named Artaxerxes or Darius.[19] In the absence of substantial and precisely dated bodies of evidence from the provinces, and with the importance of the Greek material (particularly Plutarch, Xenophon, and Diodorus), narrative history focused on western affairs once again takes precedence. Even in that particular area uncertainty reigns, however, especially with respect to the evidence for the satrapal revolts, which has always held a decisive place in the evaluation of the empire's relative strength or fragility in the course of the fourth century.[20]

Confronting the Greek sources with those from the Achaemenid world does not always yield decisive results, since the relevance of a certain comparison is sometimes hard to demonstrate.[21] As to the economic and commercial revival occasionally deduced from Artaxerxes III's mintings (Mildenberg 1998, 1999), the proposed interpretation is both disputable and less original than it appears.[22] In some cases the ambiguities in our documentation are such that we are, for example, still neither capable of telling whether the new Egyptian revolt under pharaoh Khababbash was put down by Darius III,[23] nor of reconstructing the conditions under which the land again came to be governed by the satrap Sabaces who, like his predecessor Mazdaces, is known from the coins he struck in Egypt.[24]

Some of the imperial lands are very well known. Such is the case for Babylonia (Briant and Joannès 2006: 17–306) and Asia Minor (Briant 2006a). Other regions elude detailed analysis on account of lacunae in the documentary record (Egypt).[25] Fortunately, our knowledge of the Achaemenid world is not fixed, but expanded by an evolving corpus of new discoveries and publications.[26] As a result, two regions of very different importance, Bactria and Idumea, merit revisiting.

The recently (but not completely) published corpora from the vast Central Asiatic satrapy and the little Palestinian district are both parts of archives written in Aramaic and brought to light by illegal excavations. With the exception of a few texts,[27] they were drafted in a time frame defined by the last decades of Achaemenid history and the beginnings of the Hellenistic age: from Artaxerxes III to Alexander (358[28]–324) in Bactria, and from Artaxerxes II (362) to Ptolemy (post 306) in Idumea.[29] Incidentally, it may be noted that, thanks to the Bactrian corpus, the number of texts dated after the last Darius has grown spectacularly.[30]

The space reserved in this survey for the Aramaic documents from Bactria and Idumea can easily be justified by simple reference to an appropriate methodological remark made by Eph'al during the presentation of a preliminary synthesis of the new Palestinian sources:

> A historical picture based on non-literary sources may be likened to a mosaic, put together from tiny stones, rather than large blocks, as it is generally the case with literary sources ... A meticulous analysis of the entire corpus should help to accord the Persian period its proper place in the history of Palestine and its environs, as a substantial link between the Ancient Near East and the Hellenistic period.
>
> (Eph'al 1998: 109, 119)

Such documentation enables the historian to leave political and dynastic history for what it is and to concentrate on history from below. As has been remarked by another editor of the corpus (Lemaire 2002: 232–3), the Idumean documentation invites a modest kind of history, 'a social and economical history on a local level where a small group of tax collectors and scribes do their best to manage levies in kind and in silver from taxpayers who, for the most, are peasants.' What is true for the Idumean documents also pertains to the Bactrian corpus, with the difference that the latter is more readily accessible since it includes texts in literary (epistolary) format. Documents of that type are completely absent from the minute accounts written and abbreviated on the Idumean ostraca.

2 From Bactria to Idumea

2.1 Bactria–Sogdiana from Artaxerxes III to Alexander

Recently acquired from London dealers and purportedly coming from Afghanistan, the Khalili collection[31] includes thirty documents written on parchment and eighteen on 'wooden sticks' (small wooden boards), all inscribed in Aramaic; nine additional documents have up to this point come to light – of which five are usable and date to the same period – but these texts so far remain unedited (Shaked 2006). All are dated to the third regnal year of Darius III (333/2). The wooden boards carry brief inscriptions and are acknowledgments of debts (*ADAB*, Dl–18, pp. 31–3, 231–57). The parchment documents, on the other hand, are letters and lists of allocations. One recognizes the names of the leading officials of the satrapy such as Bagavant, whose designation is *pehat* (governor) of the town of Khulmi (modern Khulm) and who corresponds with his superior Akhvamazda. The latter could be considered the satrap in Bactria, but no text confers that title on him. An elusive reference to a treasurer/*ganzabara* is found on a fragment (B10).[32] The name of Bactra is twice attested, again in fragmentary texts (A7, A8). As the corpus testifies, the responsibilities of Akhvamazda and Bagavant were not limited strictly to Bactria.[33] Bagavant's assignment was to administer the collection of crop revenues in storages, and, additionally, the distribution of rations to various groups; additional duties included the maintenance of buildings and the construction of fortifications in Sogdiana. In 348 or 347, Bagavant, at this time in Khulmi, received a letter from Akhvamazda, telling him that he had been assigned a contingent from the local troops (*hyl' mt*) in order to construct a wall and a ditch in the town of Nikhshapaya (A4, pp. 93–9). Another letter, sent to Bagavant and to other officials, conveys Akhvamazda's renewed insistence that his orders be carried out strictly and that the wall be constructed in conformity with regulations. This time the letter is to be delivered by a messenger (*zgnd'*; compare Gk. ἀστάνδης and Akhvamazda's foreman (*frataraka-*); it concerns the town of Kiš (A5). Other texts mention more individuals and toponyms and allow tentative descriptions of the status of the garrison troops, apparently part-soldier, part-peasant.[34]

The range of different rations in document C1 (Shaked 2003: 1522–4; 2004: 40–2; *ADAB* 177–85) allows glimpses of the richness of the production in livestock (sheep, goats, cattle, donkeys, geese, chicken),[35] animal products (cheese, milk), crops, and agricultural products (fruits, spices, flour of various qualities, oil, spices, vinegar), as well as the magnitude of the reserves kept in the administration's storehouses (fodder; see also A10a). In addition, this document is part of a group of texts that yield pertinent details on the organization of official missions and the rations given to travelers at state-run halting places (C5). One finds a technical terminology known from the Aramaic documents from Egypt and the Elamite tablets from Persepolis (e.g., *baššabara* = **pasābara-*, 'travel provisions' – *ADAB* 197). Other documents again list products, such as barley, wheat, and millet disbursed as rations (*ptp*) to laborers and to the administration's personnel; the quality of the products allocated is clearly a function of the social rank of the recipient (B2). As for the term used for 'ration,' *ptp*, it is the same that is found at Elephantine as well as at Persepolis, in Babylonia (*HPE*, index, 1174) and now in Idumea (see below). One of the suppliers of rations holds an Iranian designation, rendered in Aramaic as *ptpkn* (< **piθfakāna-*).[36]

In the Bactrian corpus, one also discerns clearly the transfer of commodities from one locality to another, by means of the officials that collect them and transport them to those responsible for its distribution (C4, dated to year 7 of Alexander: *ADAB* 203–12). The meticulousness of the accounting of commodities entering and leaving the storehouses seems to equal procedures known from Persepolis (e.g., C3).

Apart from donkeys (C1, B4, B6), camels were reared (B8) and used for transports. Some of these animals were labeled 'camels of the king' (A1 :3: *gmln zy mlk'*), again an expression known from Persepolis, where it is used to refer to king's assets per se (as opposed to the institution's assets in general).[37] The situation undoubtedly was the same in Bactria. Camel-keepers (**uštrapāna-*) enjoyed a special fiscal status and were exempt from certain taxes. One letter relates that, at one occasion, they were unjustly surcharged, and even detained by Bagavant, his foreman (**frataraka-*) and the magistrates (*dyny'*), upon which Akhvamazda had to intervene on several occasions in order to make sure that his orders were followed by Bagavant and the other officials of the district (*ADAB* 68–75, A1). The document also gives some specifications on the taxes (here: *ḥlk*). In an unfortunately broken context, another document refers to 'the king's tribute' (*mndt'mlk'*: A8: 2).[38]

Akhmavazda himself seems to have owned property in the province under his control. One text refers to commodities taken out 'from [his] house' (*byt'zylk*: A2), but it is possible that the expression relates to assets that are *ex officio* under the satrap's control (see *HPE* 463). In another letter (A6), Akhvamazda reproaches Bagavant, this time for not having followed his instruction (*handarz*) to roof two old houses (located in two villages), and to bring wheat and sesame for sowing as seed to the granary in accordance with his instructions. If Bagavant remains reluctant to effectuate the order, he risks having to pay for the whole amount 'from your own house' (*byt'*). Here again, Akhvamazda refers to the buildings, the houses, and the granary as belonging to him. Are these his private property, or domains of which he, in his capacity as satrap, was the usufruct, like Aršama a century before in Egypt? Note that, like his Egyptian colleague, Akhvamazda had a steward (*paqdu*) who managed his assets, and who denounced Bagavant's culpable behavior (A6: 1). As to the threat that hangs over the latter's head, the expression used ('from your own house'), is reminiscent of the expenditures by other administrators or Persian military commanders, whose responsibility makes them liable, if necessary, 'from their own possessions' (ἐκ τῶν ἰδίων: *HPE* 595–6).

The new documentation also yields information on religious practices (Shaked 2004: 42–47; *ADAB* 35–7) and on Old Iranian onomastics (partly from local origin, such as the names built on the base *wḥšw* (**vaxšu-*), the name of the river known in Greek as the Oxus: *ADAB* 57–60). One even finds, on a rolled document (C2), the impression of a magnificent Achaemenid seal: a horseman holds up a lance and faces a rampant lion; he is accompanied by a second figure on foot who, his head covered by a *bashlyk*, holds a pike, ready to help the horseman if necessary.

A first encounter with the said documentation inspires amazement at the fact that it was found in a region that, until now, was a little-known territory that appeared in two quite disparate groups of sources: the Greco-Roman corpus of Classical and Hellenistic texts on the one hand, and the massive amount of data gathered in years of surveys in northern Afghanistan on the other. Archaeologists have always insisted on the 'particularly Bactrian' character of the hydraulic structures attested in the area since the third millennium. From their point of view, the extent of these structures and their continuity into the Achaemenid period suggest the existence, persisting during the reigns of the Great Kings, of what is invariably referred to, with a somewhat hazy description, as a 'Bactrian entity,' or a 'pre-Achaemenid Palaeo-Bactrian entity.' In this model, the focus lies on Bactrian continuities still existing after the Achaemenid conquest, which, by contrast, would not have left conspicuous traces.

This view raises several questions. That the construction of systems of irrigation canals was a phenomenon occurring throughout the third, second, and first millennia is not to be doubted. But should one deduce from the existence of an inherited "characteristically Bactrian" technique – and from that alone – that, after the Persian conquest, the Achaemenid administration never intervened in this complex? Would that not be an overinterpretation of the absence of Achaemenid textual evidence? For many reasons (including the find of an Elamite Persepolis-type administrative tablet in the Achaemenid layers of Old Kandahar[39]), which I have advanced since the start of the debate, the validity of such a rigid interpretation may be doubted.[40] From my point of view, it would seem preferable to leave open the possibility that, one day, a textual documentation from the Achaemenid period would come to light from this region.[41] This is exactly the point proved by the corpus currently being published. Obviously, the texts do not answer all the questions, but they will at least show that, contrary to well-established opinion, Bactria did not constitute a special case within the whole of the Achaemenid empire. The region was, unmistakably, a satrapy in the full sense of the word, a province where the royal administration carried out the same tasks that it had assigned itself in other parts of the empire. One is struck in particular by the formal and functional similarities between the Bactrian documentation on the one hand, and the Elamite tablets from Persepolis and the Aramaic documentation from Egypt on the other.

Another characteristic of the Bactrian administration is that it is written in a form of Aramaic very close in morphology, syntax, and redaction to that known from Achaemenid Egypt (Shaked 2004: 22–9; *ADAB* 39–51). It is fascinating to note that the hypothesis of a diffusion of *Reichsaramaïsch* throughout the lands of the Iranian plateau during the reigns of the Great Kings had already been posed with much vigor by Benveniste as early as 1958 in his edition of the Aramaic version of the Kandahar Bilingual, that is, on the basis of a document dating well into the Hellenistic period. There, he demonstrated the close links in terms of language and redaction, as evidenced by the presence of a host of Iranian loans, with the Elephantine documents dated to Artaxerxes I and Darius II. 'Nous sommes en réalité dans une province iranienne où s'étaient maintenues les traditions des chancelleries achéménides,' Benveniste concluded, speaking of the borders between the Iranian Plateau and the Indus lands.[42] This is precisely what the Aramaic documents from Bactria are now confirming. As the great number of Iranian terms they include shows (*ADAB* 281–3), it is absolutely clear that the use of Aramaic in the Bactrian documents should be related to the installation and functioning of the imperial administration of the Great Kings.

2.2 *Idumea, a province in the Trans-Euphrates satrapy between Artaxerxes II and Darius III*

The period discussed in the previous section is also illuminated by material from the other end of the empire: Idumea, at the frontiers of the Negev. In the context of the attack by one of Antigonus' generals against the city of Petra at the beginning of the Hellenistic era, Diodorus refers to the eparchy as well as to the satrapy of Idumea, centered on Lake Asphaltites (the Dead Sea).[43] At that point, Idumea served as a military base for the Macedonian troops (19.95.2, 98.1). Regardless of the term used for it, one observes that the area constituted the territory of a provincial government; its capital, during the Persian period, may have been Hebron or Lachish. The new Aramaic documentation, which is currently being published,[44] will give new impetus to the debate on the region's status during both the last phase of imperial Achaemenid history and the period of transition and the establishment of the Hellenistic kingdoms.

The size of the corpus is considerable;[45] however, it is mutilated as a result of the illegal character of the excavations that brought it to light and its subsequent dispersal, in smaller lots, between a number of museums and private collections (since *c.*1985). Nevertheless, the Aramaic ostraca from Idumea bring new insights into one of the least-known regions of the Achaemenid Trans-Euphratean lands.[46] The texts, which are extremely difficult to read, are very short and may be drafts of partial accounts, possibly destined to be included in longer documents that would have been kept in the regional archive.

Though some documents have no date at all, many mention a month name and some a regnal year. Fortunately, a few texts also provide a royal name: Artaxerxes, Alexander, Philip, and also Antigonus. The last three names may be those of Alexander IV (?),[47] Philip Arrhidaeus and Antigonus Monophthalmus (see also Wheatley, ch. 3 [in the original]).[48] The Achaemenid part of the chronology of the ostraca is established by the occurrence of the royal name Artaxerxes which can be associated with certain years and sometimes interpreted more precisely thanks to identification of individual dossiers within the corpus (Porten and Yardeni 2003, 2004, 2006). Given that there is a series of documents dating to years 42–46, it is certain that part of the corpus is from the reign of Artaxerxes II (the only king of that name who ruled for so many years), and that ostraca from years higher than 21 may be assigned to the reign of the same king. Identifying documents dating to Artaxerxes II's successors is often more complicated: Arses can be referred to only by his first or second regnal year, and Darius III by years 1–3 (until the loss of Syria), but years 1–3 may also refer to Artaxerxes III (which is, in fact, often the case[49]), Philip or Alexander.[50] Be that as it may, the beginning of the Aramaic Idumean documentation, as far as we know at present, may be fixed to 362, during the reign of Artaxerxes II.[51] None of the documents is explicitly dated to the reign of Darius III.

The ostraca are silent with regard to the designations and functions of those active in the region's administration,[52] but they imply that products were collected, undoubtedly as taxes, from the land, that they were registered and subsequently redistributed from storehouses[53] that must be those controlled by the provincial administration. Some of these are located at Maqqedah (Kirbet-el Qom, 14 km west of Hebron) and Maresha (well known from the Hellenistic period, from the correspondence of Zeno, among other sources).[54]

The texts are dockets that, after a date, mention one or several commodities, the quantity delivered, the measure in which it is counted, and a proper name. They supply, in the first place, information on the resources of a region that, manifestly, was being extensively developed in the period. Apart from cereals, flour, and straw, one finds wine, olive oil, wood, and hay (measured in fodder loads) as well as all kinds of livestock (camels, donkeys, cattle, sheep/goats, pigeons).[55] Some documents refer to the handling of silver (*ksp*), perhaps measured in shekels,[56] others to some form of cadastral register, or at any rate a registry of fields, which are, as elsewhere (*HPE* 414), sometimes measured by the amount of seed necessary for cultivation.[57] More than forty texts also speak of 'workers,' plausibly day laborers, each of whom was registered on a document. It is particularly difficult, however, to establish under what conditions such workers were recruited, and by which authority.[58]

The Idumean corpus also yields a good deal of information on the organization in 'clans' ('house,' *byt*) or 'families' ('son of,' *bny*), on the coexistence of populations with different origins in the same region during the Achaemenid period (Arabs, Arameans, Judeans, Phoenicians, etc.),[59] on the temples, and on the cults.[60] Finally, a few Iranian terms are recognizable in their Aramaic form, such as 'paradise, garden' (*prds*) and 'rations' (*ptp*).[61]

It is essential to compare the Idumean ostraca with other corpora discovered, in regular excavations, at other sites in southern Palestine, especially those of Arad and Beersheba.[62] The Arad ostraca, published in 1981, carry very short texts written in ink. They document deliveries of staple goods (barley, barley grits, straw) as fodder for animals (horses, donkeys). The texts are not dated, but may be situated, on palaeographic grounds, in the middle of the fourth century, that is, in the late Achaemenid period (Naveh 1981). The same is true for the Beersheba ostraca, which do, however, mention regnal years (from 1 to 12) that belong either to Artaxerxes II or to Artaxerxes III (the latter is more likely according to the editor: Naveh 1979). Some twelve documents may be considered as dockets that register deposits of certain quantities of barley and wheat, and that mention proper names (as in Idumea and Arad): these texts may pertain to the delivery to a central storage facility of taxes collected from farms scattered in the countryside. Based on such evidence, it appears that Beersheba must, at this date, have been one of the most importance centers (perhaps the capital?) of the Negev.

Even though the ostraca currently being published are silent on the ranks of the administration, there is no doubt that the circulation of commodities as evidenced by these tiny documents bears witness to a system well known from Persepolis, that is, that of levies, storage, and redistribution.[63] As to the utilization of the reserves, the Arad ostraca may give a possible answer: the rations given to animals and their caretakers can probably be related to the disposition of guard posts (with an organization in contingents (*degelin*), as in Elephantine), as well as to the existence of official halting stations along a road (Naveh 1981: 175–6)[64] – these are elements well known from the Persepolis tablets, from a famous Aramaic document from Egypt, and from the Greco-Roman sources (*RTP* 505; *HPE* 364–5).[65]

The Idumean ostraca now accessible illustrate imperial realities that, though situated in a micro-region, are far from insignificant. The chronological convergence of the various text groups seems to allow for the conclusion that the region was being reorganized during the later part of the reign of Artaxerxes II, resulting in a relatively dense occupation of the available space under the aegis of the imperial authorities and their local representatives.[66] It is therefore possible that our documentation bears witness to the origin of the province of Idumea as attested later by Diodorus when using the terms *satrapeia* and *eparchia*. We can scarcely go beyond that conclusion, though it is tempting to establish a link with the strategic situation of this region within the empire at the time, until 343, that the Achaemenid armies were led in counter-offensives against Egypt.[67]

3 From Halicarnassus to Sidon, via Xanthus and Tarsus: two Achaemenid satraps between Artaxerxes III and Darius III

It is not a novel observation that an inventory of satrapies constituting the empire of Darius III and a list of holders of satrapal positions can be given on the basis of Greco-Roman accounts of Alexander's expedition.[68] Yet, even when connected to episodes from earlier periods, these texts yield limited concrete and precise evidence on either the regular or the special missions of Achaemenid satraps. As shown by the Egyptian and Babylonian examples (sixth to fourth centuries) and that of Akhvamazda in Bactria during the reign of Artaxerxes III, those persons whom we would term 'satraps' are not necessarily designated as such in documents pertaining to regular administrative practice.[69] Moreover, it is much less from the Classical texts than from Achaemenid evidence (textual or numismatic; Elamite, Akkadian, Aramaic, etc.) that we may gather pieces of information on the specifics and the nature of the satraps' interventions in the daily life in the provinces, as well as on the prerogatives granted to them by the central authorities in times both of peace and war. What is true for the satraps of Egypt,[70] Babylonia, or Bactria applies also to the satraps of Asia Minor and Syria under the last Achaemenid kings. This is demonstrated by the examples of Pixodaras and Mazaeus/Mazday, selected here because of the variety of available sources and the insights they offer on how the provincial administrations represented and managed the imperial interests.

3.1 *Pixodarus at Xanthus: satrapal power and local elites*

In contrast to the case of the satrap Mausolus, whose links to the crown can be studied on the basis of a number of (largely epigraphical) sources,[71] the same type of research was rather difficult in the case of Pixodarus until recently.[72] The youngest son of Hecatomnus and brother of Mausolus, Artemisia, Hidrieus, and Ada (the last being the famous dynast/satrap of Caria), Pixodarus was born *c*.400; he died in 336/5, shortly after the accession of Darius III. Pixodarus was succeeded, as satrap in Caria, by Orontobates, who was sent not long before to Halicarnassus by the Great King and had married his predecessor's daughter, Ada the Younger.[73] The literary sources also inform us on the obscure episode of negotiations with Philip II ('the Pixodarus affair').[74]

Apart from a few inscriptions that illustrate his administrative measures in Caria and Lycia (*HPE* 709), Pixodarus used to be known particularly for his remarkable coin issues, struck in his own name.[75] He has become even more well known, however, since the French mission at Xanthus uncovered, in 1973, and published the now famous trilingual inscription, a document that continues to arouse divergent, if not conflicting interpretations.[76] Though technically a trilingual inscription (Lycian, Greek, Aramaic), the stele in fact carries the text of *two* resolutions: first, the decision taken by the inhabitants of Xanthus, expressed in Lycian and Greek, inscribed on the sides of the monument; second, the intervention of the satrap Pixodarus documented in an Aramaic text on the edge of the stele.

The evidence can be summarized as follows: the Xanthians decided to institute a regular cult for Basileus Kaunios and Arkesimas. Accordingly, appropriate measures were taken concerning the erection of an altar (βωμός?), the selection of a priest (ἱερεύς) both for the present and for the future, an exemption from taxes (ἀτέλεια) for the priest, and the allocation of land, the revenues of which would finance the cults. Furthermore, the income of the sanctuary would be provided by an annual sum levied from the Xanthians and a tax incumbent on freed slaves. The inscription ends with a traditional curse formula aimed at any future violator of the rules; the text also includes a direct appeal to Pixodarus, who is to punish anyone who violates the 'law' (*datah*):[77] 'May Pixodarus be its guarantor!' (Πιξώταρος δὲ κύριος ἔστω).

The trilingual document poses some formidable problems in terms of satrapal chronology and imperial history, which will be touched on only briefly. The Aramaic text opens with an absolute dating formula: 'In the month of Sivan in year 1 of King Artaxerxes, in the citadel of Orna, Pixoda[ro] son of Katomno, the satrap of Caria and Lycia, said … ' In the eyes of the editors, this could refer only to Artaxerxes III, that is, in the year 358. In an attempt to solve certain difficulties, Badian (1977) has, however, proposed to date the text to the first regnal year of Artaxerxes IV, that is, according to the author, Arses, in 337. Despite the critique expressed by the editors vis-à-vis this view (*FdX* 166 n. 1), Badian's proposal has been accepted by a number of scholars.[78] If correct, it would imply that the Xanthus Trilingual is the only official text dated to Artaxerxes IV[79] – the existence of this king has hitherto not unambiguously been confirmed by the Babylonian texts.[80] According to a third hypothesis (Maddoli 2006), the chronology behind the carving of the different versions of the text is more complex than previously assumed: in summary, Pixodarus would have become satrap of Lycia *only* in the first regnal year of Artaxerxes III (358)[81] while Mausolus was still satrap of Caria and would only later, from 341 onward, control Caria as well (the situation known from other sources).

Regardless of how the dating issue is to be solved, the exceptional document at any rate informs us on what constituted a 'satrap' in the period between Artaxerxes III and Darius III in a micro-region of the empire, on his prerogatives and capacity to intervene in the local affairs of the territories of his assignment. Given the evident intricacies of jurisdictions involved in the decision to introduce a new cult at Xanthus, the Trilingual bears an exceptional contribution to the debate on the relationship between imperial authority and local rule.

All this explains why, throughout the last quarter-century, the document has more or less been adopted by specialists of postexilic Judah. This tradition is actually older than the discovery of the Trilingual, since in 1896 Eduard Meyer had already used the *Letter from Darius to Gadatas* (published 1888) as an argument supporting the purported authenticity of the decrees contained in the book of Ezra (Briant 2003b: 110–11). As the number of archaeological discoveries and textual publications increased, the case of Judah gradually became integrated in a dossier containing a documentation as varied as the *Cyrus Cylinder* (Akkadian), the Aramaic papyri from Egypt, the hieroglyphic inscriptions of Udjahorresnet, the correspondence of Pherendates with the authorities of the temple of Khnūm (Demotic and Aramaic), the 'Decree of Cambyses,' and the codification of Egyptian laws at the initiative of Darius (Demotic). In one and the same assemblage, one finds, from Asia Minor, the *Letter from Darius to Gadatas* as well as (since the 1970s) the inscription of Droaphernes at Sardes and the Xanthus Trilingual, but also some other epigraphical documents from Lydia (the so-called 'Inscription of Sacrileges'), from Ionia (arbitration by Struses: *HPE* 495,646) and from Caria, and even a passage from Herodotus on the tribute reforms by Artaphernes (*HPE* 494–7). It is on the basis of this dossier that, in recent years, the status of Judah has been reexamined, often in the light of the Xanthus Trilingual. In an attempt to clarify the texts by means of other texts in the same corpus, they have been included in more general interpretations at the level of the empire, resulting in sharply contrasting views: either that of an extremely potent and interventionist empire of the kind defined by Eisenstadt,[82] or an empire that grants local communities far-reaching autonomy and that even lends its 'imperial ratification' (*Reichsautorisation*) to decisions taken locally (see Frei 1996, 1996²). As a result of this debate on the status of Judah, the Xanthus Trilingual has acquired the rank of an essential comparative reference.[83] It shares this position with some other epigraphical documents from Asia Minor, including texts of doubtful authenticity[84] or of debatable relevance for the discussion at hand.[85]

In itself, approaching a problem at the level of the empire is a perfectly sound method. At the same time, it should be observed that an all-encompassing comparatist view tends to construct or postulate a global model that in turn is applied, without the necessary precautions, to a regional or micro-regional case to the detriment of its specific traits. The consequence is, all too often, that the epigraphical material from Asia Minor is used within a 'dossier' that is so heterogeneous that one risks pushing the independent voice of individual inscriptions into deadlocked generalizations.[86]

A more fruitful approach would be to revisit the historical and institutional context of the Xanthus Trilingual, a context that can explain its genesis and that shows its particularities. To start with: what relations existed between the satrap and the city of Xanthus? Two possible answers, which are not mutually exclusive, suggest themselves. First, it may be reiterated that there should be no doubt that Lycia and Xanthus were subjected: Pixodarus appointed two *archontes* in the land, and an ἐπιμελητής at Xanthus. In addition, it was the satrap's prerogative to impose certain taxes (customs) or to proclaim a fiscal exemption (TL 45).[87] Furthermore, though referred to as πόλις in the Greek version (1.12), Xanthus appears, under its Lycian name Orna, as a *birtha* in the Aramaic version of the Trilingual; *birtha*, 'citadel,' appears as a generic term in several Aramaic corpora of the imperial administration (Elephantine, Samaria, Sardes, Kiršu-Meydancikkale, and even Persepolis: Briant 1993a: 21; *HPE* 433).

At the same time, Xanthus is not defined by its status as subject city alone. The decision to found a new sanctuary, to organize the performance and material conditions of the cult, was actually taken by 'the Xanthians and the *perioeci*' (ἔδοξε δὴ Ξανθίοις καὶ τοῖ περιοίκοις); it is this community that 'selects a priest' (εἵλοντο ἱερέα) and that makes an oath to effect all that it has pledged in the stele. Also, it is the πόλις that allocates (ἔδωκαν) lands and fields (ἀγρόν) for the support of the new cult. It can therefore not be denied that, whatever the precise institutional contexts, the text refers to a community that exerts some kind of autonomy. As to the closing formula, 'May Pixodarus be its guarantor!' (κύριος ἔστω), it certainly does not imply that the whole process, from the beginning to the end, is placed under the satrap's supervision. Already under the threat of divine wrath, the offenders will also have to account for their acts before the satrap, if the Xanthians decide to refer a complaint to his authority. From that moment onward, it is the satrap's responsibility to preserve or restore the sanctuary's interests, including the economic conditions that insure its sustenance.[88]

In the eyes of several commentators, however, the formula κύριος ἔστω, well attested in Greek cities, could not have had the same meaning in a Lycian context, since Xanthus was not a democratic Greek city.[89] The objections seem hardly decisive (*BHAch* II. 179–82). In fact, both the concept and the reality of a 'deliberating community,' whatever the basis of the selection of the 'citizens,' are not exclusively Greek,[90] and in this case it is clearly 'the Xanthians and the *perioeci*.' In addition, the recently published Carian–Greek document from Caunus demonstrates that the Caunians were perfectly able to develop a political vocabulary and political concepts without slavishly adopting a Greek model (Marek 2006: 122–3).

The Xanthus Trilingual also informs us about the coexistence of Lycians and Greeks in Lycia in the second half of the fourth century and the preservation of the local language. It is certainly remarkable that it was on the basis of the Lycian text that the Greek version could be restored, and not the other way around. Despite the advance of Greek as the preferred language for official inscriptions in Lycia, Lycian remained very much present throughout the period of Achaemenid domination. Recently enriched by the Caunus Bilingual, evidence of the intercultural and interlingual contacts in southern Asia Minor at the end of the Achaemenid period keeps expanding and grows more promising – all this despite the uncertain datings which complicate interpretation (Briant 2006a: 322–7).

3.2 'Mazday who is over Trans-Euphrates and Cilicia'

Attention may be drawn to another satrap of Darius III, a man known from the Classical sources as Mazaeus, a grecism of the Persian Mazday, as found on coins. There is no doubt that this individual enjoyed a very high prestige in the king's entourage.[91] Nothing can be said about his family background, but we do know that he had already been charged with certain responsibilities under Artaxerxes III. In his long and rather imprecise description of the revolts of the lands between Syria and Egypt,[92] Diodorus notes that Artaxerxes himself took supreme command and that, on the march from Babylonia to Phoenicia, he was joined, 'by Belesys, satrap of Syria, and by Mazaeus, governor of Cilicia [Βέλεσυς ὁ τῆς Συρίας σατράπης καὶ Μαζαῖος ὁ τῆς Κιλικίας ἄρχων], who had opened the campaign directed against the Phoenicians' (16.42.1). As so often with a testimony from Diodorus, we find ourselves confronted with several difficulties: one relating to its terminology, the other to its chronology.

What, then, was the division of authority between Belesys (I) and Mazday? Was it just that of different provinces: Trans-Euphrates (Belesys) and Cilicia (Mazday)? Or was it a difference in rank (σατράπης/ἄρχων) within the same administrative division? Nothing is known of Belesys, but it is tempting to connect him with a homonymous individual who, around 400, governed Syria (τοῦ Συρίας ἄρξαντος) and who, on the basis of that position, could dispose of a residence (βασίλεια) and a paradise (παράδεισος) at the sources of the Dardas (near Aleppo).[93] The latter Belesys (IIa) is certainly the same person who, in the Babylonian sources, has a Babylonian name (Belšunu; IIb) and patronymic (Bēl-usuršu), who, from 407 to 401, held the title of 'governor (*pīḫātu*) of Ebir-Nāri' and who, under Darius II (between 421 and 414), held the title of 'governor (*pīḫātu*) of Babylon' (Stolper 1987). Another (?) Belšunu has the title of satrap (*aḫšadrapanu*) in a text dated to 429? (IIc). This text, among others, attests that Babylonian terminology for satrap/governor is as variable as that found in Greek texts, but the document does not allow the conclusion that the 'satrap' Belesys (IIc) is identical to the Belesys (IIb) who is qualified as 'governor of Syria' (Βέλεσυος ... τοῦ Συρίας ἄρξαντος) by Xenophon (Stolper 1989a: 291; *HPE* 601–2, 981). Apart from the hypothesis of his Babylonian origins, the anthroponyms and the terminology used tell us nothing about the identity and functions of the Belesys (I) of Diodorus. One cannot therefore reliably interpret his Greek titulature (τῆς Συρίας σατράπης) in the light of one of the titles of the Babylonian Belšunu (*pīḫātu* of Ebir-Nāri; IIa). Nor is it possible to advance a hypothesis on the functions assigned to Mazday in Cilicia: whether it is that of a plenipotentiary governor, or that of a subordinate of Belesys.[94]

It is only on the basis of numismatic evidence that we can proceed from here, but only with due caution since the interpretive uncertainties are impressive and persistent. Series of coins struck at Tarsus, already known for a long time, often display on the obverse a seated figure on a throne at right and an Aramaic inscription at left: 'Baal of Tarsus.' The reverse has the well-known theme of lion and prey (very familiar in Achaemenid art). Certain series also have an Aramaic inscription above the lion that may be translated as 'Mazday who is over (governing) Trans-Euphrates and Cilicia.'[95] Comparison with the situation deduced from Diodorus' testimony suggests that, at some point, Mazday united Cilicia and Trans-Euphrates under a single governorship,[96] and that Belesys disappeared from the scene (or our sources).

Unfortunately, the chronology of the mintings is highly uncertain as a result of divergent dates (355 or 346) assigned to the revolt and the surrender of Sidon to Artaxerxes III and his generals. The latter event is fixed to year 4 or 14 of Artaxerxes on the basis of a Babylonian chronicle, which cites the arrival of Sidonian prisoners in the royal palace at Babylon at that time.[97] Finally, the entire argument is connected to mintings by Mazday at Sidon; the coins from these mintings bear his name in Aramaic (MZD) on the reverse, sometimes accompanied by an official scene representing the king or the city god in a chariot.[98] There are some disagreements, however, on the counting system used by the satrap on the coins: if we are dealing with year numbers from the reign of Artaxerxes III (years 1–21: 353–333?), his mintings could indicate that Mazday became satrap of Cilicia and Trans-Euphrates in 356, and kept his post until 333.[99]

In any case, there is scarcely any doubt that Mazday was, as a governor, assisted by a host of local subordinates such as, possibly, his son Brochubelus in Syria proper.[100] There were, additionally, a governor of Damascus,[101] local dynasts at Sidon (Elayi 2005), Jerusalem, or Samaria (Dušek 2007), and no doubt also a governor of Idumea.

3.3 From Lycia to Cilicia: the imperial hold

On a general level, the examples from Lycia and Cilicia are remarkably instructive concerning the empire that Darius III inherited. In Cilicia, leaving aside the chronological debate, the literary (Diodorus) and especially the numismatic evidence demonstrates two essential facts. One is that a new, vast administrative division was created, encompassing Cilicia and Trans-Euphrates. This measure was not without logic since Cilicia had long been oriented toward Syria and Mesopotamia, and its culture included a number of common and similar characteristics. In addition, Mazday was not the first imperial grandee to have struck coins in Cilicia: his predecessors, Persian military commanders, minted coins in the context of short-term military operations in the region. But Mazday was the first to coin silver as a standing territorial responsibility in his capacity as 'governor of Cilicia and Trans-Euphrates.' He was also the first to include his name and titulature on the coinage. Simultaneously, yet without abolishing the royal coinages, Mazday introduced his name on a series of mintings at Sidon – another means of asserting, even more distinctly, Achaemenid sovereignty over the region.

As for Lycia, the Xanthus Trilingual fits in the history of Carian–Lycian relations since at least the reign of Mausolus, and illustrates the constant tendency of the lords of Halicarnassus to extend their sway to Lycia. It is possible that the introduction of divinities whose origins lie in Caria (more precisely in the border region with Lycia) corresponded, at least partially, with the wishes of the Hecatomnid satrap. Yet, in these circumstances, the introduction of Hecatomnid power in the region was not brought about against the empire's interests. Quite the contrary: it was rather to strengthen control over Lycia that, under Artaxerxes III, the region was first defined as an autonomous satrapy and confined to Pixodarus, and subsequently included in a larger Carian–Lycian satrapy from 341 onward. When one takes into consideration that Pixodarus' harmonious relations with the central court brought Orontobates to Halicarnassus and that the latter succeeded him upon his death (336/5), one discerns in the developments described a reinforcement of Achaemenid imperial hold on the southwestern regions of Asia Minor between Artaxerxes III and Darius III (see *HPE* 666–73, 707).

The case of Cilicia is thus joined by that of Lycia, in the sense that one witnesses the disappearance of local dynasts: in the course of Artaxerxes III's reign, Lycia and Caria were, as it were, "satrapized" to a greater extent than before. Changes in the territories assigned to satraps were a frequent and constant feature in these regions: hence, it is quite possible that the death of Pixodarus led Darius III to take measures to effect a territorial and tributary organization in Lycia and the adjacent regions.[102] Altogether, if we add the cases of Bactria and Idumea (§2.1–2), the Lycian and Cilician examples (§3.1–2) confirm the reality of Achaemenid imperial domination, both in its unity (e.g., the use of Aramaic) and in its regional diversity.

4 At the Empire's center: indications of dynastical and imperial continuity

Greek texts abound in details on the dynastic conflicts that took place between Artaxerxes III and Darius III, on the 'decadent luxury' of Darius III's court.[103] The documentation on the center of the empire as such is less informative, even though there are some particularly important insights into the daily administrative organization of life at court.[104]

According to Plutarch (*Alex.* 69.1–2), Artaxerxes III never went to Pasargadae in order to avoid the royal custom that demanded that at such occasions the king gave Persian women a piece of gold. Evidently, the anecdote has been reworked by Plutarch (Stadter 1965: 53–6), who wanted to contrast Alexander and Artaxerxes and to portray the former as the one who revitalized the tradition of the 'giving king.' At the same time, Arses and Darius III may not have left any material or epigraphical trace at

Persepolis or any other residence,[105] but their immediate predecessors certainly did. The royal tombs (V and VI) overlooking the platform and seen by Diodorus' source (17.71.7) are attributed to Artaxerxes II and Artaxerxes III. Though we do not know the reasons prompting their choice of Persepolis rather than Naqš-i Rustam, the site of the four earlier royal tombs, it is at any rate clear that the later tombs followed a model that had been used without interruption since the first rock tomb, that of Darius I (Schmidt 1970: 99–107). With the exception of a few details, the motif of subject peoples represented as throne bearers and identified by means of captions (A^3Pb) is repeated exactly. The same loyalty to dynastic traditions can be observed in an inscription by Artaxerxes III (A^3Pa), found in different fragmentary copies on that part of the Persepolis platform where early constructions (Artaxerxes I) had become dilapidated (Palace G).[106] As he himself records, Artaxerxes III ordered the construction of a staircase and the execution of reliefs, the sequencing of which evinces a development from earlier models of representing delegations of subject peoples.[107] The inscription A^3Pb (on his tomb) reproduces (ll. 1–8) part of the inscription that may be described as the "Prince's Own Mirror" and was carved on the tomb of Darius I (DNa), and it proceeds according to the well-known model of the royal genealogy (ll. 8–21). The captions that identify the thirty throne bearers on Artaxerxes III's tomb duplicate almost exactly the captions of inscription DNe, at Naqš-i Rustam. It may also be noted that, as Artaxerxes II had done before him, Artaxerxes III explicitly included Mithra among the gods whose protection he implores for himself and his constructions. Despite the persistent uncertainties involved, it is clear that the royal inscriptions attest that ideological-religious traditions continued, but underwent evolution and adaptation throughout the Achaemenid period (HPE 676–9, 998–1001). Several testimonies by the Alexander biographers show that Darius III still invoked the protection of Mithra in his prayers (HPE 243, 253).

The persistence of religious and dynastic traditions during the reign of Darius III is also shown by the descriptions given by the classical authors of Alexander's second visit to Pasargadae after his return from India. One detail in these reports, as given by Arrian, that demonstrates the importance that the tomb and the memory of Cyrus the Great had for Alexander (RTP 386–393) should be singled out:

> Within the enclosure and by the ascent to the tomb itself there is a small building (οἴκημα σμικρόν) put up for the Magians who used to guard Cyrus' tomb, from as long ago as Cambyses, son of Cyrus (ἔτι ἀπὸ Καμβύσου τοῦ Κύρου), an office transmitted from father to son (παῖς παρὰ πατρὸς ἐκδεχόμενος). The king used to give them a sheep a day, a fixed amount of meal and wine, and a horse each month to sacrifice to Cyrus (καὶ τούτοις πρόβατόν τε ἐς ἡμέραν ἐδίδοτο ἐκ βασιλέως καὶ ἀλεύρων τε καὶ οἴνου τεταγμένα καὶ ἵππος κατὰ μῆνα ἐς θυσίαν τῷ Κύρῳ).
>
> (6.29.7; trans. P. A. Brunt)

This passage not only shows unequivocally the continuity of the dynastic and religious tradition in Fārs under Darius III (and even five years after the death of the last Great King), but it also, and especially, informs the debate on the economic bases of the monarchy at this period. In fact, the testimony of Arrian evokes in a compelling way the functioning of a 'royal economy' as we know it from the reigns of Darius I, Xerxes, and Artaxerxes I thanks to the Persepolis archives (HPE 422–71). Part of this documentation deals with the allocation of various commodities (flour, cereals, livestock) to officiants administering different cults. These allocations are made, on the orders of the king and the highest representatives of the crown, from the institution's stores and/or from the House of the King (Henkelman 2003, 2006). Such is certainly the case here, in the context described by Arrian.[108]

The testimony just cited and the commentary to be added to it on the basis of the Persepolis material open up a different approach for historians of the reign of Darius III. In the absence of any Achaemenid documentation in the proper sense, the Greco-Roman texts on Alexander and the Diadochi, when analyzed against the background outlined above, indicate the persistence of an institutional economy, with its organized means of production and intricate administration, in Fārs throughout the Achaemenid period. Echoes of Achaemenid administrative practice are, for example, clearly discernible in an anecdote (set in 322) related by Plutarch in his *Life of Eumenes* (8.5).[109] Another example, pertaining to a few years earlier (325/4) and this time situated in Babylonia, is that of the financial stratagems recorded in the *Oeconomica* of Ps.-Aristotle (2.2.38), which introduce a certain Antimenes. This individual was undoubtedly Alexander's director of finances[110] and it is in this capacity that he issues orders to satraps.[111] He reminds them that their task is to retain a constant level of reserves (ἀναπληροῦν) in the supply stations situated along the royal roads (τοὺς θησαυροὺς τοὺς παρὰ τὰς ὁδοὺς τὰς βασιλικάς) – the places where traveling groups on official business could receive rations, doubtless upon presentation of an authorized travel voucher. The striking similarity with the well-known organization of the road system at the time of the Great Kings unmistakably shows that the orders given by Antimenes were not an innovation; rather, they reflect an Achaemenid heritage (cf. κατὰ τὸν νόμον τὸν τῆς χώρας).[112] The same is true for another measure taken: Antimenes imposed the tithe on all caravans entering Babylon, including "those who bring numerous presents (δῶρα πολλά) <to the king>." In doing so, he reintroduced a regulation that had existed for a long time in Babylon (νόμου ... ἐν Βαβυλωνίᾳ παλαιοῦ), but that had fallen into disuse (2.2.34). A third measure (2.2.34), another of Antimenes' expedients to replenish Alexander's funds, was to demand that slave owners in the armies register the value of their slaves (ἀνεγράψατο) and pay a specific tax. It is tempting to relate this information to what we know about the taxes levied on slave sales in Babylonia since the reign of Darius I: here too, the royal registries (*karammaru ša šarri*) were in charge of controlling the slave rolls and levying the tax.[113]

Such connections allow the deduction that the material, productive, and administrative basis of taxation and redistributions had continued in more or less the same form into the reigns of the last Great Kings. Only the sustaining (even if only partially) of these traditions, administrative modes, and practices makes it possible to understand how, at the end of the Achaemenid period, the richness and the prosperity of the Persian lands struck eyewitnesses in the way they did: the agricultural wealth was not simply the result of advantageous climatic conditions, but rather that of organized development.[114] This is also the only context that allows us to appreciate how the kings of the fourth century could continue with their building programs, as well as with the reconstruction and maintenance of Persepolis and other royal residences (*HPE* 734–5), or how Alexander could gather enormous herds of pack animals for the transport of the royal treasure.[115] As the measures taken by Antimenes reveal, it was evidently in the best interest of the conqueror to retain in force all the traditions and regulations, since he was the de facto heir of the Persian House of the King (*ulhi sunkina*) in the economic sense that the expression already had in Achaemenid context (*HPE* 463–71, 445–6, 945–7).[116]

Against the above background, one can better understand the episode of the herdsman who, in the winter of 331/30, guided Alexander round the Persian Gates. Plausibly, the son of a mixed marriage and deported to Persia after a Lycian defeat against the Persians, the herdsman is but one of many individuals who constituted the labor force in the service of the institutional economy, those whom the Persepolis tablets call, in generic terminology, the *kurtaš*. These *kurtaš* were recruited from all the empire's populations (one of the most frequently mentioned ethnonyms is that of the *Turmilap* (Τερμίλαι). A number of them were active in the administration's craft centers where production was organized and closely supervised (*HPE* 433). If we disregard the romantic overtones of the contexts in which they appear, the status of the Greeks 'liberated' by Alexander from the *ergastula* of Persepolis seems perfectly comparable.[117] Other *kurtaš* worked on the fields and on pastures. The tablets also provide documentation on flocks of livestock and their herdsmen (*batera*) whose status undoubtedly was the same as that of the Lycian who guided Alexander at the end of the year 331 through the Persian mountains.[118]

One simply cannot avoid acknowledging that what has been called the 'sudden interruption' of the Persepolis archives is an illusory phenomenon, a distorting perspective due to the intrinsically uncertain history of the modes of archiving.[119] It is, at any rate, certainly not the expression of an abrupt annihilation of the 'royal economy' evidenced by the texts. Other bureaucratic methods (involving more perishable documents? *HPE* 423) and/or chance preservation suffice to explain 'archival silence' after 458.

Once reunited in a single dossier, the texts cited above, as well as others, allow the conclusion that, under Darius III, there was, on the regional level of the Persis as well as on the general level of the empire, still an economic and administrative organization with a logical coherence that was comparable overall with the elaborately documented structures in place during the reign of Darius I.[120] It is thanks to the ample documentation of those 'bureaucratic' systems (*RTP* 209) inherited by later kings that we are able to pinpoint their echoes in the Greco-Roman sources on the reigns of Darius III and Alexander. Altogether the daily and/or monthly allocations to the magi at Pasargadae are only the tip of an iceberg of Achaemenid documentation that will, perhaps, one day be revealed more completely.

5 From Darius to Alexander: empire(s) in transition

As observed by one of the editors of the Idumean ostraca, 'the arrival of Alexander did not result in a sudden disruption of economic life in this region. Aramaic continued to be used and one only replaced the name of the Persian king with that of Alexander.'[121] The Aramaic documents from Bactria invite a similar reflection: a list of rations (C4) documents, for a period of three months (June–August), the allocation of cereals (barley, millet, wheat) to various groups. The text itself is dated to 'the 15th of Sivan, year 7 of Alexander,' that is, July 324; it constitutes one of the proofs that, from one domination to another, the administrative processes and their textual and linguistic expression remained the same, at least in the short term.[122] In this sense, these documents on economic practice nourish the discussion on the continuities and adaptations that mark the transition from the administration of the Great Kings to that of Alexander.

Let us, in conclusion, return to Mazday. At the time that this individual continued to fight at Darius' side (November 333 to November 331), Alexander had his first imperial coinage struck at Tarsus: a coinage that displays undisrupted continuity from the coinages struck by Darius' satrap, if not the rehiring of artists from the satrapal workshops.[123] Thanks to a now celebrated astronomical tablet (*ADRTB*-330), we know that about a month after Gaugamela, and after negotiations with the Babylonians, Alexander appeared before the walls of the imposing Mesopotamian metropolis (November 331). Arrian and Curtius, each in his own style, describe the welcome organized for the conqueror outside the city walls, with representatives of the local elites as well as the Persian leaders: Bagophanes, the *custos* of the royal fortune, and Mazaeus/Mazday. Having fled to the city after the battle, Mazday met Alexander 'as a suppliant, with his mature children, and surrendered the city and himself.'[124] Next, Mazday was given the post of satrap in Babylonia, the first appointment of this kind, which was, at the same time, a sign of the continuity of an Iranian policy conceived by Alexander from the moment he embarked on his expedition.[125]

The poorly documented satrapal administration of Mazday (331–328) does not concern us directly in this context, except for one point: numismatic evidence shows not only that, among Alexander's satraps, Mazday was the only one to have minted his own coinage in the province under his control, but also that the types used copied those from the earlier coin series he had struck at Tarsus at the time of the Great Kings. The Babylonian tetradrachms of Mazday bear, on the reverse, his name in Aramaic (MZDY), inscribed over a lion; on the obverse, one finds again a Tarsian motif, that of a figure seated on a throne and the name of the god (Baaltars) inscribed in Aramaic (BLTRZ). Only the standing censer (*thymiaterion*) of the Cilician coinages has disappeared.[126] In other words: these Babylonian mintings provide most eloquent comments on the question of the transition of the empire(s) from Darius to Alexander, and they bear witness to the intermediary role played by a man like Mazday.

Notes

1 My warmest thanks to Wouter Henkelman (Collège de France) who translated my text into English.

2 See below, ch. 9.

3 Cf. Briant 2005c: 26 [=1974: 27], 36, 39–4; also Briant 2003a: 567–8. The necessity of presenting the Achaemenid empire in courses on the history of Alexander is sometimes explicitly acknowledged (e.g., Flower 2007: 420), but has not really been taken into account in more recent syntheses.

4 See, e.g., Seibert 1988; Badian 2000b; Garvin 2003 and compare the earlier publication by Murison 1972 (followed by Briant 1974: 50 n. 2). See also Nylander 1993 (with my remarks in Briant 2003a: 242–4, 530–1, 577).

5 See Briant 2003a: 85–130, 567–9.

6 'This man of demonstrated courage ... found himself facing one of the greatest military leaders. What might have sufficed against an Agesilaus proved totally inadequate against Alexander.'

7 Briant 2003a: *passim*.

8 Briant 2003a: 126–30; Briant 2005c: 49–62.

9 Mayrhofer 1976; the same scholar participated in the premier edition: *FdX* 181–5.

10 I sensed this approach already in *CAH*[2] vi (1994), which includes several chapters that are excellent syntheses, but lacks chapters on the regions beyond Mesopotamia. The very recent case of the *Cambridge Economic History of the Graeco-Roman World* (2007) is distinctly worse. The chapter 'The Persian Near East' (Bedford 2007) is included in a volume the tide of which clearly announces its Aegeocentric orientation. Despite the deceptive map (304–5), an incomprehensible editorial bias has in fact reduced 'the Persian Empire' to Mesopotamia and Syria-Palestine, i.e., to the Near East, in an extraordinarily restrictive sense that excludes Asia Minor and Egypt, as well as the regions east of the Tigris. Furthermore, recently published documentation (such as

the Idumean ostraca; cf. 312–13, 315–16) [is] neither mentioned nor used. As to the Persepolis tablets, these are barely referred to in the course of a bibliographical note (315, with n. 47). Against the background of the *longue durée* of Achaemenid historiography, such a chapter and the conception that informed it represent a perplexing step backward.

11 Extensive discussions of the subject are already to be found in *HPE* 691–871, 1007–50; updates are given in *BHAch* I. 57–63 and II. 92–100.

12 Military operations as such need not be discussed again within this perspective, except where they can clarify the structural analysis (see *HPE* 817–71, 1042–50).

13 See Briant 1976 and 1982: 57–112 (*HPE* 726–33, 1022: Zagros); *HPE* 1019–20 and Briant 2006c, 2008 (καταρράκται). Compare also, on the Uxians and Cossaeans and their connections with the royal administration, the interesting proposals by Henkelman 2005: 159–64.

14 See Briant, *RTP* 141–5, 491–506, the resolved methodological reminder in *HPE* 693–5 and chs. 16–17, devoted to a detailed analysis of the empire. See also Briant 1999: 1131–8 and 2003a: 16–18; cf. below §4.1 cannot see why Garvin (2003: 89 n. 11) would assume that I dismissed 'the Greek sources on account of their biases,' or why Brosius (*Gnomon* 2006), in a very positivist review of Briant 2003a, assumes that I have denied any reality to the Greek and Latin literary texts about Alexander. The method that I have consistently promoted and defended is rather more complex and elaborate (see, e.g., Briant 2006c and 2008 on the καταρράκται of the Tigris): it is not about simplistically reasoning by exclusives (yes/no), but about understanding that the literary Classical tradition is *at the same time* useful and deforming.

15 The thesis that holds the contrary finds its origins in Macedonian circles (*HPE* 842–3 and esp. Briant 2003a: 177–81); via the biased lens of the *Alexander Romance* the idea was redeveloped in medieval Arab-Persian literature in order to make an 'evil king' out of Darā (2003a: 461–3, 475–86).

16 See *HPE*, *passim*, esp. 389–90, 451–6, and index, 1125–6; see also below §4 and the numerous studies on the subject by Descat, the latest being 2006: 365–71. The recent commentary by Zoepffel 2006 is, unfortunately, badly informed on current debates in Achaemenid and Hellenistic history.

17 It is to these three reigns that the documents from Persepolis are dated (*HPE* 422–3, 938–9). On the unequal spread of the sources, see also *HPE* 8–10, 518, 569–70, 612–15.

18 On Susa, see the surveys by Boucharlat 2006: 443–50 and forthcoming.

19 *HPE* 613–14, 675–81, 986–7, 998–1003; see also Boiy 2006: 45–7.

20 See *HPE*, chs. 14–15, with the corresponding notes (972–1006); see also Briant 1984: 76–80 (Bactria).

21 With regard to the revolt of Datames, the Babylonian explanation suggested by Van der Spek 1998: 253–5 seems very speculative to me (see *BHAch* II. 93–5). The postulated connection between Datames and the Tarkumuwa known from Cilician mintings has met with skepticism from several scholars, myself included (*BHAch* I. 59–61; II. 94–5).

22 See the doubts expressed by Le Rider 2001: 223–6. On the traditional glorification of the figure of Artaxerxes III, in contrast to the negative image of Darius (so Mildenberg 1998: 283), see Briant 2003a: 108–12.

23 On the Satrap Stele, see the bibliography and discussion in *HPE* 1017–18; *BHAch* I. 58; and Briant 2003a: 65–70, 563; most recently: Schäfer, forthcoming.

24 See Nicolet-Pierre 1979 (*HPE* 1017) and, most recently, Van Alfen 2002; images in Briant 2003a: 76–7.

25 The influx of new material (see Briant 2003c: 39–46) does not pertain to the period under discussion. On the documents relating to the second Persian domination (between 343 and 332), see Devauchelle 1995; on the documents from the transition period see Chauveau and Thiers 2006.

26 See *HPE* 693–768, 1007–32, particularly the comments on 1029–32, as well as the updates in *BHAch* I and II, and the synthesis in Briant 2003b.

27 Two texts from Bactria are palaeographically dated to the fifth century (Shaked 2004: 13, 22; 2006; *ADAB* 16 [B10]); two ostraca of Maresha are dated to the same century (Kloner and Stern 2007: 142).

28 The date depends on the dating of text C1. The dating formula reads, 'In the month of Kislev, in year 1 of king Artaxerxes.' As the editors read the name of 'Bessus,' receiving 'supplies as he

went from Bactra to Varnu,' they conclude that the texts is from the first regnal year of Bessus-Artaxerxes V or November–December 330 (Shaked 2003; 2004: 16–17; *ADAB* 180). The interpretation seems disputable, however (on this point I share the skepticism expressed by Lane Fox 2007: 297), since, apart from the difficulties in the reading 'Bessus,' I fail to see how, in one and the same document, the same individual could be referred to as 'king' and as private person receiving travel rations. If the text indeed dates to the first year of a certain ruler, it may pertain to year 1 of Arses-Artaxerxes IV (336/5) or, more plausibly, to year 1 of Artaxerxes III, i.e., 358 (this hypothesis is considered but rejected by Shaked 2003: 1521 on the basis of arguments that do not seem to be decisive).

29 A recently published ostracon (Ahituv and Yardeni 2004: 9, 19–20) dates to Ptolemy ('Talmaios the king'), but see cautioning remarks on the identity of this Ptolemy by Lemaire 2006c: 417 n. 96: 'Cet ostracon fragmentaire devra être revu et interprété … pour savoir s'il faut le rattacher au groupe principal ou aux ostraca du IIIe siècle.'

30 On the few Babylonian documents dating to Darius III, see Joannès 2001: 250, 255 and Boiy 2006: 45–7; see also Dušek 2007: 118–19 (Samaria; accession year of Darius, corresponding to the second regnal year of his predecessor, i.e., March 335).

31 See the preliminary but precise presentations in Shaked 2003, 2004, who kindly entrusted me with an advance copy of the premier edition (*ADAB*, forthcoming): I express my warmest thanks to him and his co-author.

32 Text dated to the middle of the fifth century by palaeographical criteria (*ADAB* 16). On administrative structures and practices, see *ADAB* 22–6, 27–9.

33 As stressed by Shaked (2003: 1528–30), it is certainly remarkable that the administration's authority stretched into Sogdiana, across the Oxus: the two regions seem to form a single unit, as was the case during Darius III (cf. Berve ii. 267–8; I am not sure whether I understand correctly the construction suggested by Jacobs 1994: 213–14 in this regard). On the strategic responsibilities of the satrap of Bactria, see also Briant 1984: 71–6.

34 This is at any rate what is suggested by text A4 (letter from Akhvamazda to Bagavant at Khulmi): upon the request to that effect received from 'Spaita, the magistrates and others (of) the garrison' of Nikhshapaya, Akhvamazda gives his authorization to interrupt their construction work temporarily so that the 'troops' may return to gather the harvest under threat of a locust plague; after having completed harvesting, 'they will build that wall and ditch.'

35 See the list of animal and plant species in *ADAB* 33–5.

36 See *ADAB*, C4: 10; 28, 55.

37 See discussion in *HPE*, 463–71 and 945–7; Henkelman, forthcoming.

38 On the different meanings of *mandattu*, see *HPE* 385 (a tax levied on commercial cargo entering the Nile); 405, 462 (taxes levied on Egyptian domains); 441 (in a Treasury text from Persepolis); 942.

39 Briant 1984: 59; *HPE* 753, 764; most recently *BHAch* II. 73, and Stolper-Tavernier, www.achemenet.com/document/2007.001-Stolper-Tavernier.pdf). Note that recent archaeological research has identified new important sites dating to the Achaemenid period (communication by Roland Besenval).

40 On the debate with archaeologists, see Briant, *RTP* 314–18, and esp. Briant 1984; cf. *HPE* 752–4, 1027–8; Gardin 1997; Lyonnet 1997: 118–19; Francfort and Lecomte 2002: 659–66 – the last three adopting a more flexible approach, with recognition of the limits of the archaeological documentation. See also *BHAch* II. 162–4 and Briant 2002a (where the future publication of the Aramaic documents from Bactria and their integration in the ongoing debate is announced: 522 n. 20).

41 See Briant 1984, esp. ch. 2, where, objecting to the *argumentum a silentio*, I introduced the idea and the conviction that 'les autorités achéménides de Bactriane maniaient les archives avec autant de constance et de persévérance que leurs collègues des régions babyloniennes et égéennes' (59; on satrapal archives see *RTP* 209); see also *HPE* 754: 'It is safe to say that the discussion is not over.'

42 References in Briant 1984: 59–60 (see n. 7 on the Aramaic documents found at Ai-Khanum); see also my introduction to Shaked 2004: 5–8. Benveniste's study is, surprisingly, not mentioned by Graf 2000.

43 The expression found in D.S. 19.98.1, 'in the middle' (κατὰ μέϑην τὴν σατραπείαν), does not have a strictly geographical meaning: cf. Bartlett 1999: 106; on the excavation see the survey in Stern 2001: 443–54 as well as Grabbe in Lipschits et al. 2007: 125–44.

44 The new documentation is briefly introduced in *BHAch* I. 31; II. 56–7, and announced in *HPE* 1017. Three volumes, comprising 201, 199, and 384 texts, have been published: one by Eph'al and Naveh (1996), and two by Lemaire (1996, 2002). The publications of Lemaire 1996 and Eph'al and Naveh 1996 have been discussed also by, e.g., Amadasi-Guzzo 1998: 532–8. Since these publications, a number of isolated documents have been published in various articles partial list: see esp. Lozachmeur and Lemaire 1996; Lemaire 1999b, 2006a; Ahituv and Yardeni 2004; Porten and Yardeni 2003, 2004, 2006 (these last three articles contain the most sophisticated interpretation of the archives). A great number of documents, dispersed over various private and public collections, are yet to be edited (a history of the successive discoveries is found in Porten and Yardeni 2003: 207–9; 2006: 457–9); an encompassing publication with continuously numbered texts, under the direction of Porten, is in preparation (see Porten and Yardeni 2003). Among (necessarily provisional) syntheses see, e.g., Eph'al 1998; Lemaire 1999a; 2006a; 2006b: 416–19; and Kloner and Stern 2007.

45 According to the latest estimate by Porten and Yardeni 2006: 458, 1,900 items, of which about 1,700 are legible.

46 On Trans-Euphrates in this period, see *HPE* 716–17, 1016–7, as well as the regular surveys published in *Transeuphratène* (Elayi and Sapin 2000; *Transeuphratène* 32 [2006], 191–4) and, most recently, Lemaire 2006c.

47 There are some differences in opinion with regards to this Alexander: contrary to Eph'al and Naveh 1996, Lemaire argues that he cannot be Alexander IV, but must be Alexander the Great. To support this, he has devised the hypothesis that there was a different year count in Palestine in this period (1996: 41–5; 2002: 199–201; repeated in 2006b: 418 n. 98). Anson 2005a chooses Lemaire's chronology without hesitation, whereas Porten and Yardeni 2006: 484–6 seem to remain undecided. That the documents refer to Alexander IV is forcefully asserted by Boiy 2006: 58–61; see also his reflections in Boiy 2005 (on the Lydian inscriptions).

48 On the chronology of the ostraca dated to Antigonus, see now Boiy 2006: 73–4.

49 See the chronological charts in Porten and Yardeni 2006: 462–3, 468–70; see also Porten and Yardeni 2003 and 2004.

50 See the remarks of Eph'al and Naveh 1996: 16–17 and Lemaire 1996: 11–13.

51 See Lemaire 2002: no. 1 (pp. 11, 199): a document dated to Tammuz 27, year 43, i.e., July 20, 362.

52 It may be mentioned, however, that Lemaire 2002: 227–8 proposes to read the term GZBR' (**ganzabara*, 'treasurer') on an ostracon found at Tel 'Ira.

53 From this perspective, the documentation under discussion presents a number of functional resemblances with the Aramaic texts from Persepolis (see the remark by Eph'al and Naveh 1996: 14–15).

54 On the history of Maresha in the Achaemenid period on the basis of the ostraca, see the remarks by Eshel 2007. On Zeno's voyages in the region, see Durand 1997.

55 Eph'al and Naveh 1996: 10–13; Lemaire 1996: 142–6; 2002: 203–8, 223–9.

56 See the interpretations suggested by Lemaire 2002: 223–9.

57 Eph'al and Naveh 1996: 13; Lemaire 2002: 206.

58 On this point, see esp. the exposition by Porten and Yardeni 2006: 473–82; see also Lemaire 2006b: 443, who raises the question of forced labor.

59 Kloner and Stern 2007: 142–3; a small number of Iranian anthroponyms have been noted (see table on p. 143 [of Kloner and Stern]); on Maresha, see Eshel 2007.

60 See, e.g., Lemaire 2002: 221–3.

61 Lemaire 2002: 208 (the term *ptp* is known from Bactria, Elephantine, Babylonia, and Persepolis).

62 So already Eph'al and Naveh 1996: 11. Note that the reconstruction of administrative processes in Idumea, as proposed by Lemaire (1996, 2002), is clearly directly inspired by the model drawn by Naveh for Arad and Beersheba.

63 *HPE*, ch. 11; these are the 'revenues' (εἰσαγώγιμα) and 'expenses' (ἐξαγώγιμα) of Ps.-Arist. *Oec.* 2.1.2 (*HPE* 452–3, 943–4).

64 This interpretation by Naveh has met with some opposition (see *HPE* 928).

65 On the strategic aspect of fodder reserves in this region (and certainly in others too, e.g., in Bactria: *ADAS*, A10, C1, C3), compare the famous travel voucher given by the Egyptian satrap Aršāma to his intendant (*HPE* 362–3) or the measures taken by the Sidonian rebels against the Persians (D.S. 16.41).

66 On this point, see also *HPE* 716–17; 1016–17.

67 So Lemaire 1996: 151; 2002: 231–2; see also Sapin 2004.

68 See Berve i. 253–73, and the name entries in vol. ii; cf. Jacobs 1993. On the functions of satraps, see Berve i. 273–83 and, recently, Klinkott 2005; Henkelman, forthcoming, esp. §5. On the satraps and satrapies in Asia Minor, see the recent synthesis by Debord 1999, whose analysis has the merit of integrating numismatic sources in all their diversity and complexity. To my knowledge, Casabonne 2004 is the only recent monograph on Achaemenid Cilicia.

69 See Stolper 1987 and 1989b (Babylonian terminology); Briant 2000c: 268 (Aramaic and Demotic terminology).

70 On the coins struck by the last two satraps in Egypt under Darius III, see Nicolet-Pierre 1979 and Van Alfen 2002.

71 See Hornblower 1982: 137–70; *HPE* 667–70, 995; on his double status ("king of the Carians" and satrap), see *HPE* 767–8, 1032.

72 Overview of the sources in Berve ii, no. 640; see also Ruzicka 1992: 100–55 and Debord 1999: 400–6.

73 Arr. *Anab.* 1.23.7–8; Str. 14.2.17; on the name Orontobates (written Rhoontopates on the coins), see Schmitt 2006: 257–60; on the later history of this individual see also *HPE* 1043–4.

74 See Plu. *Alex.* 10.1–5 (eg., Ruzicka 1992: 120–34).

75 See Konuk 1998: 161–83 (gold coinage: 178–83); 2002.

76 Since its preliminary presentation in *CRAI* 1974 and its premier edition in 1979 (*FdX*), the document has provoked a considerable number of studies, listed and discussed in 1996: 707–9 (text on 708), 1011–12, and particularly in my specialized study, Briant 1998 (and, subsequently, in *BHAch* II. 179–82). In this context I refer only to the most recent studies. Text of the Lycian version: Melchert 2000; text of the Aramaic version: Kottsieper 2002.

77 On the term (used in the Aramaic version and in many other imperial corpora), see *HPE* 510–1, 956–7; *BHAch* I. 96–7; ii. 143, 177; Briant 1999: 1135.

78 See, e.g., Briant 1998: 305–6 n. 3.

79 An Aramaic document from the Wadi Daliyeh, published by Cross in 1985 and republished by Gropp in 1986 (*HPE* 1033) and Dušek (2007: 118–19), is dated to the accession year of Darius (III) and the second regnal year of his predecessor (March 19, 335); unfortunately neither his personal name (Arses) nor his throne name are mentioned.

80 See recently Boiy 2006: 45–7, whose argumentation on the basis of the unique and only decisive tablet reveals that the 'fact' is still to be established firmly.

81 On the date formula that opens the Lycian and the Greek version (ἐπεὶ Λυκίας ξαδράπης ἐγένετο Πιξώδαρος), see discussion in Briant 1998: 320–5, and the meticulous study by Cau 1999–2000.

82 A thesis defended throughout by Fried 2004 (see 4–5), following Eisenstadt 1969 (frequently cited). On the subject, see my remarks in *BHAch* II. 184–5 n. 396 (on the basis of the 2000 typescript, published largely unaltered, as Fried 2004).

83 See esp. Frei 1996: 39–47; in the first edition of this book (1983), the Trilingual already held a strategic importance. See also Fried 2004: ch. 4 (140–54 on the Trilingual); Watts 2001 (see index, 222, and the high number of references to the Trilingual in the papers of the contributors); Bedford 2001: 132–57 (143–5 on the Trilingual); Kratz 2002: 174, 194; Grabbe 2004: 107–9; 213–4; Grabbe in: Lipschits and Oeming 2006: 538–9.

84 On the *Letter of Darius to Gadatas*, see Briant 2003b; Lane Fox 2006 does not respond to any of the arguments and analysis advanced in it (despite his postscript, 169–71); the same is true for Fried 2004: 108–19.

85 See, on the Droaphernes inscription, my remarks in *BHAch* II 177–9, and, on the 'Inscription of Sacrileges,' Briant 2000a: 242 n. 32 and *BHAch* II. 179.

86 See on this problem Kuhrt 1987 and 2001: 171–2, where she stresses the 'crucial' character of the Trilingual in Frei's argumentation and reaches the conclusion that 'in sum, then, none of Frei's examples provides instance of *Reichsautorisation* in the sense needed to sustain the

argument.' On the risks of comparative history, see also Briant 2000a: 'L'histoire comparatiste ne peut aboutir à des résultats fondés que si chacun des exemples … a été minutieusement étudié préalablement *per se*' (242); cf. *BHAch* II. 157–9.

87 See *HPE* 709, and compare other Achaemenid texts such as the papyrus on the custom duties of Egypt: *HPE* 384–7, 930.

88 I have developed this interpretation in Briant 1998, esp. 330–6; it has, basically, been followed by Maddoli 2006: 607.

89 See, independently, Fried 2004: 151–2 and Le Roy 2005; see also Debord 1999: 66–7 (the comparison with the Droaphernes inscription seems unfortunate: *BHAch* II. 153).

90 See Briant 1993a: 19–23, on Sardis and its internal organization, with a comparison with the case of Xanthus (21–2); see also the connections rightly established between the Xanthus Trilingual and the Caro-Greek Bilingual from Caunus (SEG xlvii: no. 1568; Marek 2006: 120–1). In both cases, what I call the 'civic version' (a terminology accepted by Frei) is introduced by ἔδοξε Καυνίοις/Ξανθίοις καὶ τοῖς περιοίκοις. See most recently Briant 2006a: 322, and compare Debord 1999: 67, who also speaks of a 'décision politique … consistant en la création d'un culte poliade.' A firm stand to the same effect is also taken by Domingo Gygax (2001): 102–3, 195–9; see the discussions summarized in *SEG* li: no. 1824, and *SEG* lii: no. 1424–5.

91 Μαζαίου δὲ τοῦ μεγίστου παρὰ Δαρείῳ γενομένου (Plu. *Alex.* 39.9); he was one of the Friends (τῶν φίλων) of the king (D.S. 17.55.1) and a *vir illustris* who became even more celebrated on account of his behavior at Gaugamela (Curt. 5.1.18).

92 On the enormous difficulties in the reconstruction and interpretation of Diodorus narrations, see *HPE* 656–75, 993–8 (Artaxerxes II); 681–8, 1003–5 (Artaxerxes III).

93 Xen. *Anab.* 1.4.10.

94 A host of different hypotheses was already extensively analyzed by Leuze 1935: 193–235, without any real progress.

95 Ever since Six 1884, Mazday's coinage has often been studied; see Mildenberg 1990–1; Debord 1999: 412–16; Le Rider 2001: 211–3, 226–8; Casabonne 2004: 207–23. In these publications detailed analyses are given for each minting. On the Aramaic titulature, see Lemaire 2000: 134–8, and my own remarks in Briant 2000c: 268.

96 A coin, published in 1998, from Menbig in Syria (the coinage of which is otherwise well known) has the Aramaic inscription 'Mazday who is over Ebir-Nāri.' The document has engendered quite some conflicting interpretations (*BHAch* I. 29; Lemaire 2000: 135–7; Casabonne 2004: 210). Much caution remains warranted and this includes reckoning with the possibility of a fake (so Elayi and Sapin 2000: 173–5).

97 *HPE* 683–4, 1004 (year 345); since then, Elayi 2005: 129–32 has reaffirmed his conviction that the date is indeed year 4 of Artaxerxes III, i.e., 355.

98 The historical implications are debated: is it a purely Sidonian scene (Elayi and Elayi 2004b; 2005: 6974), or one that marks the Great King's imprint on the city *(HPE* 606–8, 983, with caution)?

99 Such is the position defended by Elayi and Elayi 2004b and Elayi 2005: 132–5, 139–41; a number of questions remain unanswered, however.

100 See Curt. 5.13.11: *Brochubelus, Mazaei filius, Syriae quondam praetor* (*HPE* 1013).

101 Curt. 3.12.3: *praefectus Damasci*.

102 Arr. *Anab.* 1.24.5, with my comments in *HPE* 706 and 1011.

103 See Briant 2003a: 347–419.

104 Esp. Polyaen. *Strat.* 4.3.32, on which see *HPE* 286–92, 921, as well as the recent seminal study by Amigues 2003.

105 On Darius III, see Briant 2003a: 40–52.

106 See esp. Tilia 1972: 243–4; Roaf 1983: 127–31, 140–1.

107 See Calmeyer 1990a: 12–13; *HPE* 734. The inscriptions A^3Pa and A^3Pb have been edited by Schmitt 1970: 114–22 (with specialized bibliography).

108 As demonstrated in *HPE* 95–6 and 895; 734–6; my interpretation was subsequently followed and elaborated by Henkelman 2003: 152–4, who also comments (153) on a slightly divergent passage in Str. 15.3.7.

109 See my comments in *RTP* 209 and *HPE* 452.

110 In *Oec.* 2.2.34, Ps.-Aristotle calls him ἡμίολος (conj.; ἡμιόδιος ms.), an appellative that has long been disputed (e.g., Zoepffel 2006: 629–30). Based on the context of his activities, Le Rider 2003: 304–5 has proposed considering him as the official charged with the finances of Babylonia after Harpalus' flight. Müller 2005, in turn, based his analysis on recently published inscription from Asia Minor (*SEG* xlvii: no. 1745) and concludes that Antimenes was Alexander's director of finances. The tentative comparison suggested (381), with the position of Parnakka in the Fortification texts from Persepolis, is a bit bold, but certainly suggestive in terms of possible continuities between Achaemenid financial administration and that of Alexander.

111 See *Oec.* 2.2.38: ἐκέλευε τοὺς σατράπας. Similarly 2.2.34: Antimenes orders the satraps to recover runaway slaves (ἐκέλευε τὸν σατράπην ...).

112 See *HPE* 364–5; 406 (on the term θησαυροί); 364–5 and 453 (on the ambiguous role of Antimenes – but the passage merits a detailed reevaluation); see also Le Rider 2003: 304–10 (analysis of each of the stratagems related in the *Oeconomica*), and 316–19 (Antimenes and the coinage of Alexander).

113 The existence of this tax in Babylonian has been demonstrated by Stolper 1989b (see *HPE* 413, 935). Comparison with this material allows, in my view, a better understanding of the passage in Ps.-Aristotle, including the clause on the flight of slaves. In a very rigid line of argumentation that, necessarily, is not made explicit, Lane Fox 2007: 290 decides that there has been no continuity, erroneously assuming that the tax was only imposed under Darius I (undoubtedly he misread *HPE* 413). In fact, Stolper's unmistakably shows that the tax is especially known from texts postdating Darius (probably from the reigns of Artaxerxes II and III: 82 n. 2), and that it is subsequently amply attested in the Seleucid period. As the author demonstrates very clearly, we are dealing with a remarkable case of Achaemenid–Hellenistic continuity via Alexander (90–1).

114 See esp. D.S. 17.67.3; 19.21.3; Arr. *Ind.* 40.2–3; Str. 15.3.6 (*RTP* 338, *HPE* 733–4). On Arr. *Ind.* 42.5; cf. Briant, forthcoming: 70.

115 See, e.g., Plu. *Alex.* 37.4; D.S. 17.71.1 (on the numbers see de Callataÿ, *REA* 1989: 263); the pack animals partly came from the royal herds, and partly from subject peoples (cf., e.g., Arr. *Anab.* 3.17.6, with the comments by Henkelman 2005: 159–64).

116 As Arr. *Anab.* 3.18.11 remarks (through Parmenion), that a lasting conquest cannot be defined by military victories and plundering alone: Alexander would also have to let the economical and fiscal heritage of Darius, to which his victories had given him access, yield profit since he now possessed these as 'his own property' (αὐτοῦ κτήματα), both in the present and in the future.

117 *RTP* 223 n. 353; 329 n. 161; 344 n. 73; *HPE* 735–6.

118 On the *kurtaš*, see *HPE* 429–39, 456–63; on the episode with the Lycian herdsman, see my suggestions in *RTP* 343–4; cf. *HPE* 735.

119 Pending the publication of the international Paris symposium on the Persepolis archives (Briant et al., forthcoming), see the reflections of Henkelman 2006: 96–116, who suggests that the excavated part of the archive was already dormant during the Achaemenid period (and preserved precisely because of that circumstance).

120 See already my explicit reflections to this regard in *RTP* 208 and 223 n. 353; 344; 329 (the documentation 'suggère le maintien (total ou partiel) de l'organisation sociale et économique achéménide dans le Fārs du vivant d'Alexandre'); see *HPE* 734–6.

121 Lemaire 1996: 152; the remark remains valid, independent of the identity of the "Alexander" of the ostraca; see also my remarks in *BHAch* I. 62.

122 Shaked 2003: 1526–9; 2004: 17–8; *ADAB* 202–12. Paradoxically, to say the least, the very same document is advanced by Lane Fox 2007: 297 as support for his skepticism on the assumed continuities between the Achaemenids and Alexander!

123 See Le Rider 2003: 161–5, with my comments in Briant 2006a: 312–17.

124 Curt. 5.1.17; on the circumstances of Alexander's entry into Babylon, see *HPE* 840–2, 845–50, 1045–6. Despite Lane Fox 2007: 275–7, 297–8 n. 60, the available documentation, when taken together, does indeed show clearly that there had been negotiations (see also Le Rider 2003: 275–6). As to the official entrance into Babylon and other places (HPE 189–95), this was, again despite Lane Fox (2007), surely an Achaemenid ceremonial protocol, which in turn was adapted from an Assyro-Babylonian model (Kuhrt 1990). The necessary logistics are clearly referred to in a Babylonian text (official entrance of Artaxerxes II at Susa in 398; text in Joannès 2004: 217–18;

see Briant, forthcoming. On the use of the image of Mazday in the Napoleonic period, see Calmeyer 1990b (see Briant 2003c: 33).

125 Briant 1993a and *HPE* 842–4.

126 On this complex, see the remarkable study by Nicolet-Pierre 1999; see also Le Rider 2003: 274–6 (Mazday himself, in the course of the negotiations that resulted in his coming over to Alexander's side, obtained from the latter the right to coin money with his own name and his own mint types), and Mildenberg 1990–1 = 1998: 9–23. After 328, the motifs are still the same, but they have been partially Hellenized: Babylonian documents from the time of Antigonus refer to the coins as 'lion staters.'

References

Ahituv and Yardeni 2004 = S. Ahituv and A. Yardini, 'Seventeen Aramaic Texts on Ostraka from Idumea: The Late Persian Period to the Early Hellenistic Perdiods', *Maarav* 11/1 (2004), pp. 7–23.

Amadasi-Guzzo 1998 = M.G. Amadasi-Guzzo, 'L'Idumée entre la fin de l'époque perse et la début de la période héllenistique: nouveaux ostraca araméens', *Orientalia* 67 (1998), pp. 532–538.

Amigues 2003 = S. Amigues, 'Pour la Table du Grand roi', *Journal des Savants* (2003), pp. 3–59.

Anson 2005a = E.M. Anson, 'Idumaean Ostraca and Early Hellenistic Chronology', *JAOS* 125 (2005), pp. 263–266.

Badian 1977 = E. Badian, 'A Document from Artaxerxes IV?', in K.H. Kinzl (ed.), *Greece and the Eastern Mediterranean in Ancient History and Prehistory* (Berlin: 1977), pp. 40–50.

Badian 2000a = E. Badian, 'Conspiracies', in A.B. Bosworth and E.J. Baynham (eds),*Alexander the Great in Fact and Fiction* (Oxford: 2000), pp. 50–95.

Badian 2000b = E. Badian, 'Darius III', *HSCPh* 100 (2000), pp. 241–268.

Bartlett 1999 = J.R. Bartlett, 'Edomites and Idumeans', *PEQ* 131 (1999), pp. 102–114.

Bedford 2001 = P.R. Bedford, *Temple Restoration in Early Achaemenid Judah* (Leiden: 2001).

Bedford 2007 = P.R. Bedford, 'The Persian Near East', in W. Scheidel, I. Morris, and P.R. Saller (eds), *The Cambridge Economic History of the Greco-Roman World* (Cambridge: 2007), pp. 302–329.

BHAch I = P. Briant, *Bulletin d'Histoire Achéménide* 1 (Paris: 1997).

BHAch II = P. Briant, *Bulletin d'Histoire Achéménide* 2 (Paris: 2001).

Boiy 2005 = T. Boiy, 'Alexander Dates in Lydian Inscriptions', *Kadmos* 44 (2005), pp. 165–174.

Boiy 2006 = T. Boiy, 'Aspects chronologiques de la période de transition (350–300)', in P. Briant and F. Joannès (eds), *La Transition entre l'empire achéménide et les royaumes hellénistiques (v. 350–300), Persika 9* (Paris: 2006), pp. 37–100.

Boucharlat 2006 = R. Boucharlat, 'Le Destin des résidences et sites perses d'Iran dans la seconde moitié du IVe siècle av. J.C.', in P. Briant and F. Joannès (eds), *La Transition entre l'empire achéménide et les royaumes hellénistiques (v. 350–300), Persika 9* (Paris: 2006), pp. 433–470.

Briant 1974 = P. Briant, *Alexandre le Grand* (Paris: 1974).

Briant 1976 = P. Briant, '"Brigandage", conquête et dissidence en Asie achéménide et hellénistique', *DHA* 2 (1976), pp. 163–259.

Briant 1982 = P. Briant, *États et pasteurs au Moyen-Orient ancien* (Paris: 1982).

Briant 1984 = P. Briant, *L'Asie centrale et les royaumes proche-orientaux du premier millénaire* (Paris: 1984).

Briant 1993a = P. Briant, 'Alexandre à Sardes', in J. Carlsen, B. Due, O.S. Due, and B. Poulsen (eds), *Alexander the Great: Reality and Myth* (Rome: 1993), pp. 13–27.

Briant 1998 = P. Briant, 'Cités et satrapes dans l'empire achéménide: Xanthos et Pixôdaros', *CRAI* (1998), pp. 305–340.

Briant 1999 = P. Briant, 'L'Histoire de l'empire achéménide aujourd'hui: l'historien et ses documents', *Annales HSS* 5 (1999), pp. 1127–1136.

Briant 2000a = P. Briant, 'Histoire impériale et histoire régionale: à propos de l'histoire de Juda dans l'empire achéménide', in A. Lemaire and M. Sæbø (eds), *Congress Volume Oslo 1998* (Leiden: 2000), pp. 235–245.

Briant 2000c = P. Briant, 'Numismatique, frappes monétaires et histoire en Asie mineure achéménide (quelques remarques de conclusion)', in O. Casabonne (ed.), *Mécanismes et innovations monétaires dans l'Anatolie achéménide: numismatique et histoire* (Istanbul: 2000), pp. 265–274.

Briant 2002a = P. Briant, 'L'État, la terre et l'eau entre Nil et Syr-Darya: remarques introductives', *Annales HSS* 57/3 (2002), pp. 517–529.

Briant 2002b = P. Briant, 'Guerre et succession dynastique chez les Achéménides: entre "coutume perse" et violence armée', in A. Chianotis and P. Ducrey (eds), *Army and Power in the Ancient World* (Stuttgart: 2002), pp. 39–49.

Briant 2003a = P. Briant, *Darius dans l'ombre d'Alexandre* (Paris: 2003).

Briant 2003b = P. Briant, 'Histoire et archéologie d'un texte: la *Lettre de Darius à Gadatas* entre Perses, Grecs et Romains', in M. Giorgieri, M. Salvini, M.C. Trémouille, and P. Vanicelli (eds), *Licia e Lidia prima dell'ellenizzazione* (Rome: 2003), pp. 107–144.

Briant 2003c = P. Briant, 'New Trends in Achaemenid History', *AHB* 17 (2003), pp. 33–47.

Briant 2005c = P. Briant, *Alexandre le Grand* (Paris: 2005).

Briant 2006a = P. Briant, 'L'Asie mineure en transition', in P. Briant and F. Joannès (eds), *La Transition entre l'empire achéménide et les royaumes hellénistiques (v. 350–300), Persika 9* (Paris: 2006), pp. 309–51.

Briant 2006c = P. Briant, 'Retour sur Alexandre et les *katarraktes* du Tigre: l'histoire d'un dossier (*première partie*)', *Studi Ellenistici* 19 (2006), pp. 9–75.

Briant 2008 = P. Briant, 'Retour sur Alexandre et les *katarraktes* du Tigre: l'histoire d'un dossier (*suite et fin*)', *Studi Ellenistici* 20 (2008), pp. 155–218.

Briant and Joannès 2006 = P. Briant and F. Joannès (eds), *La Transition entre l'empire achéménide et les royaumes hellénistiques (v. 350–300), Persika 9* (Paris: 2006).

Briant forthcoming = P. Briant, 'Suse et l'Élam dans l'empire achéménide', in J. Perrot (ed.), *Le Palais de Darius à Suse* (Dijon).

Briant, *RTP* = P. Briant, *Rois, tributs et paysans* (Paris: 1982).

Briant et al., forthcoming = P. Briant, W.F.M. Henkelman and M.W. Stolper (eds), *Les Archives des Fortifications de Persépolis dans le contexte de l'empire achéménide et de ses prédecesseurs* (Paris: 2008).

Brosius *Gnomon* 2006 = M. Brosius, 'Review of Briant 2003a', *Gnomon* 78 (2006), pp. 426–430.

Calmeyer 1990a = P. Calmeyer, 'Die Orientalen auf Thorwaldsens Alexanderfries', *AchH* 5 (1990), pp. 91–120.

Calmeyer 1990b = P. Calmeyer, 'Das Persepolis der Spätzeit', *AchH* 4 (1990), pp. 7–36.

Casabonne 2004 = O. Casabonne, *La Cilicie à l'époque achéménide* (Paris: 2004).

Cau 1999–2000 = N. Cau, 'L'uso delle formule di datazione nelle iscrizioni licie', *EVO* 22–3 (1999–2000), pp. 179–188.

Chauveau and Thiers 2006 = M. Chauveau and C. Thiers, 'L'Égypte en transition: des Perses aux Macédoniens', in P. Briant and F. Joannès (eds), *La Transition entre l'empire achéménide et les royaumes hellénistiques (v. 350–300), Persika 9* (Paris: 2006), pp. 375–404.

de Callataÿ, *REA* 1989 = F. de Callataÿ, 'Les Tresors achéménides et les monnayages d'Alexandre: espèces immobilisées ou espèces circulantes?', *REA* 91 (1989), pp. 259–264.

Debord 1999 = P. Debord, *L'Asie Mineure au IVème siècle (412–323): pouvoirs et jeux politiques* (Bordeaux: 1999).

Descat 2006 = R. Descat, 'Aspects d'une transition. L'Économie du monde égeen (350–300)', in P. Briant and F. Joannès (eds), *La Transition entre l'empire achéménide et les royaumes hellénistiques (v. 350–300), Persika 9* (Paris: 2006), pp. 353–373.

Devauchelle 1995 = D. Devauchelle, 'Réflexions sur les documents égyptiens datés de la deuxième domination perse', *Trans.* 10 (1995), pp. 35–43.

Domingo Gygax 2001 = M. Domingo Gygax, *Untersuchungen zu den lykischen Gemeinwesen in klassischer un hellenistischer Zeit* (Bonn: 2001).

Durand 1997 = X. Durand, *Des Grecs en Palestine au IIIe siècle av. J.C.: le dossier syrien des archives de Zénon de Caunos (261–252)* (Paris: 1997).

Dušek 2007 = J. Dušek, *Les Manuscrits araméens du Wadi Daliyeh et la Samarie vers 450–332 av. J.C.* (Leiden: 2007).

Eisenstadt 1969 = S. Eisenstadt, *The Political System of Empire* (New York: 1969).

Elayi 2005 = J. Elayi, *Le Monnayage d' 'Abd' Aštart Ier/Straton de Sidon: un roi phénicien entre Orient et Occident* (Paris: 2005).

Elayi and Elayi 2004b = J. Elayi and A.G. Elayi, 'La Scène du char sur les monnaies d'époque perse', *Trans.* 27 (2004), pp. 89–108.

Elayi and Sapin 2000 = J. Elayi and J. Sapin (eds), *Quinze Ans de recherche (1985–2000) sur la Transeuphratène à l'époque perse* (Paris: 2000).

Eph'al 1998 = I. Eph'al, 'Changes in Palestine during the Persian Period in Light of Epigraphic Sources', *IEJ* 48 (1998), pp. 106–119.

Eph'al and Naveh 1996 = I. Eph'al and J. Naveh (eds), *Aramaic Ostraca of the Fourth Century BC from Idumaea* (Jerusalem: 1996).

Eshel 2007 = E. Eshel, 'The Onomasticon of Mareshah in the Persian and Hellenistic Periods', in O. Lipschits, G.N. Knoppers, and R. Albertz (eds), *Judah and the Judeans in the Fourth Century B.C.E.* (Winona Lake: 2007), pp. 145–156.

FdX = H. Metzget et al., *Fouilles de Xanthos 6: La Stèle trilingue du Létôon* (Paris: 1973).

Flower 2007 = M. Flower, 'Not Great Man History: Reconceptualizing a Course on Alexander the Great', *CW* 100 (2007), pp. 417–423.

Francfort and Lecomte 2002 = H.P. Francfort and O. Lecomte, 'Irrigation et société en Asie centrale des origines à l'époque achéménide', *Annales HSS* 57/3 (2002), pp. 625–663.

Frei 1996 = P. Frei, 'Zentralgewalt und Lokalautonomie im Achämenidenreich', in P. Frei and K. Koch (eds), *Rechsidee und Reichsorganisation im Perserreich* (Freiburg-Göttingen: 1996), pp. 5–131.

Fried 2004 = L. Fried, *The Priest and the Great King: Temple–Palace Relations in the Persian Period* (Winona Lake: 2004).

Gardin 1997 = J.C. Gardin, 'À Propos de l'entité politique bactrienne', *Topoi* 1 (1997), pp. 263–277.

Garvin 2003 = E.E. Garvin, 'Darius III and Homeland Defense', in W. Heckel and L.A. Tritle (eds), *Crossroads of History: The Age of Alexander* (Claremont: 2003), pp. 87–111.

Grabbe 2004 = L. Grabbe, *A History of the Jews and Judaism in the Second Temple Period* 1: *Yehud: A History of the Persian Province of Judah* (London: 2004).

Graf 2000 = D. Graf, 'Aramaic on the Periphery of the Achaemenid Realm', in *Iberien (Königreich Kartli) und seine Nachbarn in achaimenidischer und nachachaimenidischer Zeit* (2000), pp. 75–92.

Henkelman 2003 = W. Henkelman, 'An Elamite Memorial: The *Šumar* of Cambyses and Hystaspes', in W. Henkelman and A. Kuhrt (eds), *A Persian Perspective: Essays in Memory of Heleen Sancisi-Weerdenburg* (Leiden: 2003), pp. 101–172.

Henkelman 2005 = W. Henkelman, 'Animal Sacrifice and "External" Exchange in the Persepolis Fortification Tablets', in H.D. Baker and M. Jursa (eds), *Approaching the Babylonian Economy* (Münster: 2005), pp. 137–165.

Henkelman 2006 = W. Henkelman, *The Others Gods Who Are: Studies in Elamite–Iranian Acculturation based on the Persepolis Fortification Texts* (Leiden: 2006).

Henkelman forthcoming = W. Henkelman, 'Consumed before the King: The Table of Darius, that of Irdabama and Irtaštuna, and that of his Satrap Karkiš', in B. Jacobs and R. Rollinger (eds), *Der Achämenidenhof* (Stuttgart).

Hornblower 1982 = S. Hornblower, *Mausolus* (Oxford: 1982).

HPE = P. Briant, *From Cyrus to Alexander: A History of the Persian Empire* (Winona Lake: 2002).

Jacobs 1993 = B. Jacobs, 'Die Stellung Lykiens innerhalb der achämenidish-persischen Reichsverwaltung', in J. Borchhardt and G. Dobesch (eds), *Akten des II. Internationalen Lykien-Symposions* 1 (Vienna: 1993), pp. 63–69.

Jacobs 1994 = B. Jacobs, *Die Satrapienverwaltung im Perserreich zur Zeit Darius' III* (Wiesbaden: 1994).

Joannès 2001 = F. Joannès, 'Les Débuts de l'époque hellénistique à Larsa', in P. Briant (ed.), *Irrigation et drainage dans l'Antiquité: qanats et canalisations souterraines en Iran, en Égypte et en Iran* (Paris: 2001), pp. 249–264.

Klinkott 2005 = H. Klinkott, *Der Satrap: Ein persischer Amtsträger und seine Handlungsspielräume* (Frankfurt: 2005).

Kloner and Stern 2007 = A. Kloner and I. Stern, 'Idumea in the Late Persian Period (Fourth Century B.C.E.)', in O. Lipschits, G.N. Knoppers, and R. Albertz (eds), *Judah and the Judeans in the Fourth Century B.C.E.* (Winona Lake: 2007), pp. 145–156.

Konuk 1998 = K. Konuk, 'The Coinage of the Hekatomnids of Caria' (D.Phil., Oxford: 1998).

Kottsieper 2002 = I. Kottsieper, 'Zum aramäischen Text der "Trilingue" von Xanthos und ihrem historischen Hintergrund', in O. Loretz et al. (eds), *Ex Mesopotamia et Syria Lux: Festschrift für Manfried Dietrich zu seinem 65* (Münster: 2002), pp. 209–243.

Kratz 2002 = R.G. Kratz, *Religion und Religionskontakte im Zeitalter der Achämeniden* (Gütersloh: 2002).

Kuhrt 1987 = A. Kuhrt, 'Review of Frei-Kock, *Rechsidee*', *BiOr* 44 (1987), pp. 199–205.

Kuhrt 1990 = A. Kuhrt, 'Alexander and Babylon', *AchH* 5 (1990), pp. 121–130.

Kuhrt 2001 = A. Kuhrt, 'The Persian Kings and their Subjects: A Unique Relationship?', *OLZ* 96/2 (2001), pp. 167–174.

Lane Fox 2006 = R. Lane Fox, 'The Letter to Gadatas', in *XAIKON ΣΥΜΠΟΣΙΟΝ ΕΙΣ ΜΝΗΜΗΝ W.G. Forrest* (Athens: 2006), pp. 149–171.

Lane Fox 2007 = R. Lane Fox, 'Alexander the Great: "Last of the Achaemenids"?' in C. Tuplin (ed.), *Persian Responses: Political and Cultural Interaction with(in) the Achaemenid Empire* (Swansea: 2007), pp. 267–311.

Lemaire 1996 = A. Lemaire, *Nouvelles Inscriptions araméennes d'Idumée au Musée d'Israël* (Paris: 1996).

Lemaire 1999a = A. Lemaire, 'Der Beitrag idumäischer Ostraka zur Geschichte Palästinas um Übergang von der persischen zur hellenistischen Zeit', *ZDPV* 115/1 (1999), pp. 12–23.

Lemaire 1999b = A. Lemaire, 'Quatre Nouveaux Ostraca araméens d'Idumée', *Trans.* 18 (1999), pp. 71–74.

Lemaire 2000 = A. Lemaire, 'Remarques sur certaines légendes monétaires ciliciennes (Ve–IVe s. av. J.C.)', in O. Casabonne (ed.), *Mécanismes et innovations monétaires dans l'Anatolie achéménide: numismatique et histoire* (Istanbul: 2000), pp. 129–142.

Lemaire 2002 = A. Lemaire, *Nouvelles Inscriptions araméennes d'Idumée II* (Paris: 2002).

Lemaire 2006a = A. Lemaire, 'Administration in Fourth-Century B.C.E. Judah in Light of Epigraphy and Numismatics', in O. Lipschits and M. Oeming (eds), *Judah and the Judeans in the Persian Period* (Winona Lake: 2006), pp. 53–74.

Lemaire 2006b = A. Lemaire, 'New Aramaic Ostraca from Idumea and their Historical Interpretation', in O. Lipschits and M. Oeming (eds), *Judah and the Judeans in the Persian Period* (Winona Lake: 2006), pp. 413–456.

Lemaire 2006c = A. Lemaire, 'La Transeuphratène en transition', in P. Briant and F. Joannès (eds), *La Transition entre l'empire achéménide et les royaumes hellénistiques (v. 350–300), Persika 9* (Paris: 2006), pp. 405–441.

Le Rider 2001 = G. Le Rider, *La Naissance de la monnaie: pratiques monétaires de l'Orient ancien* (Paris: 2001).

Le Rider 2003 = G. Le Rider, *Alexandre le Grand: monnaie, finances et politique* (Paris: 2003).

Le Roy 2005 = C. Le Roy, 'Vocabulaire grec et institutions locales dans l'Asie mineure achéménide', in U. Bultrighini (ed.), *Democrazia et antidemocrazia nel mondo antico* (Alexandria: 2005), pp. 333–344.

Leuze 1935 = O. Leuze, *Die Satrapieneinteilung in Syrien und im Zweistromlande von 520 bis 320. Schriften der Königsberger Gelehrten Gesellschaft* (Halle: 1935).

Lipschits and Oeming 2006 = O. Lipschits and M. Oeming (eds), *Judah and the Judeans in the Persian Period* (Winona Lake: 2006), pp. 53–74.

Lipschits et al. 2007 = O. Lipschits, G.N. Knoppers and R. Albertz (eds), *Judah and Judeans in the Fourth Century Century BCE* (Winona Lake: 2007).

Lozachmeur and Lemaire 1996 = H. Lozachmeur and A. Lemaire, 'Nouveaux orstraca araméens d'Idumée', *Semitica* 46 (1996), pp. 123–142.

Lyonnet 1997 = B. Lyonnet, *Prospections archéologiques en Bactriane orientale (1974–1978) sous la direction de J.C. Gardin* (Paris: 1997).

Maddoli 2006 = G. Maddoli, 'Pixodaros di Hekatòmnos e la datazione della Trilingue del Letôon', *Athenaeum* 94/2 (2006), pp. 601–608.

Marek 2006 = C. Marek, *Die Inschriften von Kaunos* (Munich: 2006).

Mayrhofer 1976 = M. Mayrhofer, 'Kleinasien zwischen Agonie des Perserreiches und hellenistischem Frühling. Ein Inschriftenfund des Jahres 1973', *Anzeiger d. OÄW* 112 (1976), pp. 274–282.

Melchert 2000 = H.C. Melchert, 'The Trilingual Inscription of the Létôon: Lycian Version', www.achemenet.com/pdf/lyciens/letoon.pdf (2000).

Mildenberg 1990–1 = L. Mildenberg, 'Notes on the Coin Issues of Mazday', *INJ* 11 (1990–1), pp. 9–23.

Mildenberg 1998 = L. Mildenberg, 'Money Supply under Artaxerxes III Ochus', in R. Ashton and S. Hurter (eds), *Studies in Greek Numismatics in Memory of M.J. Price* (London: 1998), pp. 277–284.

Mildenberg 1999 = L. Mildenberg, 'Artaxerxes III Ochus (358–338 B.C.). A Note on the Maligned King', *ZDPV* 115 (1999), pp. 201–227.

Müller 2005 = H. Müller, 'Hemiolios: Eumenes II, Toriaion und die Finanzorganisation des Alexanderreiches', *Chiron* 35 (2005), pp. 355–384.

Murison 1972 = C.L. Murison, 'Darius III and the Battle of Issus', *Historia* 21 (1972), pp. 399–423.

Naveh 1979 = J. Naveh, 'The Aramaic Ostraka from Tell Beer-Sheeba (Seasons 1971–76)', *Tel-Aviv* 6 (1979), pp. 182–195.

Naveh 1981 = J. Naveh, 'The Aramaic Ostraka from Tell-Arad', in Y. Aharoni (ed.), *Arad Inscriptions* (Jerusalem: 1981), pp. 153–176.

Nicolet-Pierre 1979 = H. Nicolet-Pierre, 'Les Monnaies des deux derniers satrapes d'Égypte avant la conquête d'Alexandre', in O. Mørkholm and N.M. Waggoner (eds), *Greek Numismatics and Archaeology. Essays in Honor of Margaret Thompson* (Wetteren: 1979), pp. 221–230.

Nicolet-Pierre 1999 = H. Nicolet-Pierre, 'Argent et or frappés en Babylonie entre 331 et 311 ou de Mazdai à Séleucos', in M. Amandry and S. Hurter (eds), *Travaux de numismatique grecque offerts à G. Le Rider* (London: 1999), pp. 285–305.

Nylander 1993 = C. Nylander, 'Darius III, the Coward King: Point and Counterpoint', in J. Carlsen, B. Due, O.S. Due, and B. Poulsen (eds), *Alexander the Great: Reality and Myth* (Rome: 1993), pp. 145–159.

Porten and Yardeni 2003 = B. Porten and A. Yardeni, 'In Preparation of a Corpus of Aramaic Ostraca from the Land of Israel: The House of Yehokal', in R. Deutsch (ed.), *Shlomo: Studies in Epigraphy, Iconography, History and Archaeology in Honor of Shlomo Moussaief* (Tel Aviv: 2003), pp. 207–223.

Porten and Yardeni 2004 = B. Porten and A. Yardeni, 'On Problems of Identity and Chronology in the Idumean Ostraca', in M. Heltzer and M. Mahul (eds), *Tshûrôt LaAvishur: Studies in the Bible and the Ancient Near East, in Hebrew and Semitic Languages* (Tel Aviv: 2004), pp. 161–183.

Porten and Yardeni 2006 = B. Porten and A. Yardeni, 'Social, Economic and Onomastic Issues in the Aramaic Ostraca of the Fourth Century B.C.E.', in O. Lipschits and M. Oeming (eds), *Judah and the Judeans in the Persian Period* (Winona Lake: 2006), pp. 457–488.

Roaf 1983 = M. Roaf, *Sculptures and Sculptors at Persepolis* (London: 1983).

Ruzicka 1992 = S. Ruzicka, *Politics of a Persian Dynasty: The Hecatomnids in the Fourth Century B.C.* (Norman: 1992).

Sapin 2004 = J. Sapin, 'La "frontière" judéo-araméenne au IVe siècle av. J.C.', *Trans.* 27 (2004), pp. 109–154.

Schmidt 1970 = E. Schmidt, *Persepolis 3: The Royal Tombs and Other Monuments* (Chicago: 1970).

Schmitt 2006 = R. Schmitt, *Iranische Anthroponyme in der erhaltenen Resten von Ktesias' Werk* (Vienna: 2006).

Seibert 1988 = J. Seibert, 'Dareios III', in W. Will and J. Heinrichs (eds), *Zu Alexander dem Grossen* (Amsterdam: 1988), pp. 437–456.

Shaked 2003 = S. Shaked, 'De Khulmi à Nikhšapaya: les données des nouveaux documents araméens de Bactres sur la toponymie de la région (IVe siècle av. n.è.)', *CRAI* (2003), pp. 1517–1532.

Shaked 2004 = S. Shaked, *Le Satrape de Bactriane et son gouverneur: documents araméens du IVe siècle av. n.è.* (Paris: 2004).

Shaked 2006 = S. Shaked, 'Are the Aramaic Documents from Ancient Bactria Part of an Archive?', in *Papers Presented to the Conference 'Les Archives des Fortifications de Persépolis dans le contexte de l'empire achéménide et de ses prédécesseurs', Collège de France November 6th–7th 2006* (Paris: 2006).

Six 1884 = J.P. Six, 'Le Satrape Mazaios', *NC* 4 (1884), pp. 97–159.

Stadter 1965 = P.A. Stadter, *Plutarch's Historical Methods: An Analysis of the Mulierum Virtutes* (Cambridge: 1965).

Stern 2001 = E. Stern, *Archaeology of the Land of the Bible* 2: *The Assyrian, Babylonian and Persian Periods (732–332 B.C.E.)* (New York: 2001).

Stolper 1987 = M.W. Stolper, 'Bēlšunu the Satrap', in R. Rochberg-Halton (ed.), *Language, Literature and History: Philological and Historical Studies presented to Erica Reiner* (New Haven: 1987), pp. 389–402.

Stolper 1989a = M.W. Stolper, 'The Governor of Babylon and Across-the-River in 486 B.C.', *JNES* 48/4 (1989), pp. 283–305.

Stolper 1989b = M.W. Stolper, 'Registration and Taxation of Slave Sales in Achaemenid Babylonia', *ZA* 79 (1989), pp. 80–101.

Strauss and Ober 1990 = B.S. Strauss and J. Ober, 'Darius III of Persia: Why He Lost and Made Alexander Great', in *The Anatomy of Error: Ancient Military Disasters and Their Lessons for Modern Strategists* (New York: 1990), pp. 103–131.

Tilia 1972 = A.B. Tilia, *Studies and Restorations at Persepolis and Other Sites of Fārs* (Rome: 1972).

Van Alfen 2002 = P.G. Van Alfen, 'The "Owls" from the 1989 Syria Hoard with a Review of Pre-Macedonian Coinage in Egypt', *AJN* 14 (2002), pp. 1–57.

van der Spek 1998 = B. van der Spek, 'The Chronology of the Wars of Artaxerxes II in Babylonian Astronomical Diaries', in M. Brosius and A. Kuhrt (eds), *Studies in Persian History: Essays in Memory of David M. Lewis* (Leiden: 1998), pp. 239–256.

Watts 2001 = J.W. Watts, *Persia and Torah: The Theory of Imperial Authorization of the Pentateuch* (Atlanta: 2001).

Zoepffel 2006 = R. Zoepffel, *Aristoteles: Oikonomika* (Berlin: 2006).

ALEXANDER'S SETTLEMENTS IN CENTRAL ASIA

Frank L. Holt

In rugged and still remote regions of Central Asia lie the scattered remains of a remarkable episode in the history of ancient Greece. Silent cities and countless coins bear witness there to kings and colonists who broadened the Greek world beyond Bactria. Alexander's settlements in Central Asia were the source for this development, but the survival of these colonies as a Hellenistic kingdom must not obscure their difficult origins. During Alexander's lifetime and soon thereafter, these settlements showed few signs of permanent success. In fact, to the extent that Alexander's colonies were meant to insure this king's control over Bactria-Sogdiana, they were one of the worst failures of Macedonian foreign policy in the fourth century B.C.

In the most recent studies of Alexander's campaigns in this region, scholars have done much to clarify the problems which plagued the king.[1] The general conclusion has been that Alexander overcame all obstacles and achieved complete success through his policy of founding cities.[2] It has not been pointed out, therefore, that Alexander's settlements were themselves a large part of his political and military problems in the east.[3] These colonies did not complete the conquest of Bactria-Sogdiana, nor enforce a permanent peace. To the contrary, they caused three major revolts against Macedonian rule in the east – one by the Barbarians of Sogdiana and Scythia, and two by the Greek settlers themselves.

The familiar claim that these colonies brought peace to the region must therefore be reconsidered; it will be suggested instead that Alexander's settlements in Central Asia were a source of unrest and insurrection. It is important to realize in this regard that Alexander and his army marched completely across Bactria and Sogdiana before meeting any major military resistance. No battle was fought in the Macedonian invasion of Bactria because the threat from Bessus never materialized. In fact, the troops collected under Bessus' command deserted and disbanded to their native villages, while the principal Bactrian cities – including the satrapal capital itself – opened their gates to the invaders.[4] When Alexander later advanced into Sogdiana, Bessus was betrayed by his last supporters, including Spitamenes.[5] Traversing all of Sogdiana, Alexander reached the Jaxartes River without serious opposition.[6]

The success of this long march is startling in light of later events, and one must wonder whether the natives had really been rallied by Bessus to a 'national war of resistance'. There is no evidence to suggest that there was strong native opposition to Alexander's nominal rule over the region; yet, at the *end* of the king's march through these satrapies a major revolt did erupt. The question is, why, and why there? The circumstances suggest that the planned settlement of Alexandria-Eschate, Alexander's first city-foundation anywhere in Bactria-Sogdiana, may have finally provoked a native attack on the Macedonian army. It was, in fact, after the site had been selected and the initial planning begun that the immediate area rose up in revolt, so that Alexander was temporarily diverted from the project by the sudden outbreak of fighting.[7] When the king was able to return to this site, the city's walls were hurriedly raised to a defensible height in the face of enemy opposition.[8] Indeed, the principal aim of those dwelling on the opposite shore of the Jaxartes was to destroy the offending city and to drive off those settled there.[9] It seems quite clear that the sudden outbreak of hostilities must be associated with Alexander's first attempt to found settlements in Bactria Sogdiana. The rebellion was aimed not against Alexander as king or conqueror, but against Alexander as colonizer. The presence of a Macedonian king and his army could be tolerated, as already shown, but sudden changes in the socio-economic structure of the region was another matter. It was Alexander's purpose, according to our sources, to build the city as a bulwark against the Scythian nomads who inhabited the trans-Jaxartes.[10] He hoped, therefore, to inhibit the traditional intercourse between Sogdiana and Scythia by militarizing the Jaxartes under direct Macedonian control.[11]

The establishment of Alexandria-Eschate merely provoked for the present what Alexander wished to prevent for the future – an active and hostile confederacy of Scythians and Sogdians. The diverse populations living along both sides of the Jaxartes immediately resisted this effort to create an artificial march state between them.[12] Thus, in spite of praises past and present, Alexander's settlement policy led to provocation rather than peace. The king raided Scythia, but this did not inhibit its support of the Sogdians – much less pacify Asia as Curtius claimed.[13] The king fortified Alexandria-Eschate and hoped to strengthen his rule over the neighboring population, but even massacre and *andrapodismos* had little effect beyond increasing the turmoil which had precipitated the crisis.[14] If the natives of this area were unable to pursue the political, social, and economic patterns of life to which they were accustomed, they were certainly not thereby pacified. Indeed, the problem was self-perpetuating since Alexander's counter-measures (political and military) only contributed to the original causes of the revolt. Thus, as the king was forced to carry his campaigns throughout much of Sogdiana, Spitamenes with his Sogdian and Scythian cavalry widened the war as far south as Bactria.[15]

In the valleys of southeastern Sogdiana, Alexander established additional military colonies.[16] It was while operating in this region that the king may have selected the now-famous site of Ai Khanoum for settlement.[17] Paul Bernard, the French excavator of this city, has argued that it was Alexander's obvious intention to seal this frontier against Scythian nomads.[18] If so, the king was indeed embarked upon a systematic effort to rid Sogdiana of Scythian influence.[19]

This policy of Alexander was certainly not well rewarded since the influence of the nomadic Scythians was never eliminated from Sogdiana by Alexander or his successors. Furthermore, his efforts to colonize the area seemed to complicate the task of establishing firm Macedonian control. The bitter struggle made it impossible for Alexander to reconcile the population to foreign rule, so that the means of establishing order was also the cause of continued fighting. Thus peace and prosperity were hardly the result of these settlements in Central Asia.

It was conciliation rather than colonization which brought Alexander some success in Sogdiana, as his treatment of Oxyartes, Chorienes, and Sisimithres suggests.[20] This does not mean, however, that matters were finally resolved or that Macedonian control was secure. Alexander's only immediate achievement lay in the fact that he was able, after two difficult years, to extricate himself from a problem for which his settlements were no solution.

Even as the king marched on to India, he was forced to leave an army of over 13,000 to occupy this 'pacified' area.[21] Soon thereafter, there were said to be some 23,000 settlers distributed among Alexander's new colonies in Sogdiana.[22] Even during the worst years of the rebellion, Alexander had considered a force of 3,000 sufficient to hold Sogdiana, so one must wonder whether order had yet been imposed.[23] In any case, to whatever extent the area had been secured under Macedonian rule, these settlements soon again undermined Alexander's aims.

The men left behind by Alexander were many, but they were in no mood to provide either peace or permanent Macedonian rule; in fact, many were openly mutinous.[24] Disaffected and determined to abandon the settlement of Bactria-Sogdiana, many of these Greek colonists rose up in rebellions whenever the opportunity arose. One uprising occurred when it was rumored that Alexander had been killed in India, a second when the king actually expired at Babylon in 323 B.C.[25] In the first case, by the time it was learned that Alexander had survived his injury in India, matters had gone too far in Bactria and Sogdiana. Among several rival Greek factions, the most audacious was led by one Athenodorus, who had seized the poorly-guarded citadel of Bactra.[26] He then urged the barbarians to join the revolt, and even took the title of king.[27] Yet another faction-leader was Biton, a fellow countryman of Athenodorus.[28] This Biton plotted the assassination of Athenodorus, a deed carried out by a Bactrian named Boxus as the new 'king' reclined at a banquet; however, the removal of Athenodorus was no remedy at all. The Greeks were divided on the question of the assassination, and those who disapproved were not easily deterred from killing Biton in return.[29]

Alexander's settlements were already in chaos while the Macedonian king was still in the East, yet matters grew even worse. As Biton plotted against those who had saved his life, he was seized in turn with Boxus. The Bactrian was executed summarily while Biton was sentenced to torture as well as execution. In the midst of torture, however, Biton was rescued by another faction and his oppressors were forced to flee.[30] Biton and his followers were thus able to evacuate Bactria-Sogdiana and, so Curtius claims, made their way back to Greece.[31] Diodorus, whose account is much less detailed, does report that a band of 3,000 marched homeward with great difficulty, but they were later massacred by the Macedonians after the death of Alexander.[32]

These events make it certain that Bactria-Sogdiana was in great turmoil by the time of Alexander's death. Revolts and assassinations had become the sad sequel of the king's effort to colonize this region. When the king in fact died at Babylon in June 323, the eastern settlers collected together a veteran force of more than 20,000 infantry and 3,000 cavalry under the command of Philon of Aeniania.[33]

The response of Perdiccas to this second settlers' revolt was to dispatch from Babylon an army under the command of Pithon, a former bodyguard of Alexander and an early supporter of Perdiccas' ascendancy.[34] Pithon was given 3,800 Macedonian soldiers, with an additional 18,000 troops to be supplied en route by other satraps; the expeditionary force reached Bactria at a full strength of some 21,800 (13,000 infantry and 8,800 cavalry).[35] Perdiccas allegedly instructed Pithon to kill 'all' whom he conquered and to distribute the spoils among his soldiers. The reason for such severity, explains Diodorus, was that Perdiccas suspected that Pithon would try to win over the rebels and unite them with his expeditionary army, enabling him to establish independent rule over the eastern satrapies.[36]

There is a problem, of course, since none of these troops were interested in remaining in the east, a notable flaw in Pithon's 'plan'. There is, too, the question of Perdiccas' wisdom in ordering a wholesale slaughter of all settlers just to thwart Pithon's alleged ambitions. In any event, could 23,000 rebels be totally annihilated by an army somewhat smaller in size? Although a massacre did indeed take place, there is no reason to assume (as some have done) that all 23,000 of the rebellious colonists were killed.[37] Diodorus, in fact, describes in fair detail what actually transpired. We are told that Pithon subborned Letodorus, a commander of 3,000 of the rebellious colonists, through the agency of a certain Aenianian.[38] During the battle between Pithon and Philon, this Letodorus and his troops withdrew to a hillside and refused to fight. As a result, the rebels under Philon were thrown into confusion and so fled the battlefield.[39]

With the battle won, Pithon sent a herald to those defeated, ordering them to disarm and return to their own colonies. After an exchange of pledges, the Greeks were intermingled with the Macedonians. Pithon's troops, however, recalled Perdiccas' orders and so set upon the Greek prisoners in spite of their oaths. All the Greeks were killed and their possessions were confiscated as plunder.[40]

In view of these events, it seems clear that the massacre of rebels involved the 3,000 with Letodorus, not all who fled the battle.[41] That Pithon had hoped to spare these particular rebels for services rendered may account for the story of Perdiccas' suspicions and pre-emptive orders. But whatever Perdiccas' exact orders, they were interpreted by the Macedonian troops with an eye toward money and revenge. Service in Bactria, whether temporary or not, seldom brought out the best in men from the Mediterranean. These Macedonians, after all, had developed first-hand only a few years before a great repugnance for Bactria. Having returned west as far as Babylon, and eager to continue on to Macedonia, they had suddenly been ordered instead to march again to Bactria. Letodorus and his like were the reason for this onerous duty, so it is little wonder that the mood of the Macedonians was murderous.[42] There may also have been some vengeance taken if the Macedonian satrap had indeed been killed earlier; his successor Philip, appointed at Babylon in 323, is also missing in our accounts of the second revolt and may have been killed as well.

Pithon's expedition did not end in the extinction of Greek colonies or colonists in Bactria. At least 3,000 were killed, but perhaps a great number remained. For these survivors of the second revolt, however, the situation could hardly have seemed worse. They were prisoners more than pioneers, men unhappy to be in Bactria but unable to fight their way back west. Thus, there is little positive evidence that Bactria-Sogdiana ever became a pacified part of Alexander's ephemeral empire: four satraps had been variously assigned since Alexander's arrival (the 'retired' Artabazus, the murdered Cleitus, and the 'missing' Amyntas and Philip). There are three major revolts setting barbarians against Greeks and Macedonians, Greeks against Greeks, and Greeks against Macedonians. What settlement (if any) had been imposed by Pithon remains a mystery. The next known appointment of a satrap (Stasanor of Soli) occurs several years later in 320 B.C. as part of the administrative arrangements of Antipater at Triparadeisos.[43]

The over-all picture of eastern affairs during this troubled period is one of waning Macedonian control. The extent to which the Macedonians were able to maintain rule over this region was limited to the coercion of rebellious Greek colonists, and even that at a great distance by dispatching a punitive expedition. By 320 B.C., the satrap sent to administer this restless province was a Greek, not a Macedonian. As the Macedonians became more pre-occupied with their power struggles in the west, this Stasanor and his Greek settlers were left more and more to their own devices.

To argue, therefore, that Alexander's settlements in Central Asia were the agents of Macedonian rule and permanent peace seems altogether unwarranted. Whether the fault of the king or his colonists, these settlements may instead be considered one of the most frustrating failures of Macedonian foreign policy in the fourth century B.C.[44]

Notes

1   The following publications of A.B. Bosworth and Pierre Briant are especially noteworthy: Bosworth, 'Alexander and the Iranians', *JHS* 100 (1980): 1–21: Bosworth, 'A Missing Year in the History of Alexander the Great', *JHS* 101 (1981): 17–39; Briant, '"Brigandage", dissidence et conquête en Asie achéménide et hellénistique', *DHA* 2 (1976): 163–258: Briant, 'Colonisation hellénistique et populations indigènes: la phase d'installation', *Klio* 60 (1978): 57–92. Also important are N.G.L. Hammond's fine biography, *Alexander the Great: King, Commander and Statesman* (Noyes: Park Ridge, N.J., 1980), and Donald Engels' study entitled *Alexander the Great and the Logistics of the Macedonian Army* (Berkeley: Univ. of California Press, 1978).

2   This view of Alexander's final triumph in the east has long prevailed, in spite of continuing research into the problem: *cf.* E. Badian, 'The Administration of the Empire', *Greece and Rome* 12 (1965): 177.

3   Briant (above, note 1) comes closest to such a conclusion, but his analysis is primarily social and so falls short of a strong political or military judgement on this issue. I nevertheless owe much to his pioneering work.

4   For Bessus' troop-strength, see Curtius 6.6.13, 7.4.20, 7.4.30, and Arrian 3.28.8. Rather than contest Alexander's invasion while the Macedonians were struggling across the Hindu Kush, Bessus decided upon a scorched-earth policy (Curtius 7.4.1–19; Arrian 3.28). The Bactrian troops then deserted, Bessus retreated into Sogdiana, and Alexander advanced unopposed through the area (Curtius 7.4.19–21; Arrian 3.29).

5   Curtius 7.5.19–26, 36–43; Arrian 3.29–30. 6; Diodorus 83.8–9. Again, the Macedonian army had been vulnerable to attack since the desert crossing from Bactria to the Oxus was a considerable disaster: Curtius 7.5.1–18; Arrian 3.28.8. Yet, even though Bessus had planned to hold the Oxus (Curtius 7.4.5), Alexander found no opposition there and could afford to dismiss 900 veterans (Curtius 7.5.27; Arrian 3.29– 4.5).

6   Alexander's cavalry was resupplied with horses from the area and his forces passed through heavily fortified Maracanda, the chief city of the region, without incident: Arrian 3.30. 6; *cf.* Curtius 7.6.10 for the defenses of Maracanda. This passage in Curtius (which mentions hostilities) has created much unnecessary confusion, and must here be clarified. The context of Curtius' remarks is not Alexander's (uneventful) march *to* the Jaxartes, but a later episode. This should be clear from Curtius' previous statement (7.5.36) that Alexander had already reached the Tanais (Jaxartes). There is nothing in Curtius' statement which contradicts Arrian, who himself places the Maracandan conflict after Alexander had reached the Jaxartes: Arrian 4.5.2 and 4.6.4, which (like Curtius) states that Alexander reached Maracanda *from* the Jaxartes on the fourth day.

7   Alexandria-Eschate: Arrian 4.1.3–4, 4.4.1; Curtius 7.6.13, 25–27: Justin 12.5.2. The revolt: Arrian 3.30.10, 4.2–4; Curtius 7.6. The native resistance spread quickly and easily because the Macedonians, and their numerous garrisons, were caught by surprise after so little hostility had hitherto been encountered.

8   Arrian 4.4.1.

9   Curtius 7.7.1.

10 Arrian 4.1.3–4; Curtius 7.6.13. The city was to be a military base from which Sogdiana could be defended and the Scythians attacked, as Alexander did when the foundation was established: Arrian 4.4.2–4, 5.1 and Curtius 7.7.5–29, 7.8.1–7.9.17.

11 Alexander had previously warned the Scythians not to cross the Jaxartes without his permission: Curtius 7.6.12.

12 Alexander's animosity toward the Scythians may be easily understood. These nomadic peoples were generally perceived by Greeks as uncivilized predators who endangered sedentary societies (*cf.* Curtius 7.8.8–30; Arrian 4.17.5). On this classical stereotype, see F. Hartog, 'La question du nomadisme: les scythes d'Herodote', *AAASH* 27 (1979): 135–148, and his book *Le miroir d'Herodote: Essai sur la representation de l'autres* (Paris: Gallimard, 1980). P. Briant, too, has done much to improve our understanding of this particular problem (see above, note 1). He argues

that the nomad menace was one of Alexander's own making; otherwise, the Jaxartes was a natural meeting place of nomads and settled peoples, not a perpetual 'march state'. In fact, this traditional interaction was precisely what Alexander feared: Arrian 4.3.6: 4.5.4–6.2; 4.16.4–17.2; Curtius 6.6.13; 7.4.6; 7.7.1, 31; 8.1.3; 8.3.1; Strabo 11.8.8 (513).

13 Curtius 7.9.17, who then contradicts himself by continuing his description of prolonged native resistance.

14 Arrian 4.2–4.4; Curtius 7.6.16–23.

15 The events of this year (328 B.C.) have now been examined at length in a study by A.B. Bosworth, 'A Missing Year in the History of Alexander the Great', *JHS* 101 (1981): 17–39. Favoring Curtius' narrative over that of Arrian, Bosworth has revised both chronological and geographical details. I concur for the year 328 B.C., but cannot agree with his conclusions for 327 and lament that he did not examine the causes of the conflict in 329.

16 Curtius 7.10.15 mentions six foundations in Margania, which Bosworth ('Missing Year', pp. 24–29) locates not in the oasis of Margiana, but the hills of Tadzhikistan.

17 The possibility is mentioned by Bosworth, 'Missing Year', p. 29; see also P. Bernard's tentative identification of the city as Alexandria-Oxiana in Sogdiana: P. Bernard and H.-P. Francfort, *Études de géographie historique sur la plaine d'Ai Khanoum* (Paris CNRS, 1978), pp. 5–9.

18 P. Bernard, 'Ai Khanoum on the Oxus: A Hellenistic City in Central Asia', *PBA* 53 (1967): 74–75, 89; Bernard. 'Ai Khanoum: Ville coloniale grecque', *DA* 5 (1974): 102.

19 Briant suggests that Alexander sought to limit the powers of the semi-independent Sogdian chieftains by converting their territories into *chora basilike*: 'Colonisation', *Klio* 60 (1978): 72–73.

20 *Ibid.*, pp. 73–74. Unable to eliminate such leaders, Alexander co-opted them. This policy proved far more conducive to peace than direct Macedonian control through military colonies. In fact, as shown below, the colonies continued to cause unrest.

21 Curtius 8.1.19; 8.2.14; Arrian 4.17.3 and 4.22.

22 On Alexander's colonies and garrisons, see Strabo 11.11.4; Justin 12.5.13; Curtius 8.1.3; 10.2.8; Arrian 3.29.1; 4.5.2; and 4.16.4–5. Diodorus 18.7.2 mentions 23,000 disgruntled settlers.

23 Curtius 7.10.10.

24 Justin 12.5.13.

25 The first revolt (326/5 B.C.): Diodorus 17.99.5–6; Curtius 9.7.1–11. The Second Revolt (323): Diodorus 18.7.1–9. These revolts have rarely been treated at length, although passing references to the unrest of the Bactrian settlers are common in general histories. The only recent study of the revolts is by G.A. Koshelenko, 'The Revolt of the Greeks in Bactria and Sogdiana in Light of Fourth Century Social and Political Theory', *VDI* 119 (1972): 59–78. Koshelenko attributes the revolt to an ideological clash between Macedonian and Greek (Aristotelian) political theory, but his argument has little evidence to support it.

26 Both Curtius 9.7.1 and Diodorus 17.99.5 make it clear that the settlers were Greeks, no doubt mercenaries. Few Macedonians, except those disabled in combat, were left behind by Alexander. The satrap Amyntas may have commanded some fellow-Macedonians at Bactra, but the disappearance of Amyntas suggests that he and any such troops were killed when Athenodorus stormed the citadel of Bactra. By 323, the satrap is Philip (Diodorus 18. 33), but he also disappears in the course of the second settlers' revolt soon after Alexander's death. Other Macedonian satraps in the east were killed by Greek mercenaries as well: Arrian 6.27, *cf.* 6.15.

27 Curtius 9.7.2–3. Athenodorus assumed the title 'non tam imperii cupidine quam in patriam revertendi cum eis qui auctoritatem ipsius sequebantur'.

28 Curtius 8.7.4–11. The native city of Biton and Athenodorus unfortunately is not identified.

29 Curtius 9.7.5–6. Biton claimed that he was defending himself against a plot set by Athenodorus.

30 Curtius 9.7.7–10. These events, and the shifting factions which shaped them, were not easily explained by Curtius: 'incertum ob quam causam'.

31 Curtius 9.7.11.

32 Diodorus 17.99.6. The demise of these men may be linked to the massacre of those who revolted in 323, since the number 3,000 is given there as well: Diodorus 18.7.6.

33 Diodorus 18.7.1. This large force has often been questioned, but the size of the army sent against it (below, note 34) lends credibility to Diodorus here. Briant, 'Colonisation', *Klio* 60 (1978): 85 considers 23,000 a conservative figure.

34 Diodorus 18.4.8 and 18.7.1–9. In events of this period and the major persons involved, see R.M. Errington, 'From Babylon to Triparadeisos: 323–320 B.C.'. *JHS* 90 (1970): 49–77, although Errington pays scant attention to eastern affairs.

35 Diodorus 18.7.3, 5.

36 Diodorus 18.7.4–5.

37 See F.W. Walbank, *The Hellenistic World* (Cambridge, Mass.: Harvard University Press, 1982), pp. 44–5.

38 Diodorus 18.7.5. Philon, the leading general of the rebel army, was himself from Aeniania (Diod. 18.7.2). It seems that Pithon was exploiting native Greek loyalties, just as Antiochus the Great tried to do later in Bactria. The Aenianians were one of the twelve tribes in the Delphic Amphictyony and inhabited the Spercheus River Valley.

39 Diodorus 18.7.6.

40 Diodorus 18.7.7–9.

41 Whether Diodorus 17.99.6 also refers to Letodorus' men is uncertain. The recurrence of the number 3,000 may be a doublet; but, if so, the problem may lie in the first reference (Book 17) rather than the second (Book 18).

42 This particular point has been made by P. Briant, 'D'Alexandre le Grande aux Diadoques: Le cas d'Eumene de Kardia', *REA* 75 (1973): 63, in order to explain Eumenes' struggle against the prevailing wish of Macedonian soldiers to return home. As he notes, the desire of the Greeks to return west was no different during this tumultuous period.

43 Diodorus 18.39.6: Arrian *FGH* 156 F9. This Stasanor may be the Stasanor mentioned in Justin 41.4.1 who had reportedly been satrap of Parthia because 'no Macedonian would accept the position'.

44 Although important work continues on this problem, the notes of this paper reflect only those published prior to September 1983, the date of the Symposium.

ALEXANDER THE GREAT, NATION BUILDING, AND THE CREATION AND MAINTENANCE OF EMPIRE

Ian Worthington

Alexander the Great (356–23) fought strategically brilliant battles and laid sieges against numerically superior foes to establish one of the greatest geographic empires of antiquity, from Greece in the west to what the Greeks called India (modern Pakistan) in the east. When he died he was ready to undertake an invasion of Arabia, and plausibly after that he would have moved against Carthage. He created his empire in a little over a decade, invading Asia in 334 and dying in Babylon in 323. Not even the Romans, who boasted the largest empire of antiquity, could attribute their empire to just one man, and it took centuries to reach the extent it did before it fell. Alexander's campaigns also facilitated the spread of Greek culture in the areas through which he and his army marched, and they opened new trading avenues and possibilities between West and East, which forever changed relations between Greece and Asia.

This chapter shows how Alexander established his empire, discusses the problems he faced in ruling a large, multicultural subject population, and examines the approaches and strategies he took to what might be called nation building. In doing so, it allows us also to praise and critique his actions. Alexander's experiences in Asia arguably can inform present makers of modern strategy and shed light on contemporary problems in this or any culturally different region of the world. At the same time, the argument can be made that Alexander's failings (sometimes his fault, at other times not) show how little the modern world learns from, or even ignores, the past.

Alexander succeeded to the Macedonian throne on the assassination of his father, Philip II, in 336. He had already proved himself on the battlefield. In 340, when he was sixteen, his father appointed him regent of Macedon, and during his tenure of power Alexander successfully marched against and defeated the Maedians on the upper Strymon River. Philip was impressed, for two years later, in 338, he gave his son the command of the Macedonian left flank, and of the Companion Cavalry, no less, at the Battle of Chaeronea. This was the battle by which the Greeks lost their autonomy and in the following year became members of the so-called League of Corinth, which was headed by the Macedonian king and used to enforce Macedonian hegemony. In fierce fighting at Chaeronea, Alexander distinguished himself by helping to annihilate the famous 300-strong Theban Sacred Band.

When Alexander became king, he immediately had to deal with a number of problems, not least a revolt of the Greeks from Macedonian rule, which he easily ended. Afterward he revived his father's League of Corinth, and with it his plan for a pan-Hellenic invasion of Asia to punish the Persians for the suffering of the Greeks, especially the Athenians, in the Greco-Persian Wars and to liberate the Greek cities of Asia Minor. However, it was not until the spring of 334 that Alexander led an army of some 48,000 infantry and 6,000 cavalry, supported by a fleet of 120 warships, from Greece to Asia. Before landing, the story goes, he threw a spear into Asian soil to indicate he regarded all of Asia as his spear-won territory.[1]

In three major battles against far numerically superior Persian armies (at the Granicus River in 334, Issus in 333, and Gaugamela in 331), Alexander defeated the Persians. He did so thanks to a better trained army, inherited from his father Philip II, than the

Persian one, and by a combination of strategic brilliance, daring, and luck.[2] Darius III, the Great King, had not been present at Granicus (the Persian side was commanded by Arsites, the satrap of Hellespontine Phrygia), but he fought Alexander at Issus and Gaugamela, and on both occasions Alexander, the heart of his strategy being to kill or capture him, had forced him off the battlefield. The demoralizing effect this had on the Persian troops had turned the tide of battle in favor of Alexander both times. Also demoralizing, and taking place before both Issus and Gaugamela, must have been Alexander's visit to Gordium (close to the modern Ankara) in 333. Here was the wagon dedicated by Midas, son of Gordius, who allegedly left Macedon and became king of Gordium. The wagon was famous for the knot made of cornel wood on its yoke, and the accompanying prophecy that whoever untied it would rule Asia. Needless to say, the king undid it, either by slashing it with his sword or by unraveling it.[3] His visit to Gordium, then, was political: to show everyone he was the next ruler of Asia.

In between Granicus and Issus, Alexander had marched down the coastline of Asia Minor and Syria, in some cases receiving the immediate surrender of the cities, in other cases having to besiege them (his most famous sieges are probably at Halicarnassus, Tyre, and Gaza). In 332 he had entered Egypt, where the satrap, Mazaces, immediately surrendered the capital, Memphis, and hence all Egypt to him. Mazaces had no choice, for the Egyptians were tired of Persian rule and welcomed the Macedonian army as liberators; if Mazaces had resisted, the Egyptians would have risen up against him. While in Egypt, Alexander made his famous trek to consult the Oracle of Zeus-Ammon at the Siwah oasis in the Libyan Desert to obtain confirmation that he was the son of Zeus.[4] His pretensions would, however, lead to his undoing later (see below).

Alexander's success at Gaugamela meant that the Persian Empire was to all intents and purposes no more. It would not be long before its more important and wealthier royal capitals were in Macedonian hands. These included Babylon, Ecbatana, Susa, and finally Persepolis, home of the palace of Darius and Xerxes, the 'most hated city in Asia.'[5] Shortly before the Macedonian army left Persepolis in spring 330, the palace burned to the ground. Whether this was accidental or deliberate is not known with certainty, but the symbolism of its burning, as with the Gordian knot, was exploited: the peoples of the Persian Empire no longer would pay homage to the Great King but to Alexander as Lord of Asia.

The burning of Persepolis meant, in effect, that the original aims of the invasion of Asia — punishment of the Persians and freeing of the Greek cities of Asia Minor — had been achieved, and the men in the army evidently thought they would now be going home.[6] But Alexander did not turn westward. He needed to hunt down Darius once and for all, and so set off after him. He caught up with him at Hecatompylus, only to find him dead and that Bessus, satrap of Bactria, one of the men who had deposed Darius and had had a hand in his murder, had proclaimed himself Great King as Artaxerxes V. Again Alexander's men expected their king to give orders to start the long march home,[7] and again they were disappointed, as Alexander gave orders to pursue Bessus.

Although the army had wanted to return home at Persepolis and at Hecatompylus, Alexander was right to see the need to depose Bessus in order to maintain stability in his new Asian empire. Nevertheless, the Macedonian invasion had entered a different phase, one of conquest for the sake of conquest. Also different was how Alexander treated those people who defied him as he marched eastward, with mass slaughter and even genocide becoming something of a norm.

Bessus was quickly joined by Satibarzanes, satrap of Areia, and Bactrian chieftains such as Oxyartes (the father of Roxane) and Spitamanes, who commanded substantial numbers of men, and especially first class cavalry. To counter this threat, Alexander invaded Bactria and Sogdiana. The speed with which he moved caused these leaders to fall back beyond the Oxus, and not long after Alexander crossed this river, Oxyartes and Spitamanes betrayed Bessus to Alexander, who ordered his execution. Again, the removal of one leader meant nothing, for Spitamenes came to the fore, and the Macedonians were now faced with fierce guerrilla warfare in this different and hostile part of Central Asia. By 327, though, the resistance was over, Spitamenes was dead, and Alexander added cavalry contingents from the two areas to his army.

During the Bactrian campaigns, two potentially major conspiracies against Alexander were revealed. The first, the so-called Philotas affair, was in 330 at Phrada, capital of Drangiana. Although Philotas, commander of the companion cavalry and son of Parmenion, had nothing to do with the affair, his criticisms of Alexander's orientalism and pandering to Persian nobility led to his undoing. He was accused of complicity in the conspiracy and put to death. Alexander then gave orders for the killing of the equally critical Parmenion, who was at Ecbatana at the time and had no knowledge of any conspiracy. Then in 327 at Bactria a conspiracy involving some of the royal pages was discovered. Callisthenes, the court historian, who had defied Alexander's attempt to introduce *proskynesis* (the Asian custom of prostration before the Great King), was implicated and put to death, yet no evidence existed against him. If Alexander's likely manipulation of these conspiracies to rid himself of critics were not bad enough, Alexander also murdered his general Cleitus at Maracanda (Samarkand) in 328 after the two men got into a furious drunken row. There is no question that the Bactrian campaign was a turning point in Alexander's deterioration as a king and as a man.

After pacifying Bactria (or so he thought), Alexander pushed eastward into India. Here he fought only one major battle, against the Indian prince Porus at the Hydaspes River in 326. It was another Macedonian victory, but it was the high point militarily of Alexander's campaign in India. The men had expected to be returning home as early as 330 following the burning of Persepolis, but Alexander was showing no signs of that, and the campaign in India was the final straw. After seventy days of marching through drenching monsoon rains toward the Ganges, the army mutinied at the Hyphasis (Beas) River, forcing Alexander to turn back. One of Alexander's ambitions in India was to sail down the Indus River and out into the Southern (Indian) Ocean. He would achieve this (along the way almost losing his life at the siege of Malli), and his voyage was one of the highlights of his time in India.

Leaving India, Alexander led a contingent of his troops westward through the Gedrosian Desert. His reason was personal: Dionysus, with whom Alexander was by then identifying himself, had traveled through the desert, while Cyrus the Great of Persia had tried but failed. Alexander's ill-fated march saw about a third of the men with him die because of the hostile natural conditions. This mattered less to the king than the personal glory of marching through the desert.[8]

In the meantime, Bactria and Sogdiana revolted, and India followed suit. Alexander had mistakenly believed that defeated in battle meant conquered, but the Afghans were (and are) not conquered by anyone. The Pashtun tribes of the present northwest frontier of Afghanistan are constantly fighting each other, and there is a saying today that they are only united when they face a common enemy. That is exactly what Alexander was in the 320s, just as the British in the nineteenth century and the Russians in the twentieth were, and the same holds true today. This time there was little that Alexander could do.

Two years later, in 324, at Opis, a second mutiny occurred over Alexander's policy to discharge his veterans, although his plans to invade Arabia did not help — nor did his adoption of a combination of Persian and Macedonian clothing[9] or his belief in his own divinity, as the men's mocking 'you and your father Zeus can go to Arabia if you want' indicates. His powers of persuasion were unable to end this mutiny, and after three days he was successful only when he shamed the men into giving in by transferring Macedonian commands to Persians. In other words, he played on the men's racial hatred of the Persians to end the mutiny. A year later, in Babylon, in June 323, on the eve of his Arabian expedition, Alexander the Great died, a few months shy of his thirty-third birthday. He left behind no heir (his wife Roxane, a Bactrian princess, was pregnant when he died), and when asked to whom he left his empire, he enigmatically replied, 'to the best.' Thus began a thirty-year round of bloody wars between his generals that saw the carving up of the Macedonian Empire and the emergence of the great kingdoms of the Hellenistic period.

It is important to remember that Alexander's empire was never static but continually shifting its frontiers and absorbing new peoples. There was never an instance when Alexander fought that one final battle; there was never a time when he ruled his empire peacefully, and he was faced with opposition all the time he was in Asia, from the Persian Great King to the chieftains of Central Asia and the princes of India to the aristocratic families, all of whom naturally saw Alexander as a threat to their power and prestige. After the Granicus River battle in 334, a goodly number of the survivors fled to Miletus to defy Alexander. When Miletus fell after a short siege, many from there fled to Halicarnassus, forcing Alexander to wage yet another siege. And so the years and resistance wore on. Against the background of the unabating opposition, the undoing of the Gordian knot makes even more sense, as Alexander strove to show everyone he was the new ruler of Asia, not merely by conquest but according to prophecy.

We might expect the political exploitation of this religious symbolism to be effective, and Alexander probably thought it would be, given the religious nature of the people. However, he was a conqueror, and despite attempts to endear himself to the aristocracy by involving them in his administration (see below), no one likes to be conquered. Even after the turning-point defeat of Darius at Issus, the Great King was able to regroup and bring Alexander to battle at Gaugamela. Alexander's victories were hard-won, the enemy always outnumbered him, and Darius, in addition to his enormous resources (far greater than those of Alexander), was a skilled strategist and commander.[10] And he never said die: after Issus, he gathered together another army, and after Gaugamela he was determined to fight Alexander again, this time with an army principally made up of his easternmost subjects. His failures in battle proved too much, though, and he was deposed and murdered.

Even then the resistance to Alexander did not fall apart but continued in the leadership of Bessus, forcing Alexander into Bactria and Sogdiana. Bessus was quickly joined by Satibarzanes, whom Alexander had appointed the satrap of Areia but who now sided with Bessus against the invader. This type of disloyalty was something Alexander would encounter time and again.

At first Alexander gained the upper hand in Bactria, as seen in the betrayal of Bessus to him, but Spitamenes, who succeeded Bessus, was far more dangerous and tactically cunning. Using the barren, desolate, and rocky topography that he and his people knew so well but the invading army did not, he forced Alexander into more than two years of intense guerrilla fighting and bloody siege warfare. Alexander was forced to deal with all this and with growing opposition from his senior staff as well as from the rank and file of his army, opposition that exploded in 326 at the Hyphasis, forcing him to turn back. If the army had not revolted, he would have reached the Ganges, and if he had not died in Babylon, he would have invaded Arabia.

Thus at no time did Alexander rule a fixed geographic area, at no time did he appear to want to rule an empire with fixed borders, as his continual campaigning shows, and at no time were all his subjects passive and supportive of his presence among them. All these factors made administering his empire in some longer-term uniform and efficient fashion and persuading his men to continue marching and fighting doubly difficult.[11]

The Persian kings had realized the impossibility of one man trying to rule the large and diverse kingdom they had created. That was why Darius I (522–486) divided his empire into twenty satrapies (administrative regions), personally appointing a satrap (governor) over each one. Apart from paying annual taxes to the Great King and furnishing troops for the Persian army, the satraps wielded all the power in their satrapies, although the Great King was at the top of the administrative hierarchy, and he ruled absolutely.

The satrapal system remained in existence because of the relative autonomy of the satraps and their acceptance of the Great King. While Alexander might call himself Lord of Asia, that was very different from being the Great King, and many of the satraps had fought in battle against him. Alexander as invader would have cause to question their loyalty, but he recognized the value of the satrapal system, so he kept it, with some changes.[12] In the earliest stages of his Asian campaign he placed his own men in charge of the western satrapies — for example, Calas was made satrap of Hellespontine Phrygia, Antigonus of Phrygia, Asander of Lycia, and Balacrus was made satrap of Cilicia. However, as Alexander's territories increased eastward, especially after Gaugamela, Alexander began to involve the aristocratic Persian families in his administration and appoint some as satraps. The first of these was really Mazaeus, who was appointed satrap of Babylonia in 331. Others included Abulites, satrap of Susa, Phrasaortes, satrap of Persis, and Artabazus, satrap of Bactria and Sogdiana. Alexander's action would help smooth the path of a new, 'transition' regime (so he hoped) by nullifying opposition from these influential families whose power he was eroding. Besides, he needed these people for their knowledge of the language and customs of their people. The last point is important, because by being part of the administrative hierarchy, they would help to reconcile the mass of the people to his rule, the plan being to help him maintain a peaceful occupation.

The danger, of course, was that a conquered people could not be left to its own devices. Alexander could not afford an insurrection, so he made some important modifications to the satrapal system. Native satraps continued to have some civil authority and to levy taxes in their satrapies. However, they were little more than titular figureheads, for Alexander appointed Macedonians to be in charge of the treasury and the military forces of each satrapy. Thus, real power in the satrapies now lay with his men. The change extended the precedent he had set, for example, in Caria, where Ada continued as its satrap but Ptolemy was in charge of military affairs,[13] or in Egypt, where a Persian Doloaspis was governor of sorts but was dominated by Cleomenes, a

Greek from Naucratis, who used his position as collector of taxes and overseer of the construction of Alexandria to seize the reins of power. The new system continued throughout the reign, although in 325, when Alexander returned from India, he punished many disloyal satraps (and generals of mercenary armies) with death and appointed as their successors both Persians and Macedonians; for example, Peucestas was made satrap of Persis (he was the only Macedonian who learned Persian and immersed himself in Persian customs, which pleased the people greatly, according to Arrian).[14]

While Alexander allowed the satraps to continue collecting taxes, he created the post of imperial treasurer at some point before (or in) 331. His boyhood friend Harpalus oversaw all imperial finances (first from Ecbatana and eventually from his headquarters in Babylon). Alexander seems to have put the Greek cities of his empire in a special category, for taxes from those in Asia Minor were to be collected by Philoxenus and those in Phoenicia by Coeranus.[15]

Alexander's men did not expect the enemy to retain any positions of influence, and needless to say, the satraps would have resented losing control of their armies and treasuries. The military might of the Macedonians held them in check, but it is no surprise that native satraps were disloyal when Alexander was in India, and that in Central Asia the satrapies of Bactria and Sogdiana revolted twice. Bactria proved to be such a problem area that when Artabazus resigned his post in 328, Alexander appointed Cleitus, co-commander of the Companion Cavalry, as its satrap, although Alexander killed him before he could take up this position. In his place he appointed another Macedonian, Amyntas, who would head the largest contingent of troops in any one satrapy.[16]

Such disloyalty is also part and parcel of imperial power being held by one man, and an invader at that. When Alexander was present with his superior army, resistance was not an option, but when he left it was a different matter. Bactria shows this, as does India. Here, Alexander confirmed the power of many of the local princes who submitted to him, for example Taxiles east of the Indus, and after the battle of the Hydaspes, Porus was allowed to retain his power (although he became a vassal of Alexander); however, once the king left India, the rulers reverted to their old ways and paid him only lip service.

Diodorus tells us another way that Alexander intended to manage his empire. In his account of Alexander's so-called last plans, he says that Alexander planned to found cities and to transplant people from Asia to Europe and vice versa, to bring "the biggest continents into a common unity and to friendship by intermarriages and family ties."[17] Alexander did not embark on any transpopulation policy, but he did found a large number of settlements, apparently as many as seventy. However, the majority of these were not actual poleis with developed constitutions, gymnasia, theaters, and all the attributes of a city but instead were more garrison posts, often inhabited by veteran soldiers and local peoples to keep a particular area in check.[18] Alexander probably founded only a dozen actual cities, the most famous being Alexandria in Egypt.[19]

Founding cities for strategic reasons was not novel. Philip II had done the same thing along his northwest frontier with the troublesome Illyrian tribes in 345, and Alexander's borrowing this leaf out of his father's book shows us he realized that using native satraps would not be enough to placate his subject peoples. Philip had conquered the various Illyrian tribes, unified Macedon as a result, and then incorporated them into the new

Macedonian army. Even so, he was forced to monitor them continuously throughout his reign.[20] So Alexander also could not afford to assume his satrapal arrangements would be enough. Hence he took care to pepper the garrison settlements throughout the areas of his empire where he expected the most resistance — unsurprisingly, the greatest concentration was in the eastern half of the empire. Even so, these would not prove to be enough in Bactria and Sogdiana.[21]

The new settlements also facilitated trade and communications, although they rose to economic prominence only after Alexander. Thus, Alexandria (in Egypt) became the cultural center and an economic power in the Hellenistic period after Ptolemy I made it the capital.[22] The real advantage of using cities to help maintain rule over huge empires is shown by the later Seleucid rulers of Syria. It is no coincidence that Seleucus, the first of these rulers, and the first to make city foundations deliberate policy, was one of Alexander's generals. He had learned well by example.

Diodorus also talks about a 'common unity' between the western and eastern halves of Alexander's empire and intermarriages. This sort of line, compounded by Plutarch's presentation of Alexander as a philosopher and idealist in his rhetorical treatise *On the Fortune or the Virtue of Alexander*, has led to a belief that Alexander wanted to create a brotherhood of mankind as a means of ruling his empire. There is, of course, merit to a policy that tries to make foreign rule acceptable not by enforcing it but by promoting equality and commonality among everyone, and some of Alexander's actions throughout his reign seem to support the belief that he was striving to achieve such an equality. Prominent among his actions here were the integration of foreigners into his army and administration, his marriage in spring 327 to the Bactrian princess Roxane, his attempt to enforce *proskynesis* at his court, the mass wedding at Susa in 324, at which he and ninety members of his senior staff married Persian noblewomen, and finally a reconciliation banquet at Opis in 324, at which he prayed for harmony between everyone.

Yet there was no such thing as a unity-of-mankind 'policy' on Alexander's part.[23] None of the above actions was ideological in purpose, but, like Alexander himself, all were pragmatic and no different from, say, founding cities to maintain Macedonian control. For example, foreigners in his army, such as specialist troops from Iran or the Bactrian cavalry, were kept apart in their own ethnic units until 324, when Alexander incorporated them into the army for tactical reasons before the Arabian expedition.[24] Native satraps, as already noted, were merely figureheads, the powerful families being given some semblance of their former station to secure their support.

For Alexander, Roxane may well have been 'the only woman he ever loved,' but the marriage was political.[25] Her father Oxyartes had been one of Alexander's toughest opponents; the marriage, Alexander would have hoped, was to secure his support, and hence Bactria's passivity, and in return Alexander made him satrap of Parapamisadae. Hence, Alexander's marriage was no different from his father's first six marriages, undertaken to help consolidate Macedon's borders — and provide an heir. Roxane had a child who died in 326 at the Hydaspes,[26] thus giving us a motive for Alexander's marriages in 324 to two Persian princesses: to solidify his rule and to produce heirs on the eve of his Arabian campaign (Roxanne became pregnant soon after).

Proskynesis set Persians apart from Greeks, who thought the act was akin to worship. Alexander's attempt to enforce it on his own men looks like he was trying to fashion some common social protocol between the races, to get West to meet East. Yet he was brought up to believe in the traditional gods and still performed the traditional sacrifices as king in the last days of his life, so he must have known his men saw the act as sacrilegious. Even the posture was unacceptable, as Greeks commonly prayed standing up with their arms upraised, whereas slaves lay on the ground. More likely, then, is that Alexander now thought of himself as divine, and *proskynesis* reflected that.

The symbolism of the interracial mass marriage at Susa seems obvious, but it is important to note that no Greek women were brought out from the mainland to marry Asian noblemen, which we would expect if Alexander was sincere about fusing the races by intermarriage. What Alexander was doing was polluting the bloodline to ensure that children from these marriages would never have a claim to the Persian throne. Moreover, his men were against the marriages, and after Alexander's death, they all, apart from Seleucus, divorced their wives.

Finally, the prayer to harmony after the Opis mutiny: Alexander ended the mutiny by playing on his men's hatred of the Persians. At a reconciliation banquet the same evening the seating order sought to emphasize the superiority of the invaders: Macedonians sat next to Alexander, then came the Greeks, and then all others. Moreover, the prayer to concord was about unity in the army, not unity of mankind, because Alexander planned to invade Arabia, and so dissension in the ranks was the last thing he needed.

Aristotle, his personal tutor from the age of fourteen to sixteen, had advised Alexander 'to treat the Greeks as if he were their leader and other people as if he were their master; to have regard for the Greeks as for friends and family, but to conduct himself towards other peoples as though they were plants or animals.'[27] Aristotle may well have influenced Alexander's scientific curiosity to find out about the natural resources of the areas through which he traveled,[28] but Alexander did not follow Aristotle's advice about his Asian subjects. At the same time, Alexander knew he had to regard the conquered populations with suspicion; hence everything he did was for a political reason.

Another area that might throw light on Alexander's relationship with the conquered people, and hence the maintenance of his empire, is the spread of Greek culture. Hellenization became something of a staple in Alexander's nation building. To a large extent, the spread of Greek civilization was inevitable simply as an effect of Alexander's army marching through new areas and exposing the people there to things Greek. Alexander was an avid reader of Homer (especially the *Iliad*) and of Greek tragedy (Euripides was his favorite), and his men would have shared his tastes. Thus, when the army returned to Tyre from Egypt in the summer of 331, Alexander held a celebratory festival to Heracles, complete with games and dramatic performances. Among the performers were the celebrated actors Thessalus (a personal friend of Alexander) and Athenodorus, who reneged on a contract to perform at the culturally important festival of the city Dionysia in Athens to be at Tyre. For this he was fined, but Alexander paid the fine for him.

These sorts of cultural events would have been lost on his men if they did not appreciate them, and they must have had an effect on local peoples. Indeed, his fostering of Greek culture led later authors such as Plutarch to speak of him as the bringer of civilization to foreign peoples.[29] However, one might argue that the spread of Greek culture was not simply an offshoot of his campaigns but that he saw the political benefits to be gained from cultural change. The problem was, he made little attempt to tolerate local customs and religious practices, and he would end customs that Greeks condemned or that he personally disliked.

For example, Greeks were appalled that in Persia, brothers would marry sisters and sons married their mothers.[30] On the other hand, these practices might be overlooked because the Macedonians had marital customs that other Greeks condemned, specifically polygamy (later in Ptolemaic Egypt the practice of ruling brothers marrying sisters began with Ptolemy II Philadelphus and his sister, Arsinoë). However, the Scythians' practices of sacrificing their elderly parents, drinking the blood of their first human kill, and using as much of a corpse as possible in their everyday lives were another thing.[31] So too was the Bactrians' custom in regard to their elderly: 'those who became infirm because of old age or sickness are thrown out alive as prey to dogs, which they keep specifically for this purpose, and in their native tongue they are called "undertakers". While the land outside the walls of the city of the Bactrians looks clean, most of the land inside the walls is full of human bones.'[32]

We, like the Greeks back then, find this custom shocking, but nevertheless it was a traditional local custom. However, that did not stop Alexander ending it, and he had no business to do so. It was this type of disruption to established social practices that could only fuel discontent in the affected areas and encourage locals to resist the Macedonians, and it gave rise to an anti-Greek sentiment. This is very much in evidence with the Ptolemaic kings of Egypt, for example, who segregated the native Egyptians in society and precluded them from taking part in state administration. The feelings of exploitation had grown to explosive levels by the reign of Ptolemy IV (221–203), and Egypt was split by civil war that tested Ptolemaic rule to its utmost.

On the other hand, Alexander was more tolerant of religious beliefs, but then the equivalents of Greek gods were everywhere. For example, Alexander identified the local god Melqart at Tyre with Heracles; at Siwah there was an oracle of Zeus-Ammon, and at Nysa in India the local god Indra or Shiva was deemed the equivalent of Dionysus. Religion is a powerful tool for bringing about unity, and the king used it as and when he saw fit, though not always properly understanding what religion meant to different people. Thus, in Egypt he took care to sacrifice to Apis at Memphis and in Babylon he gave orders to rebuild the temple to Bel, which Xerxes had destroyed. He spared the lives of the people of Nysa in 326 (a deviation from what had by then become his modus operandi of wholesale slaughter of native tribes) because they claimed descent from those who had traveled with Dionysus through the region, Nysa was the name of Dionysus's nurse, and Alexander was convinced a local plant was ivy, Dionysus's symbol.

However, Alexander could be far more myopic. In 332, after the people of Tyre had surrendered to him, Alexander expressed his wish to worship in their temple. The temple was to Melqart, the local equivalent of Heracles, who was one of Alexander's ancestors. The temple, then, was not to Heracles but to Melqart, and for Alexander to worship there was sacrilegious to the Tyrians, who refused, asking him to worship on the mainland opposite (in antiquity, Tyre was an island). Rather than recognizing the political advantage he had just gained from the Tyrians' surrendering to him (it was essential for him to control Tyre to prevent the Phoenician navy using it as a base) and accepting the compromise because of its religious nature, Alexander took the rebuff as a personal affront. Furious, he gave orders for Tyre to be besieged. When it fell to him after a difficult and lengthy siege, he put many of its citizens to death and sold the rest into slavery. As an example to other places that might defy him, he ordered the crucified bodies of 2,000 Tyrians to be set up along the coastline. This act merely stiffened resistance to him, for the next town he approached, Gaza, refused to open its gates to him. After a short siege Gaza fell, and Alexander punished the people harshly, including dragging the garrison commander Batis behind a chariot around the walls of Gaza until he died.

As a king and at times even as a general, Alexander had flaws, but he was impossible to beat. He was, then, 'his own greatest achievement.'[33] However, it is common to transfer his failings as a king and a man to his plans for the building of a single empire. He did not have a conscious economic policy, if such a term is not too modern, for the empire as a whole, although he recognized the economic potential of the areas through which he traveled and which he next targeted – one of the reasons for invading Arabia had to have been its lucrative spice trade. His continual marching east until his men forced him back leads one to conclude he knew nothing else but fighting.[34] Yet Alexander did give thought to how he could deal with the problems that faced him and manage his empire so as to maintain Macedonian rule over it. He introduced administrative measures to this end, such as streamlining the satrapal system and creating the office of imperial treasurer. He involved the powerful Persian aristocratic families, whose support he needed, in his administration, and he started wearing Persian dress and the upright tiara (in 330 after Darius III was killed) to endear himself to the Persians and to offset the threat from Bessus and Artaxerxes V.[35]

These factors help us to see how Alexander's exploits more than two millennia ago highlight the dilemma of modern nation building. It is easy for us to think of ways he could have endeared himself to his subject peoples more. For example, he could have worked to understand different customs, religious beliefs, and even cultures and maintain them on an equal basis with his own. While it was perfectly fine to expose the Asians to Greek culture, their own culture should not have been ignored, condemned, or reduced because the Greeks thought theirs was better (whatever that means). Then again, perhaps to achieve this 'equality' was impossible in the real world. What Alexander did (or did not do) shows us that the dilemma of Western nation building was as alive in antiquity as it is now – or conversely, that Alexander's inherent problems in nation building set a trend for the centuries that followed and into the modern era that has not yet been reversed.

Thus, to persuade his men to keep marching, to keep conquering, and thus to keep expanding his empire, Alexander was forced to argue the benefits that hellenization would bring to the peoples of the former Persian Empire, as well as the advantages (economic and otherwise) that the conquest and maintenance of Asia would bring to Macedon. These benefits were worth fighting for – and dying for – although the material benefits of booty would not have been lost on the army. At the same time, he had to reconcile his rule with the native peoples and so rule his empire with minimum opposition. These peoples, however, might be attracted to aspects of his brand of Hellenism, but not at the expense of their own culture and, even more important, their freedom. Using powerful families in his administration, allowing natives to be satraps, involving natives in his army, and adopting Asian dress were some of the ways in which Alexander might have appealed to his subjects.

His methods, however, alienated his own men and were transparent to the locals: no native satrap could have thought for a moment that nothing had changed from the days of the Great King. The fact that Macedonians were in charge of the army and treasury in his satrapy was a daily reminder that a new regime existed. Thanks to the Macedonian army's continued victories, Alexander's position as Lord of Asia was as secure as it ever could be. However, the problems increased as he marched farther eastward, intent on expanding his empire. The intense fighting in Bactria and Sogdiana was a turning point in Alexander's relations with his own men, who up to that point had loyally followed their king. The fighting in these regions and then in India, together with Alexander's orientalism, proved too much, as seen in the mutiny at the Hyphasis. This event marked a decline in Alexander's control of Asia as a whole. That military success was the basis of his power, and not hellenization or empire building, is proved by the revolts of India, Bactria, and Sogdiana as he left, and by the activities in the west of the satraps, generals, and imperial treasurer in his absence. And it is significant that before the burning of Persepolis, the story goes, Parmenion warned Alexander about the possible native backlash from the palace's destruction. None came, a testimony not so much to the acceptance of Alexander's rule as to the military might of the conquering army.

No one wants to be conquered, and in the end, only military power, not idealism, can maintain a conqueror's power. Alexander's empire did not survive him, but that was probably its fate anyway. He established an empire that was for a time without parallel, but its very size and cultural diversity made it impossible for one man or one regime to govern it effectively. These factors alone led to the failure of his attempts to maintain it. At the same time, without Alexander, there would not have been the great Hellenistic kingdoms and the cultural capitals at Alexandria, Antioch, and Pergamum. These great centers arose from the spread of Greek civilization that began with Alexander and continued with the Hellenistic kings, as shown by the ease with which the Ptolemaic kings in Egypt and the Seleucid kings in Syria, whose dynasties were founded by Alexander's generals in the disintegration of his empire, were able to attract Greeks from the west to live and work in their empires.

Further reading

Dozens of accounts of Alexander's reign were written during and shortly after his lifetime (the so-called primary sources), but only fragments of these survive. The extant narrative histories of Alexander's reign that we have (the secondary sources) were written centuries after his death, beginning with Diodorus Siculus in the first century BC, Quintus Curtius Rufus sometime in the mid- to later first century AD, Arrian in the second century AD, and Justin's epitome of an earlier work by Pompeius Trogus (now lost), which he copied in either the second or the third century AD. Of these, Arrian is commonly accepted as the most reliable source, principally because of his critical and balanced approach to the primary sources and his reliance on the eyewitness account of Ptolemy. To these later sources may be added the biography of Alexander by Plutarch (second century AD) and his treatise *On the Fortune or the Virtue of Alexander*, though this is a rhetorical, not historical, work. Ian Worthington, *Alexander the Great: A Reader* (London: Routledge, 2003), includes a wide selection of translated primary sources, and Waldemar Heckel and J. Yardley, *Alexander the Great: Historical Sources in Translation* (Malden, MA: Blackwell, 2003), contains a selection of mostly secondary sources in translation.

There is an abundance of modern books about Alexander, from scholarly biographies to glossy coffee-table ones. Michael Wood's *In the Footsteps of Alexander* (Berkeley and Los Angeles: University of California Press, 1997) is recommended as a general introduction to Alexander and especially for its photographs of the areas through which he marched since Wood himself followed his route. More recent biographies that can be singled out include Peter Green, *Alexander of Macedon 356–323 B.C.: A Historical Biography* (Harmondsworth, UK: Penguin, 1974); Robin Lane Fox, *Alexander the Great* (London: Penguin, 1973); A.B. Bosworth's *Conquest and Empire: The Reign of Alexander the Great* (Cambridge: Cambridge University Press, 1988), the best scholarly biography, together with his *Alexander and the East* (Oxford: Oxford University Press, 1996); Major General J.F.C. Fuller, *The Generalship of Alexander the Great* (New Brunswick, NJ: Rutgers University Press, 1960); N.G.L. Hammond, *Alexander the Great: King, Commander and Statesman* (Bristol: Bristol Press, 1989), to be preferred over his later *The Genius of Alexander the Great* (London: Duckworth, 1997); Paul Cartledge, *Alexander the Great: The Hunt for a New Past* (London: Routledge, 2003); and Ian Worthington, *Alexander the Great: Man and God*, rev. ed. (London: Pearson, 2004). Some collections of scholarly articles that deal with different aspects of Alexander's reign are A.B. Bosworth and E.J. Baynham, eds., *Alexander the Great in Fact and Fiction* (Oxford: Oxford University Press, 2000); Guy T. Griffith, ed., *Alexander the Great: The Main Problems* (Cambridge: Cambridge University Press, 1966); Joseph Roisman, ed., *Brill's Companion to Alexander the Great* (Leiden: Brill, 2003); Waldemar Heckel and Lawrence A. Tride, eds., *Crossroads of History: The Age of Alexander* (Claremont, CA: Regina Books, 2003); and Worthington, *Alexander the Great: A Reader*. For the Persian Empire, the best book is still Pierre Briant, *From Cyrus to Alexander: A History of the Persian Empire*, trans. Peter D. Daniels (Winona Lake, IN: Eisenbrauns, 2002).

Notes

1 Diodorus 17.17.2; Justin 11.5.10.
2 On Philip's army reforms, see Ian Worthington, *Philip II of Macedonia* (New Haven, CT: Yale University Press, 2008), 26–32; on Alexander's army, see A.B. Bosworth, *Conquest and Empire: The Reign of Alexander the Great* (Cambridge: Cambridge University Press, 1988), 266–77.
3 Aristobulus, *FGrH* 139 F7 (Arrian 2.3.7); Plutarch *Alexander* 18.4.
4 Cf. Plutarch *Alexander* 27.3–6.
5 Diodorus 17.70.
6 Plutarch *Alexander* 38.6–7.
7 Q. Curtius Rufus 6.2.15–16.
8 Note Arrian 3.3.2 implies that Alexander made the long and arduous trek to Siwah in Egypt to emulate his ancestors Perseus and Heracles.
9 Diodorus 17.77.7; Q. Curtius Rufus 6.6.9–12.
10 For a reappraisal of Darius, see Ernst Badian, "Darius III," *HSCP* 100 (2000): 241–68.
11 See Ernst Badian, "The Administration of the Empire," G&R2 12 (1965): 166–82, and W.E. Higgins, 'Aspects of Alexander's Imperial Administration: Some Modern Methods and Views Reviewed," *Athenaeum* 58 (1980): 29–52.
12 On Alexander's satrapal appointments and arrangements, see in more detail Bosworth, *Conquest and Empire*, 229–41, and Badian, 'Administration of the Empire,' 166–82. On the Indian arrangements, see A.B. Bosworth, 'The Indian Satrapies under Alexander the Great,' *Antichthon* 17 (1983): 37–46.
13 Arrian 1.23.6.
14 Arrian 6.30.2–3.
15 On Alexander's financial administration, see in more detail Bosworth, *Conquest and Empire*, 241–45.
16 Arrian 4.22.3.
17 Diodorus 18.4.4.
18 Cf. Diodorus 17.111.6.

19   On Alexander's cities, see P.M. Fraser, *Cities of Alexander the Great* (Oxford: Oxford University Press, 1996), who argues that, excluding Alexandria in Egypt, Alexander founded only eight cities.

20   See further A.B. Bosworth, 'Philip II and Upper Macedonia,' *CQ*2 21 (1971): 93–105.

21   Justin 12.5.13 says that Alexander founded twelve cities in Bactria and Sogdiana, but he does not name them.

22   See Arrian 4.1.3–4 on the potential of Alexander-Eschate (Alexandria-on-the-Jaxartes, the modern Leninabad) as security against future Scythian attacks.

23   Much has been written on this topic, but for excellent arguments against the unity of mankind, see Ernst Badian, 'Alexander the Great and the Unity of Mankind,' *Historia* 7 (1958): 425–44, and A.B. Bosworth, 'Alexander and the Iranians," *JHS* 100 (1980): 1–21, citing previous bibliography.

24   See Bosworth, *Conquest and Empire*, 271–73.

25   Plutarch *On the Fortune or the Virtue of Alexander* 338d.

26   Metz *Epitome* 70.

27   Plutarch *On the Fortune or the Virtue of Alexander* 329b. On what Hellenism constituted, bound up with speaking Greek, see Herodotus 8.1442 and Thucydides 2.68.5, with J.M. Hall, *Hellenicity: Between Ethnicity and Culture* (Chicago: University of Chicago Press, 2002), 189–98.

28   See Ernst Badian, 'Alexander the Great and the Scientific Exploration of the Oriental Part of His Empire,' *Ancient Society* 22 (1991): 127–38.

29   Plutarch *On the Fortune or the Virtue of Alexander* 328b.

30   See, e.g., Herodotus 3.32.4 on Cambyses marrying his sister; Strabo 15.3.20 on sons marrying their mothers. See A.M. Schwarts, 'The Old Eastern Iranian World View According to the Avesta,' in *Cambridge History of Iran*, ed. I. Gershevitch, vol. 2 (Cambridge: Cambridge University Press, 1985), 656.

31   Sacrificing elderly parents: Herodotus 1.126; using corpses: Herodotus 4.64.1–65.

32   Onesicritus, *FGrH* 134 F 5 (Strabo 11.11.3).

33   See C.B. Welles, 'Alexander's Historical Achievement,' *G&R*2 12 (1965): 216–28; quotation at 228.

34   Cf. Arrian 7.19.6.

35   Cf. Bosworth, 'Alexander and the Iranians,' 6.

7

ALEXANDER, INDIA
AND THE GEDROSIAN DESERT

Introduction

Alexander did not face the same types of military problems in India as in Persia,[1] and there was only the one great battle at the Hydaspes river in 326 against the prince of that region, Porus (Sources 72–75).[2] However, the Indian campaign is characterized by the excessive slaughter of local peoples, and it is the bloodiest part of Alexander's entire expedition.

In spring 327 Alexander marched from Bactra through the Hindu Kush and advanced towards the plain of the Indus. He split the invasion force into two, one half under the command of Hephaestion and Perdiccas, which was to march to the Indus via the Hindu Kush and secure the main communications route, and the second under himself, which marched east through Laghman into the Swat. The massacres began almost immediately, for when Alexander encountered the Assaceni in the Lower Swat Valley he killed so many of them that the survivors took refuge on the 10,000 foot high mountain fortress of Aornus (Pir Sar). Undaunted, Alexander besieged the 'Rock of Aornus', which soon fell to him. The Macedonian forces met at the Indus in spring 326, and after bridging it, Alexander moved to the capital Taxila. When news came that a neighbouring prince, Porus, refused to yield to Alexander, the king set out immediately to meet him and the two sides did battle at the Hydaspes river. Alexander crossed the river against no small adversity (cf. Source 21), and once on its opposite bank quickly and decisively defeated Porus. This was a significant victory for him, although propaganda exaggerated it, and Alexander celebrated it by founding two new cities, Nicaea and Bucephala, after his horse Bucephalus, who had died from exhaustion following the battle (Arr. 5.19.4–5, Plut. *Alex*. 61.1): see Sources 74 and 75. He also struck special commemorative coinage at the mint in Babylon. Porus was confirmed king of his subjects but as a vassal to Alexander, and his elephant corps integrated into the Macedonian army. The Battle of the Hydaspes was the high point of Alexander's invasion of India. Rather than return to Taxila to wait for the monsoon rains to pass he continued eastwards. By the time he reached the Hyphasis river, some 390 miles from the Hydaspes,[3] it had been raining for 70 days (Diod. 17.94.3; cf. Source 61); the men had had enough, and led by Coenus they refused to go further (Arr. 6.2.1, Curt. 9.3.20): Source 76. Alexander was forced to turn around, and by late September 326 he was back at the Hydaspes. Little had been accomplished by this part of the campaign, and although the environmental and climate conditions were the straw that broke the camel's back, arguably the origins of the mutiny can be found at Hecatompylus in 330 when the men expected to return to Greece, and Alexander persuaded them to march into Bactria after Bessus. Alexander was determined to sail down the Indus river to the Southern (Indian) Ocean, and this deed he accomplished in 325. Earlier, he had prosecuted the siege of Malli, where he had been so badly wounded when an arrow pierced a lung that his men had thought he was dead and slaughtered everyone in the town. Thus Alexander left India on something of a high note, having sailed the Indus and sacrificed to Poseidon in the Southern Ocean to set another boundary of the Macedonian empire. However, any successes he had won in India evaporated almost as soon as he left, as the native peoples shrugged off Macedonian 'rule' and returned to the *status quo* (the same is true in Bactria and Sogdiana). Rather than return west by the same route, Alexander chose to emulate and outdo certain predecessors by taking part of his army with him across the Gedrosian desert. That march is a disastrous epilogue to the Indian campaign, for it cost him dearly in manpower because of the harsh environment, lack of food and water, and sudden flash flooding (see Sources 77–80). It is hardly a surprise that those who survived the march through this desert celebrated in drunken fashion in a week's march (or more probably stagger) through Carmania.

Of note during Alexander's time in India were his encounter with the Brahman philosophers (one of them, Calanus, accompanied him until his death, by ritual burning; Sources 65–68), and Nearchus' great voyage from India along the Makran coast, with its fascinating description of the geography and peoples. The longer fragments from Nearchus' work deal with this expedition, the basis of the full account of Arrian's *Indica*.

India presented Alexander with arguably wider-ranging problems when it came to administration than Persia (on Alexander's administrative measures in Persia, see Chapter 6). At the same time, the Indian campaign presents us with more worrying traits in Alexander's character. For example, his motive in besieging the Rock of Aornus was less strategic than to outdo Heracles, for in mythology Heracles had besieged the rock and failed to take it. Alexander thus had a chance to eclipse Heracles, and he seized it with both hands rather than weighing the pros and cons of the logistics of the siege. It is also in India that Alexander distances himself from Heracles as a heroic ancestor to emulate and begins to identify himself with Dionysus. The march across Carmania, during which Alexander dressed himself as Dionysus and rode on an elevated platform, is arguably the most overt example of this.

Ancient sources

Geography

60   Ctesias the Cnidian says that India is equal to the rest of Asia, but he talks nonsense; and so does Onesicritus (*FGrH* 134 – now *BNJ* 134 – F 6), saying that it is the third part of all the earth. Nearchus says that it is a journey of four months through the plain alone of India. To Megasthenes the distance from the east to the west … He says that where it is shortest it extends 16,000 stades, and that from north to south … it extends 22,300 stades, where it is the narrowest (Nearchus, *FGrH* 133 – now *BNJ* 133 – F 5 = Arrian, *Indica* 3.6, Strabo 15.1.12).

61   Aristobulus says that only the mountains and their foothills have both rain and snow, but that the plains are free alike from rain and snow, and are inundated only when the rivers rise; that the mountains have snow in the winter-time, and at the beginning of spring-time the rains also set in and ever increase more and more, and at the time of

the Etesian winds the rains pour unceasingly and violently from the clouds, both day and night, until the rising of Arcturus; and that, therefore, the rivers, thus filled from both the snows and the rains, water the plains. He says that both he himself and the others noted this when they had set out for India from Paropamisadae, after the setting of the Pleiades, and when they spent the winter near the mountainous country in the land of the Hypasians and of Assacanus, and that at the beginning of spring they went down into the plains and to Taxila, a large city, and thence to the Hydaspes river and the country of Porus; that in winter, however, no water was to be seen, but only snow; and that it first rained at Taxila; and that when, after they had gone down to the Hydaspes river and had conquered Porus,[4] their journey led to the Hypanis[5] river towards the east and then back again to the Hydaspes, it rained continually, and especially at the time of the Etesian winds; but that when Arcturus rose, the rain ceased; and that after tarrying while their ships were being built on the Hydaspes river, and after beginning their voyage thence only a few days before the setting of the Pleiades, and, after occupying themselves all autumn and winter and the coming spring and summer with their voyage down to the seacoast, they arrived at Patalene at about the time of the rising of the Dog Star; that the voyage down to the seacoast therefore took ten months, and that they saw rains nowhere, not even when the Etesian winds were at their height, and that the plains were flooded when the rivers were filled, and the sea was not navigable when the winds were blowing in the opposite direction, and that no land breezes succeeded them.

Now this is precisely what Nearchus (*FGrH* 133 – now *BNJ* 133 – F 18) says too, but he does not agree with Aristobulus about the summer rains, saying that the plains have rains in summer but are without rains in winter. Both writers, however, speak also of the risings of the rivers. Nearchus says that when they were camping near the Acesines river they were forced at the time of the rising to change to a favorable place higher up, and that this took place at the time of the summer solstice; whereas Aristobulus gives also the measure of the height to which the river rises, forty cubits, of which cubits twenty are filled by the stream above its previous depth to the margin and the other twenty are the measure of the overthrow in the plains. They agree also that the cities situated on the top of mounds become islands, as is the case also in Egypt and Aethiopia, and that the overflows cease after the rising of Arcturus, when the waters recede; and they add that although the soil is sown when only half-dried, after being furrowed by any sort of digging instrument, yet the plant comes to maturity and yields excellent fruit. The rice, according to Aristobulus, stands in water enclosures and is sown in beds; and the plant is four cubits in height, not only having many ears but also yielding much grain; and the harvest is about the time of the setting of the Pleiades, and the grain is winnowed like barley; and the rice grows also in Bactria and Susis, as also in Lower Syria (Onesicritus, *FGrH* 134 – now *BNJ* 134 – F 15).

Aristobulus, comparing the characteristics of this country that are similar to those of both Egypt and Aethiopia, and again those that are opposite thereto, I mean the fact that the Nile is flooded from the southern rains, whereas the Indian rivers are flooded from the northern, enquires why the intermediate regions have no rainfall; for neither the Thebais as far as Syene and the region of Meroe nor the region of India from Patalene as far as the Hydaspes has any rain. But the country above these parts, in which both rain and snow fall, are cultivated, he says, in the same way as in the rest of the country that is outside India; for, he adds, it is watered by the rains and snows. And it is reasonable to suppose from his statements that the land is also quite subject to earthquakes, since it is made porous by reason of its great humidity and is subject to such fissures that even the beds of rivers are changed. At any rate, he says that when he was sent upon a certain mission he saw a country of more than a thousand cities, together with villages, that had been deserted because the Indus had abandoned its proper bed, and had tuned aside into the other bed on the left that was much deeper, and flowed with precipitous descent like a cataract, so that the Indus no longer watered by its overflows the abandoned country on the right, since the country was now above the level, not only of the new stream but also of its overflows (Aristobulus, *FGrH* 139 F 35 = Strabo 15.1.17–19).

Customs and people

62   All the Indians wear their hair long and dye it with a sable or saffron colour. Their particular luxury is gems. They make no display at funerals. Besides, as has been made known in the works of Kings Juba and Archelaus, the dress is as varied as the customs of the people. Some dress in linen robes, others in woollen ones; some are nude, others cover their private parts only and several are just girded with flexible bark fibres. Some tribes are so tall that with a very easy leap they clear an elephant as they would a horse. Many are wont neither to kill an animal nor to eat meat; most of them subsist on fish alone and depend on the sea for food. There are some who kill their parents and nearest kin just as they would victims of sacrifice, before age or disease emaciate them; then they banquet on the entrails of the slain; this is not considered a crime there, but an act of piety. There are even those who on falling sick withdraw into hidden places far from other people and wait for death with equanimity (Archelaus, *FGrH* 123 F 1 = Solinus 52.18–23).

63   The Indians use linen clothing, as says Nearchus, made from the flax taken from the trees, about which I have already spoken. And this flax is either whiter in colour than any other flax, or the people being black make the flax appear whiter. They have a linen frock reaching down half-way between the knee and the ankle, and a garment which is partly thrown round the shoulders and partly rolled round the head. The Indians who are very well off wear earrings of ivory; for they do not all wear them. Nearchus says that the Indians dye their beards various colours; some that they may appear white as the whitest, others dark blue; others have them red, others purple, and others green. Those who are of any rank have umbrellas held over them in the summer. They wear shoes of white leather, elaborately worked, and the soles of their shoes are many-coloured and raised high, in order that they may appear taller. The Indians are not all armed in the same way; but their infantry have a bow equal in length to the man who carries it. Placing this downward to the ground and stepping against it with the left foot, they discharge the arrow, drawing the string far back. Their arrows are little less than three cubits long; and nothing can withstand one shot by an Indian archer, neither shield nor breast-plate nor anything else that is strong. They carry on their left arms targets of raw ox-hide, narrower than the men who carry them, but not much inferior in length. Others have javelins instead of arrows. All wear a sword which is broad, and not less than three cubits in length. When the battle is at close quarters, a thing which very rarely happens to be the case between Indians, they bring this sword down upon the antagonist with both hands, in order that the blow may be a mighty one. The cavalry have two darts, like the darts called *saunia*, and a target smaller than that of the infantry.

Their horses are not saddled or bridled like those of the Greeks or Gauls; but a piece of raw ox-hide stitched is fastened right round the front of the horse's mouth, and in this there are brass or iron spikes not very sharp, turned inwards. The rich men have ivory spikes. In the mouth their horses have a piece of iron, like a spit, to which the reins are attached. When therefore they draw the rein, the spit curbs the horse and the spikes which are fastened to it prick him and do not allow him to do anything else than obey the rein. The Indians are spare in body and tall and much lighter than other men. Most of the Indians ride camels, horses, and, asses, and those who are well off, elephants. For among the Indians royal personages ride on elephants. Next to this in honour is the four-horsed chariot, third camels. It is no honour to ride on horseback. Their women who are very chaste and would not go astray for any other reward, on the receipt of an elephant have communication with the donor. The Indians do not think it disgraceful for them to prostitute themselves for an elephant, and to the women it even seems an honour that their beauty should appear equal in value to an elephant. They marry, neither giving nor receiving any dowry, but the fathers bring forward the girls who are of marriageable age and station them in a public place for the man who wins the prize for wrestling, boxing, or running, or who has been adjudged winner in any manly contest, to make his choice. The Indians are bread-eaters and agriculturalists, except those who live in the mountains. These live upon the flesh of wild animals. I have copied the very well-known statements made by Nearchus and Megasthenes, two esteemed authors (Nearchus, *FGrH* 133 – now *BNJ* 133 – F 11 = Arrian, *Indica* 16–17).

64   Crates of Pergamus calls the Indians, whose age exceeds one hundred years, by the name of Gymnetae; but not a few authors style them Macrobii. Ctesias mentions a tribe of them, known by the name of Pandare, whose locality is in the valleys, and who live to their two hundredth year … On the other hand, there are some people joining up to the country of the Macrobii, who never live beyond their fortieth year … This circumstance is also mentioned by Agatharchides, who states, in addition, that they live on locusts, and are very swift of foot. Cleitarchus and Megasthenes give these people the name of Mandi, and enumerate as many as three hundred villages which belong to them. Their women are capable of bearing children in the seventh year of their age, and become old at forty (Cleitarchus, *FGrH* 137 F 23 = Pliny, *Natural History* 7.28–29).

Calanus and the Brahmans

65   Onesicritus says that he himself was sent to converse with these sophists; for Alexander had heard that the people always went naked and devoted themselves to endurance, and that they were held in very great honour, and that they did not visit other people when invited, but bade them to visit them if they wished to participate in anything they did or said; and that therefore, such being the case, since to Alexander it did not seem fitting either to visit them or to force them against their will to do anything contrary to their ancestral customs, he himself was sent; and that he found fifteen men at a distance of twenty stades from the city, who were in different postures, standing or sitting or lying naked and motionless till evening, and that they then returned to the city; and that it was very hard to endure the sun, which was so hot that at midday no one else could easily endure walking on the ground with bare feet. Onesicritus says that he conversed with one of these sophists, Calanus, who accompanied the king as far as Persis and died in accordance with the ancestral custom, being placed

upon a pyre and burned up (*FGrH* 134 – now *BNJ* 134 – F 18). He says that Calanus happened to be lying on stones when he first saw him; that he therefore approached him and greeted him; and told him that he had been sent by the king to learn the wisdom of the sophists and report it to him, and that if there was no objection he was ready to hear his teachings; and that when Calanus saw the mantle and broad-brimmed hat and boots he wore, he laughed at him and said: 'In olden times the world was full of barley-meal and wheaten-meal, as now of dust; and fountains then flowed, some with water, others with milk and likewise with honey, and others with wine, and some with olive oil; but, by reason of his gluttony and luxury, man fell into arrogance beyond bounds. But Zeus, hating this state of things, destroyed everything and appointed for man a life of toil. And when self-control and the other virtues in general reappeared, there came again an abundance of blessings. But the condition of man is already close to satiety and arrogance, and there is danger of destruction of everything in existence.' And Onesicritus adds that Calanus, after saying this, bade him, if he wished to learn, to take off his clothes, to lie down naked on the same stones, and thus to hear his teachings; and that while he was hesitating what to do, Mandanis, who was the oldest and wisest of the sophists, rebuked Calanus as a man of arrogance, and that too after censuring arrogance himself; and that Mandanis called him and said that he commended the king because, although busied with the government of so great an empire, he was desirous of wisdom; for the king was the only philosopher in arms that he ever saw, and that it was the most useful thing in the world if those men were wise who have the power of persuading the willing, and forcing the unwilling, to learn self-control; but that he might be pardoned if, conversing through three interpreters, who, with the exception of language, knew no more than the masses, he should be unable to set forth anything in his philosophy that would be useful; for that, he added, would be like expecting water to flow pure through mud ... (Onesicritus, *FGrH* 134 – now *BNJ* 134 – F 17a = Strabo 15.1.63–64).

66   They (the Brahmans) never jump into the fire. Onesicritus, Alexander's pilot, saw Calanus burn himself and, according to him, when the pyre has been made ready, they stand motionless, resting in front of it. Then they climb on top and there they sit, smouldering away in a dignified manner (Onesicritus, *FGrH* 134 – now *BNJ* 134 – F 18 = Lucian, *De mort. Peregr.* 25).

67   As soon as the men to whom the duty had been assigned set fire to the pyre (of Calanus), Nearchus says the trumpets sounded, in accordance with Alexander's order, and the whole army raised the war-cry as it was in the habit of shouting when advancing to battle. The elephants also chimed in with their shrill and warlike cry, in honour of Calanus (Nearchus, *FGrH* 133 – now *BNJ* 133 – F 4 = Arr. 7.3.6).

68   Chares of Mytilene, in his *Tales of Alexander*, says of Calanus ... that he threw himself on a funeral pyre which he had built, and so died, and he says that at his tomb Alexander got up a contest in athletic games and in a musical recital of his praises. 'He,' Chares says, 'because of the love of drinking on the part of the Indians, also instituted a contest in the drinking of unmixed wine, and the prize for the winner was a talent, for the second-best thirty minas, for the third ten minas. Of those who drank the wine, thirty-five died immediately of a chill, and six others shortly after in their tents. The man who drank the most and came off victor drank twelve quarts and received the talent, but he lived only four days more; he was called "Champion"' (Chares, *FGrH* 125 F 19a = Athen. 10.437a-b).[6]

Nysa

69   That Dionysus fought and defeated Indians is told by Dionysius and Aristodemus in the first of the Theban epigrams and by Cleitarchus in the *History of Alexander*, who adds to the account that there is a Mt. Nysa in India and a plant similar to ivy is planted there, called scindapsos ... (Cleitarchus, *FGrH* 137 F 17 = Scholiast on Apollonius, *Argonautica* 2.904).

The siege of Malli

70   Among the Malli Alexander was wounded with an arrow two cubits in length, that went in at his breast and came out at his neck, as Aristobulus relates (Aristobulus, *FGrH* 139 F 46 = [Plut.] *Mor.* 341c).

71   Alexander himself also was wounded with an arrow under the breast through the breast-plate in the chest, so that Ptolemy says air was breathed out from the wound together with the blood (Ptolemy, *FGrH* 138 F 25 = Arr. 6.10.1).

The battle of the Hydaspes river

72   But Ptolemy, son of Lagus, with whom I agree, gives a different account. This author also says that Porus dispatched his son, but not at the head of merely sixty chariots; nor is it indeed likely that Porus hearing from his scouts that either Alexander himself or at any rate a part of his army had effected the passage of the Hydaspes, would dispatch his son against him with only sixty chariots. These indeed were too many to be sent out as a reconnoitring party, and not adapted for speedy retreat; but they were by no means a sufficient force to keep back those of the enemy who had not yet got across, as well as to attack those who had already landed. Ptolemy says that the son of Porus arrived at the head of 2,000 cavalry and 120 chariots; but that Alexander had already made even the last passage from the island before he appeared. Ptolemy also says that Alexander in the first place sent the horse-archers against these, and led the cavalry himself, thinking that Porus was approaching with all his forces, and that this body of cavalry was marching in front of the rest of his army, being drawn up by him as the vanguard. But as soon as he had ascertained with accuracy the number of the Indians, he immediately made a rapid charge upon them with the cavalry around him. When they perceived that Alexander himself and the body of cavalry around him had made the assault, not in line of battle regularly formed, but by squadrons, they gave way; and 400 of their cavalry, including the son of Porus, fell in the contest. The chariots also were captured, horses and all, being heavy and slow in the retreat, and useless in the action itself on account of the clayey ground (Ptolemy, *FGrH* 138 F 20 = Arr. 5.14.5–15.2)

73   Aristobulus says that the son of Porus arrived with about sixty chariots before Alexander made his later passage from the large island, and that he could have hindered Alexander's crossing, for he made the passage with difficulty even when no one opposed him, if the Indians had leaped down from their chariots and assaulted those who first emerged from the water. But he passed by with the chariots and thus made the passage quite safe for Alexander; who on reaching the bank discharged his horse-archers against the Indians in the chariots, and these were easily put to rout, many of them being wounded. Other writers (Ptolemy, *FGrH* 138 F 20) say that a battle took place ... (Aristobulus, *FGrH* 139 F 43 = Arr. 5.14.3).

74   The horse of King Alexander was called 'Bucephalas' because of the shape of his head. Chares wrote that he was bought for thirteen talents and given to King Philip … It seemed a noteworthy characteristic of this horse that when he was armed and equipped for battle, he would never allow himself to be mounted by any other than the king. It is also related that Alexander in the war against India, mounted upon that horse and doing valorous deeds, had driven him with disregard of his own safety, too far into the enemies' ranks. The horse had suffered deep wounds in his neck and side from the weapons hurled from every hand at Alexander, but though dying and almost exhausted from loss of blood, he yet in swiftest course bore the king from the midst of the foe; but when he had taken him out of range of the weapons, the horse at once fell, and satisfied with having saved his master breathed his last, with indications of relief that were almost human. Then King Alexander, after winning the victory in that war, founded a city in that region and in honour of his horse called it 'Bucephalon' (Chares, *FGrH* 125 F 18 = Gellius 5.2.1–5).

75   After the battle with Porus, too, Bucephalas died – not at once, but some time afterwards – as most writers say, from wounds for which he was under treatment, but according to Onesicritus, from old age, having become quite worn out; for he was thirty years old when he died (Onesicritus, *FGrH* 134 – now *BNJ* 134 – F 20 = Plut. *Alex.* 61.1).

The Hyphasis mutiny

76   Having said this, Alexander retired into his tent,[7] and did not admit any of the Companions on that day, or until the third day from that, waiting to see if any change would occur in the minds of the Macedonians and Grecian allies, as is wont to happen as a general rule among a crowd of soldiers, rendering them more disposed to obey. But on the contrary, when there was a profound silence throughout the camp, and the soldiers were evidently annoyed at his wrath, without being at all changed by it, Ptolemy, son of Lagus, says that he none the less offered sacrifice there for the passage of the river, but the victims were unfavourable to him when he sacrificed. Then indeed he collected the oldest of the Companions and especially those who were friendly to him, and as all things indicated the advisability of his returning, he made known to the army that he had resolved to march back again (Ptolemy, *FGrH* 138 F 23 = Arr. 5.28.3–5).

The Gedrosian desert

77   They say that Alexander pursued this route, not from ignorance of the difficulty of the journey – Nearchus, indeed, alone says that he was ignorant of it – but because he heard that no one had hitherto passed that way with an army and emerged in safety, except Semiramis, when she fled from India. The natives said that even she emerged with only twenty men of her army; and that Cyrus, son of Cambyses, escaped with only seven of his men. For they say that Cyrus also marched into this region for the purpose of invading India, but that he did not effect his retreat before losing the greater part of his army, from the desert and the other difficulties of this route. When Alexander received this information he is said to have been seized with a desire of excelling Cyrus and Semiramis. Nearchus says that he turned his march this way, both for this reason and at the same time for the purpose of conveying provisions near the fleet (Nearchus, *FGrH* 133 – now *BNJ* 133 – F 3a = Arr. 6.24.2).

78 If, however, one should dismiss these accounts and observe the records of the country (India) prior to the expedition of Alexander, one would find things still more obscure. Now it is reasonable to suppose that Alexander believed such records because he was blinded by his numerous good fortunes; at any rate, Nearchus says that Alexander conceived an ambition to lead his army through Gedrosia when he learned that both Semiramis and Cyrus had made an expedition against the Indians, and that Semiramis had turned back in flight with only twenty people and Cyrus with seven; and that Alexander thought how grand it would be, when those had met with such reverses, if he himself should lead a whole victorious army safely through the same tribes and regions. Alexander, therefore, believed these accounts. But as for us, what just credence can we place in the accounts of India derived from such an expedition made by Cyrus or Semiramis? And Megasthenes virtually agrees (Nearchus, *FGrH* 133 – now *BNJ* 133 – F 3b = Strabo 15.1.5).

79 Most of the historians of Alexander's reign assert that all the hardships which his army suffered in Asia were not worthy of comparison with the labours undergone here. They say that Alexander pursued this route, not from ignorance of the difficulty of the journey – Nearchus (*FGrH* 133 – now *BNJ* 133 – F 3a), indeed, alone says that he was ignorant of it – but because he heard … The scorching beat and lack of water destroyed a great part of the army, and especially the beasts of burden; most of which perished from thirst and some of them even from the depth and heat of the sand, because it had been thoroughly scorched by the sun. For they met with lofty ridges of deep sand, not closely pressed and hardened, but such as received those who stepped upon it just as if they were stepping into mud, or rather into untrodden snow. At the same time too the horses and mules suffered still more, both in going up and coming down the hills, from the unevenness of the road as well as from its instability. The length of the marches between the stages also exceedingly distressed the army; for the lack of water often compelled them to make the marches of unusual length. When they travelled by night on a journey which it was necessary to complete, and at daybreak came to water, they suffered no hardship at all; but if, while still on the march, on account of the length of the way, they were caught by the heat, the day advancing, then they did indeed suffer hardships from the blazing sun, being at the same time oppressed by unassuageable thirst.

The soldiers killed many of the beasts of burden of their own accord; for when provisions were lacking, they came together, and slaughtered most of the horses and mules. They ate the flesh of these, and said that they had died of thirst or had perished from the heat. There was no one to divulge the real truth of their conduct, both on account of the men's distress and because all alike were implicated in the same offence. What was being done had not escaped Alexander's notice; but he saw that the best cure for the present state of affairs was to pretend to be ignorant of it, rather than to permit it as a thing known to himself. The consequence was, that it was no longer easy to convey the soldiers who were suffering from disease, or those who were left behind on the roads on account of the heat, partly from the want of beasts of burden and partly because the men themselves were knocking the wagons to pieces, not being able to draw them on account of the depth of the sand; and because in the first stages they were compelled on this account to go, not by the shortest routes, but by those which were easiest for the carriages. Thus some were left behind along the roads on account of sickness, others from fatigue or the effects of the heat, or from not being able to bear up against the drought; and then was no one either to lead them or to remain and tend them in their sickness. For the expedition was being made with great urgency; and the care of individual persons was necessarily neglected in the zeal displayed for the safety of the army as a whole. As they generally made the marches by night, some of the men also were overcome by sleep on the road; afterwards rousing up again, those who still had strength followed upon the tracks of the army; but only a few out of many overtook the main body in safety. Most of them perished in the sand, like men getting out of the course at sea. Another calamity also befell the army, which greatly distressed men, horses, and beasts of burden; for the country of the Gadrosians is supplied with rain by the periodical winds, just as that of the Indians is; not the plains of Gadrosia, but only the mountains where the clouds are carried by the wind and are dissolved into rain without passing beyond the summits of the mountains. On one occasion, when the army bivouacked, for the sake of its water, near a small brook which was a winter torrent, about the second watch of the night the brook which flowed there was suddenly swelled by the rains in the mountains which had fallen unperceived by the soldiers. The torrent advanced with so great a flood as to destroy most of the wives and children of the men who followed the army, and to sweep away all the royal baggage as well as all the beasts of burden still remaining. The soldiers, after great exertions, were hardly able to save themselves together with their weapons, many of which they lost beyond recovery. When, after enduring the burning heat and thirst, they lighted upon abundance of water, many of them perished from drinking to excess, not being able to check their appetite for it. For this reason Alexander generally pitched his camp, not near the water itself, but at a distance of about twenty stades from it, to prevent the men and beasts from pressing in crowds into the river and thus perishing, and at the same time to prevent those who had no control over themselves from fouling the water for the rest of the army by stepping into the springs or streams.

Here I have resolved not to pass over in silence the most noble deed perhaps ever performed by Alexander, which occurred either in this land or, according to the assertion of some other authors, still earlier, among the Parapamisadians. The army was continuing its march through the sand, though the heat of the sun was already scorching, because it was necessary to reach water before halting. They were far on the journey, and Alexander himself, though oppressed with thirst, was nevertheless with great pain and difficulty leading the army on foot, so that his soldiers also, as is usual in such a case, might more patiently bear their hardships by the equalization of the distress. At this time some of the light-armed soldiers, starting away from the army in quest of water, found some collected in a shallow cleft, a small and mean spring. Collecting this water with difficulty, they came with all speed to Alexander, as if they were bringing him some great boon. As soon as they approached the king, they poured the water into a helmet and carried it to him. He took it, and commending the men who brought it, immediately poured it upon the ground in sight of all. As a result of this action, the entire army was reinvigorated to so great a degree that anyone would have imagined that the water poured away by Alexander had furnished a draught to every man … The following adventure also occurred to the army in that country. At last the guides declared that they no longer remembered the way, because the tracks of it had been rendered invisible by the wind blowing the sand over them. Moreover, in the deep sand which had been everywhere reduced to one level, there was nothing by which they could conjecture the right way, not even the usual trees growing along it, nor any solid hillock rising up; and they had not practised themselves in making journeys by the stars at night or by the sun in the daytime, as sailors do by the constellations of the Bears – the Phoenicians by the Little Bear, and other men by the Greater Bear. Then at length Alexander perceived that it was necessary for him to lead the way by declining to the left; and taking a few horsemen with him he advanced in front of the army. But when the horses even of these were exhausted by the heat, he left most of these men behind, and rode away with only five men and found the sea. Having scraped away the shingle on the sea-beach, he lighted upon water fresh and pure, and then went and fetched the whole army. For seven days they marched along the sea coast, supplying themselves with water from the shore. Thence he led his expedition into the interior, for now the guides knew the way (Aristobulus, *FGrH* 139 F 49a = Arr. 6.24).

80　But Alexander was in great distress throughout the whole journey, since he was marching through a wretched country; and from a distance, likewise, he could procure additional supplies only in small quantities and at rare intervals, so that his army was famished; and the beasts of burden fagged out, and the baggage was left behind on the roads and in the camps; but they were saved by the date palms, eating not only the fruit but also the cabbage at the top. They say that Alexander, although aware of the difficulties, conceived an ambition, in view of the prevailing opinion that Semiramis escaped in flight from India with only about twenty men and Cyrus with seven, to see whether he himself could safely lead that large army of his through the same country and win this victory too.

In addition to the resourcelessness of the country, the heat of the sun was grievous, as also the depth and the heat of the sand; and in some places there were sand-hills so high that, in addition to the difficulty of lifting one's legs, as out of a pit, there were also ascents and descents to be made. And it was necessary also, on account of the wells, to make long marches of two hundred or three hundred stades, and sometimes even six hundred, travelling mostly by night. But they would encamp at a distance from the wells, often at a distance of thirty stades, in order that the soldiers might not, to satisfy their thirst, drink too much water; for many would plunge into the wells, armour and all, and drink as submerged men would; and then, after expiring, would swell up and float on the surface and corrupt the wells, which were shallow; and others, exhausted by reason of thirst, would lie down in the middle of the road in the open sun, and then trembling, along with a jerking of hands and legs, they would die like persons seized with chills or ague. And in some cases soldiers would turn aside from the main road and fall asleep, being overcome by sleep and fatigue. And some, falling behind the army, perished by wandering from the roads and by reason of heat and lack of everything, though others arrived safely, but only after suffering many hardships. And a torrential stream, coming on by night, overwhelmed both a large number of persons and numerous articles; and much of the royal equipment was also swept away; and when the guides ignorantly turned aside so far into the interior that the sea was no longer visible, the king, perceiving their error, set out at once to seek for the shore; and when he found it, and by digging discovered potable water, he sent for the army, and thereafter kept close to shore for seven days, with a good supply of water; and then he withdrew again into the interior (Aristobulus, *FGrH* 139 F 49b = Strabo 15.2.5–7).

Modern works

In the following selections, A.K. Narain, formerly Principal of the College of Indology at Banaras Hindu University, deals with Alexander's Indian campaign as a whole, making observations on Alexander's aims, battles and accomplishments. A.B. Bosworth, Emeritus Professor of Classics at the University of Western Australia, examines problems that Alexander had already encountered in Asia, namely how to administer India.

1   A.K. Narain, 'Alexander and India', *Greece and Rome*[2] 12 (Cambridge University Press 1965), pp. 155–165.[8]
2   A.B. Bosworth, 'The Indian Satrapies under Alexander the Great', *Antichthon* 17 (Australasian Society for Classical Studies 1983), pp. 37–46.[9]

Additional reading

E. Badian, 'The Administration of the Empire', *Greece and Rome*[2] 12 (1965), pp. 166–182.

A.B. Bosworth, 'Calanus and the Brahman Opposition', in W. Will (ed.), *Alexander der Grosse: Eine Welteroberung und ihr Hintergrund* (Bonn: 1998), pp. 173–203.

——, The Indian Campaigns, 327–325 BC', in J. Roisman (ed.), *Brill's Companion to Alexander the Great* (Leiden: 2003), pp. 159–168.

P. Briant, 'The Empire of Darius III in Perspective', in W. Heckel and L. Tritle (eds), *Alexander the Great. A New History* (Oxford: 2009), pp. 141–170 (reprinted in Chapter 6).

P.A. Brunt, *Arrian, History of Alexander*, Loeb Classical Library 2 (Cambridge and London: 1983), pp. 435–474.

W. Heckel, 'Resistance to Alexander the Great', in L. Tritle (ed.), *The Greek World in the Fourth Century* (London: 1997), pp. 189–227.

——, 'Alexander the Great and the "Limits of Civilised World"', in W. Heckel and L. Tritle (eds), *Crossroads of History. The Age of Alexander* (Claremont: 2003), pp. 147–174 (reprinted in Chapter 3).

W.E. Higgins, 'Aspects of Alexander's Imperial Administration: Some Modern Methods and Views Reviewed', *Athenaeum* 58 (1980), pp. 129–152.

F.L. Holt, 'The Hyphasis Mutiny: A Source Study', *Ancient World* 5 (1982), pp. 33–59.

A.N. Oikonomides, 'The Real End of Alexander's Conquest of India', *Ancient World* 18 (1988), pp. 31–34.

P.O. Spann, 'Alexander at the Beas: Fox in a Lion's Skin', in F.B. Titchener and R.F. Moorton (eds), *The Eye Expanded. Life and the Arts in Greco-Roman Antiquity* (Berkeley and Los Angeles: 1999), pp. 62–74.

R. Stoneman, 'Naked Philosophers: The Brahmans in the Alexander Historians and the *Alexander Romance*', *Journal of Hellenic Studies* 105 (1995), pp. 99–114.

B. Strauss, 'Alexander: The Military Campaign', in J. Roisman (ed.), *Brill's Companion to Alexander the Great* (Leiden: 2003), pp. 133–156.

Notes

1   See Chapter 6.

2   Diod. 17.87–89.3, Arr. 5.14–18, Plut. *Alex*. 60, Curt. 8.13–14. On Alexander's generalship, see Chapter 4.
3   On distances, see Sources 1, 36, 37; cf. 60.
4   The Battle of the Hydaspes river in 326.
5   The Hyphasis river, at which Alexander's men mutinied and forced him to turn back.
6   On Alexander's drinking, see Sources 85–90, 117–119.
7   The context is the mutiny at the Hyphasis river in 326.
8   Reprinted with the permission of Cambridge University Press.
9   Reprinted with the permission of the author and the Australasian Society of Classical Studies.

ALEXANDER AND INDIA

A.K. Narain

No army leader has become more famous in history than Alexander. He has been praised and admired as well as blamed and cursed. But even if blemishes can be found in his career and character, no one can deny his 'daemonic' strength of will and leadership, which alone are sufficient to mark him out as one of the greatest generals history has seen. Opinions may, however, differ as to whether he was more than that.

We are told Alexander's invasion of Persia was a pan-Hellenic war of revenge and he was elected as the leader of the League of Corinth for the purpose. It is said he was influenced by Isocrates' *Philippus*; if so, he should have envisaged the conquest of Asia Minor only. And Tarn would have us believe that Alexander did not cross the Dardanelles with any definite design of conquering the whole of the Persian empire (Tarn, i. 9). But when it comes to Alexander's invasion of India, he states, 'India had been part of the empire of Darius I; and Alexander's invasion was only the necessary and inevitable completion of his conquest of that empire. It had nothing to do with any scheme of world conquest; indeed it could not have, for in the far East the 'world', like 'Asia', only meant the Persian empire; nothing else was known' (ibid. i. 86–87). He goes one step further and adds, 'possibly the Beas [= Hyphasis] had been the boundary of Darius I; it would agree with what happened. For at the Beas the army mutinied and refused to go farther' (Tarn, i. 98). Tarn would not like Alexander to dream of more than he actually achieved. For nothing succeeds like success and a fulfilled dream is the perfection of success.

But Alexander was certainly more ambitious than that; perhaps his ambition had no end. Describing the return march of Alexander, when he reached the Pasargadae and Persepolis, Arrian pauses to remark 'that Alexander had no small or mean conceptions, nor would ever have remained contented with any of his possessions so far, not even if he had added Europe to Asia, and the Britannic islands to Europe; but would always have searched far beyond for something unknown, being always the rival if of no other, yet of himself'.[1] Even if Alexander dreamt of more than Isocrates recommended he might very well have stopped with the collapse of the power of Darius III or when the latter died, and he would still be remembered as the glorious Captain of the League who succeeded not only in avenging the prestige of Hellas but also in bringing the Achaemenid era to an end. But he did not stop. He dragged his war-weary army to Sogdiana and the Punjab. He could have even taken them beyond the Beas, but he was fortunate, as he was in his death (cf. Tarn, i. 121), that the army refused to listen to him.

Of course, it serves no purpose to speculate what would have happened if Alexander had not retreated from the Beas, just as it does not help to discuss what would have happened if Napoleon had not marched into Russia. But certainly there is no evidence to extend the empire of Darius I east of the Indus and certainly not as far as the Beas. Even if it was Alexander's *mission* to conquer the whole of the Persian empire, whether to Hellenize it or for *Homonoia*, he had no justification in crossing the Indus, for 'the Indus river was the boundary between India and Ariana, which latter was situated next to India on the west and was in the possession of the Persians at that time'.[2] Doubtless therefore Alexander did nourish an ambition to conquer India, perhaps even to reach the 'Eastern ocean' (Tarn, i. 99). Otherwise the crossing of the Indus was meaningless. Of course, Alexander hardly invaded India within its present boundaries because the point he reached at the Beas is only a few miles within the Indian Union. India, as his contemporaries knew it, did not end at the Beas either, and it was reported to him that the main power of India was really beyond this river. But the conquest of India remained an unfulfilled dream of Alexander. However, even what remains of Alexander's story would be shorn of all its romance and glory if his campaigns in Sogdiana and the Punjab were deleted and if there were no Spitamenes and Porus, Scythians and the Malloi.

It is beyond the scope of the present paper to give a detailed account of Alexander's conquest. But we can make a summary review of Alexander's march from Kabul to the Beas and from the Beas to the lower Indus. Alexander took almost two years to cover this area, which is proportionately a longer time for a lesser space than in his other campaigns, and the battles fought were as dangerous, as glorious, as full of bravery and adventure.

It was early summer of 327 when Alexander recrossed the Hindu Kush and divided his army. He sent Hephaestion and Perdiccas with the baggage and part of the army through the Khyber pass to the Indus and himself followed the old route through Laghman, ascended the Kunar river, and crossed into Swat. The people of these mountain tracts were called the Aspasians, Gouraians, and Assakenians by Arrian (iv. 23. 1). They were brave people and it was hard work for Alexander to take their strongholds, of which Massaga and Aornus need special mention. At Massaga, Alexander massacred 7,000 mercenaries because they refused to join him against their own countrymen (A. iv. 27.3 ff.; D. 84). What makes this massacre 'a foul blot on Alexander's martial fame'[3] is his treachery to the mercenaries who had capitulated, and the account given by Diodorus of the desperate fight which both the men and the women gave to meet a glorious death 'which they would have disdained to exchange for a life with dishonour'[4] is really heart-rending. At Aornus, the fighting was at once fierce and dangerous. Ptolemy, who had taken a vantage point at the far end of the fortress by surprise, was cut off there for two days and hard pressed before the main body under Alexander could break through to him (A. iv. 29). The valley of the Swat was thus subjugated.

After these prodigious encounters, Alexander had a pleasant relief when he reached Nysa. The leader of the Nysaeans, Acuphis, not only offered submission but claimed kinship on account of their Greek origin and traditional association with the mythical Dionysus (A. v. 1–2; C. viii. 10. 7 ff.). It pleased the fancy of Alexander and his army. The Nysaeans were left undisturbed in their rule and Alexander gave his army licence to fraternize and enjoy Bacchanalian revelry.

Alexander joined Hephaestion at the Indus. Hephaestion had already bridged the river at Ohind, sixteen miles above Attock.[5] He crossed the Indus and was welcomed by Ambhi and lavishly entertained in Taxila for three days. Alexander also made return presents to Ambhi, enjoyed the hospitality there and allowed Ambhi and those who were unable to defend themselves to live in peace.[6] But the ambition of the impetuous and aggressive Alexander as well as the brave warrior in him did not wander so far only to enjoy stale luxury in the company of cowards and those who did not value freedom. He appointed Philippus as a satrap and left a garrison there (A. v. 8. 3) and proceeded to the Jhelum (= Hydaspes) without wasting more time, for he was getting restive to meet Porus, perhaps more because he wanted to test his mettle than to help Ambhi in his designs.

Alexander had learnt that Porus was ready at the far side of the Hydaspes with all his army, determined to prevent his crossing or at least to attack him, should he attempt it.[7]

Although hemmed in by enemies, cowards, and traitors, both in front and rear, the undaunted spirit of Porus refused to submit. We are told, when envoys went to him to summon him to meet Alexander, he proudly replied that he would indeed meet him, but at his frontiers and in arms.[8] This was a sufficient challenge for Alexander and he reached the Jhelum in early June 326. He found Porus ready with his forces on the opposite bank [. . .]. Both sides made active preparation for the inevitable war, of which the details of strategy and movements are so well known that we need not repeat them.[9] The part played by the rains also need not be gainsaid. Porus fought bravely, and even when he saw his army had almost perished, 'he did not copy the example of the great king Darius and set his own men an example of flight, but so long as any part of the Indian troops held their ground in the fight, so long he battled bravely', but having been wounded in the right shoulder 'he wheeled his elephant and retreated'. 'Alexander having seen him play a great and gallant part in the battle desired to save him' (A. v. 18). First Ambhi was sent with Alexander's message, but, when Porus saw him coming, he once again turned his elephant and rode up to pierce him with a javelin and Ambhi could save himself only with great difficulty and returned. Alexander sent others in relays and finally Meroes who had long been a friend of Porus. 'But Porus, hearing Meroes' message, and being also much distressed by thirst, halted his elephant and dismounted; and after drinking, and recovering his strength, bade Meroes conduct him at once to Alexander. Porus was then conducted to Alexander, who, learning of his approach, rode a horse and met him in advance of the line with a few of the Companions; then halting his horse, he admired the great size of Porus, who was over five cubits in height, and his handsomeness, and the appearance he gave of a spirit not yet tamed, but of one brave man meeting another brave man after an honourable struggle against another king for his kingdom.'[10] We need not repeat again the very well known conversation between Alexander and Porus. Porus was not only reinstated but further territories were added to his kingdom. Alexander thus became greater in peace than in war; according to Indian codes he acted as a *Dharmavijayi*[11] like Samadragupta, the great king of the Magadhan empire, who behaved in this way towards the kings of South India in the middle of the fourth century A.D.[12]

Alexander then proceeded further and crossed the Chenab and the Ravi (= Acesines and Hydraotes) and on the way defeated another Porus[13] and also obtained the submission of Abhisares.[14] He then crossed the Ravi and entered the country of the Cathaeans (Kathas),[15] who were among the best fighters of the Punjab and first among 'the self-governing Indians'; they gave Alexander some of the toughest experiences of his campaign.[16] He did capture Sangala, the hill fortress of the Kathas, by assault in which 'there perished some seventeen thousand of the Indians, and over seventy thousand were captured, with three hundred waggons, and five hundred horsemen'; however, Alexander had at one time to leap down from his horse and lead the Phalanx on foot, and over twelve hundred, including several of the officers and Lysimachus, were seriously wounded besides those who were slain (A. v. 24. 5–8). Alexander razed the city of Sangala to the ground and advanced towards the Beas.

Phegeus, a near-by king who submitted to Alexander without resistance in order that his subjects might attend to the cultivation of their fields according to their needs, told Alexander about the extent and power of the Nanda empire east of the Beas, and Porus also confirmed his statements.[17] Of course, such statements whetted Alexander's eagerness to advance further; but his troops, especially the Macedonians, had begun to lose heart at the thought of the distance they had travelled from their homes, and the hardships and the dangers they had been called upon to face after their entry into India. Alexander's exhortations and the reply of Coenus, which form a classic dialogue between a general and his army, are well known.[18] The army mutinied and refused to march further. It was a severe blow to Alexander. He saved his face by offering a sacrifice preliminary to crossing the river, and, finding the omens unfavourable, as expected, he proclaimed his decision to return.[19] The army received the announcement with tears of joy and grateful shouts. They hardly realized what was still in store for them. For Alexander had yet to fight some of his fiercest and most dangerous battles. From the bank of Beas he returned to the Jhelum, handed over all the country between the Jhelum and the Beas to Porus, and sailed down the Jhelum on his return journey.

Below the confluence of the Jhelum and the Chenab the armies of Alexander camped and he prepared for his last important campaign against the Malloi (Malavas).[20] Unlike the monarchical states of the Punjab, the 'republican' states had the sense to unite against the common aggressor. The spectacle of Alexander's success did not deter them. The Cathaeans fought alone and failed. The Malloi therefore made a confederacy with the Oxydracae (Kshudraka) and planned to defend themselves together. But by his quick movements Alexander prevented the Oxydracae from joining the Malloi[21] and the latter had to face the aggression alone, and it is clear from the accounts that they fought bravely. In fact, among Alexander's campaigns this is unique in its dreadful record of mere slaughter. Indeed, it was the least creditable of the campaigns, and the deep wound Alexander got in his chest as a result of his desperate expedient in the fight with the Malloi left him weakened and indirectly hastened his end. The Oxydracae, who could not join the Malloi, had no alternative but to submit after the collapse of their confederates the Malloi.

'The progress of the flotilla down the Chenab and the Indus cannot be traced, nor the places mentioned be identified, because all the rivers, more especially the Indus, have since altered their course many times' (Tarn, i. 103). But obviously more 'peoples' and kings fought with him. The most important among them were the Brahmanas and a king called Musicanus.[22] About the end of July 325, Alexander reached Patala. Here the Indus bifurcated and Alexander halted to prepare for the last stage of his journey out of India and back to Hellas (Tarn, i. 104).

How did contemporary India react to his invasion? The following information about 'the wise men' and 'philosophers' of ancient India is significant in this connexion:

Arrian refers to Indian wise men, some of whom, the story goes, were found by Alexander in the open air in a meadow, where they used to have their disputations, and who, when they saw Alexander and his army, did nothing further than beat with their feet the ground on which they stood. Then when Alexander inquired by interpreters what this action of theirs meant, they replied: 'O king Alexander, each man possesses just so much of the earth as this on which we stand; and you being a man like other men, save that you are full of activity and relentless, are roaming over all this earth far from your home troubled yourself, and troubling others. But not so long hence you will die, and will possess just so much of the earth as suffices for your burial' (A. vii. 1.5 ff.).

Plutarch says that, 'the philosophers gave him (Alexander) no less trouble . . . because they reviled the princes who declared for him and encouraged the free states to revolt from his authority. On this account he hanged many of them'.[23]

Plutarch[24] also refers to a certain Indian 'philosopher', Kalanus, as showing Alexander a symbol of his (Alexander's) empire. Kalanus threw down on the ground a dry and shrivelled hide and planted his foot on the edge of it. But when it was trodden down in one place, it started up everywhere else. He then walked all round it and showed that the same thing took place wherever he trod, until at length he stepped into the middle, and by doing so made it all lie flat. This symbol was intended to show Alexander that he should control his empire from its centre, and not wander away to its distant extremities.

There is again a reference[25] to the capture of ten of the 'gymnosophists', who had been principally concerned in persuading Sabbas (?) to revolt and who had done much harm to the Macedonians in other ways. They were all to be executed for this, but before their execution they were asked certain questions. One of them was asked for what reason he had induced Sabbas to revolt. He answered, 'Because I wished him to live with honour or die with honour.'[26]

The contemporary Indian observations made above are at once philosophical and patriotic. They indicate two things. First, there was an emotional love of freedom and a patriotic sense of honour. Second, India, with her peculiarly philosophical attitude, was not at all overawed by the greatness of Alexander and not only regarded the Indian campaign as most unjustifiable, but also anticipated its futility. The astute Brahman politician Chanakya[27] and the youthful Kshatriya commoner Chandragupta,[28] who seems to have had a first-hand view of Alexander's campaign in the Punjab, and who had perhaps met and offended Alexander (J. xv. 4), understood the Indian pulse of reaction correctly. Even while Alexander was in Gedrosia, the only alien satrap appointed by him in India was murdered[29] and when Alexander was dying in Babylon, Chandragupta and Chanakya, perhaps with the help of Porus,[30] were liberating and unifying the Punjab as a prelude to the final overthrow of the great Nanda power of the Ganges valley, which the army of Alexander dreaded so much that the latter was forced to withdraw from the Beas. Alexander's campaign in India was therefore certainly not a political success. And it is also true that it left no permanent mark on the literature, life, or government of the people. The name of Alexander is not found in Indian literature. Certainly, Alexander did not intend his conquests in India to be as meaningless as this. But it was so.

One Indian historian[31] feels that 'the adventure was no doubt highly creditable, but cannot be regarded as a brilliant military achievement, as he had never been brought face to face with any of the great nations of Hindusthan'. The same historian makes a note of 'the untold sufferings inflicted upon India – massacre, rapine, and plunder on a scale till then without a precedent in her annals, but repeated in later days by more successful invaders like Sultan Mahmud, Tamerlane, and Nadir Shah. In spite of the halo of romance that Greek writers have woven round the name of Alexander, the historians of India can regard him only as the precursor of these recognized scourges of Mankind'.[32] This may be an extreme statement. But so is the statement that Alexander 'proclaimed for the first time the unity and brotherhood of mankind'.[33] If the Indian historian suffers from sentiment, the western historian suffers from guilt; if one sees in Alexander's campaign an unjustified aggression, the other sees a justification for his mission, and neither of them needs to be blamed for his attitude. Shorn of these overstatements, Alexander's image remains that of an admirable army leader who suffered no defeat before he died, an image of a youthful person full of ambition and adventure curbed only by death, and above all an image of a human being who could commit crimes and atrocities and yet feel remorse and sympathy. Alexander will no doubt remain 'great', but not because of historians seeing more in him than what he actually was, but just for what he actually was.

But when all is said, we must admit two indirect results of Alexander's raid. People of the North-West, perhaps, realized that 'emotional love of independence was no match to the disciplined strength of a determined conqueror';[34] and it was felt that the existence of small states was not in the wider interests of the country. Chandragupta had probably himself witnessed the spirit of resistance, which the freedom-loving people of the Punjab had shown. He organized a disciplined army out of them and unified the Punjab and later the whole of Northern India after overthrowing the Nandas; he even added territories in the south and within a few years the first big Indian empire was established.[35] To this empire were also added the four satrapies of Aria, Arachosia, Gedrosia, and Paropamisadae, which were ceded by Seleucus to Chandragupta only a few years after the death of Alexander.[36] Seleucus I sent Megasthenes as an ambassador to the Mauryan court of Chandragupta.[37] We have no evidence to tell us whether Chandragupta sent a return embassy to Seleucus. But stray references do indicate the continuance of diplomatic exchanges between the Hellenistic kingdoms and India. Athenaeus tells us, on the authority of Hegesander, that Amitrochates, king of the Indians, wrote to Antiochus I of Syria asking that monarch to buy and send him sweet wine, dried figs, and a sophist. The Syrian king replied, 'We shall send you figs and the wine, but in Greece the laws forbid a sophist to be sold' (Ath. xiv. 652 ff.). Diodorus testifies to the great love of the king of Palibothra, apparently a Mauryan king, for the Greeks (D. ii. 60). Strabo refers to the sending of Deimachus to the court of Allitrochades, son of Sandrokottos (ii. 1. 9. 70c). Pliny mentions another envoy, Dionysius, from Ptolemy II of Egypt (NH vi. 58). Asoka's friendly relations with the Yavanas of Western Asia and Egypt are well known. The thirteenth Rock Edict, a version of which has also been found in Greek recently at Kandahar,[38] refers to the *Dhammavijaya* of Asoka in the kingdoms of Antiochus II of Syria, Ptolemy Philadelphus II of Egypt, Antigonus Gonatas of Macedonia, Magas of Cyrene, and Alexander of Corinth.[39] Asoka arranged for the medical treatment of men and cattle in the dominions of Antiochus II and his neighbours.[40] It is not unlikely that his description of himself as *Devanampriya Piyadassi* is an echo of the deification of kings current among Alexander's successors in the Hellenistic East,[41] although the style of his edicts is clearly influenced by edicts of Darius.[42] These stray references do give a cumulative impression of a continuous contact of India with the Hellenistic world. The very fact that both Megasthenes and Kautilya refer to a state department run and maintained specifically for the purpose of looking after foreigners,[43] who were mostly Yavanas and Persians, testifies to the impact created by these contacts. It also explains the occurrence of such finds as the fragmentary handle of a terra-cotta vase recovered from Taxila,[44] showing Alexander's head in lion's skin, or random finds from the Sarnath, Basarh, and Patna regions of terra-cotta pieces of distinctive Hellenistic appearance or with definite Hellenistic motifs and designs.[45] [. . .].

The second indirect result was the rise of the Yavana power in Bactria and its ultimate expansion and rule over what is now known as Afghanistan and Western Pakistan for about one hundred and fifty years.[46] I have shown elsewhere that these 'Greeks' were not necessarily Hellenistic Greeks, but mostly the descendants of earlier settlers preserving their traditions but much intermixed with the Iranian peoples and in some measure reinforced by the newcomers, the veterans of Alexander or colonists of the Seleucids.

But they no doubt got their chance owing to the invasion of Alexander and the resultant dismemberment of the Achaemenid empire. There are as many as forty-one names of men who ruled this Yavana kingdom known from coins alone.[47] It is to these kings that Strabo referred when he mentioned that 'more tribes were subdued by them (i.e. the Indo-Greeks) than by Alexander – mostly by Menander (at least if he actually crossed the Hypanis towards the east and advanced as far as the Imanus), for some were subdued by him personally and others by Demetrius, the son of Euthydemus. the King of the Bactrians . . .'. I have shown elsewhere that Menander was the most powerful among the Indo-Greek kings.[48] He is the only king who has survived in Indian literature and tradition [. . .]. He is known to have become a Buddhist and a tradition connects with Menander the origin of the most famous statue of Buddhism in Indo-China, the statue of Buddha of the Emerald, which Menander's Indian teacher Nagasena materialized out of a magic emerald by supernatural power.[49] The discussions between Menander, who is known as king Milinda in the Pali-Buddhist literature, and Nagasena are embodied in a book called *The Questions of King Milinda*. Plutarch (*Moralia* 821D–E) says that when Menander died the cities celebrated his funeral in other respects as usual, but in respect of his remains they put forth rival claims and divided the ashes equally to erect monuments on the relics, which is typical of the Buddhist custom. Numismatists believe that the occurrence of the wheel on some coins of Menander is the *Dharma Çakra*, the wheel of righteousness connected with Buddhism.[50] We also know from an inscription engraved on a Garuda pillar [. . .] found at Besnagar near Bhilsa (in the state of Madhya Pradesh) that an inhabitant of Taxila named Heliodorus, son of Dion, came as an envoy from Antialcidas, an Indo-Greek king, to the court of the Indian king, Bhagabhadra, and that Heliodorus was a follower of the Bhagawat sect of Hinduism.[51] We also know from later evidence about Greeks who adopted not only Indian religions but also Indian names. The Indo-Greeks were more influenced by Indian religion and thought than was any Hellenistic king by the faith and ideas of the land in which he lived and ruled. No Seleucid ever put Iranian or Babylonian legends on his coinage, no Ptolemy ever used Egyptian, but the Indo-Greeks introduced Indian legend in Indian scripts on their money [. . .]. They came, they saw, but India conquered.

Notes

1   A. vii. 1. 4 (Loeb translation).
2   Strabo, xv. 1. 10 (Loeb translation).
3   K.A. Nilakanta Sastri, *The Age of the Nandas and Mauryas* (Banaras, 1952), 50.
4   D. xvii. 84; see R. C. Majumdar, *The Classical Accounts of India*, 163. Majumdar has reproduced the extract from McGrindle, *The Invasion of India by Alexander the Great as described by Arrian, Quintus Curtius, Diodorus, Plutarch and Justin* (London, 1896).
5   A. v. 3. 5; D. xvii. 86. 3; C. viii. 11. 4 ff.
6   A. v. 3. 5; 8. 2 ff. ('Mophis'); all the Diodorus references are to Book xvii unless otherwise stated; C. loc. cit. ('Omphis').
7   A. v. 8. 4; D. 87; C. viii. 12.
8   C. loc. cit.
9   [. . .].
10   A. v. 18. *fin.*–19, *init.* (Loeb translation); cf. C. viii. 14; P. 60.
11   Dharmavijayi means 'conqueror through righteousness'.
12   Samadragupta was the fourth king of the Gupta dynasty. He was a great conqueror and Smith thought of him as the Indian Napoleon. An account of the campaigns of the king is inscribed on

an Asokan pillar found at Allahabad. It refers to the defeat of several kings of South India whose names are given and it says that the king reinstated all those kings after their defeat, having obtained only their allegiance. He did not annex their territories.

13   Arrian (v. 21. 2 ff.) refers to him as 'Porus, the bad one', because he was reported to have left his own province and fled. Some sources believe that this Porus was a cousin of the great Porus; cf. D. 91. 1.

14   A. v. 20. 5; C. ix. 1. 7 ff.; cf. D. 90. 4.

15   A. v. 22. 1; D. 91. 2 ff.

16   A. v. 20. 5–6; 24. 2; D. 91. 4. Cathaeans had a non-monarchical form of government and they were the 'republics' of ancient India, like the Malloi (Malavas), Oxydracae (Kshudraka), and others.

17   C. ix. 1. 36 ff.; D. 93. 1.

18   A. v. 25 ff.; C. ix. 2–3; cf. D. 94, *fin.*; P. 62.

19   Ibid.

20   A. vi. 3–11; D. 97 ff.; C. ix. 4. 15 ff.; P. 63.

21   A. vi. 11. 3 (Loeb translation): '. . . they (the Mallians) had determined to join the Oxydracae and to fight together, but Alexander reached them too quickly …'. A different account in D. 98; confused in C.

22   A. vi. 16; D. 102–3; C. ix. 8. 8 ff. ('the Musicani').

23   P. 69; see R. C. Majumdar, op. cit. 200. 24 Ibid. 65; Majumdar op. cit. 201–2. 25 Ibid. 64; Majumdar op. cit. 200–1. 26 Ibid. 27 Chanakya was a Brahman scholar of Taxila (?), who was offended by the Nanda king. He later became the Chief Minister of Chandragupta after having helped him to overthrow the Nandas. He wrote the famous treatise on Polity known as Kautalya's *Arthasastra.*

28   According to the Buddhist sources, Chandragupta was born in a self-governing Kshatriya tribe known as the Moriyas in the Nepalese Terai.

29   Philippus: A. vi. 27. 2; C. x. 1. 20.

30   According to Indian literary sources, Chandragupta and Chanakya were helped in their bid to overthrow the Nanda power by a certain Indian king named Parvartaka who ruled in the Punjab and who may be identified with Porus.

31   Radha Kumud Mukherjee, *The Age of Imperial Unity* (Bombay, 1951).

32   Ibid.

33   Tarn i. 147 cf. ii, Appendix 25. Against this, however, E. Badian, *Historia* vii (1958), 425 ff.

34   K. A. Nilakanta Sastri, op. cit. 79.

35   His empire is definitely known to have included an area from Aria to Bengal and from Kashmir to Mysore. This empire over which the Mauryas ruled up to the time of Asoka was never ruled again by any single king or power in Indian history.

36   The discovery of an Asokan inscription in Greek characters in Kandahar should dispel whatever lurking doubts some scholars might have had in this regard.

37   Strabo, ii. 1. 9, 70 c; xv. 1. 36, 702 c; A. v. 6. 2; Pliny, *NH* vi 58; Clem. Alex. *Strom.* i. 72. 5.

38   D. Schlumberger, L. Robert, etc., *Une bilingue gréco-araméenne d'Asoka* (Paris, 1958).

39   See the text of Rock Edict XIII; Hultzsch, *Inscriptions of Asoka* in *Arch. Sur. Ind.* (Calcutta and Oxford, 1925).

40   K. A. Nilakanta Sastri, op. cit. 354.

41   Ibid.

42   Ibid. 358.

43   Ibid.; see Kautilya's *Arthasastra*, ed. and trans. by Shama Sastri.

44   Marshall, *Taxila* (Cambridge, 1951), ii. 433, iii. Pl. 130.

45   L. Bachhofer, *Early Indian Sculpture* (Paris, 1929), i. Pl. 13.

46   See A. K. Narain, *The Indo-Greeks* (Oxford, 1957).

47   Ibid. 181.

48   Narain, op. cit. 97.

49   *Bulletin de l'École française d'Extrême-Orient*, xxv (1925), 112; xxxi (1931), 448.

50   Marshall, *Taxila*, i. 33–34.

51   Narain, op. cit. 118.

THE INDIAN SATRAPIES UNDER ALEXANDER THE GREAT

A. B. Bosworth

Alexander's administrative arrangements in India are an obscure and somewhat neglected subject. The obscurity is due to a crucial lacuna in the narrative sources, which take us to a crisis in government but say nothing of its resolution. Late in 325 the satrap of northern India, Philip son of Machatas, was assassinated by some of his native mercenaries. In his place Alexander appointed the native prince Taxiles to govern the territory along with Eudamus (the officer commanding the satrapal army of Thracians) until such time as he sent out a new satrap from court.[1] Nothing more is heard of a replacement or of India. The sources foreshadow an administrative change but never report the outcome. Instead we have to wait for the reports of the satrapal distributions of Babylon and Triparadeisus, in which the division of the Indian provinces is sensibly different from what it had been in Alexander's day. The change may be due to the king himself or to his successors. Both views have been stated, but the issue has never been fully argued and it is worth reopening. It has important implications for Alexander's view of empire in his last years and for the status of India in his imperial plans.

Down to late 325 B.C. Alexander's administrative acts in India are clearly reported and easy to follow.[2] When he entered India in the summer of 327, he ensured that the strategic line of communication along the Cophen valley was strongly garrisoned. Its tribal centres were placed under native hyparchs, some of them former refugees who had been at loggerheads with the previous rulers.[3] The administrative head of the area was a Macedonian satrap, Nicanor, who had general oversight between the borders of Parapamisadae and the Indus.[4] Beyond the Indus a second satrapy was established, comprising the area of the Punjab between the rivers Indus and Hydaspes and extending as far south as the confluence with the Acesines. Its nucleus was the principality of Taxiles, Alexander's most constant local ally. This second satrapy was governed by Philip son of Machatas, who had a formidable garrison force which included the entire Thracian contingent.[5] For a time at least the western satrapy also formed part of his competence. Nicanor, it seems, was assassinated by his subjects in the Cophen valley late in 326. Philip was sent to restore order there, and after a successful punitive campaign he was vested with the territory west of the Indus as far as Parapamisadae.[6] For the moment the lands between the Hindu Kush and the Acesines were in the hands of a single satrap.

Beyond the Hydaspes was the territory of Porus. Defeated in battle in the spring of 326, he attracted the conqueror's favour and benefactions by his heroism, and his realms were systematically expanded. In early 325 Porus was made vassal king of all the lands between the Hydaspes and the Hyphasis,[7] an area which Alexander had overrun but was unwilling to keep under direct Macedonian control. He may have had the technical title of satrap[8] but he was in fact plenipotentiary, exercising power without Macedonian troops or Macedonian officials. To the south of the Acesines was another Macedonian satrap, Peithon son of Agenor, who was in charge of the territory as far as the Indian Ocean.[9] The Indus and the Hydaspes now formed a continuous river frontier, its defence and administration shared between two Macedonian satraps, and there was an extensive buffer zone across the Punjab under the control of a native prince. That was the situation at the end of 325 when Philip was assassinated in the north.

The evidence begins again after Alexander's death, and it will be convenient to deal first with the reports of the distribution at Triparadeisus in 321. We have parallel narratives in Photius' digest of Arrian's *History of the Successors* and in Diodorus Siculus, which are clearly taken from the same ultimate source.[10] They list the same appointments in the same geographical order and use very similar terminology. Diodorus is the less efficient excerptor, briefer and much more careless, and his description of the Indian satrapies is perplexing at first sight: the satrapy contiguous to Parapamisadae was conferred upon Peithon, son of Agenor, while the neighbouring kingdoms were given to native rulers, that along the Indus to Porus and that along the Hydaspes to Taxiles, 'for it was not possible to move them without a royal army and a first-rate general' (Diod. 18.39.6). This account is paradoxical in several ways. Porus' territory under Alexander did not impinge on the Indus, and Peithon's satrapy had been southern India, not the western province. The problem, however, is largely relieved by the fuller excerpt of Photius/Arrian. This agrees on Peithon's appointment in the north-west and it defines the native kingdoms more explicitly: the satrapy extending along the Indus to Patala, the greatest city of the region, was ceded to Porus, that along the Hydaspes to Taxiles, 'for it did not seem easy to remove them, seeing that they had received their realms at Alexander's hands and maintained considerable armies'.[11] There are two additions of importance. Porus' territory extended to Patala and both kings owed their position to Alexander. Now Patala was at the mouth of the Indus, Nearchus' departure point for his Ocean voyage, and it marked the southern limit of Peithon's old satrapy. If we accept this explicit record, it follows that Peithon was at some stage transferred to western India while Porus' realms were enlarged to include his old satrapy. This reorganization, so Photius' digest implies, took place under Alexander.

This evidence has been very variously treated in modern times. Benedictus Niese accepted Photius/Arrian at face value, but Beloch bluntly dismissed the report as incredible ('ganz unglaublich') and deterred most subsequent scholars from accepting the evidence of the sources.[12] In 1937 Helmut Berve criticized Beloch's dogmatism, based as it was upon wholly subjective criteria, and modified his own earlier treatment of the Indian satrapies, accepting the evidence of Photius/Arrian and drawing the necessary conclusion of a reorganization at the end of Alexander's life. Unfortunately his discussion was embodied in a little-read article in Pauly-Wissowa and has been generally overlooked.[13] Meanwhile Tarn returned to scepticism, arguing that Peithon only received the western satrapy at the time of the Triparadeisus distribution: between 324 and 321 Taxiles ruled the territory from Parapamisadae to the Indus and Porus his old realm between the Hydaspes and Hyphasis.[14] If the critics are correct, a gross error has been committed. Either Photius or Arrian is mistaken in asserting that the situation ratified at Triparadeisus dates back to Alexander's reign.

The easiest assumption would be garbling by Photius, either an explanatory gloss or an incompetent contraction of the original text. Fortunately we can test his technique by comparison with his treatment of a similar passage from the *History of Alexander* (cod. 91). There Photius gives a detailed summary of Arrian's list of the bridal partners at Susa. He virtually transcribes Arrian,[15] retaining his vocabulary for the most part but varying the word order. The result is a reasonably faithful rendering of the original, the last few sentences almost verbatim reproduction. Textual variants are rare, one major ('Αρσινόη for Βαρσίνη) and one trivial ('Αρτώνην for "Αρτωνιν). There are a number of omissions, most of them involving peripheral detail. The father of Rhoxane is not named and Photius does not give Arrian's explanation of the choice of Hephaestion's bride.[16] The only structurally serious omission is the sentence recording Perdiccas' marriage to the daughter of Atropates, which is a slip rather than deliberate excision. We may conclude that the excerpt is a fairly reliable reproduction. The original is pruned but not drastically, and, most importantly for our purposes, there are no glosses or intrusive explanations. In that case there is every reason to believe that his account of the Triparadeisus settlement is an accurate rendering of the original and that Arrian did in fact attribute the Indian reorganization to Alexander.

Arrian himself may be in error but there is no *a priori* reason to think so. There is also some corroborative evidence. The geographical survey of Asia at the beginning of Diodorus 18 has long been accepted as an account of the administrative divisions of the empire at the time of Alexander's death. Almost certainly it is part of a *mise en scène* which Hieronymus placed at the beginning of his history and as such is contemporary evidence.[17] This survey begins with a description of India, starting with the eastern territories and moving to the portion conquered by Alexander, the land of the five rivers. In that area, says Diodorus (18.6.2), were many kingdoms, including the realms of Porus and Taxiles, through which it happens that the Indus flows (ἥ τε τοῦ Πώρου καὶ Ταξίλου δυναστεία, δι' ἧς συμβαίνει ῥεῖν τὸν Ἰνδὸν ποταμόν). The passage seems to envisage the domains of Porus and Taxiles as a single entity covering the length of the Indus, and it is exactly the position described by Photius/Arrian.

Paradoxically Tarn used this evidence to support his conclusion that Peithon was not in western India until 321 B.C., but he could only do so by selective quotation: 'the Indus river happens to run through the realm of Taxiles'.[18] Having omitted Porus he was able to argue that Taxiles' domains covered both sides of the Indus and so included the western satrapy. This presses Diodorus' vague terminology very uncomfortably. Even if the Indus merely formed the western boundary of Taxiles' realm it would be possible to say in so general a context that the river flowed through it. In any case, if Taxiles did occupy land west of the Indus, there is no proof that his holdings included the whole of the western satrapy as far as Parapamisadae. But once we read the complete text the argument founders irretrievably. There are two alternatives. If Porus' domains comprised territory on the Indus, they extended to south India and Peithon had been replaced as satrap. If the passage is wrong about Porus there is no conceivable reason to suppose that it is right about Taxiles. Tarn cannot have it both ways. On the contrary, as it stands, Diodorus' text agrees with the situation in 321 as described by Photius/Arrian. It may be a retrojection of the later position but there is no compelling reason to believe so. Otherwise the list is perfectly compatible with the situation at Alexander's death, and the inclusion of Susiane in Persis (18.6.3) must date to the period before Triparadeisus, when Susiane had a satrap of its own once again.

The reports of the Babylon settlement are not as unanimous as those of Triparadeisus. Photius' digest of Arrian says nothing of the eastern satrapies, implying that they remained under their former rulers. That information is provided in another digest of Arrian, that of Dexippus, who wrote a *History of the Successors* on the same lines as Arrian but with a more complete record of satrapies. He states that Taxiles and Porus ruled all the Indians, Porus the peoples between the Hydaspes and the Indus and Taxiles the rest. Peithon controlled the territory bordering on theirs, except for Parapamisadae.[19] That is a repetition of the distribution of territories at Triparadeisus, except that the digest has Porus in Taxiles' kingdom – an inversion most probably due to Dexippus' own carelessness.[20] Otherwise the two native rulers control all the Indian territories except for the western satrapy, which is already in Peithon's hands. There is no explicit reference to a satrapy of south India and no note of a Macedonian commander in that area.

The other sources are even less helpful. Justin gives a typically competent satrapy list which has a similar note that the Indian and Bactrian commanders were confirmed in office. He then reports Taxiles' domains correctly as the lands between the Hydaspes and Indus, omits Porus altogether and states that Peithon son of Agenor was placed over the colonies founded in India.[21] There is a fair degree of garbling here, and the reference to the colonies is particularly difficult, for there are no known foundations in western India. Berve argued that Peithon was stationed in western India as his primary base but maintained supervision of the cities newly founded in the south of the Indus valley.[22] That would be an extraordinary division of authority between two wholly disparate areas several hundred kilometres apart. It is more likely that there is an error of contraction. Justin's list gives some indication that Pompeius Trogus (the author he abridges) annotated the bare record of appointments with historical details. Nearchus is anachronistically assigned to Lycia and Pamphylia, from which he was in fact withdrawn in 329;[23] and we can only make sense of the report if we assume that Trogus mentioned that Lycia and Pamphylia, which (as all other sources attest) were included in Antigonus' satrapy in 323, had been governed by Nearchus in the past. Justin then carelessly placed Nearchus' original appointment in the Babylon distribution and omitted the rest of the note. In the same way Trogus might first have referred to Peithon's original commission in southern India, which was to populate the cities recently fortified by Alexander,[24] and then proceeded to his appointment at Babylon. Justin then operated in his usual slovenly manner and recorded only the preliminary details. If that is true, we have no way of knowing where Trogus actually located Peithon's satrapy at the time of the Babylon settlement.

There remains Diodorus (18.3.2–3), whom many have taken to be the most reliable source for the satrapy distribution. He retains the division between eastern and western satrapies, agreeing that no change was made in the east. Like Dexippus he lists the unchanged appointments and begins with the Indian satrapies. Unfortunately the text is corrupt. The notice of the confirmation of Taxiles' and Porus' kingdoms has been displaced by seventeen lines; it occurs after Seleucus' appointment to the cavalry *agema* at a stage in the list when it is irrelevant and ungrammatical. Kallenberg's transposition is necessary and unavoidable.[25] But the corruption probably needs further surgery. Diodorus goes on to describe the western Indian satrapy, and his language is most peculiar as it is transmitted: τούτων δὲ τὴν συνορίζουσαν σατραπείαν τοῖς περὶ Ταξίλην βασιλεῦσι συνεχώρησε. Tarn took this to mean that Taxiles received the western satrapy and he has been generally followed. Unfortunately this can only be sustained by translating 'he conceded the satrapy bordering on them (sc. Porus and Taxiles) to Taxiles'. That is ungrammatical. Elsewhere συνορζειν takes the dative,[26] and the genitive τούτων can only be interpreted as possessive: 'the contiguous satrapy which belonged to them'.[27] That is not only clumsy to the last degree but also nonsensical, implying that Taxiles and Porus had some mysterious joint-ownership of western India. Given the textual disruption at this point it is fair to posit additional corruption. The traditional emendation, Πείθωνι δέ for τούτων δέ, at least restores grammar and provides a double dative construction which coheres with Diodorus' usage elsewhere.[28] The text now reads: 'he conceded to Peithon the satrapy which bordered on Taxiles' and is in exact agreement with Dexippus. Unfortunately Peithon's name depends on emendation and Diodorus cannot be taken as complete corroboration. He does, however, indicate that Porus and Taxiles had kingdoms in India proper and that there was no Macedonian control of southern India. And the most natural interpretation of the text implies that western India was under a separate command.

The only full and explicit evidence for the division of the satrapies remains that of Dexippus, who is certainly not contradicted by any other source and suggests that the situation ratified at Triparadeisus was already in force at the time of Alexander's death. It is a theoretical possibility that he has anticipated Peithon's appointment at Triparadeisus, as he seems to have done with Seleucus' appointment to Babylon.[29] But, if that were the case, we should have to assume that Peithon remained in south India, his appointment recorded in none of the sources for the Babylon settlement, except conceivably Justin. That cannot be technically disproved, but it is overwhelmingly more probable that, as Photius/Arrian implies, the southern Indian satrapy was attached to Porus' kingdom during Alexander's reign and Peithon was transferred to western India. That arrangement was approved, together with Alexander's other eastern appointments, at Babylon and again at Triparadeisus.

Alexander's final settlement amounted to a withdrawal of Macedonian control. The Indian territories were now virtually ceded to the two native princes. In fact the whole history of the Indian campaign had been turbulent and unsatisfactory. On the northwest frontier the tribes of the Cophen valley had been hard to conquer and they remained recalcitrant. The death of Nicanor had proved that their administration would be costly and dangerous. Similarly the conquest of southern India had been marked by repeated insurgency and massacre, and the pacification achieved was superficial. Even at Patala, where the Macedonian fleet was stationed, there was trouble. As soon as the king departed for the west the local tribesmen renounced his royal authority and attacked Nearchus, forcing him to take to sea prematurely.[30] Once Nearchus and the fleet were gone, the unfortunate satrap would have been in a confused vortex of hostile peoples, his writ unenforceable outside the region where his army happened to be. It was only in the northern satrapy that conditions had been relatively peaceful, under the influence of Alexander's faithful ally and subject, Taxiles, but even here the Macedonian satrap was murdered late in 325. By 324, then, it would have been painfully obvious to Alexander that India could only be fully subjugated if he returned there with his royal army and subjected it to the vicious punitive campaigns and forced resettlement that he had inflicted on the peoples of Bactria and Sogdiana. But now his military ambitions were focused on the west, with preparations for the Arabian campaign under way,[31] and a return to India was wholly unacceptable.

The alternative was reorganization – and contraction. Peithon was withdrawn from the Indus delta and transferred to the north-western satrapy. His army probably went with him, together with any European settlers left in southern India.[32] Now direct Macedonian rule was restricted to the narrow corridor between the central Hindu Kush and the Indus valley. This was garrisoned strongly, as it had been before, and governed by a Macedonian satrap with a mercenary army. It was a relatively small area, where the army could in time hope to contain and subject the local tribesmen; and it provided automatic entry into the Punjab, if Alexander should ever wish to renew his campaigns in India. To the east was a bridgehead between the Indus and Hydaspes, governed by a native prince of proven loyalty with a European army under a Macedonian commander.[33]

On its frontiers were the new cities founded by Alexander, Nicaea and Bucephala on opposite sides of the Hydaspes and an Alexandria at the great confluence of the Acesines and the Indus, now garrison centres marking the limit of empire. Beyond the Hydaspes was a vast buffer zone from the foothills of the Himalayas to the Indian Ocean, all under the nominal rule of Porus. In that territory even Porus' control may have been largely theoretical outside his own domains, and the peoples of southern India were in effect left to their own devices. This was a tactical retreat without parallel in the reign. Alexander tacitly recognized that his conquests were untenable. He retained nominal suzerainty, but over vast tracts of India he abdicated any attempt to maintain military control. For all the ostensible victories and all its dreadful carnage the campaign in India had proved a failure in the end.

Notes

1 Arr. 6.27.2; Curt. 10.1.20-1.
2 Cf. P. Julien, *Zur Verwaltung der Satrapien unter Alexander dem Grossen* (Leipzig 1914), 44–50; H. Berve, *Das Alexanderreich auf prosopographischer Grundlage* (Munich 1926), 1.268–73. There is a good short account by E. Badian, *Greece & Rome* 12 (1965), 178–80.
3 Cf. Arr. 4.22.8 (Sangaeus); Arr. 4.30.4 (Sisicottus).
4 Arr. 4.28.6. Nicanor had come fresh from his supervision of Alexandria in Caucaso, the new foundation in neighbouring Parapamisadae.
5 Arr. 5.8.3; 6.15.2. For full references see Berve (above, n. 2) 2.384–5, no. 780.
6 Arr. 5.20.7: a report from Sisicottus, 'satrap' of the Assaceni, that the tribesmen had killed their hyparch. The victim is not named, but he is usually identified as Nicanor, who disappears from history after 326 and is replaced by Philip son of Machatas by the time of the Indus voyage (Arr. 6.2.3). Arrian's terminology is very loose. Sisicottus, previously attested garrison commander at Aornus (Arr. 4.30.4), is here termed satrap and we must assume that Nicanor, previously attested satrap, is the unnamed hyparch. There are parallels. Arrian often uses hyparch as a synonym of satrap (cf. Bosworth, *CQ* 24 [1974], 56–7) and occasionally refers to city commanders as satraps (cf. 7.6.1: οτ σατράπαι οἱ ἐκ τῶν πόλεων). But the exchange of titles at 5.20.7 is perverse and misleading, and the text may be garbled.
7 Arr. 5.29.2; 6.2.1.
8 So Plut. *Alex.* 60.15. B. Niese, *Geschichte der griech. und mak. Staaten* (Gotha 1893), 1.502, accepted the statement but found little support. It makes no difference what Porus' official title was. To his subjects he remained their monarch and to Alexander he was a vassal.
9 Arr. 6.15.4; cf. Berve (above, n. 2) 2.310, no. 619; *RE* 19.219.
10 This has been generally agreed since Kallenberg, *Philologus* 36 (1877), 318–21. E. Will, *AC* 29 (1960), 376–86, concedes that there is a common source but modifies the theory considerably, arguing that Arrian conflated two different traditions. His argument is excessively complex and has evoked dissent: cf. F. Bizière, *REG* 87 (1974), 369–74; J. Hornblower, *Hieronymus of Cardia* (Oxford 1981), 51–3.
11 Phot. 71 b 40 ff. = Arr. *Succ.* F 1.36 (Roos): τὴν μὲν παρὰ τὸν Ἰνδὸν ποταμὸν καὶ Πάταλα, τῶν ἐκείνῃ Ἰνδῶν πόλεων τὴν μεγίστην, Πώρῳ τῷ βασιλεῖ ἐπεχώρησε, τὴν δὲ παρα τὸν Ὑδάσπην ποταμὸν Ταξίλῃ.
12 Niese (above, n. 8) 1.505. For the rebuttal see J. Beloch, *Griechische Geschichte* 4².2.316, who seems to believe that Porus was never given the south Indian satrapy and airs the possibility of confusion in the common source. Julien (above, n. 2) 49–50 accepted Beloch's general argument but suggested that Peithon had a dual command, in north-west India and in the Delta.
13 *RE* 19.219 (Peithon [2]). Berve's earlier treatment (above, n. 2) had avoided the question of Alexander's final reorganisation, and his biographies of Peithon (no. 619) and Porus (no. 683) briefly endorsed Beloch's views, retaining Peithon in southern India until Alexander's death. It does not seem to have been noticed that he changed his mind; the later treatment was apparently unknown to H. Schaefer when he wrote the Pauly article on Porus (*RE* 22.1228).

14 W. W. Tarn, *Alexander the Great* (Cambridge 1948), 2.310–13, briefly accepted by Badian (above, no. 2) 180 with references to Berve's unmodified views.

15 Phot. 68 b 5–18 = Arr. 7.4.4–6.

16 Photius also excises the brief reference to the offices of Ptolemy and Eumenes (68 b 12); and, more importantly, he omits Arrian's note (7.4.4) that Aristobulus was his authority for Alexander's second marriage at Susa. The same occurs at 68 b 37–9, where a reference to Aristobulus is the only omission in an otherwise verbatim excerpt of Arr. 7.28.1. Any citation of sources in the *History of the Successors* is likely to have been automatically suppressed by Photius.

17 See now Hornblower (above, n. 10) 80–7, rightly rejecting Tarn's view that the geography is taken from a contemporary gazetteer.

18 Tarn (above, n. 14) 2.310. The passage is fully quoted somewhat earlier (2.276 n. 1), where Diodorus' 'additions' are printed in square brackets. Porus' name does not appear in parenthesis.

19 Phot. 64 b 10–11 = *FGrH* 100 F 8: ἦσαν δὲ ἄρχοντες Ἰνδῶν μὲν ἀπάντων Πῶρος καὶ Ταξίλης· ἀλλ' ὁ μὲν Πῶρος οἵ ἐν μέσῳ Ἰνδοῦ ποταμοῦ καὶ Ὑδάσπου νέμονται. Ταξίλης δὲ τῶν λοιπῶν. Πείθων δέ τις τούτοις ὁμόρων ἡγεῖτο πλὴν Παρ<οπ>αμισαδῶν.

20 The error recurs at *Metz Epitome* 121, whereas the Alexander Romance proper seems to have the facts right (cf. R. Merkelbach, *Die Quellen des gr. Alexanderromans* 249).

21 Justin 12.4.20: *terras inter amnes Hydaspen et Indum Taxiles habebat, in colonias in Indis conditas Pithon mittitur.*

22 Berve, *RE* 19.219 (this is in fact a revival of Julien's suggestion of a divided satrapy [see above, n. 12]).

23 Justin 13.4.15. For Nearchus' earlier command and recall see Arr. 3.6.6; 4.7.2. The historical notes on the appointments may be ultimately derived from Hieronymus himself. Eumenes' assignment in Cappadocia is usually reported with a brief note on the area's history under Alexander (Diod. 18.3.3; Plut. *Eum.* 3.3; Curt. 10.10.3) and the résumé presumably derives from the common source, Hieronymus, who was evidently interested in Cappadocia (App. *Mithr.* 8.25 = *FGrH* 154 F 3).

24 Arr. 6.17.4, 20.2. Niese (above, n. 8) 1.504 n.6 had already seen the connexion.

25 Hornblower (see above, n. 10) 96 has argued for the retention of the tradition, suggesting that Diodorus rearranged the appointments and became muddled doing so. This does not explain the disruption of grammar and the lone intrusive infinitive (ὁμοίως εἶναι).

26 18.3.1: Εὐμένει δὲ Παφλαγονίαν . . . καὶ πάσας τὰς συνοριζούσας ταύταις χώρας. 18.39.6: τῆς δὲ Ἰνδικῆς τὰ μὲν συνορίζοντα Παροπανισάδαις Πείθωνι.

27 Goukowsky's Budé translation reads: 'quant à la satrapie limitrophe de ces royaumes, il l'accorda au roi Taxile.' That is ambiguous, leaving it undecided whether or not the satrapy was part of the kingdoms.

28 Another approach, which is perhaps preferable, is to retain τούτων as a partitive genitive referring to the totality of the satrapies mentioned in the previous sentence and to add Peithon's name at the end of the clause (συνεχώρησε <Πείθωνι>): 'it was resolved to leave the satrapies under the same commanders (likewise that Taxiles and Porus should be masters of their own kingdoms, as Alexander himself had ordained). Of these satrapies he assigned to Peithon the one contiguous with Taxiles".

29 *FGrH* 100 F 8.6 (Archon of Pella was actually satrap of Babylonia in 323). Carmania is also falsely attributed to Neoptolemus instead of Tlepolemus, perhaps through scribal error. The supposed muddle over Susiana (cf. Tarn 2.313 ff.) is a red herring; the manuscript reading is Σογδιανῶν and the traditional emendation to Σουσιανῶν is wholly unjustified (cf. *CP* 78 [1983], 160).

30 Strabo 15.2.5 (721) = *FGrH* 133 F 1a.

31 The preparation of the fleet for Arabia was well under way by the spring of 323 (Arr. 7.19.3–6; Strabo 16.1.11 [741]). Tarn's view (2.394–6) that the expedition was for exploration not conquest is at total variance with the sources and has only curiosity value. Interestingly Tarn stresses Alexander's ceding of territory to Porus as a crucial turning point, the move from conquest to exploration, and somewhat contentiously states: 'those who wish to rule the world do not of themselves give away hard won provinces' (2.398). 'Of themselves' is the vital point. Alexander's renunciation of territories in India was an acknowledgement that he could not hold them with

his present forces and present ambitions. He had certainly not given up imperial aspirations elsewhere. *Reculer pour mieux sauter* is the best description of his final arrangements in India.

32 There is no evidence that the embryonic foundations at the Indus mouth continued their existence (for the scanty testimonia see V. Tscherikower, *Die hellenistischen Städtegründungen* [*Philologus* Suppl. 19: Leipzig 1927], 109). Tarn (above, n. 14) 2.239 went so far as to dispute whether Alexander founded any cities as such in southern India.

33 Eudamus remained in India until 317, when he returned to the war in the west, taking with him the 120 elephants acquired by his assassination of Porus (Diod. 19.14.8).

8

FROM MASS MARRIAGE
TO DEATH

Introduction

With the horrors of the Gedrosian march behind them, the Macedonian army arrived in Susa in March 324. From there Alexander issued his Exiles Decree, and also held a mass marriage in which he and 91 members of his court married Persian noble women (see Sources 96 and 97), an event that has often been seen as an attempt to unite the races.[1] Not long after, Alexander left Susa, and by summer he was at Opis, where he announced the discharge of his wounded and veterans. We would image this 'honorable discharge' would have been met with widespread applause, but instead his men mutinied on him. It appears that Alexander's orientialism and his belief in his own divinity, which intensified in the last years of his reign (see Sources 105 and 106), proved too much – for one thing, the men mockingly referred to his association with 'his father Zeus'. So also a factor was the arrival in Susa earlier of 30,000 foreign soldiers called *epigonoi* ('successors'), which were incorporated into the army. Alexander faced the men's refusal to back down for three days, until finally he began to transfer Macedonian military titles and commands to Persians. His men gave in, and to celebrate the end of the mutiny and his forgiving them, he held a great banquet of reconciliation and prayed for concord.[2]

From Opis Alexander marched to Ecbatana, where his lifelong friend, lover and second-in-command Hephaestion died. Alexander was inconsolable for days, and he ordered the whole empire to be in mourning and ordered various honours for Hephaestion, including a heroic (semi-divine) cult.

In early 323 Alexander and his army arrived at Babylon, despite various warnings and portents that indicated his life was in danger (Sources 81, 82 and 83). Here, he dealt with embassies from various peoples (apparently including the Romans), of which those from Greece were concerned with the problem of their returning exiles. Alexander had by now drawn up plans to invade Arabia, and intended to launch that campaign from Babylon. He would never live to see Arabia.

At the end of May Alexander developed a fever, which soon confined him to his bed; after lapsing into a brief coma he died on 10 or 11 June 323, at the age of thirty-two years and eight months. Typhoid has been suspected, or liver collapse given Alexander's drinking habits (Sources 85–90, 117–119), perhaps even a combination of both. There is also a belief that Alexander was poisoned, presumably by some of his generals (Sources 91–93), including Antipater in Greece, who felt threatened by Alexander summoning him from Pella to his court. The problem with this theory is that the enmity that his generals felt towards each other meant that they would never unite in loyalty under one of their own. That is proved by the way that, for example, after they carved up Alexander's empire among themselves, Perdiccas quickly wrecked any settlement and brought about decades of civil war, a bloody start to the Hellenistic period.

We can say with certainty that the true reason for Alexander's death may never be known, but that it was exploited by ambitious generals for their own advancement.

Ancient sources

The end is nigh?

81   When Alexander had crossed the river Tigris with his army, and was marching to Babylon, he was met by the Chaldaean philosophers; who, having led him away from his Companions, besought him to suspend his march to that city. For they said that an oracular declaration had been made to them by the god Belus, that his entrance into Babylon at that time would not be for his own good. But he answered their speech with a line from the poet Euripides to this effect: 'He is the best prophet that guesses well'. But the Chaldaeans said: 'O king, do not at any rate enter the city looking towards the west nor leading the army advancing in that direction; but rather go right round towards the east.' But this did not turn out to be easy for him, on account of the difficulty of the ground; for the deity was leading him to the place where entering he was doomed soon to die (Aristobulus, *FGrH* 139 F 54 = Arr. 7.16.1).

82   Having thus proved the falsity of the prophecy of the Chaldaeans, by not having experienced any unpleasant fortune in Babylon, as they had predicted, but having marched out of that city without suffering any mishap, he grew confident in spirit and sailed again through the marshes, having Babylon on his left hand. Here a part of his fleet lost its way in the narrow branches of the river though want of a pilot, until he sent a man to pilot it and lead it back into the channel of the river. The following story is told. Most of the tombs of the Assyrian kings had been built among the pools and marshes. When Alexander was sailing through these marshes, and, as the story goes, was himself steering the trireme, a strong gust of wind fell upon his broad-brimmed Macedonian hat, and the band which encircled it. The hat, being rather heavy, fell into the water; but the band, being carried along by the wind, was caught by one of the reeds growing near the tomb of one of the ancient kings. This incident itself was an omen of what was about to occur, and so was the fact that one of the sailors swam off towards the band and snatched it from the reed. But he did not carry it in his hands, because it would have been wetted while he was swimming; he therefore put it round his own head and thus conveyed it to the king. Most of the biographers of Alexander say that the king presented him with a talent as a reward for his zeal, and then ordered his head to be cut off; as the prophets had expounded the omen to the effect that he should not permit that head to be safe which had worn the royal head band. However, Aristobulus says that the man received a talent; but also received a scourging for placing the band round his head. The same author says that it was one of the Phoenician sailors who fetched the band for Alexander; but there are some who say it was Seleucus, and that this was an omen to Alexander of his death and to Seleucus of his great kingdom. For that of all those who succeeded to the sovereignty after Alexander, Seleucus became the greatest king,[3] was the most kingly in mind, and ruled over the greatest extent of land after Alexander himself, does not seem to me to admit of question (Aristobulus, *FGrH* 139 F 55 = Arr. 7.22).

83   But Alexander's own end was now near. Aristobulus says that the following occurrence was a prognostication of what was about to happen. He was distributing the army which came with Peucestas from Persia, and that which came with Philoxenus and Menander from the sea, among the Macedonian lines, and becoming thirsty he retired from his seat and thus left the royal throne empty. On each side of the throne were couches with silver feet, upon which his personal Companions were sitting. A certain man of obscure condition (some say that he was even one of the men kept under guard without being in chains), seeing the throne and the couches empty, and the eunuchs standing round the throne (for the Companions also rose up from their seats with the king when he retired), walked through the line of eunuchs, ascended the throne, and sat down on it. According to a Persian law, they did not make him rise from the throne, but rent their garments and beat their breasts and faces as if on account of a great evil. When Alexander was informed of this, he ordered the man who had sat upon his throne to be put to the torture, with the view of discovering whether he had done this according to a plan concerted by a conspiracy. But the man confessed nothing, except that it came into his mind at the time to act thus. Even more for this reason the diviners explained that this occurrence boded no good to him (Aristobulus, *FGrH* 139 F 58 = Arr. 7.24.1–3).

Alexander's death

84   Alexander died in the hundred and fourteenth Olympiad, in the archonship of Hegesias at Athens. According to the statement of Aristobulus, he lived thirty-two years, and had reached the eighth month of his thirty-third year (Aristobulus, *FGrH* 139 F 61 = Arr. 7.28.1).

85   Moreover, in the *Ephemerides* there are recorded the following particulars regarding his sickness. On the eighteenth of the month Daesius he slept in the bathing-room because he had a fever. On the following day, after his bath, he removed into his bed-chamber and spent the day at dice with Medius. Then, when it was late, he took a bath, performed his sacrifices to the gods, ate a little, and had a fever through the night. On the twentieth, after bathing again, he performed his customary sacrifice; and lying in the bathing-room he devoted himself to Nearchus, listening to his story of his voyage and of the great sea. The twenty-first he spent in the same way, and was still more inflamed, and during the night he was in a grievous plight, and all the following day his fever was very high. So he had his bed removed and lay by the side of the great bath, where he conversed with his officers about the vacant posts in the army, and how they might be filled with experienced men. On the twenty-fourth his fever was violent and he had to be carried forth to perform his sacrifices; moreover he ordered his principal officers to tarry in the court of the palace, and the commanders of divisions and companies to spend the night outside. He was carried to the palace on the other side of the river on the twenty-fifth, and got a little sleep, but his fever did not abate. And when his commanders came to his bedside, he was speechless, as he was also on the twenty-sixth; therefore the Macedonians made up their minds that he was dead, and came with loud shouts to the doors of the palace, and threatened his companions until all opposition was broken down; and when the doors had been thrown open to them, without cloak or armour, one by one, they all filed slowly past the couch. During this day, too, Python and Seleucus were sent to the temple of Serapis to enquire whether they should bring Alexander thither; and the god gave answer that they should leave him where he was.

And on the twenty-eighth (Daesius), towards evening, he died. Most of this account is word for word as written in the *Ephemerides* (*FGrH* 117 F 3b = Plut. *Alex.* 76–77.1; cf. Arr. 7.25.1–26.3).

Alexander's death: alcohol

86   But Alexander, after returning from the funeral pyre[4] and assembling many of his friends and officers for supper, proposed a contest in drinking neat wine, the victor to be crowned. Well, then, the one who drank the most, Promachus, got as far as four pitchers; he took the prize, a crown of a talent's worth, but lived only three days afterwards. And of the rest, according to Chares, forty-one died of what they drank, a violent chill having set in after their debauch (Chares, *FGrH* 125 F 19b = Plut. *Alex.* 70.1–2).

87   And Nicobule, or whoever ascribed to her the compilations, says that when Alexander was dining with Medeius of Thessaly he pledged the health of everyone at the dinner, there being twenty in all, and accepted the same number of toasts from all; he then left the party and soon after went to sleep (Nicobule, *FGrH* 127 F 1 = Athen. 10.434c).

88   But Nicobule says, that 'while he was at supper all the morris dancers and athletes studied to amuse the king; and at his very last banquet, Alexander, remembering an episode in the *Andromeda* of Euripides, recited it in a declamatory manner, and then drank a cup of unmixed wine with great eagerness, and compelled all the rest to do so too' (Nicobule, *FGrH* 127 F 2 = Athen. 12.537d)

89   The things about Alexander that are not good. They say that on the fifth of the month Dius he drank at Eumaeus', then on the sixth he slept from the drinking; and as much of that day as he was fresh, rising up, he did business with the officers about the morrow's journey, saying that it would be early. And on the seventh he was a guest at Perdiccas' and drank again; and on the eighth he slept. On the fifteenth of the same month he also slept, and on the following day he did the things customary after drinking. On the twenty-fourth he dined at Bagoas'; the house of Bagoas was ten stades from the palace; then on the twenty-eighth he was at rest. Accordingly one of two conclusions must be true, either that Alexander hurt himself badly by drinking so many days in the month or that those who wrote these things lie. And so it is possible to keep in mind henceforth that the group of which Eumenes is a member ... makes such statements (*Ephemerides*, *FGrH* 117 F 2a = Aelian, *Varra Historia* 3.23).

90   Proteas of Macedon, also, drank a very great deal, as Ephipppus says in his work *On the Funeral of Alexander and Hephaestion* ... Alexander, for example, once called for a six-quart cup and after a drink proposed the health of Proteas. He took the cup, and when he had sung the king's praises he drank, to the applause of everybody. A little while afterwards Proteas demanded the same cup, and again drinking, pledged the king. Alexander took it and pulled at it bravely, but could not hold out; on the contrary, he sank back on his cushion and let the cup drop from his hands. As a result, he fell ill and died, because, as Ephippus says, Dionysus was angry at him for besieging his native city, Thebes (Ephippus, *FGrH* 126 F 3 = Athen. 10.434a–b).

Alexander's death: poison

91   Others have stated that Medius, being a lover of Iollas, took part in the deed (of Alexander's poisoning); for he it was who induced the king to hold the revel (Medius, *FGrH* 129 T 4 = Arr. 7.27.2).

92 (the poisoning of Alexander at the banquet of Medius): The guests present were twenty: Perdiccas, Meleager, Pytho, Leonnatus, Cassander, Peucestas, Ptolemy, Lysimachus, Philip the physician, Nearchus of Crete, Stasanor. ... Of these, Perdicass, Ptolemy, Olcias, Lysimachus, Eumenes and Asander did not know what was going to happen, but all the others were accomplices in the plot (Nearchus, *FGrH* 133 – now *BNJ* 133 – T 10(d) = [Callisthenes], *History* 3.31.8).

93 Neither Aristobulus nor Ptolemy has given an account differing much from the preceding. Some authors, however, have related that his Companions asked him to whom he left his kingdom; and that he replied: 'To the best.' Others say, that in addition to this remark, he told them that he saw there would be a great funeral contest held in his honour. I am aware that many other particulars have been related by historians concerning Alexander's death, and especially the poison that was sent to him by Antipater ... (Ptolemy, *FGrH* 138 F 30 = Arr. 7.26.3).

Modern works

In the selection below, A.B. Bosworth, Emeritus Professor of Classics at the University of Western Australia, looks at the events leading up to Alexander's death, and tests the accounts in the sources, especially the *Alexander Romance* and the *Ephemerides*, to argue that Alexander was murdered

A.B. Bosworth, 'The Death of Alexander the Great: Rumour and Propaganda', *Classical Quarterly*[2] 21 (Cambridge University Press 1971), pp. 112–136.[5]

Additional reading

E. Badian, Conspiracies', in A.B. Bosworth and E.J. Baynham (eds), *Alexander the Great in Fact and Fiction* (Oxford: 2000), pp. 50–95.

E.N. Borza and J. Reames-Zimmermann, 'Some New Thoughts on the Death of Alexander', *Ancient World* 31 (2000), pp. 22–30.

A.B. Bosworth, 'Ptolemy and the Will of Alexander', in A.B. Bosworth and E. Baynham (eds), *Alexander the Great in Fact and Fiction* (Oxford 2000), pp. 207–241.

——, *The Legacy of Alexander. Politics, Warfare and Propaganda under the Successors* (Oxford: 2002).

L. Depuydt, 'The Time of Death of Alexander the Great', *Welt des Orients* 28 (1997), pp. 117–135.

D.W. Engels, 'A Note on Alexander's Death', *Classical Philology* 73 (1978), pp. 224–228.

A.W. Erskine 'Life after Death: Alexandria and the Body of Alexander', *Greece and Rome*[2] 49 (2002), pp. 163–179.

N.G.L. Hammond, 'The Royal Journal of Alexander', *Historia* 37 (1988), pp. 129–150.

——, 'Aspects of Alexander's Journal and Ring in his Last Days', *AJPh* 110 (1989), pp. 155–160.

——, 'The Macedonian Imprint on the Hellenistic World', in P. Green (ed.), *Hellenistic History and Culture* (Berkeley and Los Angeles 1993), pp. 12–23.

W. Heckel, *The Last Days and Testament of Alexander the Great* (Stuttgart: 1998).

——, 'The Earliest Evidence for the Plot to Poison Alexander', in W. Heckel, L. Tritle and P. Wheatley (eds), *Alexander's Empire: Formulation to Decay* (Claremont: 2007), pp. 265–275.

J. Reames-Zimmerman, 'The Mourning of Alexander the Great', *Syllecta Classica* 12 (2001), pp. 98–145.

Notes

1   See Chapter 9.
2   Arr. 7.8.1–12.3, Diod. 17.109.2–3, Plut. *Alex.* 71.2–9, Curt. 10.2.3 ff., Justin 12.11; see also Chapter 9.
3   The founder of the Seleucid dynasty, which was the largest and most powerful of the Hellenistic kingdoms.
4   Of Calanus, the Indian philosopher: see Sources 65–68.
5   Reprinted by permission of Cambridge University Press.

THE DEATH OF ALEXANDER THE GREAT: RUMOUR AND PROPAGANDA

A.B. Bosworth

I

Propaganda and history are often inseparable. Most governments are in a position to control the dissemination of evidence, and if an event is embarrassing or damaging, the relevant evidence is certain to be distorted or withheld. Moreover the writers of history, however innocent their motives, cannot disregard the official apologia of their rulers. One notes with interest that the learned authors of the official Soviet history of the world portray the invasion of eastern Poland on 17 September 1939 as a crusade of liberation.[1] Of course it might be true that the people liberated by the Red Army were glad to be rid of 'the arbitrary despotism of the Polish Pans' and that in the subsequent elections there was absolute freedom of choice and overwhelming support for union with the Ukraine, but the fact remains that it was impossible for members of the Moscow Academy to contradict their government's justification of the invasion.

Few ancient writers were proof against this type of pressure, at least when they wrote contemporary history. Even non-contemporary history had its perils. *Antiquis scriptoribus rarus obtrectator* is by no means universally true, as Livy found to his cost when faced with the unwelcome and unanimous source tradition that a military tribune won the *spolia opima* at Fidenae. He had no choice but to accept the counter-evidence of the corselet of Cossus, obligingly supplied by Augustus.[2] Indeed in the case of Augustus one sees the supreme instance of a smooth, impenetrable façade deliberately constructed to mislead posterity. Throughout his long reign he could effectively suppress recalcitrant pamphleteers like T. Labienus,[3] and his successors were disinclined to blacken the memory of the founder of their dynasty. After Actium the stream of hostile memoirs was dammed and the historical record channelled to uniformity.

Fortunately few men have been in the enviable position of imposing their will on historical tradition. Propaganda usually has two sides. Rivals for empire broadcast conflicting slanders, and not every monarch has an interest in preserving the immaculate purity of his predecessor's reputation. This was particularly the case in the decade after the death of Alexander, when the Hellenistic world was split between warring coalitions variously aiming for satrapal independence or for the assertion of centralized royal authority. Each side appealed to the intentions and dispositions of the dead king, and the suspicious circumstances of his death became a weapon of party invective. Literature was necessarily affected, and traces of the propaganda war can easily be detected, notably in the accusations of poisoning directed against Antipater and his family. But propaganda is not always clearly labelled, and it can be difficult to detect, particularly when politically biased interpretations are swallowed as factual by secondary sources. Now it must be emphasized that the earliest consecutive account of the death of Alexander and its sequel is given by Diodorus Siculus, who wrote as long after the events as 45 B.C., and the probability of our extant sources being fouled by propaganda is very high. This paper is an attempt to strip away some of the layers of fabrication from our confused record of the transmission of power at Babylon; only then can one begin to disentangle the complicated web of intrigue that surrounded the death of Alexander.

Alexander died in Babylon on 10 June 323[1] after an illness of some ten days. Rumours immediately burgeoned, destined to be ignored or relegated to footnotes by ancient and modern historians of Alexander. Droysen merely mentions what he calls 'senseless conjectures', and his abrupt dismissal set the pattern.[2] However, the rumours of poison played an important part in the subsequent dynastic conflict and were consistently used to harass the family of Antipater. In 317 Alexander's mother, Olympias, returned from exile in Epirus. Immediately she purged Macedon of a large number of her political enemies, among whom was Nicanor, younger son of Antipater, and her justification was that she was avenging the death of Alexander μετερχομένη, καθάπερ ἔφησε, τὸν Ἀλεξάνδρου θάνατον. Iolaus, who had been cup-bearer to Alexander, was expelled from his grave and his ashes cast to the winds – again a son of Antipater. The source is Diodorus,[3] at this point universally agreed to be excerpting Hieronymus of Cardia, a contemporary of the events described. This is solid evidence that Antipater's family was suspected very early of having contrived Alexander's death and that the suspicion was fostered by politically interested parties. Olympias was not the first to make capital out of the rumours. According to the *Lives of Orators* attributed to Plutarch, Hypereides moved a decree ironically proposing honours for Iolaus, the supposed poisoner of Alexander (*Mor.* 849 F). Whether or not the actual wording of the decree mentioned poison cannot be determined from our text of the *Lives*, but it is clear enough that Antipater was extremely sensitive to the implications. After the Lamian War Hypereides was treated with exceptional savagery; the weight of evidence is that his tongue was cut out before execution and his body refused burial at Athens.[4] Antipater bore him a personal grudge, which should surely be based on allegations implicit or explicit that he had murdered his king. This is of course no proof that Alexander *was* murdered; Antipater's extreme sensitivity shows that the rumours were damaging, not that they were true. What we can say is that the rumours reached mainland Greece very quickly. The Lamian War ended by July 322,[5] and with it ended the possibility of Athenian statesmen making capital out of the rumours. Within a year of Alexander's death there were allegations in mainland Greece that he had been poisoned.

The sources give a whole compendium of stories, more or less scandalous. Plutarch, Arrian, Curtius, and Justin are, however, unanimous over the main lines of the story. Cassander brought the poison to court (in a mule's hoof), to be administered by Iolaus at a banquet held at the house of Medius of Larissa.[1] That is the basis for subsequent variants. Plutarch mentions rumours that it was Aristotle who advised Antipater to commit the murder, and that he made the poison in person from ice-cold water gathered at the stream of Nonacris.[2] The story is attributed to a certain Hagnothemis, who in turn had picked it up from Antigonus. Antigonus, it may be added, would have welcomed the propaganda to further his intrigues against Cassander. Not only Cassander. Slanders against Aristotle would also damage the famous Peripatetic statesman, Demetrius of Phalerum, who governed Athens in close co-operation with Cassander. In 307/6 he was expelled from Athens by Demetrius Poliorcetes and escaped to Egypt from fear of Antigonus.[3] This story of the philosopher playing tyrannicide is amusing indeed, but nevertheless an elaboration upon a myth, the myth of enmity between Aristotle and his former pupil.[4] The Aristotle stories moreover are detachable from the corpus of rumours, a secondary layer worked up from the known friendship between the philosopher and the family of Antipater.[5] The earliest rumour (corroborated by the Hypereides decree) is that the plot was hatched by Antipater, transmitted by Cassander, and executed by Iolaus. What truth, if any, is in it?

The main sources do not encourage the suspicion of poison. Arrian expresses extreme scepticism, while Plutarch claims that most writers considered the stories fabricated.[6] However, he adduces as proof the alleged fact that Alexander's body stayed fresh and fragrant several days after death – hardly very compelling evidence. We find different causes of death alleged very early. Ephippus of Olynthus held that at Medius' celebrated banquet Alexander took to drinking the company's health in a twelve-pint cup.[7] The effort was too much for him, and as a result he fell ill and died, 'thanks to the wrath of Dionysus on account of the sack of his homeland Thebes'. The bias is hostile to Alexander and the reference to Thebes reminiscent of Cassander's restoration of the city in 316. Cassander would have welcomed insinuations that Alexander died from drink, and Ephippus may consciously have served his interests. The story is elaborated in the sensational tract produced by some writer unknown masquerading under the name of Nicobule.[8] Here it was maintained that Alexander managed to pledge the whole company of twenty guests at Medius' banquet. This tradition must have gained very wide circulation, for we find the notoriously apologetic Aristobulus reacting against it. Alexander, he maintained, only drank heavily at Medius' banquet because he *already* had a fever, and his potations were only to quench the thirst it generated.[1] But elsewhere Aristobulus took pains to gloss over Alexander's wildly intemperate drinking habits,[2] and like Tarn he would have found displeasing the allegation that his hero drank himself to death. Most probably he reversed the original causal sequence, and placed the fever deliberately before the symposium. It is interesting moreover that even where Alexander's death is put down to intemperance, the centre of the drama is the banquet of Medius. Something must have happened there, either the marathon drinking or the alleged crime. Diodorus' narrative is especially intriguing. Though he himself is sceptical, he mentions the reports of some writers that Alexander drank a draught of poison. In his earlier report of the banquet he makes Alexander drain a large cup and cry aloud as though struck a violent blow.[3] I suspect that his source (Cleitarchus?) gave a stock report of the banquet and then followed it up with the poisoning stories. In that case the violent shock after drinking comes from a non-tendentious source. Moreover it is a standard motif, recurring in Plutarch, Justin, and Arrian (a rumour);[4] it might even be fact.

At this point I come to a most peculiar document – a tract on Alexander's death with an elaborate testament forming an appendix. It occurs in several versions of the Alexander Romance and also as a continuation of the Metz Epitome.[5] I follow Merkelbach in treating it as an independent pamphlet and I shall refer to it as the *Liber de Morte*. In the various versions of the pamphlet there are divergences of detail, but the core of the story is identical, a full and lurid exposé of an assassination plot by Antipater and his family. Sensational though the details are, there are elements which must be very early. The story places extraordinary emphasis on the person of Perdiccas, who is represented as the foremost of the marshals, and even in one version given Egypt in preference to Ptolemy.[6] This propaganda is only relevant to 321 B.C., when Perdiccas invaded Egypt and opened hostilities with Antipater.[7] In the pamphlet the poisoning rumours are given in full in their most damaging form, and clearly Perdiccas was using the same techniques as Hypereides in attempting to alienate Antipater from his Macedonian following. There are, however, extensive interpolations. Merkelbach convincingly proves that there are considerable additions in the interests of Rhodes, inserted some time after 305.[8] However, he goes too far in postulating only one set of interpolations. Much of the poisoning story and the testament is inappropriate to the propaganda war of 321. In particular, if the pamphlet was produced by the Perdiccan faction, the favourable treatment Ptolemy enjoys throughout is inexplicable.[1] There must be several layers of interpolation, deriving from the various stages of the propaganda war against Cassander. But originally the allegations of poisoning came from the Perdiccan faction, slandering Antipater and claiming that Perdiccas' pre-eminence was sanctioned by Alexander.

In the Latin version of the pamphlet there is a remarkable statement that it is proper to the narrative to include the names of persons who were passed over by Onesicritus to avoid arousing powerful enmities.[2] The writer then gives a list of guests at Medius' banquet and explicitly exculpates six of them from the charge of poisoning; these are Perdiccas, Eumenes, Ptolemy, Lysimachus, Asander, and the enigmatic Holcias,[3] who in this source alone appears as an intimate of Alexander. The names as they appear in our texts cannot, *pace* Merkelbach, be propaganda of the Perdiccan faction. Peithon, for instance, is alleged to have been privy to the conspiracy, but he was in the forces of Perdiccas until the very end, spearheading his assassination in Egypt.[4] His previous behaviour may have been suspect, but he was still an adherent and it would have been madness to alienate him with accusations of regicide. What matters for our purposes is that Onesicritus must have hinted that Alexander was poisoned, otherwise there would have been no motive for the tract-writer's claim to superior knowledge. Now Onesicritus was a first-hand authority, the head-steersman of Nearchus' fleet[5] and presumably present with him in Babylon. Admittedly he had the reputation of a trader in sensationalism,[6] but one can safely assume that this was scandal which he transmitted rather than scandal of his own invention. If it is true that his work was produced shortly after Alexander's death,[7] we have further positive evidence that rumours were abroad very early in both Europe and Asia that the king was poisoned.

II

If the rumours were widespread and originated close to Alexander's death, it is at first sight puzzling why modern historians have ignored or dismissed them so confidently. But the unanimity stems from reliance on a document known as the Royal Ephemerides which is cited by both Arrian and Plutarch.[1] When they come to record the death of Alexander both authors refer to a day-by-day account of the progression of the illness to be found in the Royal Ephemerides; Plutarch indeed claims to give an almost verbatim copy (τὰ πλεῖστα κατὰ λέξιν). In our extant literature there are five other references to these Ephemerides. According to Athenaeus they were composed by Eumenes of Cardia and Diodotus of Erythrae, while in a textually corrupt passage Aelian appears to repeat the attribution to Eumenes.[2] Now before promotion to a cavalry hipparchy Eumenes had been chief secretary to Alexander, during the Indian campaign at least,[3] and it was primarily the weight of his name which gave rise to the hypothesis that the document attributed to him was an official day-to-day diary of Alexander's activities, compiled from official records of the same type as the *hypomnematismoi* of functionaries in Roman Egypt.[4] This daybook, it was held, was used extensively by Ptolemy, whose writings were therefore surrounded with a unique aura of authenticity.[5]

This hypothesis was long canonical, but there have always been difficulties. Most important is the problem why both Plutarch and Arrian present the document as an unambiguously reliable record of Alexander's death, but elsewhere ignore it, Arrian completely and Plutarch almost so.[6] The standard explanation, most fully developed by Kornemann,[7] is that the Ephemerides were used only by Ptolemy and our citations come at second hand. Now Arrian concludes his extract with the words οὐ πόρρω δὲ τούτων οὔτε Πτολεμαίῳ οὔτε Ἀριστοβούλῳ ἀναγέγραπται. This phrase can be interpreted in two ways, either 'nothing was recorded beyond this point' or 'their accounts were no different from this'.[8] If one accepts the first interpretation, there is no inconsistency in the hypothesis that Arrian took his account from Ptolemy. But then the problem remains why Plutarch should have used Ptolemy as an intermediary source. An intermediary source is indeed likely, despite Plutarch's claim to be quoting verbatim. His library at Chaeronea he admits was limited (*Demosth.* 3.1), and it may well not have contained a work as obscure as Eumenes' Ephemerides. However, if Plutarch drew on an intermediary, it is unlikely to have been Ptolemy; there is no evidence that Plutarch consulted his work directly.[9] Athenaeus too refers to the Ephemerides[10] and there is no sign that he had ever read Ptolemy. If the hypothesis of Ptolemy's privileged access is to hold, one has to postulate that Athenaeus got his material at third hand from an unnamed source, who in turn was derived from Ptolemy. That is too much to swallow; it is far simpler to deny the privileged access. Plutarch and Arrian will have obtained their material either from the original or by different transmissions. In that case why are the Ephemerides so rarely cited?

It is best to grasp the nettle and concede that the document only existed as a record of the last few months of Alexander's life. Most recently A.E. Samuel suggested that the document is a posthumous compilation from Babylonian public records, which certainly did give mundane details of the daily life of kings resident in the city.[1] Moreover the records relevant to Alexander would have covered only the last few months of his life. Now it is true enough that the language would have presented no obstacle to Eumenes, for he could concoct a fake letter in *Syria grammata* during the campaign of 317/16,[2] and his staff was certainly in a position to raid the archives of Babylon. It is, however, an enigma why they should have done so. Eumenes would surely not have considered these records any more reliable than his own memory and possibly his own memoirs. Moreover, if the city archives were used to give a spurious air of authenticity, it is inexplicable that no source mentions this ground for the document's reliability. I conclude that the Babylonian records are as superfluous an entity as Occam's razor has ever pared away. The jejune entries Samuel cites are vague and general references to royal illnesses; there is nothing like the precise description of the progression of the illness that we find in the Ephemerides. Moreover it is inexplicable how Babylonian records should have come to mention a consultation of *Sarapis* unless Alexander actually founded a temple in Babylon, which is unlikely to the last degree.[3]

At first sight Pearson's solution is more attractive: 'a literary production, composed in later times and based in part on the works of historians like Ptolemy, Aristobulus and their contemporaries'.[4] He even identifies the forger, a certain Strattis of Olynthus, who according to a desperately corrupt entry in the *Suda* composed five books of Ephemerides or about Ephemerides; the manuscripts permit either reading.[5] This is a superfluous hypothesis. If the Ephemerides are a late fabrication, fathered on Eumenes and Diodorus for the sake of corroborative verisimilitude, the name of the author is of no great moment. However, the hypothesis of a purely literary forgery seems to me unconvincing. Pearson's major argument centres on the celebrated crux of the temple of Sarapis, which we find mentioned in the excerpts of Plutarch and Arrian as the place visited by senior Macedonian officers on the eve of Alexander's death.[1] Now the cult of Sarapis is usually assumed to have been founded in Egypt by Ptolemy Soter, probably some time before 312,[2] and the reference to a pre-existing temple in Babylon looks like a glaring anachronism. But another problem immediately arises. Why should a late forger have invented a temple to an Egyptian god in Babylon? There is no conceivable motive, unless with Kornemann[3] one suggests that Ptolemy somehow doctored the archives at Babylon with propaganda for his new god. We are faced with a dilemma: either the Ephemerides are a late fabrication and a motiveless fabrication, or Ptolemy interpolated the record in his own interests, in which case the fabrication is early. It might be possible to slip between the horns and argue that it was Alexander who established the cult of Sarapis and with it a temple in Babylon. But no evidence before the Alexander Romance links the Ptolemaic cult with Alexander,[4] and there is no record of any major building activity by the king in Babylon beyond the reconstruction of the great state temple of E-sagila. The picture was not changed by the discovery of an inscription by the south-east corner of the Caspian Sea dealing with the manumission of a slave and his dedication to Sarapis.[5] It is dated to the reign of Antiochus I (281–61), and the surprisingly early provenance in such a distant part of the Seleucid empire led C.B. Welles to the hypothesis that the cult of Sarapis was founded and promulgated by Alexander. The arguments are inconclusive; recently Fraser[6] suggested that the foundation in Hyrcania was the work of a settlement of Egyptian soldiers. Nor can we postulate consistent hostility between the two empires inhibiting the spread of the cult of Sarapis. We know that it was being disseminated in the period 305–1,[7] the time of the great alliance against Antigonus; then Seleucus might well have favoured the establishment of shrines to Sarapis, the deity so honoured by his ally.

But what of the temple of Sarapis mentioned by the Ephemerides? Wilcken's researches have made it almost certain that the cult of Sarapis under the Ptolemies originated in the late Pharaonic worship of the Memphis underworld god, Osiris-Apis (Wśr-ḥp), whose name is used in Ptolemaic bilingual inscriptions as a transliteration of Sarapis.[1] Now this underworld god had been worshipped and approached by the Greeks of Memphis before the Macedonian conquest,[2] and the Macedonian troops resident there over the winter 332/1 must have been familiar with his great sanctuary. Arrian[3] mentions a sacrifice to the Apis bull, the earthly incarnation of Osiris, and there is no good reason to deny that the Macedonians were acquainted with the worship of the deceased Apis in the form of the underworld god, Oserapis. Moreover the sacrifice to Apis was a necessary act of conciliation after the sacrileges of the Persian reconquest of Egypt ten years before,[4] and Alexander must have paid due respect to all the major deities of Memphis. In that case there must have been a striking resemblance between Oserapis and Bel-Marduk, the bull god of Babylon; indeed the Macedonians could well have regarded them as twin manifestations of the same deity, just as the Greek Zeus and the Libyan Ammon had been regarded as identical since the fifth century.[5] In that case the temple of Bel-Marduk in Babylon might have been described as belonging either to Belus or to Oserapis, and a reference to Oserapis would inevitably have been altered by later writers to the more familiar form Sarapis. Now, if this interpretation is correct, it would follow that the reference to a temple of Sarapis at Babylon must be early. After Ptolemy's reshaping of the Memphis cult with the addition of elements from Greek religion[6] the identification of Bel-Marduk with (O)serapis would no longer be feasible; the representations of the Ptolemaic Sarapis with the modius-crowned head of Zeus would have borne no resemblance to the bull god of Babylon. The reference to Sarapis in the Ephemerides, far from proving the document a late fabrication, is inexplicable unless it was made before the reconstitution and broadcasting of the Memphis underworld cult by Ptolemy Soter.

There is another peculiarity: the versions of the Ephemerides given by Plutarch and Arrian contain discrepancies. In particular Arrian[7] mentions repeated briefing sessions for the forthcoming Arabian expedition, whereas Plutarch knows nothing of them. The only comparable conference he mentions is with Nearchus to discuss his recent voyage in the Indian Ocean; in Arrian this turns into another briefing.[1] Plutarch also has a meeting to discuss army appointments,[2] which is either ignored by Arrian or unknown to him. Lastly the officers whom Plutarch makes consult Sarapis/Marduk are Seleucus and an otherwise unknown Python. In Arrian Python is replaced by the more celebrated Peithon and four more names are added. Further the plain visit in Plutarch becomes a (non-Babylonian) incubation, and the response of the god is slightly different.[3] Some of these divergences are radical, and the texts used by our two authors must have been different. If Arrian, as is likely, got his version from Ptolemy, the king either added his own embellishments or used a fuller text. Now this phenomenon of progressive elaboration is very reminiscent of the *Liber de Morte*, in which we can detect several layers of propaganda. The initial references to Perdiccas' salutation as regent[4] and his assignment to Egypt[5] have been extruded in later versions and replaced by variants. Moreover there are manifest later interpolations in favour of Ptolemy and Rhodes. Similarly, if the Ephemerides were used as propaganda, they would have been progressively altered as the political climate changed. In Arrian's version two of the names added to the list of officers consulting Sarapis are men branded as poisoners in the Alexander Romance, Peithon and Peucestas.[6] It is at least possible that here we have a counterblast to detailed accusations of poisoning. The accused, so the propagandist maintains, did all they could to ensure Alexander's recovery and were in no way to blame for his death. Similarly Arrian's repeated briefings for the Arabian expedition could be designed to show Alexander active during his illness, so as to discount stories of poisoning at Medius' banquet.

III

Now if the Ephemerides were an original propaganda document some very interesting conclusions emerge. Apart from the extracts about the last illness, the quotations surviving from the Ephemerides refer almost exclusively to Alexander's excessive drinking. The most substantial extract, from Aelian, gives a day-to-day account of the king's drinking during the month of Dios, some seven months before his death.[7] What results is a continuous record of carousing with the frequent story that the king slept solidly for one or even two days after his excesses. This last detail is taken up by Athenaeus and Plutarch[8] (in the *Quaestiones Conviviales*), who speak of frequent entries "τήνδε τὴν ἡμέραν ἐκ τοῦ πότου καθεύδων", ἔστι δ'ὅτε, "καὶ τὴν ἐφεξῆς". Aelian even says that from the extracts he gives one can judge the tone of the whole work.[1] So either the testimonia are to be rejected out of hand or we must face the conclusion that the

Ephemerides recorded a drinking marathon unique in history, in which the king spent his life alternately drinking himself to insensibility and sleeping off the results. Clearly this is the story of Ephippus and Nicobule, who attributed Alexander's death to his excesses at Medius' banquet. In the Ephemerides the final illness seems anticipated by a string of comparable debauches,[2] and the impression to be fostered is no doubt that Alexander ruined his constitution by his drinking and so succumbed easily to the illness thereby induced.

Tarn, who believed with Aristobulus that Alexander sat up to talk, not to carouse, claimed that the king drank to quench the thirst he had from a fever developed *before* Medius' banquet, and he held that the Ephemerides support this assertion.[3] But, needless to say, Arrian's version (Plutarch's begins later) states that after a carouse lasting well into the night Alexander bathed and slept in the bathroom ὅτι ἤδη ἐπύρεσσεν;[4] this is as clear a statement as one could wish for that the fever came on after the drinking. As in the *Liber de Morte* the crucial time is the feast of Medius, but the Ephemerides make him develop a fever, not the symptoms of poisoning, and that fever is eminently well anticipated by a long record of similar potations. No doubt the author hoped to eliminate all suspicion of foul play. The picture given of Alexander may not have appealed to Aristobulus and Tarn, but Antipater would have been very appreciative.

Athenaeus and Aelian attribute the composition to Eumenes of Cardia, and indeed the name of the ex-secretary of Alexander would make the ideal heading to a purported piece of archival material if one wished to give it an authentic appearance. But the Ephemerides are an early production, and it is not improbable that Eumenes *was* the author. In that case the original document can be given a very precise date of composition. The work exculpates Antipater, and such a work could hardly be composed in 321, when Eumenes commanded the Perdiccan forces in Asia Minor against the invading army of Antipater and Craterus. Nor could it have been written in the years of Eumenes' exile at Nora, condemned to death *in absentia* thanks to Antipater and Antigonus. The years in which he was a royal general in Asia, down to his death in 316, are likewise excluded, for the arch-enemies of the regime he supported were the sons of Antipater.[5] The only possible period would be the eighteen months of coexistence between the death of Alexander and the opening of hostilities between Antipater and Perdiccas in the winter of 322/1. Rumours of poisoning spread from Asia immediately after Alexander's death, and at first it was in the interests of all the generals to scotch them. Eumenes would have been the first choice to produce a quasi-official document giving a day-to-day account of Alexander's illness and implicitly ruling out poison as a cause of death.[6] This document will have been a standard propaganda weapon in Antipater's arsenal and modified as circumstances required. It must have been widely circulated, for it came by different routes to be used by Plutarch and Arrian. Moreover Plutarch makes it clear that the account of the Ephemerides was widely accepted,[1] and the authority of the name of Eumenes must have been as high in antiquity as it has been in recent years. Curtius Rufus, however, was sceptical, pointing out that Antipater controlled Macedonia and therefore Macedonian opinion, and he sums up in a phrase worthy of Tacitus himself: '*haec, utcumque sunt, credita eorum quos rumor asperserat mox potentia exstinxit*'.[2] This writer of the early principate could judge the value of official apologetic better than most of his successors.

Analysis of the sources for Alexander's last illness leads to an impasse. The king died in early June after a protracted illness, but the causes of the illness are unknown.

The Ephemerides build up a moving and edifying picture, culminating in the army's ceremonial parade past the bedside of their dying king. On the other hand persistent rumours, fostered by Perdiccas and Antigonus for their own purposes, hinted at collusion by a group of generals to poison Alexander. The question how Alexander died will probably remain for ever insoluble, inextricably confused by conflicting propaganda. Other problems, however, are less intractable. We can examine the situation before and after the king's death, and see whether the result of his sudden demise was to introduce new dangers or to resolve existing ones. The behaviour of the senior generals at Babylon is also open to probing for evidence of collusion. Was Alexander's death a wholly unexpected thunderbolt, or were there already plans to meet the succession crisis? Questions such as these should yield the evidence to judge which of the rival stories is the more credible.

IV

The year before Alexander's death was a time of crisis. The king's return from India had brought with it a spate of executions in which nearly a dozen officials, satraps and military commanders lost their posts and their heads.[3] The motives for the purge were complex. The recent disaster in Gedrosia necessitated finding a scapegoat, and the incumbents of Susiana and Paraetacene were obvious victims.[1] But the terror went further than the provinces adjacent to Gedrosia, and the motives were more profound. When Alexander moved into India most of mankind must have thought him gone for ever,[2] and many satraps will have taken the opportunity of carving out for themselves quasi-independent baronies. In Media Cleander, son of Polemocrates, and Harpalus, son of Machatas, controlled between them the holding forces and the central treasury of the empire. Both came from the Macedonian mountain province of Elimiotis,[3] and in all probability they had co-operated to exercise virtual control over the central satrapies, the heartland of the empire, thanks to the absence of any effectual supervision. The army commanders of Media dutifully escorted reinforcements to Carmania, and on their arrival were accused of misgovernment. Curtius[4] gives a vivid picture of Alexander listening to accusations of the most lurid atrocities, substantially repeated in Arrian, and finally adding his own verdict; 'ab accusatoribus unum et id maximum crimen esse praeteritum, desperationem salutis suae; nunquam talia ausuros, qui ipsum ex India sospitem aut optassent reverti aut credidissent reversurum' (10.1.7). This rings true; arbitrary behaviour from subordinates would be feared and resented by a Macedonian monarch, well aware of the dangers of an uncontrolled nobility.[5] Above all by Alexander, whose very existence had been threatened by the family of Attalus.[6] The man who had so carefully exterminated Parmenion's family was not likely to tolerate another group's attaining comparable eminence in any sector of the army or the administration. Harpalus had certainly adopted regal airs, if one can place any reliance on the extracts preserved by Athenaeus from Theopompus' letters to Alexander.[7] In these symbouleutic treatises he accused Harpalus of allowing his mistress, Glycera, to stay in the royal palace of Tarsus and to bear the title of βασίλισσα. Whether or not the charges are true,[1] they must represent popular rumour and shed some light on the pretensions and aspirations of Harpalus. Alexander's reactions must have been predictable to his treasurer, who was wise to flee – especially after the clear signal given by the execution of Cleander.

In Macedonia too Antipater and his family had consolidated their influence throughout the ten years of the king's absence, and the laurels won at Megalopolis were as yet untarnished. Any action against dangerously independent satraps must have included him, and indeed Curtius claims that his supposed regal pretensions were denounced by Alexander.[2] After the purge in Carmania it can hardly have caused surprise that in summer 324 Craterus was sent with 10,000 veterans of Opis to take over the regency of Macedonia, Thrace, and Thessaly, and – a pleasant euphemism – to champion the liberty of Greece.[3] It is possible to argue that Antipater would have surrendered his command and conducted the new Macedonian levies to Asia without breaking the peace,[4] but the objections are to my mind insuperable. In June 323 Craterus was no further west than Cilicia,[5] and in Cilicia he remained until mid 322. Moreover it was Leonnatus who first moved to Greece to help Antipater in the crisis of the Lamian War despite his orders from Babylon to assist Eumenes in the recovery of Cappadocia.[6] Craterus had ignored an earlier appeal by Antipater for help,[7] and his behaviour gives the impression that he was waiting for an opportunity to intervene decisively and to dictate his terms to Antipater.[8] This is all the more surprising when one reflects that the troops under his command had mutinied at Opis because of their intense yearning for home.[9] Craterus had a mandate from his king to return them to Macedonia, and it is inexplicable that they were inactive so long unless they were confident that Antipater would fight to retain his command. We need a very solid deterrent, much more than the moral quarantine suggested by G.T. Griffith;[10] orders to delay until Antipater's reinforcements had left for Asia would not have impressed the veterans of Opis.

There are too statements in the sources which imply a considerable rift between Antipater and Alexander. Admittedly Arrian is sceptical, but his wording is cautious and repays examination. After a very sober statement of Craterus' mission he continues, λόγος δέ τις οὗτας ἐφοίτα ἀφανὴϑ παρὰ τοῖς τὰ βασιλικὰ πράγματα, ὅσῳ ἐπικρύπτεται, τοσῷδε φιλοτιμότερον ἐξηγουμένοις.[11] This is not a typical *legomenon* of Arrian, that is, an extract from a late subsidiary source. What it is is a factual report from a major narrative source (possibly Aristobulus) that there were rumours of alienation between Alexander and his general in Europe. The rumours are historical, and Arrian's emphatic disapproval is no argument against their authenticity. The correspondence with Olympias, who consistently attacked and slandered Antipater, is irrelevant to the situation in 324. If Arrian is right, Alexander chafed at the price Olympias demanded for his ten-month lodging,[1] and the battle had been won by Antipater as early as 330, when the queen mother retired to nurse her grievances in Epirus.[2] Her complaints may have been renewed effectively six years later, but, if so, some additional factor must have come into play. It is interesting that the *Liber de Morte* begins with a statement that Alexander was instigated to remove Antipater by letters from Olympias.[3] If there was a rift between Alexander and Antipater, the correspondence of Olympias would naturally have been adduced as its cause, but it is unlikely that a rift would have been inferred from the correspondence and the mission of Craterus alone. Indeed the fact that the poisoning stories sprang up so early is confirmation that Antipater had most to gain from the death of Alexander.

The only remaining evidence against the hypothesis of hostility between the king and his regent is the mission of Cassander.[4] Would Antipater deliberately send his eldest son to court as a hostage to fortune? One cannot say how soon Antipater realized his position was threatened. The obvious move on learning of the executions in Carmania was to send a representative to explain his own behaviour, and who better than his eldest son?[5] When it became known that Craterus was to control Macedonia and Alexander's ferocious reception of Cassander had confirmed the initial suspicions, he could only take defensive moves.[6] Antipater's replacement fits precisely into the pattern of moves against satraps of key areas, and the summons to court must have looked sinister given the political context. Perhaps he was not marked for liquidation, as was rumoured,[7] but he was to be stripped of *potestas* and *auctoritas*. The gulf between the regency of Macedonia and leading levies to an uncertain future is too great for him to have submitted tamely. Craterus had his suspicions, surely justified.

The imminent peril of Antipater was not the only cloud on the horizon. Alexander had been showing disturbing signs of megalomania,[8] and there were ominous hints that he had hard and indefinite fighting planned for the immediate future. Greece was in a state of acute unrest thanks to the imminent influx of exiles from the disbanded satrapal armies in Asia.[9] Athens and Aetolia were determined to resist attempts to restore exiles to Samos and Oeniadae, and Alexander was equally determined to crush resistance.[1] Justin claims that Alexander had plans to crush Athens,[2] and according to the tendentious account of Ephippus a certain Gorgus of Iasus promised weapons and ammunition on a fantastic scale for the siege of Athens.[3] The proposal was made at Ecbatana in late 324, so hostilities were envisaged nearly a year before Alexander's death. Probably few Macedonians would have objected to a war limited to Athens, but there was a far more ominous shadow. It seems certain that Alexander had hatched grandiose schemes of conquest in the west. Even the sober Aristobulus admitted that the king was insatiable of conquest, and Arrian endorsed his verdict.[4] It would have caused no surprise when Perdiccas produced ὑπομνήματα by his dead master, advocating conquest of the south Mediterranean to the Atlantic.[5] Senior officers must have discussed these plans with their king, and given the army's morale at Opis they would have had their apprehensions about the troops' reaction. Certainly Perdiccas knew what he was about when he selected the provisions for the army to decide upon![6]

In 323 then there was the immediate prospect of localized war in Greece and the high probability of a large-scale war of expansion in the west. In addition Alexander's staff faced the perpetual hazard of an unbalanced king, neurotically suspicious of independent achievement. The future was black, and Alexander's sudden death in June 323, at the early age of 33, must have been nothing less than providential. That is no proof that he was murdered; his welcome demise could have been coincidence, the happy result of endemic malaria.[7] Before inferring foul play we must examine the settlement at Babylon for evidence that the king's death was anticipated and the necessary arrangements made in advance.

V

The succession crisis of 323 was unique. Not only was the extent of Macedonian power infinitely greater than in 336, but there was no successor to the throne. Alexander's initial security measures had ensured that the Argead house was virtually extinct. One descendant of Philip survived, his son by Philinna of Larissa, possibly illegitimate and certainly a half-wit;[1] his behaviour in Curtius is no positive argument to the contrary, for Curtius here embroiders his source material with motifs from early imperial history.[2] Alexander's wife, Rhoxane, was pregnant, but there was no guarantee of the sex of her child, and, even if she bore a son, the Macedonians cannot have been expected to welcome

261

a king who was half Bactrian.[3] In such a situation there were clear historical parallels; when Archelaus was murdered in 400/399 there followed a decade of usurpation and civil war,[4] and even Amyntas despite his sons did not avert succession intrigues. All through Alexander's reign the danger was acute that he himself would be killed and his kingdom dismembered by conflicting pretenders. Parmenion's advice to produce an heir before exposing himself to danger proves how acutely the lack of a legitimate successor was felt.[5] When Alexander in fact died, the extraordinary thing is that no serious disputes are recorded in the period immediately following. Admittedly the only source to give a detailed account of the succession debate is Curtius, who patently contaminates his work with motifs from Roman imperial history. In particular Perdiccas' reluctance to assume the ring of Alexander is extremely evocative of the behaviour of Augustus and Tiberius before the senate.[6] The fact that Perdiccas received Alexander's ring, attested by all sources but Arrian,[7] is embroidered for dramatic effect; hesitation to shoulder the *moles imperii* would be a gambit familiar enough to a Roman audience. Similarly the preliminary negotiations between the generals are staged before the whole army, not in private conclave, as is overwhelmingly probable.[8] However, despite the rhetorical overlay basic facts can be extracted.

It seems that the generals had worked out a plan whereby the unborn child of Alexander should succeed, and, if the Curtian narrative is not fiction at this point, that the empire should be governed by a junta of regents.[9] This peculiar arrangement not unnaturally was vehemently opposed by the phalanx regiments, who, instigated by Meleager, opted for the mentally deficient Arrhidaeus and secured his proclamation as king.[1] Now the interesting thing is not that there was opposition but that it was led by a man as insignificant as Meleager. He commanded a battalion of the phalanx and was the obvious person to foment discontent in that quarter,[2] but he was certainly not the equal of the great marshals, Perdiccas, Leonnatus, and Ptolemy. Moreover the cavalry stood firm behind their leaders. Arrian lists eight commanders of the utmost distinction backed by the cavalry, whereas Meleager alone is mentioned as supporting the infantry in their demands.[3] He was clearly an opportunist taking advantage of the discontent of his own troops to reinforce his position. His action provoked no split in the cavalry leadership, which though prepared to accept Arrhidaeus as king would not tolerate either mutiny in the phalanx or supremacy for Meleager. The food supplies were requisitioned, and a reconciliation took place with understandable promptness.[4] The ringleaders of the conspiracy in the phalanx were liquidated and Meleager himself disappeared soon afterwards.[5]

Meleager's bid for power was soon crushed, within a week of the king's death,[6] and the only result of the phalanx agitation was that Arrhidaeus as well as Alexander's unborn child achieved regal status. This was immaterial; Arrhidaeus' mental condition necessitated a protector as much as the infancy of Alexander's son-to-be.[7] The crucial question was who was to be regent; the kings were figureheads, and their actual status was puzzling even to contemporaries. Generally documents were dated by the regnal years of Arrhidaeus,[8] but the custom took time to solidify. The Thersippus decree, passed by the island league in 321, regards the kings as equal for dating purposes. It is quite certain that the young Alexander bore the title of βασιλεύς; our sources refer frequently to 'the kings'[9] and their testimony is now confirmed by a recently discovered dedication at Samothrace.[10] The legality of the situation is irrelevant; the Macedonians had no written constitution. What was far from irrelevant was the regentship, for the regent manipulated the kings.

Now it has become one of the most vexed questions of Hellenistic scholarship whether Perdiccas or Craterus was appointed regent at Babylon.[11] The discussion centres on source criticism, and here modern scholars have been perfectly unscrupulous in their methods. There are three roughly contemporary writers definitely known to have dealt with the period of the succession. Hieronymus of Cardia was the lieutenant of Eumenes, and is highly respected as a historian.[12] On the other hand we have Duris of Samos, one of Schwartz's 'tragic historians',[1] execrated by writers ancient and modern, and the enigmatic Diyllus of Athens, of whose works three fragments survive.[2] Now by ingenious manipulations the diametrically opposed conclusions of, say, Fontana and Schwahn have been made to emanate from Hieronymus and any variants from Duris and Diyllus. One finds strange assumptions: Beloch[3] for instance enunciates the admirable principle that one must base one's conclusions on the best source, but he goes on to state that the best source is Arrian, failing to add that our knowledge of Arrian's work on the Successors is based on Photius' summary, which reduces five books of Arrian to three pages of Teubner text.[4] One desperately needs a sure basis for criticism, and the only source amenable is Diodorus. It is as certain as any result in this field can be that Hieronymus is the direct source of large parts of Diodorus 18–20,[5] and the most likely hypothesis is that the preamble of book 18 is Hieronyman material, drastically abridged in Diodorus' characteristic manner.[6] One can then isolate what was probably the earliest version and contrast it with the variants elsewhere.

Diodorus' account is straightforward. After the reconciliation by the chief officers[7] Arrhidaeus was made king and Perdiccas *epimeletes* of the kingdom. All satraps appointed were to obey the king and Perdiccas. Next comes the distribution of satrapies, with Macedonia assigned to Antipater alone,[8] and after the distribution there is a reference to Craterus in Cilicia with 10,000 veterans (Diod. 18.4.1). Now Diodorus later mentions Antipater's appeal to Craterus in the crisis of the Lamian War and adds in parenthesis a recapitulation of the instructions of Alexander.[9] It is often argued that the first passage is a doublet from another source, but wrongly; this passage is an important pivot in the narrative. Diodorus' satrapy list had one notable omission: Craterus, one of Alexander's most powerful generals, was left without a post, and Hieronymus will have explained the reason. When the king died, Craterus was stranded in Cilicia and his interests were not represented at Babylon. He was cut off from office and left to be eliminated at the earliest opportunity. Craterus, however, had orders from Alexander to displace Antipater, and Diodorus in the celebrated ὑπομνήματα excursus explains that Perdiccas took elaborate pains to quash all Alexander's last plans, in particular the instructions to Craterus.[10] Antipater was the chief beneficiary – his deposition was now revoked – and the fact that Perdiccas took such pains to help him is a clear hint of collusion. The general picture in Diodorus is clear. Perdiccas becomes regent, Antipater retains his sphere of influence, while Craterus is discarded and left to fend for himself.

This picture, however, is not uniform, and the only source to reproduce it fully is the Heidelberg Epitome of the history of the Successors, which because of its brevity is useless as a control source.[1] Elsewhere, though there is unanimity on the position of Antipater, there is considerable divergence about Perdiccas and still more about Craterus. The main discrepancy is in Photius/Arrian,[2] where one learns that the terms of the reconciliation between infantry and cavalry were that Antipater should be general in Europe, Craterus should be champion of Arrhidaeus' kingdom (οστάτης τῆς Ἀρριδαίου βασιλείας), Perdiccas should have the chiliarchy which Hephaestion had held, which involved the administration of the entire empire (τὸ δὲ ἦν ἐπιτροπὴ τῆς ξυμπάσης βασιλείας). Substantially the same story recurs in Dexippus, a writer of the third century A.D., whose narrative according to Photius was largely derived from Arrian.[3] According to Photius' summary[4] he gave Craterus κηδεμονία καὶ προστασία τῆς ἀρχῆϑ (which is glossed as the most important position among the Macedonians), and Perdiccas had the chiliarchy of Hephaestion. This concurrence is at first sight impressive, but there are inconsistencies within the accounts of both authors. In Arrian's version of the satrapy list[5] Craterus is made to share the government of Macedonia with Antipater, while at the beginning of the extract from Dexippus[6] there is a statement that the government devolved upon the kings and Perdiccas, who by the vote of the Macedonians administered the empire for them. Now Dexippus' variant can easily be explained away by supposing that the government administration and the regentship were distinct and separate offices.[7] However, the joint command in Arrian is recalcitrant, and has to be explained away as an intrusive gloss.[8] This is a desperate expedient, and it neglects the rest of the tradition that a joint command in Macedonia was intended by the generals at Babylon.[9] Indeed why should one emend away apparent variants in Arrian? The recording of variants was part of his historical technique and cannot have been confined to the *Anabasis*. Moreover his treatment of the events at Babylon was very ample[10] and would have incorporated divergent traditions as a matter of course. It need cause no anxiety that Photius' summary leaves the divergences unlabelled. What matters is the statement that Craterus was to become προστάτηϑ τῆϑ βασιλείας, and on this the argument must rest.

Arrian and Dexippus both maintain that Perdiccas was given the chiliarchy of Hephaestion, which Arrian glosses as the administration of the empire. Now under the Achaemenids the commander of the élite battalion of the Persian army, the 10,000 Immortals, was known as the chiliarch.[1] He was second only to the king,[2] and beside his military functions he had a major role at court. There are several ceremonial duties attested, such as ushering embassies[3] or even supervising executions.[4] The chiliarch was an important but to us shadowy figure. Only once does any of them achieve prominence in our sources. In 395 Artaxerxes II commissioned Tithraustes, his chiliarch,[5] to execute the delicate diplomatic task of liquidating Tissaphernes in Caria. Tithraustes performed his mission efficiently, paid off the arrears due to Conon's sadly neglected fleet, and returned to court after a short stay at Sardes.[6] The chiliarch then could be entrusted with confidential state business, and this was no doubt due to his close proximity to the king at court as well as to the distinction of his military command. There is no evidence of any specific administrative role; the chiliarch was a confidential agent who might be used in emergencies. Together with other Persian paraphernalia this office was absorbed into Alexander's court, and it reappears in 319, when Antipater made his son Cassander chiliarch under the regentship of Polyperchon.[7] Now under Alexander the chiliarchy fell to Hephaestion, commander of the first cavalry hipparchy, and Chares' description of the *proskynesis* scene in Bactria probably shows him performing his office's ceremonial functions.[8] After Hephaestion's death Perdiccas succeeded to the chiliarchy. Plutarch states categorically that after Hephaestion's death Perdiccas took over his hipparchy and Eumenes moved into the vacant place.[9] The objections to this firm statement of fact are based on Arrian, who claims that after Hephaestion died Alexander appointed nobody to his chiliarchy so that his name would not disappear 7.14.10). But it is to the last degree implausible that a major cavalry unit was left without a commander; Arrian goes on to say that the battalion continued to bear Hephaestion's name and badge, and no doubt this is behind his statement that no commander was appointed. We need not doubt that Perdiccas was chiliarch in Alexander's lifetime; Ptolemy's hostility is sufficient reason for the omission of his promotion in Arrian.[10]

A further difficulty is that in Diodorus' account *Seleucus* is appointed chiliarch in Babylon, and the same statement recurs in Appian's brief sketch of Syrian history under the Successors (γίγνεται δ' εὐθὺς Ἀλεξάνδρου μεταστάντος ἡγεμὼν τῆς ἵππου τῆς ἑταιρικῆς, ἧς δὴ καὶ Ἡφαιστίων ἡγήσατο Ἀλεξάνδρῳ καὶ ἐπὶ Ἡφαιστίωνι Περδίκκας),[11] and Appian's source for this period, whether directly or indirectly used, was Hieronymus.[1] Now, if one accepts that Seleucus was appointed at Babylon, the chiliarchy of Perdiccas becomes very nebulous indeed. Bengtson[2] goes so far as to postulate a split in the functions of the chiliarchy, Seleucus dealing with the military side and Perdiccas administering the empire. This means conflating inconsistent source data, a method always suspect; no source mentions chiliarchies held by *both* Perdiccas and Seleucus. Moreover, if my argument is right, the chiliarchy was never primarily an administrative post, and Perdiccas was definitely not reduced to a non-military court superintendent. Justin and Curtius regard him as the most powerful man in Asia, and Justin[3] explicitly gives him overriding military command. He must have been regent; Plutarch too clearly implies it – ἦν γὰρ ἐκεῖνος εὐθὺς ἐν δυνάμει μεγίστῃ τόν Ἀρριδαῖον ὥσπερ δορυφόρημα τῆς βασιλείας ἐφελκόμενος (*Al.* 77.7).

Craterus' standing is even more perplexing. If he was προστάτης, his forces of 10,000 men, no matter how battle-hardened, were no match for Perdiccas or for the man he had orders to depose. The 'champion of the royal house' was in a desperate position, and it passes belief that he and not Perdiccas was appointed guardian of the kings in Babylon. Hieronymus' version that he was passed over is by far the most convincing. The variant in Arrian that he and Antipater were to share Macedonia has won some acceptance.[4] Craterus, however, never makes any move to claim this inheritance from Alexander. His attitude to Antipater is consistently deferential, even though he brought vital reinforcements, postponed until the last minute. There are no signs that he was entitled to a joint command, and Antipater easily dispensed with him after the Lamian War. Even before the breach with Perdiccas we find him marrying Antipater's eldest daughter, Phila, and preparing for his return into Asia.[5] It seems to have been recognized that Craterus was to seek his future in Asia; Alexander's *acta* had been annulled and with them any claims he might have on Macedonia. Now Craterus' allocation to Macedonia recurs in the testament of Alexander given in the *Liber de Morte*,[6] where Craterus is appointed to Macedonia and Antipater given a vague overriding command in the territory west of the Halys.[7] Such provisions fit in beautifully with Perdiccan propaganda in 321, when Alexander's last orders could be resuscitated and used against Antipater. There is no difficulty in the propaganda having reached Arrian; we do not know that he believed it. The *prostasia* of Craterus belongs to the same world of propaganda and with it the spurious chiliarchy of Perdiccas and the omission of Seleucus. When Perdiccas insinuated that Antipater's tenure of Macedonia was illegitimate, the obvious counter was to query the basis of Perdiccas' own position. Accordingly he was portrayed as a usurper, the subordinate of Craterus who appropriated the regentship by force of arms. Such propaganda might well have been effective among the many combatants who had not participated in the Babylon distribution, and after 321 Antipater and Ptolemy could with impunity foster the myth of the Perdiccan usurpation. Perdiccas was accordingly demoted to chiliarch at Babylon, and Ptolemy studiously avoided all reference to his promotion after Hephaestion's death. Partisan or uncritical writers will have transmitted the fictions for Arrian to collect in his great work on the Successors. We can only regret that Photius' summary was not more extensive.

VI

I conclude that Perdiccas was made regent at Babylon, so becoming *de facto* head of the Macedonian empire and representing the king himself. Macedonia had known regents before, and the precedents were ominous; there was a natural tendency for the protector to push aside his ward and assume the throne himself. The examples of Ptolemy Alorites and Philip, son of Amyntas, would have been fresh in men's minds, and few would have believed that Perdiccas could be restrained from displacing the mentally deficient Arrhidaeus. Perdiccas had been the choice of the officers at Babylon, but Antipater had not been represented, and he might well have felt that the regentship should be his. There were no objections from Macedonia, no doubt because Antipater was enmeshed in the Lamian War and in no position to press home any claims. He may, however, have come to some agreement with Perdiccas in the last months of Alexander's life, confirming tenure for himself and conceding the regentship. Perdiccas would then have honoured his agreement by negotiating the cancellation of Alexander's last plans, thereby isolating Craterus.

In winter 332/1 Antipater was forced to break off his invasion of Aetolia by the startling news that Perdiccas was about to seize the kingship and displace him from Macedonia.[1] The first part of Perdiccas' plan could have been foreseen, but under existing circumstances, if he had made himself king, it would have been as husband to Antipater's daughter, Nicaea. In late 322 Iolaus and Archias had arrived in Asia with Perdiccas' bride-to-be,[2] and the coalition seemed at least firm. But Perdiccas had been intriguing with Cleopatra, daughter of Philip and sister of Alexander, and by the winter he had decided to discard Nicaea and, with her, Antipater.[3] Now it was brutally clear that Perdiccas' *subsidia imperii* were to be not Antipater and his house but Cleopatra and the charisma of Alexander. The regent had made his bid to succeed Alexander, and immediately broke the pre-existing coalition.

It is then probable that an agreement between Perdiccas and Antipater antedated the king's death, and Cassander could have executed the diplomatic negotiations during his stay at court. There is one passage of Diodorus which gives this hypothesis more than probability. The context is Perdiccas' marital intrigues, and Diodorus gives an introductory *mise en scène*.[1] 'Perdiccas had previously decided upon co-operation with Antipater, and for this reason he had pressed his suit when his position was not yet firmly supported; but when he had achieved control of the royal forces and the guardianship of the kings, he altered his calculations.' This passage has always caused difficulties. Schwahn, who found it particularly troublesome, shrugged it off on to the shoulders of Diyllus of Athens[2] and discarded it with an easy conscience. The problem is that Diodorus, here as usual following Hieronymus, talks of a period of κοινοπραγία, which Perdiccas terminated after having gained custody of the kings. Accordingly scholars who believe in the chiliarchy of Perdiccas and the *prostasia* of Craterus find here confirmation of a Perdiccan *usurpation* of the regent's powers and functions, this causing the civil war of 321.[3] It is, however, perfectly clear that what Hieronymus and Diodorus thought led to war was the abandonment of Antipater's family for Alexander's; this is explicitly separated from his obtaining the regent's powers. Moreover on no sensible interpretation of the evidence can one talk of a 'non-military grand viziership of Perdiccas'. When Diodorus speaks of assuming the royal powers and the championship of the kings, he must mean the Babylon settlement of June 323.[4] The consequence is that the κοινοπραγία can only have been before the settlement and therefore before Alexander's death. Then Perdiccas' affairs could be described as not yet firmly supported, and co-operation with Antipater would have been cemented through Cassander. One would dearly like to have the original of Hieronymus and see what exactly lies behind Diodorus' phraseology, but it seems unavoidable that he knew of an agreement between Perdiccas and Antipater shortly before Alexander's death. If so, it is certain that his informant was Eumenes of Cardia, chief lieutenant of Perdiccas himself.

There may be another hint by Hieronymus of a conspiracy in the last days of Alexander. In 316, when Seleucus was about to break with Antigonus, he was dunned by the new regent for accounts of his administration, and replied that he was not bound to submit accounts for Babylonia, which the Macedonians had given him for his services during the lifetime of Alexander.[5] Whatever the legality of Antigonus' demands, Seleucus is claiming that his services in the reign of Alexander put him above interference by the present regime. Now Seleucus had not been especially outstanding under Alexander,[6] and the donation of Babylonia at Triparadeisus can only have been the reward for his behaviour in the war of 321; his claim to Antigonus is therefore somewhat startling. It is, however, conceivable that he played a leading part in the coalition which engineered Alexander's death, and the rejoinder put in his mouth by Diodorus would then have been very pointed irony. Seleucus' great services were to remove Alexander from the land of the living!

The hypothesis built up is that Antipater, threatened with replacement and perhaps extinction, took the counter-offensive through his son, Cassander, at court. There the chiefs of staff formed a coalition and parcelled out the empire between themselves. In due course Alexander was removed, and the empire he had conquered passed with the minimum of fuss into the hands of his successors. The equilibrium subsisted for a year and was abruptly shattered by Perdiccas' bid for supremacy. Complete proof is impossible, but the probability is that Alexander was murdered. Given the fact that propaganda is at the root of all accounts of his death, one can only assess the prevailing situation. That is that a despot died at a providential moment, that despite the lack of a designated successor the throne passed over without rifts among the successors, and that there is evidence of a junta being formed before Alexander's death. All this points to a successful *coup d'état*, cleanly and ruthlessly executed. It may be a less romantic and uplifting picture than the traditional view of an Alexander worn out by fatigue and wounds dying among grieving friends, but I think it truer to the evidence. Paradoxically the Alexander Romance is nearer to the truth than the Royal Ephemerides.

Notes

1 *Weltgeschichte* x (Berlin, 1968 = Moscow, 1965), pp. 94–5.

2 Livy, 4.20.5–11. On this intriguing passage see Ogilvie's commentary ad loc., and, most recently, E. Mensching, *Museum Helveticum* xxiv (1967), 12 ff.

3 Seneca, *Contr.* 10, praef. 4 ff.; cf. Peter, *HRR*, ii. c–ci.

1 For the date see A.J. Sachs, *Late Babylonian Astronomical and Related Texts* (Rhode Island, 1955), nr. 209, cited by A.E. Samuel, *Historia* xiv (1965), 8.

2 Droysen, i³, 465, n. 1; Beloch, iv². 1.62 and Berve, *Alexanderreich* ii. 184, also dismissed the rumours very abruptly. Grote at least gave the matter serious thought: 'It is quite natural that fever and intemperance{…}should not be regarded as causes sufficiently marked and impressive to explain a decease at once so unexpected and so momentous' (xii. 78, n. 2.).

3 Diodorus 19.11.8; Plut. *Al.* 77.1.

4 [Plut.] *Vit. Or.* 849 B. Hermippus alleged that Hypereides' tongue was cut out in Macedonia, others said at Cleonae. The story that he bit off his tongue to avoid divulging secrets of Athens seems romantic embroidery. It is difficult to see what secrets of Athens would have been important to Antipater after the city surrendered. Cf. Plut. *Demosth.* 28.

5 The battle of Crannon is dated by Plutarch to 7 Metageitnion (late July) – *Camill.* 19.5.

1 Plut. *Al.* 77, Arr. 7.27, Curt. 10.10.9–20, Justin 12.14.

2 Plut. 77.3, Arr. 7.27.1.

3 Diod. 20.45.3, Dion. Hal. *De Dinarch.* 3 (= *FGrH* 328 F 66), Diog. Laert. 5.78: cf. Jacoby, *FGrH* ii D. 642 ff.

4 The rift between Aristotle and Alexander is a speculative construction, based primarily on the relationship between the philosopher and Callisthenes (cf. Berve ii. 72 ff., Jaeger, *Aristotle*, pp. 318 f.). It is clear, however, that too much stress has been laid on the family connection, and there is no adequate evidence that Callisthenes' fall had repercussions for Aristotle. Cf. my article to be published shortly in *Historia*.

5 Pausanias 6.4.8 attests Aristotle's influence with Antipater, which is corroborated by an apothegm of Alexander (Plut. *Al.* 74.5). Antipater is further mentioned as executor in Aristotle's will (Diog. Laert. 5.12 f.).

6 Arr. 7.27.3, Plut. *Al.* 77.5.

7 Athenaeus 10.434 A–B = *FGrH* 126 F 3.

8 *FGrH* 127 F 1. A general discussion of the fragments of Ephippus and Nicobule is to be found in L. Pearson, *The Lost Histories of Alexander the Great*, pp. 61–8.

1 Plut. *Al.* 75 = *FGrH* 139 F 59.

2 Arr. 7.29.4 (F 62); Plut. *Al.* 23.1; cf. Schwartz, *RE* ii. 917 f. = *Griechische Geschichtsschreiber* (Leipzig, 1959), p. 129.

3 Diod. 17.117.5 ff. for the poisoning stories, 117.2 for the shock motif.

4 Plut. *Al.* 75.5, Justin 12.13.8–9, Arr. 7.27.2.

5 The parallel texts of this document are most conveniently given by R. Merkelbach, *Die Quellen des griechischen Alexanderromans* (Zetemata, ix [Munich, 1954]), pp. 220–1.

6 Ps.-Call. 3.33.15, cf. Metz Epitome, 117.

7 Fully argued by Merkelbach, op. cit. pp. 124 ff., building on the conclusions reached by Ausfeld, *Rh. Mus.* 1 (1895), 357 ff. and lvi (1901), 517 ff.

8 Merkelbach, pp. 145 ff. Diod. 20.81.3 knows of a testament of Alexander allegedly deposited in Rhodes.

1 In our extant texts Ptolemy has prominence equivalent to that of Perdiccas – cf. Metz Epitome, 111; only the variant that Perdiccas was to hold Egypt, Ptolemy Libya (Ps.-Call. 3.33.15), hints at an earlier version.

2 Metz Epitome, 97–8 = *FGrH* 134 F 37.

3 Cf. Berve ii, nr. 580. Merkelbach, p. 128 n. 3, may be correct in suggesting that Holcias was the original author of the tract.

4 Diod. 18.36.5; cf. Merkelbach, p. 129. It is also relevant to the argument that Medius is accused of complicity in the poisoning (Metz Epitome, 97). Now Medius was a lieutenant in Perdiccas' forces, commanding the mercenary troops for the Cyprus expedition in early 321 (Arr. *Succ.* F 24.6 = *FGrH* 156 F 10.6). Again Perdiccas seems to be accusing one of his own adherents.

Merkelbach, p. 130, suggests that Medius promptly turned his coat (he reappears in 314 as an admiral of Antigonus – Diod. 19.69.3, etc.), but there is a difficulty. Asander, satrap of Caria, is exculpated explicitly from the murder (Metz Epitome, 98, Ps.-Call. 3.31.9). Now Asander deserted to Antigonus in the vanguard of the invasion of Asia Minor, again in early 321 (Arr. *Succ.* F 25.1–2). If all the list of poisoners is Perdiccan propaganda, it can only have been written if Medius changed his allegiance before the defection of Asander; otherwise Perdiccas would be incriminating an adherent and exculpating a traitor. Unfortunately our only source for these incidents is the Vatican palimpsest, universally assigned to Arrian's history of the Successors, and we have no absolute chronological placings. However, Asander must have deserted at the very opening of the campaign in Asia, and Medius was still commanding Perdiccan forces at the beginning of the campaigning season. It seems unlikely that he deserted (if he did desert) before Perdiccas' defeat in Egypt, and almost impossible that his desertion came before Asander's.

5 *FGrH* 134 T 5.
6 Strab. 15.1.28 (698) = *FGrH* 134 T 10 ὃν οὐκ Ἀλεξάνδρου μᾶλλον ἢ τῶν παραδόξων ἀρχικυβερνήτην προσείποι τις ἄν.
7 So Strasburger, *RE* xviii. 465, T.S. Brown, *Onesicritus*, pp. 5 ff.
1 Arr. 7.25–6, Plut. *Al.* 76. The extant fragments of the Ephemerides are conveniently printed by Jacoby, *FGrH* 117.
2 Athenaeus 10.434 в, Aelian *VH* 3.23.
3 Plut. *Eum.* 1, Nepos *Eum.* 1.4–6.
4 The foundation article was produced by Wilcken, *Philologus* 53 (1894), 81. His discussion of the technical meaning of Ἐφημερίδες has been expanded by A.E. Samuel, *Historia* xiv (1965), 1–3.
5 For one of many statements of this view see Berve i. 50 f.
6 In his *Life of Alexander* Plutarch refers to the Ephemerides once more for the trivial detail that Alexander often disported himself hunting foxes and birds (*Al.* 23.5).
7 E. Kornemann, *Die Alexandergeschichte des Königs Ptolemaios I*, p. 37.
8 Arr. 7.26.3; cf. L. Pearson, *Historia* iii (1955), 437 f. (now *Alexander the Great, the main problems*, ed. G.T. Griffith [Cambridge, 1966], pp. 9–10).
9 In the whole corpus of Plutarch's writings there are only two references to Ptolemy, both in lists of authorities (*FGrH* 138 F 4, 28a). There is no evidence that he was ever used directly.
10 Athenaeus 10.434 в = *FGrH* 117 F 2b.
1 *Historia* xiv (1965), 10–12.
2 Diod. 19.23.3, Polyaen. 4.8.3. Arrian (6.30.3) implies that Peucestas was the only Macedonian dignitary to learn the Persian language, but this is clearly exaggerated. He himself notes that Laomedon, brother of Erigyius of Mytilene, was bilingual (3.6.6 δίγλωσσος{...}ἐς τὰ βαρβαρικὰ γράμματα). Members of Alexander's staff at all levels would have been competent to read Aramaic script.
3 Arr. 7.26.2, Plut. *Al.* 76.9. There is another embarrassment: Aelian mentions entries in the Ephemerides from the Macedonian month of Dios (Oct./Nov.). There is no evidence that Alexander reached Babylon until the Cossaean campaign of winter 324/3 was finished (Arr. 7.15.4). In that case either Aelian's text is corrupt (the reference being to some month other than Dios), or the record is of Alexander's earlier stay at Babylon after Gaugamela (Oct./Nov. 331). In the latter case what was the motive in conflating two brief extracts from the Babylonian archives, some 7½ years apart?
4 *Historia* iii (1955), 439; *Lost Histories*{...}, p. 260.
5 *FGrH* 118 T 1. Even if this mysterious Strattis entitled his work Ἐφνμερίδες he may not have been unique in this. The *Suda* has an entry about Aeschrion of Mytilene, an epic poet friendly with Aristotle and in the train of Alexander. Tzetzes and the scholiast to Lycophron cite romantic details from a work by him called the Ἐφημερίδες (ἐν ζ †Ἐφεσίδων Σ Lyc. *Al.* 688). Strattis' work may have been more like Aeschrion's fantasy than the dry record of Plutarch and Arrian. Cf. *FGrH* iii в (Text), p. 742.
1 Arr. 7.26. 2, Plut. *Al.* 76.4, Pearson, pp. 438 f.
2 Macrob. *Sat.* 1.20.16. Even if the oracle here given is a relatively late fabrication (M.P. Nilsson, *Geschichte der griechischen Religion*, ii. 148, n. 6), there must have been some connection between Nicocreon of Cyprus and the Ptolemaic cult of Sarapis. A bogus oracle could be added to a

genuine historical context, whereas it is very unlikely that a forger would have chosen a person as obscure as Nicocreon to receive an invented oracle.

3 Kornemann, *Ptolemaios*{…}, p. 37; Wilcken, *UPZ* i. 82.

4 The literary evidence is amassed by C.B. Welles, *Historia* xi (1962), 272–89, and discounted by P.M. Fraser, *Opuscula Atheniensia* (Acta Instituti Atheniensis Regni Sueciae, Series in 4°) vii (1967), 32–4 (especially n. 49).

5 First published by L. Robert, *Hellenica* xi (1960), 85 ff. (photograph, plate V).

6 Welles, op. cit., pp. 290–2, Fraser, op. cit., pp. 30–1.

7 Even if the Halicarnassus inscription (*OGIS* 16) is to be placed after 270 (N. Greipl, *Philologus* 85 (1930), 159 ff.), the cult of Sarapis must have been widely promulgated in Egypt in the last decade of the fourth century. The fragment, certainly of Menander, calling Sarapis a σεμνὸς Θεός (F 139, Körte; Fraser, n. 78) implies that the cult was accepted all over the Greek world by the time of Menander's death, around 293/2 (*IG* xiv. 1184 – the chronological data on the stone are inconsistent, but the limits for his death are 293 and 290 B.C. Cf. Körte, *Menander*, p. 1 = T 3). Demetrius of Phalerum allegedly wrote paeans celebrating the restoration of his sight by Sarapis (Diog. Laert. 5.76), but this proves nothing. They could have been written at any time between his arrival in Egypt about 307 and his death in disgrace under Philadelphus.

1 Wilcken, *UPZ* i. 79–82.

2 A prayer to Oserapis by the Hellenomemphite woman, Artemisia, dates from the mid fourth century B.C.: Wilcken, *UPZ* i. 97–104.

3 Arr. 3.1.4.

4 The Persians are said to have perpetrated every kind of sacrilege in the invasion (Diod. 16.51.2), and Ochus is said to have committed the supreme desecration of killing the Apis bull (Ael. *VH* 4.8, 6.8, Plut. *de Is. et Serap.* 11 (355 C). Cambyses may not have anticipated the atrocity (Olmstead, *History of the Persian Empire*, 89 f.), but Alexander would have read his Herodotus and taken note.

5 The equation of Zeus and Ammon had been made by the fifth century. Despite Tarn's indignant disclaimer (ii. 349) Herodotus 2.55 is conclusive corroboration, if corroboration is needed, of Pindar (*Pyth.* 4.16, F 36 (Snell)). An amazing example of syncretism is found in a late inscription from Cius in Bithynia (*CIG* 3724): 'I hail Osiris{…}he is Zeus Cronides, he is the mighty Ammon, the deathless king, and highly honoured as Sarapis.'

6 Cf. Roeder, *RE* IA. 2418 ff.

7 Arr. 7.25.2–6.

1 Plut. *Al.* 76.3 καὶ κατακείμενος ἐν τῷ λοντρῶνι τοῖς περὶ Νέαρχον ἐσχόλαζεν, ἀκροώμενος τὰ περὶ τὸν πλοῦν καὶ τὴν μεγάλην θάλατταν; Arr. 7.25.4 λούσασθαι καὶ λουσάμενον θῦσαι. Νεάρχῳ δὲ καὶ τοῖς ἄλλοιϑ ἡγεμόσι παραγγεῖλαι τὰ ἀμφὶ τὸν πλοῦν, ὅπως ἔσται ἔς τρίτην ἡμέραν.

2 Plut. *Al.* 76.5.

3 Arr. 7.26.2, Plut. *Al.* 76.9.

4 The archipresbyter Leo preserves a unique passage in which Alexander on his death-bed commends his empire and wife to Perdiccas, the unanimous choice of his generals. The Metz Epitome (100) and Ps.-Callisthenes (3.32.3) replace the incident with a lame doublet, an obvious piece of surgery to excise a passage embarrassingly favourable to Perdiccas. Cf. Merkelbach, *Die Quellen des{…}Alexanderromans*, pp. 131 ff., 230 f.

5 The donation of Egypt to Perdiccas occurs only in Ps.-Callisthenes (3.33.15). Here Ptolemy is confined to Libya, while Perdiccas has Egypt. The Metz Epitome (117) excises the donation to Perdiccas. Ps.-Callisthenes must represent the earliest version; after 321 such propaganda would have been pointless (Merkelbach, pp. 142 ff.).

6 Ps.-Call. 3.31.8. The parallel list in the Metz Epitome (97) is extremely corrupt, but clearly there are variants. The list of poisoners may have varied with the political climate.

7 Ael. *VH* 3.23 = *FGrH* 117 F 2a.

8 Athen. 10.434 B, Plut. *Q.C.* 1.6 (623 E) = *FGrH* 117 F 2 b and c.

1 ἔξεστι δὲ ἐκ τούτων ἐννοεῖν καὶ τοῦ λοιποῦ Χρόνου τὰ ὅμοια αὐτοὺς λέγοντας.

2 If we accept Aelian's apparent dating to the month of Dios, the record of drinking went back at least seven months. Gessner's emendation of the MS. reading δι' οὖμηνός το Δίου μηνός seems inescapable.

3 Tarn, *Alexander* ii. 41; cf. Aristobulus, *FGrH* 139 F 62.

4 Arr. 7.25.1.

5 For the career of Eumenes cf. Kaerst, *RE* vi. 1083 ff., H. D. Westlake, *Bull. John Rylands Library* 37 (1954), 309 ff.

6 Berve ii, p. 184 refers to 'den einwandfreien Krankenbericht der Ephemeriden, der eine Vergiftung als Todesursache ausschliesst'. That hits the nail squarely on the head!

1 Plut. *Al.* 77.5 οἱ δὲ πλεῖστοι τὸν λόγον ὅλως οἴονται πέπλασθαι τὸν περὶ φαρμακείας.

2 Curtius 10.10.18. Diod. 17.118.2 and Justin 12.13.10 make the same obvious point that Cassander was in a position to stifle broadcasting of the rumours in Macedonia.

3 E. Badian, *JHS* lxxxi (1961), 17 ff. (= Griffith, pp. 207 ff.), gives full details, but probably exaggerates the extent of the terror. In particular he seems to lay excessive stress on the arrivals of satraps at court, inferring that a summons to court meant danger for the man invited. The details hardly support the hypothesis. Stasanor we know arrived at court in Carmania with the doomed army commanders of Media (Arr. 6.27.3). However, Arrian says quite explicitly that Stasanor was sent back to his province before the departure for Pasargadae (6.29.1); if suspected, he was soon acquitted. According to the *Liber de Morte* he was one of the guests at Medius' banquet (Ps.-Call. 3.31.8, Metz Epitome 97), but this list of poisoners is patent propaganda and is certainly not reliable evidence for the actual composition of the banquet. Even if he was at Babylon in June 323, it might have been for a routine report or even to deliver a batch of ἐπίλονοι, as Berve suggests (ii. 362). The arrival of Peucestas, Philoxenus, and Menander was only a month or two before the king's death (Arr. 7.23.1). They were bringing a large and important consignment of reinforcements, and there is no evidence that Alexander intended to replace them as satraps. The fact that they were still at Babylon when Alexander died is hardly significant.

1 Plut. *Al.* 68.7, Arr. 7.4.2. Despite Badian's arguments (*CQ* N.S. viii [1958], 147 f.) I do not think Apollophanes was in this category. In a list of appointments at the Gedrosian capital of Pura Arrian says (6.27.1) that Apollophanes was deposed for neglect. However, Apollophanes was killed in a battle against the Oreitae and his death unimpeachably attested by Nearchus (Arr. *Ind.* 23.5). Badian believes that he was to have been the first scapegoat for the Gedrosian disaster, and that he was deposed before news of his death reached Pura (cf. Curt. 9.10.19). Then Alexander turned against other satraps of the area. However, Apollophanes can never have made a satisfactory scapegoat. Arrian (6.22.2) says that he was left midway on the desert journey and told to work in conjunction with Leonnatus. If there were recriminations to be made in that sector, one would expect Leonnatus to have been implicated too. However, the high honours accorded him prove that he was not (Arr. *Ind.* 42.9). On the other hand the obvious scapegoat for the disaster was Astaspes, satrap of Carmania, who certainly *was* deposed and executed at this point (Curt. 9.10.21–9). Now Arrian is completely unaware of Astaspes' fate, and it seems highly probable that Ptolemy made a slip and conflated Apollophanes and Astaspes (so Berve ii. 57, nr. 105), misled by the close proximity of the death of the one and the deposition of the other.

2 Arr. 7.4.2, Plut. *Al.* 68.3.

3 Cf. Berve ii. 215, Badian, *JHS* lxxxi (1961), 22.

4 Curt. 10.1.1–8, Arr. 6.27.4.

5 The use of πεζέταιροι as a title for the *phalanx* (Anaximenes, *FGrH* 72 F 4) implies that at some point the Macedonian foot was built up as a counterweight to the noble ἑταῖροι, a central core of the army loyal to the royal house. Similarly Philip's institution of a corps of royal pages bears far more resemblance to a permanent pool of hostages than to an officer training school (Arr. 4.13.1). The institution was developed by Alexander, who instituted a permanent corps of Asians. These 30,000 *Epigonoi* are succinctly described by Curtius as '*obsides simul{ ... }et milites*' (8.5.1).

6 Plut. *Al.* 9, Justin 9.7.3 ff., Satyrus *op.* Athen. 13.557.

7 Athen. 13.586 c, 595 A–E = *FGrH* 115 F 253–4.

1 Berve (ii, nr. 365) and Jacoby (*FGrH* ii D. 390) go too far in representing Theopompus as an official agent of Alexander in Chios, who sent regular reports to Asia. These letters are surely modelled on the sundry exhortations of Isocrates, interspersed with the vindictiveness to individuals so typical of Theopompus' writing. There is no reason to think that the denunciations of Harpalus were written before his flight.

2 Curt. 10.14, *saepe certe audita est vox Alexandri, Antipatrum regium affectare fastigium maioremque esse praefecti opibus ac titulo Spartanae victoriae inflatum, omnia a se data asserentem sibi.* cf. Justin 12.14.3.

3 Arr. 7.12.4.

4 So Berve ii. 50–1, G.T. Griffith, *PACA* viii (1965), 12 ff.

5 Diod. 18.4.1, Badian, *JHS* lxxxi (1961), 35–6.

6 Diod. 18.14.4–5, cf. Plut. *Eum.* 3.

7 Diod. 18.12.1.

8 He did not move until mid 322 after the death of Leonnatus, and when Antipater's fortunes were at their nadir (Diod. 18.16.4).

9 Arr. 7.8.3; 9.1, Curt. 10.2.12–19. Interestingly Craterus' troops were whittled down to 6,000 by the time he left for Europe (Diod. 18.16.4); it can only have been through desertions.

10 See above, n. 4.

11 Arr. 7.12.5.

1 Arr. 7.12.6, cf. Plut. *Al.* 39.11.

2 According to Livy 8.24.17 Olympias and her daughter Cleopatra received the bones of Alexander the Molossian, which had been sent to Epirus via Metapontum. The date of his death is roughly fixed by Aeschines (*Ctes.* 242), who mentions (in mid 330) a recent embassy to Cleopatra, consoling her on the death of her husband.

3 Ps.-Call. 3.31.1, Metz Epitome, 87. cf. Diod. 17.118.1, Justin 12.14.1–3.

4 Plut. *Al.* 74, Berve ii, nr. 414.

5 Phratapharnes, satrap of Hyrcania, sent a son to Carmania (Arr. 6.27.3), presumably to give a detailed report. Both his sons were selected for the élite mixed hipparchy (Arr. 7.6.5), maybe as hostages for their father's good behaviour.

6 Cassander's arrival at court cannot be dated precisely. Shortly before Alexander's death Plutarch speaks of him as newly arrived (ἀφῖκτο μὲν νεωστί); this is consistent with departure from Macedonia before Craterus' mission was published.

7 Curt. 10.10.15.

8 Cf. J. R. Hamilton, *CQ* N.S. iii (1953), 156–7.

9 Cf. Badian, *JHS* lxxxi (1961), 29 ff.

1 Note the apophthegm in Plutarch (*Al.* 49.15): οὐκ Οἰνιαδῶν ἔφη παῖδας ἀλλ' αὐτὸν ἐπιθήσειν δίκην Αἰτωλοῖς.

2 Justin 13.5.1–8; cf. Curt. 10.2.2.

3 Athen. 12.538 B = *FGrH* 126 F 5. Whatever the value of the rest of the information, the proposal by Gorgus is eminently reasonable. He was a friend of the Samians and honoured by them in a decree passed after the restoration, a decree which incidentally confirms his crowning of Alexander at Ecbatana (*SIG*³ 312).

4 Arr. 7.19.6 τὸ δ' ἀληθές, ὡς γέ μοι δοκεῖ, ἄπληστος ἦν τοῦ κτᾶσθαί τι ἀεὶ Ἀλέξανδρος. Despite Arrian's qualification the verdict was Aristobulus'. Strabo repeats the judgement in a passage explicitly taken from Aristobulus 16.1.11 (74.1), τὸ δ' ἀληθὲς ὀρεγόμενον πάντων εἶναι κύριον); cf. Jacoby, FGrH 139 F 56.

5 Diod. 18.4.4. The authenticity of these ὑπομνήματα has often been impugned, the most recent doubter being M.J. Fontana, *Le Lotte per la Successione di Alessandro Magno dal 323 al 315* (Palermo, 1960), p. 280. However, it seems certain that the relevant passage of Diodorus is from the same source as the rest of the opening chapters of book 18 – Hieronymus of Cardia (cf. Schachermeyr, *JÖAI* lxi (1954), 120–4 (= Griffith, pp. 324 ff.), Badian, *Harvard Studies* lxxii (1967), 184–9), and there is no valid reason to rule out as late fabrication any of the provisions quoted by Diodorus. Certainly Alexander's schemes of western conquest are credible enough. Justin 12.1.5 claims that he was jealous of his uncle, Alexander of Epirus, and if the latter's remark is historical that his nephew in Asia had merely raided a harem (Gell. *NA* 17.21.33, Curt. 8.1.37), it is quite possible that Alexander intended to overshadow his uncle's successes.

6 Cf. Badian, *Harvard Studies* lxxii (1967), 200 ff.

7 So Schachermeyr, *Alexander der Grosse*, n. 290.

1 Satyrus, *ap.* Athen. 13.557D, Plut. *Al.* 77.7, Diod. 18.2.2.

2 Cf. G.V. Sumner, *AUMLA* xv (1961), 30 f., endorsed by Badian, *Studies in Greek and Roman History*, p. 263.

3 Curtius 10.6.13 makes Ptolemy indignantly inveigh against an Asian king: 'Roxanes vel Barsinae filius, cuius nomen quoque Europam dicere pigebit'.

4 Cf. Momigliano, Filippo il Macedone, p. 29.

5 Diod. 17.16.2 (advice before the crossing into Asia), Plut. Al. 21.7 = FGrH 139 F 11 (advice to marry Barsine).

6 Curt. 10.6.18 haerebat inter cupiditatem pudoremque et, quo modestius, quod expectabat, appeteret, pervicacius oblaturos esse credebat.

7 Diod. 17.117.4; 18.2.4, Curt. 10.5.4, Justin 12.15.2, also the Liber de Morte (Metz Epitome, 112). The omission in Arrian's Anabasis is not significant; Ptolemy would not have wished to broadcast the fact that his rival had virtually been designated Alexander's successor.

8 Curt. 10.6.24–7.1. 10.6.2 is clear evidence that originally the debate was private; the disagreement before the army is superimposed (10.6.4 ff.). Compare Meleager's dramatic appeal to the infantry in Curtius (10.7.1 ff.) with the more sober account of Diodorus 18.2.3 and Justin 13.3.2, who make Meleager join a delegation to confront the troops and then side with the men he was intended to placate.

9 This was Perdiccas' proposal (Curt. 10.6.9), reinforced by Aristonous (10.6.16–18) and contested by Meleager (6.21 ff.). Peithon drafted the final compromise that Perdiccas and Leonnatus should be tutors of the future king, Craterus and Antipater jointly administer Europe. There may be some Perdiccan propaganda here, but one can hardly doubt that the initial proposal was for the succession of Alexander's unborn child. Justin gives a different account of the debate but the same conclusion (13.2.14). For discussion see Fontana, Le Lotte{...}, pp. 112 f.

1 Curt. 10.7.2 ff., Arr. Succ. 1.1, Diod. 18.2.2, Justin 13.3.

2 Cf. Berve ii, nr. 494. He had been a taxis leader throughout Alexander's reign ('niemals mit einem grösseren Kommando betraut'). Justin 13.3.2 makes his fellow officer Attalus an accomplice in the agitation; his importance, however, is much less.

3 Arr. Succ. F 1.2.

4 Curt. 10.8.8–23, Diod. 18.2.3–4, Arr. Succ. 1.3.

5 Curt. 10.9.10–21, Arr. Succ. 1.4, Diod. 18.4.7, Justin 13.4.8–9.

6 Curt. 10.10.9.

7 Cogently argued by Badian, Studies{...}, pp. 263 f.

8 SIG³ 311, p. 530, OGIS 8; cf. Schwahn, Klio xxiv (1931), 312 f.

9 Diod. 18.23.2; 29.1; 55.1.

10 Hesperia xxxvii (1968), 222 (cf. plate 66) Βασιλεῖς Φίλιππος [καὶ Ἀ]λ[εξαν]-δ[ρος]. Another Samothracian inscription from the reign of Lysimachus mentions a dedication of sacred land by οἱ βασιλεῖς Φί[λιππος] καὶ Ἀλέξανδρος (Hesperia vol. cit. 220 f.). This is unlikely to indicate a dedication by Philip II confirmed by Alexander.

11 A summing-up of earlier literature in Bengtson, Die Strategie in der hellenistischen Zeit, i. 64 f.; cf. Fontana, Le Lotte{...}, p. 145, Badian, Studies{...}, pp. 264 ff.

12 Schubert, Quellen zur Geschichte der Diadochenzeit, pp. 6 ff.

1 FGrH 76 T 8; cf. Schwartz, RE v. 1853 ff. (= GG, pp. 27 ff.).

2 FGrH 73.

3 GG iv². 2.308.

4 The discovery of the Vatican palimpsest (Arr. Succ. F 24–5 = FGrH 156 F 10) proved that Photius totally omitted large portions of the original.

5 Jacoby, RE viii. 1548; Fontana, Le Lotte{...}, pp. 273 ff.

6 The counter-arguments are basically those of Tarn, JHS xli (1921), 1 ff., which I find far from cogent. The basic props are the omission of Perdiccas' chiliarchy and the alleged Craterus doublet.

7 οἱ χαριέστατοι τῶν ἀνδρῶν (Diod. 18.2.4). This is a pretty certain reference to Eumenes (cf. Plut. Eum. 3), so the favourable bias in Diodorus is a fair indication of Hieronyman authorship.

8 Diod. 18.3.2.

9 Diod. 18.12.1.

10 Diod. 18.4.1 ff.; cf. Badian, Harvard Studies lxxii (1967), 202–3.

1 FGrH 155 F 1, 1–2; cf. Jacoby, FGrH ii D. 548 ff.

2 Arr. Succ. F 1.3.

3 *FGrH* 100 F 8.8 καὶ τὰ ἄλλα διέξεισι ἐν πολλοῖς, ὡϑ κ'ἂν τούτοις, Ἀρριάνῳ κατὰ τὸ πλεῖστον σύμφωνα γράφων.

4 *FGrH* 100 F 8.4.

5 Arr. *Succ.* F 1.1 τὰ δὲ ἐπέκεινα τῆϑ Θρᾴκης ὡς ἐπὶ ἰλλυρίους καὶ Τριβαλλοὺς καὶ αὐτὴ Μακεδονία καὶ ἡ Ἤπειροϑ ὡϑ ἐπὶ τὰ ὄρη τὰ Κεραύνια ἀνήκουσα καὶ οἱ Ελληνες σύμπαντες Κρατέρῳ καὶ Ἀντιπάτρῳ ἐνεμήθη.

6 *FGrH* 100 F 8.1 ἡ τῶν Μακεδόνων ἀρχὴ περιέστη...καὶ ἐς τοὺς ἀμφὶ Περδίκκαν, ἶ κρίσει τῶν Μακεδόνων ἐπετρόπευον αὐτοῖς τὴν ἀρχήν.

7 Fontana, pp. 144 f., even supposes two distinct regentships; Perdiccas had 'la tutela del nascituro', while Arrhidaeus with surprising far-sightedness demanded a guardian antagonistic to Perdiccas, so that Craterus was appointed; 'scelto a reppresentare e proteggere la parte più tradizionalista e conservatrice del suo popolo e, in questo senso, il regno di Arrideo'.

8 Jacoby, *FGrH* ii D. 558, explains away Κρατέρδω as a marginal note absorbed into the text by scribal error.

9 Curt. 10.7.9 – the abortive proposal of Peithon; the fictitious will of Alexander (Ps.-Call. 3.33.13) also appointed Craterus directly to Macedonia.

10 Photius' summary of the first five books ends with the defeat of Ariathes in late 322 (Arr. *Succ.* F 1.12).

1 Artabanus, murderer of Xerxes, is called both chiliarch (Plut. *Them.* 27.2) and ἀφηγούμενοϑ τϕων δορυφόρων (Diod. 11.69.1).

2 Nepos, *Conon* 3, Diod. 11.69.1.

3 Diod. 16.47.3, Hesych. s.v. ἀζαραπατεῖσοί παρὰ Περσαῖς εἰσαγγελεῖς. Cf. Marquardt, *Philologus* lv (1896), 227 f., P. J. Junge, *Klio* xxxiii (1940), 12 ff., esp. 32 ff. Junge's hypothesis (pp. 24–8) that the chiliarch (hazarapatiš) was head of the treasury and therefore of the royal chancellery is pure speculation and totally unconvincing.

4 Hdt. 3.34.30.

5 The only evidence that Tithraustes was chiliarch is given by Nepos (*Con.* 3.2), who erroneously attributes the fall of Tissaphernes to Conon's initiative (Barbieri, *Conone* [Rome, 1955], pp. 128 f.), but there is no reason to doubt that Tithraustes was Artaxerxes' chiliarch: the office can hardly be an invention.

6 *Hell. Ox.* 19.3 (Bartoletti) περιμείνας ὀλίγον χρόνον ἐν ταῖς Σάρδεσιν ἀνέβαινεν ὡς βασιλέα.

7 Diod. 18.48.5.

8 Plut. *Al.* 54 = *FGrH* 125 F 14a.

9 Plut. *Eum.* 1, τὴν Περδίκκον παραλαβεῖν (sc. Εὐμένης) (ἱππαρχίαν ὅτε Περδίκκας ἀποθανόντος Ἡφαιστίωνος εἰς τὴν ἐκείνου προῆλθε τάξιν: cf. Appian, *Syr.* 57.292.

10 Strasburger, *Ptolemaios und Alexander*, p. 47, Kornemann, *Ptolemaios*, p. 195.

11 Diod. 18.3.4; App. *Syr.* 57.292.

1 In the *Mithridates* (8.25) there is one of the very few citations of Hieronymus by name (*FGrH* 154 F 3), and elsewhere there is a close correlation between his narrative and that of Diodorus.

2 Bengtson, *Strategie*, i. 66.94 f.

3 Justin 13.4.5, castrorum et rerum (regum ?) cura Meleagro et Perdiccae adsignatur.

4 Schwahn, *Klio* xxiv (1931), 324 f., endorsed by Badian, *Studies*, p. 266.

5 Diod. 18.18.7, ὁ δ' Ἀντίπατρος...τὴν εἰς τὴν Ἀσίαν ἐπάνοδον συγκατεσκεύασεν.

6 Ps.-Call. 3.33.12–15, Metz Epitome, 117, cf. Merkelbach, p. 141.

7 The succession debate in Curtius may be tinged with Perdiccan propaganda. Peithon's motion proposes that Craterus and Antipater together administer Europe (10.7.9); Ptolemy is given a speech favouring satrapal independence and government by common consent (10.6.13–15).

1 Diod. 18.25.3, cf. Arr. *Succ.* F 1.26.

2 Arr. *Succ.* F 1.21 dated after the subjugation of Cappadocia by Diodorus 18.23.1: cf. J. Seibert, *Historische Beiträge zu den dynastischen Verbindungen, Historia Einzelschriften* x (1967), 13 ff.

3 Diod. 18.23.3, Arr. *Succ.* F 1.21 and 26, Justin 13.6.4–6. A dialogue on papyrus (*P. Berl.* 13045) contains a purported speech by Deinarchus claiming that Nicaea was betrothed by Alexander. This may be Antipater's reply to claims in hostile propaganda that Rhoxane was bequeathed to Perdiccas (Ps.-Call. 3.33.15, Metz Epitome, 118).

1 Diod. 18.23.2, ὁ δὲ Περδίκκας πρότερον μὲν ἦν κεκρικὼς κοινοπραγίαν καὶ διὰ τοῦτο τὴν μνηστείαν ἐπεποίητο μήπω τῶν κατ' αὐτὸν πραγμάτων βεβαίως ἐστερεωμένων, ὡς δὲ

παρέλαβε τάς τε βασιλικὰς δυνάμεις καὶ τὴν τῶν βασιλέων προστασίαν, μετέπεσε τοῖς λογισμοῖς.

2 Schwahn, *Klio* xxiv (1931), 329: 'Der Satz steht in einem längeren Abschnitt aus Diyllos über den Lamischen Krieg und die daran anschliessenden Ereignisse.' In fact the passage comes directly after the subjugation of Cappadocia in a self-contained excursus on the rival machinations of Perdiccas and Antigonus.

3 So Bengtson, *Strategie*, i. 73: 'Dieses Verhältnis zwischen den beiden Machthabern musste sich natürlich nach der Usurpation der προστασία τῶν βασιλέων durch Perdiccas verschieben'; Fontana, p. 153.

4 Badian, *Studies*, p. 265, argues that his control over the royal forces was not secure until Craterus' attitude was assured. The point of security is allegedly given in Diod. 18.4, but on this interpretation there is an amazingly short interval between the wooing of Antipater and the *volte face*. It may also be observed that Diodorus says nothing of *firm* control of the royal forces. For him Perdiccas' position is secure when he becomes guardian of the kings.

5 Diod. 19.55.3 ἣν Μακεδόνες δεδώκασι διὰ τὰς γεγενημένας ἐξ αὐτοῦ χρείαϑ Ἀλεξάνδρου ζῶντος.

6 Note Berve's summary (ii, nr. 700); 'unter Al. durch nichts hervorragend'.

9

ALEXANDER AND THE 'UNITY OF MANKIND'

Introduction

Several events in Alexander's reign involving non-Macedonians and Greeks have sometimes been cobbled together and viewed as something akin to a 'policy' of the fusion of races or brotherhood of mankind. Actions and events which have been singled out in particular are Alexander's integration of foreigners into his army and administration, his marriage to Roxanne of Bactria in 327, the attempt in 327 to introduce *proskynesis* (genuflection) at Bactra (see Sources 94 and 95),[1] the mass marriage in 324 at Susa (see Sources 96 and 97), at which Alexander and 91 of his court married Persian noble women (Alexander taking two wives) in a Persian ceremony which lasted for five days,[2] and the banquet of reconciliation and prayer for concord amongst the races (Arr. 7.11.9) after the mutiny at Opis in 324.[3]

Consequently, Alexander has been viewed as a philosophical idealist, striving to create a unity of mankind, and so even more worthy of being called 'Great'.[4] This view still materializes today (see, for example, the 2003 movie *Alexander* written and directed by Oliver Stone). However, there was no fusion of the races 'policy', and Alexander was always the pragmatist. Thus he rarely integrated foreigners into his army, and when he did so he kept them in their own, ethnic units. Also, when he used them in his administration it was for their local knowledge and linguistic expertise, and to act as liaisons of sorts between himself and the people to help promote Macedonian rule, for Macedonians and Greeks significantly always controlled the army and the treasury. Pragmatics rather than idealism influenced Alexander. That can certainly be seen in his marriage to Roxanne of Bactria, the daughter of one of his opponents, Oxyartes. Here he was taking a leaf out of his father's book with this political marriage to gain Oxyartes' support at the end of the Bactrian revolt and so ensure the passivity of Bactria and Sogdiana while he marched into India.

Alexander's attempt to adopt the Asian custom of *proskynesis* (a long-standing social act which involved subjects prostrating themselves before their king in an act of subservience) may be seen as a way of uniting his own men and foreigners in a common social protocol. However, given the religious connotations associated with the act, which he knew his men could not accept, it is more plausible to connect the attempt with his belief in his own divinity.[5]

Likewise, too much has been read into the mass wedding at Susa, for no Macedonian or Greek women were brought out from the mainland to marry Persian noblemen. Moreover, the marriages were forced onto his men (cf. Arr. 7.6.2), for after Alexander's death all but one of the men divorced their wives. Most likely is that Alexander could not afford these noblewomen to marry their own races and thus provide the potential for revolt, something mixed marriages with his own court might offset. As for the reconciliation banquet at Opis and prayer for harmony, it is important to note that in order to end the mutiny Alexander played on the hatred between the Macedonians and the Persians, and that it was the Macedonians who were seated next to him at the banquet in order to emphasize their racial superiority. That seating order clearly separated the conquerors from the subjects. Furthermore, we would also expect a prayer for future harmony after a mutiny and as a prelude to the upcoming invasion of Arabia (cf. Source 106).

Ancient sources

Proskynesis

94   Chares of Mytilene says that once at a banquet Alexander, after drinking, handed the cup to one of his friends, and he, on receiving it, rose up so as to face the household shrine, and when he had drunk, first made obeisance to Alexander, then kissed him, and then resumed his place upon the couch. As all the guests were doing this in turn, Callisthenes took the cup, the king not paying attention, but conversing with Hephaestion, and after he had drunk went towards the king to kiss him; but Demetrius, surnamed Pheido, cried: 'O King, do not accept his kiss, for he alone has not done thee obeisance.' So Alexander declined the kiss, at which Callisthenes exclaimed in a loud voice: 'Well, then, I'll go away the poorer by a kiss' (Chares, *FGrH* 125 F 14a = Plut. *Alex.* 54.4–6).

95   The following account has also been given: Alexander drank from a golden goblet the health of the circle of guests, and handed it first to those with whom he had concerted the ceremony of prostration. The first who drank from the goblet rose up and performed the act of prostration, and received a kiss from him. This ceremony proceeded from one to another in due order. But when the pledging of health came to the turn of Callisthenes, he rose up and drank from the goblet, and drew near, wishing to kiss the king without performing the act of prostration. Alexander happened then to be conversing with Hephaestion, and consequently did not observe whether Callisthenes performed the ceremony completely or not. But when Callisthenes was approaching to kiss him, Demetrius, son of Pythonax, one of the Companions, said that he was doing so without having prostrated himself. So the king would not permit him to kiss him; whereupon the philosopher said: 'I am going away only with the loss of a kiss' (Chares, *FGrH* 125 F 14b = Arr. 4.12.3–5).

The mass marriage

96   And Chares, in the tenth book of his *History of Alexander*, says: 'When he took Darius prisoner, he celebrated a marriage feast for himself and his companions,[6] having had ninety-two bedchambers prepared in the same place. There was a house built capable of containing a hundred couches; and in it every couch was adorned with wedding paraphernalia to the value of twenty minae, and was made of silver itself; but his own bed had golden feet. And he also invited to the banquet which he gave, all his own private friends, and those he arranged opposite to himself and the other bridegrooms; and his forces also belonging to the army and navy, and all the

ambassadors which were present, and all the other strangers who were staying at his court. And the apartment was furnished in the most costly and magnificent manner, with sumptuous garments and cloths, and beneath them were other cloths of purple, and scarlet, and gold. And, for the sake of solidity, pillars supported the tent, each twenty cubits long, plated all over with gold and silver, and inlaid with precious stones; and all around these were spread costly curtains embroidered with figures of animals, and with gold, having gold and silver curtain-rods. And the circumference of the court was four stades. And the banquet took place, beginning at the sound of a trumpet, at that marriage feast, and on other occasions whenever the king offered a solemn sacrifice, so that all the army knew it. And this marriage feast lasted five days. And a great number both of barbarians and Greeks brought contributions to it; and also some of the Indian tribes did so. And there were present some wonderful conjurors – Scymnus of Tarentum, and Philistides of Syracuse, and Heraclitus of Mitylene; after whom also Alexis of Tarentum, the rhapsodist, exhibited his skill. There came also harp-players, who played without singing – Cratinus of Methymne, and Aristonymus the Athenian, and Athenodorus the Teian. And Heraclitus the Tarentine played on the harp, accompanying himself with his voice, and so did Aristocrates the Theban. And of flute-players accompanied with song, there were present Dionysius of Heraclea, and Hyperbolus of Cyzicus. And of other flute-players there were the following, who first of all played the air called The Pythian, and afterwards played with the choruses – Timotheus, Phrynichus, Caphesias, Diophantus, and also Evius the Chalcidian. And from this time forward, those who were formerly called Dionysio-colaces, were called Alexandro-colaces, on account of the extravagant liberality of their presents, with which Alexander was pleased. And there were also tragedians who acted – Thessalus, and Athenodorus, and Aristocritus; and of comic actors there were Lycon, and Phormion, and Ariston. There was also Phasimelus the harp-player. And the crowns sent by the ambassadors and by other people amounted in value to fifteen thousand talents (Chares, *FGrH* 125 F 4 = Athen. 12.538b–539a).

97 In Susa also he celebrated both his own wedding and those of his companions. He himself married Barsine, the eldest daughter of Darius, and according to Aristobulus, besides her another, Parysatis, the youngest daughter of Ochus (Aristobulus, *FGrH* 139 F 52 = Arr. 7.4.4).

Modern works

In the following selections, W.W. Tarn, a lawyer by profession and a brilliant scholar of Alexander, puts forward the idea of a brotherhood of mankind 'policy' based largely on his interpretation of Plutarch's *On the Fortune or Virtue of Alexander*.[7] (The attack on Tarn's view began properly with E. Badian, in his classic article 'Alexander the Great and the Unity of Mankind' in 1958 – see additional reading – but Alexander and the unity of mankind is still a subject of discussion.) A.B. Bosworth, Emeritus Professor of Classics at the University of Western Australia, argues persuasively against such a notion and shows that Alexander's motives were anything but idealistic. E.N. Borza, Emeritus Professor of History at Pennsylvania State University, extends Bosworth's arguments by arguing that Alexander did not even favour Greeks in his administration (only Macedonians), but used Greeks only for cultural purposes at his court.

1   W.W. Tarn, *Alexander the Great* 1 (Cambridge University Press: 1948), Chap. II, 'The Conquest of the Far East', 'the Susa wedding', pp. 110–111, 'the mutiny at Opis', pp. 115–117, Chap. III, 'Personality, Policy and Aims', 'the policy of fusion', pp. 137–138 and 145–148.[8]

2   A.B. Bosworth, 'Alexander and the Iranians', *Journal of Hellenic Studies* 100 (Hellenic Society 1980), pp. 1–21.[9]

3   E.N. Borza, 'Ethnicity and Cultural Policy at Alexander's Court', *Ancient World* 22 (Arcs Publishers, Inc. 1991), pp. 21–25.[10]

Additional reading

E. Badian, 'Alexander the Great and the Unity of Mankind', *Historia* 7 (1958), pp. 425–444.

——, 'Alexander the Great and the Loneliness of Power', in E. Badian, *Studies in Greek and Roman History* (Oxford: 1964), pp. 192–205 (reprinted in Chapter 11).

H.C. Baldry, *The Unity of Mankind in Greek Thought* (Cambridge: 1965), pp. 113–140.

W.W. Tarn, 'Alexander the Great and the Unity of Mankind', *Proceedings of the Cambridge Philological Society* 19 (1933), pp. 123–166.

——, *Alexander the Great* 2 (Cambridge: 1948), pp. 434–449.

C.G. Thomas, 'Alexander the Great and the Unity of Mankind', *Classical Journal* 63 (1968), pp. 258–260.

R.A. Todd, 'W.W. Tarn and the Alexander Ideal', *The Historian* 27 (1964), pp. 48–55.

Ian Worthington, 'Alexander the Great, Nation-building, and the Creation and Maintenance of Empire', in V.D. Hanson (ed.), *Makers of Ancient Strategy: From the Persian Wars to the Fall of Rome* (Princeton: 2010), pp. 118–137 (reprinted in Chapter 6).

Notes

1   Arr. 4.10.5–7, Plut. *Alex.* 54.3–6, Curt. 8.5.9–12.
2   Arr. 7.4.1–8, Diod. 17.107.6, Plut. *Alex.* 70.3, Justin 12.10.9–10.
3   Arr. 7.8.1–12.3, Diod. 17.109.2–3, Plut. *Alex.* 71-.2–9, Curt. 10.2.3 ff., Justin 12.11.
4   On his justifying the epithet, see Chapter 12.
5   On which, see Chapter 10.
6   At Susa in 324.
7   On the sources, see Chapter 1.
8   © Cambridge University Press 1948. Reprinted with the permission of Cambridge University Press.
9   Reprinted with the permission of Council of the Society for the Promotion of Hellenic Studies.
10 Reprinted by permission of Arcs Publishers, Inc. and the author.

THE SUSA WEDDING

W. W. Tarn

At Susa too a great feast was held to celebrate the conquest of the Persian empire, at which Alexander and 80 of his officers married girls of the Iranian aristocracy, he and Hephaestion wedding Darius' daughters Barsine and Drypetis. It was an attempt to promote the fusion of Europe and Asia by intermarriage. Little came of it, for many of the bridegrooms were soon to die, and many others repudiated their Asiatic wives after Alexander's death; Seleucus, who married Spitamenes' daughter Apama, probably an Achaemenid on her mother's side, was an honourable and politic exception. At the same time 10,000 of the troops married their native concubines. Alexander undertook to pay the army's debts, and invited all debtors to inscribe their names. It is significant of the growing tension between him and his men that they at once suspected that this was merely a trick to discover those who had exceeded their pay; he thereon paid all comers in cash without asking names. But the tension grew from another cause. The governors of the new cities came bringing for enrolment in the army the 30,000 native youths who had received Macedonian training; this inflamed the discontent already aroused among the Macedonians by several of Alexander's acts, the enrolment of Asiatic cavalry in the Hipparchies and of Persian nobles in the *agemā*, and the Persian dress worn by himself and Peucestas. Alexander, they felt, was no longer their own king, but an Asiatic ruler.

THE MUTINY OF OPIS

W. W. Tarn

It was soon afterwards, at Opis, that the discontent in the army came to a head. Alexander was not trying to oust the Macedonians from their ancestral partnership with him, but they thought he was; he only wished to take it up into something larger, but they distrusted the changes entailed by a new world, and especially his Persian policy. The occasion was his proposal to send home with Craterus any veterans past service. The Macedonians took this to mean that he intended to transfer the seat of power from Macedonia to Asia, and the whole army except his Guard, the *agema* of the Hypaspists, broke into open mutiny; all demanded to go home, and told him to go and campaign with his father Ammon. Alexander's temper rose; after ordering his Guard to arrest the ringleaders, he passionately harangued the troops[1] and ended by dismissing the whole army from his service. 'And now, as you all want to go, go, every one of you, and tell them at home that you deserted your king who had led you from victory to victory across the world, and left him to the care of the strangers he had conquered; and no doubt your words will win you the praises of men and the blessing of heaven. Go.' Then, after shutting himself up for two days, he called the Persian leaders to him and began to form a Persian army, whose formations were to bear the old Macedonian names.[2] This broke down the Macedonians; they gathered before his quarters, crying that they would not go away till he had pity on them. He came out and stood before them, with tears running down his face; one began to say 'You have made Persians your kinsmen', and he broke in 'But I make you all my kinsmen.' The army burst into wild cheers; those who would kissed him; the reconciliation was complete. Those veterans who desired (10,000) were then sent home with large presents under Craterus' leadership.

But before they went, Alexander's reconciliation with the army had been followed by a greater reconciliation.[3] He made a vast banquet – traditionally there were 9,000 guests – to celebrate the conclusion of peace; at his own table there sat Macedonians and Persians, the two protagonists in the great war, together with representatives of every race in his Empire and also Greeks, who were part of his world though not under his rule. The feast ended, all at his table drew wine for the libation from a huge silver crater which had once belonged to Darius, the crater which Eratosthenes or his informant was to figure as a loving-cup of the nations, and the whole 9,000 made libation together at the sound of a trumpet, as was Macedonian custom, the libation being led by Greek seers and Iranian Magi. The libation led up to, and was followed by, Alexander's prayer, in which the ceremony culminated. A few words of summary, and a brief allusion, are all that have reached us; but he prayed for peace, and that Macedonians and Persians and all the peoples of his Empire might be alike partners in the commonwealth (i.e. not merely subjects), and that the peoples of the world he knew might live together in harmony and in unity of heart and mind – that *Homonoia* which for centuries the world was to long for but never to reach. He had previously said that all men were sons of one Father, and his prayer was the expression of his recorded belief that he had a mission from God to be the Reconciler of the World. Though none present could foresee it, that prayer was to be the crown of his career; he did not live to try to carry it out.

Notes

1   On the genuineness of the essential parts of this speech, notably the conclusion, see Appendix 15 [in Tarn].
2   There is nothing to show that such an army was ever formed.
3   This paragraph is a brief summary of App. 25, vi [of Tarn], to which I refer.

THE POLICY OF FUSION

W. W. Tarn

Next, Alexander's policy of the fusion of races. It was a great and courageous idea, which, as he planned it, failed. He might indeed fairly have supposed that his experiment in mixed marriages would be successful, for he only applied it to Asia and it only meant marriage between different branches of the white race. Greek blood had once been mixed with Anatolian with good results in Miletus and many other cities, as with Libyan (Berber) blood in Cyrene; Herodotus and Themistocles were half-breeds, while the intermarriage of Macedonian and Iranian was to produce that great organiser Antiochus I; but speaking broadly, the better-class Greeks and Macedonians now refused to cooperate.[1] And it is doubtful whether, even had he lived, he could have carried out his idea of a joint commonwealth; for his system of Iranian satraps had broken down before he died. Of eighteen appointed, two soon died, one retired, and two are not again heard of; but ten were either removed for incompetence or executed for murder of subjects or treason, and were replaced by Macedonians. The three who alone held office when Alexander died were doubtless good men; nevertheless Atropates certainly, and Oxyartes possibly,[2] ended by founding independent Iranian kingdoms, while from Phrataphernes' satrapy of Parthia-Hyrcania came later the main Iranian reaction. In fact, Alexander had come into conflict with the idea of nationality, which was exhibited, not merely in the national war fought by Sogdiana, but in the way in which, even during his lifetime, independent states like Cappadocia and Armenia under Iranian rulers arose along the undefined northern limits of his empire. But of course, owing to his death, his policy never had a fair trial. The Seleucid kings indeed, half Sogdian in blood, were a direct outcome of that policy, and they did carry out parts of it; they transferred Europeans to Asia, employed, though sparingly, Asiatics in high position, and produced a marvellous mixture of east and west. But it was not done on Alexander's lines or in his spirit; the Macedonian meant to be, and was, the dominant race. What Alexander did achieve was again done through the cities, both his own and those which he inspired Seleucus to found, and it was a great enough achievement; the cities radiated Greek culture throughout Asia till ultimately the bulk of the upper classes over considerable districts became partially hellenised, and Demetrius of Bactria led Greeks for a second time beyond the Hindu Kush, to succeed for a moment where Alexander had failed and rule northern India for a few years from Pātaliputra to Kathiawar. What Alexander did succeed in ultimately giving to parts of western Asia was not political equality with Greece, but community of culture.

[...]

The real impression that he left on the world was far different; for, whatever else he was, he was one of the supreme fertilising forces of history. He lifted the civilised world out of one groove and set it in another; he started a new epoch; nothing could again be as it had been. He greatly enlarged the bounds of knowledge and of human endeavour, and gave to Greek science and Greek civilisation a scope and an opportunity such as they had never yet possessed. Particularism was replaced by the idea of the 'inhabited world', the common possession of civilised men; trade and commerce were internationalised, and the 'inhabited world' bound together by a network both of new routes and cities, and of common interests. Greek culture, heretofore practically confined to Greeks, spread throughout that world; and for the use of its inhabitants, in place of the many dialects of Greece, there grew up the form of Greek known as the *koinē*, 'common speech'. The Greece that taught Rome was the Hellenistic world which Alexander made; the old Greece counted for little till modern scholars re-created Periclean Athens. So far as the modern world derives its civilisation from Greece, it largely owes it to Alexander that it had the opportunity. If he could not fuse races, he transcended the national State; and to transcend national States meant to transcend national cults; men came to feel after the unity which must lie beneath the various religions. Outwardly, this unity was ultimately satisfied in the official worship of the Roman Emperor, which derived from the worship of Alexander after his death; but beside this external form there grew up in men's hearts the longing for a true spiritual unity. And it was Alexander who created the medium in which the idea, when it came, was to spread. For it was due to him that Greek civilisation penetrated western Asia; and even if much of the actual work was done by his successors, he broke the path; without him they would not have been. Consequently, when at last Christianity showed the way to that spiritual unity after which men were feeling, there was ready to hand a medium for the new religion to spread in, the common Hellenistic civilisation of the 'inhabited world'; without that, the conquests made by Christianity might have been as slow and difficult as they became when the bounds of that common civilisation were overpassed.

But if the things he did were great, one thing he dreamt was greater. We may put it that he found the ideal State of Aristotle, and substituted the ideal State of Zeno. It was not merely that he overthrew the narrow restraints of the former, and, in place of limiting men by their opportunity, created opportunities adequate for men in a world where none need be a pauper and restrictions on population were meaningless. Aristotle's State had still cared nothing for humanity outside its own borders; the stranger must still be a serf or an enemy. Alexander changed all that. When he declared that all men were alike sons of one Father, and when at Opis he prayed that Macedonians and Persians might be partners in the commonwealth and that the peoples of his world might live in harmony and in unity of heart and mind,[3] he proclaimed for the first time the unity and brotherhood of mankind. Perhaps he gave no thought to the slave world – we do not know; but he, first of all men, was ready to transcend national differences, and to declare, as St Paul was to declare, that there was neither Greek nor barbarian. And the impulse of this mighty revelation was continued by men who did give some thought to the slave world; for Zeno, who treated his slave as himself, and Seneca, who called himself the fellow-slave of his slaves, would (though Alexander might not) have understood St Paul when he added 'there is neither bond nor free'. Before Alexander, men's dreams of the ideal state had still been based on class-rule and slavery; but after him comes Iambulus' great Sun-State, founded on brotherhood and the dignity of free labour. Above all, Alexander inspired Zeno's vision of a world in which all men should be members one of another, citizens of one State without distinction of race or institutions, subject only to and in harmony with the Common Law immanent in the Universe, and united in one social life not by compulsion but only by their own willing consent, or (as he put it) by Love. The splendour of this hopeless dream may remind us that not one but two of the great lines of social-political thought which until recently divided the world go back to Alexander of Macedon. For if, as many believe, there was a line of descent from his claim to divinity, through Roman Emperor and medieval Pope, to the great despotisms of yesterday, despotisms 'by the grace of God', there is certainly a line of descent from his prayer at Opis, through the Stoics and one portion of the Christian ideal, to that brotherhood of all men which was proclaimed, though only proclaimed, in the French Revolution. The torch Alexander lit for long only smouldered; perhaps it still only smoulders to-day; but it never has been, and never can be, quite put out.[4]

Notes

1   The attitude of the Greeks in Asia to mixed marriages is discussed, Tarn, *Bactria and India*, pp. 34–8.
2   A. de la Fuye, Revue *Numismatique*, 1910, pp. 281 sqq. (Now very doubtful; for a more probable suggestion of what happened to the Paropamisadae, see Tarn, J.H.S. LIX, 1939, p. 322, reviewing E. T. Newell, *The coinage of the Eastern Seleucid mints*.)
3   See App. 25, VI [in Tarn] and pp. 116–17 ante.
4   I have left the latter part of this paragraph substantially as written in 1926. Since then we have seen new and monstrous births, and are still moving in a world not realised; and I do not know how to rewrite it.

ALEXANDER AND THE IRANIANS*

A. B. Bosworth

The last two decades have seen a welcome erosion of traditional dogmas of Alexander scholarship, and a number of hallowed theories, raised on a cushion of metaphysical speculation above the mundane historical evidence, have succumbed to attacks based on rigorous logic and source analysis. The brotherhood of man as a vision of Alexander is dead, as is (one hopes) the idea that all Alexander sources can be divided into sheep and goats, the one based on extracts from the archives and the other mere rhetorical fantasy. One notable theory, however, still flourishes and has indeed been described as one of the few certainties among Alexander's aims.[1] This is the so-called policy of fusion. As so often, the idea and terminology go back to J. G. Droysen, who hailed Alexander's marriage to Rhoxane as a symbol of the fusion (*Verschmelzung*) of Europe and Asia, which (he claimed) the king recognised as the consequence of his victory. At Susa the fusion of east and west was complete and Alexander, as interpreted by Droysen, saw in that fusion the guarantee of the strength and stability of his empire.[2] Once enunciated, Droysen's formulation passed down the mainstream of German historiography, to Kaerst, Wilcken, Berve and Schachermeyr, and has penetrated to almost all arteries of Alexander scholarship.[3] Like the figure of Alexander himself the theory is flexible and capable of strange metamorphoses. In the hands of Tarn it developed into the idea of all subjects, Greek and barbarian, living together in unity and concord in a universal empire of peace.[4] The polar opposite is an essay of Helmut Berve, written in the heady days before the Second World War, in which he claimed that Alexander, with commendable respect for Aryan supremacy, planned a blending of the Macedonian and Persian peoples, so that the two racially related (!) *Herrenvölker* would lord it over the rest of the world empire.[5] On Berve's interpretation the policy had two stages. Alexander first recognised the merits of the Iranian peoples and placed them alongside the Macedonians in his court and army hierarchy. Next came the '*Blutvermischung*', the integration of the two peoples by marriage.[6]

Most scholars have tacitly accepted Berve's definition and take it as axiomatic that Alexander did recognise the merits of the Iranians and did try to integrate them with the Macedonians. The extent of the fusion is disputed, some confining it to the two aristocracies, but few have denied that Alexander had a definite policy. The loudest voice crying in the wilderness has been that of Franz Hampl.[7] Hampl has repeatedly emphasised the arbitrary and speculative nature of most discussions of the subject and the absence of concrete evidence in the ancient sources, and he categorically denies the existence of any policy of fusion. The protest is a valuable warning but in itself it is insufficient. The fact that there is no reliable ancient attestation of the policy of fusion does not prove that no such policy existed; it merely makes the case more complex. The attested actions of Alexander may still be explicable only on the assumption that he had some definite policy of integration. This is a viable hypothesis, but it must be tested rigorously. We need to examine precisely what the ancient sources say and not interpolate them with our own interpretations or wishful thinking; and above all the evidence needs to be treated in its historical context, not thrown together haphazardly to buttress some abstract concept which attracts us for sentimental reasons.

There are two passages in the sources that suggest that Alexander had some ideas of fusing together the Macedonians and Persians. Foremost comes the famous prayer of reconciliation after the Opis mutiny (late summer 324). According to Arrian Alexander held a sacrifice at which all participants, Macedonians, Persians and representatives of other nations, sat around Alexander while he and his entourage poured libations from the same vessel. The king made a prayer whose main burden was 'concord and community in empire for Macedonians and Persians' ὁμόνοιάν τε καὶ κοινωνίαν τῆς ἀρχῆς Μακεδόσι καὶ Πέρσαις).[8] The two concepts, concord and community, are tied together grammatically and contextually. The background of the prayer was mutiny, a mutiny caused in part at least by Macedonian resentment of Persians and crushed by Alexander turning towards his Persians and creating a new court and army structure composed totally of Persians.[9] The stratagem had been entirely successful and the Macedonians capitulated as soon as Alexander began his distribution of army commands to notable Persians. There was certainly Macedonian fear and resentment of the Persians around Alexander and the king played upon these emotions to destroy the mutiny. There was every reason under the circumstances for a ceremony of reconciliation and a prayer for concord. Concord is associated with community in empire, and there is no doubt that Arrian means the sharing of command in Alexander's empire.[10] The terminology is vague and imprecise, as so often with Arrian, but there is no reason to give the prayer a universal significance. Alexander may be referring to the satrapies of the empire which had been and were to continue to be governed both by Macedonians and Iranians.[11] There may even be a reference to the army commands recently conferred upon Persians and a covert threat that he would repeat his action if there were further trouble. The prayer and its context are primary evidence for bad blood between Macedonians and Iranians and Alexander's desire to use some at least of both races in the administration of the empire. They do not give any support for a general policy of fusion.[12]

Diodorus is more explicit. In the context of the notorious *hypomnemata*, the alleged last plans of Alexander presented to the Macedonian army by Perdiccas, came a proposal to synoecise cities and transplant populations from Europe to Asia 'to bring the continents to common unity and friendly kinship' by means of intermarriage and ties of community.[13] We have here two things, a proposal to found cities and transplant populations, and an interpretation of that proposal. The interpretation is unlikely to have been embodied in the original plans submitted by Perdiccas, and like the puerile note a few sentences later (that the Pyramids were accounted among the Seven Wonders) it is most probably a comment either by Diodorus or his source.[14] Now there is little or no evidence that Diodorus had a personal interest in Alexander as an apostle of international unity[15] and the overwhelming probability is that the comment comes from his immediate source, Hieronymus of Cardia.[16] Hieronymus was a contemporary of Alexander but his history was written towards the end of his prodigiously long life and covered events at least to 272.[17] His recollections of Alexander were now distant and his views of the king's motives perhaps affected by fifty years of experience and reflection. He may have considered that Alexander's shifts of population were designed to bring about greater community between races,[18] but nothing suggests that Alexander shared his views. What is more, the authenticity of the *hypomnemata* is a notorious crux. It is certainly possible that Perdiccas included fictitious proposals which he knew would antagonise the army in order to induce them to revoke the whole of Alexander's *acta*.[19] If so, those proposals would have been couched in the most provocative terms. There is, then, no certainty that even the original proposal to transplant populations emanates from Alexander, let alone the parenthetical comment. And the force of the comment is that Alexander envisaged a general spirit of unity among all his subjects, Greek and barbarian; it is not in any sense a plan to combine Macedonians and Persians as a joint ruling class. The only connection with the Opis prayer is the fact that the concept of ὁμόνοια occurs in both passages!

The next relevant observation comes from Eratosthenes, who observed that Alexander ignored advice to treat the Greeks as friends and barbarians as enemies, preferring to welcome all possible men of fair repute and be their benefactor.[20] On the surface Eratosthenes' comment has nothing to do with any policy of fusion: it is merely the just observation that Alexander was catholic in his benefactions and did not treat the conquered peoples with hostility. There is no hint here of a proposed union of races. But discussion has been unforgivably confused by the belief that Eratosthenes lies at the base of Plutarch's exposition in the first of his speeches *de Alexandri fortuna*. As is well known, this essay is the prime source for the view of Alexander as the reconciler of mankind. In a famous passage of rhetoric Plutarch tells of the rejection of Aristotle's advice to treat the Greeks ἡγεμονικῶς; Alexander blended all men together, mixing their lives, marriages and ways of life in a *krater* of friendship and making his only distinction between Greek and barbarian a man's virtue or vice.[21] After the recent analyses by Badian and Hamilton[22] there should be no question that the whole shaping of the passage is Plutarch's own, designed to show that Alexander achieved in fact the single polity which Zeno advocated. He may have drawn on Eratosthenes, but nothing suggests that the passage as a whole is an extract or summary. In particular there is no reason to believe that Eratosthenes used the metaphor of mixing.

There is still a tendency to argue that Eratosthenes described a policy of fusion. Two chapters later Plutarch explicitly cites him on the subject of Alexander's court dress, a mixture of Persian and Macedonian elements.[23] He goes on to explain that the object was to win the respect of the subject peoples and further the aim of a single law and polity for all mankind. But there is nothing to suggest that Plutarch's interpretation of the mixed dress comes from Eratosthenes. The whole passage is designed to buttress the paradoxical thesis that Alexander was a philosopher in arms and seeking the reconciliation of mankind which was merely preached as an ideal by conventional philosophers. The concrete examples of the Susa marriages and the adoption of mixed court dress are chosen as examples of his achievement of κοινωνία and the choice is Plutarch's own. The reference to Eratosthenes seems thrown in as a passing remark, just as in chap. 3 he interlaces his exposition with casual references to Onesicritus, Aristobulus, Anaximenes and Duris. Eratosthenes, we may be sure, described Alexander's court dress, but we cannot assume that he gave it an ecumenical significance. What matters is Plutarch's mode of procedure. His task is to prove the thesis that Alexander was a philosopher in practice[24] and both the examples and their rhetorical embellishment are carefully geared to that end. His general view may derive ultimately from Onesicritus' story of Alexander and the gymnosophists,[25] but, if so, the original is totally transformed. Onesicritus' view is of an Alexander who still has sympathy for the search for wisdom even in the cares of empire; but for Plutarch Alexander not only sympathises with philosophical theories, he embodies and perfects them in his actions. In the same way the interpretation he gives to the Susa marriages and the assumption of court dress need owe nothing to previous writers. Once he had propounded his theme he was limited in his choice of material and his interpretation was predetermined. Other rhetoricians with other theses to prove would adapt their viewpoint accordingly. One need only compare Aelius Aristides' *Roman Oration*. Here Rome is exalted as Plutarch exalts Alexander. She is the civilising power, breaking down the old distinction of Hellene and barbarian by the conferment of citizenship upon all deserving men. Against that background Alexander can only be presented as a meteoric failure, who acquired empire but had no time to establish a permanent system of law, taxation and civil administration.[26] If Rome was the great reconciler, Alexander could only appear as an ephemeral conqueror. In these pieces of epideictic rhetoric it is the thesis adopted for debate which determines both the choice of material and the interpretation put upon it,[27] and it is a possibility, if no more, that the whole topic of racial fusion in Alexander's reign was a creation of the rhetorical schools of the early Empire. In Plutarch himself there is only one reference in the *Life of Alexander* (47.3) to Alexander's efforts to achieve κοινωνία and ἀνάκρασις, and the examples he chooses are different from those in the earlier speech – the creation of the *Epigoni* and the Marriage to Rhoxane. And there is virtually no reference to racial fusion outside Plutarch. Only Curtius places in Alexander's mouth a speech commemorating the Susa marriages as a device to remove all distinction between victor and vanquished.[28] This speech was allegedly delivered to the Iranian soldiers during the Opis mutiny, and once again the circumstances determine the content of the speech. The subject matter, as often in Curtius, may be derived from his immediate source; but the speech is composed in generalities with none of the interesting points of authentic detail found in other Curtian speeches, and it seems to me that the observations on the fusion of Macedonian and Iranian tradition are most likely to be embellishments by Curtius himself. Even so, it is interesting that the idea of fusion occurred to Curtius as a natural theme for a speech of Alexander during the Opis crisis. The *topos* of fusion existed in the early empire and there were regular *exempla* – court dress, dynastic marriages, and the assimilation of Iranians in the national army. Not surprisingly these are the areas in which modern discussion of the 'policy of fusion' has tended to centre – and there is the possibility that the rhetoricians of the early empire and modern scholarship are correct in their interpretation. But forensic eloquence is no substitute for analytic evaluation of the evidence, and the various *exempla* need to be assessed both in their historical detail and historical context.

We may begin with the assumption of Persian court ceremonial. This is most fully described by the vulgate sources,[29] especially Diodorus who mentions five aspects. Alexander introduced court chamberlains of Asiatic stock (ῥαβδοῦχοι Ἀσιαγενεῖς) and a bodyguard of distinguished nobles including Darius' brother Oxyathres. Secondly he adopted some aspects of Persian court dress – the diadem, the white-striped tunic and the girdle.[30] Next he distributed scarlet robes and Persian harness to his companions, and finally took over Darius' harem of 360 concubines. Curtius has much the same detail but adds that Alexander used Darius' ring for his correspondence in Asia. The sources assess these moves variously. The vulgate sources unanimously regard them as a decline towards barbarian τρυφή as indeed does the normally uncritical Arrian (later he suggests on his own initiative that the adoption of mixed dress was a σόφισμα to win over the barbarians).[31] Plutarch in his life represents the mixed dress as either an adaptation to native custom or anticipation of the introduction of *proskynesis*. It is only in the *de Alexandri fortuna* that he represents it as a means to bring about friendship between victor and vanquished.[32] There is no indication that any of the ancient sources had direct information about Alexander's motives for the innovation. It should be emphasised that the adoption of Persian court protocol was fairly extensive, not confined to Alexander's choice of a mixed court dress. On the one hand he used Persians in ceremonial positions, but he also issued his ἑταῖροι with the traditional purple robes of the Achaemenid courtiers.[33] The new king had his *purpurati*, but they were Macedonians. As yet there was no attempt to integrate the two nobilities. Diodorus implies quite clearly that they formed separate groups. The Persians might be given posts as chamberlains and selected nobles formed into a corps of δορυφόροι, but Alexander showed clearly by his distribution of purple that the courtiers of the new Great King were his Macedonians.[34] In his dress and court ceremonial Alexander adopted Achaemenid practices but he kept Persians and Macedonians distinct and the Macedonians were in a privileged position.

The date of the innovation is also important. Plutarch states explicitly that Alexander first assumed mixed dress during the rest period in Parthia after the Hyrcanian expedition, that is, in autumn 330.[35] It is precisely at this point that the vulgate sources place the episode, and we cannot doubt the accuracy of the chronology.[36] Now Alexander's claims to be the legitimate king of the Persian empire go back at least to the Marathus correspondence of early 332, when he demanded that Darius acknowledge him as overlord. After Gaugamela he was solemnly pronounced King of Asia and furthered his claims by solemnly occupying the throne of Darius in Susa.[37] It is possible (though it cannot be proved) that Alexander was never formally consecrated in Pasargadae, and he seems never to have used the title 'King of Kings' in his dealings with the Greek world.[38] But his claims to be the legitimate king of the Persian empire were absolute. Yet, even so, Alexander did not adopt Achaemenid court protocol until at least six weeks after the death of Darius. What was the importance of the period in Parthia? The answer is that Alexander now had a rival. It was precisely at the time that he returned to Parthia that Alexander learned that Bessus had declared himself Darius' successor, assuming the jealously guarded royal prerogative, the *kitaris* or upright tiara, and also the regnal name Artaxerxes.[39] The news, according to Arrian, reached Alexander on his return to Parthia and the vulgate sources place Bessus' usurpation in the context of Alexander's new court protocol. Now the threat from Bessus should not be underestimated. He was related by blood to Darius[40] and could be seen by some as his legitimate successor. He also commanded the resources of Bactria and Sogdiana, whose cavalry had retired practically undefeated from the field of Gaugamela. It was also a period at which Alexander's military resources were at a low ebb. The Greek allied troops had been demobilised from Ecbatana, probably at the news of Darius' death.[41] More seriously Alexander had left behind 6,000 of his phalanx troops at the Median border for the escort of his vast bullion train, and they were to remain detached from his main force until he entered Arachosia in early 329.[42] He had also transferred his Thracian troops and a large body of mercenaries for the garrison of Media.[43] Alexander was caught with a greatly reduced army and he suffered for it. Satibarzanes, once a regicide and Alexander's first governor of Areia, immediately revolted and forced Alexander to return from his march on Bactria.[44] His intervention brought only temporary relief. No sooner had he moved south to Drangiana and Arachosia than Satibarzanes returned with reinforcements from Bessus, and his uprising was not crushed until the summer of 329.[45] At the same time Bessus' forces invaded Parthia and tried to establish a certain Brazane as satrap.[46] The disaffection was widespread and it lasted almost a year. It was late 329 before Bessus was captured and the last rebels were brought from Parthia and Arcia to meet the judgement of Alexander. There had been almost a year of challenge and insurrection, and it is difficult to believe that Alexander did not foresee trouble when he first heard of Bessus' usurpation.

The adoption of court protocol had an obvious propaganda value in these circumstances. Alexander demonstrated that he was genuinely King of Kings, not a mere foreign usurper, and the bodyguard of noble Persians was crucial to his claim. At his court in a position of high honour was none other than Oxyathres, brother of the late king. Not only was Alexander the self-proclaimed successor to Darius, but Darius' brother recognised the claim and supported Alexander's court ceremonial. This had been one of Alexander's assertions as early as 332, when he boasted that the Persians in his encourage followed him out of free choice.[47] At the same time Alexander adopted some items of Persian court dress, not the more obtrusive regalia (the tiara, and the purple trousers and long-sleeved *kandys*) but the diadem, the royal tunic and girdle, which he wore with the broad-brimmed Macedonian hat (*kausia*) and the Macedonian cloak.

Even this caused serious discontent among the Macedonian army – and Macedonian resistance to things oriental is one of the persistent factors of Alexander's reign. All sources stress the hostility to Alexander's adoption of mixed dress and it is prominent in the list of grievances which led to the Opis mutiny in 324.[48] The cleft widened among Alexander's officers, and the disagreements between Craterus and Hephaestion were notorious; Craterus, we are told, steadfastly adhered to Macedonian tradition.[49] Now the popularity of Craterus is one of the best-attested facts of the period after Alexander's death. His short marriage to Phila made the lady a desirable bride for Demetrius.[50] So strong was the devotion of the phalangites that Eumenes in 321 went to extraordinary lengths to conceal the fact that Craterus led the opposing army, in the belief that no Macedonian would fight against him.[51] The reason Plutarch gives (excerpting Hieronymus) is that Craterus often incurred Alexander's hatred by opposing his inclination to Persian excess and protecting ancestral customs from erosion.[52] Now it is notable that in the latter years of Alexander's reign Craterus was sent repeatedly on lengthy missions away from court, almost assuming the mantle of Parmenion. In particular he led the army division of Macedonian veterans first from India to Carmania in 325/4 and then from Opis to the coast.[53] The veterans were the men most closely bound to him but his popularity was universal and the reason was his championship of ancestral custom. Macedonian kings were said to rule by custom rather than force (οὐδὲ βίᾳ ἀλλὰ νόμῳ)[54] and the sight of a Heraclid and Argead in the trappings of the Great King, the paradigm of despotism, must have been deeply shocking. All the more so since the march from Babylon, which had been a triumphal progress, marked by the sacking of Persepolis and the burning of the palace and finally the ignominious death of the last Achaemenid at the hands of his subjects. Now the victor was assuming the protocol of the vanquished, acting the part of Great King and declaring his intentions of remaining as lord of Asia – a matter of weeks after his troops had come near mutiny in their desire to end the campaign and return home.[55]

The autumn of 330 was a time of crisis when Alexander was under strong and conflicting pressures. On the one hand the challenge from Bessus and his temporary shortage of troops forced him to propaganda, demonstrating to his subjects that he was not merely a foreign conqueror but the true Great King, supported by the old nobility of Darius. On the other he could not antagonise his Macedonians by too outrageous a breach of custom. The mixed dress was a compromise, taking on the very minimum of Persian attire compatible with his pretentions: and at the same time Alexander's Macedonian companions were given the purple robes of courtiers. This involved them in some of the odium of breach of custom and at the same time marked them out as the friends and satraps of the Great King. It was a limited experiment, and Diodorus is probably right that Alexander used the new ceremonial fairly sparingly.[56] We hear little of it in the years after 330. The Persian ushers figure among Cleitus' complaints at Maracanda, but only in Plutarch's version and then only as a peripheral attack.[57] The complaints re-emerge in Curtius' speeches on the occasion of the Pages' Conspiracy (327). They are raised briefly by Hermolaus and answered by Alexander.[58] The material may come from Curtius' sources, as do several details in these speeches, but the formulation is vague and consistent with the limited experiment implied by Diodorus. Polyaenus also indicates that Alexander reserved his Persian ceremonial receptions of his barbarian subjects during the campaigns in Bactria, Hyrcania and India,[59] but, as we shall see, his information is garbled to some extent and mostly refers to the last years of the reign. Nothing, however, contradicts the pattern of the evidence, which suggests that Alexander's first introduction of Persian ceremonial was a limited gesture, designed to capture the allegiance of his barbarian subjects at a time of crisis.

The court ceremonial was far more obtrusive after the return from India in 325/4. Alexander's court dress figured prominently in the complaints made by his Macedonian troops before the Opis mutiny, and, far from confining it to his appearances before barbarian subjects, he now wore it every day, the Macedonian cloak with the Persian white-striped tunic and the Macedonian *kausia* with the Persian diadem. The source admittedly is Ephippus of Olynthus, who was markedly hostile to Alexander, but there is no reason to doubt what he says.[60] In any case it is not the day-to-day costume of the king that he is out to pillory but the outrageous charades that he staged at banquets, dressing as Ammon, Hermes, Heracles and even Artemis. Ephippus' evidence moreover fits in well with what is otherwise known of the extravagance of Alexander's court during his last year. There is a famous description, deriving from the third century author Phylarchus, which deals with the day-to-day splendour of Alexander's court. Three versions survive (in Athenaeus, Aelian and Polyaenus) and they are complementary.[61] All these sources indicate that the court scene described was regular in Alexander's later days, but it is clear that the description refers primarily to the five-day period of the Susa marriages. The vast tent with its 100 couches and 50 golden pillars corresponds to the description of the Susa marriage hall provided by Alexander's chamberlain, Chares of Mytilene,[62] and it is hard to see how such a mammoth structure could have accompanied Alexander on all his travels. Similarly Polyaenus refers to a group of 500 dignitaries from Susa who formed a group outside the tent[63] and there is no reason why such a group should have been present when the court was not at Susa. The description, then, refers to a limited period, but the arrangements described are interesting. The court was arranged in concentric circles around Alexander and his σωματοφύλακες, that is, the eight supreme marshals of the Macedonian nobility. The first circle comprised 500 Macedonian *argyraspides*, selected for their physique; next came 1,000 archers in multi-coloured costumes, and on the outer circle of the tent 500 Persian *melophoroi*, the old infantry guard of the Achaemenid court with the distinctive golden apples on their spear butts. Alexander now had two royal guards, one the traditional Macedonian *agema* of hypaspists (the equation with *argyraspides* is certain)[64] and the other the traditional Achaemenid guard, but the two forces were kept distinct – the Macedonians closest to the king and the Persians separated by a girdle of archers. The division was continued outside the tent where the *agema* of elephants was stationed together with 1,000 Macedonians in Macedonian dress and in the final outer circle 10,000 Persians in Persian costume and scimitars. This was a brilliant display of Persian and Macedonian ceremonial, but the two races were kept rigidly separated. There was no attempt at integration – or even of '*Gleichstellung*', for the Macedonians were invariably closer to the king. Again we have no reason to doubt the main details of this description. The arrangement with its concentric circles was clearly imitated in Peucestas' great state banquet at Persepolis in 317 B.C., only here it was the closeness to Philip and Alexander which was emphasised by the division and at the centre Persian dignitaries occupied couches alongside Macedonians.[65]

Some degree of integration had taken place by the end of the reign. After the great mutiny of 324 Alexander introduced 1,000 Persians into the court guard of hypaspists. Both Diodorus and Justin agree on the fact but differ over whether it came after or during the mutiny.[66] Either it was part of Alexander's moves to bring his Macedonians to heel or it was a consequence of the mutiny, a permanent reminder of his threat to recruit his guard from Persians alone. But even so there is no evidence that the two races were intermingled in the guard and some that they were not. The panels on Alexander's sarcophagus portrayed the elaborate progress of the king in the last part of his life. Alexander rode in a chariot, preceded by an advance guard and surrounded by his regular court guard. This guard was divided into two separate bodies, one Macedonian armed in Macedonian style and the other Persian *melophoroi*.[67] Now the two races stood side by side, but they were brigaded in separate and identifiable corps. There was no attempt to integrate them into a unified body; if anything, it looks like deliberate design to balance one against the other.

It is clear that Alexander's court had become much more pretentious in the last two years of his life. The mixed dress was a more permanent feature and there was an increasing use of Persian *melophoroi* as court guards. The pomp and circumstance fits well the increasing megalomania of Alexander's last years which, as is well known, rose to a climax after the death of Hephaestion.[68] The increase in Persian ceremonial was doubtless caused by the fact that in 325/4 Alexander was travelling consistently between the old Achaemenid capitals (Persepolis, Susa, Ecbatana and Babylon) and needed to display himself to his oriental subjects as the new Great King. What is more, his absence in India between 327 and 325 had brought renewed insubordination and insurrection. The satraps of Carmania, Susiana and Paraetacene were executed when Alexander returned to the west and replaced by Macedonians.[69] More seriously, when he reached Persia proper he discovered that Orxines, apparently a lineal descendant of Cyrus the Great who had commanded the Persian contingent at Gaugamela, had established himself as satrap without any authorisation by Alexander.[70] There had also been trouble in the inner satrapies, for Craterus needed to arrest an insurgent, Ordanes, during his progress through southern Iran; and in Media a certain Baryaxes had assumed the upright tiara and laid claim to the throne of the Medes and Persians.[71] Alexander must have felt that there was widespread reluctance among his Iranian subjects to accept his regal authority,[72] and his parade of all the magnificence of the Achaemenid court including the old bodyguard of *melophoroi* is perfectly understandable. But while Alexander increased the Persian complement in his immediate entourage he appears to have reduced their political influence away from court. The end of the reign saw only three Iranians governing satrapies – Alexander's own fatherin-law in distant Parapamisadae, the impeccably loyal Phrataphernes in Parthia/ Hyrcania, and Atropates in Media, the satrapy with the most formidable garrison of Hellenic troops. There are many aspects to Alexander's behaviour. We may plausibly argue a desire to flaunt ostentatiously the splendour of his court, to impress his Iranian subjects with his military power and legitimacy as Great King; and there are signs that he used his promotion of Iranians to crush discontent among his Macedonian army. What we cannot as yet assume is any serious policy of assimilating and fusing the two races. The reverse seems the case.

We must now turn to the theme of mixed marriage, which was the original inspiration for Droysen's idea of 'Verschmelzungspolitik'. For almost the first ten years of his reign Alexander avoided marriage with remarkable success.[73] After Issus the majority of the Persian royal ladies were in his power. Alexander scrupulously cultivated the Queen Mother, Sisygambis as his 'Mother' and promised dowries to Darius' daughters.[74] Taking over Darius' functions as son and father he buttressed his claims to be the genuine King of Asia. But he stopped short of actual marriage, contenting himself with a liaison with Barsine, the daughter of Artabazus and descendant of Artaxerxes II.

This liaison was protracted and from it came a son, Heracles, born in 327,[75] but there was no question of marriage until the last days of Alexander's campaign in Bactria/ Sogdiana. Then came his meeting with Rhoxane and almost immediate marriage. The circumstances whereby Rhoxane came into his hands cannot be elucidated here, for they involve one of the most intractable clashes of authority between Arrian and the vulgate tradition,[76] but fortunately there is unanimity about the date of the wedding (spring 327) and equal unanimity that it was a love match. There is, however, no suggestion of a policy of fusion. Curtius merely accredits him with a statement that it was conducive to the stability of the empire that Persians and Macedonians were joined in marriage; the arrogance of the victors and shame of the vanquished would both be reduced.[77] This is a far cry from the symbolic union of races which many have seen in the marriage.

There is, however, a point to be stressed. Alexander married Rhoxane whereas he had only formed a liaison with Barsine. If all that was at issue was physical attraction, there was no reason for a formal marriage, unless we believe that Alexander's chivalry had improved since Issus. There were undoubtedly political reasons as well. Rhoxane married Alexander in spring 327 on the eve of his march into India. The previous two years had seen unremitting warfare caused by repeated insurrections inside Bactria/ Sogdiana and invasions from the Saka nomads of the steppes. Alexander's response had been increasingly savage repression. During the first stage of the uprising, summer 329, his orders included the massacre of all male defenders of conquered cities and the enslavement of women and children.[78] Later we hear a dark story of the crucifixion of defenders who actually capitulated[79] and the index of Diodorus hints at wholesale massacre.[80] At the same time Alexander founded a network of military settlements with a nucleus of Greek mercenaries and discharged Macedonian veterans together with settlers from the barbarian hinterland.[81] The relationship between Greek and barbarian is hard to elicit in this instance, but both Curtius and Justin suggest that the barbarians involved in the foundation of Alexandria Eschate were survivors from the recently conquered cities, especially Cyropolis.[82] In that case they can hardly have acted in any other role than that of native serfs.[83] Curtius adds that the survivors from the rock of

Sogdiana were distributed to the colonists of the new foundations, as additional slaves.[84] Some of the barbarians may have participated as volunteers on a more privileged basis, but the Greek settlers certainly formed a governing élite and their numbers were such that they could keep their barbarian subjects under military control. Outside the colonies the principal fortresses were occupied by Greco-Macedonian garrisons[85] and both colonies and fortresses had commandants directly imposed by Alexander. Finally the satrapy of Bactria/Sogdiana was in the overall control of a Macedonian, Amyntas son of Nicolaus.[86] In no other satrapy of the east was Macedonian military strength so firmly entrenched in the permanent establishment. Though there remained small pockets of independence such as the districts of Sisimithres and Chorienes,[87] Hellenic military settlements dominated the bulk of the countryside and the hierarchy was exclusively Greco-Macdonian.

The marriage to Rhoxane marks the final act of the settlement, and Curtius may be justified in viewing it as an act of conciliation after two years of warfare and devastation. But there is another aspect. The taking of a bride from the Iranian nobility of Bactria underlined Alexander's claims to be the legitimate lord of the area. In 336 he had had a painful object lesson in his wooing of the daughter of Pixodarus of Caria and the result of that episode had been the demonstration that with the princess went the satrapy.[88] He himself had taken care to venerate the elderly Hecatomnid princess Ada as 'Mother' to support his claims to Caria.[89] It was natural that after demonstrating his military supremacy to the Bactrians and Sogdians he married one of their princesses, cementing his rule by the wedding. There is a tradition moreover that Alexander also persuaded some of his friends to marry Bactrian ladies.[90] If it is true (and there is no contrary evidence), his fellow bridegrooms may well have been the satrap and garrison commanders left behind after the march on India. The new lords of the region would now have native wives.

Finally we come to the palladium of Alexander's alleged policy of fusion – the mass marriage at Susa at which Alexander and 91 of his Companions took Iranian brides. The weddings were celebrated with the utmost splendour in the Iranian mode[91] and Alexander commemorated the event by distributing gifts to Macedonian soldiers who had taken native wives, to the number of 10,000.[92] Without doubt this was a ceremony of unparalleled pomp with important political implications, but the sources leave us totally uninformed of those implications. In the speech *de Alexandri fortuna* Plutarch represents the marriage as a means of uniting the two imperial peoples, as does Curtius in the speech he attributes to Alexander;[93] but, as we have seen, both statements reflect the rhetorical interpretations of the first century A.D. rather than any authentic tradition from the time of Alexander. But if we look at the recorded facts, one feature stands out starkly—so starkly that it is incredible that it was first noted by Hampl in 1954.[94] The marriages were totally one-sided. Persian wives were given to Macedonian husbands, but there is no instance of the reverse relationship.

Admittedly Alexander's court was not well endowed with noble ladies of Greek or Macedonian extraction, but, if his aim was really to place the two imperial races on an equal footing, it would have been relatively easy for him to import the necessary brides from mainland Greece and delay the ceremony until they arrived. In fact there is nothing attested except Persian women married to Greco-Macedonian men.[95] The names as recorded are striking. Alexander and Hephaestion both married daughters of Darius, Craterus a daughter of Darius' brother, Oxyathres. The other wives whose names are recorded came from prominent satrapal families – daughters of Artabazus, Atropates of Media, and even Spitamenes, the leader of the insurgent Sogdians during 329 and 328.[96] This was an integration of sorts, but its effect was to mark out Alexander's Companions as the new rulers of the Persian Empire. They already had the scarlet robes of Persian courtiers; now they were married into the most prominent satrapal families. Nothing could have made it clearer that Alexander intended his Macedonians to rule with him as the new lords of the conquered empire.

It is also debatable how far Alexander intended his Macedonians to be assimilated into Persian ways. The traditional view is that Alexander wished the Macedonian nobles to adapt themselves to Persian customs but was frustrated by the Macedonians' tenacious adherence to their ancestral tradition. This theory rests primarily upon Arrian's account of Peucestas' installation as satrap of Persis in early 324. As soon as he was appointed he affected Median dress and became the only Macedonian to do so and learn the Persian language. Alexander commended him for his actions and he became popular with his Persian subjects, correspondingly unpopular with the mutinous Macedonian rank-and-file.[97] Peucestas' adoption of Persian customs is an unchallengeable fact, but it remains to be seen whether his behaviour was unique. In the first place he was not the only person in Alexander's entourage to learn an oriental language. We are told explicitly that Laomedon of Mytilene (brother of Erigyius) was a bilingual, or at least could understand Semitic script, and Eumenes could concoct a letter in Aramaic, the *lingua franca* of the eastern world.[98] If Arrian's credit be retained, we must assume either that Peucestas was the only foreigner to learn Persian (as opposed to Aramaic) or that he excluded the Greeks and referred only to true Macedonians. But Diodorus gives another perspective when he explains Peucestas' popularity with his subjects in 317 B.C. Alexander, so it was said, made a concession. Only Peucestas was *allowed* to wear Persian dress, so that the favour of the Persians could be secured.[99] If we accept the text as it stands (and nothing in Arrian contradicts it) we must conclude that as a general rule Macedonian nobles were not permitted to assume the full Persian dress.[100] The satrap of Persis was the one exception Doubtless Alexander had laid to heart the lesson of Orxines' usurpation and concluded that in Persis his satrap had to conform and be seen to conform to the local *mores*. And in the case of Peucestas there was no reason to suspect his personal loyalty; he had saved the king in the Malli town and owed his promotion to Alexander's favour.[101] He could therefore be encouraged to adapt himself to Persian tradition and ingratiate himself with his subjects. In other satrapies Alexander might have felt it prudent to drive a wedge between the satraps and their subjects. The rulers were marked out by their dress as aliens and were accordingly most unlikely to develop the accord with their subjects which they would need to revolt from the central authority. The evidence of Diodorus suggests that Peucestas was not meant to be a paradigm for other governors but rather an exception to the general rule.

It is difficult to trace any admission of Persian nobles into the Macedonian court hierarchy. Before 324 the only certain example is Oxyathres, brother of Darius, who was admitted to the ranks of the ἑταῖροι immediately after his brother's death.[102] It is hazardous to argue from silence, given the defective nature of all Alexander histories, but there is some evidence that Persians were initially excluded from the court hierarchy. In 329 Pharnuches, apparently an Iranian domiciled in Lycia,[103] found himself in titular command of a force of mercenaries thanks to his competence in the local dialects. When his force was ambushed, he attempted (so Aristobulus claimed) to cede his command to

Macedonian officers on the grounds that he was a barbarian while they were Macedonians and ἑταῖροι of the King. The account in general is confused and tendentious, but the clear distinction between barbarians and ἑταῖροι is fundamental to it.[104] Admittedly the text does not state that there were no barbarian ἑταῖροι, but it does support the argument from silence. Nearchus' list of trierarchs for the Indus fleet takes us further. The Macedonians of Alexander's court are listed according to their domicile, as are the Greeks. There are two representatives of the regal families of Cyprus, and finally one solitary Persian – Bagoas, son of Pharnuches.[105] The rarity of the patronymic virtually guarantees that Bagoas was the son of the Lycian Pharnuches. Unlike his father, he achieved a status commensurate with the Macedonian ἑταῖροι, and he was probably the Bagoas who entertained Alexander at Babylon.[106] But at the time of the Indus voyage he was the only Persian among the ἑταῖροι (Oxyathres had retired to Ecbatana to supervise Bessus' execution); otherwise it is inconceivable that his fellow Iranians did not compete as trierarchs.

By 324 there were more Iranians among the ἑταῖροι. Arrian gives the names of nine nobles who were drafted into the élite cavalry *agema*, the king's guard. The list is intended to be exhaustive, and what makes the first impression is its brevity.[107] Not only is the list short but the families are well known – a group selected by Alexander for especial distinction. There is a son of Artabazus, two sons of Mazaeus, two of Phrataphernes and finally Itanes, brother of Alexander's wife Rhoxane.[108] The fathers were all satraps and their loyalty was impeccable throughout the reign. Two names, Mithrobaeus and Aegobares, are totally unknown,[109] but the leader of the group, Hystaspes of Bactria, was connected by marriage to the house of Artaxerxes III Ochus, and he may have been a descendant of the son of Xerxes who ruled Bactria in the fifth century.[110] The lineage of these nobles was beyond reproach and, given their small numbers, one may assume that Alexander was forming an élite within the Persian nobility. One can only guess at his motives, but there were two clear results from his actions. The small group of nobles incorporated in the *agema* were effectively isolated from their father's satrapies. They were trained and armed in Macedonian style and doubtless identified with the conquerors by their people. At the same time they acted as hostages for their parents, as did the Macedonian pages around Alexander's person.[111] These adlections to the *agema* seem a parallel phenomenon to Alexander's satrapal appointments. The Iranian satraps were reduced to a handful – Phrataphernes, Oxyartes and Atropates – and their sons were attached to Alexander's own court, separated by distance and culture from their roots in the satrapies.

The evidence so far has produced little or nothing that suggests any policy of fusion. Alexander's actions when viewed in their historical context seem rather to indicate a policy of division. There was no attempt to intermix the Macedonian and Persian nobilities, if anything an attempt to keep them apart. In particular the Macedonians seem to have been cast as the ruling race. It is they who monopolise the principal commands, civil and military, they who marry the women of the Persian aristocracy, they who dominate court life. Even when Alexander adopted Persian ceremonial his Macedonians were marked out as his courtiers and his chiliarch (or grand vizier) was no Persian but his bosom friend Hephaestion. By contrast apart from a small, carefully chosen élite the Persians had no positions of power at court and the Iranian satraps were inexorably reduced in numbers as the reign progressed. The factor which dominated everything was Alexander's concept of personal autocracy. From early 332 to the end of his life he declared himself King of Asia. He acknowledged no equal and all were his subjects. Against that background the traditional recalcitrance of the Iranian satraps was totally unacceptable and, I believe, Alexander's actions can largely be explained as a demonstration of the fact of conquest. His court ceremonial underlined that he alone was the Great King and the mass marriages made it patently obvious that he and his nobles were the inheritors of the Achaemenids. As for the Persians, they were gradually extracted from the satrapies in which they had been prematurely confirmed in the years after Gaugamela and only a small group was left, tied by marriage to the Macedonian conquerors and with sons virtual hostages at court. This is a far cry from any policy of fusion. The only counter evidence comes from the Opis mutiny, when Alexander turned to his Iranians in order to crush disaffection among the Macedonians. Afterwards Alexander was able to pray for community of command, but the prayer was demonstrably affected by the recent events. In effect there is no hint that Alexander gave positions of power to Iranians during his last year; the hierarchy of command remained stubbornly Macedonian.

If there is no trace of any planned integration of the Macedonian and Persian aristocracies, it might be thought that the fusion took place at a lower level. By the end of his reign Alexander certainly possessed a mixed army, in which Persians and Macedonians fought side by side both in the phalanx and Companion cavalry. But did the mixture come about by policy or by military necessity? And how rigorous was the fusion? Were the two races divided into separate sub-units or did they fight side by side in integrated companies and with common weaponry? These questions are fundamental and once again require close examination of the evidence.

According to orthodox dogma Alexander began to use oriental cavalry at an early stage. In his description of the Hyrcanian campaign (late summer 330) Arrian notes that the king now had a body of mounted javelin-men (ἱππακοντισταί).[112] These troops were used repeatedly in the campaign in central Iran and Bactria, and it is universally assumed that they were a select Iranian squadron, recruited to give extra flexibility to his cavalry.[113] But there is no hint in any of the ten references in Arrian that these troops were Iranians. In fact they are invariably grouped with regular units of the Macedonian army, the Agrianians, and the Companions. What is more, ἱππακοντισταί formed the nucleus of the garrison of Areia in 330 and they were massacred during Satibarzanes' first revolt.[114] It is surprising that Iranians were chosen for such an exposed position, more surprising that they remained loyal. One should certainly admit the possibility that these troops were Macedonians. Now one of Alexander's principal cavalry units, the Scouts (πρόδρομοι) is not mentioned after the pursuit of Darius. Instead the ἱππακοντισταί appear precisely in the role formerly cast for the Scouts,[115] and in Sogdiana they are used alongside σαρισσοφόροι, who previously belonged to the Scouts.[116] It is possible that Alexander reorganised the Scouts in the year after Gaugamela and turned them into two formations, one using the ponderous *sarisa* and the other light missile javelins.[117] At Gaugamela the Scouts had been mauled by the cavalry of the eastern satrapies, and Alexander perhaps thought it prudent to variegate his cavalry before moving east. The year 330 was one of reorganisation, the year that hipparchies are first mentioned in Ptolemy's campaign narrative,[118] and it is perfectly credible that Alexander trained some of his Scouts as a unit of javelin-men.[119] There is no reason to assume that he was using an Iranian squadron in conjunction with his Macedonian troops as early as 330.

The first unequivocal reference to use of oriental troops comes in the Sogdian revolt of 328/7, when we are told that Bactrians and Sogdians fought in the satrapal forces of Amyntas.[120] When he left Bactria for India Alexander had with him large numbers of Iranian cavalry, from Bactria, Sogdiana, Arachosia and Parapamisadae. There were also Saka cavalry from the northern steppes.[121] These troops fought alongside the Macedonians at the Hydaspes but they were brigaded in separate formations and outside the battle narrative they are not individually mentioned. There is one exception, the squadron of horse-archers (ἱπποτόξοται) which first emerges during the march on India and is mentioned repeatedly in Arrian's campaign narrative.[122] The horse-archers are usually employed alongside Macedonian units in relatively light formations, performing the same functions, it seems, as did formerly the Scouts and ἱππακοντισταί (who are mentioned once only after the invasion of India). These horse-archers seem to have been recruited from the Dahae, who are specifically designated the horse-archers at the Hydaspes,[123] and it looks as though they formed a *corps d'élite* corresponding to the Agrianians in the infantry. The first appearance of these Iranian troops is significant. After the protracted campaign in Bactria/Sogdiana Alexander was leaving the area altogether and moving to invade India. The Iranian cavalry were being employed outside their home territory where there was little chance of disaffection. Alexander could safely draw upon them to strengthen his own cavalry, and at the same time they served as a great pool of hostages, exactly as had the troops of the Corinthian League during the first years of the campaign. They fought in national units and there was as yet no attempt to combine them with his Macedonian troops.

The combination took place, in the cavalry at least, after Alexander's return to the west in 325. The only evidence unfortunately is a single passage of Arrian which is at best unclear and most probably corrupt. In his list of Macedonian grievances at Susa Arrian gives superficially detailed information about the use of barbarians in the cavalry (vii 6.2–5); this he summarises two chapters later as an admixture of heterogeneous cavalry into the ranks of the barbarians.[124] What kind of admixture is meant? Arrian divides the Macedonians' grievance into three parts. In the first place he mentions that certain Iranians, selected for their social distinction and physique, were assigned to the Companion cavalry. There were three categories, carefully marked off: first Bactrians, Sogdians and Arachosians; next Drangians, Areians and Parthyaeans; and finally an obscure group of Persians termed the 'Euacae'. As Brunt saw, these groups correspond to the cavalry taken from Bactria in 327, the troops which arrived in Carmania in late 325, and finally cavalry levied in Persis in early 324.[125] The incorporation of the last two groups was a relatively recent occurrence, but it is possible that the Bactrian cavalry had been integrated with the Companions as early as the campaign in Southern India. The verb Arrian used to describe the incorporation (καταλοχισθέντες) is unfortunately flexible. In its technical sense it denotes the division of an amorphous body of troops into distinctive files or λόχοι,[126] but it is most often used in the most general sense as a synonym of καταλέγειν. What it does not mean is assignment of extra troops to existing units.[127] Arrian makes the situation clearer in his next phrase. Besides these Iranians assigned (καταλοχισθέντες) to the Companion cavalry there was a fifth hipparchy which was not entirely barbarian. The phrase implies clearly that there were four hipparchies consisting wholly of Iranian cavalry,[128] and a fifth which was only partially so. It must be emphasised that the passage says nothing about the number of Macedonian hipparchies at this period (although it has frequently been taken to do so).[129] What is at issue is the reaction of the Macedonians to Persian involvement in the Companion cavalry, and their grievances are presented in ascending order. First comes the objection that the Iranians were organised in separate hipparchies within the cavalry body, next the more serious complaint that there was a mixed hipparchy, in which Iranians and Macedonians served together and finally the crowning outrage that there was a troop of Persian nobles inside the élite *agema*. The organisation of the Macedonians was irrelevant to the grievances, and we must assume that there was an unspecified number of Macedonian hipparchies *in addition to* the four Persian hipparchies and the mixed hipparchy.[130] The total number at this period cannot even be guessed at.

Arrian says virtually nothing about the process of infiltration. He merely adds an obscure parenthesis remarking that the fifth mixed hipparchy had originated at a time when the entire cavalry body was expanded. The date of the expansion is not given, but it is a reasonable (and popular) assumption that it came after the crossing of the Gedrosian desert, which certainly caused great loss of life and greater loss of livestock, especially horses.[131] Probably Alexander reformed his cavalry during his stay in Persis, regrouping the Macedonians and adding the recent arrivals from central Iran. The supernumeraries, both Macedonian and Iranian, were grouped together in a single hipparchy, the only unit apart from the *agema* in which the two races were combined. The basic reorganisation, then, seems to have occurred in 325/4, but there is a possibility that the Bactrians and Sogdians had served inside the Companion cavalry before this date. We have noted that they fought at the Hydaspes in separate national units and it is a striking fact that they are never again mentioned in the campaign narrative for Southern India. Once more it is possible that the omission is purely fortuitous, but there is nothing against the hypothesis that some of the Iranian cavalry had been brigaded in hipparchies as early as 326.

If the evidence of Arrian is strictly interpreted, it indicates that, apart from one hipparchy, Macedonians and Iranians served in separate units within the body of the Companion cavalry. In other words, the Iranian cavalry shared the title of ἑταῖροι. This has often been doubted, but Arrian's terminology seems unambiguous: they were assigned to the Companion cavalry. Alexander's actions at Opis are not contrary evidence. There he began to create new formations of Persians bearing the Macedonian names, including a fresh cavalry *agema* καὶ ἡ τῶν ἑταίρων ἵππος.[132] This does not imply that all Companions had previously been Macedonians, rather that in future he intended to have a corps of Companions who were exclusively Persian. That is quite compatible with a situation before the mutiny in which Macedonians and Iranians served together in a single body of Companions. And the single reference in Arrian to Macedonian Companions does not exclude there having been Persian Companions also.[133] A curious picture therefore emerges. The Iranian cavalry largely served in separate hipparchies, and they retained their national weapons (it is only the group of nobles in the *agema* who are said to have exchanged their javelins for Macedonian lances). Nevertheless they served in the Companion cavalry and presumably bore the title ἑταῖροι. It would seem that Alexander was using the traditional policy of Macedonian kings. The title *pezhetairoi* (Foot Companions), as a name for the entire phalanx infantry, appears to have been introduced as a deliberate measure to place the infantry on terms of equality with the cavalry.[134] The King named all his infantry his Companions and emphasised their close ties to him, thus setting them up as a group parallel and opposed to the aristocratic cavalry, the group which had previously monopolised the title of Companion. Alexander, it seems, did the same with his cavalry, establishing a body of Iranian Companions in the same organisation as the Macedonians. This development fits well into the period after the Hyphasis mutiny, when Alexander was faced with disaffection or, at best, lack of enthusiasm among his own troops. The admission of Iranian Companions made it clear that he was not limited to his Macedonians and could find support elsewhere. It was an implicit threat, which was nearly fulfilled at Opis. There is, then, no trace of a policy of fusion. Once again the tendency seems to have been to keep Iranians and Macedonians separate and even mutually suspicious. Each served as a check and balance on the other.

The pattern is further exemplified in Alexander's use of Iranian infantry. First and foremost is the formation of 30,000 *Epigoni*, Iranian youths armed in Macedonian fashion and trained in phalanx discipline. All sources agree that the *Epigoni* arrived during Alexander's stay in Susa and aroused the jealousy and fear of the Macedonians by their brilliant display.[135] Plutarch alone says that the institution was designed to promote a mixture (ἀνάκρασις) and harmony;[136] the vulgate sources see much more sinister motives. For Diodorus the formation was Alexander's reaction to the recalcitrance of his Macedonian troops ever since the Hyphasis mutiny (he speaks of the Ganges!). The king needed an ἀντίταγμα for his Macedonian phalanx. Pierre Briant has recently elucidated the sense of ἀντίταγμα; it was a counter-army, 'face à une phalange macédonienne et contre elle'.[137] Elsewhere Diodorus uses the word to describe the force of mercenaries raised by Thrasybulus of Syracuse to counter his citizen forces and Plutarch describes as an ἀντίταγμα the force of cavalry which Eumenes in 322/1 built up to counter and crush the phalanx infantry of Neoptolemus.[138] When applied to Alexander's *Epigoni* the word has a sinister ring. Alexander intended the Persians not only to balance his Macedonian forces but also to be thrown against them if necessary.

Curtius describes the origins of this new counter-infantry, claiming that Alexander gave orders for the levy of 30,000 youths before he left Bactria in 327, intending them to be conveyed to him when trained, to act as hostages as well as soldiers.[139] His order is presented as a security measure – a measure against the Iranians not the Macedonians. Some of this coheres with other evidence. Arrian claims that the *Epigoni* were raised by satraps from the newly-founded cities and the rest of the conquered territories.[140] His terminology is loose, using σατράπης to refer to the city commandants whom he elsewhere terms ὕπαρχοι,[141] but it is clear that the new foundations of the east were the prime recruiting grounds for the *Epigoni*. These foundations were concentrated most densely in Bactria/Sogdiana and, as we have seen, the conquered peoples formed a large pool of second-class citizens. They were an obvious area for recruits; young men were closely concentrated and it would be a prudential step to remove those who were outstanding and most likely to be discontented with their lot. Originally, then, Alexander's intention might have been to skim away the most outstanding youths of the central satrapies, train them in effective infantry tactics and then isolate them from their cultural background. As the morale and obedience of his Macedonians declined he saw the potential of his new infantry phalanx and deliberately used the new force to balance and intimidate his Macedonians. It was essential that the two infantry bodies were kept distinct – an obvious and permanent exception to any policy of fusion.

According to Justin there was a second body of *Epigoni*, the offspring of mixed marriages between Macedonian soldiers and Asiatic wives. Justin states that Alexander began to encourage these unions in 330, at the time when he first adopted Persian dress.

Two motives are given – to reduce his troops' longing for domestic life in Macedonia and to create an army of mixed race whose only home was the camp.[142] Justin is fuller than usual and not apparently garbled; and there is corroborative evidence. Arrian agrees that more than 10,000 mixed marriages had been contracted by the time of the celebrations at Susa and the veterans of Opis had produced a fair number of offspring by their native wives, enough for Alexander to retain them, promising to train them in Macedonian style and to reunite them with their fathers when they reached manhood.[143] The evidence is consistent and indicates that Alexander had long- and short-term objectives. In the first place the legitimisation of his troops' liaisons with native women gave them an inducement to remain in Asia which was stronger than mere concubinage and politically desirable in 330, when there was agitation in the army to conclude the campaign and return to Macedonia.[144] The ultimate aim, however, was to produce a corps of troops without roots in Europe or permanent home in Asia, the janissaries of the new Empire, whose loyalty would be to Alexander alone.[145] The two bodies of *Epigoni* were alike in their close attachment to the court and their training in Macedonian discipline. In both cases Alexander was attempting to create a supra-national army, but his motives were grounded in practical politics and military considerations were paramount.

So far the evidence has indicated that Alexander kept Iranians and Macedonians separated in both cavalry and infantry and that he used the two races to counterbalance each other. There is, however, one instance of a combined force of Persians and Macedonians. Shortly before Alexander's death Peucestas arrived in Babylon with a force of 20,000 Persians, reinforced with mountaineers from the Zagros and Elburz.[146] The king commended this new force and assigned them to the Macedonian ranks (κατέλεγεν ἐς τὰς Μακεδονικὰς τάξεις). The details of this reorganisation are given, for once, and they are interesting. This new composite infantry was organised into files (δεκάδες) of sixteen, twelve Persians to four Macedonians. Each file was commanded by a Macedonian, backed by two other Macedonians in second and third place. The Persians then filled out the centre of the phalanx and a Macedonian brought up the rear. The four Macedonians were armed in traditional style (with the *sarisa*) and were given preferential rates of pay, whereas the Persians retained their native bows and javelins. The result was a curiously heterogeneous phalanx, packed with Persians untrained in Macedonian discipline. The Macedonians formed an élite, the first three ranks using *sarisae* and bearing the brunt of any attack. Even in the old phalanx there was hardly space for more than the first three ranks to use sarisae in couched position. In Polybius' day, when *sarisae* were longer, only the first five ranks were able to thrust with their weapons; the rest added weight and held their *sarisae* vertically as a screen against missiles.[147] The Persians in the new phalanx added weight and numbers and no doubt they were intended to shoot arrows and javelins over the heads of the Macedonian ranks, much in the same way as the λογχοφόροι were to operate in Arrian's legionary phalanx of A.D. 135.[148] This new phalanx could only be used in frontal attacks. There was no possibility of complex manoeuvres or changes of front and depth on the march which had been the hallmark of the old Macedonian phalanx and had been displayed so prominently in the Illyrian campaign of 335 and the approach to Issus.[149] This reorganisation was in fact a means to make the best use of untrained manpower and also to husband the trained Macedonian phalangites. It is strong *prima facie* evidence that Alexander's native Macedonian troops were in short supply by 323.

There is every reason to believe that the main army was drained of Macedonians. Curtius (x 2.8) implies that Alexander was thinking of leaving a moderate holding army in Asia after the departure of Craterus' veterans, an army comprising 13,000 infantry and 2,000 cavalry. These are superficially high figures, but none the less misleading. There is no reason to think that only Macedonians are understood.[150] The explicit context is the size of the force to be left in Asia (he had recently threatened to attack Athens and the Arabian expedition was in preparation);[151] it is specifically a holding force and presumably contained a relatively small proportion of Macedonians.[152] After Opis Alexander deliberately drained his infantry forces, sending with Craterus 6,000 of the veterans present at the Hellespont in 334 and 4,000 of the troops conveyed in later reinforcements.[153] There is no statement how many remained, but one may assume that the fighting in India and the Gedrosian desert march took a heavy toll of life, and there is little trace of reinforcements. Only Curtius speaks of 8,000 *Graeci* sent to Sogdiana in 329/8 and 5,000 cavalry (*sic*) sent from Thrace in 326.[154] There is no trace in the sources of Macedonian reinforcements and it seems that Antipater did not have the necessary manpower resources to cater for Alexander's demands. Diodorus says explicitly that Macedonia was drained of national troops in 323 because of the numbers of reinforcements sent to Asia, so that he could not cope with the initial crisis of the Lamian War.[155] The forces who remained in Babylon can only be guessed at. The *argyraspides*, 3,000 in number, were present in Perdiccas' invasion force in 321, and, since their baggage train contained their wives and children, we can assume that they were not sent with Craterus' column in 324.[156] Alexander must have retained them in Babylon together with an unspecified number of phalingites.[157] They were also veterans for the most part. The evidence for the *argyraspides* is unanimous that they had all fought through the campaigns of Philip and Alexander. The statement that the youngest of the corps were sixty years old may be an exaggeration, but it is common to Diodorus and Plutarch and presumably derives from Hieronymus.[158] And we should not forget the exploits of Antigonus at Ipsus and Lysimachus and Seleucus at Corupedium: *in hac aetate utrique animi iuveniles erant.*[159] It seems then that Alexander was left with a nucleus of Macedonian veterans. He had ordered Antipater to bring prime troops from Macedonia to replace Craterus' army column but they could not be expected for some time after Craterus reached Macedon – and he was travelling with prudent slowness.[160] But Alexander was about to embark on the Arabian expedition, and shortly before his death the advance orders for the departure of both land and naval forces had been given.[161] There was no alternative but to make the best of his Macedonian veterans – to distribute them among the front-rank positions and fill up the phalanx in depth with Persian infantry. The mixture was patently forced upon Alexander by military necessity. Had the fresh levies from Macedon ever arrived, he would certainly have removed the Iranian rank and file and replaced them with the trained manpower from Macedon.[162]

Nothing remains of the policy of fusion. As regards his military organisation Alexander was reacting to a series of problems. To begin with, his use of Iranians from the central satrapies was determined by his need for auxiliaries in the Indian campaign and the obvious desirability of removing crack fighting men from their native satrapies, where they would be fuel for any revolt against his regal authority. The next stage was to use his Iranian auxiliaries as a counter-weight to his increasingly mutinous Macedonian troops, and finally, when the Macedonians were decimated and cowed, they were used as a pool of manpower to supplement the trained Macedonian cadres. There is nothing here remotely resembling a deliberate policy to fuse together the two peoples into a single army. If there is any policy it is *divide et impera*. We have seen Alexander at work at two levels. Firstly the continuous and traditional recalcitrance of his Iranian nobles forced him to proclaim his pretensions as the heir of the Achaemenids with increasing pomp and splendour and to make it increasingly obvious that his Greco-Macedonian nobles had in fact supplanted the Iranians as a ruling class. On the other hand the increasing disaffection of his Macedonian rank and file forced him to rely more on Iranian infantry and cavalry. If there is any consistent element it is Alexander's categorical claim to personal autocracy and the reciprocal demand for total obedience from his subjects at all levels of society. The resistance to that claim appeared in different forms and Alexander's response was accordingly different. There is little that can be said to approximate to careful premeditated policy: rather Alexander seems to have reacted promptly to the various challenges confronting him during his reign. The result is piecemeal and certainly less romantic than a visionary policy of fusion and conciliation but it is far truer to the evidence as it stands.

Notes

* This paper was delivered at the annual meeting of the American Association of Ancient Historians, held at Boulder, Colorado in May 1978, and at seminars in Berkeley and Oxford. I am grateful for the comments made on those occasions and acknowledge liability for the remaining errors.

1   G. T. Griffith, *JHS* lxxxii (1963) 74.
2   J. G. Droysen, *Geschichte des Hellenismus* i² (Gotha 1877) 2.83 f. = i³ (Basel 1952) 307; i² 2.241 f. = i³ 404.
3   For a bibliographical survey see J. Seibert, *Alexander der Grosse* (Darmstadt 1972) 186–92. The references which are definitive for German scholarship are J. Kaerst, *Geschichte des Hellenismus* i³ (Berlin/Leipzig 1927) 471; U Wilcken, *Alexander the Great*, ed. E. N. Borza (New York 1967) 248 f.; F. Schachermeyr, *Alexander der Grosse: Das Problem seiner Persönlichkeit und seins Wirkens* (*SÖAW Wien* cclxxxv: 1973) 355, 472, 479–83 (exposition unchanged from the first edn: Graz 1949). For recent statement of orthodoxy see F. Altheim–R. Stiehl, *Geschichte Mittelasiens in Altertum* (Berlin 1970) 212 ff., esp. 217; H. E. Stier, *Welteroberung und Weltfriede im Wirken Al. d. Gr. (Rhein.-Westfäl. Akad. Wiss.* Vorträge G 187: 1972) 38–41. For the diffusion of the idea outside its German context see G. Radet, *Alexandre le Grand* (Paris 1931) 342 f.; W. W. Tarn, *Alexander the Great* (Cambridge 1948) 1 111, 137 f.; J. R. Hamilton, *Alexander the Great* (London 1973) 105, 163.
4   *Op. cit.* (n. 3) ii 399–449 (the definitive statement). Tarn separated the two ideas of brotherhood and fusion, but he used precisely the same evidence to argue for universal brotherhood that others had used to support the policy of fusion. For the counter-arguments, which are conclusive, see E. Badian, 'Alexander the Great and the Unity of Mankind', *Historia* vii (1958) 425–44 with P. Merlan, *CPh* xlv (1950) 161–6.
5   H. Berve, 'Die Verschmelzungspolitik Alexanders des Grossen', *Klio* xxxi (1938) 135–68. Berve took his view to extreme lengths, even arguing that the concubines in Alexander's army train were exclusively Iranian (158 f.)
6   *Cf.* Berve (n. 5) 136 for the full definition.
7   F. Hampl, 'Alexander der Grosse und die Beurteilung geschichtlicher Persönlichkeiten', *La Nouvelle Clio* vi (1954) 115–23; cf. *Studies presented to D. M. Robinson* ii (Washington 1953) 319 f. For some pragmatic recent views which I would largely endorse, see E. Badian, *Studies in Greek & Roman History* (Oxford 1964) 201; P. Green, *Alexander of Macedon* (1974) 446.
8   Arr. vii 11.8–9. For the grammatical structure see the discussion of Badian (n. 4) 430 f.
9   For the Macedonian resentment see Arr. vii 6.1–5; 8.2. For the crushing of the mutiny see Arr. vii 11.1–4; Curt. x 3.5–6; Diod. xvii 109.3; Plut. *Al.* 71.4; Justin xii 12.1–6.

10 Cf. Arr. iii 21.5: καὶ διασῴζειν ἐς τὸ κοινὸν τὴν ἀρχήν (the regicides with Bessus).

11 For examples of ἀρχή as a synonym of satrapy see Arr. i 17.7, 23.8; vi 29.1. In Arrian ἀρχή implies rule over subjects (cf. iv 20.3 where the Persian empire is described as Περσῶν τε καὶ Μήδων τὴν ἀρχήν, rule over Persians and Medes). I cannot see how the Opis prayer can imply anything other than that the Persians and Macedonians were to rule jointly over subject peoples. The distinctions hitherto made between ἀρχή as 'rule' and ἀρχή as 'realm' are meaningless: Tarn (n. 3) ii 443 f.; F. Wüst, *Historia* ii (1953) 429; cf. Badian (n. 4) 431.

12 Arrian makes it clear that the participants at the feast were clearly divided by their national origins. Far from intermingling the Persians and Macedonians were separated from each other and the Macedonians alone were in the king's entourage (ἀμφ' αὐτὸν μὲν Μακεδόνων, ἐν δὲ τῷ ἐφεξῆς τούτων Περσῶν). Cf. Badian (n. 4) 429 f.

13 Diod. xviii 4.4: ὅπας τὰς μεγίστας ἠπείρους ... εἰς κοινὴν ὁμόνοιαν καὶ συγγενικὴν φιλίαν καταστήσῃ.

14 So Badian, *HSCP* lxxii (1968) 194–5. Even if the proposals did contain statements of intent, those statements were transmitted by Perdiccas and cannot be directly attributed to Alexander himself. Cf. Schachermeyr, *Alexander in Babylon* (SÖAW Wien cclxviii. 3: 1970) 192: 'natürlich hat Perdikkas am Heer nicht ganz Schriftsätze vorgelesen, sondern das meiste einfach paraphrasiert'.

15 At xvii 110.2 he refers to the mixed phalanx of Persians and Macedonians as κεκραμένην καὶ ἁρμόζουσαν τῇ ἰδίᾳ προαιρέσει, but there is no other reference to any deliberate policy of fusion.

16 Cf. Schachermeyr, *JÖAI* xli (1954) 120–3; Badian (n. 14) 183 ff., both conclusive against Tarn (n .3) ii 380.

17 Cf. F. Jacoby, *RE* viii 1542 f.; Schachermeyr (n. 14) 106 f.

18 Cf. R Andreotti, *Saeculum* viii (1957) 134, arguing that Hieronymus may have had a pacifist ideology after his experience of the devastation wrought by the Successors (but cf. Schachermeyr [n. 14] 194 n. 188). If so, he may have placed a romantic interpretation upon Alexander's projected colonisation in order to preach a sermon to his own generation.

19 Cf. Badian (n. 14) 198 f., 203 f. Schachermeyr (n. 14) 193 f. places too much faith in the incorruptibility of Eumenes and takes it for granted that Hieronymus both had inside information and revealed nothing but the truth. Perdiccas read the *hypomnemata*, but he acted on a group decision and, if there were forgeries, Eumenes would have been privy to them and acquiesced.

20 Strabo i 4.9 (66).

21 Plut. *de Al. for.* i 6 (329a–c). The attribution to Eratosthenes began with E. Schwartz, *RhM* xl (1885), 252–4: briefly and dogmatically stated but subsequently accepted as dogma (cf. Tarn (n. 3) ii 437).

22 Badian (n. 4) 434–40; J. R. Hamilton, *Plutarch Alexander* (Oxford 1969) xxix–xxxiii. See now P. A. Brunt, *Athenaeum* lv (1977) 45–7. 23 *de Al. for.* i 8 (330a) = *FGrH* 241 F 30.

24 The thesis to be proved is expounded at i 4 (328b), and it is regularly pointed by contrasts between philosophical principle and Alexander's actions in practice (328c–e, 329a–b, 330c).

25 Strabo xv 1.64 (715) = *FGrH* 134 F 17; cf. Hamilton (n. 22) xxxi.

26 For the characterisation of Alexander see Ael. Arist. xxvi (εἰς Ῥώμην) 24–7. By contrast under Rome there is no distinction of Europe and Asia (60), ἀλλὰ καθέστηκε κοινὴ τῆς γῆς δημοκρατία ὑφ' ἑνὶ ἄρχοντι καὶ κοσμητῇ, and there has developed a single harmonious union: καὶ γέγονε μία ἁρμονία πολιτείασ ἅπαντασ συγκεκληκυῖα (66).

27 One may compare the orations of Dio of Prusa. In the first Alexander appears briefly as the type of an immoderate ruler, in the second he is the defender and emulator of an idealised Homeric kingship, and in the fourth he is presented as the youthful interlocutor of Diogenes, basically sound but in need of Cynic deflation. See A Heuss, *Antike und Abendland* iv (1954) 92 f.

28 Curt. X 3. 12–14: cf. 14, 'omnia eundem ducunt colorem. Nec Persis Macedonun morem adumbrare nec Macedonibus Persas imitari decorum. Eiusdem iuris esse debent qui sub eodem victuri sunt' (the continuation is lost in a lacuna).

29 Diod. xvii 77.4–7; Curt. vi 6.1–10; Justin xii 3.8–12; *Metz Epitome* 1–2. Cf. Plut. *Al.* 45.1–4; Arr. iv 7.4–5. For full discussion see H.-H. Ritter, *Diadem und Königsherrschaft* (Vestigia vii: 1965) 31–55, superseding Berve (n. 5) 148–52.

30   Arrian iv 7.4 (and the derivative *Itinerarium* 88) claim that Alexander adopted the upright tiara (*kitaris*) of the Persian king. Berve (n. 5) 148–50 therefore argued that Alexander alternated full Persian dress with a more conservative mixed costume, and scholars have been reluctant to reject Arrian's statement. But there is no corroboration (apart from the passing remark of Lucian, *Dial. Mort.* 14.4), and it conflicts with the explicit statements of the other sources. In fact Arrian's report of the Persian costume is a parenthesis, a further example of Alexander's barbarism tacked onto the punishment of Bessus, and Arrian may have added it from his own memory – in which case he could easily have made a slip (*cf.* iii 22.4 where he refers casually to the battle of 'Arbela' despite his fulminations at vi 11.4). Certainly his passing comment cannot stand against the rest of the tradition (so Ritter [n. 29] 47).

31   Arr. iv 7.4; *cf.* vii 29.4.

32   Plut. Al. 45.1; cf. *de Al. for.* i 8 (330a).

33   The Achaemenid courtiers are regularly termed φοινικισταί or *purpurati*; *cf.* Xen. *Anab.* i 2.20; 5.7–8; Curt. iii 2.10; 8.15; 13.13 f. M. Reinhold, *Purple as a Status Symbol in Antiquity* (Coll. Latomus cxvi: 1970) 18–20.

34   The lesson was underlined when Alexander selected as his chiliarch or Grand Vizier (Persian *hazarapatis*) his closest friend, Hephaestion: Berve, *Das Alexanderreich* (Munich 1926) ii 173 no. 357; Schachermeyr (n. 14) 31–7. The date of this appointment is not known, but it presumably followed his elevation to the command of the Companion cavalry in late 330 (Arr. iii 27.4), some time after Alexander first introduced Persian court ceremonial.

35   Plut. *Al.* 45.1; *cf.* Diod. 77.4; Curt. vi 6.1, etc.

36   Arrian places it in his narrative of 329/8, but the context is a timeless digression (above n. 30) and there is no basis for chronological arguments: *cf.* Ritter (n. 29) 47–9.

37   Arr. ii 14.8–9; Curt. iv 1. 1–14; Plut. *Al.* 34.1 (cf. *FGrH* 532 F 1. C 38); Plut. *Al.* 37.7, 56.2; *de Al. for.* 329d; Diod. 66.3; Curt. v 2.13. Altheim (n. 3) 195–202 is totally unconvincing when he argues that Alexander had no pretentions to be king of Asia before the death of Darius.

38   The arguments of Ritter (n. 29) 49 ff.

39   Arr. iii 25.3; *cf.* Curt. vi 6.12–13; *Metz Epit.* 3. For the royal monopoly of the upright tiara see Ar. *Birds* 487 with scholia; Xen. *Anab.* ii 5.23; Plut. *Artax.* 26.4 and, in general, Ritter (n. 29) 6 ff.

40   Arr. iii 21.5, 30.4; *cf.* Diod. 74.1.

41   Arr. iii 19.5–6; Plut. *Al.* 42.5; Diod. 74.3–4; Curt. vi 2.17; Justin xii 1.1. *Cf.* Bosworth, *CQ* xxvi (1976) 132–6 for the chronology.

42   Arr. iii 19.7–8. For the reunification in Arachosia see Curt. vii 3.4. R. D. Milns, *GRBS* vii (1966) 165 n. 34 (so R. Lane Fox, *Alexander the Great* [London 1973] 532) has argued that the whole army was united in Parthia, but the argument rests on a misinterpretation of Arr. iii 25.4. The forces there said to be united are patently the several army columns used separately during the Elburz campaign (*cf.* iii 22.2, 24.1). It is clear that even the cavalry from the Median contingent only caught up when Alexander was on his way to Bactra (iii 25.3); the infantry must have followed at a considerable interval.

43   *Cf.* Arr. iii 19.7. The mercenaries and Thracians commissioned to Parmenion were earmarked for the abortive Cadusian expedition, but they clearly remained as the garrison of Media. Parmenion's lieutenants and murderers are known to have held commands over mercenary troops and Thracians: cf. Berve (n. 34) nos 8, 422, 508, 712.

44   Arr. iii 25.5–7; Diod. 78.1–4; Curt. vi 6.20–34. The vulgate tradition is fuller and more credible than Arrian.

45   Arr. iii 28.2–3; Diod. 81.3; Curt. vii 3.2 (renewed revolt when Alexander was in Ariaspian territory: Jan. 329); Diod. 83.4–6; Curt. vii 4.32 ff. (revolt crushed before Alexander reached Bactra: summer 329).

46   Arr. iv 7.1: Brazanes and his fellow rebels were captured by Phrataphernes and conveyed to Bactra/Zariaspa during the winter of 329/8. At the same time Arsaces, Alexander's second satrap of Areia, was arrested for connivance in Satibarzanes' revolt: ἐθελοκακεῖν at iii 29.5 implies dereliction of duty (*cf.* iv 18.3; *Tact.* 12.11 – the word is Herodotean) rather than actual rebellion (Berve [n. 34] nos 146, 179). There was trouble in the central satrapies apparently as late as 328/7, when Alexander felt it necessary to dismiss his satraps in Drangiana and Tapuria (Arr. iv.

18.3; Curt. viii 3.17; *cf.* x 1.39). The details and chronology of these dismissals are obscure, but the fact is certain.

47 Arr. ii 14.7 (at this stage the only Persian noble known to have been with Alexander was Mithrines: Berve [n. 34] no. 524).

48 Diod. 77.7; Curt. vi 6.9–12; Justin xii 4.1; *cf.* Arr. vii 6.2, 8.2.

49 *Cf.* Plut. *Al.* 47.7–12; *de Al. for.* ii 4 (337a).

50 Plut. *Demetr.* 14.2: διὰ τὸ προσυνωκηκέναι Κρατέῳ τῷ πλείστην εὔνοιαν αὐτοῦ παρὰ Μακεδόσι τῶν Ἀλεξάνδρου διαδόξων ἀπολιπόντι.

51 *Cf.* Plut. *Eum.* 6–7; Nepos *Eum.* 3.4–5; Arr. *Succ.* F 1.27 (Roos) (*cf.* F 19=Suda s.v Κράτερος, contrasting Craterus' popularity with the unpopularity of Antipater).

52 Plut. *Eum.* 6.3 This explicit statement has been queried (cf. Berve [n. 34] ii 226; Hamilton [n. 22] 131), mainly on the strength of Alexander's farewell at Opis (τὸν πιστότατόν τε αὐτῷ καὶ ὅντινα ἴσον τῇ ἑαυτοῦ κεφαλῇ ἄγει). But the king had given an equally moving (and permanent) farewell to Coenus shortly after his determined opposition at the Hyphasis (Arr. vi 2.1; Curt. ix 3.20; *cf.* Badian, *JHS* lxxxi [1961] 25), and in the case of Craterus the public statement of confidence and friendship does not exclude there having been bitter wranglers in private. Curtius describes Craterus as *regi carus in paucis* (vi 8.2), but the comment comes in the context of Philotas' trial, before there can have been concerted opposition to Alexander's Medism.

53 See the detailed exposition of Berve (n. 34) ii 222–4 (no. 446).

54 *Cf.* Arr. iv 11.6: the context is Callisthenes' speech against *proskynesis*, which presumably owes much to Arrian's own shaping, but the sentiment is convincing enough.

55 Curt. vi 2.15 ff.; Diod. 74.3; Justin xii 3.2–4. The episode is omitted by Arrian, probably because his sources were reluctant to stress the discontent in the army.

56 Diod. 77.7: τούτοις μὲν οὖν τοῖς ἐθισμοῖς Ἀλέξανδρος στανίοσ ἐχρῆτο, τοῖς δ ἐπρουπα ἄρχουσι κατὰ τὸ πλεῖστον ἐνδιέτριβε.

57 Plut. *Al.* 51.2; *cf.* 71.3.

58 Curt. viii 7.12: *Persarum te vestis et disciplina delectat: patrios mores exosus es. Cf.* viii 8.10–13.

59 Polyaen. iv 3.24.

60 *FGrH* 126 F 5 (Athen. xii 537e–f). His description of the mixed dress coheres with the other evidence, particularly that of Eratosthenes (nn. 23, 29), and Aristobulus seems to confirm that Alexander wore the *kausia* with the diadem as his day-to-day dress (Arr. vii 22.2 = *FGrH* 139 F 55). *Cf.* Ritter (n. 29) 57–8, accepting the material from Ephippus despite his misgivings about the value of the source.

61 Athen. xii 539d = *FGrH* 81 F 41; Ael. *VH* ix 3; Polyaen. iv 3.24.

62 *FGrH* 125 F 4: 100 couches and 20 cubit pillars covered with gold and silver leaf.

63 ἐπὶ τούτοις πεντακόσιοι Σούσιοι πορφυροσχήμονες. This group of 500 is also mentioned by Athenaeus, but Polyaenus alone says that they came from Susa.

64 *Cf.* Diod. 57.2; Curt. iv 13.27 with Arr. iii 11.9. According to Justin xii 7.5 the name originated in 327 when Alexander began his march into India and had his men's shields silvered for the occasion – and Harpalus allegedly sent 25,000 items of equipment chased with silver and gold (Curt. ix 3.21). The *argyraspides* also appear in the list of units named at the Opis mutiny in the place of the hypaspists (Arr. vii 11.3). This evidence cannot be dismissed as fantasy and anachronism (*pace* R. D. Lock, *Historia* xxvi [1977] 373–8. After the Indian campaign the hypaspists could also be known as *argyraspides*. The fact that the famous corps of Teutamus and Antigenes is called solely *argyraspides*, never hypaspists, is easy to explain. After Alexander's death the Successors set up their own bodyguards of hypaspists (Polyaen. iv 6.8; Diod. xix 28.1; Polyaen. iv 9.3) and hypaspist was no longer an exclusive title. Accordingly the veterans of Alexander used their second title *argyraspides* to distinguish themselves from the hypaspists of the other generals, who had not served under Alexander.

65 Diod. xix 22.2.

66 Diod. 110.1 f. (after the mutiny); Justin xii 12.4 (during). Both sources conflate the expansion of the guard with the formation of a mixed phalanx, which only occurred in mid 323 (p. 224). The common source (Cleitarchus) may well have given a summary of Alexander's various experiments with mixed infantry forces and tacked them onto the report of the great mutiny. Arr vii 29.4 speaks in the most general terms of the admixture of μηλοφοροι into the Macedonian ranks, corroborating the fact but giving no indication of chronology.

67 Diod. xviii 27.1: περὶ τὸν βασιλέα μία μὲν ὑπῆρχε θεραπεία καθωπλισμένη Μακεδόνων, ἄλλη δὲ Περσῶν μιλοφόροων.

68 Cf. J. R. Hamilton, CQ iii (1953) 156 f.; Schachermeyr (n. 3) 514 f.

69 Curt. ix 10.21, 29 (Carmania); Arr. vii 4.1; Plut. Al. 68.7 (Susiana/Paraetacene). See further Badian (n. 52) 17; Bosworth, CQ xxi (1971) 124; Schachermeyr (n. 3) 477 f.

70 Arr. vi 30.1–2; Curt. x 1.24 ff. For Orxines' lineage see Curt. iv 12.8. Curtius states that he had the overall command of the Persians at Gaugamela; Arrian (iii 8.5) gives him the command of the forces of the Red Sea, but there is almost certainly a lacuna in his text – all reference to the Persian national contingent is omitted.

71 Arr. vi 27.3; 29.3. Curtius ix 10.19 mentions two rebels, Ozines and Zariaspes, who were arrested by Craterus; the former at least seems identical with Arrian's Ordanes: Droysen (n. 2) i² 2.199 n. 1; but cf. Berve (n. 34) no. 579.

72 Plut. Al. 68.3: καὶ ὅλως διέδραμε σάλος ἁπάντων καὶ νεωτερισμός; cf. Curt. x 1.7.

73 Note the wrangle with Antipater and Parmenion in 335 (Diod. 16.2); the story is circumstantial and there is no reason to doubt it.

74 Diod. 37.6; Curt. iii 12.24 f.; cf. Diod. 38.1; 67.1; Curt. v 2.18 ff.; Arr. ii 12.5.

75 Plut. Al. 21.7; Eum. 1.7; Diod. xx 20.1; 28.1; Justin xi 10.2 f.; xii 15.9; Tarn's attempt to disprove the existence of the captive Barsine and her son Heracles (ii 330–7) is now a mere historical curiosity; cf. Schachermeyr (n. 14) 22 n. 32a; P. A. Brunt, RFIC ciii (1975) 22–34; R. M. Errington, JHS xc (1970) 74.

76 Arrian iv 18.4 says that the family of Oxyartes was captured on the rock of Sogdiana in spring 327. Curtius says nothing about Oxyartes and his family in the context of the Sogdian rock, whose capture he dates to spring 328 (vii 11.1). Rhoxane first appears in a banquet given by 'Cohortandus' in spring 327 (viii 4.21–30). That is the order of events in the index of Diodorus (the narrative proper is lost) and the Metz Epitome (15–18, 28–31). Strabo xi 11.4 (517) claims that Alexander met Rhoxane not on the rock of Sogdiana but on the rock of Sismithres, the next to be captured. The source conflict is obstinate and can only be settled by careful analysis of all sources in context, with particular emphasis on chronology. Fortunately all sources place the actual marriage immediately before the march on India.

77 Curt. viii 4.25; cf. Plut. Al. 47.7 with Hamilton (n. 22) 129 f.

78 Arr. iv 2.4: ὅυτως ἐξ Ἀλεξάνδρου προστεταγμένον; 3.1; Curt. vii 6.16.

79 Curt. vii 11.28 (Metz Epit. 18 has a variant); the story is omitted by Arrian but not contradicted (cf. iv 19.4).

80 Diod. xvii index κγ′ (p. 3 Budé; 110 Loeb): ὡς Ἀλέξανδρος ἀποστάντας τοὺς Σογδιανού ς κατεπολέμησε καὶ κατέσφαξεν αὐτῶν πλείους τῶν δώδεκα μυριάδον.

81 Cf. Arr. iv 4.1. At Alexandria in Caucaso there were 7,000 locals to 3,000 Hellenic troops (Diod. 83.2; Curt. vii 3.23). There is no indication that the number of settlers or the racial proportion was consistent throughout Alexander's foundations.

82 Curt. vii 6.27; Justin xii 5.12 f. Cf. P. Briant, Klio lx (1978) 74–7.

83 So Berve (n. 34) i 299. The excavations at Aï Khanoum are illustrating with ever increasing fullness the stubbornly Hellenic nature of that foundation. Cf. Seibert (n. 3) for bibliography, to which add Sir M. Wheeler, Flames over Persepolis (London 1968) 75 ff. and the successive reports by P. Bernard in CRAI 1974–6. Note particularly the new discoveries relating to the theatre and theatrical performances: CRAI 1976, 307–22.

84 Curt. vii 11.29: multitudo deditorum incolis novarum urbium cum pecunia capta dono data est.

85 Arr. iii 29.1 (Aornus); Metz Epit. 7–8; Arr. iv 5.2 (Maracanda), 16.4–5; Curt. viii 1.3 (Attinas, phrurarch of an unknown fortress).

86 Berve (n. 34) no. 60. He was appointed satrap either in winter 328/7 (Arr. iv 17.3) or in summer 328 (Curt. viii 2.14).

87 For Sisimithres see Curt. viii 2.32; 4.20; Metz Epit, 19; for Chorienes Metz Epit. 28; Curt. viii 4.21 (Alde's emendation Oxyartes for 'Cohortandus' is unacceptable). Arrian (iv 21.9) conflates the two figures.

88 For the story of Pixodarus see Plut. Al. 10.1–5; cf Badian Phoenix xvii (1963) 244 ff. with Hamilton (n. 22) 24 ff. For the outcome of the episode see Arr. i 23.8; Strabo xiv 2.17 (657).

89 Plut. Al. 22.7; Arr. i 23.8. For the eastern tradition of descent through the female line see H. Gelzer, RhM xxxv (1880) 515–17.

90 *Metz Epit.* 31; Diod. xvii index λ΄· τῶν φίλον πολλοὺς ἔπεισε γῆμναι.

91 Arr. vii 4.6 (*cf.* Plut. *Al.* 70.3; *de Al. for.* 7 [329d–e]; Diod. 107.6; Justin xii 10.10; Chares *FGrH* 125 F 4). The Persian ritual was what irked the Macedonian rank and file (vii 6.2); the marriage to Rhoxane had been celebrated in Macedonian mode according to Curtius (vii 4.27), and there is no reason to dispute his statement (*cf.* M. Renard and J. Servais, *Ant. Class.* xxiv [1955] 29–50).

92 Arr. vii 4.8; Plut. *Al.* 70.3. See further p. 224.

93 Plut. 329e: κοινωνίαν σουνιῶσι τοῖς μεγίοτοις καὶ δυνατωτάτοις γένεσι; *cf.* Curt. x 3.11–14.

94 *Cf.* Hampl (n. 7) 119.

95 Artabazus (Berve [n. 34] no. 152) had married a sister of Mentor and Memnon of Rhodes but that marriage had taken place by 362: Dem. xxiii 154, 157; *cf.* Brunt, *RFIC* ciii (1975) 25.

96 Arr. vii 4.5–7. For the role of Spitamenes see iii 28.10, 29.6; iv 3.6 ff.; 17.7. Full references in Berve (n. 34) ii 359–61 (no. 717).

97 Arr. vi 30.2 f.; vii 6.3, 23.3.

98 Arr. iii 6.6 (Laomedon); Diod. xix 23.1–3; Polyaen. iv 8.3 (Eumenes). Note, however, the use of an Iranian interpreter in Sogdiana (Arr. iv 3.7).

99 Diod. xix 14.5: φασὶ καὶ τὸν Ἀλέξανδρον αὐτῷ μόνῳ Μακεδόνον συγχωρῆσαι Περσικὴν φορεῖν στολήν, χαρίζεσθαι βουλόμενον τοῖς Πέρσαις καὶ διὰ τούτου μονίζοντα κατὰ πάνθ᾽ ἕξειν τὸ ἔθνος ὑπήκοον.

100 Arrian states that one of Peucestas' qualifications to govern Persis was his general sympathy with the barbarian life-style (τῷ βαρβαρικῷ τρόπῳ τῆς διαίτισ; vi 30.2). This does not imply that he had already adopted Persian dress. Leonnatus, for instance, is said to have attached himself to the lifestyle of the conquered peoples in Alexander's lifetime; he only assumed items of Persian dress after the king's death: Suda s.v. Λεοννατος = Arr. *Succ.* F 12 (Roos).

101 Peucestas was trierarch with his brother in 320 (Arr. *Ind.* 19.8), but at the Malli town he is merely styled 'one of the hypaspists' (Diod. 99.4; but *cf.* Arr. vi 9.3). He seems to have held no position of command before his elevation to the Bodyguard in Carmania (Arr. vi 28.3). See further Berve (n. 34) no. 634.

102 Plut. *Al.* 43.7; Curt. vi 2.11. He remained at court for a little over a year, returning to Ecbatana to supervise the execution of Bessus (Diod. 83.9; Curt. vii 5.40; Justin xii 5.11).

103 Arr. iv 3.7. For the persistence of Iranian families in southern Asia Minor throughout the Hellenistic and Roman periods see L. Robert, *Opera Minora Selecta* iii (Amsterdam 1969) 1532 ff.; *CRAI* 1975, 326–30. For the specifically Lycian evidence see E. Benveniste, *Titres et noms propres en iranien ancien* (Paris 1966) 101–3.

104 Arr. iv 6.1 = *FGrH* 139 F 27. For the general bias of this account see L. Pearson, *The Lost Histories of Alexander the Great* (1960) 167 f. Curtius vii 6.24, 7.34 ff. says nothing about Pharnuches and makes Menedemus sole commander (so *Metz Epit.* 13).

105 Arr. *Ind.* 18.8 = *FGrH* 133 F 1a.

106 Ael. *VH* iii 23 = *FGrH* 117 F 2a. Berve (n. 34) no. 195 and Badian, *CQ* viii (1958) 156, prefer to identify this Bagoas as the notorious eunuch.

107 Arr. vii 6.4–5. For the textual problems (not relevant here) see the *Appendix*, [below, p. 312].

108 Some had already given service to Alexander: Cophes had negotiated the surrender of Ariomazes (Curt. vii 11.22 ff.), Phradasmenes had brought succour to the army in Carmania (Arr. vi 27.3) and Artiboles had played a role in the pursuit of Darius (iii 21.1; but *cf.* Curt. v 13.11; Berve (n. 34) nos. 82, 154).

109 There is a possibilbity that they are the sons of Atropates, the third Iranian satrap surviving in 324 (Berve (n. 34) no. 124); his two colleagues, Phrataphernes and Oxyartes, had supplied sons for the *agema*, and he had visited Alexander at Pasargadae, shortly after the arrival of Phradasmenes and Phrataphernes (Arr. vi 29.3; *cf.* 27.3).

110 *Cf.* Curt. vi 2.7, adding that Hystaspes was both a relative of Darius and a military commander under him. For the fifth-century Hystaspes see Diod. xi 69.2. Given his Bactrian connexions and his relationship to Darius there is some chance that he was a relative of Bessus!

111 Arr. iv 13.1; Curt. viii 6.2–6; *cf.* Berve (n. 34) i 37–9.

112 Arr. iii 24.1; *cf.* 25.2–5, 29.7; iv 4.7, 23.1, 25.6, 26.4, 29.7; vi 17.4.

113 Berve (n. 34) i 151; Brunt, *JHS* lxxxiii (1963) 42; Griffith, *JHS* lxxxiii (1963) 69 f.

114 Arr. iii 25.2, 5. The remaining ἱππακοντισταί were used on Alexander's punitive expedition (25.6).

115 Compare Arr. iii 25.6 with 20.1.

116 Arr. iv 4.6–7. *Cf.* Brunt (n. 113) 27 f.; R. D. Milns, *JHS* lxxxvi (1966) 167; M. M. Markle, *AJA* lxxxi (1977) 337.

117 It is possible that even before 330 the σαρισσοφοροι used their special weapon only in pitched battle (Arr. i 14.1; Curt. iv 15.13); it would have been an unnecessary encumbrance: *cf.* Markle (n. 116) 334–6.

118 Arr. iii 29.7. The date and nature of the reorganisation is disputed (*cf.* Brunt (n. 113) 28–30; Griffith (n. 113) 70–73) and the subject badly needs a thorough investigation. But the year 330 was undoubtedly a time of military innovation: *cf.* iii 16.11 (cavalry *lochoi*), iii 18.5 (a mysterious and unique cavalry *tetrarchia*).

119 The javelin was a traditional weapon of the Macedonian cavalry, illustrated on the coinage of Alexander I (*cf.* Markle (n. 116) 337 n. 59); the Companions may have fought with a javelin as well as their thrusting lance (Diod. 60.2; Arr. i 2–6; but *cf.* i 15.6).

120 Arr. iv 17.3; *cf.* Griffith (n. 113) 69.

121 Arr. v 11.3 (cavalry from Arachosia and Parapamisadae serving alongside Craterus' hipparchy); v 12.2 (Bactrians, Sogdians and Saka, including Dahian horse archers).

122 Arr. iv 24.1, 28.8; v 14.3, 15.1, 16.4, 18.3, 20.3 22.5; vi 5.5, 6.1, 21.3, 22.1.

123 Arr. v 12.2 καὶ Δάας τοὺς ἱπποτόξοτας. They were apparently 1,000 strong (v 16.4); see further Altheim (n. 3) 210 f.

124 vii 8.2: ἀνάμιξις τῶν ἀλλοφύλων ἐς τὰς τῶν ἑταίρων τάξεις. Griffith (n. 113) 68, 72 f., made absurdly heavy weather of this passage and denied that Arrian is summarising his previous exposition. Instead he argues that Arrian refers to a reorganisation during the Indian campaign, in which Orientals were added to the hipparchies; see the convincing rebuttal of Badian, *JHS* lxxxv (1965) 160.

125 Brunt (n. 113) 43. For the arrival of Drangians, Areians and Parthyaeans see Arr. vi 27.3. The Euacae are only known from Arrian, but they may be a picked unit, the cavalry equivalent of the *Kardakes* of the infantry (Arr. ii 8.6; Nepos *Dat.* 8.2; Hsch. s.v.; Tarn (n. 3) ii 180–2 should be discounted).

126 So Arr. *Tact.* 5.2–4: πλῆθος ἀνθρώπον ἀθρόον καὶ ἄτακτον ἐς τάξιν καὶ κόσμον καταστῆσαι - τὸ δ' ἔστιν καταλοχίσαι τε καὶ ξυλλοχίσαι. Compare Arr. vii 24.1 where he describes the division of Peucestas' Persians into phalanx files; at vii 23.3 he uses καταλέγειν as a synonym (*cf.* Diod. xviii 70.1).

127 So Griffith (n. 113) 72: his second interpretation 'one λοχος of each *ile* now became a λοχος of picked Iranians' is not impossible, but again it reads too much into the wording. The word anticipates κατελέγησαν and προσκαταλεγέντες immediately below and, as at vii 24.1, it is used as a conscious variant in the most general sense.

128 I do not understand how Brunt (n. 113) 44 can say that it 'might mean that it was more or less Oriental than the other four'.

129 E.g. Berve (n. 34) i 111 f.; Tarn (n. 3) ii 164 f.; Brunt (n. 113) 43 f.; Griffith (n. 113) 72–4.

130 There were eight hipparchies in addition to the *agema* between 328 and 326 (*cf.* Arr. iv 24.1 with 22.7, 23.1; vi 6.4 with 7.2 and 6.1; Brunt [n. 113] 29 has miscalculated by one). There must have been serious losses in Gedrosia but we have no basis for speculation.

131 For the casualties see H. Strasburger, *Hermes* lxxx (1952) 486 f. (15,000 survivors out of 60,000/70,000). For the livestock see Arr. vi 25.1: τῶν ἵππων τοὺς πολλοὺς ἀποσφάζοντες.

132 Arr. vii 11.3; *cf.* Griffith (n. 113) 72: 'this must imply that hitherto its members have been all Macedonians'.

133 Arr. vi. 17.3; vi 14.4 does not explicitly exclude Iranians.

134 Anaximenes *FGrH* 72 F 4; on which see most recently P. A. Brunt, *JHS* xcvi (1976) 150–3; R. D. Milns in *Entr. Hardt* xxii (1976) 89 ff.

135 Arr. vii 6.1; Diod. 108. 1–3; Plut. *Al.* 71.1.

136 Plut. *Al.* 47.6.

137 P. Briant, *RÉA* lxxiv (1972) 51–60, esp. 55 – an excellent summary, but slightly misleading in that Briant (57) seems to think that Alexander actually conferred the title *pezhetairoi* upon his

Iranian infantry at Opis. Arrian suggests that Alexander made a threat only; there is not hint that he fully carried it out.

138 Diod. xi 67.5 (*cf.* Plut. *Cleom.* 23.1); Plut. *Eum.* 4.2–3: *pace* Briant (n. 137) 58 it does not appear that Eumenes created an ἀντίταγμα against his own troops. After the victory against Ariarathes Neoptolemus was left to continue operations in Armenia with a large nucleus of Macedonian troops (Briant, *Antigone le Borgne* [Paris 1973] 152 n. 8). According to Plutarch Perdiccas had his suspicions of Neoptolemus' loyalty and commissioned Eumenes to control him – hence the need for the Iranian cavalry to be used against Neoptolemus' phalanx (*Eum.* 4.3, *cf.* 5.4). There is no indication that Eumenes had Macedonians of his own in any numbers (*cf.* Diod. xviii 29.5).

139 Curt. viii 5.1: *obsides simul habiturus et milites.* Justin xii 4.11 dates the formation of the *Epigoni* to the same period but conflates them with the soldiers' children who were also trained in Macedonian style (*cf.* Arr. vii 12.2).

140 vii 6.1: οἱ σατράπαι οἱ ἐκ τῶν πόλεων τῶν νεοκτίστων καὶ τῆς ἄλλης γῆς τῆς δοριαλώτου. At v 20.7 Sisicottus, previously named phrurarch of Aornus (iv 30.4), is termed satrap. For the interchangeability of the terms satrap and hyparch see Bosworth, *CQ* xxiv (1974) 55–7.

141 E.g. iv 22.4.

142 Justin xii 4.2–10: Berve (n. 5) 157–9 valiantly attempts to prove that the women of these marriages were predominantly Iranian.

143 Arr. vii 4.8 (*cf.* Plut. *Al.* 70.3); vii 12.2.

144 Diod. xvii 74.3; Curt. vi 2.15–4.1; Justin xii 3.2–4; Plut. *Al.* 47.1–2.

145 *Cf.* Badian (n. 7) 201: 'his purpose, ultimately, was the creation of a royal army with no fixed blood or domicile – children of the camp who knew no loyalty but to him'.

146 Arr. vii 23.1–4; *cf.* Diod. 110.2 (wrongly assigned to Susa 324).

147 Plb. xviii 30.1–4; *cf.* Arr. *Tact.* 12.10.

148 Arr. *Ect. c. Alanos* 15–17, 26 f. For full discussion see Bosworth, *HSCP* lxxxi (1977) 238–47.

149 Arr. i 6.1–3; ii 8.2 (*cf.* Plb. xii 19.5 f.; Curt. iii 9.12).

150 So Brunt (n. 113) 38; Griffith, *G&R* xii (1965) 130–1 n. 4. Berve (n. 34) i 134, was more cautious (Curtius gives a total of Macedonians *and Greeks* without giving their relative proportions).

151 *Cf.* Curt. x 2.2; Justin xiii 5.7 (Athens). For the Arabian expedition see Schachermeyr (n. 3) 538–46.

152 Even so the possibility of being chosen led to panic (Curt. x 2.12).

153 Diod. xviii 16.4. The figure 10,000 is standard; Arr. vii 12.1; Diod. xvii 109.1; *cf.* Justin xii 12.7 (11,000, presumably including the 1,500 cavalry).

154 Curt. vii 10.11 f.; ix 3.21. Alexander had sent a recruiting expedition from Sogdiana in winter 328/7 (Arr. iv 18.3) but there were no results before 323, when the cavalry with Menidas at Babylon *may* have come from Macedonia (vii 23.1; *cf.* Berve [n. 34] no. 258, Badian [n. 52] 22 n. 39). Justin also suggests that the shortage of Macedonians was becoming apparent by 327 (xxii 4.5).

155 Diod. xviii 12.2. *Pace* Griffith (n. 150) 130 f., the forces of Antipater in 323 cannot be estimated from Diodorus' figures, for Μακεδόνες at 12.2 patently means 'the forces on the Macedonian side', doubtless including Illyrians and Thracians as well as mercenaries: *cf.* M. Launey, *Recherches sur les armées hellénistiques* (Paris 1949) 292 f. We should remember that Antipater was in similar difficulties at the time of Agis' War yet was able to raise a force of 40,000: Diod. 63.1; *cf. Phoenix* xxix (1975) 35–8. Similarly we have no idea how many of the 20,000 foot raised by Leonnatus (Diod. xviii 14.4–5) were native Macedonians. The only thing certain is that the forces with Craterus in 321 were 20,000 in number and 'mostly Macedonians' (Diod. xviii 30.4; *cf.* 24.1), but, once again, the nucleus must have been the veterans he had brought from Opis.

156 For their presence with Perdiccas see Arr. *Succ.* F 1.35 (Roos) and for their famous ἀποσκευή see Diod. xix 43.7; Plut. *Eum.* 16; Justin xiv 3.3 ff.

157 Peithon in 323 had 3,000 infantry and 800 cavalry selected by lot from the Macedonians (Diod. xviii 7.3) and Neoptolemus had an unspecified number of Macedonians in Armenia (above, n. 138); but we have no criteria for calculating the total. Berve's estimate of 4,000–5,000 (i 185) is the merest guess (see also Schachermeyr [n. 14] 14 f: 5,000–6,000 phalangites and hypaspists).

158 Diod. xix 30.6, 41.1–2; Plut. *Eum.* 16.7–8.

159 Justin xvii 2.10 f.; for Antigonus see Hieronymus, *FGrH* 154 F 10.

160 Arr. vii 12.4; on this matter see Badian (n. 52) 38 f.; Bosworth (n. 69) 125.

161 Arr. vii 25.2 (from the *Ephemerides*); *cf.* Plut. *Al.* 76.3 with Hamilton's notes.

162 Contrast Berve (n. 5) 157: 'Und es kann kaum einem Zweifel unterliegen, dass Alexander auch den aus Makedonien zu erwartenden Nachschub mit iranischen Elementen ... in ähnlicher Weise zu verbinden beabsichtigte.'

APPENDIX: ARRIAN VII 6.4

καὶ πέμπτη ἐπὶ τούτοις ἱππαρχία προσγενομένη, οὐ βαρβαρικὴ πᾶσα, ἀλλὰ ἐπαυξηθέντος γὰρ τοῦ παντὸς ἱππικοῦ κατελέγησαν ἐς αὐτὸ τῶν βαρβάρων.

'. . . and a fifth hipparchy added in addition to these, not entirely barbarian (but partially), for when the entire cavalry was expanded some barbarians were assigned to it.'

The difficulty is in the parenthesis. It purports to explain the existence of the fifth hipparchy but instead talks of the entire cavalry. The fact that some barbarians were assigned to the cavalry is a mere summary of the preceding phrases not an explanation of the formation of the fifth mixed hipparchy. There have been two recent attempts at emendation:

(i) Brunt, *JHS* lxxxiii (1963) 44, deletes the following phrase (τῷ τε ἀγήματι προσκαταλεγέντες) as a gloss and emends ἐς αὐτὸ to ἐς αὐτήν. The effect of this is to identify the fifth hipparchy as the *agema* (or rather, to remove the *agema* altogether) and contrast a fifth, barely infiltrated, hipparchy with four more heavily Oriental hipparchies. The gloss presupposed is difficult. Explanatory glosses in Arrian are usually rudimentary, whereas here we have a very sophisticated inference by the scribal commentator, identifying the fifth hipparchy with the *agema*. Nor is the τε 'curiously unemphatic'; it is the regular connective used to denote the last item in a series (Denniston, *Greek Particles*² 500 f.)–and the reorganisation of the *agema* is patently the last of the Macedonians' grievances.

(ii) Badian, *JHS* lxxxv (1965) 161, suggests the simple supplement <μόνον> οὐ βαρβαρικὴ ἡ πᾶσα. This creates the impression that the fifth hipparchy contrasted with the other four by its preponderance of barbarians. But the parenthesis remains curiously unhelpful. The idiom ἀλλά . . . γὰρ is extremely frequent in Arrian and in all cases it combines an adversative with an explanation (*cf.* e.g. v 13.2: οὐκ ἐς βέβαιον χωρίον ἐκβὰς . . . ἀλλὰ ἐς νῆσον γὰρ – 'not onto sure ground but the reverse, for it was an island'). The negative prepares the way for the explanation and cannot be emended away.

The difficulty lies in ἐς αὐτό, which is pleonastic and vacuous. What is needed is an explanation why the fifth hipparchy was not wholly barbarian, as opposed to the four wholly Iranian hipparchies. Any attempt to solve the problem involves quite drastic surgery, but I would tentatively suggest ἐς <τ>αὐτο, or more explicitly ἐς <τ>αὐτο <τοῖς Μακεδόσι> and translate 'not entirely barbarian but partially, for when the entire cavalry was expanded some barbarians were assigned to the same unit as Macedonians'. (For Arrian's use of ἐς ταὐτό see v 25.3; *Ind.* 3.9; 10.9.) But, whatever the original sense of the parenthesis, Arrian's presentation of the Macedonian grievances is clear and logical; first the existence of hipparchies comprised wholly of Iranians and then, much worse, the fifth hipparchy in which they served with the barbarians.

ETHNICITY AND CULTURAL POLICY
AT ALEXANDER'S COURT

E.N. Borza

In the more than half a century since William Woodthorpe Tarn proclaimed the 'Brotherhood of Mankind,'[1] there has been a narrowing interpretation of Alexander the Great's vision. Recent scholarship has replaced most of Alexander's Grand Plans with 'minimalist' interpretations.

Tarn's conception of *homonoia* was never accepted by some scholars, and within five years of its publication in the *Cambridge Ancient History*, Ulrich Wilcken attacked it as unsupported by the evidence.[2] Despite Wilcken's criticism, Tarn's views of Alexander as a social philosopher settled into the public consciousness, and into some scholarly opinion, as well.[3]

It was not until the 1950s and 1960s that the full force of criticism turned on Tarn. The 'revisionist' school of Alexander historiography, led by Ernst Badian, was characterized by severe source criticism and proved that the 'homonoic' vision of Alexander was mainly a product of Tarn's unacceptable squeezing of sources. An analysis of the *language* of Arrian at 7.11.9 — the famous prayer of reconciliation at Opis — shows that, in comparison with uses of similar constructions elsewhere in Arrian, the 'concord' or 'harmony' referred to in Alexander's prayer[4] is limited to the Persians and Macedonians and is not inclusive of the whole human race.[5]

What was left of Alexander's Grand Plan was an idea introduced by Wilcken in 1931 to replace Tarn's World Brotherhood.[6] Wilcken argued that, while the king had no intention of uniting all the races of Europe and Asia into a great concord, he did, in fact, attempt to join the ruling peoples of those continents — the Macedonians and Persians — into a commonality of shared power. This view — called 'Fusion' — has persisted for more than a half century, generally accepted at one time by many persons, myself included.

But in 1978 A.B. Bosworth presented a paper at a meeting of the Association of Ancient Historians, the full version of which appeared in the *Journal of Hellenic Studies* (1980) under the title 'Alexander and the Iranians.' Bosworth argued persuasively that there was little evidence even for a fusion between Persians and Macedonians. In an analysis of Alexander's activities toward the end of his life — where most of the evidence for fusion has seemed to reside — Bosworth showed, for example, that nearly all the Iranian auxiliaries incorporated into the army were kept as separate units. The Asians were used mainly as a political counterweight to threaten Macedonians who were disaffected from their king. Other evidence for uniting the races of Europe and Asia must be seen as *ad hoc* solutions to immediate problems, not as a part of a general policy.[7]

I accept the views of Bosworth on this issue. But what are we left with? Has the position about Alexander's Grand Scheme become so minimalist as to leave nothing but a piece of military history and a serendipitous adventure story?

There is, in fact, one surviving theme that runs through the literature and is also one of the most enduring public views of the great king's achievement: Alexander spread Greek civilization by means of his passage through Asia. It is this perception of Alexander's mission that forms the subject of the present essay.

Caution must be the methodological byword. One must make a clear distinction between what our ancient sources believed was Alexander's thinking on the matter of hellenism, and what Alexander himself actually accomplished. Ancient writers, like modern ones, wrote with the advantage of hindsight. They understood that western Asia was transformed as the result of Alexander's passage. They also knew that Alexander and his court were in many respects quite highly hellenized. It was thus easy to connect the two in a cause-and-effect relationship. (On this issue, scholarly method seems not to have advanced very much during the past eighteen centuries.)

Let us, therefore, set aside for the moment our recognition of Alexander's great achievement of conquest, and our knowledge that his passage resulted in, among other things, the establishment of Greek culture in its Hellenistic form around the eastern rim of the Mediterranean, and that this remained an enduring cultural feature of the region until the Islamic conquests. Let us, instead, review the evidence to see precisely what Alexander *intended* in the way of hellenization, and what he consciously instituted as policy.

First, the matter of the Hellenic origins of the Macedonians: Nicholas Hammond's general conclusion (though not the details of his arguments)[8] that the origin of the Macedonians lies in the pool of proto-Greek speakers who migrated out of the Pindus mountains during the Iron Age, is acceptable. As for the Macedonian royal house, the Argead dynasty was probably indigenous, the story of their Temenid Greek origin being part of the prohellenic propaganda of King Alexander I. This is a position I have already argued in print and do not wish to take up further here.[9]

Whatever the truth about the origins of the Macedonian people and their royal house, it does not affect what follows. We have suspected from literary sources for some time that the Macedonian court had become highly hellenized at least by the time of King Archelaus at the end of the fifth century B.C. And now the recent remarkable discoveries of Greek archaeologists working at Vergina and elsewhere confirm the cultural debt owed by the Macedonian gentry to the Greeks who lived in the south. There can be no remaining doubt about the degree to which at least some Macedonians on the highest levels shared a version of Greek culture.

Moreover, Alexander himself, tutored by Aristotle and raised in a court in which a manifestation of hellenism was a component of diplomacy, was a lover of Greek culture. But we must make a distinction between Alexander's personal predilections – his cultural baggage, as it were – and what he intended as policy.

Whether Alexander had a strategic policy for his empire is a matter that cannot be considered here. The question is complex and tangled in source problems, and one often despairs that it can ever be answered. But it may be possible to examine the evidence for hellenization. That is, did Alexander consciously attempt to hellenize, keeping in mind, of course, the distinction mentioned above between his personal cultural attitudes and what he intended for others to do?

Of the cultural features of Alexander's court, very little need be said. The king's train included a number of Greeks, and court practices were often hellenized,[10] resulting from the influence of Greeks in the king's train and also from those features of Macedonian life already hellenized. Although it is undeniable that a Macedonian court somewhat hellenized may have influenced policy and helped spread Greek culture, it is difficult to prove. One suspects that the extent to which Greek culture was propagated in this manner was as a byproduct of imperial conquest and administration rather than as the result of direct policy. On this point we look forward to the development of Greek frontier studies comparable to the successful accomplishments of our colleagues in Roman frontier studies. The recent work of Frank Holt on the Bactrian frontier, for example, suggests that Greek culture in the early Hellenistic period did not permeate native traditions very deeply, a conclusion similar to that reached by Stanley Burstein in his study of Egyptian Meroë.[11]

None of this adds up to a *policy* of hellenization. Perhaps we can see something in the relationship between Alexander and the Greeks themselves. There is one feature of Alexander's administration that has not been much examined, and that is the ethnicity of the persons who surrounded the king. If, for example, it could be shown that Greeks were often selected to hold important posts in imperial administration, one might conclude that that very selection and Alexander's dependence upon those Greeks were tantamount to a policy of hellenization.

What was the role of the Greeks associated with Alexander during his Asian campaign? What military or administrative assignments were they given? How close were they to the king? Of needs we turn to that magisterial data bank of Alexander's reign, the *Das Alexanderreich* of Helmut Berve, published nearly seven decades ago, but still the most useful compilation of prosopographical evidence relating to the Macedonian conqueror. What follows is based on a computer-assisted study of Alexander's associates, using the data from Berve, with some corrections and modifications. The computer was used to organize several categories of information about these persons, such as ethnic background and *cursus honorum*. A simple sort and list routine enabled the extraction of information about the individuals according to category. The two categories of information used here are: (1) ethnic origin, and (2) the offices or commands held by persons according to ethnicity.

What follows are some of the conclusions arising from this study of ethnicity, with the following caveats: first, there are a number of persons in Berve's list whose origin is uncertain. I have taken this problem into account, although the number is too small to affect much the outcome of the study. Second, I believe that one can make valid ethnic distinctions among the peoples of antiquity. The ancient authors themselves did so regularly, and such distinctions are a necessary component of my method.

On the matter of distinctions between Greeks and Macedonians in particular, I accept the general view expressed by Ernst Badian in his paper 'Greeks and Macedonians.'[12] Badian showed that in antiquity, neither Greeks nor Macedonians considered the Macedonians to be Greek. The ethnic distinctions in the present study are: mainland Greek, Asian and island Greek, Macedonian, other Balkan, Persian, other Asian, and a small miscellaneous category for the remainder.

Of the nearly 850 persons listed by Berve, 275 are either certainly or probably ethnic Greeks. Of this number, 126 persons are not associated with Alexander's train, and thus outside present concerns. Of the 149 which remain, sixty-nine – nearly half – are court figures not associated with administration. They are there mainly for what one might call 'cultural' reasons. They include sophists, physicians, actors, athletes, musicians, jugglers and other entertainers, and a variety of hangers-on.

Eighty names remain. Of these three are of uncertain ethnic origin. Twenty-four Greeks serve the king in a variety of administrative tasks: some are envoys, some are clerks, some financial officers, some act as the king's agents in local places. They pop in and out of the historical record as Alexander sees the need to employ them. More of these Greeks are Asian than European. Beyond that there is no pattern or apparent policy. The king uses these people because he finds it expedient to exploit individual skills.

The remaining fifty-three Greeks serve specific military functions. Of these, the extraordinary number of twenty-two names are attached to a single unit, the allies from Orchomenos, who are dismissed along with the other Greek allies in 330 B.C. Fourteen other Greeks hold naval appointments, either as ship commanders on the Hydaspes fleet, or in conjunction with Nearchus' ocean voyage.

Four Greeks are in charge of mercenary units, and nine others have unspecified, low-level military assignments. Seven have duties that did not take them beyond Egypt, where a number remained to carry on administrative tasks.

In summary, of the 149 known Greeks with official connections to the king, only thirty-five to forty held positions of rank – some as officers, some as administrators, but only a handful in top positions.

A look at Alexander's satrapal appointments reveals a similar pattern. We know of fifty-two different persons who held satrapies in Alexander's empire over a dozen years. Of these, twenty-four were Persians and Asians, a number of them continuing in posts held earlier under Darius. Twenty-three Macedonian satrapal appointments were made, nearly the same number as Asians. There are only five Greeks who held satrapies. Of these, Nearchus (Berve #544) and perhaps Sibyrtius (#703) were Cretan, Stasenor (#719) was a Cypriote, Cleomenes (#431) was from Naucratis in Egypt, and Thoas (#376) was from Magnesia on the Meander. No mainland Greek ever held a satrapy in Alexander's empire.

An examination of the satrapal offices held at the time of Alexander's death shows that of the twenty-four known satraps, six were easterners, fifteen were Macedonian and three were Greek, in this case – stretching the ethnic definition – Nearchus (#544) and Sibyrtius (#703) of Crete, and Cleomenes (#431) of Egypt. The pattern is clear: the trend toward the end of the king's life was to install Macedonians in key positions at the expense of Asians, and to retain very few Greeks.

Similarly, of the twenty-four garrison commanders mentioned in Arrian, twenty-one are Macedonian, two are Indian and only one is Greek – Lycidas (#475), who was left in charge of mercenaries in Egypt.

Alexander's inner circle, his *hetairoi*, would appear to replicate the pattern. Of the sixty-five or so men named as *hetairoi*, nine are Greek, including three mainlanders. Of the nine, four owed their positions to life-long connections with Macedon: Nearchus (#544) and the brothers Erygius (#302) and Laomedon (#464) were in fact raised as Macedonians, and Demaratus (#253) of Corinth had been associated with the court since the time of Philip II.

Thus we look in vain for the evidence that Alexander was heavily dependent upon Greeks either in quantity or quality. We learn that rather few Greeks beyond the sycophants and entertainers at court were associated with the king either in his inner circle or in important military and administrative positions.[13] There is one exception, however, the faithful and competent Greek *grammateus* Eumenes (#317) of Cardia, but he may be the exception that proves the rule. And if there were any doubt about the status of Greeks among the Macedonians, the tragic career of Eumenes in the immediate Wars of Succession should put it to rest. The ancient sources are replete with information about the ethnic prejudice Eumenes suffered from Macedonians.[14]

There is one other aspect of Alexander's Greek policy, and that is his formal relationship with the Greek cities of Europe and Asia. In European Greece Alexander continued and reinforced Philip II's policy of rule over the city-states, a rule resulting from conquest. As for the island Greeks and the cities of Asia Minor, their status under the reigns of Philip and Alexander has been much debated.[15] Fortunately, for my purposes, the status of these cities, whether as members of Philip II's panhellenic league or as independent towns, is not crucial, as they were in fact all treated by Alexander as subjects. Much of the debate on the issue, while interesting and occasionally enlightening, has sometimes obscured a simple reality: Greeks on both sides of the Aegean were subject to the authority of the king of Macedon.

The conclusion is inescapable: there was a largely ethnic Macedonian imperial administration from beginning to end. Alexander used Greeks at court for cultural reasons, Greek troops (often under Macedonian commanders) for limited tasks and with some discomfort, and Greek commanders and officials for limited duties. Typically, a Greek would enter Alexander's service from an Aegean or Asian city through the practice of some special activity: he could read and write, keep figures or sail, all of which skills the Macedonians required. Some Greeks may have moved on to military service as well. In other words, the role of Greeks in Alexander's service was not much different from what their role had been in the service of Xerxes and the third Darius.

If one wishes to believe that Alexander had a policy of hellenization – as opposed to the incidental and informal spread of Greek culture – the evidence must come from sources other than those presented here. One wonders – archaeology aside – where this evidence would be.

We have seen that not only has the idea of World Brotherhood been put to rest and the idea of a Fusion of Persian and Macedonian ruling classes made doubtful, but that the value of Greeks to Alexander for policy reasons cannot be sustained by evidence. In short, there is no World Brotherhood, no fusion, and no evidence of a *policy* of hellenization, if that hellenization were intended to be accomplished through the medium of ethnic Greeks.

Notes

1 Tarn in *CAH* 6 (1926), *Proc. of the British Academy* (1933), and *Alexander the Great* (Cambridge, 1948), esp. 2: 399 ff.
   Earlier versions of the present paper were presented at the 1989 annual meeting of the Friends of Ancient History in Baltimore, and at the 1990 meetings of the Pacific Coast Branch of the American Historical Association in Salt Lake City. I wish to thank Ernst Badian, Ian Morris, and Edward Anson, who were commentators at those meetings, for their suggestions, criticism and encouragement. What appears here is part of a continuing larger study of ethnicity in the administration of Alexander. I am pleased to offer it in its present form as a tribute to my teacher, Stewart Oost, who neither admired Alexander nor believed he had any impulse beyond conquest.

2 E.g., *Alexander der Grosse* (1931), English trans., by G.C. Richards, notes by E.N. Borza (New York, 1967), 221.

3 E.g., C.A. Robinson, 'The Extraordinary Ideas of Alexander the Great,' *AHR* 62 (1957) 326–44.

4 The publication by Stadter and Boulter of a microform concordance to Arrian has greatly simplified textual analysis of this type.

5 The version Arrian gives us probably is verbatim or near-verbatim of what Alexander actually said. Of course, one must consider seriously that whatever Alexander said may not have been what he intended, which is one of the main points of the present paper.

6 *Alex. the Great* (1967) 246–56.

317

7   Bosworth's views have not persuaded everyone, especially those for whom old habits die hard; e.g. N.G.L. Hammond in *Alexander the Great. King, Commander and Statesman* (1980) and elsewhere.

8   As expressed in *History of Macedonia* I and II (Oxford, 1972–79) *passim*, and more recently in *The Macedonian State* (Oxford 1989) chap. 1.

9   See my 'Origins of the Macedonian Royal House,' *Hesperia*, Suppl. 19 (1982) 7–13 [see article 5 in the original], and *In the Shadow of Olympus. The Emergence of Macedon* (Princeton, 1990) 80–84 and 110–13.

10 E.g., the Macedonian version of the symposium; see my 'The Symposium at Alexander's Court,' *Archaia Makedonia* 3 (1983) 45–55, [see article 9 in the original] and 'Anaxarchus and Callisthenes. Academic Intrigue at Alexander's Court,' *Ancient Macedonian Studies in Honor of Charles F. Edson* (Thessaloniki, 1981) 73–86 [see article 10 in the original].

11 F.L. Holt, *Alexander and Bactria, Mnemosyne* Suppl. 104 (Leiden, 1988), and the papers of Holt and Burstein in *Hellenistic History and Culture*, ed. Peter Green (Berkeley and Los Angeles, 1992).

12 *Macedonia and Greece in Late Classical and Early Hellenistic Times.* Studies in the History of Art 10, ed. B. Barr-Sharrar and E.N. Borza (Washington, 1982) 33–51.

13 There are limits to such a statistics-based argument. We are prisoners of the evidence that has survived, and my use of statistics in this fashion recognizes that the tiny number of Greeks who played important roles in Alexander's court is relative to the total number of names that *have survived.* Some persons friendly to my conclusions have suggested that I should consider using some modern statistical techniques to determine the possible *total* number of those who served Alexander in administrative and other capacities by extrapolating from the evidence we have. I have thought seriously about this, but am unable to develop a sound historical method by which I can make something from nothing. I do not know whether the ethnicities of those who served Alexander would be the equivalent of what was determined from Berve's prosopography, should I attempt to establish some total numbers. Only in the case of the satrapal appointments can we be reasonably certain that we have close to total numbers; *in the case of the satrapies the pattern of a tiny number of Greeks relative to the total is confirmed.* One must act prudently on this issue and report what the evidence says, while admitting that it is difficult, if not impossible, to determine the extent to which the surviving evidence is an accurate reflection of the actual total numbers.

14 E.g., Plut. *Eum.* 3.1; 8.1; 18.1; Diod. 18.60.1–3, 62.7 and 19.13.1–2. For present purposes I have not cited several pieces of anecdotal evidence from the sources on Alexander that establish the continuing tension at court between Greeks and Macedonians, tension that the ancient authors clearly recognized as ethnic division. A fuller version of this study will consider these incidents to support my view that Greeks and Macedonians did not get along very well with one another and that this ethnic tension was exploited even by the king himself.

15 E. Badian, 'Alexander and the Greeks of Asia,' *Ancient Society and Institutions. Studies Presented to Victor Ehrenberg* (Oxford, 1966) 37–96. Also see, e.g., V. Ehrenberg, *Alexander and the Greeks* (Oxford, 1938) 1–51; Tarn, *Alexander* 2: App. 7; and A.J. Heisserer, *Alexander the Great and the Greeks. The Epigraphic Evidence* (Norman, 1980), conclusions at 230–37.

10

ALEXANDER
AND DEIFICATION

Introduction

One of the most controversial aspects of Alexander's life is his apparent belief in his own divinity. The figure of the Macedonian king was semi-divine while alive,[1] and it is possible that Philip II was deified on his death in 336. As Alexander's reign progressed, he strove to outdo his father's achievements, and deification while alive was clearly one way to do so. Perhaps at first Alexander sought to be recognized as a god in an effort to maintain the conquered peoples' unity and loyalty to him. However, as his megalomania grew in the later part of his reign, he seems to have held the belief that he was divine, dressing in imitation of various deities, having incense burned in honour of him (Source 105), and even thinking that his exploits outstripped those of Dionysus, as one of his motives for invading Arabia reveals (Source 106).

The road to Alexander's deification began in winter 332 when he visited the Oracle of Zeus Ammon in the oasis of Siwah in Egypt, guided there in miraculous fashion (Sources 98–103).[2] Here, the priest apparently told him (we have only Alexander's word for it, for he met with him in private) that he was a son of Zeus. This was the turning point in his belief, and from then on he referred to himself in this way (for example before the Battle of Gaugamela in 331: Source 104).

In 327, he tried to have the Asian custom of *proskynesis* (prostrating oneself before the person of the king in an act of subservience) adopted by his men at his court in Bactra (Sources 94 and 95).[3] To them, prostration before a ruler was tantamount to worship, hence blasphemous, and Callisthenes led the resistance. Alexander was forced to abandon the attempt. While his aim may have been to create a form of social protocol common to Macedonians, Greeks and Persians, he must have been aware of the religious connotations associated with the act and the hostile reaction it would provoke among his men. Hence the only plausible explanation is that his attempt was a means of having his divine status recognized by all men in public (Arr. 4.9.9, Curt. 8.5.5).

Then in 323 the Greeks of the mainland were discussing divine honours for Alexander,[4] although there was resistance to it.[5] It has sometimes been thought that by this stage Alexander wanted all Greeks to worship him and issued a decree ordering this, but that is unlikely. Equally mistaken is the view that Alexander claimed divinity because his Exiles Decree, which flouted the autonomy of the Greek cities, would be rejected by the League of Corinth as an unconstitutional measure – but not if it came from a god!

Alexander's deification had repercussions for him and his kingship. The Greeks accepted that Alexander was a descendant of Zeus through Heracles, but descendant of

Zeus was different from Alexander calling himself an actual son of Zeus, and this the people did not accept. The *proskynesis* attempt caused widespread dissatisfaction of the army with him, which Alexander must have anticipated but chose to ignore. Certainly, the wishes and beliefs of his men meant little to him, for a year later he was back to claiming divine status (Arr. 7.2.3), and during the Opis mutiny his men mocked their king's association with Zeus Ammon (Arr. 7.8.3). Finally, there was widespread resistance to Alexander's proposed deification among the Greeks and even more significantly among the Macedonians on the mainland, Alexander's own people.[6] Yet the question still remains: to what extent was Alexander exploiting divinity for political reasons, or did he really believe he was a god on earth?

Ancient sources

The oracle of Zeus Ammon

98   Hence the oracle of Ammon, which was formerly held in great esteem, is now nearly deserted. This appears chiefly from the historians who have recorded the actions of Alexander, adding, indeed, much that has the appearance of flattery, but yet relating what is worthy of credit. Callisthenes, for instance, says that Alexander was ambitious of the glory of visiting the oracle, because he knew that Perseus and Heracles had before performed the journey thither. He set out from Paraetonium, although the south winds were blowing, and succeeded in his undertaking by vigour and perseverance. When out of his way on the road, he escaped being overwhelmed in a sand storm by a fall of rain, and by the guidance of two crows, which directed his course. These things are stated by way of flattery, as also what follows: that the priest permitted the king alone to pass into the temple in his usual dress, whereas the others changed theirs; that all heard the oracles on the outside of the temple, except Alexander, who was in the interior of the building; that the answers were not given, as at Delphi and at Branchidae, in words, but chiefly by nods and signs, as in Homer: 'the son of Kronos nodded with his sable brows', the prophet imitating Zeus. This, however, the man told the king, in express terms, that he was the son of Zeus. Callisthenes adds (after the exaggerating style of tragedy) that when Apollo had deserted the oracle among the Branchidae, on the temple being plundered by the Branchidae (who espoused the party of the Persians in the time of Xerxes) and the spring had failed, it then reappeared (on the arrival of Alexander); that the ambassadors also of the Milesians carried back to Memphis numerous answers of the oracle respecting the descent of Alexander from Zeus, and the future victory which he should obtain at Arbela,[7] the death of Darius, and the political changes at Sparta. He says also that the Erythraean Athenais, who resembled the ancient Erythraean Sibyl, had declared the high descent of Alexander. Such are the accounts of the historians (Callisthenes, *FGrH* 124 F 14a = Strabo 17.1.43).

99   ... ravens appeared and assumed direction of their march, flying swiftly in front of them when they followed, and waiting for them when they marched slowly and lagged behind. Moreover, what was most astonishing of all, Callisthenes tells us that the birds by their cries called back those who straggled away in the night, and cawed until they had set them in the track of the march (Callisthenes, *FGrH* 124 F 14b = Plut. *Alex.* 27.3–4).

100   Ptolemy, son of Lagus, says that two serpents went in front of the army, uttering a voice, and Alexander ordered the guides to follow them, trusting in the divine portent.

He says too that they showed the way to the oracle and back again. But Aristobulus (*FGrH* 139 F 14), whose account is generally admitted as correct, says that two ravens … (Ptolemy, *FGrH* 138 F 8 = Arr. 3.3.5).

101   Alexander then was struck with wonder at the place, and consulted the oracle of the god. Having heard what was agreeable to his wishes, as he himself said, he set out on the journey back to Egypt, by the same route, according to the statement of Aristobulus (*FGrH* 139 F 15); but according to that of Ptolemy, son of Lagus, he took another road, leading straight to Memphis (Ptolemy, *FGrH* 138 F 9 = Arr. 3.4.5).

102   After these transactions, Alexander was seized by an ardent desire to visit Ammon in Libya, partly in order to consult the god, because the oracle of Ammon was said to be exact in its information, and Perseus and Heracles were said to have consulted it, the former when he was despatched by Polydectes against the Gorgon, and the latter, when he visited Antaeus in Libya and Busiris in Egypt. Alexander was also partly urged by a desire of emulating Perseus and Heracles, from both of whom he traced his descent. He also deduced his pedigree from Ammon, just as the legends traced that of Heracles and Perseus to Zeus. Accordingly he made the expedition to Ammon with the design of learning his own origin more certainly, or at least that he might be able to say that he had learned it. According to Aristobulus, he advanced along the sea shore to Paraetonium through a country which was a desert, but not destitute of water, a distance of about 1,600 stades. Thence he turned into the interior, where the oracle of Ammon was located. The route is desert, and most of it is sand and destitute of water. But there was a copious supply of rain for Alexander, a thing which was attributed to the influence of the deity; as was also the following occurrence. Whenever a south wind blows in that district, it heaps up sand upon the route far and wide, rendering the tracks of the road invisible, so that it is impossible to discover where one ought to direct one's course in the sand, just as if one were at sea; for there are no landmarks along the road, neither mountain anywhere, nor tree, nor permanent hills standing erect, by which travellers might be able to form a conjecture of the right course, as sailors do by the stars. Consequently, Alexander's army lost the way, as even the guides were in doubt about the course to take. Ptolemy, son of Lagus (*FGrH* 138 F 8), says that two serpents went in front of the army … But Aristobulus, whose account is generally admitted as correct, says that two ravens flew in front of the army, and that these acted as Alexander's guides …

The place where the temple of Ammon is located is entirely surrounded by a desert of far-stretching sand, which is destitute of water. The fertile spot in the midst of this desert is not extensive; for where it stretches into its greatest expanse, it is only about forty stades broad. It is full of cultivated trees, olives and palms; and it is the only place in those parts which is refreshed with dew. A spring also rises from it, quite unlike all the other springs which issue from the earth. For at midday the water is cold to the taste, and still more so to the touch, as cold as cold can be. But when the sun has sunk into the west, it gets warmer, and from the evening it keeps on growing warmer until midnight, when it reaches its warmest point. After midnight it goes on getting gradually colder: at daybreak it is already cold; but at midday it reaches the coldest point. Every day it undergoes these alternate changes in regular succession. In this place also natural salt is procured by digging, and certain of the priests of Ammon convey quantities of it into Egypt. For whenever they set out for Egypt they put it into little boxes plaited out of palm, and carry it as a present to the king, or some other great man. The lumps of this salt are large, some of them being longer than three fingers' breadth;

and it is clear like crystal. The Egyptians and others who are respectful to the deity use this salt in their sacrifices, as it is clearer than that which is procured from the sea. Alexander then was struck with wonder at the place, and consulted the oracle of the god. Having heard what was agreeable to his wishes, as he himself said, he set out on the journey back to Egypt by the same route, according to the statement of Aristobulus; but according to that of Ptolemy, son of Lagus (*FGrH* 138 F 9), he took another road, leading straight to Memphis (Aristobulus, *FGrH* 139 FF 13–15 = Arr. 3.3–4).

103   On arriving at the shrine and finding out that there was an oracle in it, Alexander wished to consult it. The priest and the prophet said that it was impossible for them to give out an oracle on that day. Alexander insisted. To his pressing demand the seer replied: 'Lad, you are irresistible.' At this Alexander was delighted. Then the seer at once told him that he was not Philip's son but the son of Zeus Ammon himself. Alexander recalled the account of his mother Olympias that a dragon once prevailed over her just about the birth of Alexander. So he trusted oracles all the more and prospered the most by these acts of his (*Anonymous History of Alexander*, *FGrH* 151 F 10).

Before Gaugamela

104   On this occasion he made a very long speech to the Thessalians and the other Greeks, and when he saw that they encouraged him with shouts to lead them against the Barbarians, he shifted his lance into his left hand, and with his right appealed to the gods, as Callisthenes tells us, praying them, if he was really sprung from Zeus, to defend and strengthen the Greeks (Callisthenes, *FGrH* 124 F 36 = Plut. *Alex.* 33.1).

Acting the part?

105   And Ephippus tells us that Alexander used to wear even the sacred vestments at his entertainments; and sometimes he would wear the purple robe, and cloven sandals, and horns of Ammon, as if he had been the god; and sometimes he would imitate Artemis, whose dress he often wore while driving in his chariot; having on also a Persian robe, but displaying above his shoulders the bow and javelin of the goddess. Sometimes also he would appear in the guise of Hermes; at other times, and indeed almost every day, he would wear a purple cloak, and a tunic shot with white, and a cap which had a royal diadem attached to it. And when he was in private with his friends he wore the sandals of Hermes, and the petasus on his head, and held the caduceus in his hand. Often also he wore a lion's skin, and carried a club, like Heracles … And Alexander used to have the floor sprinkled with exquisite perfumes and with fragrant wine; and myrrh was burnt before him, and other kinds of incense; and all the bystanders kept silence, or spoke only words of good omen, out of fear. For he was a very violent man, with no regard for human life; for he appeared to be a man of a melancholic constitution.

And on one occasion, at Ecbatana, when he was offering a sacrifice to Dionysus, and when everything was prepared in a most lavish manner for the banquet, and Satrabates the satrap, feasted all the soldiers … But when a great multitude was collected to see the spectacle, says Ephippus, there were on a sudden some arrogant proclamations published, more insolent even than Persian arrogance was wont to dictate. For, as different people were publishing different proclamations, and proposing to make Alexander large presents, which they called crowns, one of the keepers of his armory, going beyond all previous flattery, having previously arranged the matter with Alexander, ordered the herald to proclaim that 'Gorgos, the keeper of the armory, presents Alexander, the son of Ammon, with three thousand pieces of gold; and will also present him, when he lays siege to Athens, with ten thousand complete suits of armour, and with an equal number of catapults and all weapons required for the war' (Ephippus, *FGrH* 126 F 5 = Athen. 12.537e–538b).

Self-divinity and Arabia

106   The common report is that he heard that the Arabs venerated only two gods, Uranus and Dionysus; the former because he is himself visible and contains in himself the heavenly luminaries, especially the sun, from which emanates the greatest and most evident benefit to all things human; and the latter on account of the fame he acquired by his expedition to India. Therefore he thought himself quite worthy to be considered by the Arabs as a third god,[8] since he had performed deeds by no means inferior to those of Dionysus (Aristobulus, *FGrH* 139 F 55 = Arr. 7.20.1).

Modern works

In the following selections, W.W. Tarn argues the point that Alexander proclaimed himself a god for political reasons in order to ensure the acceptance of the Exiles Decree (Tarn's view was persuasively attacked by J.P.V.D. Balsdon – see additional reading – but should still be considered in case Alexander used divinity for political reasons). Ian Worthington, Professor of History at the University of Missouri, outlines many of the events that took place to argue that Alexander did think himself divine. E.A. Fredricksmeyer, Emeritus Professor of Classics at the University of Colorado, looks at the traditions and beliefs in the age of Alexander, along with the king's divine birth and achievements, to argue that Alexander's claim to divinity was justified.

1   W.W. Tarn, *Alexander the Great* 2 (Cambridge University Press: 1948), Appendix 22, 'Alexander's Deification', Sec. III, '324 BC', pp. 370–373.[9]
2   Ian Worthington, *Alexander the Great, Man and God*, rev. ed. (Pearson: 2004), pp. 2273–2283.[10]
3   E.A. Fredricksmeyer, 'Alexander's Religion and Divinity', in J. Roisman (ed.), *Brill's Companion to Alexander the Great* (Brill: 2003), Chap. 10, pp. 253–278.[11]

Additional reading

E. Badian, 'The Deification of Alexander the Great', in H.J. Dell (ed.), *Ancient Macedonian Studies in Honour of C.F. Edson* (Institute for Balkan Studies, Thessaloniki: 1981), pp. 27–71.
——, 'Alexander the Great between Two Thrones and Heaven: Variations on an Old Theme', in A. Small (ed.), *Subject and Ruler: The Cult of the Ruling Power in Classical Antiquity* = *JRA* Suppl. 17 (1996), pp. 11–26.
J.P.V.D. Balsdon, 'The "Divinity" of Alexander', *Historia* 1 (1950), pp. 363–388.
A.B. Bosworth, 'Alexander and Ammon', in K. Kinzl (ed.), *Greece and the Ancient Mediterranean in History and Prehistory* (Berlin: 1977), pp. 51–75.

——, 'Alexander, Euripides and Dionysos: The Motivation for Apotheosis', in W. Wallace and E.M. Harris (eds), *Transitions to Empire. Essays in Honor of E. Badian* (Norman: 1996), pp. 140–166.

G.L. Cawkwell, 'The Deification of Alexander the Great: A Note', in Ian Worthington (ed.), *Ventures into Greek History. Essays in Honour of N.G.L. Hammond* (Oxford: 1994), pp. 293–306.

L. Edmunds, 'The Religiosity of Alexander', *Greek, Roman, and Byzantine Studies* 12 (1971), pp. 363–391.

E.A. Fredricksmeyer, 'Three Notes on Alexander's Deification', *American Journal of Ancient History* 4 (1979), pp. 1–9.

——, 'On the Background of the Ruler Cult', in H.J. Dell (ed.), *Ancient Macedonian Studies in Honour of C.F. Edson* (Institute for Balkan Studies, Thessaloniki: 1981), pp. 145–156.

——, 'On the Final Aims of Philip II', in W.L. Adams and E.N. Borza (eds), *Philip II, Alexander the Great, and the Macedonian Heritage* (Lanham: 1982), pp. 85–98.

——, 'Alexander, Zeus Ammon, and the Conquest of Asia', *Transactions of the American Philological Association* 121 (1991), pp. 199–214.

D. Gilley, 'Alexander and the Carmanian March of 324 BC', *Ancient History Bulletin* 20 (2006), pp. 9–14.

J.R. Hamilton, 'Alexander and his "So-called" Father', *Classical Quarterly*² 3 (1953), pp. 151–157.

A.N. Oikonomides, 'The Deification of Alexander in Bactria and India', *Ancient World* 12 (1985), pp. 69–71.

Notes

1 On the powers of the Macedonian kingship and Alexander's relations with Philip II, see Chapter 2.

2 Strabo 17.1.43, Arr. 3.3–4, Plut. *Alex.* 27.8–10, cf. Diod. 17.51, Curt. 4.7.25, Justin 11.11.2–12.

3 Arr. 4.10.5–7, Plut. *Alex.* 54.3–6, Curt. 8.5.9–12; see Chapter 9.

4 Athen. 12.538b; cf. Hyp. 5.31–32, Diod. 18.8.7, Curt. 10.2.5–7, Justin 13.5.1–6. On Alexander and the Greeks, see Chapter 5.

5 Polybius 12. 12b3, [Plut.] *Mor.* 219e, 804b, 842 and Aelian, *Varra Historia* 5.12.

6 On the issue of Alexander's 'greatness', see Chapter 12.

7 The Battle of Gaugamela in 331: see Chapter 6.

8 Alexander had planned an invasion of Arabia, but died in 323 before he could conduct it; cf. Source 106.

9 © Cambridge University Press 1948. Reprinted with the permission of Cambridge University Press.

10 Reprinted by permission of Pearson.

11 Reprinted by permission of Brill.

ALEXANDER'S DEIFICATION

W. W. Tarn

324 B.C.

In 324, at Susa, Alexander was faced by a new problem. In old Greece there was a mass of exiles from every city, many of them democrats exiled by Antipater or his governments. Some had taken service as mercenaries with Alexander's satraps while he was in India; when he made the satraps disband their private armies, they had returned to Greece with their arms and without occupation. The position in that overcrowded country had become difficult; at best the exiles were a focus for every kind of discontent, at worst a possible menace. Alexander saw that, if he were to have the peace in his world (not merely in his Empire, for Greece was not in his Empire) which soon after he was to pray for at Opis, the exiles must be restored to their cities and their cities must receive them. But his difficulty was that the cities were those of the League of Corinth, and as its President he had sworn to the Covenant of the League, which forbade him to interfere in the internal affairs of the cities; yet it was very necessary to interfere. In these circumstances he issued to the cities of the League[1] a decree ordering them to receive back their exiles (which he had no constitutional power to issue) and also a request for his own deification (which probably came first); for the Covenant bound Alexander the king but did not, and would not, bind Alexander the god, and he could therefore set it aside without losing his self-respect. To us this may seem a quibble, but no one can say it was a quibble to him, or that his careful observance throughout life of the outer forms of religion meant that they were nothing to him but forms. It has been objected that deification did not actually give him any new powers, but that is not the point; he had all the power he wanted, but he had not the right to use it; and to be a god gave him a juridical standing in the cities which he could not otherwise have got, for there was no place for a king in the constitution of a Greek city. The cities of the League granted his request and deified him[2], thereby (in form) condoning his breach of the Covenant; for while Alexander was thinking of a way of escape from the Covenant which bound him, the cities and States of the League were thinking primarily of the exiles decree which hit some of them hard, notably Athens and Aetolia, and was disturbing to them all; and they were hoping to appease Alexander by granting his request for deification, which by comparison seemed to them of little importance. Calling him a god did not mean that they were going to worship him; no cult of him was set up anywhere, and in fact there is no sign that, Egypt apart, anybody ever did worship him till after his death; the first known case is that of Eumenes and his Macedonian troops in the Alexander-tent. His request for deification, then, was a limited *political* measure for a purely political purpose, and nothing else. It is well known that some scholars have long believed this,[3] while others have strenuously denied it; I trust that what I have written in this study will show that the view which I follow is not only true but inevitable. His deification showed that he meant to stand above parties and factions, for many of the exiles, banished by Antipater or by the governments he supported, were Macedonia's enemies; it also showed that he had no intention of adopting Aristotle's view that such as he were above the law and that he could break the Covenant of the League at his pleasure. That his deification was purely political seems to be further supported by two facts: one is that he never put his own head on his coinage, as he must have done had he been a god in the sense in which many of the kings who followed him were gods; and the other is that his request for deification did not (so far as is known) extend to the Greek cities of Asia Minor, who were his free allies and who were not members of the League of Corinth.[4] There may have been no exiles problem there; but had there been he could have settled it without being their god, for he was not bound to them by any covenant which forbade him to interfere in their internal affairs. His deification, therefore, in 324 B.C., like his preliminary attempt at Bactra, was entirely a political matter, but this time limited to the cities of the League of Corinth; and it only remains to consider two modern objections to this view.

Professor Berve's pupil A. Heuss has put forward the view,[5] if I understand him rightly, that a political *Herrschaft* – say kingship – was always compounded of two independent elements, a political and a religious, and that you cannot abolish the religious element and make the political element do the work of both. He said there was warrant enough for this view in history, but did not say what it was; as I understand the matter, one need go no further than the Macedonian and Epirote monarchies to see that Heuss' view is untenable, and that there were plenty of kings whose kingship had no religious element; indeed I doubt if one could find any king in Alexander's day and in his sphere whose kingship *had* any religious element, putting aside Egypt and the little priest-kings of Asia Minor. Heuss makes a point that the deified kings (he includes Alexander) never mention their divine powers in their letters to the cities, where one would expect it. Why one should expect it I cannot imagine, seeing that they never mention their temporal powers either, any more than is ever done by kings or presidents to-day.

The other objection is one made in 1931 by Wilcken in his *Alexander der Grosse*. After discarding offhand the view that Alexander's deification in 324 was a political measure (though he had taken the scene at Bactra to be a political measure) he said (p. 201) that both the decree for the recall of the exiles and Alexander's request to the Greek cities of the League for deification had their roots in Alexander's psychology, and that that psychology was not only an outcome of his amazing success but was connected with, or conditioned by, his desire and plans for world-dominion; for he had been conscious for years that he *was* the son of Zeus-Ammon (p. 198) and history will go wrong if it neglects this inner religious experience. I trust I have given full weight to Alexander's inner religious experience (Ammon), fuller, possibly, than, even if not quite in the same way as, my predecessors; but this can have nothing to do with his deification in 324. There are several things to be said about Wilcken's view; the first and most obvious is that he has refuted it himself by his repeated statement that, as was indeed the fact, Alexander's request for deification in 324 was confined to the Greek cities of the League of Corinth, who were not even his subjects; what has that to do with the psychology of world-rule? The second is that, before it is possible to talk of Alexander's plans for world-dominion, some one has got to refute my demonstration (App. 24 [of Tarn 1948]), based on evidence, that his supposed plans in that behalf are a late invention; this has never been done, and I greatly doubt if it can be. As to Alexander's psychology in the matter of deification, I should be sorry to claim exact knowledge; but I have been considering it throughout this study, and as there is no reputable evidence that he ever called himself the son of any god, let alone a god, or that he even alluded to the descent of his line from Zeus, it is only fair to suppose that he did not believe that he was a god or even the son of one; and if those about him called him a son of Zeus, or even intimated that he ought to be a god, that has no bearing on his own thoughts or beliefs. Wilcken made one other point: his deification in 324 cannot have been political, or the Greek cities would never have granted it in the casual way they did. Certainly the cities did not take it to be a political move; but the only sign of casualness, I think, is the contemptuous remark attributed to Demosthenes, which is none too certain (p. 363 n. 2). I have already explained why the cities granted deification; but, quite apart from that, no city could afford to refuse. There was a great struggle at Athens over the proposal, but Demosthenes finally gave in, and those who desired appeasement and peace carried the day; Sparta, bled white at Megalopolis, was helpless; and probably most of the cities, great and small, acted as they did largely through fear of Alexander, for the moment that that fear was removed by his death they tore up the Covenant of the League of Corinth and started war against Macedonia, led by Athens, who punished Demades for having moved the proposal that Alexander should be a god.[6]

Notes

1   To the cities of the League only, for Antipater was to be executant, Diod. XVIII, 8, 4, and he had no authority on the mainland of Asia; see App. 7, 1, p. 202 n. 4 [in Tarn]. The Greek cities of Asia Minor, who were not in the League (App. 7, 11 [in Tarn]), were not affected. See [n. 4].

2   The story that at Athens he became a particular god, Dionysus, has long been exploded; see A. D. Nock, 'Notes on ruler-cult I–IV', *J.H.S.* XLVIII, 1928, p. 21. Some had rejected it before, e.g. Ed. Meyer, *Kleine Schriften*, 1, 1910, p. 331; P. Perdrizet, *R.E.A.* XII, 1910, p. 227 n. 6. There was a good deal of difference between becoming a god and becoming a particular god. 3 Ed. Meyer, *Kleine Schriften*, 1, pp. 283 *sqq.*, 312, 331; W. S. Ferguson, *Amer. Hist Rev.* 1912, p. 32; *Greek Imperialism*, 1913, pp. 147 *sqq.*; *C.A.H.* VII, 15.

4   See App. 7, II [in Tarn]. Wilcken, who so long championed the view that they were in the League of Corinth, finally abandoned it, 1938, p. 302 [7] n. 5, and in doing so he left it open (*ib.*) whether Alexander's request for deification was directed to them also or not. It seems certain that it was not; there is no evidence that the request was sent to any mainland city of Asia Minor, and the reason against it given [. . .] n. 1 *ante* should be conclusive; also no mainland city took any part in the Lamian war.

5   Stadt und *Herrscher des Hellenismus*, Klio, Beiheft XXVI, 1937, pp. 188 sq.

6   Athen. VI, 251B; Aelian, V.H. v, 12.

MAN AND GOD

Ian Worthington

Question: 'How can a man become a god?'
Answer: 'By doing something a man cannot do.'[1]

This question was one of several that Alexander asked of several Indian philosophers, who were reputed for their terse answers, in an effort to catch them out. Other questions included: Which are the more numerous, the living or the dead? (answer: the living, for the dead no longer exist); Which is the most cunning of animals? (answer: the one not yet discovered by man); and How can a man make himself most beloved? (answer: if he has supreme power but does not inspire fear). The question about how a man might become a god is the one that best explains Alexander's motives for what he did – and thus how he saw himself:

> Alexander used to wear sacred clothes at his parties. Sometimes he would wear the purple robe, and cloven sandals, and horns of Ammon, as if he had been the god. Sometimes he would imitate Artemis, whose dress he often wore while driving in his chariot; having on also a Persian robe, but displaying above his shoulders the bow and javelin of the goddess. Sometimes also he would appear as Hermes; at other times, and almost every day, he would wear a purple cloak, and a tunic shot with white, and a cap that had a royal diadem attached to it. And when he was in private with his friends he wore the sandals of Hermes, and the petasus on his head, and held the caduceus in his hand. Often also he wore a lion's skin, and carried a club, like Heracles. ... And Alexander used to have the floor sprinkled with exquisite perfumes and with fragrant wine; and myrrh was burned before him, and other kinds of incense.[2]

Ephippus, the contemporary writer who describes the above, makes it plain that Alexander went beyond merely dressing up as a god in disguise. He is describing a scene towards the end of Alexander's reign. Incense was burned in Alexander's presence, and a reverential silence was preserved. Both these observances show that there was a cult to him at his court. By the end of his reign, then, he was worshipped, and while alive. By tracking the significant events in the development of Alexander's divine pretensions throughout his reign, we can see a pattern to how his vision of himself changed, and why.[3]

Philip was deified on his death, and Alexander could reasonably be expected to follow in this 'tradition'. However, Alexander sought divine honours for himself while still alive. Was he making a break with tradition or had his father been deified at the end of his reign, while still alive?[4] The day after his daughter's wedding to the King of Epirus at Aegae in 336, as we have seen, Philip held games and dramatic contests to celebrate the event (see Chapter 2 [of the original]). The day began with a religious procession into the theatre where the people had already gathered to watch the events. The royal procession entered the theatre carrying statues of the 12 Olympian gods, and a statue of Philip that was on a par with the others in terms of size and adornment. On the same day, Philip was assassinated.

Philip's statue is interesting, for to have it carried in this procession and next to the statues of the gods may have indicated that he saw himself as divine. He had certainly done more for his state than any other Macedonian king, and he aimed to continue to do more, as his plans to invade Asia revealed. Had he done enough, though, to be regarded as a god on earth? Ephesus had erected a statue of Philip II in its temple when the advance force under Parmenion invaded Asia in 336. In Eresus (on the island of Lesbos) there was an altar to Zeus Philippios. Here, though, the link is with Zeus's role as Philip's protector, not with Philip's being seen as Zeus by the people.[5] Was Alexander trying to build on the lead of Ephesus and to exploit the association at Eresus?

Philip's divine leanings are overshadowed by those of his son. However, a common factor in both cases would be the reaction of the people. Worship of a living man was considered blasphemy. At the end of the fifth century, the Spartan general Brasidas was revered as a hero in Amphipolis. However, he was dead by then, and a hero cult was not the same as a divine one. It made the dead man merely a demigod. Yet in the same period it appears that the Spartan Lysander was worshipped as a god while alive on the island of Samos, and he had a festival in his honour. Dion of Syracuse a little later may also have been worshipped as a god by his people while still alive.

The explanation for the apotheosis of these living men is unknown. However, Samos was not the Greek mainland, and Syracuse was on Sicily in the western Mediterranean, somewhat alien to the Greeks of the eastern Mediterranean. Moreover, Lysander and Dion certainly did not set a trend, for there were no other men revered in this way (that we know of) until the late fourth century, with Alexander. If anything, the worship of the living Lysander *stopped* what might have become a trend for several decades.

In Philip's case, what happened at Ephesus (again, not on the mainland but in Asia Minor) seems to have been an anomaly, a knee-jerk reaction by the people that showed more their distaste of Persian rule and the hope that this would end. Also, it is made plain that the people were not bestowing divine honours on him, merely placing his statue in the temple as a thanks offering. At Eresus (on an island, and well away from the orthodoxy of the mainland) he was connected with a local cult, not worshipped alone.

Philip may well have *wanted* to become divine, and his planned invasion of Persia may have been the stepping stone to that. Then again, if he had sought divine honours at the end of his reign, we would expect the reaction of the people to have been far different from the adulation in which they clearly held him. His reign showed that he knew how to read people and how to handle them in order to achieve his objectives (see Chapter 2 [of the original]). He had given his own people a feeling of nationalistic pride and he had established a unity that Macedonia had never had before. At the core of all of this was the army. He never lost touch with the rank and file of his army (as Alexander would do), and he was, to put it bluntly, too savvy to do something that would risk everything.

It is unlikely that the appearance of Philip's statue in the theatre of Aegae that day meant that he was divine. More probably, it reflected his glory as a great king and his piety. It is important to remember that when he fought in the Sacred War he did so as the Saviour of Delphi, the Liberator of Apollo. He and his men wore white wreaths in their hair in the battles against the Phocians to show they were fighting for Apollo. The Sacred War was the turning point for the formal expansion of Philip's power in Greece. His intervention in it led to its end in 346 and the liberation of Delphi. After it, Macedonia was granted a seat on the hallowed Amphictyonic Council, a religious body charged with maintaining the Oracle of Apollo at Delphi, but one which also had much political influence in Greece. He was also elected President of the Pythian Games for 346.

As we have seen, Philip continued to advance into Greece and eventually defeated the Greeks at the Battle of Chaeronea in 338. That gave him control of Greece, and the League of Corinth gave him the legal means to enforce and ensure Macedonian rule. Yet what happened in 346 set up Philip's future moves. By 346, in less than 15 years after being acclaimed king, the 'barbarian' had come from nowhere to great prominence in terms of his power in Greece and in Greek religious events. His statue next to those of the gods in the procession emphasised this, and thus his piety. Perhaps also the white cloak he wore to the theatre that day evoked the white wreath he wore when fighting for Apollo in the Sacred War.

As has been said (see Chapter 3 [of the original]), Alexander's admiration of his father changed to resentment, especially in the last two years of his father's reign. The young heir was eager for glory himself. He had his nose (and aspirations) put out of joint when Philip told him he intended to leave him behind as regent while he campaigned against the Persians. Whether Alexander had a hand in Philip's murder or not, he pushed ahead with his father's plan to invade Asia once he became king. But he did not just want to conquer like his father. He wanted to do more, to establish an absolute monarchy and to be worshipped as a god while he was alive. That would propel him far ahead of his father.

Alexander's boyhood had been normal – or as normal as that of the heir to the Macedonian throne could be. However, once he left Macedonia things were quite different, and he took on a very different persona. This was part of his policy to eclipse his father, of course. The divine element increased dramatically when Alexander was in Asia. It really began with the story of the Oracle of Apollo at Didyma that had been silent since the Persian Wars of the early fifth century (see Chapter 5 [of the original]). When Alexander arrived at Didyma in autumn 334, Apollo suddenly found his voice, and started speaking again. Perhaps not at this time, but when the king was in Egypt the following year, he proclaimed that Alexander was born of Zeus.

Before Didyma, Alexander's dealings with gods and dead heroes had been for pious reasons and for the good of his mission. At Elaeus, for example, he sacrificed at the tomb of Protesilaus, and then as he crossed the Hellespont to Poseidon and the Nereids. These sacrifices combined political symbolism with heroic symbolism (see Chapter 4 [of the original]). So too did his sacrifice at Achilles' tomb, and to the Trojan Athena and Priam, in the Temple to Athena, at Troy. Didyma, however, was different. He had actually detoured somewhat to go there after the siege of Miletus and before pressing on to Halicarnassus. It seems clear, then, that he wanted to use Apollo's silence and his breaking of it to his own advantage.

His visit had done something that Philip never did: it had brought an oracle back to life. It showed his piety – and his power. That power was confirmed by Zeus himself (apparently) when Alexander severed the Gordian knot at Gordium in spring 333 (see Chapter 5 [of the original]). A violent thunderstorm happened that night as Zeus greeted the man who would rule Asia. Alexander sacrificed to him the next morning. The gods, then, were on the side of Macedonia in the invasion of Asia, and the future blossomed rosy for Alexander. As the king, he could look forward to great conquests, to great wealth and to the expansion of the Macedonian empire. All of that would give him the great reputation that he desperately needed. By now he had defeated the Persians at Granicus and Issus (after which battle Darius fled), controlled all of Asia Minor, the Levant and Egypt, and marched further than Philip had ever done.

Then he went to Egypt, and that changed everything (see Chapter 7 [of the original]). At Siwah, in 331, Alexander the man became also Alexander the god. Siwah is thus the real turning point in his quest for divine status.[6] Alexander was probably not crowned Pharaoh, but by virtue of his control of the country he assumed all the titles and powers of that office. That meant he was a god on earth, and worshipped by his Egyptian subjects. He was also only 24 years old. It is not surprising that everything he had done so far (and would do) went to his head. After all, he was only human, and it was easy to become deluded.

Like Philip, Alexander could trace his ancestry back to Zeus and Heracles. His own people and those of Asia worshipped both, sometimes in other forms (for example, at Tyre Heracles was Melqart). But now the Egyptians were worshipping Alexander. And now, I suggest, the Didyma visit was exploited for another, more ominous, reason. At some point after Alexander arrived in Egypt came the 'news', manufactured by the king, that Apollo at Didyma had said that he was a son of Zeus. On top of this were the stories, which I suggest were put out at this time, by Alexander, or at least had his official sanction about the divine nature of his birth. Artemis had delivered him and his real father was Zeus, who had appeared as an incarnation of a snake and impregnated Olympias (see Chapter 3 [of the original]). Alexander was setting himself up as divine even from the day he had been born. He had begun to see himself not merely as a descendant of Zeus, but as a son.

However, Zeus's greeting at Gordium did not mean the future ruler of Asia was his son. That explains why Alexander visited the Oracle of Zeus Ammon at Siwah in 331. Apollo at Didyma had told him he was Zeus's son; now Alexander needed to hear that from Zeus himself. With Didyma 'on line', it was necessary to go to Siwah. It is significant that Alexander wanted to go there. There was a temple to Zeus Ammon at Aphytis in the Chalcidice, not so far from Macedonia itself. Alexander certainly knew about it and most likely visited it. After all, his ancestor Heracles had done so. There was also the story that he had been conceived by a snake that had sex with Olympias – a snake that was the incarnation of Zeus Ammon himself. There were thus plenty of reasons for going to Zeus Ammon. As a boy, he would simply have worshipped at his shrine. In 332, with two defeats of the Persian army under his belt and Egypt subjected, he was a very different person.

We do not know what the priest of Zeus told Alexander at Siwah as the king met him in private and we have only his word for what happened. Not that it matters in the end. It is significant that we hear from a contemporary source that he went there to learn 'his own origin more certainly, or at least that he might be able to say that he had learned it'.[7] In other words, it did not really matter what the priest told him. Alexander believed he was Zeus's son, and that was what he told everyone. From that time, he referred to himself as son of Zeus, not descendant of Zeus.

One event that stands out in Alexander's promotion of his personal divinity is *proskynesis*. At Bactria in 327 he tried to make everyone at his court perform this Asian custom of prostration before him. When Callisthenes refused – and the majority of his court seems to have followed suit – Alexander had to abandon the plan (see Chapter 10 [of the original]).

Why did Alexander want to introduce *proskynesis* at his court? He may have wanted to establish a common social protocol between Greeks and Asians so that all would greet him in the same way. He did now rule over several races of people, who all had their different customs and beliefs. He called himself Lord of Asia, thus establishing a common form of address. Therefore it made sense to have a common custom for his subjects to greet him. However, the Greeks disliked this custom, principally because they saw it as blasphemous. It implied worship of a living man, and they only worshipped gods or dead heroes. Alexander was brought up to believe in the traditional gods, and traditional worship. He must have known that his men would react in this way, and that they would resent and resist it. Anaxarchus's argument (if indeed he did say this), that since Alexander was going to be worshipped when he was dead, he may as well be worshipped while alive, was hardly a convincing one.

The only explanation that makes sense is that Alexander now thought of himself as a god. Thus, *proskynesis* was a logical vehicle for all of his subjects to recognise his divine status in public. His action shows that he had lost touch with his men, for he was well aware of the religious connotations associated with the act. It shows that he had also lost touch with the religious beliefs on which he had been raised. Alexander had performed great deeds, and he would have been deified on his death, as his father had been. For Alexander, however, that was not enough now. Certainly, he would not eclipse Philip if he stayed a 'mere mortal'. He had already taken that extra step, and believed himself divine. Siwah had 'proved' that to him. He was prepared to ignore his men's religious orthodoxy. The army followed him into battle and into new lands. Now it needed to follow a new lead. The Asians already performed *proskynesis* before him, so too should the Greeks and Macedonians. Alexander was now man and god.

As we have seen, Callisthenes was later implicated in the Conspiracy of the Pages and executed. Indeed, those who disagreed with Alexander's policies and the way that he viewed himself – men such as Philotas, Parmenion, Callisthenes, Cleitus and perhaps Craterus – were either killed or sent far away from court. That did not mean that Alexander the man and god came to be accepted. When the army mutinied at Opis in 324, the men sarcastically told him to continue his campaign with his father Ammon (see Chapter 12 [of the original]). Alexander's mortality had shown itself every time he had been wounded. In particular, he had almost died of a fever after his swim in the River Cydnus and of loss of blood after his chest wound against the Malli. Gods are supposed to be immortal. It is a sign of Alexander's megalomania and then belief in his own godhead that he never seems to have recognised the implications of his wounds.

Of course, there is a difference between divine pretensions and actually thinking of oneself as a god. Did Alexander really think he was a god, or was he just a megalomaniac, exploiting ruler cult for the political advantages it offered? In 324 the Greeks of the mainland were discussing divine honours for him, and they sent embassies to him that wore gold crowns and brought him gold crowns.[8] These actions were what one did to honour a god. But that does not mean they believed he was a god. Indeed, they did not believe this, as Demosthenes' contemptuous 'Alexander can be the son of Zeus and of Poseidon if he wants to be'[9] proves. What they did was all part of a diplomatic policy to get Alexander to rescind the Exiles Decree (see Chapters 12 and 13 [of the original]). Nor is there any evidence that Alexander issued a directive ordering the mainland Greeks to worship him. Some island states had worshipped him since 334, but these were few and far between. They were doing so as a mark of gratitude, no different from Ephesus and Philip II. The Greeks were simply pandering to Alexander, and we get the impression he would have known this.

However, there are two indications towards the end of Alexander's reign that show that megalomania had given way to the belief that he actually was a god. The first is one of his motives for invading Arabia (see Chapter 12 [of the original]). He had several, including trade and further conquest, but a contemporary source reveals the following. The Arabs worshipped only two gods, Uranus and Dionysus:

> The former because he is himself visible and has in himself the stars of heaven, especially the sun, from which comes the greatest and most evident benefit to all mankind. The latter on account of the fame he won by his expedition to India. Therefore he thought himself quite worthy to be considered by the Arabs as a third god, since he had performed deeds by no means inferior to those of Dionysus.[10]

Second, and more important, is the heroic cult to Hephaestion. When he died in 324, the king heaped many honours on him and requested a heroic cult for his dead friend from Zeus Ammon (see Chapter 12 [of the original]). In May 323 Zeus agreed. The cult meant that Hephaestion was now a demigod, as Alexander intended. However, if he were a demigod, that made Alexander a god on earth. Hephaestion was not the king's equal, and Alexander could not elevate his friend to the same divine level as himself. That meant he must have seen himself as a living god if he arranged for Hephaestion to be a demigod.

As his reign progressed, Alexander came to think of himself as a god. This is shown especially by the *proskynesis* incident at Bactria, his relationship to the dead Hephaestion, his decision to conquer Arabia in order to be worshipped as a third god, Ephippus's account with which we started this chapter, and even by his coinage, especially after Issus (see Chapter 6 [of the original]). Alexander was worshipped by the Egyptians, he wanted to be worshipped by the Arabs, and attempts such as *proskynesis* showed that he wanted to be worshipped by his own people. At no time did he shirk his duties as king, which included the daily sacrifices on behalf of the state, but now he was sacrificing for his state to equals, not as a mortal king to the gods.

'How can a man become a god?' 'By doing something a man cannot do.' Alexander had done a great many things as he expanded the empire and outdid his father. In the process, the warrior king fell victim to megalomania, and then to a belief in his own divinity. After his death, many of the Hellenistic rulers assumed divine status and exploited ruler cult for their own political ends. So too did the Roman emperors. Both of those worlds were entirely different from that of Alexander, and the attitude to divinity was different. Or, as time continued, was it?

Notes

1 Plutarch, *Alexander* 64.9.
2 Ephippus, *FGrH* 126 F 5 = Athenaeus 12.537e.
3 See too L. Edmunds, 'The Religiosity of Alexander', *Greek, Roman, and Byzantine Studies* 12 (1971): 363–91.
4 See further, E.A. Fredricksmeyer, 'Divine Honors for Philip II', *Transactions of the American Philological Association* 109 (1979): 39–61 and 'On the Background of the Ruler Cult', in H.J. Dell (ed.), *Ancient Macedonian Studies in Honour of C.F. Edson* (Thessaloniki, 1981), 145–56.

5   Cf. E. Badian, 'The Deification of Alexander the Great', in H.J. Dell (ed.), *Ancient Macedonian Studies in Honour of C.F. Edson* (Thessaloniki, 1981), 41.

6   E.A. Fredricksmeyer, 'Alexander's Religion and Divinity', in J. Roisman (ed.), *Brill's Companion to Alexander the Great* (Leiden, 2003), 253–78, argues that it was not surprising that Alexander thought himself to be a god given his background, divine ancestry and visit to Siwah.

7   Aristobulus, *FGrH* 139 FF 13–15 = Arrian 3.3–4.

8   For the episode, see now G.L. Cawkwell, 'The Deification of Alexander the Great: A Note', in Ian Worthington (ed.), *Ventures into Greek History: Essays in Honour of N.G.L. Hammond* (Oxford, 1994), 293–306 and E. Badian, 'Alexander the Great between Two Thrones and Heaven: Variations on an Old Theme', in A. Small (ed.), *Subject and Ruler: The Cult of the Ruling Power in Classical Antiquity* (Ann Arbor, 1996), 11–26.

9   In Hyperides' speech *Against Demosthenes* at Section 31.

10 Aristobulus, *FGrH* 139 F 55 = Arrian 7.20.1.

ALEXANDER'S RELIGION AND DIVINITY

E A. Fredricksmeyer

Alexander was extremely avid for honor ... and most conscientious in his devotion to the gods.

(Arrian 7.28.1)

What we may call Alexander's religion has two major aspects, one, his relationship as an individual and as king to the world of the gods, the other, his relation to Zeus as his father, and his own divinity. As for the former, the ancient sources provide more information about it than on any other person in antiquity. This is not just an accident of our tradition, but also reflects Alexander's personal faith and values. There exists no comprehensive treatment of this subject, and the purpose of the first part of this study is to provide it. The other aspect of Alexander's religion, his divine sonship and his divinity, touches on Alexander's inmost beliefs and values, his very identity, and no other subject of his career has been so extensively discussed and so hotly debated by modern scholars. I have tried to present a critical treatment of it which draws on the best of modern scholarship, and also expresses what I consider most plausible. Not everyone will agree with my assessment, but it is firmly based on the evidence, and speculation has been kept to a minimum. Finally, I have tried to consider Alexander's religion, as far as possible, from his own perspective and that of his age, rather than from that of our own.

Part I

1 Early influences

Alexander early learned the virtues of religious piety (*eusebeia*, *eulabeia*) and of martial valor (*aretē*) from his parents. Both were acknowledged descendants of the gods, Philip from Heracles the son of Zeus, Olympias from Achilles the son of Thetis.[1] After his victory over Olynthus, Philip showed his gratitude to the gods by lavishly celebrating the festival of Olympian Zeus at Dium (Diod. 16.55.1; cf Arr. 1.11.1). He prosecuted a 'Sacred War' as champion of Apollo against the sacrilegious Phocians, and after their defeat punished them as executor of divine justice (Diod. 16.35.6; Just. 8.2.3–7). He was awarded the presidency of the next Pythian Games, and gave appropriate thanks to Apollo for the victory. Diodorus (16.60.4; cf. 16.64.3) says that Philip returned to Macedonia with a high reputation for his piety. Both Speusippus and Isocrates in their letters to Philip encouraged his martial ambitions by stressing his descent from Heracles.[2] It comes as no surprise that Philip featured on his coins the images of Zeus, Apollo, and Heracles.[3]

After his triumph at Chaeronea, Philip announced that he wished to lead the Greeks against the barbarians, to punish them for the injuries they inflicted on the Greeks, and especially their desecration of Greek temples, in their invasion of 480/79.[4] This panhellenic slogan advertised Philip's piety and discouraged Greek opposition. Then, wishing to enter the war with the gods' approval, Philip consulted Apollo's oracle at Delphi and received a response which he took as prediction of his conquest of the Persian king (Diod. 16.91.2–4). It was not to be. On the last day of his life, at the celebration of his daughter's wedding and the opening of the campaign against Persia, Philip displayed in a solemn procession to an assembled multitude his own precious statue on a par with those of the Twelve Gods as 'enthroned with them' (*synthronos*) (Diod. 16.92.5; 95.1). Moments later, the assassin struck.

We may wonder if Philip intended to use this occasion to obtain formal recognition as a god. There were precedents for the deification of mortals in their lifetime, for the greatness of their achievements, power, and abilities. Even so, at this point Philip probably wished only to suggest that he deserved to be honored on a level with the gods, if not on this very occasion, then surely after his crowning achievement of conquering the Great King. The procession marked the opening of the war against Persia, Apollo had predicted, as Philip thought, his conquest of the Great King, and Isocrates had said in an open letter to him that after the conquest of the King nothing would be left for him 'but to become a god' (*Ep.* 3.5). Whatever Isocrates meant by this statement, it is not unlikely that Philip took it as encouragement for his deification after conquering the Persian king.[5] Alexander was present on that fateful day at Aegae, and we may be sure that the significance of Philip's demonstration was not lost on him.

Olympias' influence on Alexander's religious development no doubt also was considerable. Most important, it is possible that she suggested to Alexander that his father was not Philip, but a god. At the same time, she no doubt emphasized Alexander's descent through her from the 'brilliant' Achilles, and thus reinforced Philip's influence in encouraging Alexander's ambition to emulate his heroic ancestors. Apparently she influenced the choice of Alexander's early tutors. One of them, Leonidas, was her kinsman, and another, Lysimachus, encouraged Alexander's emulation of Achilles by identifying him with Achilles, Philip with Peleus, and himself with Phoenix, and he earned praise for this.[6]

Alexander's main tutor Aristotle, appointed by Philip, influenced Alexander's religious education not with his philosophy, of which there is no hint, but by stressing the heroic ethos and thus reinforcing the influence of his other mentors. So in his *Hymn to Excellence* (*Aretē*), he singled out Alexander's ancestors Heracles, Achilles, and Aias as heroic models. At the center of Alexander's studies, he placed the tale of the *Iliad* as a handbook of martial valor, and Alexander is said to have learned it by heart.[7] His veneration of Achilles lasted throughout his life.[8]

Because of these early influences, as well as by his unique personality make-up, Alexander became the most charismatic and successful, but also the most complex, problematic and controversial, champion of an ancient warrior code, embraced in Macedonia even in the 4th c., which considered as the greatest glory to which a hero could aspire supremacy in war and conquest, because by this, as Homer and the poets taught, he might approximate the gods, and win immortal fame.[9]

2 Patrios nomos. Foreign gods

As King of the Macedonians Alexander was also their high priest and intermediary in their dealings with the gods. The Macedonians considered themselves descended from Macedon, son of Zeus, and the Argead kings were acknowledged as descendants of Heracles son of Zeus through Temenus, king of Argos in the Peleponnese (Baege 1913: 1; Hdt. 8.137; Thuc. 2.99).[10] In the exercise of his religious functions, Alexander was assisted by his (half) brother Arrhidaeus, son of Philip (Curt. 10.7.2),[11] and a staff of experts in supplicating and thanking the gods, divining their will and intentions, purifying from pollution, conducting funerals, and organizing festivals, processions and contests in honor of the gods. Alexander performed most of these functions in accord with the 'ancestral tradition' (*patrios nomos*), both on a daily basis (with the first sacrifice at dawn), and at all special events, such as campaigns, battles, victories, escape from dangers, foundations of cities, crossing of rivers and straits, banquets, and so on. Many sacrifices were part of elaborate services, with dedications, as at Ephesus and Tyre, processions, sometimes with the whole army in battle array, races, and literary and athletic contests, preferably at established festivals and sanctuaries, as at Dium and Ephesus, but also in the field.[12]

Alexander worshipped the gods either individually or in a traditional canon of Twelve (Diod. 16.92.5), as at the Hellespont (Just. 11.5.4) and at the Hyphasis (Arr. 5.29.1–2; Diod. 17.95.1; Curt. 9.3.19; cf. Strabo 3.5.5; Plut. *Alex.* 62.8). In Alexander's time the canon apparently consisted of Zeus, Athena, Heracles, Dionysus, Apollo, Artemis, Asclepius, Posidon, Helios, Selene, and Ge.[13] Various expressions of devotion by Alexander are on record to all these, and other, gods, as well as to Heroes. So he sacrificed to Zeus Olympius and the Muses at their festival at Dium (Diod. 17.16.3; Arr. 1.11.1); Artemis at her famous sanctuary in Ephesus;[14] Asclepius at Soli (Arr. 2.5.8; Curt. 3.7.3), Epidaurus (Arr. 7.14.6), and Gortys in Arcadia (Paus. 8.28.1); Posidon, Oceanus, and other sea divinities;[15] Selene, Helios, and Ge at the eclipse of the moon before the battle at Gaugamela (Arr. 3.7.6); Helios in India (Diod. 17.89.3; Curt. 9.1.1); the Dioscuri;[16] and Phobos before Gaugamela (Plut. *Alex.* 31.9).

To the Heroes, Alexander sacrificed usually at their graves or tombs, as to Protesilaus at the Hellespont, not to begrudge him a more auspicious crossing (Arr. 1.11.5; cf. Horn. *Il.* 2.695–708); the Homeric heroes in the plain of Troy, especially Alexander's ancestors Achilles and Aias;[17] Priam, an apotropaic sacrifice to purge the sacrilege of Alexander's ancestor Neoptolemus (Arr. 1.11.8); Amphilochus in Cilicia because of their shared connections with Argos (Arr. 2.5.9; Strabo 14.5.17); Alexander's friend and *alter ego* Hephaestion after ordering an empire-wide hero cult for him by permission of Zeus Ammon (who disallowed divine honors), with an immense funerary monument in Babylon and two magnificent shrines in Alexandria;[18] and we hear of Alexander's intention to found a posthumous cult for Olympias (Curt. 9.6.26; 10.5.30). The dispositions for Hephaestion and Olympias attest to Alexander's passionate personal attachment to them. All the other expressions of Alexander's piety were also in accord with 'ancestral tradition.'

It may be appropriate here to note Alexander's relations to non-Greek deities. The Greeks had always, of course, acknowledged a divine element in foreign gods, often identifying them with their own, and were willing to pay tribute to them. According to Curtius (3.8.22; 9.9.27) it was 'ancestral custom' (*patrius mos*) for Alexander to sacrifice to the gods of the locale or region (*dis praesidibus loci; praesidibus et maris et locorum dis*) wherever he found himself. But it is noteworthy that apart from sacrifices to these gods, who seem to have represented elements of nature, and his religious activities in Egypt and Babylon, which were politically motivated, we have no knowledge of any sacrifices by Alexander to clearly non-Greek deities.[19] In Memphis in 332, Alexander sacrificed to Apis, 'the sacred bull of Ptah,' his 'incarnation,' 'soul,' 'herold,' 'life,' and 'son' (Arr. 3.1.4).[20] This sacrifice may have been obligatory for Alexander at his enthronement as Pharaoh in the temple of Ptah (Ps. Call. 1.34.2).[21] We know that Alexander performed the sacred duties of Pharaoh, such as ordering the restoration of Egyptian temples, and several of his Pharaonic titles have been preserved.[22] At the founding of Alexandria, Alexander designated both the temples for Greek gods, and one for Isis in the Egyptian district (Arr. 3.1.5). In Babylon in 331, Alexander carried out all the recommendations of the [Babylonian] priests concerning the temples, and in particular he sacrificed to Bel according to their instructions (Arr. 3.16.5). It is not unlikely that, as in Egypt, Alexander had himself enthroned as native king in Babylon, and that he performed all sacred functions in this capacity, as he ordered in particular the reconstruction of the great pyramid temple Etemenanki in the temple complex Esagila of Bel, as well as of other temples in a bad state of repair (Arr. 3.16.4–5; 7.17.1–3; Strabo 16.1.5; Joseph, *c. Ap.* 1.192).[23]

Alexander's measures in Egypt and Babylon contrast with those of the later Achaemenid kings, who attempted to suppress the native religions by committing various outrages against the native gods, even killing Apis and abducting the statue of Bel.[24] While in both countries Persian rule was resented, Alexander courted the good will of the people and their powerful priesthoods.

It is the more remarkable, therefore, that in Persia, Alexander destroyed the sacred capital Persepolis (330), the high citadel of Ahuramazda, the supreme deity of the Achaemenid empire and its kings as deputies of the god on earth.[25] By this act Alexander fulfilled his religious obligation to the Greek gods, to which he had committed himself, of exacting vengeance from the Persians for their sacrilege of 480/79. But beyond this, there is reason to believe that, since Alexander attributed his own kingship of Asia, as promulgated after his conquest of Darius at Gaugamela (331), to his own prowess and the support of his gods, he considered the near-monotheistic Ahuramazda creed of the Achaemenid kings incompatible with the cult of his own gods, and that by destroying Persepolis he meant to signal that, along with the ancien régime, the dynastic cult of Ahuramazda was to be superseded by a new imperial cult of the Graeco-Macedonian gods.[26]

Apart from this Graeco-Macedonian religious superstructure, however, Alexander apparently meant to grant religious toleration to all peoples of his realm.[27] In 324, after crushing the Macedonian mutiny at Opis, Alexander staged a feast of reconciliation which he used also to promote Macedonian–Persian cooperation. Appropriately, Greek seers initiated the ceremony for the Macedonians and Persian magi for the Persians, but Alexander himself sacrificed to the gods "to whom it was his custom (*nomos*) to sacrifice," that is, to his Graeco-Macedonian gods (Arr. 7.11.8–9).[28]

3 The great patron gods

Alexander adopted from Philip the slogan of a war as a religious crusade to punish the Persians for their sacrilege against the Greek gods in their invasion of 480/79.[29] At the same time, like Philip, he embarked on the campaign also as a war of conquest for his own ends. It appears that he considered five gods as his main champions in the undertaking: Zeus, Athena, Heracles, Dionysus, and Apollo. While still in Macedonia, he issued his new imperial coinage featuring on his silver tetradrachms the head of Heracles on one side, and Zeus Basileus, with eagle and scepter, on the other, and on his gold staters the helmeted head of Athena on one side, and the figure of Nike (as attribute of Athena) on the other.[30] In 334, on crossing the Hellespont from Europe to Asia, Alexander dedicated altars to Zeus, Athena, and Heracles (Arr. 1.11.7), as he did again after his victory at Issus (Curt. 3.12.27; cf. Diod. 17.40.1; Cic. *Fam.* 15.4.9), and no doubt on other strategic occasions.[31]

Alexander interpreted various portents as sent by Zeus, Athena, or Heracles to give him aid and directions. So at Gordium in Phrygia he undid the famous Gordian Knot and took this to mean, in accord with an ancient oracle, that Zeus Basileus vouchsafed him the rule over Asia.[32] In Memphis, he honored Zeus Basileus with an elaborate sacrifice, including a parade of his army and athletic and literary contests (Arr. 3.5.2), probably in thanksgiving for the god's prediction at Gordium, and its confirmation by Zeus Ammon at Siwah.[33] Before the battle at Gaugamela, which he expected to decide the kingship of Asia (Arr. 3.9.6), Alexander supplicated Zeus with Athena Nike for victory (Curt. 4.13.15). At the Hydaspes in India, he sacrificed to Zeus Ammon, along with Heracles and other gods, in supplication for a successful expedition to the Indian Ocean (Arr. 6.3.2). In Carmenia, he performed lavish thanksgiving sacrifices to Zeus Soter, with Heracles, Apollo Alexikakos, and Posidon for the successful naval expedition of Nearchus from India (Arr. *Ind.* 36.3). In Babylon in 323, Alexander received a number of sacred embassies in the order of the prestige of their sanctuaries, with one from Zeus Olympius at Elis first, and one from Zeus Ammon at Siwah second (Diod. 17.113.3–4). And shortly before his death, Alexander planned magnificent temples for Zeus at Dium and at Dodona (Diod. 18.4.5). By far the closest of all the gods to Alexander personally was Zeus in his manifestation as Ammon at Siwah, and we will consider him shortly.

Athena was probably the tutelary goddess of Alexander's Hellenic (Corinthian) League.[34] She had been the personal champion of Heracles and Achilles, and she assumed (or confirmed) this role for Alexander at Ilium, when his chief diviner Aristander interpreted a portent as vouchsafing the goddess's help in the future. In thanksgiving Alexander made a lavish sacrifice, dedicated his armor to her in return for a sacred shield from her temple, and thereafter had it carried before him in battle. In India, it was to save his life.[35] Alexander worshipped Athena, alone or with other gods, throughout his career with sacrifices of supplication and thanksgiving, and with generous dedications at her sanctuaries when possible.[36] One of his last projects was to build magnificent temples for Athena at Ilium and in Macedonia (Diod. 18.4.5; Strabo 13.1.26).[37]

Alexander worshipped *Heracles* as his divine ancestor and heroic model, either alone or with other gods, especially Zeus and Athena.[38] He is said to have kept on his table throughout his career a statuette of Heracles (the original *Herakles Epitrapezios* of Lysippus) with which (whom) he used to commune and to whom he appealed for success in battle (Stat. *Silv.* 4.6.59–74; cf. Mart. 9.43.6–8). In negotiations with the Thessalians in 336, he appealed to their common connections with Heracles to gain their allegiance (Diod. 17.4.1). After the fall of Thebes, a certain Cleades (otherwise unknown) is said by Justin (11.4.5–7) to have tried to avert the destruction of the city, claimed by the Thebans as the birthplace of Heracles, by appealing to his devotion to the god, but unsuccessfully. One reason no doubt was the Thebans' disloyalty to the Greek cause not only at this time but also in the Persian War, while Alexander was hoping to lead a panhellenic crusade against the Persians as the common enemy of the Greeks.[39] Even so, as Polybius (5.10.7) observes, Alexander was careful not to offend against religion, and took the utmost precautions against even involuntary damage done to the temples or any part of the sacred enclosures. Also the priests and priestesses, as well as the houses of Pindar and some friends of the Macedonians, were spared (Arr. 1.9.9; Plut. *Alex.* 11.12).

Alexander accepted citizenship from the Megarians at their claim that before him only Heracles had been so honored (Plut. *Mor.* 826G; cf. Sen. *Ben.* 1.13.1–2); at Ephesus he increased the sacred *temenus*, the area of asylum of the temple of Artemis, perhaps in emulation of Heracles, who was said to have done the same (Strabo 14.1.23; Tac. *Ann.* 3.61); and at Mallus in Cilicia he remitted the city's tribute because of their common connections to Heracles (Arr. 2.5.9; cf. Strabo 14.5.17). At Tyre, Heracles came to special prominence when the Tyrians refused Alexander's request to sacrifice in the city to their main god Melcart, whom Alexander considered to be Heracles.[40] Alexander decided to take the city by force. Aristander interpreted Alexander's dream of Heracles inviting him into the city to mean that he would take the island fortress, reputedly impregnable, but with great exertion (*ponos*), the mark of Heracles.[41] At the city's fall Alexander meted out terrible punishment to the people but spared those, including the king, who had sought asylum in Heracles' temple (Arr. 2.24.5; Curt. 4.4.13).[42] Alexander sacrificed to Heracles lavishly for his aid in the city's fall, with parades on land and sea, an athletic contest, torch race, dedication of the engine that breached the wall, rededication of the Tyrian sacred ship with a new inscription, and other votive gifts, and on his return from Egypt in the following year he honored Heracles similarly.[43]

Alexander named his son by Barsine Heracles,[44] and in Bactria and Sogdiana he is said, no doubt because of the hardships of the campaign, to have named some of his new settlements Heraclea.[45] At the Hindu Kush and in India (328–6), the Macedonians came to think that they were following in the tracks of Heracles.[46] Alexander's decision to conquer the huge rock fortress Aornus in N.W. India was inspired by the claim of the natives (so he understood) that before him even Heracles had tried but failed to conquer the rock.[47] And both at the Jaxartes in Sogdiana and at the Hyphasis in India, Alexander erected altars in emulation of Heracles and Dionysus to mark the termini of his Eastern conquests.[48] Throughout his career, but especially on the grueling campaigns in Afghanistan and India, Alexander was driven by an obsession to surpass the heroic achievements of Heracles and Dionysus, and he appealed to their example to inspire his troops.[49]

The cult of *Dionysus* was ancient in Macedonia, and in Philip's and Alexander's time seems to have played a major role in the Macedonian state religion.[50] Alexander's mother worshipped Dionysus with special fervor.[51] Although Alexander's reasons for the destruction of Thebes, reputedly the home of Dionysus, were no doubt compelling, he is said later to have been remorseful, and to have felt the god's anger over the destruction (Plut. *Alex.* 13.4; Arr. 2.15.2–3). It is possible that after his victory at Gaugamela, Alexander assumed a diadem derived from the iconography of the god as the badge of his newly proclaimed kingship of Asia, and because of the legend of the god's campaigns in the East, he may have regarded him (since Heracles at this time had not yet been taken to the East) as inspiration for his conquest of Asia.[52] At the firing of Persepolis, he conducted a 'victory procession' (*epinikion kōmon*) in honor of Dionysus (Diod. 17.72.4). In Sogdiana and India, Alexander's cult of Dionysus intensified when the Macedonians found traces of the god's campaigns and felt challenged to surpass them.[53] At the Jaxartes and the Hyphasis rivers, as noted, Alexander set up altars in rivalry with Dionysus and Heracles, and on their return from India, the Macedonians are said to have celebrated their survival from the Gedrosian desert with an extended *kōmos* in honor of the god.[54]

Alexander's rivalry with Dionysus and Heracles soon became a rhetorical commonplace in which fact and fiction became inextricably fused.[55]

To turn to *Apollo*. Alexander apparently launched the invasion of Persia with an oracle from the god at Delphi, taken over from Philip, which predicted, as he wished to believe, the demise through him of the Great King (Diod. 16.91.2–3).[56] Accordingly, when on first landing on Asian soil Alexander claimed Asia as 'gift of the gods' (Diod. 17.17.2), and when he made the same claim again in his letter to Darius after the battle at Issus (Arr. 2.14.7), he no doubt based this confidence on the oracle of Apollo at Delphi.

At Tyre, Alexander attributed the city's fall, after a seven months' bloody siege, to the aid of Apollo as well as of Heracles. When he came in the city upon a statue of Apollo chained to its pedestal, he was told that it was a gift of the Carthaginians (a colony of Tyre) who had robbed it from the people of Gela in Sicily; that the Tyrians identified the god with one of their own, but during the siege someone had a vision of the god announcing that he was about to go over to Alexander. To prevent this, the Tyrians, calling him an 'Alexandrist' (Plut. *Alex.* 24.7), chained him to his pedestal. Alexander now freed him from his bonds, directed that he should henceforth be called 'Apollo Philalexandros' (Diod. 17.46.6), and celebrated him with great splendor.[57]

In 331, from the miraculously reactivated oracle at Didyma near Miletus, the god among other utterances renewed his prediction at Delphi of the death of the Great King, and also seemed to confirm Alexander's identification by Zeus Ammon at Siwah as the son of Zeus.[58]

Years later, in 329 in Sogdiana, Alexander had an opportunity to return the god's favors when he came upon a community of Greeks whose ancestors had desecrated and betrayed Apollo's temple at Didyma to Xerxes, and then followed him East to escape the wrath of their countrymen. Alexander now extirpated them.[59] Some scholars have rejected this abhorrent report, but it is quite plausible.[60] We remember Alexander's massacres in Sogdiana and India, and other acts of savagery, which balance his equally memorable acts of gallantry. In this case, Alexander acted as champion of the god, as avenger of sacrilege, as Philip had done when he killed hundreds of Phocians for their sacrilege against Apollo at Delphi (Diod. 16.35.6; Just. 8.2.3–7).

Alexander continued to honor Apollo, as in Carmania for the safe return of Nearchus and his fleet from India (Arr. *Ind.* 36.3; cf. 3.27.5); in 323 in Babylon he received envoys from Delphi as ranking only after Elis (Zeus Olympius) and Siwah (Zeus Ammon) (Diod. 17.113.4); and one of his last plans was the construction of two magnificent new temples for Apollo, at Delos and at Delphi (Diod. 18.4.5).

4 Portents and divination

The gods gave to humans directions, encouragements, warnings, and hints of the future through their seated oracles as at Delphi and Siwah, and in many other ways such as the entrails of sacrificial animals, the flight and behavior of birds, phenomena of the weather, dreams, and any other occurrences which did not have a known explanation. It is not surprising that in the course of such momentous events as Alexander's conquest of the East, in vast and unknown lands, fraught with ever-present dangers, Alexander and his men greatly depended on these signs from the gods and their correct interpretation. The seers advised Alexander on what gods to propitiate and what rites to employ, and they interpreted the condition of sacrificial victims and omens of all kinds.[61] The fact that Alexander was usually successful facilitated their task. We hear mostly of favorable pronouncements, which came true. Except that Alexander naturally desired reports which supported his designs, he seems seldom to have tried to pressure or manipulate his seers.[62] They showed considerable independence. We hear of one instance, at the Jaxartes (329), when Aristander declared the omens unfavorable and refused to come up with better ones but, provoked by the enemy's taunts, Alexander finally proceeded across the river against the omens. He fell seriously ill from dysentery, and thus vindicated the seer (Arr. 4.4.3, 9).[63]

At the Hyphasis, when Alexander's exhausted troops frustrated his desire to proceed further, Alexander took the omens but they were unfavorable. At this, he gave orders to turn back.[64] It has been said that Alexander had made up his mind, and so the sacrifices naturally were unfavorable.[65] But Alexander always was able somehow to impose his will on his men. It is not unlikely, especially after the experience at the Jaxartes, that the omens really did influence Alexander's decision.[66]

Our sources report a number of bad omens shortly before Alexander's death, some of them distorted or fabricated *ex eventu*, some probably true.[67] They reinforced each other to cause Alexander concern. So at his approach to Babylon, the local priests warned Alexander against entering the city by appealing to an oracle from Bel, but despite well-founded suspicions of the priests' motives, Alexander at first tried to comply with their request at least to enter the city from the West, rather than directly from the East, and he entered only when this proved impossible because of the nature of the terrain. Even so, Alexander was troubled by his failure to comply.[68] When on his arrival in the city Alexander was informed that a seer named Peithagoras had obtained a bad omen about him, and when on being questioned the seer confirmed the report, Alexander accepted this, but when shortly thereafter occurred two more disturbing portents, a sailor innocently donning Alexander's diadem (when it had fallen onto a reed in a swamp and the sailor swam out to retrieve it), and an unknown person unaccountably taking a seat on Alexander's momentarily empty throne, Alexander followed the seers' advice to have the men put away, to avert disaster from himself.[69] The importance which Alexander attached to portents and divination can be gauged also from the fact that while in the earlier days of his final illness he performed his 'customary' (*nomitzomena*) sacrifices, on his last four days he performed 'assigned' (*tetagmena*) sacrifices, that is, sacrifices prescribed by the seers (Arr. 7.25.2–5).

In his later years, Alexander increasingly assumed the ways of Eastern despotism, but there is no good reason to believe that at that time the seers were predominantly Orientals.[70] Alexander's Greek and Macedonian seers no doubt were quick enough to adapt themselves to the changing times. The deputation which consulted a Babylonian healing god for Alexander *in extremis* consisted of five distinguished Macedonian officers and, significantly, two priests, both Greek (Arr. 7.26.2). The crucifixion after Philip's assassination of the seer who presumably had declared the omens favorable[71] suggests that we need not look for Orientals to advise Alexander on divination in his last period.

Of the many additional portents listed by our sources, we can mention here only a few. At Thebes, Alexander no doubt is informed of the various portents which foretold the city's demise (Diod. 17.10.1–6). At the temple of Athena at Ilium, Aristander interprets the fallen statue of a former Persian satrap as portending victory in the coming battle and Athena's help also in the future (Diod. 17.17.6–7). At Miletus, Alexander interprets, differently from Parmenion, the appearance on the shore of an eagle, messenger of Zeus, as confirming his strategy to defeat the Persian fleet on the land by depriving it of its bases (Arr. 1.18.6, 9; 1.20.1). In Lycia, Alexander is encouraged by the discovery of a tablet allegedly predicting the destruction of the Persian Empire by the Greeks (Plut. *Alex.* 17.4). At the siege of Gaza, as Alexander sacrifices, a bird drops a pebble on his head, at which he consults Aristander, who declares that Alexander would capture the city but should beware on this day. After at first complying, Alexander joins the fray in the heat of battle and is wounded, but he is glad because the seer has foretold the city's fall.[72] At the Persian Gates, after unsuccessful attempts to obtain omens from the victims, Alexander abandons the attempt as 'untimely' (Curt. 5.4.2). During the difficult campaign against Spitamenes, there is discovered near Alexander's tent by the Oxus river a spring of water and nearby one of oil (perhaps the first petroleum ever seen by Europeans). At this prodigy Alexander sacrifices as the soothsayers direct, and Aristander declares the oil as portending victory after hardship (Arr. 4.15.7–8). According to Plutarch (*Alex.* 57.8; cf. Athen. 2.42 F), Alexander stated in a letter to Antipater that this was one of the greatest revelations vouchsafed to him by god.

Part II

1 Consultation of the oracle of Zeus Ammon at Siwah. Son of Zeus

On the occasion of his occupation of Egypt in 332–31, Alexander made a pilgrimage to the oasis of Siwah in the Libyan desert to consult the oracle of Zeus Ammon. While Darius was readying his forces for the final decision, Alexander took six weeks and several hundred miles to visit the oracle. We should think that his reasons were compelling.[73]

Ammon at Siwah was derived from the Egyptian Amon-Ra at Thebes, but the Greeks had long identified him as Zeus (e.g. Pindar, *Pyth.* 4.16), and there can be no doubt that Alexander too considered him as Zeus.[74] We can identify several motives for Alexander's trip. Ammon was already well known in the Greek world, with cults in a number of places including Macedonia and Athens, and his oracle was considered infallible (Arr. 3.3.1).[75] The tradition that Alexander's ancestors Heracles and Perseus also had consulted the oracle provided further incentive (Arr. 3.3.1–2; cf. Strabo 17.1.43). Certainly Alexander wished to consult the oracle about the future. In particular, it is likely that he hoped for confirmation of the prediction of Apollo at Delphi for his conquest of the Persian king,[76] and that of Zeus Basileus at Gordium for his rule over Asia, and to be given instructions for sacrifices along the way.[77] Most important, there is reason to think that by this time Alexander had already conceived the notion that, like Heracles and Perseus, he too was a son of Zeus, and that he now hoped for confirmation and clarification of this relationship (Arr. 3.3.2).[78] We may assume that Alexander informed the priests in advance of his visit and of his expectations.[79]

At his arrival, Alexander was conducted into the inner sanctum of the temple, and probably after some ritual act before the idol of the god posed his questions. The high priest in a secret listening chamber recorded the questions, formulated the god's responses in writing, and then communicated them to Alexander.[80] After rejoining his followers outside the temple, Alexander said that he had heard what he hoped for

(Arr. 3.4.5). This would suggest that at least at this time, Alexander did not divulge either his questions or the god's responses, except to say that the priest expressly (*rhētōs*) acknowledged him, no doubt in the name of the god, as his son, and the priest may have confirmed this statement (Callisthenes, *FGrHist* 124 F14 a = Strabo 17.1.43).[81]

When and how did Alexander first conceive the notion that he was the son of Zeus? He probably did not derive it from his status as Pharaoh in Egypt, by which he was *ex officio* son of Amon-Ra and Osiris, and god (as Horus). It is unlikely that he concerned himself with the intricacies of Egyptian theology,[82] and Arrian, on the authority either of Ptolemy or of Aristobulus, states clearly that already by now Alexander attributed his birth to Ammon (that is, Zeus), in the sense that tradition attributed the birth of Heracles and Perseus to Zeus (3.3.2). This then was a Greek, not an Egyptian, concept. Possibly it was Olympias who first suggested it to him, being as she was antagonistic to Philip, extremely ambitious for herself and her son, and, as we have noted, intensely religious. In particular, she was devoted to Dionysiac and Orphic mysteries, which may have encouraged her belief that she had conceived Alexander by a god. Plutarch (*Alex.* 2.6) says that Philip once saw a serpent in bed with Olympias, and thought that she might have been visited by a divine being. Serpents were especially prominent in the cult of Dionysus, and Olympias may have come to believe that Alexander had been fathered by a god, whether Dionysus or perhaps even Zeus, in the form of a serpent.[83] Eratosthenes (*FGrHist* 241 F 28 = Plut. *Alex.* 3.3) claims that before his departure for the war, Olympias told Alexander the secret of his begetting, and charged him to entertain thoughts worthy of it. If Olympias suggested to Alexander that he was the son of Dionysus, rather than of Zeus, he subsequently changed his mind, and imputed his birth to Zeus, and at Siwah the god confirmed the relationship.

Soon afterwards word reached Alexander that the oracle of Apollo at Didyma, and the prophetess Athenais at Erythrae, in Ionia, also had revealed Alexander's sonship of Zeus (Callisthenes, *FGrHist* 124 F14 a = Strabo 17.1.43). In an address to his Greek troops before the battle at Gaugamela, he prayed the gods for assistance if he was truly the son of Zeus (Callisthenes, *FGrHist* 124 F 36 = Plut. *Alex* 33.1).[84] Some time after the battle, probably at Babylon, Apelles painted Alexander, surely at his initiative, as wielder of the thunderbolt, that is, as son of Zeus (Plin. *NH* 35.92; Plut. *Alex.* 4.3),[85] and on Alexander's return from India, in 324, there was issued, probably at Susa, a silver decadrachma in celebration of his Indian conquest, again no doubt at Alexander's initiative, or at least his encouragement. It shows on one side Alexander in victorious combat with Indians, and on the other Alexander in full armor, being crowned by Nike, and wielding, as in the painting by Apelles, the thunderbolt of his father.[86] In 328 in Sogdiana, Alexander's general Cleitus during a drunken altercation taunted Alexander with his claim of a divine paternity (Plut. *Alex.* 50.11; Curt. 8.1.42), and in 324 at Opis the mutinous Macedonians did the same.[87] But Alexander persisted. In a letter to the Athenians, probably early in 323, he is said to have referred to Philip as his 'so-called father' (Plut. *Alex.* 28.2). If the letter is spurious, it was authored almost certainly not long afterwards by someone who believed that Alexander acknowledged a father other than Philip.[88]

After Alexander's death, there was found among his papers a plan for a monumental cenotaph for Philip (Diod. 18.4.4–6).[89] Perhaps his intention was to show that he still acknowledged Philip as his earthly father. But this show of *pietas* did not mean a lessening of Alexander's commitment to his divine father. He adhered to it in the face of the resentment of many, especially the Macedonians who saw in it a rejection of their beloved Philip.[90] Others, whether from conviction or flattery, accepted it. There is reason to believe that after his return from India in 324, Alexander hoped to be deified, at any rate at Athens, as son of Zeus Ammon,[91] and on his deathbed he requested burial, not with Philip at the traditional resting place of the Argead Kings in Macedonia, but with Zeus Ammon at Siwah.[92]

Perhaps we can probe a bit further into this remarkable obsession. Alexander's descent from Heracles, which he never disavowed (Arr. 3.3.2; 6.3.2), meant that he was the son of Philip (Arr. 7.9.2). But as we know from Arrian (3.3.2), drawing on either Ptolemy or Aristobulus, Alexander also attributed his birth to Ammon, that is Zeus, 'just as' (*kathaper*) tradition attributed the birth of Heracles and of Perseus to Zeus. This must mean that Alexander considered himself the son of both Philip and Zeus, and it clarifies Arrian's statement that Alexander attributed 'part' (*ti*) of his birth to Ammon (Arr. 3.3.2): the other part came from Philip.[93] Perhaps after changing his mind about the earlier notion of his conception from a god in form of a serpent, Alexander came to think that in fathering him, Zeus assumed the form of Philip, or that he was the product of the seed of both. Whatever the explanation, we may believe that the priest at Siwah confirmed and explained the matter to Alexander in a way that made sense to him. Shortly afterwards he wrote to his mother that he had received "'certain secret (*aporrhētous*) responses' from the oracle which he would tell her, and her alone, after his return" (Plut. *Alex.* 27.8). It is not unlikely that these responses concerned the intimate subject of Alexander's conception.[94]

We can be sure that Alexander's faith in the fatherhood of Zeus quickened his determination to validate this relationship by his achievements, and before long he came to think that on this basis he himself deserved to be honored as a god.[95]

2 Alexander the god

In the spring of 327, in Bactria, Alexander attempted to extend to the Greeks and Macedonians at his court the Persian homage to the king called (by the Greeks) *proskynesis*, which the Orientals accorded him as their new king as a matter of course.[96] It has been thought that by this device Alexander meant to introduce his cult as god of his empire.[97] But for the Persians, the king was not a god, and thus for them the act did not mean worship but was a gesture of obeisance to an absolute potentate. We should think therefore that Alexander's purpose in extending the practice to his Western followers was to establish a ritual acknowledgment of his new status as an autocrat for all his subjects alike without distinction.[98]

But there was more. To the Greeks and Macedonians, *proskynesis* had always meant or suggested divine worship, and although by now they certainly understood that this was not what it meant to the Persians, the notion persisted. Alexander must have known this, and we should think therefore that he was not averse to the traditional implication which the gesture conveyed for the Greeks and Macedonians.[99] It is not unlikely, therefore, that he hoped to apply it for the introduction of a formal cult, possibly empire-wide, at some time in the future. Meanwhile, the issue officially was the coordination of court ceremonial between Persians and Macedonians before Alexander as an absolute monarch, and although many of his subjects encouraged this affectation of Persian despotism, most others resented it. Alexander's court historian Callisthenes, a nephew of Aristotle, who celebrated Alexander as an Hellenic hero and son of Zeus,[100] but was no friend of barbarians and Oriental despotism, stood forth as their spokesman. At a rehearsal of the procedure he provocatively failed to perform, and Alexander, realizing that Callisthenes had the support of others, dropped the matter, for the time being. Callisthenes, of course, was doomed.

Alexander was not to be denied. Within a few years, with the crushing of the Macedonian mutiny at Opis in 324, he achieved absolute ascendancy over the Macedonians. Along with this grew his appetite for godhood. It had already been quickened by his successful rivalry with the reputed conquests of Dionysus and Heracles in India (Curt. 8.10.1).[101] And when after his return to Mesopotamia he was informed that the Arabs worshipped only two gods, the cosmic deity Uranus, and Dionysus for his Indian campaign, Alexander declared himself worthy to be worshipped by the Arabs as a third god, 'since his achievements were as magnificent as those of Dionysus, given that he would conquer the Arabs too, and permit them, like the Indians, to be governed by their own laws' (Aristobulus, *FGrHist* 139 F 55 = Arr. 7.20.1). The comparison with Dionysus is entirely plausible.[102] It not only confirms Alexander's avidity for divine status, but also points up the main basis on which he considered himself, as son of Zeus, entitled to it: his conquests in victorious rivalry with the greatest heroes of the past.

It is not unlikely that Alexander felt encouraged in his quest by his divine father at Siwah. Among the responses which the god communicated to him in 331 very possibly was a promise that he would be acknowledged as a god in his lifetime, most likely upon completion of his conquest of Asia.[103] We are not surprised, then, that in 324 Alexander sent word to the cities of Greece that he expected them to honor him as a god.[104] In response, early in 323 some, or possibly all, of the cities instituted cults for Alexander.[105] At some unknown date, or dates, at least some of the Greek cities of Asia Minor also founded cults for Alexander, most likely perhaps in conjunction, somehow, with the cults of the Greek homeland.[106]

At Athens, and probably elsewhere, Alexander appears to have been deified as son of Zeus Ammon.[107] While a cult which acknowledged his relationship to the god no doubt accorded with Alexander's wishes, it may well be that more than one cult title was proposed, and perhaps adopted, in any one city. So we hear of a proposal at Athens to erect a statue of Alexander as 'Unconquered God' (*Anikētos Theos*) (Hyp. *Dem.* 32). It confirms that Alexander was known to associate his godhead with his military conquests, and that he saw in these the decisive justification for his worship.[108] In May 323, shortly before his death, sacred envoys from Greece (and Asia Minor?) presented themselves in Babylon to acknowledge Alexander as a god (Ar. 7.23.2).[109]

In what sense, if at all, did Alexander consider himself a god? No doubt Alexander was aware that others in the Greek world had been honored as gods in their lifetime. We hear of such honors for Pythagoras in Italy, Empedocles in Sicily, Lysander on Samos, Clearchus at Heracleia on Pontus, and Alexander's own grandfather Amyntas in Pydna. There were also extravagant, some even perhaps divine, honors for Philip at Philippi, Amphipolis, Eresus, Ephesus, and Cynosarges at Athens.[110] Most significant for Alexander was Philip's presentation of his own chryselephantine statue (normally reserved for gods) on a par with those of the Twelve Gods on that momentous day at Aegae in 336.[111] No doubt by 324, Alexander had become convinced that he deserved to be recognized as a god more than any man before him.

Beyond this, it is possible that, encouraged by his flatterers, Alexander came to believe, even if not consistently, that unlike any of his predecessors he himself was divine not just in a metaphorical, but in an actual sense.[112] As we have noted, Olympias may have suggested that his father was a god, perhaps even Zeus, and Zeus Ammon at Siwah and Apollo at Didyma confirmed the idea. Alexander probably thought that all men before him in modern times who claimed a divine father were frauds, like the notorious Clearchus, because they had not proven it by their deeds. But Alexander had proven his godhood by the superhuman magnitude of his achievements. Precedents above all were two other sons of Zeus by mortal women, Heracles and Dionysus. Heracles joined the gods after his death, and Dionysus was a god already on earth, but Alexander surpassed them both (e.g. Arr. 5.26.5). At the same time, all through his life Alexander endeavored to avoid hubris, which offends the gods, by his assiduous devotion to them.[113] Even at the very end, no longer able to walk, he had himself carried out to perform his daily sacrifices (Arr. 7.25; Plut. *Alex.* 76). It is quite possible that Alexander came to expect that after his death on earth, he would live on as a god.

To us, Alexander's claim to divinity may seem like megalomania, even madness. But in the context of the traditions and beliefs of his own age, it could be seen by many, and it certainly was by Alexander himself, as reasonable and justified, by virtue of his divine birth, his superhuman *aretē* and achievements, and the approbation of his father Zeus.[114] At the time of his death, many Greeks and Macedonians no doubt shared the opinion expressed by Justin (12.16.1) that Alexander was a man endowed with a greatness of spirit that went beyond the limits of human ability.[115]

Notes

1 *Philip*: Isoc. 5.32, 105, 109–15, 127; Arr. 2.5.9; 3.3.2; 4.10.6; 4.11.6; 6.3.2; Diod. 17.1.5; Curt. 4.2.3; Plut. *Alex.* 2.1; *Mor.* 334 D. *Olympias*: Plut. *Alex.* 2.1; *Mor.* 334 D; Arr. 1.11.8; 4.11.6; Diod. 17.1.5; Curt. 4.6.29; 8.4.26; Just. 11.3.1; Strabo 13.1.27; Theopompus, *FGrHist* 115 F 355. I take it here as a given that in the fourth c. most Macedonians still believed in the reality of the Olympian gods and the heroes, and a fortiori Alexander himself, who moreover as king had a vested interest in this faith. Cf. Wilamowitz 1932: 265: 'Was gibt uns Veranlassung zu bezweifeln dass Alexander ebenso wie sein Volk an dem Glauben an die Götter festhielt?' Hammond *The Miracle* 1991: 150: 'Alexander was typically Macedonian in the intense religious belief which was the mainspring of his activity.' Also Edmunds 1971: esp. 368–91; Wirth 1973: 123; Kern 1963: 38–57.
2 Speus. *Epist. Socrat.* 30.3; Isoc. 5.105, 111–5, 127.
3 Hammond 1979: 663–7; 1994: 114, 158.
4 Diod. 16.89.2; cf. 17.4.9.
5 Fredricksmeyer 1979: 58–60; Borza 1992: 249–50; Baynham 'The Question' 1994: 35–43. Cf. Schumacher 1990: 434–5; Flower 2000: 121. Hammond (1999: 107) thinks that the Macedonians had already formally granted Philip divine honors and that the procession at Aegae was meant to advertise them. See also Prestianni Giallombardo 1975: 27–35. *Contra*: Balsdon 1950: 365–8; Badian 1981: 31 n. 9.
6 Plut. *Alex.* 5.8; 24.10; 25.7–8; *Mor.* 179 E–F; Plin. *NH* 12.62.
7 *Hymn to Arete*: Athen. 15.696 B–D. Study *of Iliad*: Plut. *Alex* 8.2; 26.1–2; Plin. *NH* 7.108; Strabo 13.1.27. Memorizing *Iliad*: Dio Ghrysostom. 4.39.
8 Curt. 4.6.29; 9.3.19; Arr. 5.28.3; 7.14.4; Plut. *Alex.* 15.8–9; 62.5; 72.3; Diod. 17.97.3; Ael. *VH* 7.8. Ameling 1988: 670–92; King 1987: *passim*; Stewart 1993: 78–86. Cf. Cohen 1995: 483–6; Carney, 'Artifice' 2000: 274–85.
9 Edmunds 1971: 363–91; King 1987: 1–45; Fredricksmeyer 1990: 304–6; Ameling 1988: 658–60; Stewart 1993: 81; Huttner 1997: *passim*.

10 Hammond 1979: 3–14; Edson 1970: 37–8.

11 Berve 1926: II, 385 no. 781.

12 Diod. 13.108.4; 17.16.3–4; Arr. 1.11.1; 1.18.2; 2.5.8; 2.24.6; 3.1.4; 3.5.2; 3.6.1; 3.16.9; 3.25.1; 4.4.1; 5.3.6; 5.8.3; 5.20.1; 5.29.2; 6.28.3; 7.14.1; *Ind.* 18.12; 36.3; 42.8; Curt. 3.7.3; Plut. *Alex.* 29.1–2; 63.14.

13 Baege 1913: *s.vv.*; Berve 1926: I, 87.

14 Arr. 1.17.10; 1.18.2; Strabo 14.1.22–3. Also various votive gifts to Artemis: *Anth.Gr.* 6.97, 128; Plin. *NH* 35.92. Note also, Alexander's intention, toward the end of his life, to erect a great temple to Artemis at Amphipolis. Diod. 18.4.5.

15 POxy 1798, *FGrHist* 148, 44 col. II; Arr. 1.4.5; 1.11.6; 5.28.4; 6.3.1–2; 6.19.5; *Ind.* 18.11–2; 20.10; 36.3; Diod. 17.104.1; Just. 12.10.4.

16 Arr. 4.8.2; Plut. *Alex.* 50.7; Plin. *NH* 35.93.

17 Arr. 1.12.1; 7.14.4; Plut. *Alex.* 15.8; Diod. 17.17.3; Just. 11.5.12; Philostr. *Her.* 53.16.

18 Arr. 7.14.7–10; 7.23.6–8; Plut. *Alex.* 72.2–5; 75.3; Just. 12.12.12; Diod. 17.114–5; 18.4.2; Hyp. *Epit.* 21; Ael. *VH* 7.8. On the problem of Hephaestion's pyre/tomb, see now Palagia 2000: 167–75, with refs.

19 No doubt Alexander considered the Ephesian Artemis an Hellenic deity, with Asian accretions (Diod. 5.77.6–8), just as he regarded the Tyrian Melcart as Heracles. A possible exception may be found in the account of Josephus (*Antiqu.* 11.317–45), with parallels in Ps. Callisthenes, Rec. C, and rabbinic literature, based on the same Hellenistic Jewish sources as those used by Josephus. According to Josephus (11.329–38), after the fall of Gaza in 332, Alexander was met near Jerusalem by a delegation of Jews led by their High Priest; Alexander paid obeisance to the High Priest as representative of god, and then visited Jerusalem, where he sacrificed to God in his temple. The historicity of this information has been debated by scholars for well over a century. But the weight of opinion appears to be with those who reject the account, among them F. Pfister, W.W. Tarn, V. Ehrenberg, E. Renan, E. Bickerman, M. Marcus, and V. Tscherikower. A reasonable conclusion would seem to be that while Alexander's obeisance (*proskynesis*) before the High Priest, and his visit to Jerusalem, are probably fictitious, he may well have met a delegation of Jews on his way to Egypt, and treated the High Priest with respect and even reverence. Such conduct would be entirely in character for Alexander. For good accounts of the controversy, with extensive references, see esp. Marcus 1956: 512–32, and Seibert 1994: 103–7, 271–4.

20 Kees 1931: 676; Grieshammer 1996: 847; Pietschmann 1894: 2808.

21 E.g. Koenen 1977: 31 and 53, and see Stewart in [the original]. Burstein argues that Alexander was not enthroned as Pharaoh. 1991: 139–45.

22 Fredricksmeyer 2000: 146, with refs.

23 Fredricksmeyer 2000: 146–7; Unger 1970: 191–200; Högemann 1985: 49–52. For Alexander's attitudes toward non-Greek religious beliefs see also Brosius in [the original].

24 *Egypt* Hdt. 3.27–9; Plut. *Mor.* 368 F; Diod. 16.51; Ael. *NA* 10.28; *VH* 4.8; 6.8. *Babylon*: Hdt. 1.183. Unger 1970: 39, 191, 209; 1928: 334–5; 356; 365. Both the Egyptians and the Babylonians, as represented by our Greek and Roman sources, exaggerated the Persian offenses.

25 Ms. Brosius (in [the original], p. 184, n. 24) faults me for saying, at 2000: 148, that before Alexander, Persepolis was 'barely known' to the Greeks. I wrote not 'barely' but 'little' known (there is a difference), as compared with Susa, and this is certainly true. Susa, not Persepolis, was for the Greeks the great symbol of Persian "power, aggression and arrogance" (2000: 148), and so the question remains why, in order to punish the Persians for their sacrilege of 480/79, Alexander destroyed Persepolis, not Susa. The most likely answer still seems to me that Persepolis was the ritual center of the Persian Empire under the aegis of Ahuramazda as the supreme deity of the Achaemenid dynasty. Cf. Fredricksmeyer 2000: 145, 147–50, 163, with refs. Also Dandamaev 1989: 255: 'The majority of scholars believe that Persepolis was not a center of administration or the capital of a world empire, but was rather the representative dynastic, ritual city of the Achaemenid kings.' Pope 1957: 125: 'Persepolis was a ritual city ... imbued with the peculiar virtue of royal authority, conferred by the power of Ahuramazda.' Pope 1969: 6: Persepolis was 'the most sacred spot in Persia, a veritable Holy of Holies.' Note also the comment of Cicero (*Rep.* 3.14) on the incompatibility of the Persian and Greek religions. Cf. *Leg.* 2.26; Hdt. 1.131; 8.109; Plut. *Mor.* 328 D. For an instructive discussion of Iranian, and in particular also Achaemenid, religion see Dandamaev 1989: 320–66. For the Greek perspective on the

burning of Persepolis, see e.g. Wheeler 1968: 45–59. On the religious significance of Pasargadae, see Fredricksmeyer 2000: 163, with refs.

26 It is here accepted that Alexander's firing of Persepolis was not an act of drunken impulse but of policy. See Fredricksmeyer 2000: 149–50, with n. 37.

27 Note e.g. Alexander's burial of Darius' wife 'according to the ancestral custom of the Persians' (Curt. 3.12.13; 4.10.23). Polybius (5.10.8) says that 'even when he crossed to Asia to chastise the Persians for the outrage they had perpetrated against the Greeks … he refrained from injuring anything consecrated to the gods, although it was in this respect that the Persians had offended most while in Greece.' Alexander punished severely the desecration of holy places by any of his underlings in Asia. Arr. 6.30.2; Curt. 10.1.8. On the other hand, Alexander's savage repression of Brahmans in southern India was prompted by their resistance to him. See now Bosworth 1998: esp. 196–203. Arrian (7.14.5) reports that in Ecbatana in 324, in his grief over the death of Hephaestion, Alexander ordered the temple of Asclepius (a local healing god identified with Asclepius) to be razed to the ground. Arrian does not credit the story, on the ground that this act would have been utterly out of character for Alexander. Arrian is probably right.

28 At Siwah in 331, Zeus Ammon gave Alexander instructions for sacrifices on his campaign in Asia, and especially for the occasion when he completed his conquest. We may assume that the gods whom Zeus Ammon specified were largely identical with Alexander's ancestral gods. Fredricksmeyer 1991: 199–214.

29 Diod. 11.29.3; 16.89.2; 17.4.9; Arr. 2.14.4; 3.18.12; Just. 11.5.6; Polyb. 3.6.13; 5.10.8; Hdt. 8.109; Cic. *Rep.* 3.14–15; *Leg.* 2.26; *ND* 1.115; *Verr.* 2.1.48. On the revenge motif, see Bellen 1974: 58–67. Cf. Seibert 1998: 5–58.

30 Price 1991: 29–31; 1974: 24–5, with pl. 11.60 and 63. Cf. Fredricksmeyer 2000: 144 n. 18. In 335, after crossing the Danube and dispersing the Getae, Alexander sacrificed on the bank of the river to Zeus Soter, Heracles, and Ister (Danube) (Arr. 1.4.5).

31 J.D. Bing (1991: 161–5) believes that the Zeus, Heracles, and Athena to whom Alexander according to Curtius (3.12.27) sacrificed in thanksgiving after the victory at Issus were actually the Cilician gods Ba'al Tarz/Tarhunzas, Nergal/Rasheph/Runzas, and 'Anat/Ishara. This is unlikely. They were rather the same Zeus, Athena, and Heracles whom Alexander worshipped, along with the other Graeco-Macedonian gods, at the Hellespont and throughout his career. Fredricksmeyer 2000: 143–5.

32 Fredricksmeyer 1961: 160–8.

33 Fredricksmeyer 1961: 166. Cf. Kienast 1987: 313. The opinion occasionally expressed that the god whom Alexander worshipped in Memphis was not the Graeco-Macedonian Zeus Basileus (Arrian) but the Egyptian Oserapis or Amon-Ra is unlikely. Correct: Wilcken 1967: 130; Hammond *Alexander the Great* 1980: 129.

34 Price 1991: 29; 1974: 24.

35 Diod. 17.17.6; 17.18.1; 17.21.2; Arr. 1.11.7–8; 6.9.3; 6.10.2; Plut. *Alex.* 15.7.

36 Plut. *Alex.* 16.18 = Arr. 1.16.7; Squillace 1992–4: 9–20 (Athens); Strabo 13.1.26 (Ilium); Dittenberger, *Syll.* No. 277 (Dedication of the new temple of Athena Polias at Priene); Curt. 3.7.3; Arr. 2.5.8, 9 (Soli and Magarsus); Curt. 3.12.27 (after Issus); Curt. 4.13.15 (before Gaugamela); *FGrHist* IIIB, Anagraphe von Lindos XXXVIII, p. 511 (Lindus); Curt. 8.2.32 (after surrender of Rock of Chorienes in Sogdiana); Arr. 4.22.6 (at Nicaea in the Paropamisadae to inaugurate the invasion of India); Curt. 8.11.24 (conquest of Aornus).

37 On Zeus and Athena as Alexander's patron gods in Asia, see also Prandi 1990: 345–69.

38 Arr. 1.4.5; 1.11.7; 2.24.6; 3.3.1–2; 4.30.4; 6.3.2; *Ind.* 36.3; Curt. 3.12.27; Plut. *Mor.* 326 B; 332 A–B; 334 D; 542 D. Edmunds 1971: 374–6; Huttner 1997: 86–123.

39 The Thebans had called on the Greeks together with them and the Great King to remove the tyranny of Alexander over Greece. Diod. 17.9.5. Cf. Flower 2000: 97 and 130 n. 143.

40 Arr. 2.15.7; 2.16.7; Diod. 17.40.2; Curt. 4.2.2–4; Just. 11.10.10.

41 Arr. 2.18.1; Plut. *Alex.* 24.5; Curt. 4.2.17; Huttner 1997: 98.

42 Note also Alexander's letter to Megabyxus concerning a run-away slave who had taken refuge in a sanctuary, directing him to try if possible to entice him outside, but not to lay hands on him in the sanctuary. Plut. *Alex.* 42.1; Hamilton 1969: 110.

43 Arr. 2.24.6; 3.6.1; Diod. 17.46.6; Curt. 4.8.16; Moretti 1975: No. 113.

44 Diod. 20.20.1–2; Plut. *Eum.* 1.3; Curt. 10.6.11; Just. 11.10.3; 12.15.9; 13.2.7; 15.2.3; Paus. 9.7.2. Brunt 1975: esp. 34; Carney *Women and Monarchy* 2000: 101–5, 149–50.

45 Loewe 1936: 34 and 39.

46 Arr. 4.28.1–4; 5.3.2–4; 5.26.5; *Ind.* 5.11–3; Diod. 17.83.1; 17.96.2–3; Curt. 7.3.22; 8.14.11; 9.4.1–3; Just. 12.9.2; Strabo 11.5.5; 15.1.8. Brunt 1983: 437; Bosworth *Historical Commentary* 1995, II: 213–7; Huttner 1997: 108–9.

47 Arr. 4.28.1–4; 4.30.4; 5.26.5; *Ind.* 5.10; Diod. 17.85.2; 17.96.2–3; Curt. 8.11.2; Just. 12.7.12–3; Strabo 15.1.8.

48 Plin. *NH* 6.49; Curt. 7.9.15 (Jaxartes); Strabo 3.5.5; Curt. 3.10.5; cf. Philostr. *Vit. Ap.* 2.43, of doubtful authenticity.

49 E.g. Strabo 3.5.5; Arr. 5.26.5; Curt. 3.10.5; 3.12.18; 9.2.29; 9.4.21; Plut. *Mor.* 326 B; 332 A. On the identification by the Macedonians of Indian deities with Heracles and Dionysus, see Hartman 1965: esp. 60–3.

50 Fredricksmeyer 1966: 179–82. Cf. Baynham 2000: 258–9.

51 Plut. *Alex.* 2.5; Athen. 13.560 F; 14.659 F.

52 Fredricksmeyer 1997: 97, 102–7.

53 Arr. 5.1.1–2.7; 6.14.2; 7.10.6; *Ind.* 1.4–7; 5.8–9; Diod. 1.19.7; Curt. 3.12.18; 7.9.15; 8.10.1; 8.10.7–18; 9.2.29; 9.4.21; 9.8.5; Just. 12.7.6–8; Plut. *Mor.* 326 B; 332 B; Strabo 15.1.8; 15.1.33; Clitarchus, *FGrHist* 137 F 17 = Schol. Apoll. Rhod. 2.904; Philostr. *Vit. Ap.* 2.9.

54 Arr. 6.28.1–2; Diod. 17.106.1; Curt. 3.12.18; 9.10.24–30; Plut. *Alex.* 67; Plin. *NH* 16.144. Further sacrifices to Dionysus: Arr. 4.9.5; 5.2.6; Suet. *Aug.* 94.5; Athen. 12.538A; 13.595 E; Diod. 17.117.1.

55 See Brunt 1983: 435–42. The story that Alexander considered Dionysus his ancestor is probably apocryphal. Nock 1928: 21–30. On Alexander's relations with Dionysus, see also Goukowsky 1981: *passim*; Bosworth, *Alexander and the East*, 98–132, 164–5, and *passim*; Edmunds 1971: 376–8; Seibert 1994: 204–6.

56 Alexander's application to himself of Philip's oracle explains why he himself did not obtain an oracle from Delphi. Instinsky 1949: 36–40; Hamilton 1969: 34–5. At the time of Alexander's crossing of the Hellespont, Olympias made inquiry of Apollo's oracle at Cyzicus (or perhaps Zeleia) whether Alexander would conquer 'the land of the Persians,' and received what appeared to be a favorable reply. *Anth. Gr.* 14.114. Cf. Kaiser-Raiss 1984: 40. Note also Alexander's votive offering to Apollo at Cyme in Aeolia in 334. Plin. *NH* 34.14.

57 Diod. 13.108.3–4; 17.41.7–8; 17.46.6; Curt. 4.3.21–2; Plut. *Alex.* 24.6–8.

58 Callisthenes, *FGrHist* 124 F14 a = Strabo 17.1.43.

59 Curt. 7.5.28–35; Diod. 17. Table of Contents K; Plut. *Mor.* 557 B; Strabo 11.11.4; 14.1.5; 17.1.43; Suda s.v. *Branchidae*.

60 Hammond 1998: 339–44; Holt 1988: 73–5; Bellen 1974: 63–5. *Contra* Tarn 1948: II, 272–5.

61 Arr. 4.15.8; 6.3.1; 7.22.4; 7.24.3–4; *Ind.* 18.11–2; Diod. 17.116.4, 7; 17.116.7–117.1; Plut. *Alex* 74.1. See also Greenwalt 1982: 17–25, with further refs.

62 A conspicuous exception, if true, is Alexander's rejection, in 326/5, of the warning of his seer Demophon to delay his assault on the city of the Malli, and Alexander sustained the most severe wound of his life. Diod. 17.98.3–4; Curt. 9.4.26–30.

63 Curtius (7.7.21–9) says that after Aristander declared the omens unfavorable, Alexander browbeat him, at which he took the omens again and declared that never before had they been more favorable. Obviously this information, which is part of the rhetorical fiction which marks Curtius' whole account of the episode (7.7.5–29), cannot stand against the testimony of Arrian. Cf. Greenwalt 1982: 20–4.

64 Ptolemy, *FGrHist* 138 F 23 = Arr. 5.28.4; Strabo 15.1.27.

65 Tarn 1948: I, 100.

66 Cf. Bosworth *Conquest and Empire* 1988: 133: ' ... it was the gods to whom he deferred, not his men.'

67 Arr. 7.16.5; 7.30.2; Plut. *Alex* 73; 74.1; 75.1–2; Diod. 17.112.4; 17.116.1, 4. Mederer 1936: 120–33.

68 Aristobulus, *FGrHist* 139 F 54 = Arr. 7.16.5–17.6; Plut. *Alex.* 73.2; 74.1; 75.1; Diod. 17.112; Just. 12.13.3; App. *B.C.* 2.152. Alexander's initial distrust of the Chaldaeans is shown by his response to them with a quote from Euripides that 'the best prophets are the ones who guess the

best' (Arr. 7.16.7). But, perhaps from a premonition of his coming illness, Alexander's nonchalance soon turned to anxiety. Plutarch (*Alex.* 75.1–2) says that toward the end in Babylon Alexander became extremely sensitive to all occurrences that could be taken as portents, and his palace was filled with 'sacrificers, purifiers, and diviners.'

69 Peithagoras: Arr. 7.18.1–5; Plut. *Alex.* 73.3–5; App. *B.C.* 2.152. Royal diadem and stranger on throne: Arr. 7.22.4; 7.24.1–3; Diod. 17.116.4–117.1; Plut. *Alex.* 73.7–74.1

70 But so Berve 1926: I, 92. Elsewhere (98 n. 3) Berve doubts the influence of Oriental seers on Alexander. Plutarch's remark (*Alex.* 57.4) that Alexander employed Babylonian purifiers is not attested elsewhere. According to Curtius (4.10.4), Alexander employed Egyptian seers as early as 331. Very possibly Alexander used some Oriental seers all along, but no doubt their function was secondary to that of the Graeco-Macedonian seers. Certainly no seer ever equaled the influence on Alexander of Aristander of Telmessus, who had served with distinction already under Philip (Plut. *Alex.* 2.5). Greenwalt 1982: 24–5.

71 Hammond 1994: 177, with nn. 2 and 3.

72 Arr. 2.26.4–27.4; Curt. 4.6.10–3; Plut. *Alex.* 25.4–5.

73 On the visit, see Arr. 3.3.3–4; Diod. 17.49.2–51.4; Curt. 4.7.5–8; Just. 11.11.2–12; Plut. *Alex.* 26.11–27.11; Strabo 17.1.43. *Important studies*: Bosworth 1977: 51–75; Badian 1981: 27–71; Brunt 1976: 467–80. See also Lane Fox 1973: 200–18; Green 1991: 272–5. *A good survey*: Seibert 1994: 116–25.

74 Denied by Tarn 1948: II, 348–59. But see Badian 1981: 45–6, with nn. 20 and 23; Bosworth 1977: 52; *Conquest and Empire* 1988: 282–3; Fredricksmeyer 1991: 199–200. When, as he did on one occasion, Alexander swore by 'Zeus of the Greeks and the Libyan Ammon,' he did not mean two different gods but the god whom the Greeks call 'Zeus,' the Libyans 'Ammon.' Arr. *Ind.* 35.8.

75 Classen 1959: 349–55; Baege 1913: 16.

76 This is intrinsically probable.

77 Fredricksmeyer 1991: 205–14; Edmunds 1971: 378–9.

78 Bosworth 1977: 67–75; *Conquest and Empire* 1988: 282. Cf. Taeger 1957: 192; Badian 1985: 433.

79 Justin (11.11.6) says (but no one else) that Alexander sent men ahead to bribe (*subornat*) the priests to give the responses he wished. An underhanded trick like this would have been so uncharacteristic of Alexander that we can safely dismiss it. At the very least, he was not so heavy-handed. Compare for instance Zeus Ammon allowing only heroic honors for Hephaestion even though Alexander wished for divine honors for him. Cf. Wilamowitz 1932: 265: 'Dass er den Zug zu dem Gotte nicht unternommen hat, um eine Komödie zu spielen und die Welt zu betrügen, darüber verliere ich keine Worte.'

80 Kuhlmann 1988: 144–6.

81 Alexander may have divulged some information at a later time. Fredricksmeyer 1991: 200–2. After the consultation, Alexander made generous thank offerings to the god and his priests. Diod. 17.51.4; Curt. 4.7.28; Plut. *Alex.* 27.7.

82 Bosworth *Conquest and Empire* 1988: 70; Hammond 1997: 102. On the Egyptian doctrines of Pharaonic worship, see Kuhlmann 1988: 146–54.

83 Hamilton 1969: 4–5; Wirth 1973: 120; Brunt 1976: 477; Badian 1996: 19.

84 Badian 1981: 63 n. 61; Brunt 1976: 475–6.

85 Stewart 1993: 193–7, and in [the original].

86 Lane Fox 1996: 87–108; Bosworth 1994: 831, fig. 39.

87 Arr. 7.8.3; Diod. 17.108.3; Just. 12.11.6.

88 Bosworth 1977: 67 n. 89. Cf. Högemann 1985: 135 n. 2. According to Megasthenes, Alexander advertised himself as son of Zeus also to the Indians. *FGrHist* 715 F34 a = Strabo 15.1.68. Cf. Curt. 8.10.1.

89 Fredricksmeyer 1990: 312–4.

90 Plut. *Alex.* 50.11; Curt. 4.10.3; 6.11.23; 8.7.13.

91 Fredricksmeyer 1979 [1980]: 5–7.

92 Diod. 18.3.5; 18.28.3; Curt. 10.5.4; Just. 12.15.7.

93 Bosworth 1977: 70–1; *Conquest and Empire* 1988: 282–3.

94 Cf. Lauffer 1993: 89: 'Dabei könnte es sich nur um die Frage seiner göttlichen Herkunft handeln.'

95 Cf. Wilamowitz 1932: 266: '[Since Alexander's visit to Zeus Ammon at Siwah] lebt er durch den Glauben an das Göttliche in ihm. Sein ganzes Leben und Handeln, sein Heldentum und auch seine Sünden werden begreiflich, wie ich meine, allein begreiflich durch diesen echten und heissen Glauben.'

96 Plut. *Alex.* 54; Arr. 4.9.9–12.7; Curt. 8.5.1–6.1; Just. 12.7.1–3; 15.3.3.

97 E.g. Tarn 1948: II, 359–69. Cf. Bosworth, *Alexander and the East* 1996: 109: The aim was 'the acknowledgment of Alexander's divine status and absolute monarchy.'

98 So *int. al.,* Wilcken 1967: 168–70; Brunt 1976: 536–41; Lane Fox 1973: 322–3; Will 1986: 135–7; Hamilton 1973: 105.

99 There probably were discussions of this issue at court at this time which are reflected in the later story of the mostly fictional debate on deification in Arrian (4.10.6–11.9) and Curtius (8.5.9–19). See e.g. Jacoby 1919: 1679; Brown 1949: 242; Brunt 1976: 538. Others consider the debate largely authentic. E.g. Edmunds 1971: 386–90; Bosworth *Historical Commentary* 1995, II: 77–90; *Alexander and the East* 1996: 109–12; Badian 1981: 28–32, 48–54.

100 Callisthenes, *FGrHist* 124 F14 a = Strabo 12.1.43; F 36 = Plut. *Alex.* 33. Cf. F 31.

101 Bosworth 'Alexander, Euripides' 1996: 153 and *passim; Alexander and the East* 1996: 98, 117–32.

102 Bosworth 'Alexander, Euripides' 1996: 156 and n. 85. The fact that Alexander's information was faulty (Högemann 1985: 131, 138–43) is irrelevant here.

103 Badian 1981: 66; Fredricksmeyer 1991: 206–14.

104 Din. *Dem.* 94; Hyp. *Dem.* 31–2; *Epit.* 21; Timaeus, *FGrHist* 566 F 155 = Polyb. 12.12b.3; Plut. *Mor.* 219 E–F; 408 B; 842 D; Ael. *VH* 2.19; 5.12; Athen. 6.251 B; Val. Max. 7.2 ext. 13; D.L. 6.63.

105 Habicht 1970: 28–36, 246–52; Fredricksmeyer 1979 [1980]: 3–7; Hamilton 1984: 11–2.

106 For 334, see Habicht 1970: 17–25, 243, 245. For a later date, or dates, in Alexander's lifetime, see Badian 1981: 59–63; Walbank 1987: 374; Stewart 1993: 98–102.

107 Fredricksmeyer 1979 [1980]: 1–7. Cf. Nock 1928: 28.

108 The stories that Alexander was deified at Athens as *Triskaidekatos Theos* (Ael. *VH* 5.12) and as *Neos Dionysos* (D.L. 6.63) were probably made up after his death. Nock 1928: 21–3; Habicht 1970: 29, with n. 4.

109 Fredricksmeyer 1979 [1980]: 3–7; Habicht 1970: 247–8; Walbank 1984: 90–1, with n. 98.

110 Habicht 1970: 3–16, 243–5; Fredricksmeyer 1979: 39–61; 1981: 145–56; Sanders 1991: 275–87; Hammond 1999: 109–10; Carney, 'The Initiation of Cult' 2000: 22–3, 34 n. 7. Cf. Schumacher 1990: 436–8; Borza 1999: 67–8. *Contra:* Badian 1981: 33–44; 1996: 14–5.

111 Note also Philip's commission after Chaeronea of a *tholos* building (normally reserved for gods) to house chryselephantine statues of himself, Alexander, Olympias, Amyntas, and Eurydice (Paus. 5.20.9–10). It is possible that Philip planned to found a dynastic cult. Fredricksmeyer 1979: 52–6. Cf. Borza 1992: 249–50; O'Brien 1992: 202, with n. 155. *Contra:* Schumacher 1990: 438–9.

112 That Alexander was not consistent in this belief is likely and plausible. Plut. *Alex.* 28; *Mor.* 180 E = 341 B; Athen. 6.250 F–251 A; 251 C.

113 E.g. Arr. 1.9.9; 6.27.4; 6.30.2; 7.4.2; 7.14.6; 7.19.1–2; 7.28.1; Diod. 17.113.3–4; 17.118.1; 18.4.4–5; Curt. 10.1.2–3; Plut. *Alex.* 11.12; 23.3; 34.1; *Mor.* 338 D; 342 F; 343 B, D; Polyb. 5.10.6–8. Cf. Arist. *Pol.* 1415a. Mention should be made of a statement by Athenaeus, with reference to Alexander's last period, quoting Ephippus to the effect that sometimes Alexander appeared at banquets with the attributes of gods, as of Ammon, Heracles, Hermes, and even Artemis (*FGrHist* 126 F 5 = Athen. 12.537 E–F). This is extremely doubtful. Athenaeus is often careless in quoting his sources, and Ephippus is known for his hostility to Alexander. Cf. Pearson 1960: 63–5; Stewart 1991: 207, with n. 54. Even if it is true, its significance would be hard to assess. Alexander may have wished to suggest his affinity to the gods rather than somehow identify himself with them. Whatever the explanation, in face of all the evidence to the contrary, the story cannot be taken as evidence of Alexander's impiety. Cf. Wirth 1973: 123, 127.

114 As we should expect, there was a wide range of reaction to Alexander's deification, from cynicism and indifference, to acceptance, to strong disapproval. Consider, on the one hand, the shameless (and treasonable) deification by Harpalus of his two mistresses in the expectation that Alexander would not return from India to punish him (Berve 1926: II, 212 no. 231; 338 no. 676; Carney,

'The Initiation of Cult' 2000: 30–1), and on the other, the belief that there remained an unbridgeable gulf between gods and mortals (e.g. Berve 1926: II, 50 no. 94 s.v. *Antipatros*).

115 I wish to thank Prof. Joseph Roisman for a close reading of the MS, and for several valuable suggestions. I also would like to thank Mrs. Sandy Adler, as always, for her expert typing of the MS. Any remaining faults are my own.

References

Ameling 1988 = W. Ameling, 'Alexander und Achilleus: Eine Bestandsaufnahme', in W. Will and J. Heinrichs (eds), *Zu Alexander d. Gr. Festschrift G. Wirth zum 60. Geburtstag am 9.12.86* (Amsterdam: 1988), pp. 657–692.

Badian 1981 = E. Badian, 'The Deification of Alexander the Great', in H.J. Dell (ed.), *Ancient Macedonian Studies in Honour of Charles F. Edson* (Thessaloniki: 1981), pp. 27–71.

Badian 1985 = E. Badian, 'Alexander in Iran', in I. Gershevitch (ed.), *Cambridge History of Iran* 2 (Cambridge: 1985), pp. 420–501.

Badian 1996 = E. Badian, 'Alexander the Great between Two Thrones and Heaven: Variations on an Old Theme', in A. Small (ed.), *Subject and Ruler: The Cult of the Ruling Power in Classical Antiquity* (Ann Arbor: 1996), pp. 11–26.

Baege 1913 = W. Baege, *De Macedonum Sacris* (Halle: 1913).

Balsdon 1950 = J.P.V.D. Balsdon, 'The Divinity of Alexander', *Historia* 1 (1950), pp. 363–388.

Baynham The Question 1994 = E.J. Baynham, 'The Question of Macedonian Divine Honors for Phillip II', *MedArch* 7 (1994), pp. 35–43.

Baynham 2000 = E.J. Baynham, 'A Baleful Birth in Babylon. The Significance of the Prodigy in the *Liber de Morte*. An investigation', in A.B. Bosworth and E.J. Baynham (eds), *Alexander the Great in Fact and Fiction* (Oxford: 2000), pp. 242–262.

Bellen 1974 = H. Bellen, 'Der Rachegedanke in der griechisch-persischen Auseinandersetzung', *Chiron* 4 (1974), pp. 43–67.

Berve 1926 = H. Berve, *Das Alexanderreich auf prosopographischer Grundlage* (Munich: 1926).

Bing 1991 = J.D. Bing, 'Alexander's Sacrifice dis praesidibus loci before the Battle of Issus', *JHS* 111 (1991), pp. 161–165.

Borza 1999 = E.N. Borza, *Before Alexander: Constructing Early Macedonia* (Claremont: 1999).

Bosworth 1977 = A.B. Bosworth, 'Alexander and Ammon', in K.H. Kinzl (ed.), *Greece and the Eastern Mediterranean in Ancient History and Prehistory* (New York: 1977), pp. 51–75.

Bosworth *Conquest and Empire* 1988 = A.B. Bosworth, *Conquest and Empire: The Reign of Alexander the Great* (Cambridge: 1988).

Bosworth 1994 = A.B. Bosworth, 'Alexander the Great', in D.M. Lewis, J. Boardman, S. Hornblower and M. Ostwald (eds), *The Cambridge Ancient History* 6 (Cambridge: 1994), pp. 791–875.

Bosworth 1996 = A.B. Bosworth, *Alexander and the East: The Tragedy of Triumph* (Oxford: 1996).

Bosworth *Alexander, Euripides* 1996 = A.B. Bosworth, 'Alexander, Euripides, and Dionysus', in R.W. Wallace and E.M. Harris (eds), *Transitions to Empire: Essays in Greco-Roman History, 360–146 B.C. in Honor of E. Badian* (Norman: 1996), pp. 140–166.

Bosworth *Historical Commentary* 1995 = A.B Bosworth, *A Historical Commentary on Arrian's History of Alexander* 2 (Oxford 1995).

Brown 1949 = T.S. Brown, 'Callisthenes and Alexander', *AJPh* 70 (1949), pp. 225–248.

Brunt 1975 = P.A. Brunt, 'Alexander, Barsine, and Heracles', *RFIC* 103 (1975), pp. 22–34.

Brunt 1976 = P.A. Brunt, *Arrian: History of Alexander and Indica*, Loeb Classical Library (Cambridge: 1976).

Brunt 1983 = P.A. Brunt, *Arrian, History of Alexander*, Loeb Classical Library 2 (Cambridge: 1983).

Burstein 1991 = S. Burstein, 'Pharaoh Alexander: A Scholarly Myth', *Anc. Soc.* 22 (1991), pp. 139–145.

Carney Artifice 2000 = E.D. Carney, 'Artifice and Alexander History', in A.B. Bosworth and E.J. Baynham (eds), *Alexander the Great in Fact and Fiction* (Oxford: 2000), pp. 263–285.

Carney The Initiation of Cult, 2000 = E.D. Carney, 'The Initiation of Cult for Royal Macedonian Women', *CPh* 95 (2000), pp. 21–43.

Carney *Women and Monarchy* 2000 = E.D. Carney, *Women and Monarchy in Macedonia* (Norman: 2000).

Classen 1959 = C.J. Classen, 'The Libyan God Ammon in Greece before 331 B.C.', *Historia* 8 (1959), pp. 349–355.

Cohen 1995 = A. Cohen, 'Alexander and Achilles – Macedonians and Myceneans', in J.B. Carter and S.P. Morris (eds), *The Ages of Homer: A Tribute to Emily Townsend Vermeule* (Austin: 1995), pp. 483–505.

Dandamaev 1989 = M.A. Dandamaev, *A Political History of the Achaemenid Empire* (Leiden: 1989).

Edmunds 1971 = L. Edmunds, 'The Religiosity of Alexander', *GRBS* 12 (1971), pp. 363–391.

Edson 1970 = C.F. Edson, 'Early Macedonia', *Ancient Macedonia* 1 (1970), pp. 17–44.

Flower 2000 = M. Flower, 'Alexander the Great and Panhellenism', in A.B. Bosworth and E.J. Baynham (eds), *Alexander the Great in Fact and Fiction* (Oxford: 2000), pp. 96–135.

Fredricksmeyer 1961 = E. Fredricksmeyer, 'Alexander, Midas, and the Oracle at Gordium', *CPh* 56 (1961), pp. 160–168.

Fredricksmeyer 1966 = E. Fredricksmeyer, 'The Ancestral Rites of Alexander the Great', *CPh* 61 (1966), pp. 179–182.

Fredricksmeyer 1979 = E. Fredricksmeyer, 'Divine Honors for Philip II', *TAPhA* 109 (1979), pp. 39–61.

Fredricksmeyer 1979 [1980] = E. Fredricksmeyer, 'Three Notes on Alexander's Deification', *AJAH* 4 (1979), pp. 1–9.

Fredricksmeyer 1990 = E. Fredricksmeyer, 'Alexander and Philip: Emulation and Resentment', *CJ* 85 (1990), pp. 300–315.

Fredricksmeyer 1991 = E. Fredricksmeyer, 'Alexander, Zeus Ammon, and the Conquest of Asia', *TAPhA* 121 (1991), pp. 199–214.

Fredricksmeyer 1997 = E. Fredricksmeyer, 'The Origin of Alexander's Royal Insignia', *TAPhA* 127 (1997), pp. 97–109.

Fredricksmeyer 2000 = E. Fredricksmeyer, 'Alexander the Great and the Kingship of Asia', in A.B. Bosworth and E.J. Baynham (eds), *Alexander the Great in Fact and Fiction* (Oxford: 2000), pp. 136–166.

Goukowsky 1981 = R. Goukowsky, *Essai sur les origines du mythe d'Alexandre* (Nancy: 1978–81).

Green 1991 = P. Green, *Alexander of Macedon* (Berkeley: 1991).

Greenwalt 1982 = W. Greenwalt, 'A Macedonian Mantis', *Anc. World* 5 (1982), pp. 17–25.

Grieshammer 1996 = R. Grieshammer, 'Apis', *Der neue Pauly* 1 (1996), p. 847.

Habicht 1970 = C. Habicht, *Gottmenschentum und friechische Städte* (Munich: 1970).

Hamilton 1969 = J.R. Hamilton, *Plutarch, Alexander: A Commentary* (Oxford: 1969).

Hamilton 1973 = J.R. Hamilton, *Alexander the Great* (London: 1973).

Hamilton 1984 = J.R. Hamilton, 'The Origins of the Ruler Cult', *Prudentia* 16 (1984), pp. 3–15.

Hammond *Alexander the Great* 1980 = N.G.L. Hammond, *Alexander the Great: King, Commander and Statesman* (Park Ridge: 1980).

Hammond *The Miracle* 1991 = N.G.L. Hammond, *The Miracle that was Macedonia* (New York: 1991).

Hammond 1994 = N.G.L. Hammond, *Philip of Macedon* (London: 1994).

Hammond 1997 = N.G.L. Hammond, *The Genius of Alexander the Great* (London: 1997).

Hammond 1998 = N.G.L. Hammond, 'The Branchidae at Didyma and in Sogdiana', *CQ²* 48 (1998), pp. 339–344.

Hammond 1999 = N.G.L. Hammond, 'Heroic and Divine Honors in Macedonia before the Successors', *AncW* 30 (1999), pp. 103–115.

Hartman 1965 = S.S. Hartman, 'Dionysos and Heracles in India according to Megasthenes: A counter-argument', *Temenos* 1 (1965), pp. 55–64.

Högemann 1985 = P. Högemann, *Alexander der Grosse und Arabien* (Munich: 1985).

Holt 1989 = F.L. Holt, *Alexander the Great and Bactria: The Formation of a Greek Frontier in Central Asia* (Leiden 1988).

Huttner 1997 = U. Huttner, *Die politische Rolle der Heraklesgestalt im griechischen Herrschertum* (Stuttgart: 1997).

Instinsky 1949 = H.U. Instinsky, *Alexander der Grosse am Hellespont* (Bad Godesberg: 1949).

Jacoby 1919 = F. Jacoby, 'Kallisthenes', *RE* 10 (1919), cols 1674–1677.

Kaiser-Raiss 1984 = M.R. Kaiser-Raiss, 'Philip II und Kyzikos', *SNR* 63 (1984), pp. 27–43.

Kees 1931 = H. Kees, 'Memphis', *RE* 15 (1931), cols 660–688.

Kern 1963 = O. Kern, *Die Religion des Griechen* (Berlin: 1963).

King 1987 = K.C. King, *Achilles: Paradigms of the War Hero from Homer to the Middle Ages* (Los Angeles: 1987).

Koenen 1977 = L. Koenen, *Eine agonistische Inschrift aus Ägypten und frühptolemäische Königsfeste* (Meisenheim: 1977).

Kuhlmann 1988 = K.P. Kuhlmann, *Das Ammeneion. Archäologie, Geschichte und Kultpraxis des Orakels von Siwa* (Cairo: 1988).

Lane Fox 1973 = R. Lane Fox, *Alexander the Great* (London: 1973).

Lane Fox 1996 = R. Lane Fox, 'Text and Image: Alexander the Great, Coins and Elephants', *BICS* 41 (1996), pp. 87–108.

Lauffer 1993 = S. Lauffer, *Alexander der Grosse* (Munich: 1993).

Loewe 1936 = B. Loewe, *Griechische theophore Ortsnamen* (Tübingen: 1936).

Marcus 1956 = R. Marcus, 'Alexander the Great and the Jews', in R. Marcus (ed.), *Josephus: Jewish Antiquities, Books IX–XI* (London: 1937), pp. 512–532.

Mederer 1936 = E. Mederer, *Die Alexanderlegenden bei den ältesten Alexanderhistorikern* (Stuttgart: 1936).

Moretti 1975 = L. Moretti, *Iscrizioni storiche ellenistiche* (Florence: 1975).

Nock 1928 = A.D. Nock, 'Notes on Ruler Cult', *JHS* 48 (1928), pp. 21–43.

O'Brien 1992 = J.M. O'Brien, *Alexander the Great: The Invisible Enemy* (New York: 1992).

Palagia 2000 = O. Palagia, 'Hephaestion's Pyre and the Royal Hunt of Alexander', in A.B. Bosworth and E.J. Baynham (eds), *Alexander the Great in Fact and Fiction* (Oxford: 2000), pp. 167–206.

Pearson 1960 = L. Pearson, *The Lost Histories of Alexander the Great* (London: 1960).

Pietschmann 1894 = R. Pietschmann, 'Apis', *RE* 1 (1894), cols 2807–2809.

Pope 1957 = A.U. Pope, 'Persepolis as a Ritual City', *Archaeology* 10 (1957), pp. 123–130.

Pope 1969 = A.U. Pope, *Persepolis and Archaeological Sites in Fars* (Shiraz: 1969).

Prandi 1990 = L. Prandi, 'Gli oraculi sulla spedizione asiatica di Alessandro', *Chiron* 20 (1990), pp. 345–369.

Prestianni Gialombardo 1975 = A.M. Prestianni Gialombardo, '*Philippika I:* Sul "Culto" di Filippo II di Macedonia', *SicGymn* 28 (1975), pp. 1–57.

Price 1974 = M.J. Price, *Coins of the Macedonians* (London: 1974).

Price 1991 = M.J. Price, *The Coinage in the Name of Alexander the Great and Philip Arrhidaeus* (London: 1991).

Sanders 1991 = L.J. Sanders, 'Dionysius I of Syracuse and the Origins of the Ruler Cult', *Historia* 40 (1991), pp. 275–287.

Schumacher 1990 = L. Schumacher, 'Zum Herrschaftsverständnis Philipps II von Makedonien', *Historia* 39 (1990), pp. 426–443.

Seibert 1994 = J. Seibert, *Alexander der Grosse* (Darmstadt: 1972).

Seibert 1998 = J. Seibert, 'Panhellenischer Kreuzzug, Nationalkrieg, Rachefeldzug oder makedonischer Eroberungskrieg? Überlegungen zu den Ursachen des Krieges gegen Persien', in W. Will (ed.), *Alexander der Grosse: Eine Welteroberung und ihr Hintergrund* (1998), pp. 5–58.

Squillace 1992–4 = G. Squillace, 'Alessandro e l'offerta ad Atena di trecento panoplie', *Miscellanea di Studi Storici* 9 (1992), pp. 9–20.

Stewart 1991 = A. Stewart, *Faces of Power* (Berkeley and Los Angeles 1994).

Stewart 1993 = A. Stewart, *Faces of Power: Alexander's Image and Hellenistic Politics* (Berkeley: 1993).

Taeger 1957 = F. Taeger, *Charisma: Studien sur Geschichte des antiken Herrscherkultes* (Stuttgart: 1957).

Tarn 1948 = W.W. Tarn, *Alexander the Great*, 2 vols (Cambridge: 1948).

Unger 1970 = E. Unger, *Babylon: Die heilige Stadt* (Berlin: 1970).

Walbank 1984 = F.W. Walbank, 'Ruler-Cult', *Cambridge Ancient History* 7 (Cambridge: 1984), pp. 87–96.

Walbank 1987 = F.W. Walbank, 'Könige als Götter. Überlegungen zum Herrscherkult von Alexander bis Augustus', *Chiron* 17 (1987), pp. 365–382.

Wheeler 1968 = M. Wheeler, *Flames over Persepolis: Turning-Point in History* (New York: 1968).

Wilamowitz 1932 = U. von. Wilamowitz-Moellendorf, *Der Glaube der Hellenen* 2 (Berlin: 1932).

Wilcken 1967 = U. Wilcken, *Alexander the Great* (New York: 1967).

Will 1986 = W. Will, *Alexander der Grosse* (Stuttgart: 1986).

Wirth 1973 = G. Wirth, *Alexander der Grosse* (Hamburg: 1973).

11

ALEXANDER
AND CONSPIRACIES

Introduction

Given the animosity that Alexander's men developed towards him, as seen in, for example, their mood at Hecatompylus, and most obviously in the mutinies at the Hyphasis river and at Opis, it is perhaps surprising that Alexander did not face conspiracies against his life more often. We know of only two conspiracies, that of Philotas in 328 and that of the Pages in 327, but the first one is problematic in the sense that Alexander may have implicated the critical Philotas in some attempt on his life in Phrada at that time to get rid of him and then his father Parmenion (see Source 107).[1] Hence we can say that Alexander was not above engineering conspiracies against others. Indeed, there are some grounds for implicating Alexander, when heir, in the plot to assassinate his father Philip II in 336.

While there were times in his reign when Alexander had genuine cause to fear conspiracies against him, the result of his increasing 'orientalism' that caused dissatisfaction among his closest advisers and army in general, there were times when his own paranoia came too much to the fore. Instances of this may be seen in the lead-up to his murder of Cleitus (Source 119),[2] or in the fate of Coenus, found dead shortly after the Hyphasis river mutiny in 326 (Arr. 6.2.1, Curt. 9.3.20). Both men had run foul of Alexander earlier, although no conspiracy can be attached to their names. Perhaps the same case can be made for Callisthenes, who had defied Alexander's attempt to introduce *proskynesis* at court, thereby earning the king's animosity and conveniently implicated in the Pages' Conspiracy (Sources 108–113). Alexander suspected conspiracies where they did not exist, and came to distrust those at his court and elsewhere (perhaps even as far afield as Antipater in Greece, for he summoned Antipater to him at the end of his reign, perhaps intending to replace him with Craterus). It is no surprise to hear from Ephippus, a contemporary writer, that everyone at Alexander's court lived in almost a state of fear given his disregard for human life, 'for he was a very violent man' (Source 105).

Again, however, the sources need to be carefully evaluated – as is well shown by the differing primary accounts of those who instigated the Pages' Conspiracy (see Sources 109–110) or the manner of Callisthenes' death (Sources 111–113), who had led the opposition to Alexander's *proskynesis* attempt (Sources 94 and 95). Moreover, we should not discount the influence on Alexander of the enemies of those who fell victim to conspiracies, and how this affects our opinion of Alexander and his relationship with his men.

Ancient sources

Philotas

107 Here (the palace of the Zarangaeans) also Alexander discovered the conspiracy of Philotas, son of Parmenion. Ptolemy and Aristobulus (*FGrH* 139 F 22) say that it had already been reported to him before in Egypt; but that it did not appear to him credible, both on account of the long-existing friendship between them, the honour which he publicly conferred upon his father Parmenion, and the confidence he reposed in Philotas himself. Ptolemy, son of Lagus, says that Philotas was brought before the Macedonians, that Alexander vehemently accused him, and that he defended himself from the charges. He says also that the divulgers of the plot came forward and convicted him and his accomplices both by other clear proofs and especially because Philotas himself confessed that he had heard of a certain conspiracy which was being formed against Alexander. He was convicted of having said nothing to the king about this plot, though he visited the royal tent twice a day. He and all the others who had taken part with him in the conspiracy were killed by the Macedonians with their javelins; and Polydamas, one of the Companions, was despatched to Parmenion, carrying letters from Alexander to the generals in Media, Cleander, Sitalces, and Menidas, who had been placed over the army commanded by Parmenion. By these men Parmenion was put to death, perhaps because Alexander deemed it incredible that Philotas should conspire against him and Parmenion not participate in his son's plan; or perhaps, he thought that even if he had had no share in it, he would now be a dangerous man if he survived, after his son had been violently removed, being held in such great respect as he was both by Alexander himself and by all the army, not only the Macedonian, but also that of the Grecian auxiliaries as well, whom he often used to command in accordance with Alexander's order, both in his own turn and out of his turn, with his sovereign's approbation and satisfaction (Ptolemy, *FGrH* 138 F 13 = Arr. 3.26).

The Pages and Callisthenes

108 Some say that Alexander accidentally happened to be drinking until daybreak; but Aristobulus has given the following account: A Syrian woman, who was under the inspiration of the deity, used to follow Alexander about. At first she was a subject of mirth to Alexander and his courtiers; but when all that she said in her inspiration was seen to be true, he no longer treated her with neglect, but she was allowed to have free access to him both by night and day, and she often took her stand near him even when he was asleep. And indeed on that occasion when he was withdrawing from the drinking-party she met him, being under the inspiration of the deity at the time, and besought him to return and drink all night. Alexander, thinking that there was something divine in the warning, returned and went on drinking; and thus the enterprise of the Pages fell through (Aristobulus, *FGrH* 139 F 30 = Arr. 4.13.5).

109 Aristobulus says that the youths asserted it was Callisthenes who instigated them to make the daring attempt; and Ptolemy says the same (Aristobulus, *FGrH* 139 F 31 = Arr. 4.14.1).

110 Aristobulus says that the youths asserted it was Callisthenes who instigated them to make the daring attempt; and Ptolemy says the same. Most writers, however, do not agree with this, but represent that Alexander readily believed the worst about Callisthenes, from the hatred which he already felt towards him, and because Hermolaus was known to be exceedingly intimate with him (Ptolemy, *FGrH* 138 F 16 = Arr. 4.14.1).

111   As to the death of Callisthenes, some say (Ptolemy, *FGrH* 138 F 17; see below) that he was hanged by Alexander's orders, others (Aristobulus, *FGrH* 139 F 33) that he was bound hand and foot and died of sickness, and Chares says that after his arrest he was kept in fetters seven months, that he might be tried before a full council when Aristotle was present, but that about the time when Alexander was wounded in India, he died from obesity and the disease of lice (Chares, *FGrH* 125 F 15 = Plut. *Alex.* 55.8–9).

112   Callisthenes also expired in torture, although he was guiltless of forming any design against the king's life; but he was by no means suited to a court and to the character of his flatterers. Therefore there was no one whose death roused greater hatred of the king among the Greeks, because he had not only put to death a man endowed with noble character and accomplishments, one who had called him back to life when he had resolved to die after Clitus, but had even tortured him, and without a trial (Callisthenes, *FGrH* 124 T 17 = Curt. 8.8.21–22).

113   Aristobulus says that Callisthenes was carried about with the army bound with fetters, and afterwards died a natural death; but Ptolemy, son of Lagus, says that he was stretched upon the rack and then hanged. Thus not even did these authors, whose narratives are very trustworthy, and who at the time were in intimate association with Alexander, give accounts consistent with each other of events so well known, and the circumstances of which could not have escaped their notice (Ptolemy, *FGrH* 138 F 17 = Arr. 4.14.3).

Modern works

In the following selections, E. Badian, John Moors Cabot Professor Emeritus at Harvard University, focuses on how Alexander changed as a person during his campaign, and how his feelings of isolation fuelled paranoia that led him to be suspicious of those close to him. Alexander exploited suspicions at his court and used conspiracies as a means to keep opponents in check. On the other hand, W. Heckel, Professor of Ancient History at the University of Calgary, examines the role that other generals at Alexander's court, who disliked Philotas, played in bringing about the end of Philotas. Then E.N Borza, Emeritus Professor of History at Pennsylvania State University, evaluates the role that the differing philosophies and personalities of Anaxagoras and Callisthenes played in the demise of Callisthenes after the Pages' Conspiracy, and argues that Anaxagoras influenced the king against Callisthenes.

1   E. Badian, 'Alexander the Great and the Loneliness of Power', in E. Badian (ed.), *Studies in Greek and Roman History* (Blackwell: 1964), pp. 192–205.[3]

2   W. Heckel, 'The Conspiracy *against* Philotas', *Phoenix* 31 (Classical Association of Canada 1977), pp. 9–21.[4]

3   E.N. Borza, 'Anaxagoras and Callisthenes: Academic Intrigue at Alexander's Court', in H.J. Dell (ed.), *Ancient Macedonian Studies in Honour of C.F. Edson* (Institute for Balkan Studies, Thessaloniki: 1981), pp. 73–86.[5]

Additional reading

W.L. Adams, 'The Episode of Philotas: An Insight', in W. Heckel and L.A. Tritle (eds), *Crossroads of History. The Age of Alexander* (Claremont: 2003), pp. 113–126.

E. Badian, 'Harpalus', *Journal of Hellenic Studies* 81 (1961), pp. 25–31.

——, 'The Death of Parmenio', *Transactions of the American Philological Association* 91 (1960), pp. 324–338.

——, 'Conspiracies', in A.B. Bosworth and E.J. Baynham (eds), *Alexander the Great in Fact and Fiction* (Oxford: 2000), pp. 50–95.

A.B. Bosworth, 'The Death of Alexander the Great: Rumour and Propaganda', *Classical Quarterly*[2] 21 (1971), pp. 112–136 (reprinted in Chapter 8).

——, 'The Tumult and the Shouting: Two Interpretations of the Cleitus Episode', *Ancient History Bulletin* 10 (1996), pp. 19–30.

P.A. Brunt, *Arrian, History of Alexander*, Loeb Classical Library 1 (Cambridge and London), pp. 517–521.

E.D. Carney, 'The Conspiracy of Hermolaus', *Classical Journal* 76 (1980), pp. 223–231.

W. Heckel, 'The Earliest Evidence for the Plot to Poison Alexander', in W. Heckel, L. Tritle and P. Wheatley (eds), *Alexander's Empire: Formulation to Decay* (Claremont: 2007), pp. 265–275.

——, 'King and "Companions": Observations on the Nature of Power in the Reign of Alexander', in J. Roisman (ed.), *Brill's Companion to Alexander the Great* (Leiden: 2003), pp. 197–225.

L. Prandi, 'A Few Remarks on the Amyntas "Conspiracy"', in W. Will (ed.), *Alexander der Grosse. Eine Welteroberung und ihr Hintergrund* (Bonn: 1998), pp. 91–102.

W.Z. Rubinsohn, 'The "Philotas Affair" – A Reconsideration', *Ancient Macedonia* 2 (Institute for Balkan Studies, Thessaloniki: 1977), pp. 409–420.

Notes

1 Philotas: Arr. 3.26–27, Diod. 17.79–80, Plut. *Alex.* 48–49, Curt. 6.7.1–7.2.38, Justin 12.5. 1–8. Parmenion: Arr. 3.27.3–4, Diod. 17.80.3, Plut. *Alex.* 49.13, Curt. 7.2.11–32.
2 Arr. 4.8.1–9, Curt. 8.19–51, Plut. *Alex.* 50–52.
3 Reprinted by permission of Mrs Natalie Badian.
4 Reprinted by permission of The Classical Association of Canada.
5 Reprinted by permission of The Institute for Balkan Studies, Thessaloniki.

ALEXANDER THE GREAT AND THE LONELINESS OF POWER[1]

E. Badian

Few episodes in history have fascinated as many readers and listeners as the bright star of Alexander the Great shooting across the firmament, to mark the end of an era and the beginning of another. From schoolboys wide-eyed at the great adventure to old men moralizing on philosopher kings, we all interpret the great drama in terms of our experience and our dreams. It has gained a secure standing among the Myths of Ancient Greece, ranking (one may say) with the story of Odysseus or of Oedipus. Needless to say, the history of Alexander III of Macedon has to some extent been lost underneath the myth-making, and some aspects of it can perhaps no longer be salvaged. But the tragedy of the historical Alexander is at least as fascinating as the best of both the ancient and the modern legends; and it is this that, across the fragments of the history, I want to sketch on this occasion.[2]

Macedonia, during twenty years or so in the fourth century B.C., had been raised by Philip II from a semi-barbarian feudal state on the borders of civilized Greece to the leading rank among the powers of the Greek world. But, as so often in the history of nations rising to sudden greatness, this had done little to civilize the primitive passions and ways of thought of the people and even of the ruling class. Philip had tried to Hellenize his court, where Greeks and Macedonian nobles mingled freely; but their mutual suspicions were not eliminated, particularly as the Macedonians, on the whole, provided the soldiers and administrators, while the Greeks, on the whole, provided the cultural prestige. As far as the Macedonian barons themselves were concerned, Philip had tried to curb the traditional feudal anarchy by methods not unlike those of the French crown in the seventeenth century. The nobles had to some extent been brought under the direct control of the court; but their connection with the feudal levy of their districts was not broken, and the feudal rivalries were merely transmuted into court intrigues.

One of these intrigues finally led to a serious estrangement between Philip and his wife Olympias and crown prince Alexander. Olympias, Alexander and their adherents had to leave the country; and though Alexander himself was apparently allowed to return, his chances of retaining his position were not rated very highly either by himself or by others competent to judge. Then, in 336 B.C., Philip was assassinated in very mysterious circumstances. We cannot quite penetrate the mystery; but in any case, Alexander was the one who profited.[3] Antipater (one of the most prominent nobles) had everything all prepared and at once produced the young man to the army, which swore allegiance to him. The opposing faction (led by one Attalus), which only a little earlier had carried all before it, was taken entirely by surprise. Charged with having instigated the assassination (which was absurd, in the circumstances), it was wiped out even to infants in arms, and Alexander's rule was made secure.[4]

The King was secure, but far from all-powerful. We must not think of this boy of less than twenty in terms of the great leader he turned out to be. For the moment he was a youth raised to power by a clique of powerful nobles, who no doubt expected to rule through him. So, in addition to his numerous foreign problems (barbarian invasions, Greek insurrections, and the war against Persia that Philip had already begun and from which his successor could not withdraw even if he had wanted to), Alexander, on a long view, was faced with an even more formidable internal problem: how to assert his independence and to become King in fact as well as in name.

The most powerful of all noble families was that of Parmenio. He had been Philip's most trusted general and had followed his master in turning to the faction headed by Attalus, who had, in fact, become his son-in-law. Philip's assassination took him entirely by surprise. He was away in Asia at the time, commanding the advance guard that had secured a bridgehead there, and Attalus was with him. As a result, they seem to have been a little out of touch with the intrigues at court – and this, perhaps, cost Philip his life. However, once they were confronted with the accomplished fact of Alexander's succession, they had to submit or rebel. Rebellion was dangerous, with the home army firmly won over to Alexander; and with wars to fight on all frontiers, Parmenio was probably too much of a staunch Macedonian to consider treason. Moreover, unlike Attalus (whose case was now hopeless), he was not irretrievably committed: Alexander would welcome his allegiance and be prepared to pay for it. Parmenio swiftly decided to throw his full weight behind Alexander. He personally saw to the elimination of his son-in-law Attalus and in return secured his own terms. When Alexander crossed to Asia in 334, after settling all wars and revolts in Europe, Antipater (his chief sponsor) was left behind with half the Macedonian forces to look after Europe; but Parmenio and his family and supporters were firmly entrenched in the army that went with the King. Parmenio's eldest son Philotas commanded the famous Macedonian cavalry (the 'Companions'); his second son commanded the most important infantry force (the 'hypaspists'); his brother Asander was in charge of the light cavalry; and many known adherents of the family (we need only mention Coenus, a son-in-law of Parmenio, and his brother Cleander, probably Parmenio's trusted aide) held other high posts. Parmenio himself was in charge of the whole infantry force and acted as the King's second-in-command and chief of staff. In view of his experience and Alexander's age, it was no doubt expected that he would take practical charge of the war against Persia.[5]

The loyalty of these men, in the war against Persia, was not in question. For one thing, it was their own war, begun, with their enthusiastic agreement, under Philip, and waged by Parmenio long before Alexander's accession. Alexander was merely following in his father's footsteps. Moreover, nearly all possible pretenders had now been killed off, and there was no one who could rally support in a bid for the throne. But Alexander found himself in a position intolerable to a man of his temperament. Screened off from personal command of his forces, he was the puppet of a faction of powerful nobles, ruling at their mercy.

The next few years saw Alexander's great victories, in which the main forces of the Persian Empire were defeated and Darius left a fugitive (finally killed by his own nobles), while Alexander emerged as the unchallenged ruler of the Empire west of the Euphrates and eastward well into Iran.[6] Throughout this period of his greatest glory he was ably supported by his commanders. But as he became better known and showed those qualities of courage and leadership that won him the enthusiastic allegiance of his men, he carefully used all opportunities of undermining the position of his excessively powerful subordinates. After the first victory, soon after the crossing to Asia, Parmenio's brother Asander was moved from his field command to become governor of the first province of the Empire to be taken over by the Macedonians (that of Lydia). It was, of course, a great honour; but in fact it turned out a loss rather than a gain to Parmenio. The field command was lost to him, while his brother was soon merely one governor among many and, in spite of distinguished service in his province, was before long inconspicuously removed from it and given a minor assignment. Moreover, those in Alexander's confidence now apparently began to spread rumours distinctly unfavourable to Parmenio. (These can be traced back to the Greek Callisthenes, a nephew of Aristotle and an enthusiastic admirer of Philip and Alexander, who had joined the expedition in order to sing its praises to the Greek world.) It was said that on various critical occasions Parmenio had given Alexander advice that the King had ignored – luckily for himself, as it had turned out; and that in battle Parmenio was no longer up to his old strength and had had to be rescued from defeat by Alexander. All this was far from true; but it was given a shadow of plausibility by the fact that in battle Parmenio normally had the difficult assignment of holding the enemy's main forces on one wing, while Alexander made the decisive breakthrough on the other. In this way, gradually, Alexander won the loyalty of the army away from him. At the same time, his adherents were kept under close watch: we know that Philotas' mistress was suborned to spy on her lover and report to one of Alexander's trusted officers.[7]

As the victorious advance continued into Iran, tension between Alexander and many of the great nobles increased. They had no intention of going on fighting and marching for ever. After gaining glory and plunder, they wanted to settle down to rule the conquered and enjoy the fruits of victory. Alexander, on the contrary, now claimed to be the lawful successor of the Persian kings (he even charged Darius with having been a usurper!) and would certainly not be satisfied with anything less than the conquest of the whole of the Empire up to the Indus. Moreover, he knew that he would have to conciliate his new subjects and win their support; and this applied particularly to the Persian aristocracy, who were the traditional administrators of the Empire. Above all (perhaps), he liked being Great King, with all the pomp and ceremonial that went with the title. In his relations with Asiatics (many of whom were now promoted to positions of honour and responsibility) he behaved entirely as they expected their Great King to behave. Naturally, this policy could not be fully carried out until Parmenio's power had been dealt its final blow: his family were among the most vocal objectors to it.

It is hard to separate personal antagonism from political opposition in all this. But the result, in any case, was to increase tension and make conflict inevitable. In Media Alexander took an important step: he left Parmenio behind in charge of the lengthening supply-lines. The general had no reasonable grounds for objecting to this; but it meant, in effect, that the King had got rid of his overpowering presence. Soon after, Parmenio's younger son, who had commanded the hypaspists, died. Philotas, his elder brother, had to stay behind to see to his funeral. This was clearly Alexander's chance, and he seized it at once. A few days after Philotas rejoined the camp, a 'conspiracy against the King' was discovered. The alleged instigator (a very obscure person) was killed while resisting arrest, but Philotas was somehow implicated. In a tense and anxious situation Alexander staged his *coup d'état*. We have a vivid description of it in our sources. Some of the King's trusted boyhood friends, in the meantime promoted to minor (though not yet major) commands, were detailed to surround Philotas' quarters with their own detachments. Struck out of the blue, Philotas could not resist and was arrested. The King at once put him on trial for high treason before the army. The army, of course, was stunned by the incident. Since the massacre at the beginning of the reign, there had been no outward sign of conflict among their commanders. But although no proof of Philotas' implication in the conspiracy could be produced, the King made it a question of confidence between himself and Philotas and demanded the death penalty. He thought that he could now use the army for the final overthrow of Parmenio's power. As usual, he had judged rightly. It is noticeable how in politics as in fighting Alexander's character appears consistent and unmistakable: never rushing things, always carefully planning further ahead than the enemy could see, but never missing the chance of striking the decisive blow when it presented itself, and then leaving the enemy no hope of resistance or recovery. Some of Parmenio's old adherents had been won over to abandon the declining cause. Coenus, for instance, was one of the most eager prosecutors. This must have helped to persuade the army. Philotas was condemned and at once executed.

A more delicate task remained. Parmenio could not be tried before his own men for crimes which there was no evidence that he had committed. The King could not risk failure. It was only after his death that stories of his planning treason appeared, and it was even said that Philotas had confessed this. But at the time there was only one thing to do. Fortunately Coenus (as we have seen) had been won over, and with him his brother Cleander, who was Parmenio's second-in-command in Media. This facilitated matters. A secret messenger was sent to assassinate the old general, with Cleander's co-operation. Though this provoked ominous unrest among the army, there was nothing the men could now do. Alexander had finally gained his independence. In Europe, Antipater remained, too powerful to be touched from a distance. But that could wait: at least he was too far away to interfere with the King.

There followed a series of spectacular trials of Parmenio's adherents. Not all were convicted: Alexander could not afford a wholesale slaughter of the Macedonian nobility and, as in military pursuit, he knew where to call a halt. But the final result was a clean sweep. All those who had not left the faction in time, or could be trusted to submit quietly now, were eliminated, and the King's trusted friends – especially those prominent in the *coup d'état* against Philotas – were promoted. The chief of these men, Hephaestion, whom Alexander called his *alter ego*, now became commander of half the Companion cavalry. The other half, in a characteristic gesture, went to a dour old Macedonian, Clitus.[8]

Naturally, much bitterness remained. Not long after, this erupted in an ugly incident at Samarcand. At a drinking party (such as were common at the half-barbarian court of Macedon) Clitus took offence at a casual remark of Alexander's. Tempers flared up, stimulated by alcohol, and finally Alexander killed Clitus with his own hand. The deed itself was merely manslaughter, significant (apart from the light it casts on the Macedonian court) only as a symptom of continuing tension. But what followed was of outstanding importance. It shows, more than almost any other incident, Alexander's ability to seize a chance offered and turn it to decisive advantage, even where (as in this instance) he had not planned to prepare it.[9]

Alexander now shut himself up in his tent and proclaimed overwhelming remorse for what he had done, and a determination to expiate it by fasting to death. The army was utterly thunderstruck by this. But gradually the realization began to sink in of what it would mean to them, if the King died; they would face an almost hopeless retreat from Samarcand, with no one to command them and the barbarians taking full advantage of their weakness. So, on the third day, they sent envoys to plead with Alexander to change his mind. When they passed a resolution posthumously convicting Clitus of treason, and thereby legitimizing Alexander's action, he let himself be persuaded. He now knew that he could rely on the army against anyone – and so did whoever might be concerned.

As the historian Curtius remarks, the death of Clitus was the end of freedom. Alexander now regularly wore an adaptation of Persian royal dress, and before long he married an Iranian princess. This would have been unthinkable a few months earlier.

However, he now went too far. Pressing home his advantage, he tried to unify his court ceremonial on a Persian basis. Hitherto he had had to keep up two entirely separate establishments: a traditional one, in which he was the first among peers, for Greeks and Macedonians, and an elaborate Persian one, in which he was the Great King, for Asiatics. He now tried to take the major step towards abolishing the former by making prostration (the ordinary mode of saluting the Great King) compulsory for Europeans. His friend Hephaestion undertook to arrange the first precedents informally at a dinner-party. He probably did not expect any serious opposition. But things went unexpectedly wrong. The Greek Callisthenes, now thoroughly disillusioned with Alexander, who from being the leader of the Greeks had become an Oriental despot, refused to perform the ceremony; and when the Persian nobles one after another duly performed it, falling on their faces in all their stately robes, a Macedonian officer burst out laughing. In a rage, Alexander had to call it off.[10]

It was his first serious setback. As usual, he had been quick to learn by his mistake and had cut his losses. But the defeat had been beyond disguise. Callisthenes' part was significant: it was clear that Alexander had lost the sympathy of thinking Greeks – even of those who had once hailed him enthusiastically as a divinely appointed leader. Callisthenes, of course, could not live much longer. He was soon executed on a trumped-up charge of having instigated some page-boys to assassinate the King.[11] But this, though it satisfied Alexander's resentment and demonstrated his power, merely made the hatred of most Greek intellectuals for him permanent and incurable. He was now committed to looking chiefly to Asia.

The memory of purges and murders could best be wiped out by military success. In a brilliant campaign in India, the army was reunited behind its invincible leader. He seems also now to have reorganized it in such a way that the four trusted men who had taken part in the arrest of Philotas became the marshals of the Empire. Hephaestion, the chief of them, combined the positions of second-in-command and Grand Vizier.[12] At the same time, the training of natives in the Macedonian fashion was begun.[13] This, at the time, aroused little attention. But Alexander was again thinking far ahead.

Then there came another disappointment, and a warning. After weeks of marching through the monsoon, with no end in sight, as Alexander, with the defective geographical knowledge of his age, pursued an elusive Ganges (or perhaps even the end of the inhabited earth) – after weeks of unimaginable and apparently pointless hardships, the men, one day, simply refused to go on. Alexander had discovered the limit of what he could expect of them. But there was worse still. The spokesman for the mutinous soldiers was none other than Coenus – the man who, once Parmenio's son-in-law, had helped to wipe out the power and the family of his benefactor and who, in due course, had become one of the four marshals. Coenus was clearly not a man to be trusted if things began to go wrong. The King, who had used the army to break the power of the nobles, was suddenly faced with the spectre of co-operation between the army and a scheming noble against himself. For the moment, nothing could be done. Alexander tried to threaten and browbeat; but the men, this time, would not yield: they knew that he could not do without them and that they had good support. Finally Alexander had to retreat down the Indus valley to the sea.[14] During the next few months, he gave the men harder fighting and marching than ever before, though from a military point of view it was now unnecessary.[15] And it is clear from our accounts that they no longer followed him as eagerly as before. To regain their loyalty, the King himself was always in the front line; and once, when storming a city, he was so severely wounded that no one thought he could survive. This at last brought the men back to their old worship of their leader. But Alexander never wholly recovered from the shock he had received. He had no sooner achieved his objective of gaining untrammelled power than he found that he was more than ever dependent on others, and that absolute power meant eternal vigilance.

As for Coenus, he died in action soon after. Alexander gave him a splendid funeral, but is said to have inveighed against his memory.[16] We cannot be certain as to the circumstances surrounding the death of this sinister man. But those who remember the fate of Rommel are entitled to be cynical – especially in view of what happened before long.

After Alexander regained full control of his men, he decided to test them in a march through the desert of southern Iran. He was well informed of the nature of that region; but the test turned out more severe than he had expected, and after incredible sufferings, worse than any endured in actual fighting, the remnants of the grand army straggled to safety in the cultivated land south-west of the plateau. Naturally, the King was quick to suspect treason as the cause of the disaster; and to his increasing distrust there was now added the need to find a scapegoat. The result was a bloody purge that went on for months. Among the first to suffer – and this is what makes us suspicious of the manner of Coenus' death – was Coenus' brother Cleander, who had arranged Parmenio's assassination and thus earned promotion. He and three of his associates among the army commanders were now summoned to bring reinforcements to the King. On their arrival they were arrested and soon executed on charges of maladministration. Altogether more than a third (perhaps two-thirds) of all the provincial commanders shared their fate, and one or two others seem to have barely averted it. The armies under the command of the provincial governors were dissolved (at the price of causing mass unemployment that led to grave social problems), and unknown men who owed everything to Alexander were appointed to the vacant posts.[17]

Then Alexander began to put into execution a great scheme that he had long been bearing in mind. He now realized that he could not count on the absolute submission of the present generation of nobles or men. In the spring of 324, at Susa, Alexander and eighty of his principal courtiers and commanders (chief of them Hephaestion) married Iranian princesses. What these nobles thought of it became clear after his death, when most of them repudiated their wives. But at the time they had to submit, and the marriages were celebrated with unprecedented pomp. Alexander wanted nothing less than a new ruling class of mixed blood, which would be free of all national allegiance or tradition. At the same time, 10,000 unions of Macedonian soldiers with native women were recognized as valid marriages (which meant legitimation of the children and rich wedding-presents from the King): clearly such associations were to be encouraged. That this was not from any humane motive was made clear at once. After putting the young natives trained in the Macedonian fashion through their paces, Alexander proceeded to dismiss (with rich rewards, of course) a large number of Macedonian soldiers; and he asked them to leave their native wives and children with him, in order not to cause trouble with their families in Macedon. His purpose, ultimately, was the creation of a royal army of mixed blood and no fixed domicile – children of the camp, who knew no loyalty but to him. At this point the Macedonian army rebelled. But Alexander was now ready for them: there was no major war in prospect, and he had them at his mercy. It might even be thought that he had deliberately provoked them at this point in order to see whether they would mutiny: if they did, he wanted them to do so when it suited him, so that he might avoid a repetition of his Indian experience. At any rate, he at once calmly told them that they were all dismissed and could make their way home by themselves: he would make do with Oriental troops. The men had no option but to ask his pardon – which he readily granted, since they were his best fighters. But he had won decisively, and after a grand banquet to celebrate the reconciliation he carried out his plans without change.

It is clear that the failures in India and in the desert had caused a severe psychological reaction in Alexander. He had discovered the insecurity of power, which all his successful scheming could not overcome. His success in the purges, and in the Susa marriages and his dealings with the mutineers, only increased the resulting instability. He took refuge from the insecurity of power in the greater exercise of power: like a god intervening in the affairs of mortals, he would order the fate of princes and of nations. He had always liked and encouraged the story that he was the son of the god Ammon (a Libyan god whom the Greeks identified with Zeus and whose oracle he had visited). The myth had been useful to inspire loyalty, particularly in Greeks, whose religion had a place for such things. But he now actually began to believe in his own divinity. About the middle of 324, he sent envoys to Greece demanding that he should be worshipped as a god. There are many anecdotes about the reluctance with which the Greeks complied. We have seen that educated Greek opinion was already largely estranged from him; and this act of blasphemy – for such it clearly was, even for the polytheistic Greeks, as many of our sources circumstantially assure us – would not endear him to them. Nor had he anything to gain by deification of this enforced sort: divine status would give him no significant political rights in a Greek city state,[18] and men's opinion of him would not change for the better. There is no escape from the conclusion that he wanted deification purely for its own sake, for psychological and not for political reasons. As for the Greeks, they had to obey. The famous decree passed by the Spartans and later quoted as an admired example of 'Laconic' speech expressed their feelings: 'Since Alexander wishes to be a god, let him be a god.'

One man, however, remained a danger to the King and god. Antipater, viceroy of Europe, the man who had made Alexander king, had no love for this new Persian King, who had murdered so many Macedonian nobles. And since the homeland, after ten years, knew him much better than it had ever got to know the King, he could count on a great deal of support. Alexander now sent one of his marshals home to supersede Antipater and ordered Antipater to report to him in person. At the same time he began to prepare the ground for what was inevitably to follow by listening with patience and obvious favour to the complaints of Greek embassies about Antipater's oppressive government. But Antipater was neither ingenuous nor easily frightened: he was, after all, the man who had manipulated Alexander's accession to the throne; and after the King's death he was to show himself, in his sure-handed and solid way, far abler than any of the more mercurially brilliant successors. Antipater simply refused to come, but sent his eldest son to negotiate on his behalf. In the meantime, he began to insure himself by entering into negotiations with the most powerful of the Greek states, which he knew to be hostile to the King.[19]

About this time Alexander suffered his most serious blow. In the autumn of 324, Hephaestion, the only man he fully trusted, drank himself to death. Alexander now approached more and more closely to insanity.[20] Hephaestion was made a demigod, and his memory was celebrated with incredible splendour and magnificence. But there was no one to take his place. It is significant that, although his duties had to be carried out, Alexander never again bestowed his titles on anyone. Henceforth the reign visibly declines. There is still some brilliant fighting. There are still some great schemes, befitting the King's new conception of his status. In fact, there are *too* many. We hear of plans for the conquest of the western Mediterranean, for the conquest of Arabia, for vast buildings and movement of populations. Historians have found it difficult to believe our evidence, though its source seems reliable enough. The fact appears to be that Alexander, amid the grandeur of divine dreams, had no real purpose left. He had won all the power he could. There was nothing left that was worth doing.

So the last few months dragged on until, about midsummer 323, at the age of 32, Alexander fell ill. Whatever the nature of his illness (and poison was, of course, suggested; but this can be neither proved nor disproved), he aggravated it by heavy drinking, until finally all hope was abandoned. He was urged to designate a successor; but he refused to the end. There is a story that, when he was asked for the last time whom he wanted to succeed him, he replied: 'The strongest'. Alexander was, essentially, not interested in a future without himself. And there was no one left about whose personal future he cared enough to help him succeed.

This is not, of course, the whole story of Alexander's reign. His military and political greatness is beyond question, and he retained his masterly touch in these fields to the end. But on the personal level, the story of Alexander the Great appears to us as an almost embarrassingly perfect illustration of the man who conquered the world, only to lose his soul. After fighting, scheming and murdering in pursuit of the secure tenure of absolute power, he found himself at last on a lonely pinnacle over an abyss, with no use for his power and security unattainable. His genius was such that he ended an epoch and began another – but one of unceasing war and misery, from which only exhaustion produced an approach to order after two generations and peace at last under the Roman Empire. He himself never found peace. One is tempted to see him, in medieval terms, as the man who sold his soul to the Devil for power: the Devil kept his part of the bargain, but ultimately claimed his own. But to the historian, prosaically suspicious of such allegory, we must put it differently: to him, when he has done all the work – work that must be done, and done carefully – of analysing the play of faction and the system of government, Alexander illustrates with startling clarity the ultimate loneliness of supreme power.

Notes

1 This is the text – slightly revised – of a lecture delivered at the Universities of Wellington and Canterbury in September 1961, and at the Universities of California (Berkeley) and Chicago in October 1961. The author wishes to thank the editor of *AUMLA* for his offer to print it.
2 Inevitably, much that needs detailed discussion will have to be briefly touched on or taken for granted. For detailed treatment of several relevant problems, see *TAPA* 91 (1960) 324 ff. and *JHS* 81 (1961) 16 ff.
3 [See now my discussion of this in *Phoenix* 17 (1963).]
4 Plutarch, *Alexander* 9, 4 f.; Diodorus xvi 91 f., xvii 2 f.; ps.-Callisthenes i 26.

5   See *TAPA*, art. cit. (n. 2 above) 327 f.

6   This story is told in all the standard accounts, e.g. (Sir) W. W. Tarn, *Alexander the Great*, vol. i, 15 f.

7   See *TAPA*, art. cit. (n. 2 above) 328 f.

8   On the *coup d'état* against the house of Parmenio, see *TAPA*, art. cit. (n. 1 above) 330 f.

9   On the death of Clitus, see Arrian, *anabasis* iv 8 f.; Plut. *Alex.* 50 f.; Curtius viii 1, 30 f.

10 Different versions of this story in Plut. *Alex.* 54 f.; Arr. *anab.* iv 10 5 f.; Curt, viii 5 f. It is much discussed in both ancient and modern works.

11 Arr. *anab.* iv 12, 6 f.; Plut. *Alex.* 55; Curt, viii 6 f.

12 See Tarn, *op. cit.* (n. 6 above) 82 f.

13 Diod. xvii 108, 1 f.; Arr. *anab.* vii 8, 2.

14 Curt, ix 2, 10 f.; Arr. *anab.* v 25 f.

15 On these campaigns, see Tarn, *op. cit.* 100 f.

16 Arr. *anab.* vi 2, 1; Curt, ix 3, 20 f.

17 For the great purge and the story of Alexander's last year, see *JHS,* art. cit. (n. 2 above). In view of the charges of maladministration and oppressive government that were used against most of these men, it is interesting to observe that one of the few who were never in any danger was Cleomenes, the governor of Egypt, known (from good evidence) for extortion and oppression.

18 Modern apologists have surpassed themselves in ingenious attempts to deny this. But cf. (decisively) J.P.V.D. Balsdon, *Historia* 1 (1950) 363 f.

19 On all this *see JHS*, art. cit.

20 On this see especially J.R. Hamilton, *CQ* N.S. 3 (1953) 151 f.

THE CONSPIRACY *AGAINST* PHILOTAS[1]

Waldemar Heckel

Few problems in the history of Alexander the Great have been a greater vexation to the historian than the execution of Philotas and the murder of his father, Parmenion, events that shed an unfavourable light on Alexander's character and on the relationships of his younger Macedonian generals.[2] For scholars such as W.W. Tarn and C.A. Robinson Jr., the Philotas-affair became a moral issue, its discussion, ultimately, a conscious effort to exculpate Alexander.[3] So it is with understandable regret that Tarn concludes that Parmenion's death was 'plain murder and leaves a deep stain on Alexander's reputation' (1.64). But in the last two decades the gentleman scholar and the gentleman conqueror have fallen out of favour, yielding to a new breed of sceptics. From this group E. Badian emerges as one of the most sound but, as I think, unduly suspicious in the case of the Philotas-affair.

Badian's persuasive thesis, although many of its details have met with objections,[4] has had a marked effect upon subsequent scholarship – as indeed has his entire characterization of Alexander as the ruthless, calculating opportunist[5] – and, since it is the most recent specialized study, it warrants a detailed examination. In Badian's view, the murder of Parmenion was not the result of the Philotas-affair in that it was a reaction to it, but the 'culmination' of a greater scheme aimed at the destruction of Parmenion's house. Furthermore, it represented the continuation of the 'reign of terror' that followed Philip's assassination,[6] after a lengthy period of calm. Parmenion and his associates, lulled into a false sense of security by the intervening tranquillity, were taken completely by surprise 'when the thunderbolt struck them' (326). It was the Philotas-affair that provided Alexander with the means of eliminating Parmenion, and Badian argues that, with Parmenion's death in mind, Alexander was party to a 'fabricated conspiracy' *against* Philotas. The view presupposes that Alexander had long desired the destruction of Parmenion and his adherents, that Parmenion was the ultimate target of the Philotas-affair, that the actual conspiracy *of* Philotas did not exist,[7] and that the conspiracy of Dimnos was a fabrication.[8]

I propose to show that Badian's treatment of the affair is unsatisfactory on the matters of Alexander's motives and methods; that a study of the careers of Alexander's younger generals will show that they (Hephaistion not the least of these), and not Alexander, were primarily responsible for the fall of Philotas; that the latter's own position of prominence and arrogant nature gave rise to the ill-feeling against him; and that, far from being victimized by a 'fabricated conspiracy' in the Dimnos-affair, Philotas, through his foolish handling of the matter – for it did it fact exist – gave his enemies the perfect opportunity to move against him. Consequently, this view precludes the theory that the murder of Parmenion was the culmination of Alexander's 'reign of terror,' which began after Philip's assassination, and that Philotas was the object of a protracted conspiracy, contrived by Alexander himself.

Let us begin with Parmenion, allegedly the target of Alexander's smouldering hostility. It is true that Parmenion recognized the growing power of Attalos and his faction and, in an effort to bring himself into closer alliance with Philip (as was only fitting for the foremost commander of the army to do), married one of his daughters to Attalos. But we should not read too much into Parmenion's relationship with him;

political marriages are not made in heaven.[9] Nor was Parmenion so great a fool as to fail to realize that, when Philip's assassination had brought about the fall of Kleopatra and her adherents, it was politically expedient to sacrifice his new son-in-law to Alexander's vengeance.[10] This was Parmenion's token of loyalty to the new King and there is no reason to doubt that Alexander was satisfied.[11] Hostile factions remained within the army, but assassination had been an all too common means of deposing Macedonian kings and nothing could ensure perfect security for the new monarch. Alexander secured his power by a combination of liquidation and conciliation, preferring the latter when possible.

What we know of Parmenion's actions after Alexander's accession to the throne (Berve, no. 606) suggests that he had opted for conciliation with the King, nor is there any evidence that, before the Philotas-affair, Alexander had viewed him with greater distrust than any other of Philip's generals. Certainly there are stories that cast Parmenion in an unfavourable light,[12] but they do so for two obvious reasons: pro-Alexander propaganda and *apologia*. But to say (Badian 328) that some of these stories 'go back to good sources (Ptolemy or even Callisthenes)' does not mean that they are true and, unless they can be proved to derive from Kallisthenes, they were surely written after Parmenion's death. Furthermore, any such story that derives from Kallisthenes (and only one can be assigned to him with certainty[13]) need not be attributed to a deliberate attempt to undermine Parmenion's reputation. Kallisthenes, as official historian of the crusade (Alexander's salesman to the League of Korinth, as many suggest[14]), wrote with [the] aim of enhancing the reputation of a young and ambitious king who was eager to win credit for himself and not appear to be winning battles through the skill of his father's general. Thus it was Kallisthenes' function to impress the brilliance of Alexander's personality and military skill upon the *Greeks*; in order to undermine the reputation of Parmenion, he ought to have been writing for the Macedonian soldiery, to whom alone this will have been a major concern. More likely, any notable anti-Parmenion propaganda was written after Parmenion's death. *Apologia* and the history of Alexander are inseparable; what greater need than to justify the murder of Parmenion?

Badian charges (329) that Alexander, while he was steadily 'undermining Parmenion's reputation, had also made considerable progress in extricating himself from the stranglehold of Parmenion's family and adherents.' The decline in power of Parmenion's house in the years that followed the crossing into Asia is evident. But is it fair to attach the blame for this to Alexander? Parmenion's sons, Hektor and Nikanor (Berve, nos. 295, 554), had died of natural causes, while a third member of the family, Asandros, Parmenion's brother, had received the honour of the satrapy of Sardeis.[15] Can this really have been part of a scheme to weaken Parmenion's power in the army? If Berve is correct (2.393), all this occurred after Alexander had strengthened the family's position by appointing Philotas commander of the Companion cavalry. Asandros was replaced in his satrapy by Menandros (no. 501), under what circumstances we do not know.[16] But how could Alexander have known that Parmenion's sons would die of natural causes? It is useless to speculate what he would have done had they not met such ends.

So, while fortune had taken two of Parmenion's sons, the most devastating move, as far as Philotas was concerned, was dictated by military sense. The events that followed Gaugamela made it clear that the nature of the war was to take a drastic change: the pursuit of Dareios and Bessos would require vigour and mobility. Since Parmenion's seventy years made him ill-suited for this type of warfare and since the young, and extremely capable, Krateros had been groomed by a series of commands of ever-increasing importance as Parmenion's eventual successor, the latter was sent to Ekbatana with the imperial treasures.[17] On account of the nature of the campaign, he was never recalled and took what we might today call a 'desk job' at Ekbatana, entrusted with the securing of east–west communications.[18] The appointment, while not a demotion, meant a considerable 'loss of *power*'[19] in relation to the army, but at Parmenion's age such a change of position was inevitable. While he may have resented the change, just as any commander, after a lifetime of service, resents removal from active duty, it was his son, Philotas, who was to suffer most from it.

With Parmenion at Ekbatana, Philotas found himself isolated within the Macedonian army; this proved disastrous. As a young man he had risen to his position of prominence, no doubt, through the influence of his father.[20] His prestige, coupled with his friendship with Alexander, gave rise in turn to arrogance and licence in speech. It is difficult to determine the precise nature of his relationship with Alexander, for, while the two are portrayed as boyhood friends by Plutarch (*Alex.* 10.3), Philotas' role in the Pixodaros-affair and his outspoken opposition to Alexander's orientalisms could not have raised him in the King's estimation. Nevertheless, both Ptolemy and Aristoboulos (*FGrHist* 138 F13; 139 F22) reported that the friendship and honour in which he held both Philotas and Parmenion at the time of the ἐπιβουλή in Egypt (332/1 B.C.) induced Alexander to overlook the former's sins.

The existence of this so-called conspiracy has not been seriously questioned. The ἐπιβουλή, related by Arrian (3.26.1), must certainly be the subject of the first part of Plutarch's account of the Philotas-affair (*Alex.* 48.4–49.2). At this point Plutarch speaks of a 'conspiracy *against* Philotas,' but our correct interpretation of this remark is vital to our understanding of the true nature of the conspiracy. Badian, admittedly, does not openly state that Plutarch's 'conspiracy *against* Philotas' was anything more than the activity of Krateros and Antigone (the 'prolonged espionage' [331] against Philotas) but his remark that 'Plutarch…very justly speaks of a conspiracy *against* Philotas' (326) immediately precedes a long digression that is followed by an account of the events almost two years later (the conspiracy of Dimnos) and the words: 'It seems to have been during this time [*i.e.*, during Philotas' absence in Areia] that *the plot* [my emphasis] against Philotas was hatched.'[21] Now it becomes clear that Badian believes in a protracted conspiracy against Philotas, during which time a 'file' was compiled against him. But the resulting ambiguity in Badian's discussion can only mislead the reader,[22] for it appears that, on account of Plutarch's remark, we ought to look for a 'fabricated conspiracy' in the Dimnos-affair; Badian's proposal thus wins credibility. The argument is delusive.

Plutarch's account deserves closer attention. Krateros (no. 446) had suborned Philotas' mistress, Antigone (no. 86), to inform against her lover and had reported the latest developments to Alexander. He was motivated by his strong sense of loyalty to the King, for which characteristic he won the label φιλοβασιλεύς,[23] and by his own personal ambition. Perhaps his zeal had brought him into open conflict with Philotas, just as it did on later occasions with Hephaistion.[24] But this 'prolonged espionage' revealed little that was not already known: that Philotas had been voicing his objections to Alexander's orientalisms, particularly the recent *Ammonssohnschaft*, and that he claimed a greater share of the credit for his own military achievements and those of his father. There is no question that, when Plutarch speaks of Philotas as being ignorant of the conspiracy against him, he is referring to the activities of Krateros and Antigone and not the Dimnos-affair that immediately follows in chapter 49.3–12.

The details of Dimnos' conspiracy can be briefly stated. Dimnos (Berve, no. 269), for an unknown reason, had plotted with several others against Alexander; Arrian relates that Demetrios (no. 260) and the sons of Andromenes (Amyntas, Attalos, Polemon, and Simmias)[25] were suspected of complicity, Curtius gives a suspicious list of otherwise unknown fellow-conspirators (6.7.15). Dimnos divulged the details of the conspiracy to his lover Nikomachos, who, in alarm, reported all he had heard to his brother, Kebalinos. The latter, in turn, attempted to inform Alexander through the agency of Philotas, who was in the habit of visiting the King twice daily. But Philotas, whether privy to the plot or merely favouring it,[26] failed to pass on the information. Kebalinos, perceiving that his words had fallen on deaf ears, resolved to bring the matter to Alexander's attention himself. In his second attempt, he found a more receptive ear.[27] Philotas and the conspirators were subsequently arrested.[28]

Because Dimnos 'conveniently killed himself (or was killed while resisting arrest)' (Badian 331) and because Philotas' guilt could not be proved,[29] Badian concludes that the Dimnos-affair was actually a 'fabrication' aimed at implicating Philotas, a plot that was hatched while he was attending to the funeral rites of his brother. I consider Hamilton's refutation (134–135) simple and adequate: 'how could Alexander *know* that Philotas would fail to pass on the information?' There are, of course, other almost equally devastating objections: the complexity of the plot would have made its successful execution extremely difficult.[30] But the strongest argument against the 'fabricated conspiracy' is the understanding of the true conspiracy *against* Philotas.

As we have seen, Philotas was reported to have been one of Alexander's boyhood friends. Yet it appears that he was somewhat of an outsider to this inner group, the very people who were later to rise to prominence through their jealous rivalry with one another for Alexander's affection. Perhaps Philotas' alienation from the group was due to the difference in age that, although it may not have been great,[31] was sufficient to separate him 'from the boys' at a critical time. Certainly his devotion to his father and his military position made it neither necessary nor desirable for him to go into exile when Olympias and her children fell out of favour. At that point he very likely incurred the enmity of those companions of Alexander who had.[32]

It does not appear that Alexander himself bore Philotas a grudge, for at the outset of the expedition he either retained him as commander of the Companions or promoted him to the post. But what Philotas had not done as a youth to alienate several of Alexander's young companions, he did in the early years of the campaign. His prestigious command was coveted by the younger commanders, while his arrogance (Themistios, *Or.* 19.229c–d, uses him as an exemplum of αὐθάδεια) fanned the flames of their jealousies, giving rise to a 'conspiracy' against him. Now the irony of the situation becomes apparent. For, while Parmenion, through the rejection of the party of Attalos – and this will have included the arrest of Alexandros of Lynkestis – and his loyalty, had won a reprieve from Alexander, his son, Philotas, through his own folly and unpopularity, was to bring about their downfall. Opposition was to come from another quarter. When the news of Dimnos' conspiracy broke, the cards were stacked against Philotas; his licence in speech and the suspicion of earlier treason made his complicity in the affair all the more credible. It appears that Philotas himself did not fully understand his own predicament at the time when the events of what we call the 'Philotas-affair' began to unfold. Certainly, his foolish disregard of his father's advice,[33] his arrogance, and his general unpopularity made his ultimate deposition only a matter of time. His political enemies, who had long before begun to work for his elimination, seized the opportunity presented by the Dimnos-affair. Deep-rooted animosities manifested themselves in the form of vigorous prosecution and, in the face of adversity, Parmenion, through whose influence Philotas had escaped an earlier charge of treason, was no longer present to help him.

When Philotas was confronted with the charge of complicity in Dimnos' conspiracy, he replied that he had not passed on the information because he had not taken it seriously, a peculiar attitude in a court where intrigues were common and always potentially dangerous. At another time Parmenion's mere presence might have commuted the charge from treason to excusable negligence. In the present circumstances, the implication of Philotas in the conspiracy provided his enemies with the best and, in their minds, possibly the only opportunity for securing his elimination.

Curtius' lengthy discussion of the proceedings that followed Philotas' arrest is often tiresome, offering little in the way of new details. Yet Curtius is by far our most valuable source for the Philotas-affair; it is unfortunate that his imaginative speeches and the reputation of his source, Kleitarchos, have detracted from the quality of Curtius' history.[34] Kleitarchos drew his information mainly from eye-witness reports, and this will explain some of the confused details in Curtius' narrative.[35] But Curtius was more than a skilful rhetorician: he understood the inner workings of the Philotas-affair, relating what the other *vulgate* writers did not perceive and what Ptolemy and Aristoboulos would not disclose. Curtius' Roman background had educated him in the ways of court intrigue and factional politics. One remark strikes to the heart of the matter: Philotas pronounces that the bitterness of his enemies has overcome Alexander's goodwill (*vicit…bonitatem tuam, rex, inimicorum meorum acerbitas*, Curt. 6.8.22). Furthermore, Curtius portrays Krateros and Koinos as Philotas' chief opponents, Krateros thinking that no better opportunity would present itself for destroying a detested rival and Koinos, although married to Philotas' sister, being his most outspoken assailant (6.8.4; 6.9.30). The latter, for his involvement in the affair, has been stigmatized by modern scholars as one of the most unsavoury characters in the history of this period.[36] Yet it is likely that the most serious blows to Philotas' hopes of acquittal were struck behind the scenes.

The years that intervened between the beginning of the expedition and the Philotas-affair were marked by a conspicuous lack of achievement on the part of Alexander's dearest friend, Hephaistion. Whether Hephaistion was in fact Alexander's boyhood friend is open to doubt; certainly Plutarch does not mention him among the list of friends who were exiled on account of the Pixodarus-affair.[37] Nevertheless, it is clear that at sometime very early in the campaign Hephaistion began to exert an increasingly great influence upon Alexander.[38] Certainly it would be naïve to believe that Hephaistion's sudden rise from relative obscurity to command of one-half of the Companions was not in some way related to his role in the Philotas-affair.

What we know of Hephaistion's later relationships with Alexander's commanders reveals that he was of a particularly quarrelsome nature and not reluctant to malign others to Alexander.[39] His influence is evinced by his contribution to the fall of Kallisthenes[40] and the great alarm that Eumenes felt at Hephaistion's death, lest his former enmity toward him should bring about serious consequences.[41] If any man had the power to persuade Alexander that Philotas was expendable, that man was Hephaistion. But Hephaistion's own military record provides an even greater cause for suspicion. As we have seen, his contribution to the war effort before 330 had been almost negligible; we know of only one minor naval command, in which he took the fleet from Tyre to Gaza, and of his wounding at Gaugamela.[42] Polyainos' remark (4.3.27) that Hephaistion commanded a cavalry division against Phrasaortes (a mistake for Ariobarzanes) finds no parallel in another extant account. More important, however, is Hephaistion's failure to display, during the remainder of the campaign, those qualities of military skill and leadership that would warrant his unprecedented promotion. In fact, he is never reported exercising that command. Instead he appears to have been tactfully demoted whenever the actual command of military units was concerned.[43]

We must therefore view Hephaistion's rise with suspicion. This is especially true in view of his vehement advocacy of the use of torture against Philotas, behaviour that is not out of character and that reflects a rivalry with Philotas on both a personal and official level (Curt. 6.11.10). Not only did he advocate torture but he took a personal lead in the act itself; Plutarch (*Alex.* 49.12) speaks of Philotas' tormentors as τοῖς περὶ τὸν Ἡφαιστίωνα. Even more suspicious is the nature of Arrian's account (3.26.2 ff.), which derives from Ptolemy.[44] Here we are told of Hephaistion's promotion and of Ptolemy's own replacement of Demetrios the bodyguard, yet the account of the actual *Philotasprozess* is abbreviated to the point of uselessness. The Arrian-Ptolemy tradition has often been interpreted as official *apologia* for Alexander, but, as Schwahn and Errington have pointed out,[45] it protected on numerous occasions Ptolemy's own interests and, very likely, those of his friends.

The accounts of the execution of Philotas are, for the most part, brief[46] and concur in stating that Philotas was 'judicially executed'; Curtius' version is, predictably, more elaborate. Here again, while the tedious rhetoric and needless expansion of events give rise to particulars that can be dismissed as inventions, there is the important ring of verisimilitude,[47] often the best that the historian can hope for. If Plutarch's remark, ὁ μὲν οὖ Φιλώτας ἐπιβουλευόμενος οὕτως ἠγνόει (*Alex.* 49.1), leads us to suspect a conspiracy against Philotas at the time of Dimnos' treason, Curtius' account is most useful for the interpretation of it. The conspiracy *against* Philotas was not a 'transparent fabrication,' an invented conspiracy by an obscure individual named Dimnos, Alexander's means of trapping Philotas and eliminating Parmenion. It was, in fact, the Macedonian court at work, the struggle for power among Alexander's young and ambitious commanders. It entailed the undermining of Philotas' character and reputation by his most dangerous enemies: Hephaistion, Krateros, Koinos, Ptolemy, Erigyios, and others. These men realized that Philotas' isolation and his failure to pass on the information of Kebalinos presented the best opportunity for his destruction. Alexander had to be convinced that Philotas' involvement could not be overlooked or excused. When Alexander personally called for the death sentence before the Macedonian soldiers, the enemies of Philotas won the day.[48] Their efforts had secured for them commands of major importance, positions that were to bring them into conflict with one another shortly afterward. The success of their conspiracy against Philotas only helped to encourage this factional rivalry and no other individual was more prone or better able to seek promotion by winning Alexander's ear than Hephaistion. It became clear that Alexander has been too much the centre of the history of his period, with the result that a hybrid, biographical-historical literature has developed. It is all too easy to view the

Philotas-affair and similar events from Alexander's vantage-point, to assume that all things were initiated by Alexander. Should it be unreasonable to expect that Alexander was himself influenced, even manipulated at times, by those people who were closely associated with him?

There is no doubt that Alexander was not acting against his will when he allowed himself to be persuaded that Philotas must be removed. Schachermeyr is quite right to point out that the drastic steps that followed Philotas' arrest need not have been taken.[49] But Alexander, had he not been strongly influenced by his group of companions, might well have been content to take less stringent measures and to allow the house of Parmenion to lapse into the state of obscurity for which it was already destined.

We need not belabour the fate of Parmenion, nor indeed ought we take into consideration its moral implications. Parmenion's death was outright murder, quite conceivably a 'regrettable necessity,'[50] which not even Arrian-Ptolemy attempted to disguise.[51] Alexander realized that, once Philotas' death had been demanded, Parmenion's murder was inevitable: the father would not endure the son's execution. It became apparent that Parmenion must die before the news of his son's death reached him and that the murder must in some way be justified. For the immediate purpose, the alleged confession of Philotas under torture proved adequate.[52] The army, indignant at the audacity of the proposed crime, remained loyal; disciplinary measures were taken against a small dissident faction.[53] Polydamas was sent with all haste to Sitalkes, Kleandros, and Menidas, who struck Parmenion down as he read the news of his son's execution and the charges against himself. It was an act of fearful desperation. The process had advanced to the point of no return.

The fates of the 'fellow-conspirators' need be treated only briefly. They are, in fact, not a part of the conspiracy *against* Philotas but of the Dimnos-affair, the catalyst that brought about the destruction of Philotas and the subsequent murder of Parmenion. Demetrios the bodyguard remains an obscure figure; Curtius is certainly incorrect in claiming that he was executed together with Philotas and those named by Dimnos and Nikomachos (6.7.15; 11.38). Alexander of Lynkestis ended his imprisonment as the victim of a lynching, a thing characteristic of the mob when passions are aroused.[54] Amyntas and his brothers were reprieved and, despite Amyntas' death shortly afterward, their futures cannot be linked with their roles in the Philotas-affair with any certainty.[55] As for the other conspirators (Peukolaos, Nikanor, Aphobetos, Theoxenes, Iolaos and Archepolis), their existence and identities, owing to their obscurity, cannot be determined. It is true that, at that time, Alexander could ill afford a 'wholesale slaughter of the Macedonian nobility,' but it is also doubtful that he wished even as much as actually came about.

Notes

1 This is a revised version of a paper given, under the same title, at the annual meetings of the Classical Association of Canada in Edmonton in June, 1975. I thank Professors T.S. Brown, J.A.S. Evans, P.E. Harding and M.F. McGregor for reading this paper in its various stages and offering their criticisms. I am also grateful to the Journal's referees for their constructive criticisms.

2 F. Cauer, 'Philotas, Kleitos, Kallisthenes,' *Jahrbücher für classische Philologie*, Supplbd 20 (1894) 8–38; C. A. Robinson Jr., 'Alexander the Great and Parmenio,' *AJA* 49 (1945) 422 ff.; W.W. Tarn, *Alexander the Great* (Cambridge 1948) esp. 2.270–272, App. 12, 'The Murder of

Parmenion'; E. Badian, 'The Death of Parmenio,' *TAPA* 91 (1960) 324–338; J.R. Hamilton, *Plutarch, Alexander: A Commentary* (Oxford 1969) 134–135; F. Schachermeyr, *Alexander der Grosse: Das Problem seiner Persönlichkeit und seines Wirkens* (Vienna 1973) 326–336; J. Rufus Fears, 'Pausanias, The Assassin of Philip II,' *Athenaeum* 53 (1975) 111–135, esp. 132–134; and, for a survey of the major views, J. Seibert, *Alexander der Grosse: Erträge der Forschung* (Darmstadt 1972) 140–141. These works will be referred to by author's name alone.

3   In the case of Parmenion, a valiant defence is attempted by Robinson (*AJP* 58 [1937] 109) on the basis of Curtius 6.11.20:...*legem Macedonum veriti, qua cautum erat ut propinqui eorum qui regi insidiati essent cum ipsis necarentur*....Not even Tarn found this acceptable but Robinson reiterated this view in 'Alexander's Brutality,' *AJA* 56 (1952) 169–170.

4   These are collected and discussed by Hamilton, where special attention is given to Badian's 'fabricated conspiracy' and his misleading discussion of Plut. *Alex.* 49.1 (ἐπιβουλευόμενος).

5   See particularly 'Alexander the Great and the Loneliness of Power,' *Studies in Greek and Roman History* (Oxford 1964) 192–205.

6   For this see E. Badian, 'The Death of Philip II,' *Phoenix* 17 (1963) 244–250.

7   So Badian (332) comments: '[*sc.* Tarn] having introduced the story of the 'conspiracy of Philotas' (which he is the only reputable recent scholar to believe)...'

8   Badian (333): 'Moreover, since Philotas' 'treason' was a transparent fabrication, the assassination of his father was not a panic-stricken reaction to an unforeseen emergency; it must be regarded as an integral part of the same scheme, and indeed, in view of Parmenio's position, as its culmination.'

9   Fears (133, n. 77) believes that 'the alleged marriage of Philotas' sister to Attalus, found in no other source [than Curtius], is{...}an invention.' I find this piece of information more likely to be true than not. The extensive system of political alliance through marriage is aptly demonstrated by A.B. Bosworth ('Philip II and Upper Macedonia,' *CQ* 21 [1971] 93–105) for the period immediately preceding Alexander's reign (through admittedly for the royal house in particular). But cf. the marriage of Koinos, son of Polemokrates, to one of Parmenio's daughters (Curtius 6.9.30; Arr. 1.24.1; 1.29.4 and supported by epigraphic evidence, Dittenberger, *Syll.*³ 332). For the political significance of such unions in the Hellenistic period (though also applicable in Alexander's lifetime) see J. Seibert, 'Historische Beiträge zu den dynastischen Verbindungen in hellenistischer Zeit,' *Historia, Einzelschrift* 10 (1967).

10 For a slightly different approach consider Curtius 7.1.3: [*sc. Parmenio*]...*amicus et ipsi Alexandro tam fidus, ut occidendi Attalum non alio ministro uti mallet* [*sc.* Alexander]. Diod. 17.2.5–6; 5.2 says that Attalos was killed by an agent named Hekataios. See Berve, no. 292. This must have been done with Parmenion's knowledge and approval.

11 Diodoros (17.5.2) suggests that the murder of Attalos had two functions: the elimination of Attalos and the proof of Parmenion's loyalty. Cf. L. Edmonds, 'The Religiosity of Alexander,' *GRBS* 12 (1971) 367; Badian, 'Alexander the Great and the Loneliness of Power' (above, n. 4) 194.

12 Arr. 1.13.2 ff.; Plut. *Alex.* 16.3; Curt. 3.5.1 ff. and 6.10.34 f.; Plut. *Alex.* 19; Arr. 2.4.9–10; Diod. 17.54.4; Arr. 2.25.2; Plut. *Alex.* 33; Arr. 3.18.11. There are cases in which Parmenion's advice is accepted, or in which Parmenion gives good advice: Diod. 17.16; Curt. 3.7.8–10; Plut. *Alex.* 21.9; Curt. 4.10.16–17; Arr. 3.18.11; or cases in which Parmenion performs loyal service: Arr. 1.25.4 ff.; Curt. 7.1.3.

13 Plut. *Alex.* 33 = *FGrHist* 124 F 37. Kallisthenes charges that Parmenion managed affairs badly (deliberately) at Gaugamela. On this see Hamilton (89) and Jacoby (*FGrHist* IID, 429–430) who assert, quite rightly as I think, that this passage (indeed the entire hostile portrait of Parmenion) was written after Parmenion's death. Note also Lionel Pearson, *The Lost Histories of Alexander the Great* (New York 1960) 47, who suggests that the evidence that links Kallisthenes to this hostile portrait is questionable. Undoubtedly he is correct to assume that the stories were 'elaborated by later writers.'

14 W.K. Prentice, 'Callisthenes, the Original Historian of Alexander,' *TAPA* 54 (1923) 74 ff.; T.S. Brown, 'Callisthenes and Alexander,' *AJP* 70 (1949) 233 f. on the importance of Greek public opinion; L. Pearson (n. 13 above) 22 ff.; Jacoby, *FGrHist* IID, 411.

15 Badian and Schachermeyr tend to view such appointments as *Kaltstellung*, a concept somewhat similar to the Tacitean notion of *honor exilii* (cf. *Hist.* 1.21.1). In view of Asandros' career (Berve,

no. 165), his appointment to the rich satrapy of Sardeis cannot be considered in this light; certainly it was not a demotion. I see no evidence for C. Bradford Welles' suggestion (*Alexander and the Hellenistic World* [Toronto 1970] 39) that Parmenion and Asandros were cousins.

16 A certain Asandros (without patronymic) appears at Zariaspa-Baktra (Arr. 4.7.2; Curt. 7.10.12) with reinforcements from Lykia. Berve (2.87) offers several explanations for his disappearance thereafter. If this is the brother of Parmenion, Alexander's act of recalling him from Sardeis to the main camp in order to have him eliminated (so Badian 329) cannot have been politically astute. This could only have revived unpleasant memories of the Philotas-affair and accentuated the sufferings of the house of Parmenion. Perhaps the man in question is Berve's no. 164, the later satrap of Karia (323 B.C.).

17 Arr. 3.19.7; J.R. Hamilton, *Alexander the Great* (London 1973) 90 is one of the few writers to point out this obvious reason for Parmenion's removal from the army. For his age (70 years), Curt. 6.11.32. With the end of the 'Panhellenic' phase of the war, many of Parmenion's troops were sent back to Greece. This is a factor, of course, but it can hardly have been Alexander's reason for removing Parmenion.

18 Alexander may have wished to keep a watchful eye on his perfidious treasurer, Harpalos, who had earlier (before the battle of Issos) fled to the Megarid, undoubtedly after pilfering the treasury. He had, however, been reinstated. For a different view on the cause of his departure in 333 see E. Badian, 'The First Flight of Harpalus,' *Historia* 9 (1960) 246.

19 Badian acknowledges this 'loss of *power*' (his phrase, 329 n. 16) and yet maintains that 330 was a critical year in which Parmenion represented a threat to Alexander's security. In truth, his relegation to Ekbatana was proof that Parmenion's family had already suffered a great decline. Only if, as in the case of Philotas' execution, Alexander gave Parmenion a compelling reason to rebel, was the latter's position at Ekbatana a threat to the King.

20 So R. Lane Fox, *Alexander the Great* (London 1973) 287. One wonders whether the death of Attalos and the promotion of Philotas were in any way related.

21 Badian (330); but Plutarch (*Alex.* 49.3: ἐν δὲ τῷ τότε Χρόνῳ) is also vague.

22 Hamilton (135) clarifies this ambiguity.

23 Plut. *Alex.* 47.10; Diod. 17.114.1–2.

24 Plut. *Alex.* 47.9 ff., esp. 47.11. Much of this may have been due to Hephaistion's nature but, as both Badian and Schachermeyr demonstrate, such conflicts among the young nobles were common and indeed natural.

25 Arr. 3.27.1–5. See my discussion of these individuals in 'Amyntas, Son of Andromenes,' *GRBS* 16 (1975) 393–398.

26 Perhaps Philotas foolishly hoped to protect the conspirators from prosecution (especially if Amyntas, whom he considered a personal friend, was included) and thus failed to pass on the information.

27 Diod. 17.79.4 says 'a royal page;' Curt. 6.7.22 names him Metron; see Berve, no. 520.

28 Curtius' account of the arrest of Philotas and the conspirators (6.7.31 ff.) is overdramatized and is strongly influenced by the writer's Roman background (*i.e.*, not to be traced to Kleitarchos). See Badian (331–332) and R. Lane Fox ([above, n. 21] 283–284).

29 R. Lane Fox is indecisive on the extent of Philotas' guilt, supposing (288) that Philotas may have planned the conspiracy while he was returning from his brother's funeral (completely opposite to Badian [330], who supposes that he was plotted against in his absence). Then, after suggesting that Philotas' guilt consisted of negligence, Fox concludes (289): 'Nobody believed that Philotas was innocent and it is absurd to idealize him as a martyr to Alexander's ruthlessness simply because the histories explain so little.'

30 Also the news of Dimnos' plot, had Philotas not favoured it, would have given Philotas the perfect opportunity to prove his loyalty and win honour. Cf. R. Lane Fox (289) and Hamilton (135).

31 Berve (2.393) estimates that he was not much more than four years older. He may have been older still, although it appears that Philotas owed his rapid advancement more to his father's influence than to his age.

32 Plut. *Alex.* 10.4 names Harpalos, Nearchos, Erigyios and Ptolemy. Arr. 3.6.5 adds Laomedon, the brother of Erigyios. Hephaistion is curiously absent. See n. 37 below.

33 Plut. *Alex.* 48.3: ὑποψίαν (εἶχε) καὶ Φθόνον, ὥωστε καὶ Παρμενίωνά ποτ' εἰπεῖν πρὸς αὐτόν, 'ὦπαῖ, χείρων μοι γίγου.'

34 On Kleitarchos see Jacoby *FGrHist* 137; T. S. Brown, 'Clitarchus,' *AJP* 71 (1950) 134–155; L. Pearson (above, n. 13) 212–242.

35 F. Schachermeyr, *Alexander in Babylon und die Reichsordnung nach seinem Tode* (Vienna 1970) 81–92.

36 For Koinos see Berve, no. 439. Schachermeyr (327) serves as an example: 'Koinos, der beidere Haudegen.{... }Zwar Schwiegersohn des Parmenion, jedoch von betonter Loyalität.'

37 Plut. *Alex.* 10.4. Tarn 2.57 believes that they were not boyhood friends and that the Hephaistion–Patroklos parallel (which many interpret as indicative of an early intimate relationship) is the work of the poetasters. The evidence for Hephaistion's early relationship with Alexander is scanty and of questionable quality. Only Curtius (3.12.15: *cum ipso pariter educatus*) deserves serious consideration. Compare this with Diog. Laert. 5.1.27 (misprinted by Berve 2.169, n. 3), where a letter from Aristotle to Hephaistion is mentioned. Ps.-Kallisthenes 1.18 and Jul. Valer. 1.10 mention Hephaistion and Alexander sailing together as youths; admittedly an unreliable source. The evidence is at best inconclusive.

38 Two famous anecdotes attest to their close relationship during the early years of the campaign: Arr. 2.12.6 f.; Diod. 17.37.5; 17.114.2; Curt. 3.12.15 ff.; Val. Max. 4.7 ext. 2; *Itiner.* 37; *Suda s.v.* Ἡφαιστίων. Also Curt. 4.1.15–25; Plut. *de fort. Al.* 2.340c–d; Diod. 17.47 ff. It was also through the agency of Hephaistion that Demosthenes sent Aristion to Alexander in 331 (Marsyas of Pella, *FGrHist* 135 F 2; Jacoby IID, 482).

39 Plut. *Alex.* 55.1; 47.9–11; *Eumenes* 2.2; Arr. 7.12.7 f.; 7.14.9.

40 Plut. Alex. 55.1. Hephaistion told Alexander that Kallisthenes had promised to do *proskynesis* but had gone back on his word.

41 Arr. 7.14.9. Eumenes was the first to pay honour to the dead Hephaistion, fearing that their former quarrels (Arr. 7.12.7; Plut. *Eumenes* 2) would make Alexander suspect that he welcomed Hephaistion's death.

42 Curt. 4.5.10 (Tyre to Gaza); Diod. 17.61.3, Arr. 3.15.2, Curt. 4.16.32 (Gaugamela).

43 So P.A. Brunt, 'Alexander's Macedonian Cavalry,' *JHS* 83 (1963) 27–46; cf. G.T. Griffith, 'A Note on the Hipparchies of Alexander,' *JHS* 83 (1963) 68–76. I do not subscribe to R. Lane Fox's view ([above, n. 21] 535) that Hephaistion became Chiliarch shortly afterward (i.e., in Sogdiana).

44 C. A. Robinson Jr., *AJP* (1937) 109, argues against the accounts of Demetrios' arrest and Hephaistion and Ptolemy's promotions deriving from Ptolemy ('the difficulty is to decide where a quotation begins and ends'). But see my remarks, *GRBS* 16 (1975) 393, n. 5.

45 W. Schwahn, 'Die Nachfolge Alexanders des Grossen,' *Klio* 23 (1930) 211–238; R.M. Errington, 'Bias in Ptolemy's History of Alexander,' *CQ* 19 (1969) 233–242.

46 Arr. 3.26.2; Diod. 17.80.1–2; Plut. *Alex.* 49.

47 On the verisimilitude of Curtius: T.S. Brown ([above, n. 35] 148) says of Curtius' source that 'verisimilitude seems to be his chief aim as a historian.' For Curtius' style and attitude to history see E.I. McQueen, 'Quintus Curtius Rufus,' in *Latin Biography*, ed. T.A. Dorey (London 1967) 17–43.

48 The persuasion apparently took place over an extended period (note that Plutaro *Alex.* 49.8, calls them τοὺς πάλαι μισοῦντας αὐτόν but it appears that Alexander was convinced on the night when Philotas' enemies visited his (A.'s) tent; Curt. 6.8.1 *Secunda deinde vigilia, luminibus extinctis, cum paucis in regiam coeunt Hephaestio Craterus et Coenus et Erigyius, hi ex amicis, ex armigeris autem Perdiccas et Leonnatus.*

49 Schachermeyr (334–335): 'Keineswegs wäre der König genötigt gewesen, alles Äussersten zu treiben.{...}Die Schlüsse, welche der Herrscher zog, man musste sie ziehen.' Both Badian and Schachermeyr develop the portrait of rivalry among the leading individuals in Alexander's camp and yet are reluctant to reach any other conclusion than that Alexander himself perpetrated the conspiracy *against* Philotas for personal, albeit politically motivated, reasons.

50 Badian (332), paraphrasing Tarn.

51 Arr. 3.26.4. The remark that Alexander could not believe that Philotas plotted without Parmenion's complicity is feeble and could not have expected to convince. Arrian admits that fear of retaliation motivated Alexander to murder Parmenion.

52 Whether Philotas admitted to anything or not. The Hegelochos-story remains a mystery. It is generally held that the story is an invention, *apologia* written after Parmenion's death (cf. Badian 332; Fears 133, n. 77). There may be some basis for the charges, the clue to which lies in the identity of Hegelochos. I intend to argue this elsewhere.

53 Diod. 17.80.4; Justin. 12.5.4 ff.; Curt. 7.2.35 ff.
54 Berve, no. 37. On his death, Diod. 17.80.2; Curt. 7.1.8–9; Justin 12.14.1; Arrian did not mention it.
55 Amyntas' death creates the same suspicions as does the death of Koinos shortly after opposition to Alexander at the Hyphasis. One can not hope to determine the truth of it. See *GRBS* 16 (1975) 393–398, cited above, n. 26.

ANAXARCHUS AND CALLISTHENES:
ACADEMIC INTRIGUE AT ALEXANDER'S COURT

Eugene N. Borza

The following study is dedicated to one whose work on ancient Macedonia has provided an inspiration and established the standard for those who follow. Charles Edson, much of whose life has been spent in academic institutions, is a veteran of the conflicts which characterize the activity of those who profess to 'live the life of the mind'. This essay intends to probe a bit into Macedonian court life in the age of Alexander the Great by examining some aspects of the competition among intellectuals for the king's favor. More than most, Professor Edson knows that things have not changed very much.

Anaxarchus of Abdera is usually included in the list of those associated with the School of Abdera whose founder was Democritus.[1] His *floruit* is given by Diogenes Laertius (9.58) as the 110th Olympiad (340–36 B.C.), and he accompanied Alexander, whom he survived. The story of Anaxarchus' own death contributed to whatever fame he enjoyed in antiquity. It was said that once, while at Alexander's table, Anaxarchus had mocked Nicocreon, the ruler of Salamis in Cyprus. Years later it was Anaxarchus' misfortune to be forced ashore on Cyprus. Nicocreon seized the philosopher and ordered him to be pounded to death with iron pestles. Anaxarchus accepted his fate with the proverbial speech: 'Pound the pouch of Anaxarchus; you pound not Anaxarchus'.[2]

We have no way of knowing precisely when Anaxarchus joined Alexander's train. We first hear of him in the year 331. As Alexander marched out of Egypt toward Assyria he paused in Phoenicia, probably at Tyre, and there held a series of sacrifices and competitions.[3] Among the *choregi* was the Cypriot ruler, Nicocreon.[4] It was likely on this occasion that Anaxarchus delivered the insult to Nicocreon which would later cost the philosopher his life.[5] In the summer of 328 Anaxarchus was summoned to Alexander's presence to console the king in the aftermath of Cleitus' death.[6] He remained with the expedition through the Indian campaign,[7] and was among those who persuaded Alexander to enter Babylon in 323, despite the Chaldean warning to avoid the place.[8] We have no information about Anaxarchus in the period immediately following Alexander's death, although he cannot have survived Nicocreon, who died in 311–10.[9]

Anaxarchus' place in the history of Greek philosophy is as one of those associated with the transition between the school of Democritus and the rise of Epicureanism. He thus serves as a link between one of the most influential pre-Socratic schools and the rise of a cosmological and ethical system which would become [one] of the most popular in the Hellenistic and Roman eras. Anaxarchus' teacher was Diogenes of Smyrna, about whom very little is known.[10] Diogenes had studied under the influential Metrodorus of Chios, a pupil of Nessas of Chios, who trained with Democritus of Abdera himself.[11] Freeman pointed out[12] that it would be odd if Anaxarchus, a native of Abdera, should have to go abroad to study Democritean doctrines; yet there seems to have flourished along the Anatolian coast (Nessas and Metrodorus at Chios, and Diogenes at Smyrna) a lively group of Democriteans. Anaxarchus was joined by Pyrrho of Elis[13] who accompanied his teacher to India and back,[14] and later became an important Sceptic. Among Pyrrho's students was Nausiphanes of Teos (another Ionian), said to be a teacher of Epicurus[15].

One can, therefore, speak of a Democritean tradition having issued from Abdera with an important Ionian offshoot which carried through the fourth century and eventually helped train Epicurus. The modern histories of philosophy call this tradition variously the sceptical school, the atomist school, or the Democritean school. I am inclined to accept Guthrie's view[16] that we must not use 'School' in the formal sense (presumably as one would in the case of Plato or Aristotle), but rather as a description of a group of philosophers who transmitted Democritus' ideas as a basis of knowledge issuing from Abdera, each in turn training his students, and disseminating Democritean works. Thus, Anaxarchus is a link in a tradition of teacher–pupil relationships which lasted from the late fifth century down to the end of the fourth.

Few fragments of these philosophers exist, and we do not know the extent to which they were truly Democriteans. What does seem clear is that a tendency toward scepticism appeared rather early on in the 'school' and waxed. Anaxarchus seems to have shared in this sceptical attitude. Zeller pointed out that the sceptics denied every dogmatic position, believing that it was impossible to know that one external condition was preferable to another. Thus, one should pursue happiness (the goal of all philosophy) without reference to dogma. 'The real objective of this Scepticism is, therefore, a purely negative one — indifference.'[17] It will be seen that many of Anaxarchus' actions and words expressed at the court of Alexander reflected this sceptical attitude.

Athenaeus and Plutarch both refer to Anaxarchus as *eudaimonikos*, happy. Two references in Athenaeus are attributable as fragments of Hellenistic writers of biography, in one case (6.250F–251A) to Satyrus (*eudaimonikos philosophos*), the other (12.548B) to Clearchus of Soli (*eudaimonikos*). The text of Plutarch (*de Alex. fort.* 331E) is disputed, but almost certainly refers to Anaxarchus as eudaemonic.[18] But is eudaemonism a philosophical school? Diogenes Laertius (1.17) informs us that among the several schools of philosophy, some take their names from cities, some from nicknames, some from circumstances, some from their dispositions, such as the *Eudaimonikoi*. Is there such a thing as the 'Happiness School' of philosophy? In his subsequent discussion of the several schools (1.19–21), Diogenes mentions most of the famous schools, but makes no further reference to eudaemonism.

What we know of Anaxarchus' own training offers little information. His teacher, Diogenes of Smyrna, is little more than a shadow figure.[19] The fragments of Diogenes' teacher, Metrodorus of Chios, give us nothing on *eudaimonia*; they tell only of his extreme scepticism (agnosticism might be a more accurate description).[20] Yet eudaemonism, a philosophical commonplace, was indivisible from the Democritean tradition. Democritus himself had written a treatise *Peri Euthymies* (*On Cheerfulness*),[21] and a later tradition refers to him as *gelasinos*, the 'laughing' philosopher.[22] This must not be construed as a philosophy of hilarity; rather it is the art of moderation and cheerfulness, of living well (or as well as possible, since perfection in all matters is unknowable), and of exhibiting some indifference to the excesses of the world. It is a simple, undogmatic view which established Happiness as a refuge from not knowing for certain. So long as one followed the general pattern and held the general outlook, one was permitted a considerable latitude in developing a personal life style.

Thus Anaxarchus, identified as eudaemonic by the ancients, and as a sceptic by some modern commentators, was probably not an adherent to any rigid philosophical principle or system. His scepticism and eudaemonism were part of the Democritean tradition in which he was trained, although both aspects may well have described characteristics of his own temperament.

About Anaxarchus' own outlook and behavior we have more information, both from the traditions about him in the later writers of *Lives* and from the mainstream of the Alexander historians themselves. Perhaps the most telling comment about Anaxarchus is that he was said to be independent-minded in philosophy, and contemptuous of his associates.[23] It may have been this free spirit that commended Anaxarchus to Alexander, although whether as the most valuable of the king's friends, as Plutarch suggests (*de Alex, fort* 331E), or simply as entertainment in a court noted for its sociability, is open to question.[24] The personal characteristics of Anaxarchus about which all traditions agree are his wit, his scepticism and his eudaemonic outlook.

Possessing an independent mind and being unafraid to loose a sharp tongue, Anaxarchus chided the great and mean alike. We have already observed the circumstances of his insult to Nicocreon of Cyprus. With Alexander himself Anaxarchus was only slightly less acerbic. It was Anaxarchus who commented to the wounded monarch that it was blood, not ichor, that flowed from his veins.[25] On another occasion, on being pelted with apples thrown by Alexander during a dinner party, Anaxarchus retaliated with, 'One of the gods shall be struck by a mortal hand'.[26] And once when a great clap of thunder had terrified the party, Anaxarchus asked of Alexander, 'Could you, son of Zeus, thunder like that?' Alexander is said to have laughed and retorted: 'I do not wish to cause fear for my friends as you would have me do, you who hates my suppers because I supply the tables with fish, not the heads of satraps'.[27] One is, of course, tempted to put this incident at Tyre in 331, the famous dinner which produced Anaxarchus' insult to Nicocreon, but there is nothing here to insure such a chronology. The passage in Plutarch is a character study with no chronological context, and it is likely that the satrap's-head insult had become a favorite recollection at later feasts.

It is difficult to place absolute faith in the veracity of all these stories; but whatever the status of literal truth in these incidents the general contexts deserve credence. The frequent feasts and drinking parties formed the Macedonian version of the Athenian symposium, though less refined, more characterized by rough soldiers' talk and hard politics, and certainly more alcoholic. The Macedonian symposium was both a relief from the rigours of campaigning, and an outlet for the mental exercise of a court which, while not brilliant, had its charm.[28] The exercise of wit was prevalent, although it always ran the danger of becoming ugly if particular topics were treated indelicately, or if passions were aroused by too much unmixed wine. Anaxarchus would appear to be one of the continuing successes in this repartee. He had the king's confidence; his eudaemonic and sceptical outlook plus his lack of ties to any of the old-line established factions undoubtedly kept him from being considered a threat, and his acid comments were couched in the poetry of Homer and Euripides, an acceptable device on such occasions. He was, as it were, a high-level court jester, and what he said was forgivable and entertaining both because of who he was and the style in which he spoke. Politically safe and intellectually stimulating, Anaxarchus eventually emerged as one of the mainstays of the court.

While many of the accounts of Anaxarchus' activity at court tell of his wit, there was a serious side as well, also in keeping with his training in the Democritean tradition. Alexander is said to have wept upon hearing Anaxarchus speak of an infinite number of worlds, for he, Alexander, had not yet become master of even one.[29] Whatever one makes of Alexander's reply, the fact that Anaxarchus should speculate on innumerable worlds deserves credence; the subject was one of the speculative commonplaces of the period, an extension of basic atomist theory, one of whose leading proponents was Metrodorus of Chios, Anaxarchus' own teacher.[30] Anaxarchus, moreover, was characterized as a person of moderate temper who possessed the ability to bring others to their senses through reason.[31] It was through Anaxarchus' philosophical arguments that Alexander, upset and alarmed by the Chaldeans' warnings in 323 to avoid Babylon, was persuaded to disregard such prophecies and enter the city.[32] Thus, it would seem that both his wit and his serious demeanor helped endear him to Alexander who we are told honored Anaxarchus highly.[33]

A fragment of Satyrus (Athenaeus 6.250F–251A) calls Anaxarchus a flatterer (*kolax*), although one would be hard put to demonstrate that the witty insults directed at the king were flattery in the fawning sense. It has been suggested that Satyrus reflected a hostile Peripatetic view of Anaxarchus, a view made explicit by Clearchus of Soli, himself a disciple of Aristotle.[34] Clearchus condemned Anaxarchus' taste for luxury and his practice in later life of having his wine poured by a naked young girl of exceeding beauty (thus exhibiting Anaxarchus' lustful and corrupt nature), and of having his baker cover himself with gloves and mask in order to prevent sweat and breath from contaminating the dough. Both Clearchus and Satyrus were Peripatetics; this alone is thought to have made them hostile to Anaxarchus and his way of life.[35] Yet all that the evidence permits us to say is that both Clearchus and Satyrus wrote *Bioi*, and seemed interested (we can judge this only from scattered fragments) in the effect of fame, success and luxury on individuals. I suggest that the hostile Peripatetic view which attempted to contrast a dissolute Anaxarchus with (presumably) a virtuous Callisthenes goes further than the meager evidence will permit, and may, indeed, be a modern invention. Professor Badian laid to rest the 'Peripatetic tradition' as it related to Alexander,[36] and I see no reason why we should perpetuate it for the sake of Anaxarchus or, indeed, for anyone else. I myself have dealt elsewhere with the question of 'hostility' in Alexander sources,[37] and must reiterate that one should attribute a hostile attitude to an ancient author only with great care and unimpeachable evidence. The standards for measuring hostility are relative, both to the individual and to the spirit of the age.

Thus far this discussion has focused on Anaxarchus and his place in Alexander's court. Little has been said about Callisthenes, and it is not my intention to go over ground already well-covered by others.[38] Kinsman of Aristotle, and an established historian in his own right, Callisthenes of Olynthus joined the expedition to play Homer to Alexander's Achilles, and was ensconced as one of the leading intellectuals of the court. Not long into the Asian venture Callisthenes and Anaxarchus appear as rivals, a fact which should not surprise us as we have in recent years become increasingly aware of numerous jealousies and considerable intrigue among members of Alexander's entourage. Evidence for the conflict between Callisthenes and Anaxarchus may be summarized as follows:

1   After the murder of Cleitus, the grief-stricken Alexander plunged into deep mourning. His alarmed friends brought Callisthenes to him, but, using gentle methods, the philosopher/historian was unable to relieve the king's suffering. It was Anaxarchus' turn; by shaming and flattering the king he was able to rouse Alexander from his grief, while bringing royal disfavour upon Callisthenes.[39]

2   Diogenes Laertius (5.10) notes that Alexander was angry at Aristotle for having introduced Callisthenes into the court, and punished the famous philosopher by honoring *Anaximenes,* and sending gifts to Xenocrates. It is an odd story, and we are in doubt about its context. Pearson[40] suggests that by Anaximenes, Diogenes Laertius really meant *Anaxarchus*; this is an attractive idea, and the whole passage in Diogenes Laertius reflects traditions in Plutarch (*Alex.* 8 and *de Alex fort.* 331E). There is, however, nothing to suggest when (or if) Alexander became displeased with Aristotle because of the king's later dispute with Callisthenes, and it is, therefore, impossible to make any more sense of the story. But what Diogenes Laertius (or his source) recalls is the memory of a conflict between Callisthenes and Anaxarchus (if Pearson is correct), which serves as the cause of hostility felt by the king for Aristotle. This last may not deserve credence, but the *cause* is believable.

3   There is the case of the famous scene at which Callisthenes and Anaxarchus met in debate over the question of Alexander's divinity. It appears that an arrangement had been made between Alexander and the sophists that the question of *proskynesis* should be raised.[41] In Curtius' account Anaxarchus is not mentioned, and his place is taken by a certain Cleo. It is clear, however, that the Anaxarchus–Cleo figure is the same.[42] According to Arrian's account (4.10.5–11.9) Anaxarchus opened the discussion by suggesting that Alexander was more deserving of divinity than even Dionysus and Heracles. His fellow schemers agreed. Then Callisthenes interrupted the speeches and, addressing Anaxarchus directly, admonished him for taking such a stand, especially as he was attached to Alexander as a teacher and wise man (4.11.6). He continued in a moderate speech to argue against Alexander's divinity. Alexander was irritated by the turn of events, even though the rest of the Macedonians were pleased.

   Curtius' account of the debate is in substantial agreement with that of Arrian,[43] although some differences should be noted. Callisthenes' adversary is called Cleo by Curtius, and his speech favoring divinity is directed at Callisthenes. While the topic is prearranged in both accounts, Arrian has Alexander present during the debate and Curtius has the king leave the room just before Cleo (Anaxarchus) makes his opening remarks. Alexander then hid from view behind some curtains in order to hear the discussion.[44] In Curtius, as in Arrian, Callisthenes argued in direct discourse, addressing his opponent by name. In both versions of the speeches, Callisthenes suggested that Alexander himself would not want divinity, as it ran contrary to Macedonian custom.[45] Then follows the story that the guests rose one by one, drank from a common cup, prostrated themselves, and kissed Alexander. When it came Callisthenes' turn he drank from the cup and attempted to kiss the king, but one Demetrius announced that Callisthenes had failed to prostrate himself. Alexander refused the kiss, causing Callisthenes to remark, 'I shall go away poorer by a kiss'.[46]

4   The personal animosity between Callisthenes and Anaxarchus is the subject of an incident related by Plutarch (*Alex.* 52.8). The scene is a dinner; the conversation is about climate. Callisthenes' view that Asian weather was colder than Greek was vigorously opposed by Anaxarchus. Callisthenes responded by chiding Anaxarchus: 'You must admit that it is colder here than there; for there you would pass the winter in a *tribôn*, while here you recline at meals covered with three rugs'.[47] The incident is said to have increased the irritation of Anaxarchus.

5   (Plut. *Alex.* 52.7) Anaxarchus made himself very popular with Alexander, bringing
     into additional disfavor Callisthenes' relationship with the king, never very pleasant
     because of the philosopher's austerity.

It is clear that the sources have established a conflict between Callisthenes and
Anaxarchus. It remains to suggest an explanation for Anaxarchus' failure to appear in
Curtius, Diodoius and Justin until after Callisthenes' death, that is, why is there no
mention in these authors of Anaxarchus' feud with Callisthenes?[48] It may be because
they depended on a source for these incidents which did not mention Anaxarchus.
Ultimately this source may have been Callisthenes himself; it does not seem likely that
Callisthenes would have referred to a rival who finally succeeded in securing Alexander's
favor with the consequent loss of his own prestige. Conversely, the source for the
complete account of the Anaxarchus–Callisthenes feud found in Arrian and Plutarch
may be some non-Callisthenean tradition which was not averse to relating the details of
the conflict.

     Neither Curtius, nor Diodorus, nor Justin mentions Anaxarchus' role in consoling
Alexander immediately following the death of Cleitus.[49] It appears that Curtius may
have used an account of Cleitus based on Callisthenes (with its failure to mention
Anaxarchus). In his eulogy to Callisthenes later, using another source sympathetic to
Callisthenes, Curtius came across the incident of Callisthenes having saved Alexander's
life and included it only at this point.

     Both Justin and Diodorus mention Anaxarchus' role in persuading Alexander to
disregard the Chaldean warning about entering Babylon in 323 B.C.[50] Perhaps a common
source underlies this incident, but whoever it was, it was not the source used by Plutarch
and Arrian. Although the story of the warning is common to Plutarch and Arrian,[51]
Plutarch replaces Anaxarchus with Pythagoras, and Arrian mentions only the warning
and has Alexander reply to the Chaldeans by quoting a line from Euripides; there is no
reference to counselors.

     Thus we have two traditions on the role of Anaxarchus. One, that which Arrian and
Plutarch followed, described in some detail the growing antipathy between Anaxarchus
and Callisthenes which resulted in the latter's alienation from the king. The other
tradition, reflected in Curtius, Diodorus and Justin, failed to take note of any such feud.

     The feud is not writ large in the ancient literature. Those who wrote about Callisthenes
were primarily interested in the growing disaffection from the king which resulted in
his death, while those who mentioned Anaxarchus were largely concerned with his
eudaemonism, his wit, and the quality of indifference which characterized his last
moments.[52] This very lack of a full account of the rivalry permits only a tenuous
speculation about the relationship between the two men and, ultimately, about its effect
on Callisthenes' downfall.

     There are two features of the rivalry which permit some conjecture. The first is that
the antipathy between Callisthenes and Anaxarchus was in part due to a scholastic
rivalry. Hostility between philosophical schools and individual philosophers had been a
feature of intellectual life virtually since the beginning of systematic analysis and
presentation in sixth-century Ionia. Presumably Callisthenes was an Aristotelean,
although the fragments and testimonia about him offer no information about his
philosophical beliefs and methods. Moreover, the sources call him variously a
'philosopher' or 'sophist' without pattern or discrimination. Whatever the nature of his

training and philosophical views, Callisthenes' primary function was to serve Alexander as an historian, and it was in this capacity as a royal client, as well as because of his earlier reputation, that he has achieved his fame. As for Anaxarchus, it is problematic whether the loose nature of his sceptical indifference would have contributed to a formal scholastic rivalry with one whose Aristoteleanism may have been more a matter of kinship than of intellectual slavishness.[53] The evidence will not permit more than a suspicion that scholastic rivalry played much of a role in the animosity between the two men.

We are on firmer ground in suggesting that a personal rivalry characterized the relationship of Anaxarchus and Callisthenes. Part of this may have stemmed from basic differences in personality and habits: Callisthenes' austerity and Anaxarchus' propensity for luxury; Callisthenes' dour deportment and Anaxarchus' eudaemonism; Callisthenes' apparent adherence to certain ideas about the nature of the kingship and Anaxarchus' indifference and more cavalier treatment of politics in general.[54] An even more visible aspect of the rivalry was the competition for the king's favour. All the ancient sources agree that Callisthenes' downfall occurred both because of his unrelenting opposition to *proskynêsis* and Alexander's apotheosis, and his blunt manner of criticism.[55] One would err, however, to regard Callisthenes' undoing as a single stroke. Alexander's displeasure had grown over a period of time, and Anaxarchus seemed quick to exploit it for his own benefit.[56] Callisthenes became increasingly uncomfortable in a court full of flatterers;[57] he was disliked by them for having attracted young men on account of his eloquence, and older ones because of his austerity. He became a loner; rejected by the king in favor of the eudaemonic Anaxarchus, hated by his rivals because of his disapproval of their fawning servilitude toward Alexander, Callisthenes seemed to have emerged eventually as an outcast at court. It is no wonder that both Alexander and Callisthenes' detractors were ready to believe the worst about him when the 'Pages Conspiracy' (as much a conspiracy against Callisthenes as against Alexander) occurred in 327 B.C.[58]

Anaxarchus' name is nowhere linked with those who denounced Callisthenes. One searches in vain for some connection between Anaxarchus and the plot to remove Callisthenes. Anaxarchus' role in Callisthenes' downfall must be regarded as indirect. He benefited from Callisthenes' disgrace; he seems to have attempted to discredit Callisthenes in public; he was part of a group of 'sophists and flatterers' whose hostility toward the Olynthian helped precipitate Callisthenes' demise. But one must stop short of making any direct connection between Anaxarchus and the final scheme that cost Callisthenes his life; the evidence will not permit such a charge. Anaxarchus was undoubtedly a witness to the proceedings against Callisthenes; whether he was capable of active participation in the anti-Callisthenean plot is entirely problematic.

Anaxarchus survived, no mean feat in a court subject to increasingly brutal internal politics and to the ofttimes whimsical prejudices of the king. He apparently suffered no diminution of favour with Alexander, and was with the king to the end.[59] Later, after Alexander's death had deprived him of his royal patron's protection, he fell into the clutches of the long-memoried Nicocreon, and met his fate. Unprincipled in Callisthenean terms, the eudaemonic Anaxarchus suffered at the hands of later writers and propagandists. His end was grisly, but, with uncommon irony, the very indifference which made him seem base in Alexander's court, made him immortal in Nicocreon's. 'Pound the pouch of Anaxarchus; you pound not Anaxarchus'. Callisthenes' last words are nowhere recorded.

Notes

1 *Testimonia* on Anaxarchus is collected in Diels, *Frag. der Vorsokratikei*[5], No. 72. For present purposes the 11th edition of Diels by Walther Kranz (Zürich/Berlin, 1964) was used. The longest account of Anaxarchus from antiquity is in Diogenes Laertius 9.58–60; there are additional references in some of the traditional Alexander sources, in particular Plutarch, Arrian and Curtius, and notices scattered in a handful of other ancient writers. Among modern works is the succinct account of Kathleen Freeman, *The Pre-Socratic Philosophers*[3] (Oxford, 1953), 330–32, based on Diels' *Frag. der Vorsokr.*; see also, H. Berve, *Das Alexanderreich...*, II (Munich, 1926), no. 70. Kaerst's article in *RE*, I (1894), 2080, is abbreviated and of little value. On Anaxarchus' place in the history of Greek philosophy see E. Zeller, *A History of Greek Philosophy*, II, trans. S.F. Alleyne (London, 1881), 317–19, and *The Stoics, Epicureans and Sceptics,* rev. ed., trans. O.J. Reichel (reprint, New York, 1962), 518, and W.K.C. Guthrie, *A History of Greek Philosophy*, II (Cambridge, 1969), 382.

2 Diog. Laert. 9.59; also see Cic. *Tusc. Disp.* 2.22.52, and Diod. 19.59–79. The sources variously call Nicocreon king, satrap or tyrant of Salamis. It may be that Nicocreon's position was not understood, or that fourth-century traditions did not clearly distinguish among rulers' titles. On this last point see S.I. Oost, 'The Tyrant Kings of Syracuse', *Cl Phil* 71 (1976), 224–36, esp. 224–26.

3 Plut. *Alex.* 29, and *de Alex. fort.* 334E.

4 Berve, No. 568.

5 There is no direct evidence linking Anaxarchus with Nicocreon on this occasion, but Arrian (2.20.3 and 2.22.2) makes Nicocreon's father, Pyntagoras, Alexander's ally during the siege of Tyre in 332. Pyntagoras was killed in that battle (Arr. 2.22.2) or died shortly after, because in the following year Nicocreon showed up as ruler, and, undoubtedly anxious to please Alexander, was a sponsor in the dramatic competition. Although Diogenes Laertius (9.58–59) does not explicitly put Anaxarchus at this dinner, he does leave the impression that the insult to Nicocreon was direct. The scene is a banquet, and in response to an inquiry from Alexander about the quality of the feast, Anaxarchus expressed his general approval, suggesting only that the table would be improved if the head of some satrap were upon it. Diogenes states that this was directed at Nicocreon, who never forgot the insult. It would be hard to imagine that such an affront given *in absentia* would cut so deep; the scene suggests a personal remark delivered in person by one noted for a loose tongue, directed at Nicocreon, whose embarrassment promoted the hatred which resulted in Anaxarchus' grisly execution some years later.

6 Plut. *Alex.* 52.1–5 makes it clear that Alexander's friends summoned Anaxarchus; Arr. 4.9.5–7 mentions something of the nature of Alexander's friends' concern, but does not tell us who summoned Anaxarchus. Anaxarchus appears twice early in Plutarch's *Alex.* (9.4 and 28.2–3), but both passages are disquisitions on Alexander's character, and bear no relationship to the surrounding chronological context.

7 Diog. Laert. 9.61.

8 Diod. 17.112.4–5.

9 *Marm. Par.* B17 (311/10) in Jacoby, *FGrH,* No. 239; also see Diod. 20.21, with R.M. Geer's note in the Loeb edition.

10 Diels, No. 71.

11 Diels, No. 69, A1, 2; No. 70, A1; on the likelihood that Nessas brought Democritean doctrine to Chios see Freeman, p. 327, n. 1. The *Suda*, No. 447, *s.v. Dêmokritos* (ed. Adler), has the sequence of transmission conflated, and is of little value.

12 Freeman, p. 330.

13 Diog. Laert. 9.61–108; the *Suda*, No. 3238, *s.v. Pyrrôn* (ed. Adler); Berve, No. 682, and Zeller, *Stoics...*, pp. 514–27.

14 Diog. Laert. 9.61.

15 Diog. Laert. 9.61, and Diels, No. 75.

16 *Hist. of Gr. Phil.*, p. 382, n. 1.

17 Zeller, *Stoics...*, pp. 514, 525–26. Zeller (p. 518, n. 3) denied that Anaxarchus was a sceptic, yet he characterized Anaxarchus (p. 519, n. 3) as being far more indifferent about things than Democritus, and as having commended such indifference to his pupil, Pyrrho. If indifference is

a goal (and even a technique) of scepticism, then Anaxarchus qualifies as a sceptic by Zeller's own definition, although with so little evidence I am reluctant to press the definition too closely. For another story concerning Anaxarchus' indifference, see Diog. Laert. 9.63.

18 Here I follow Ménage's reading *eudaimonikon Anaxarchon*, rather than Babbit's *harmonikon Anaxarchon* in the Loeb edition; *q. v.*, Loeb *Moralia*, IV, p. 410, n. 1.

19 Diog. Laert. 9.58.

20 Diels, No. 70, B1.

21 Diog. Laert. 9.46; also see Diels, No. 68, B191 (Stob. III, 1, 210). This Democritean fragment suggests that *euthymia* can be achieved by moderation, contentment, and reasonable indifference to excess.

22 Juv. 10.33; Hor. *Ep.* 2.1.194.

23 Plut. *Alex.* 52.

24 There is a common tradition that Alexander was normally well disposed toward intellectuals in the court. Plutarch (*de Alex. fort.* 331E) speaks of Alexander's kindly attitude toward philosophers; in *Alex.* 9.4 there is a long digression on Alexander's education and his continuing yearning for 'philosophy', as evidenced by his warm feelings for Anaxarchus, Xenocrates (whom he is said to have offered fifty talents!), Dandamis and Calanus (*Alex.* 65.1 ff.). We may also recall the king's continuing interest in the Indian gymnosophists.

25 Diog. Laert. 9.60; the actual line about ichor is from the *Iliad*, 5.340. Plut. *Alex.* 28.2 also tells a version of the story, but has Alexander make the comment himself about his wound, without Anaxarchus' presence. But in the lines which follow immediately, Anaxarchus appears in two brief stories. One is tempted to suggest that it was Plutarch's error or oversight which failed to connect Anaxarchus to the ichor incident. Seneca (*Suas.* 15) has Callisthenes (!) make the comment about what flowed in the king's veins. It may in the end be impossible to make sense of this incident.

26 Plut. *Quaest. conviv.* 737A; the line is from Euripides (*Orestes* 271), the Macedonians' favorite playwright. Diog. Laert. (9.60) has Anaxarchus quote the line while raising his goblet to toast Alexander. Philodemus, *de vit.* 4 (Diels, No. 72, A7) has Anaxarchus threatening Alexander with his goblet.

27 Plut. *Alex.* 28.2–3; Athen. 6.250F–251A. See my 'The Symposium at Alexander's Court', forthcoming in *Archaia Macedonia,* III.

28 Some examples: Plut. *de Alex. fort.* 331–335.

29 Plut. *de tranq. anim.* 446D.

30 See F.M. Cornford, 'Innumerable Worlds in Pre-Socratic Philosophy', *Cl Quart* 28 (1934) 1–16, esp. p. 13. This scientific theory rests on a series of rhetorical proofs leading to a logical conclusion, and not on the observation of natural phenomena. One may suggest that this procedure marked Anaxarchus and his 'school' as different from Aristotle and his followers, but the point cannot be pressed.

31 Diog. Laert. 9.60.

32 Just. 12.13.5; Diod. 17.112.1–5. Diodorus (or his source) obviously approved of the victory of Greek reason over eastern sooth-saying.

33 Plut. *de Alex. fort.* 331E.

34 Athen. 7.275B.

35 For example, see J.R. Hamilton, *Plutarch: Alexander: A Commentary* (Oxford, 1969), 74–75.

36 E. Badian, 'The Eunuch Bagoas', *Cl Quart* N.S. 8 (1958) 154–56.

37 'Cleitarchus and Diodorus' Account of Alexander', *Proc. African Class. Assn.* 2 (1968), 36–43.

38 E.g., T.S. Brown, 'Callisthenes and Alexander', *Amer. Jour. Phil.* 70 (1949) 225–48; Lionel Pearson, *The Lost Histories of Alexander the Great* (New York, 1960) 22–49, *passim*; testimonia and fragmenta in F. Jacoby, *FGrH*, IIB, No. 153; also Berve, No. 408; for additional bibliography see J. Seibert, *Alexander der Grosse* (Darmstadt, 1972) 233–35, 285.

39 Arr. 4.9.7–9; Plut. *Alex.* 52.3–7.

40 *Lost. Hist.,* p. 244, n. 2. Also see Plut. *Alex.* 55.7, who speaks of Alexander's plan to punish those who sent Callisthenes to him (with Hamilton's commentary, *loc. cit.*).

41 Arr. 4.10.5; Curt. 8.5.10. I have also considered the possibility that the paired speeches in our sources may be a literary device used to illuminate some major issues at the court. The extent to which the use of such a literary technique may have influenced our understanding of both the

debate scenes and the protagonists is a complex issue which I hope to deal with at another time. A useful analysis of the *proskynêsis* debate is that of Lowell Edmunds, 'The Religiosity of Alexander the Great', *Gr. Rom. Byz. Stud.* 12 (1971) 386–90.

42 The name 'Anaxarchus' never appears in Curtius' text; see the note by J.C. Rolfe in the Loeb edition at 10.4.3.

43 Curt. 8.5.9–12.

44 J.P.V.D. Balsdon, 'The Divinity of Alexander the Great', *Historia* 1 (1950), 377, calls this story absurd.

45 Curt. 8.5.14; Arr. 4.11.4.

46 This incident occurs in Plut. *Alex.* 54.6 (Chares) and in Arr. 4.12.5. The versions are similar. Curtius does not mention the kiss, although the question of prostration by Persians alone occurs at the end of the account of the banquet at 8.5.22–24.

47 The *tribôn* was a simple, threadbare cloak worn by Spartans and by some philosophers as a sign of austerity. See Hamilton's commentary on the passage, *loc. cit.*

48 Unfortunately the great lacuna in Diodorus' text includes the period of the quarrel with Cleitus and the arrest and death of Callisthenes.

49 In his eulogy to Callisthenes Curtius (8.8.21–23) mentions that Callisthenes' death roused a great hatred of the king among the Greeks, not only because of the philosopher's noble nature and good works, but also because he had called Alexander back to life when the king was resolved to die after Cleitus' death. In his account of Alexander's mourning following the murder of Cleitus, however, Curtius fails to mention Callisthenes (8.2.11–12).

50 Just. 12.13.5; Diod. 17.112.4–5. Curtius' text is broken at this point.

51 Arr. 7.16.5–8; Plut. *Alex.* 73.1–2; also see Hamilton's commentary, *loc. cit.*

52 Everything we know about the Callisthenes–Anaxarchus rivalry rests mainly on two sources: Arrian and Plutarch. Diogenes Laertius (5.10), who hints at the rivalry, but may not have understood it, derived at least some of his information about Anaxarchus from Plutarch; see D.L. 9.60.

53 For a discussion of scholastic rivalry in the fourth and third centuries see Felix Grayeff, *Aristotle and his School* (London, 1974), pp. 57–68. For Athenian schools in particular, see John P. Lynch, *Aristotle's School. A Study of a Greek Educational Institution* (Berkeley and Los Angeles, 1972), pp. 47–67.

54 Although see note 58 below.

55 E.g., Jacoby, *FGrH*, no. 124, TI, 7, 8, 18ff., F5, 6. It is not my intention to trace in detail the prosecution of Callisthenes beyond his relationship with Anaxarchus. For full accounts of Callisthenes' end see note 38 above.

56 E.g., Plut. *Alex.* 53.7.

57 Curt. 8.8.21–22; Plut. *Alex.* 23.7–08; also see *Mor.* 65 C–E for the flatterers, although Anaxarchus himself is not mentioned. For an analysis of the flatterers' activities see Peter Green, *Alexander of Macedon* (Harmondsworth, 1974), pp. 374–5.

58 Arr. 4.12.7; Plut. *Alex.* 55.1–2.

59 Green (pp. 452, 457, 549 n. 12) argues that Anaxarchus continued to maintain an important role at court as a flatterer and propagandist for Alexander's projects and activity. It is an attractive idea, although I am inclined to use the evidence more cautiously pending a closer prosopographical analysis of the court intelligentsia.

12

ALEXANDER:
THE 'GREAT'?

Introduction

Alexander III is called 'Great' for many reasons: in little more than a decade he journeyed further than any single person before him (on distances, see Sources 1, 36, 37; cf. 60), he defeated opposing forces on a vast scale, he established a huge empire which stretched from Greece in the west to India in the east, he spread Greek culture and education in that empire, he stimulated trade and the economy, he died young (Source 84), and had he lived he would have embarked on a campaign to Arabia. Even the Romans (apparently) sent an embassy to him in recognition of his achievements and stature (Sources 12 and 115). There is no question that Alexander was a brilliant general, strategist and tactician; however, he was not merely a general; he was also a king. As such, it is necessary to consider the entire 'package' of him as king, general and statesman. When we do so, we see there is a downside to Alexander's reign and to him as a man, aspects of which have been outlined in the works of some modern scholars in the preceding chapters, and that there is a great difference between the mythical Alexander, in other words the image we have today, and the historical.

In part, the mythical Alexander is due to the nature of our source material and Alexander's own propaganda, which make any objective evaluation of him difficult (cf. Source 1).[1] At the same time, there has been a tendency to accept the 'greatness' of Alexander at face value because of what he achieved in the military sphere or was said to have done. As has been said, Alexander's military abilities are beyond question,[2] yet let us not forget that his army mutinied on him twice (cf. Source 76), that his march through the Gedrosian desert was a dreadful and costly mistake (Sources 77–80), and that he often put himself in peril without thought as to who would lead his army were he to die (Sources 11, 23, 70 and 71) – and certainly the Macedonians made it plain that they needed Alexander as leader in the Far East (cf. Arr. 6.12.1–3). His preference for constant warfare rather than long-term administration and his failure to provide an heir resulted in confusion as to his successor (cf. Source 93 – who was 'the best'?), and his empire exploding on his death in 323 in a three-decades long bloody civil war waged by his generals. The Macedonian throne in that time became a prize in the wars of his successors, and stability was not restored to it until the Antigonid dynasty firmly took root in the 280s.

Conspiracies were hatched either against Alexander by others or by him because of his paranoia,[3] and he was held in fear by those with him (Source 105). There was reaction against him among his people on the mainland, especially over his megalomania that led to his belief in his own divinity.[4] Alexander's excessive drinking not only wasted his body but also clouded his reason on occasions (Sources 59, 85–90, 117–119), and it was a criticism levelled against him by a contemporary author (see Source 117). At the same time, it must be said that Alexander was never incapacitated by alcohol when it mattered, such as in battle or indeed planning campaigns. He drank copiously at symposia and other parties, but it was acceptable to do so at such gatherings. Yet it was alcohol that led to his murdering Cleitus. As a man, let alone a king, Alexander can thus be found failing to live up to any heroic ideal or code of honour as exemplified by those on whom he modelled himself.

The question is raised whether Alexander knew anything else but conquering, in itself echoing what Quintus Curtius Rufus at 6.2.1 writes: 'Alexander could cope better with warfare than peace and leisure'. This might not be completely true, as it has been shown (in Chapter 6) that Alexander was concerned with the administration of his empire. However, his thirst for fighting and ambition were continuous (cf. Source 116), and he showed no sign of bringing his campaigning to an end, for he was prepared to invade Arabia when he died (cf. Sources 106 and 116). With the new army that he had created and new sights that he was setting himself, one wonders if he would have ever stopped, and how different Macedonian kingship would become from what it was traditionally. Perhaps it is hardly a surprise that the empire he created came to a end, and not just because Alexander did not properly provide an heir for it. Macedonia became a shadow of its former self, a stark contrast to how Philip had left it for his son in 336. Hence the legacies of Philip and of Alexander must be borne in mind in any assessment of Alexander as king,[5] and a question that a modern scholar posed should be considered carefully: was Alexander 'his own greatest achievement'?[6]

Ancient sources

Alexandria

114   In his desire to overtake Darius he started in his pursuit. But again he came to Egypt and saw a site naturally suited for the erection of a city. He wanted to build one; at once he ordered his architects to trace the circuit of the city to be founded. But as they had no clay to do so, he happened to see a threshing-floor with wheat on it and ordered them to place the grains around and use them instead of clay in marking he circuit. They did so. The following night fowls came and picked up the grain. This seemed to be a sign: some said it portended ill (the city to be founded would be captured); Alexander however said it was a good omen (though it was made clear that many would be fed by that city) and at once built a large city there, which he called Alexandria, after his own name. Then he advanced in pursuit of Darius (*Anonymous History of Alexander*, *FGrH* 151 F 11).

Alexander and Rome's greatness

115   Of the men who have written the history of Alexander, Aristus and Asclepiades alone say that the Romans also sent an embassy to him, and that when he met their embassy, he predicted something of the future power of Rome, observing both the attire of the men, their love of labour, and their devotion to freedom. At the same time, he made urgent enquiries about their political constitution. This incident I have recorded neither as certainly authentic nor as altogether incredible; but none of the Roman

writers have made any mention of this embassy ... nor of those who have written an account of Alexander's actions, has either Ptolemy, son of Lagus (*FGrH* 138 F 29), or Aristobulus (*FGrH* 139 F 53) mentioned it (Aristus, *FGrH* 143 F 2 = Arr. 7.15.5).[7]

'Insatiably ambitious'?

116   Aristobulus says that he found at Babylon the fleet with Nearchus, which had sailed from the Persian Sea up the river Euphrates; and another which had been conveyed from Phoenicia ... Near Babylon he made a harbour by excavation large enough to afford anchorage to 1,000 ships of war; and adjoining the harbour he made dock-yards. Miccalus the Clazomenian was despatched to Phoenicia and Syria with 500 talents to enlist some men and to purchase others who were experienced in naval matters. For Alexander designed to colonize the seaboard near the Persian Gulf, as well as the islands in that sea. For he thought that this land would become no less prosperous than Phoenicia. He made these preparations of the fleet to attack the main body of the Arabs, under the pretext that they were the only barbarians of this region who had not sent an embassy to him or done anything becoming their position and showing respect to him. But the truth was, it seems to me, that Alexander was insatiably ambitious of ever acquiring fresh territory (Aristobulus, *FGrH* 139 F 55 = Arr. 7.19.3–6).

'The things ... that are not good'?

117   The things about Alexander that are not good. They say that on the fifth of the month Dius he drank at Eumaeus', then on the sixth he slept from the drinking; and as much of that day as he was fresh, rising up, he did business with the officers about the morrow's journey, saying that it would be early. And on the seventh he was a guest at Perdiccas' and drank again; and on the eighth he slept. On the fifteenth of the same month he also slept, and on the following day he did the things customary after drinking. On the twenty-fourth he dined at Bagoas'; the house of Bagoas was ten stades from the palace; the on the twenty-eighth he was at rest. Accordingly one of two conclusions must be true, either that Alexander hurt himself badly by drinking so many days in the month or that those who wrote these things lie. And so it is possible to keep in mind henceforth that the group of which Eumenes is a member ... makes such statements (*Ephemerides*, *FGrH* 117 F 2a = Aelian, *Varra Historia* 3.23).

118   Alexander also drank a very great deal, so that after the spree he would sleep continuously for two days and two nights. This is revealed in his *Ephemerides* written by Eumenes of Cardia and Diodotus of Erythrae (*Ephemerides*, *FGrH* 117 F 2b = Athen. 10.434b).[8]

119   Aristobulus does not say whence the drunken quarrel originated, but asserts that the fault was entirely on the side of Cleitus, who, when Alexander had got so enraged with him as to jump up against him with the intention of making an end of him, was led away by Ptolemy, son of Lagus, the confidential bodyguard, through the gateway, beyond the wall and ditch of the citadel where the quarrel occurred. He adds that Cleitus could not control himself, but went back again, and falling in with Alexander who was calling out for Cleitus, he exclaimed: 'Alexander, here am I, Cleitus!' Thereupon he was struck with a long pike and killed (Aristobulus, *FGrH* 139 F 29 = Arr. 4.8.9).

Modern works

In the following selections, the late N.G.L. Hammond, formerly Professor of Greek at the University of Bristol, lauds Alexander and his achievements, and so gives us the 'rosy' image of the king that many people have today. While acknowledging Alexander's achievements, Ian Worthington, Professor of History at the University of Missouri, examines the comparison of Diodorus and Justin on Philip and Alexander, and argues that they held Philip in higher esteem that Alexander and thought him to be the better king; as a result, the epithet 'Great' gives a false impression of the historical Alexander.

1   N.G.L. Hammond, *Alexander the Great: King, Commander and Statesman*[2] (Bristol Classical Press: 1989), pp. 269–273 and 306 (notes).[9]
2   Ian Worthington, 'Worldwide Empire vs Glorious Enterprise: Diodorus and Justin on Philip II and Alexander the Great', in E.D. Carney and D. Ogden (eds), *Philip II and Alexander the Great: Lives and Afterlives* (Oxford University Press: 2010), pp. 165–174 (notes on pp. 289–291).[10]

Additional reading

J.E. Atkinson, 'On Judging Alexander: A Matter of Honour', *Acta Classica* 50 (2007), pp. 15–27.

E. Badian, 'Alexander the Great and the Loneliness of Power', in E. Badian, *Studies in Greek and Roman History* (Oxford: 1964), pp. 192–205 (reprinted in Chapter 11).

——, 'Alexander the Great and the Scientific Exploration of the Oriental Part of his Empire', *Ancient Society* 22 (1991), pp. 127–138.

——, 'Conspiracies', in A.B. Bosworth and E.J. Baynham (eds), *Alexander the Great in Fact and Fiction* (Oxford: 2000), pp. 50–95.

R. Billows, *Kings and Colonists* (Leiden: 1995), pp. 183–212.

A.B. Bosworth, 'Alexander the Great and the Decline of Macedon', *Journal of Hellenic Studies* 106 (1986), pp. 1–12.

——, 'Alexander and the Iranians', *Journal of Hellenic Studies* 100 (1980), pp. 1–21 (reprinted in Chapter 9).

——, *The Legacy of Alexander. Politics, Warfare and Propaganda under the Successors* (Oxford: 2002).

E.D. Carney, 'The Death of Clitus', *Greek, Roman, and Byzantine Studies* 22 (1981), pp. 149–160.

——, 'Macedonians and Mutiny: Discipline and Indiscipline in the Army of Philip and Alexander', *Classical Philology* 91 (1996), pp. 19–44.

——, 'Women in Alexander's Court', in J. Roisman (ed.), *Brill's Companion to Alexander the Great* (Leiden: 2003), pp. 227–252.

E.A. Fredricksmeyer, 'Alexander's Religion and Divinity', in J. Roisman (ed.), *Brill's Companion to Alexander the Great* (Leiden: 2003), Chap. 10, pp. 253–278 (reprinted in Chapter 10).

D.L. Gilley and Ian Worthington, 'Alexander the Great, Macedonia and Asia', in J. Roisman and Ian Worthington (eds), *The Blackwell Companion to Ancient Macedonia* (Oxford: 2010), pp. 186–207.

N.G.L. Hammond, 'The Macedonian Imprint on the Hellenistic World', in P. Green (ed.), *Hellenistic History and Culture* (Berkeley & Los Angeles 1993), pp. 12–23.

W. Heckel, 'King and "Companions": Observations on the Nature of Power in the Reign of Alexander', in J. Roisman (ed.), *Brill's Companion to Alexander the Great* (Leiden: 2003), pp. 197–225.

——, 'Alexander the Great and the "Limits of Civilised World"', in W. Heckel and L. Tritle (eds), *Crossroads of History, The Age of Alexander* (Claremont: 2003), pp. 147–174 (reprinted in Chapter 3).

F.L. Holt, 'The Hyphasis Mutiny: A Source Study', *Ancient World* 5 (1982), pp. 33–59.

——, 'Alexander the Great Today: In the Interests of Historical Accuracy?', *Ancient History Bulletin* 13.3 (1999), pp. 111–117.

——, 'The Death of Coenus', *Ancient History Bulletin* 14.1–2 (2000), pp. 49–55.

S. Müller, 'In the Shadow of his Father: Alexander, Hermolaus, and the Legend of Philip', in E.D. Carney and D. Ogden (eds), *Philip II and Alexander the Great: Lives and Afterlives* (Oxford: 2010), pp. 25–32.

J. Roisman, 'Honor in Alexander's Campaigns', in J. Roisman (ed.), *Brill's Companion to Alexander the Great* (Leiden: 2003), pp. 279–321.

B. Strauss, 'Alexander: The Military Campaign', in J. Roisman (ed.), *Brill's Companion to Alexander the Great* (Leiden: 2003), pp. 133–156.

L. Tritle, 'Alexander and the Killing of Cleitus the Black', in W. Heckel and L.A. Tritle (eds), *Crossroads of History. The Age of Alexander* (Claremont: 2003), pp. 127–146.

C.B. Welles, 'Alexander's Historical Achievement', *Greece and Rome*² 12 (1965), pp. 216–228.

Ian Worthington, 'How "Great" was Alexander?', *Ancient History Bulletin* 13.2 (1999), pp. 39–55.

——, 'Alexander the Great and the "Interests of Historical Accuracy": A Reply', *Ancient History Bulletin* 13.4 (1999), pp. 136–140.

——, 'Alexander the Great, Nation-building, and the Creation and Maintenance of Empire', in V.D. Hanson (ed.), *Makers of Ancient Strategy: From the Persian Wars to the Fall of Rome* (Princeton: 2010), pp. 118–137 (reprinted in Chapter 6).

Notes

1 On the sources and the problems associated with the source material, see Chapter 1.
2 See Chapter 4.
3 See Chapter 11 on conspiracies.
4 See Chapter 10.
5 On Philip, see Chapter 2. On legacies and differences, cf. Ian Worthington, *Philip II of Macedonia* (New Haven and London: 2008), pp. 194–208, and the reprinted articles below.
6 C.B. Welles, 'Alexander's Historical Achievement', *G&R*² 12 (1965), p. 228.
7 See also Source 12, where an embassy from Rome is queried.
8 On Alexander's drinking, see also Sources 85–90 and 117–119.
9 Reprinted by permission of Bloomsbury.
10 Reprinted by permission of Oxford University Press.

AS A PERSONALITY

N.G.L. Hammond

Ancient and modern writers have studied various aspects of Alexander's personality. His sexual life, for instance, has been the subject of wild speculation. Some have supposed that his closeness to his mother and his continence in the presence of Darius' mother, wife, and daughters were signs of sexual impotence; others just the opposite, that he travelled with a harem which provided him with a different girl each night of the year; and others that he had homosexual affairs with herds of eunuchs, Hephaestion, Hector, and a Persian boy. The truth is not attainable nor of much importance; for in the Macedonian court homosexual and heterosexual attachments were equally reputable, and the sexual life of Philip, for instance, seems to have had no effect on his achievements in war and politics. Disappointingly for sensationalist writers Alexander's relations with women seem to have been normal enough for a Macedonian king: three or four wives at the age of thirty-two and two or perhaps three sons – Heracles by Barsine, widow of the Rhodian Memnon and daughter of the Persian Artabazus (P. 21.7–9 and Plut. Eum. 1 fin.; C. 10.6.11–13; J. 13.2.7; Suidas s.v. Antipatros); by the Bactrian Roxane a boy who died in infancy (*Epit. Metz* 70) and a boy born after Alexander's death, who became Alexander IV.[1]

Alexander's relations with his parents have been interpreted in differing ways. Some have held him guilty of patricide, planned in advance with the connivance of his mother; others have pictured him publicly disowning his 'so-called father,' Philip; and others have made him praise the services of Philip to his country and plan to raise a gigantic memorial over Philip's tomb. If we consider these matters from the viewpoint not of the twentieth century but of the fourth century BC, we should note that patricide, being the most heinous crime in Greek religion, was hardly conceivable in a man of strong religious faith; that to believe one was the son of a god was not to disown one's human father (whether Amphitryon or Joseph); and that praise of Philip was natural in every Macedonian and not least in the successor to his throne. Indeed if the first unplundered tomb at Vergina is that of Philip, as I believe, its unparalleled splendour is a measure of Alexander's affection for and admiration of his father. He was always loving and loyal to his mother, Olympias. Her tears meant more to him than any triumph, and in taking her side he endangered his own chances of the succession to the throne. When he went to Asia, he made her guardian of the kingship and his representative in the performance of state religion and ceremonial in Macedonia, and he sent to her, partly in that capacity, his regular despatches and a part of the spoils of war. As son and king, he seems to have had full control over her.[2]

In the course of the narrative we have described many facets of Alexander's personality: his deep affections, his strong emotions, his reckless courage, his brilliance and quickness of mind, his intellectual curiosity, his love of glory, his competitive spirit, his acceptance of every challenge, his generosity and his compassion; and on the other hand his overweening ambition, his remorseless will, his passionate indulgence in unrestrained emotion, his inexorable persistence, and his readiness to kill in combat, in passion, and in cold blood and to have rebellious communities destroyed. In brief, he had many of the qualities of the noble savage. What is left to consider is the mainspring of his personality, his religious sense. The background is essential. Members of the Macedonian royal house worshipped the Olympian gods of orthodox Greek religion in the orthodox way; participated in the ecstatic religions of Orpheus, Dionysus, and the Cabiri (in Samothrace); consulted oracles, apparently with credulity, for instance of Zeus Ammon at Aphytis in Chalcidice, Apollo at Delphi, and Trophonius at Lebadea in Boeotia; and believed in omens and their interpreters. Further, they had at Aegeae and Pella their particular worship of Heracles Patroüs as their heroic ancestor and semidivine exemplar; for Heracles himself was a 'son of god,' even of Zeus.

To emulate, even to surpass his father Philip, or the conquering prototype, Cyrus the Great; to rival the journeys and achievements of Heracles and Dionysus; and in his turn to win 'divine honours', was probably Alexander's youthful ambition. Europe had been the scene of Philip's triumphs, and Italy was to be invaded by the Molossian Alexander; so Asia was the continent for Alexander. But would the gods give it to him? As he landed in the Troad Alexander gave expression to his faith: 'from the gods I accept Asia, won by the spear.' He reaffirmed this after his victory at Gaugamela, when he dedicated spoils as 'Lord of Asia' in thanksgiving to Athena of Lindus and wrote to Darius, 'the gods give Asia to me.' And in the end he was to see himself, and others – even the remote Libyans – were to see him as 'King of all Asia' (A. 7.15.4; *Ind*. 35.8).

But in 334 BC, he must have asked himself whether he was indeed a 'son of god,' capable of such heroic achievement. The answers came unambiguously from oracles and priests in whose words he had belief: in 332 BC the priests of Egypt greeted him as 'Son of Ra'; the priest of Ammon at Siwah probably led him and certainly led others to think he was 'Son of Ammon,' and then the shrines of Didyma and Erythrae declared him to be a 'Son of Zeus.' It was tempting to put such faith to the test, and his prayer at Gaugamela did so. The victory there reassured him that he was indeed 'descended from Zeus.'

Many signs and wonders – some self-evident, others interpreted by seers – showed that the gods were on his side. There is no doubt that he and his men believed in them implicitly. We must remember that Alexander's preferred readings were the Iliad, the plays of the three great tragedians, and dithyrambic poetry, in all of which the gods revealed their purposes to men in a variety of ways – signs and wonders being among them.[3] Of those which happened to Alexander Arrian, drawing on Ptolemy and Aristobulus, mentions the following: the swallow at Halicarnassus, the knot at Gordium untied by the future 'ruler of Asia,' the thunder and lightning there, the dream before the attack on Tyre, the bird of prey at Gaza, the grain marking the bounds of Alexandria, the rain and the crows on the way to Siwah, the soaring eagle at Gaugamela, the adverse omen at the Jaxartes, the Syrian clairvoyant in Bactria, the springs of oil and water by the Oxus, and the oracle of Belus (Ba'al) before the entry into Babylon (A. 7.16.5–17.6). Even when death was overshadowing him Alexander might have said, like old Oedipus, 'in all the signs the gods themselves have given me, they never played me false.'

The gods were the authors also of all success in the opinion of Alexander (Plut. *Mor.* 343B), and to them he gave the credit and the thanks. He was constantly engaged in religious acts; he sacrificed every morning of his adult life, on any evening of carousal with his Companions, on starting any enterprise, crossing any river, entering battle, celebrating victory, and expressing gratitude. He was more self-effacing in his devoutness than his father. For example, whereas Philip had portrayed himself on his coins taking the salute, probably at a victory parade, and advertising his successes at the Olympic games, Alexander showed gods only on his regular coin issues. In the famous sculptures of Alexander by Lysippus he was represented with a melting and liquid softness of the eyes 'looking up towards the heavens,' and this was interpreted at the time as looking up towards Zeus, from whom his inspiration came. In his early years, for instance on landing in Asia, he paid special honour to Athena Alcidemus (the Macedonian war-goddess who protected Philip and Alexander according to Pliny NH 35.114),[4] Zeus the King ('of gods and men') and Heracles, ancestor of the royal house; and throughout his reign he showed them, and them alone, on his gold and silver coins. It is only on the Porus medallion that the figure of Alexander appeared: diminutive in a symbolic combat. On the reverse his face is not thrown into relief. [. . .]

After the pilgrimage to Siwah he put Zeus Ammon, or Ammon of the Libyans (in contrast to Ammon at Aphytis), or just Ammon on the same level as Athena, Zeus, and Heracles in his regard; for instance, on meeting Nearchus he called to witness 'Zeus of the Greeks' and 'Ammon of the Libyans' (*Ind.* 35.8). The thunderbolt which is carried by Alexander on the Porus medallion was probably the weapon of Zeus Ammon, with which he had armed Alexander to win the Kingdom of Asia. In the paintings by Apelles, Alexander was portrayed wielding the thunderbolt, probably as King of Asia. It was the oracle of Zeus Ammon, not an oracle in Greece, that Alexander consulted about the honouring of Hephaestion, and at the mouth of the Indus, for instance, he made two sets of sacrifices with the rituals and to the gods prescribed by the oracle of Ammon.

He sacrificed occasionally to other non-Greek deities, such as Tirian Melkart (identified with Heracles), Apis and Isis in Egypt, and Belus (Ba'al) in Babylon, whose temple he intended to rebuild. And his readiness to turn to Greek and non-Greek gods alike for help is shown by his consulting not only Greek seers but also those of Egypt, Persia (the Magi), and Babylon (the Chaldaeans). It was no doubt because of his faith in these divine powers that during his last illness Sarapis was consulted; that his corpse was embalmed by Egyptians and Chaldaeans; and that the ram's horn, the emblem of Ammon, was added to the head or Alexander on the coins of Lysimachus. It is evident that Alexander did not think in terms of his national gods defeating those of other races, as the Greeks and the Hebrews for instance had done; rather he was ready to accord respect and worship to the gods of other peoples and to find in some of those gods an excellence equal to that of the Macedonian and Greek gods.

That Alexander should grow up with a sense of mission was certainly to be expected. For he was descended from Zeus and Heracles, he was born to be king, he had the career of Philip as an exemplar, and he was advised by Isocrates, Aristotle, and others to be a benefactor of Macedonians and Greeks alike. His sense of mission was inevitably steeped in religious associations, because from an early age he had been associated with the king, his father, in conducting religious ceremonies, and he was imbued with many ideas of orthodox religion and of ecstatic mysteries. Thus two observations by Plutarch (*Mor.* 342 A and F) have the ring of truth. 'This desire (to bring all men into an orderly system under a single leadership and to accustom them to one way of life) was implanted in Alexander from childhood and grew up with him'; and on crossing the Hellespont to the Troad Alexander's first asset was 'his reverence towards the gods.' Already by then he planned to found a Kingdom of Asia, in which he would rule over the peoples, as Odysseus had done, 'like a kindly father' (*Odyssey* 5.11). He promoted the fulfilment of that plan 'by founding Greek cities among savage peoples and by teaching the principles of law and peace to lawless, ignorant tribes.' When he had completed the conquest of 'Asia' through the favour of the gods and especially that of Zeus Ammon, he went on to establish for all men in his kingdom 'concord and peace and partnership with one another' (*Mor.* 329 F).

This was a practical development, springing from a religious concept and not from a philosophical theory (though it led later to the philosophical theory of the Cynics, who substituted for Asia the whole inhabited world and talked of the brotherhood of all men), and it came to fruition in the banquet at Opis, when he prayed in the presence of men of various races for 'concord and partnership in the ruling' of his kingdom 'between Macedonians and Persians.'

What distinguishes Alexander from all other conquerors is this divine mission. He had grown up with it, and he had to a great extent fulfilled it, before he gave expression to it at the banquet at Opis in such words as those reported by Plutarch (*Mor.* 329 C). 'Alexander considered,' wrote Plutarch, 'that he had come from the gods to be a general governor and reconciler of the world. Using force of arms when he did not bring men together by the light of reason, he harnessed all resources to one and the same end, mixing the lives, manners, marriages and customs of men, as it were in a loving-cup.' This is his true claim to be called 'Alexander the Great': that he did not crush or dismember his enemies, as the conquering Romans crushed Carthage and Molossia and dismembered Macedonia into four parts; nor exploit, enslave or destroy the native peoples, as 'the white man' has so often done in America, Africa, and Australasia; but that he created, albeit for only a few years, a supra-national community capable of living internally at peace and of developing the concord and partnership which are so sadly lacking in the modern world.

Notes

1 See the first edition of this volume n. 114 for ancient evidence for and against Alexander being given to paederasty, which was the normal form of homosexual relationship in Greek antiquity (rather than between consenting adults). Statements about his heterosexual practices varied in ancient authors from near-impotence to gross excess. Modern authors have indulged in similar speculations, notably M. Renault, *The Nature of Alexander* (1975).
2 She probably held the *prostasia*; see Hammond, *A* 474 ff. and *HM* 3.90 f.
3 P. 8.2–3.
4 The head of this Athena was represented on the iron helmet in Philip's tomb at Vergina; see M. Andronikos in *AAA* 10 (1977) 47 and *Vergina* 141.

References

Andronikos, *Vergina* = M. Andronikos, *Vergina: The Royal Tombs* (Athens: 1984).
Hammond, *A* = N.G.L. Hammond, 'Some passages in Arrian concerning Alexander', CQ2 30 (1980), pp. 455–476.
Hammond, *HM* = N.G.L. Hammond and F.W. Walbank, *A History of Macedonia 3* (Oxford: 1988).

'WORLDWIDE EMPIRE' VERSUS 'GLORIOUS ENTERPRISE': DIODORUS AND JUSTIN ON PHILIP II AND ALEXANDER THE GREAT

Ian Worthington

At the end of his comparison of the good and bad qualities of Philip II and Alexander III (the Great) of Macedonia, Justin has this to say: *Quibus artibus orbis imperii fundamenta pater iecit, operis totius gloriam filius consummauit* – 'with such qualities did the father lay the basis for a worldwide empire and the son bring to completion the glorious enterprise' (9.8.21).[1] At first sight the quotation is an apt summary of the key achievements of their reigns. From disunited chaos, economic ruin, and military weakness, Philip II (r. 359–36) turned Macedonia into the super-power of the fourth century, established an empire, created a first-class army (and an engineering *corps* that pioneered the torsion catapult), and framed the plans for the invasion of Asia.[2] Alexander built on his father's legacy and in little over a decade as king (r. 336–23) he brought the planned invasion of Asia to spectacular fruition. On his death in 323, the Macedonian empire, stretching from Greece to India (modern Pakistan), was as close to worldwide as one could get in antiquity.

It is easy to understand why Alexander has come to be the household name he is, in his time and down to the present day, and why he is the subject of far more books than Philip (although the paucity of ancient evidence that we have today for Philip, compared to Alexander, is a factor).[3] Philip lives in the shadow of his famous son, given that he did not wage anything like the spectacular battles and sieges that Alexander did, and while Philip did more for the actual kingdom of Macedonia than any of its other kings, he did not oversee a Macedonian empire that was as expansive as that of Alexander. The difference between the reigns of these two kings is apparently also reflected in how ancient writers saw them. In the case of Philip, we have only two narrative sources for his reign, Diodorus (book 16), of the first century B.C., and Justin (book 7.6–9), himself writing in later imperial times, but who epitomized Pompeius Trogus' *Historiae Philippicae,* which was also written in the first century B.C.[4] Philip is praised for such things as his diplomatic and military skills, his achievements in Macedonia, and the reorganization of the army, but our ancient writers seem to wax the more lyrical over Alexander in their narratives of his reign, principally for his spectacular exploits in Asia, as the opening quotation indicates.[5]

It is the contention of this paper, however, that the impression that Diodorus and Justin favor Alexander is a misleading one. It can be argued that Justin's lengthy comparison of the two kings (9.8) and Diodorus' personal comments on Philip (16.95) and Alexander (17.117) actually elevate Philip over Alexander, not the other way around. This view has implications about the standards on which they based their evaluations, especially in light of the Roman perceptions of Alexander at the time when they were writing, and by extension it further distances Diodorus from being merely a summarizer of his sources, especially Ephorus.[6] Further, it plays a role in how we today ought to view Philip and Alexander.

I begin with Justin 9.8, a comparison of Philip and Alexander made at the end of his narrative of Philip's reign:

(1) Philip … was a king with more enthusiasm for the military than the convivial sphere; (5) in his view his greatest treasures were the tools of warfare. (6) He had a greater talent for acquiring wealth than keeping it, and thus despite his daily pillaging he was always short of funds. (7) His compassion and his duplicity were qualities which he prized equally, and no means of gaining a victory would he consider dishonourable. (8) He was charming and treacherous at the same time, the type to promise more in conversation than he would deliver, and whether the discussion was serious or lighthearted he was an artful performer. (9) He cultivated friendships with a view to expediency rather than from genuine feelings. His usual practice was to feign warm feelings when he hated someone, to sow discord between parties that were in agreement and then try to win the favour of both. (10) Besides this he was possessed of eloquence and a remarkable oratorical talent, full of subtlety and ingenuity, so that his elegant style was not lacking fluency nor his fluency lacking stylistic elegance. (11) Philip was succeeded by his son Alexander, who surpassed his father both in good qualities and bad. (12) Each had his own method of gaining victory, Alexander making war openly and Philip using trickery; the latter took pleasure in duping the enemy, the former in putting them to flight in the open. (13) Philip was the more prudent strategist, Alexander had the greater vision. (14) The father could hide, and sometimes even suppress, his anger; when Alexander's had flared up, his retaliation could be neither delayed nor kept in check. (15) Both were excessively fond of drink, but intoxication brought out different shortcomings. It was the father's habit to rush from the dinner party straight at the enemy, engage him in combat and recklessly expose himself to danger; Alexander's violence was directed not against the enemy but against his own comrades. (16) As a result Philip was often brought back from his battles wounded while the other often left a dinner with his friends' blood on his hands. (17) Philip was unwilling to share the royal power with his friends; Alexander wielded it over his. The father preferred to be loved, the son to be feared. (18) They had a comparable interest in literature. The father had greater shrewdness, the son was truer to his word. (19) Philip was more restrained in his language and discourse, Alexander in his actions. (20) When it came to showing mercy to the defeated, the son was temperamentally more amenable and more magnanimous. The father was more disposed to thrift, the son to extravagance. (21) With such qualities did the father lay the basis for a worldwide empire and the son bring to completion the glorious enterprise.

At a first reading the account gives a generally hostile view of Philip's character. Justin views him as a cruel person, deceitful, and beyond shame in his actions, and, further, says that Philip had no hesitation in plundering and selling into slavery the women and children of allied cities (8.3.1–5). Alexander is also the subject of criticism, and the passage shows that Alexander's bad qualities outweighed his good qualities.

The relationship of Justin's work to the original one by Trogus is problematic to say the least.[7] Estimates for the life of Justin span the second to the fourth century A.D.,[8] and we cannot say whether he is merely echoing Trogus or giving us his own opinion. However, his criticism of Alexander echoes that of Diodorus (see below), who was writing in first-century B.C. Rome. Diodorus, therefore, could have been roughly contemporary to Trogus. Moreover, the Romans' attitude to Alexander (and of Greek values) was hostile at this time. Alexander's reputation was really only elevated in the second century A.D. when philhellenism fell into fashion again. Both Trogus and Diodorus are a product of the Roman world and its values and beliefs, and so must have been influenced by these factors (and perhaps by the depiction of Alexander in Roman writers).[9] Since Justin was writing so much later, when Alexander was viewed more positively, we might expect his account to reflect this reevaluation more widely. While there are positive elements in it, thus reflecting Justin's times, most of it is critical, and hence reflective of the earlier negative views of Alexander. This type of contextualization thus gives us good enough grounds for accepting that Justin is following Trogus in his opinions of Philip and Alexander.

A more careful reading of this Justin passage reveals that Philip is presented as the reverse of Alexander. In other words, Philip's personal good qualities outweigh his bad ones, and hence Trogus/Justin elevates him over Alexander. For example, Justin says that Alexander 'surpassed his father both in good qualities and bad [qualities].' The latter would include emotional outbursts, for Philip 'could hide, and sometimes even suppress, his anger,' unlike Alexander, whose retaliation (when angered) 'could be neither delayed nor kept in check.' Further, Alexander was violent 'not against the enemy but against his own comrades': one thinks of the engineered demises of Philotas and Parmenion in the so-called Philotas conspiracy at Phrada in 330,[10] Callisthenes in the Pages Conspiracy at Bactra in the same year,[11] probably Coenus, who openly voiced discontent at the mutiny at the Hyphasis river in 326,[12] and of course the drunken murder of Cleitus at Maracanda in 328,[13] to which Justin must refer when he says Alexander often left 'a dinner with his friends' blood on his hands.' Nevertheless, he does end with the line that Philip laid 'the basis for a worldwide empire and Alexander brought to completion the glorious enterprise.'

The criticisms of Philip's character in the passage may, however, simply be pragmatic acknowledgments of the measures Philip was forced to take, given the situations in which he so often found himself, and hence which Trogus/Justin's Roman audience would understand. For much of his reign, Philip was fighting to unite his kingdom, given its history, to protect its borders from invasion, and to defy interference on the part of hostile Greek powers. It is hardly a surprise, then, that Philip (as Justin says) was 'charming and treacherous at the same time' and that he had to 'cultivate friendships with a view to expediency rather than from genuine feelings' and 'to feign warm feelings when he hated someone, to sow discord between parties that were in agreement and then try to win the favour of both.'

Justin puts his comparative passage at the end of Philip's reign. This is logical, although introducing Alexander into it adds an interesting and arguably unexpected dynamic. Further, it makes one wonder how Justin might deal with Alexander in a summation at the end of his account of Alexander's reign. This occurs in book 12 chapter 16, in a passage that starts with the news that Alexander died at the age of 33. Yet the majority of that chapter is about the myths associated with Olympias' impregnation and Alexander's birth, and his instruction under Aristotle. It ends as follows (12.16.11):

> So it was that he did battle with no adversary without defeating him, besieged no city without taking it, and attacked no tribe without crushing it entirely.

402

(12) In the end he was brought down not by the valour of an enemy but by a plot hatched by his own men and the treachery of his fellow countrymen.

There is no question that this is a far briefer treatment of Alexander's end than Trogus/ Justin lavish on Philip. All Alexander did was fight, it seems (albeit always successfully), and in the end his men had enough of him and he was brought down not in battle, as we might imagine he might have wanted his end to be, but as a victim of a conspiracy.[14] It is thus an inglorious death, not a Homeric/heroic one, but then so was that of Philip, cut down by an assassin's dagger at Aegae in 336 and perhaps also the victim of a conspiracy that may even have involved Alexander.[15]

Next, let us consider Diodorus. Again (as with Trogus/Justin), we have the problem that affects all of the secondary ancient sources on Alexander: to what extent do they accurately use the primary (earlier) source material, existing today only in fragments,[16] and especially do they give us views stemming from the historical and cultural backgrounds in which they wrote or do they simply reiterate those of their sources?[17] It has been convincingly demonstrated that Diodorus was not merely a 'scissors and paste historian,' virtually summarizing his sources, when it comes to his use of the sources (as has long been thought), but was his own distinctive writer and with his own opinions.[18] Since I have argued that the judgments of Diodorus and Tragus/Justin are similar, they may well reflect the Roman view of Alexander in the early empire. However, it is the concluding passages in Diodorus that I find particularly telling because before each of these passages Diodorus has given us a straightforward narrative of each king's reign. In the concluding sections what we read are his own opinions of these kings, with Philip coming off better than Alexander.

Thus, at 17.117.5, Diodorus is of the opinion that '[Alexander] accomplished greater deeds than any, not only of the kings who had lived before him but also of those who were to come later down to our time.' This is high praise, but fitting for someone who within a decade had expanded the Macedonian empire from Greece to what the Greeks called India (modern Pakistan), and could not be matched by any other king of Macedonia. However, in his concluding comments about Philip in 16.95, Diodorus has this to say:

> Such was the end of Philip, who had made himself the greatest of the kings in Europe in his time, and because of the extent of his kingdom had made himself a throned companion of the twelve gods. He had ruled twenty-four years. He is known to fame as one who with but the slenderest resources to support his claim to a throne won for himself the greatest empire in the Greek world, while the growth of his position was not due so much to his prowess in arms as to his adroitness and cordiality in diplomacy. Philip himself is said to have been prouder of his grasp of strategy and his diplomatic successes than of his valor in actual battle. Every member of his army shared in the successes that were won in the field but he alone got credit for victories won through negotiations.

The immediate reaction is that this is far better than the brief conclusion on Alexander. That Philip was the 'greatest of the kings in Europe' clearly echoes Theopompus' famous line in the *Proem* to his *Philippica* that Europe had never produced such a man as Philip.[19] Theopompus goes on to detail Philip's various character flaws and ruthlessness, such as his excessive drinking, a voracious sexual appetite for women, men, and boys, his incontinence, his inability to manage money, and his destruction of Greek cities.[20] He also states that Philip owed more to luck than anything else, and expounds on the dangers of life at the Macedonian court. There are echoes here of Demosthenes (2.18–19), who says the Macedonian court was dangerous, debauched, and full of indecent dancing and drunken revelry, and he regularly attributes the king's military successes to his use of bribes.[21] Theopompus and Demosthenes were contemporary writers and they did not like Philip (yet Demosthenes would call Philip 'the cleverest man under the sun,' Aes. 2.41). Clearly the criticisms of our later writers on Philip are far more limited in extent,[22] and in fact they dilute what the earlier sources give us in their presentation of the two kings.

Thus, Diodorus echoes what Theopompus has to say about Philip and Europe, but he decides to modify it and even ignore some of the more telling criticisms. Philip seemingly has done enough to make him a god;[23] he came from nowhere and won for himself 'the greatest empire in the Greek world.' He did so by a combination of military force and diplomacy, and he thought more of diplomacy than fighting.[24] In other words, he used other means to beat his enemies (unlike Alexander) and especially to consolidate his position, again unlike his son.

The similarity in viewpoint and especially in the placement between Diodorus' longer closing comment on Philip and shorter one on Alexander and Justin's longer closing comment on Philip and shorter one on Alexander is striking. Moreover, Trogus/ Justin turns his necrology of Philip into a long comparison between Philip and his famous son. In Alexander literature as a whole it is unique, and it extends far beyond the famous speech in 324 that Alexander allegedly delivered to his mutinous men at Opis (as Arrian gives it to us), in which he started off by lauding his father but then went on to praise his own achievements more.[25]

Justin does not appear to be giving us merely rhetorical flourish, as it has been argued that Arrian does in the Opis speech, nor was he expounding on some literary father–son topos. There is more to his necrology than a literary undertone. Like Diodorus, Trogus/ Justin's view of Philip and Alexander is based not so much on what each king did, but how each king acted in the best interests of his kingdom and especially each king's legacy. These points now need expansion, beginning with the legacies.

There is a chasm of a difference between the legacy of Alexander and that of Philip.[26] Thus, at the end of Alexander's reign in 323, when the Macedonian empire was at its greatest geographical extent, national pride back home was probably at its lowest and dissatisfaction with its king at its highest. Alexander left no undisputed heir to succeed him, and when news of his death reached the mainland, the Greeks revolted from Macedonia in the Lamian War.[27] He also depleted Macedonian manpower with his frequent demands for reinforcements to the extent that Antipater, left behind as guardian of Greece and deputy *hēgemōn* of the League of Corinth, could have been severely compromised if the Greeks had attempted a widespread insurrection.[28] Diodorus 17.16 tells us that Parmenion and Antipater had been urging Alexander from the time of his accession not to become actively involved in Asia until he had produced a son and heir, but he ignored them (admittedly, choosing a bride in his first year as king, given the problems he faced, was problematic, not least because of the relative dearth of suitable candidates). That was perhaps his biggest failing as king. Unlike his father, Alexander failed to grasp the advantages of political marriages to consolidate and maintain power — of Philip's seven marriages, the first six were *kata polemon*.[29] Alexander's marriage to Roxane of Bactria in 327 was probably political — an attempt to secure the loyalty of Bactria, as well as to have an heir.[30] By then it was a case of too little too late. Roxane did give birth to a child, who died at the Hyphasis river in 326 (*Metz Epit.* 70). She was pregnant again when Alexander died, and Alexander's answer of 'to the best' when he was asked to whom he was leaving his empire only exacerbated the tensions between his generals.[31] Alexander may well have ushered in the cultural greatness of the Hellenistic era,[32] but after his death the Macedonian throne became a bone of contention in the bloody wars waged by those generals for three decades, and the empire that Philip had worked so hard to found and Alexander to extend was no more.

Philip's legacy, on the other hand, was brilliant, and there is no question that Macedonia benefited more from his rule than from that of Alexander. We need only compare the kingdom in 359 when he became king to 336 at the time of his death for the very obvious differences. By the time he died, he had doubled Macedonia in size and population, and his empire stretched from southern Greece to the Danube. The systematic reduction of previous enemies within Upper Macedonia and elsewhere on his frontiers, Illyria, Paeonia, Thrace, and the Chalcidice, and a new, centralized government at Pella, created border security and a unified Upper and Lower Macedonian kingdom for the first time in its history. Indeed, the unification of Macedonia and the elevation of Pella as capital of the entire kingdom were arguably Philip's greatest successes, as everything he was able to do followed from them. His military and economic reforms revolutionized both army and state. He stimulated the economy as never before, and Macedonian coinage became the strongest in Europe. He left Alexander the best army in the Greek world, no external threats, the plan for the invasion of Asia, and no succession problems.[33]

Diodorus writes of Alexander as he does at the end of his narrative of that king's reign because of his military successes and the extent of the empire he forged. Alexander did accomplish 'greater deeds than anyone, not only of the kings who had lived before him but also of those who were to come later down to our time,' by which he means Alexander created a great empire that no single person could match. Not even the Romans came close to duplicating what Alexander did because no single man forged their empire, but a succession of generals in different areas, and over a far greater time frame than the decade it took Alexander. Pompey was great, but he was one of many who played a role in extending Rome's empire.

However, let us consider the difference between creating an empire (i.e., winning the battles) and administering it. Alexander did try to administer his vast empire and to reconcile his rule with the conquered peoples, especially the Persian aristocratic families, but his attempts at nation-building ultimately failed.[34] Diodorus does not distance Philip from what Alexander achieved, and nor does Trogus/Justin. Yet as Justin significantly says at the end of his necrology, quoted above, Philip 'laid the basis' (*fundamenta pater iecit*) for 'a worldwide empire' and Alexander brought to completion 'the glorious enterprise.'

The phrase *fundamenta pater iecit* ('Philip laid the basis') is important. I would argue that it shows that these authors did not merely understand that Alexander built on his father's considerable accomplishment, but also that without Philip's original plan to invade Asia, Alexander would not have been able to achieve what he did. Given the distance that Alexander traveled, as far east as present-day Pakistan, it was nothing short of a worldwide empire — even in his own time, some Greek orators depicted Alexander as reaching the end of the world.[35] The comparison between the two kings gives Philip the edge because he formed the plans to invade Asia (a glorious Panhellenic enterprise to liberate the Greek cities of Asia Minor and to punish the Persians for what the Greeks had suffered at their hands during the Persian Wars);[36] Alexander carried the enterprise out, but again, without Philip and the plan to invade Asia, there would have been no Alexander in Asia, and hence no Alexander the Great.

It was the legacy of both kings and the nature of their rules that drove our ancient writers to see them as they did. Hence, to Diodorus, Alexander might have actually done more than any king down to his day, but it was Philip who 'won for himself the greatest empire in the Greek world.' Philip never forgot what his duties as king were, never lost touch with his people, and worked to ensure the continuation of his dynasty. In his battles and sieges he lost an eye, shattered a collarbone, and suffered a near fatal wound that maimed a leg and made him limp for the rest of his life, but he took all these knocks in the pursuit of his own glory and especially for that of his kingdom — as even his harshest critic Demosthenes admits — and with no reluctance (cf. 11.22, 18.67).

Likewise, Trogus/Justin, who takes the opportunity of rounding off his account of Philip's reign to make this unique, detailed comparison between Philip and Alexander that structurally and dramatically would have been lost at the end of his Alexander narrative. It is not mere rhetoric: Justin wants us to remember the points he makes about Alexander (and about him and his father) as we read on in his account into Alexander's reign. He has set us up beforehand to be critical of Alexander. It has the same effect as Thucydides' description of Cleon as 'the most violent of the citizens' the first time he introduces him before the Mytilene debate (3.36.6). Try as we might, it is impossible to get that image out of our minds when we read about Cleon in Thucydides.

Trogus/Justin and Diodorus were preoccupied with that makes a good ruler — as the Romans of their time were. Diodorus we know concerned himself with the relationship of the individual to state,[37] and so it is no surprise that Philip receives the better press from this writer, given what he did for Macedonia, than Alexander, who was present in his kingdom only for two years of his reign, and whose death marked the disintegration of the Macedonian empire and Macedonia becoming a pawn in the wars of the successors until the Antigonid dynasty established itself in the third century. That Alexander may have been implicated in his father's assassination did not help either. At the same time, they were writing when the Romans' view of Alexander was being shaped by important changes in politics and culture that were taking place in republican and early imperial Rome. Thanks to these, Alexander had become a 'Roman construct, a product of Roman sensibilities and worldview,'[38] and he was the 'archetype for monarchy and charismatic autocracy'[39] because of Roman attitudes to Greek kingship. Although Philip himself had works written about him (Theopompus' *Philippica* being the obvious example, and of course Trogus' account of the same title), and hence was known to a Roman audience, he was not subject to the same shift of reinterpretation as his more famous son. This was because Alexander excited the imagination more, given his spectacular military achievements, which put Philip in their shadow. Diodorus and Trogus/Justin, however, rightly shone the spotlight on Philip as being the better ruler for Macedonia. The great conqueror did not make the better king.

Diodorus and Trogus/Justin constructed a deliberately styled juxtaposition of Philip and Alexander in their accounts of their reigns. Both have a higher opinion of Philip than of Alexander, which was based not so much on mere exploits, but on the nature of kingship and what makes a good king. While few people today would eulogize Alexander as the rosy, heroic figure of a Tarn or a Lane Fox,[40] especially when we consider him not as just a general but as a king, our ancient writers were also concerned with presenting and representing as correct an image of Alexander, and of his father, as historically possible — and so should we. To them (and the Roman audience), it would seem, setting up a future worldwide empire was more important than completing that glorious enterprise. Perhaps the norm of referring to the fourth century as the age of Alexander should be adjusted and it would be better to call that century the age of Philip and Alexander.

Notes

1   All translations of Justin are from Develin and Heckel 1994: 91–92.
2   On Philip, see now Worthington 2008. Also on Philip, though getting on in years, are Ellis 1976, Cawkwell 1978, Hammond 1994, and Hammond and Griffith, 1979: 203–698.
3   The number of books on Alexander is enormous, and Alexander can be lauded or condemned depending on the perspective of the author. Among the more recent biographies may be singled out Green 1974, Hammond 1989, Hammond 1997, Cartledge 2003, and Worthington 2004. The best scholarly biography is still Bosworth 1988a, and see also Bosworth 1996. For more bibliography and discussion, see the bibliographic essays at Cartledge 2003: 327–47 and Worthington 2004: 320–332.
4   See below on the date of Justin.
5   There is no need to rehearse the details of these two kings' reigns or to give copious references to all points in this essay: for these, any of the modern books cited in notes 2 and 3 (which quote further bibliography) may be consulted.
6   On the cultural and political significance of Alexander for Rome, how he may have been shaped by Roman political and cultural life, and these effects on writers of the time, see Spencer 2002. The best discussion of the problems of the sources for Alexander is Bosworth 1988b, and on this issue see further below.
7   On the relationship of Justin's work to the original work by Trogus, see Yardley 2003; cf. Hammond 1991.
8   See further, Syme 1988 (arguing for the late date).
9   Spencer 2002: 37; see also Alonso-Núñez 1987.
10   Diod. 17.79–80, Arr. 3.26, Curt. 6.7–7.2, Plut. *Alex.* 48.1–49, Justin 12.5.1–8; cf. Bosworth 1988a: 100–04, Worthington 2004: 120–24.
11   Arr. 4.13.4, Curt. 8.6.11, Plut. *Alex.* 55.9; cf. Bosworth 1988a: 117–19, Worthington, 2004: 141–43. On the conspiracies, see Badian 2000.
12   Diod. 17.94.4, Arr. 5.25.2–29, Curt. 9.2.10–3.19, Plut. *Alex.* 62.1–3, Justin 12.8.10; cf. Bosworth 1988a: 132–34, Worthington 2004: 158–61 and 208–09.
13   Arr. 4.8.8, Curt. 8.1.29–51, Plut. *Alex.* 51.8; cf. Bosworth 1988a: 114–16, Worthington 2004: 136–38.
14   See Bosworth 1988a: 171–73, Worthington 2004: 266–68; on the fabrications surrounding Alexander's death, see Bosworth 1971.
15   See Worthington 2008: 181–86, citing bibliography.
16   Currently collected together in Jacoby, *FGrH* IIB, nos. 117–53, with a German commentary in IID at pp. 403–542. (A completely new edition of *FGrH* is in progress, entitled *Brill's New Jacoby*, publication of which will continue until 2013.) Translations of all primary sources are in Robinson 1953: i; cf. Worthington 2003. For discussion, see Pearson 1960.
17   On the sources for Alexander, see Bosworth 1988b; cf. Baynham 2003.
18   See Sacks 1990 and Green 2006; see also Sacks 1994 and Hammond 1983.

19 Theopompus, *FGrH* 115 F27. On Theopompus, see Flower 1994, especially chapters 5–6 on Theopompus and Philip.

20 Many of the allegations must be taken with a pinch of salt. There is, for example, no proof that Philip was a pederast: see Worthington 2008: 70.

21 Dem. 1.5, 8.40, 19.265 and 342, 18.48, for example.

22 Cf. Diod. 16.93.3–4, Justin 8.6.5–8, 9.8.6–7.

23 This passage is one of several that has been wrongly interpreted to mean that Philip sought divine honors in his lifetime or was accorded them: see, further, Worthington 2008: 228–33.

24 On Philip's preference for diplomacy over military might, and his use of diplomacy, see Ryder 1994; cf. Cawkwell 1996.

25 Arr. 7.9.2–5; cf. Curt. 10.2.23–4.3. The historicity of the speech is suspect; cf. Bosworth 1988b: 101–13. On the background to the Opis mutiny, see Bosworth 1988a: 159–61 and Worthington 2004: 248–52.

26 For a convenient summary of their legacies, cf. Worthington 2008: 204–08; on Philip's achievements, see ibid. pp. 194–203.

27 On the Lamian War, see Hammond and Walbank 1988: 107–17, for example.

28 Cf. Bosworth 1986; *contra* Billows 1995: 183–212.

29 The phrase is difficult to translate precisely; literally it would mean 'to do with (?according to) (the) war' but the first six marriages were not the product of one military engagement. On Philip's marriages see further Tronson 1984 and Worthington 2008: 172–74, both also discussing this phrase. Very good arguments for Philip's seventh marriage to Cleopatra being for a political reason, rather than for a personal reason, as is commonly accepted, are put forward by Carney 2000: 73–74.

30 Arr. 4.19.5, Plut. *Alex.* 47.7–8; on the political nature of the marriage, see Worthington 2004: 188–90.

31 Ptolemy, *FGrH* 138 F30 = Arr. 7.26.3, Diod. 17.117.4.

32 Cf. Hammond 1993.

33 [Plutarch], *Moralia* 327c, says that 'all of Macedonia was ablaze with discontent, and was looking to Amyntas and the sons of Aeropus.' This is hardly true. Antipater immediately proclaimed Alexander king (Justin 11.1.7–10), the people quickly swore their loyalty to him (Diod. 17.2.1–2), and Alexander embarked on a purge of possible opponents: see further Worthington 2008: 187–89.

34 On these aspects, see Worthington 2010.

35 Cf. Aes. 3.165, Din. 1.34, with Gunderson 1981.

36 On Philip's reasons for the Asian expedition, see Worthington 2008: 166–71.

37 Spencer 2002: 36.

38 Spencer 2002: xv.

39 Spencer 2002: xix.

40 Tarn 1948 and Lane Fox 1973, both of whom idealistically set up Alexander as a Homeric hero type who could do next to no wrong. On the issue of Alexander's greatness, see the ancient sources and modern works in Worthington 2003: 296–325.

References

Alonso-Núñez 1987 = J.M. Alonso-Núñez, 'An Augustan World History: The *Historiae Philippicae* of Pompeius Trogus', *G&R*^{2} 34 (1987), pp. 56–72.

Badian 2000 = E. Badian, 'Conspiracies', in A.B. Bosworth and E.J. Baynham (eds), *Alexander the Great in Fact and Fiction* (Oxford: 2000), pp. 50–95.

Baynham 2003 = E. Baynham, 'The Ancient Evidence for Alexander the Great,' in J. Roisman (ed.), *Brill's Companion to Alexander the Great* (Leiden: 2003), pp. 3–29.

Billows 1995 = R. Billows, *Kings and Colonists* (Leiden: 1995).

Bosworth 1971 = A.B. Bosworth, 'The Death of Alexander the Great: Rumour and Propaganda,' *CQ*^{2} 21 (1971), pp. 112–136.

Bosworth 1986 = A.B. Bosworth, 'Alexander the Great and the Decline of Macedon', *JHS* 106 (1986), pp. 1–12.

Bosworth 1988a = A.B. Bosworth, *Conquest and Empire, the Reign of Alexander the Great* (Cambridge: 1998).

Bosworth 1988b = A.B. Bosworth, *From Arrian to Alexander* (Oxford: 1988).

Bosworth 1996 = A.B. Bosworth, *Alexander and the East* (Oxford: 1996).

Carney 2000 = E.D. Carney, *Women and Monarchy in Macedonia* (Norman, OK: 2000).

Carney 2002 = E.D. Carney, *Women and Monarchy in Macedonia* (Norman: 2002).

Cartledge 2003 = P.A. Cartledge, *Alexander the Great: The Hunt for a New Past* (London: 2003).

Cawkwell 1978 = G.L. Cawkwell, *Philip of Macedon* (London: 1978).

Cawkwell 1996 = G.L. Cawkwell, 'The End of Greek Liberty', in R.W. Wallace and E.M. Harris (eds), *Transitions to Empire: Essays in Honor of E. Badian* (Norman: 1996), pp. 98–121.

Develin and Heckel 1994 = R. Develin and W. Heckel, *Justin. Epitome of the Philippic History of Pompeius Trogus* (Atlanta: 1994).

Ellis 1976 = J.R. Ellis, *Philip II and Macedonian Imperialism* (London: 1976).

Ellis 1978 = J.R. Elis, *Philip II and Macedonian Imperialism* (London: 1978).

Flower 1994 = M.A. Flower, *Theopompus of Chios* (Oxford: 1994).

Green 1974 = P. Green, *Alexander of Macedon* (Harmondsworth: 1974).

Green 2006 = P. Green, *Diodorus Siculus Books 11–12.37.1* (Austin: 2006).

Gunderson 1981 = L.L. Gunderson, 'Alexander and the Attic Orators', in H.J. Dell (ed.), *Ancient Macedonian Studies in Honor of C.F. Edson* (Thessaloniki: 1981), pp. 183–192.

Hammond 1983 = N.G.L. Hammond, *Three Historians of Alexander the Great* (Cambridge: 1983).

Hammond 1989 = N.G.L. Hammond, *Alexander the Great: King, Commander and Statesman*[2] (Bristol: 1989).

Hammond 1991 = N.G.L. Hammond, 'The Sources of Justin on Macedonia to the Death of Philip', *CQ*[2] 41 (1991), pp. 496–508.

Hammond 1993 = N.G.L. Hammond, 'The Macedonian Imprint on the Hellenistic World', in P. Green (ed.), *Hellenistic History and Culture* (Berkeley and Los Angeles: 1993), pp. 12–23.

Hammond 1994 = N.G.L. Hammond, *Philip of Macedon* (London: 1994).

Hammond 1997 = N.G.L. Hammond, *The Genius of Alexander the Great* (London: 1997).

Hammond and Griffith 1979 = N.G.L. Hammond and G.T. Griffith, *A History of Macedonia* 2 (Oxford: 1979).

Hammond and Walbank 1988 = N.G.L. Hammond and F.W. Walbank, *A History of Macedonia* 3 (Oxford: 1988).

Lane Fox 1973 = R. Lane Fox, *Alexander the Great* (London: 1973).

Pearson 1960 = L. Pearson, *The Lost Histories of Alexander the Great* (New York: 1960).

Robinson 1953 = C.A. Robinson, *The History of Alexander the Great* 1 (Providence: 1953).

Ryder 1994 = T.T.B. Ryder, 'The Diplomatic Skills of Philip II', in Ian Worthington (ed.), *Ventures into Greek History. Essays in Honour of N.G.L. Hammond* (Oxford: 1994), pp. 228–257.

Sacks 1990 = K.S. Sacks, *Diodorus Siculus and the First Century* (Princeton: 1990).

Sacks 1994 = K.S. Sacks, 'Diodorus and his Sources: Conformity and Creativity', in S. Hornblower (ed.), *Greek Historiography* (Oxford: 1994), pp. 213–232.

Spencer 2002 = D. Spencer, *The Roman Alexander* (Exeter: 2002).

Syme 1988 = R. Syme, 'The Date of Justin and the Discovery of Trogus' *Historia*', *Historia* 37 (1988), pp. 358–371.

Tarn 1948 = W.W. Tarn, *Alexander the Great*, 2 vols (Cambridge: 1948).

Tronson 1984 = A.D. Tronson, 'Satyrus the Peripatetic and the Marriages of Philip II', *JHS* 104 (1984), pp. 116–126.

Worthington 2003 = Ian Worthington, *Alexander the Great: A Reader* (London: 1994).

Worthington 2004 = Ian Worthington, *Alexander the Great, Man and God*, rev. ed. (London: 2004).

Worthington 2008 = Ian Worthington, *Philip II of Macedonia* (New Haven and London: 2008).

Worthington 2010 = Ian Worthington, 'Alexander the Great, Nation-building, and the Creation and Maintenance of Empire', in V.D. Hanson (ed.), *Makers of Ancient Strategy* (Princeton: 2010), pp. 118–137.

Yardley 2003 = J. Yardley, *Justin and Trogus. A Study of the Language of Justin's Epitome of Trogus* (Toronto: 2003).

INDEX OF
SOURCES

Occasionally, I repeat a contemporary literary source in another chapter, and where I have done so both source numbers in this book appear in the list below. On some occasions I have 'split' a long fragment into two or more separate parts, depending on its context and the information it gives, hence some of the fragments listed below have more than one source number (e.g. Aristobulus, *FGrH* 139 F 55).

Inscriptional	*Number*
Tod, no. 184 = R–O no. 86A	26
Tod, no. 192 = R–O no. 84A	27
Tod, no. 201 = R–O no. 85	28
Tod, no. 202 = R–O no. 101	30
*SIG*³, no. 312 = R–O no. 90B	29

Literary	
Amyntas, *FGrH* 122 F 6	Chap. 6 n. 9
Anonymous History of Alexander, *FGrH* 151 F 1	42
Anonymous History of Alexander, *FGrH* 151 FF 3–5	47
Anonymous History of Alexander, *FGrH* 151 F 6	45
Anonymous History of Alexander, *FGrH* 151 F 7	52
Anonymous History of Alexander, *FGrH* 151 F 10	103
Anonymous History of Alexander, *FGrH* 151 F 11	114
Anonymous History of Alexander, *FGrH* 151 FF 12–13	54
Anonymous Relating to the History of Alexander, *FGrH* 153 T 1	16
Archelaus, *FGrH* 123 F 1	62
Aristobulus, *FGrH* 139 F 2b	35
Aristobulus, *FGrH* 139 F 3	33
Aristobulus, *FGrH* 139 F 4	20
Aristobulus, *FGrH* 139 F 5	41
Aristobulus, *FGrH* 139 F 7a	43

Aristobulus, *FGrH* 139 F 7b	44
Aristobulus, *FGrH* 139 F 11	17
Aristobulus, *FGrH* 139 FF 13–15	102
Aristobulus, *FGrH* 139 F 24	58
Aristobulus, *FGrH* 139 F 29	59, 119
Aristobulus, *FGrH* 139 F 30	108
Aristobulus, *FGrH* 139 F 31	109
Aristobulus, *FGrH* 139 F 34	9
Aristobulus, *FGrH* 139 F 35	61
Aristobulus, *FGrH* 139 F 43	73
Aristobulus, *FGrH* 139 F 46	70
Aristobulus, *FGrH* 139 F 49a	79
Aristobulus, *FGrH* 139 F 49b	80
Aristobulus, *FGrH* 139 F 52	97
Aristobulus, *FGrH* 139 F 53	12
Aristobulus, *FGrH* 139 F 54	81
Aristobulus, *FGrH* 139 F 55	25
Aristobulus, *FGrH* 139 F 55	82
Aristobulus, *FGrH* 139 F 55	106
Aristobulus, *FGrH* 139 F 55	116
Aristobulus, *FGrH* 139 F 58	83
Aristobulus, *FGrH* 139 F 61	84
Aristus, *FGrH* 143 F 2	115
Baeton, *FGrH* 119 F 2a	37
Callisthenes, *FGrH* 124 T 17	112
Callisthenes, *FGrH* 124 F 14a	98
Callisthenes, *FGrH* 124 F 14b	99
Callisthenes, *FGrH* 124 F 35	46
Callisthenes, *FGrH* 124 F 36	104
Callisthenes, *FGrH* 124 F 37	55
Chares, *FGrH* 125 F 2	38
Chares, *FGrH* 125 F 4	96

INDEX